Publisher's Note

This account is a lasting tribute to what was, undoubtedly, a much appreciated asset of the town in its time. It is especially a tribute to the men and women who worked the trolleybuses – sometimes a whole working life – amongst them all the drivers, conductors, inspectors, electricians, fitters, overhead linesmen, and the office staff. And, not least, the Transport Committees and the General Managers who shaped the history of the undertaking and made it so unique. The trolleybuses have now gone – almost a third of a century ago, back in another millennium. Fond memories of what was but isn't now. But, on the other hand, it's history – part of the social history of the town.

Doubtless, older enthusiasts will be pleased to learn that, thanks to the generosity of John Mawson, author of *Bournemouth Corporation Transport* (published May 1967), David Bowler has been able to use collected but unpublished information gathered over 30 years ago, when it was John Mawson's intention to write his second volume.

It has been a difficult history to tell, because of the system's complexity and the immense amount of information involved. Service patterns changed from year to year – and even with the seasons – while the adjacent boroughs of Christchurch and of Poole regularly put in their six-pennyworth, too! The early involvement of the company-operated tramway system in Poole, and the later co-ordination with Hants & Dorset Motor Services Ltd., also served to complicate matters.

This book – the result, hours and hours – indeed several years – of sifting, weeding, honing and polishing, have resulted in this mammoth 264-page tome. It is nearly twice the size of anything we have previously attempted. It should be twice as good!

J. R. WHITEHEAD   3, Littlecote Drive, READING RG1 6JD   *April 2001*

Bournemouth Square looking east, shortly after the Second World War, but before the March 1947 roundabout construction. Note the war damage on Richmond Hill (formerly the site of the Central Hotel), the tramway waiting rooms, the tram rails and the chocolate-coloured roofs on the trolleybuses. The gap in the central paving at the apex of Gervis Place and Old Christchurch Road indicates the position of the emergency loop line.   *Bournemouth Transport*

Preface

It will be readily apparent to any reader of this volume that the author, David Bowler, has committed a tremendous amount of time and effort to providing the most comprehensive record of Bournemouth's trolleybuses yet available. From the earliest reference to the 'trackless trolleys' to the most recent 'enthusiasts' trip', here in great detail is a survey of every major and many minor events and decisions together with an exhaustive analysis of the myriad changes in the system required by the ever-changing development of the Borough. For me, reading the draft has been a nostalgic journey back through a period in the middle of my career in public transport, a period of great change in transport and in towns themselves with the advent of one-person-operation and major alterations to the highway structure.

With the benefit of hindsight would I have sought to retain the trolleybuses in Bournemouth? I do not honestly think so. Neither the Bournemouth Council nor Ronald Cox and I in management had any inherent desire to remove the trolleybuses, but the fact remains that so many factors were stacked up against them — Government policy, economics, the demise of trolleybus manufacture in Britain, one-person-operation and relative inflexibility — that there was little choice. If we were wrong so were councils and managements of every other trolleybus operator in Britain, nor did I see any private individual or company anxious to invest funds in trolleybus operation.

None of this should detract from the merits of this splendid book. Whether the reader is more interested in the vehicles themselves or the infrastructure of the power supply, whether he wants to know all there is to know about the route changes, the service frequencies or the fare levels, he will find in this book a painstaking record of a system which was a model of its kind and is still remembered with affection by many. It is indeed a fitting epitaph.

IAN CUNNINGHAM, MBE, BSc, C Eng, MIMechE, FCIT
Deputy General Manager and Engineer, Bournemouth Corporation Transport, March 1963 – June 1964
General Manager, Bournemouth Corporation Transport, June 1964 – March 1986
Managing Director, Bournemouth Transport Limited, March 1986 – October 1989

Sunbeam MS2 trolleybus 72 (AEL 400) – the first of Bournemouth's "production" trolleybuses. This is one of a series of photos taken when the vehicle was new in 1934 to demonstrate the rear entrance/front exit layout. The location is Southcote Road, looking west.
Bournemouth Corporation Transport

Foreword

Having worked in the public transport industry for over forty years, the last thing you want to do in your spare time is to read a book on trolleybuses. I started reading David Bowler's manuscripts and, to my surprise, became quite interested to read the of developments of public transport in Bournemouth.

It is true to say, nothing really changes in public transport. The same old arguments for promoting or delaying the introduction of another route or a type of vehicle existed during the Ignatius Bulfin era as they do today. Before a decision is taken, visits to other bus companies are made and a report has to be produced on their findings; only then will the controlling authority believe that what was reported by the General Manager some six months earlier was in fact correct!

This book manages to bring out the background to the trolleybus era of Bournemouth Corporation Transport in an interesting manner. It shows how the undertaking has evolved over the last one hundred years and how mergers have led to what we have today. This is not a book full of statistics and fleet lists etc.; it is a readable prose for historians, trolleybus lovers, transport enthusiasts and people who live in and around the town of Bournemouth.

TED REID, *Managing Director, Bournemouth Transport Limited, October 1989 – September 1999*

The Bournemouth trolleybus system was famous for its turntable at Christchurch, shown here on 2nd August 1959. This view shows the conductor pulling BUT 9641T/ Weymann 250 (KLJ 350) round via one of its handrails, while simultaneously holding one of the booms down with the bamboo pole. The driver cannot be seen – presumably he is helping by pushing the vehicle on its front nearside!

J. S. King (BTS Library)

Bournemouth was also well-known for its fleet of impressive, modern-looking Sunbeam MF2B trolley-buses, with their bodywork extending ahead of the front axle. Bournemouth was one of only two British operators of the type (the other being Hull). Bournemouth's examples had an open rear entrance and a front exit, and were fitted with two staircases. This view shows 282 (YLJ 282) turning into Bath Road at the Lansdowne on 16th May 1960, en route to Westbourne.

D. L. Chalk collection

Author's Acknowledgements

How can I begin to thank the small group of individuals who have helped me in my research to document the story of Bournemouth's trolleybuses without my words reading the same as those at the start of any other book? Quickly overflown and forgotten! But please not on this occasion, for the next few paragraphs express my inadequate gratitude to all of them for their hours of work on my behalf. Trolleybuses left the streets of Bournemouth over thirty years ago, yet I feel it is essential that their history should be committed to paper before those generations who still remember them as a part of the everyday scene have also vanished. Without the endeavours of those mentioned below it would have been impossible for me to complete my research.

In particular, there are two persons who have invested much time and effort in helping me prepare this book. Tremendous help and support has been given by local transport historian David Chalk, who has interests varying from paddle-steamers to trolleybuses. David is one of those fortunate individuals who has been able to combine career and hobby, with a career with Bournemouth Corporation Transport and its successor, Yellow Buses, lasting 44 years; he retired in May 2000. It was he who prepared a brief history of the erstwhile trolleybus system, *Silent Service*, for the Omnibus Society in 1961, and who has written the undertaking's several commemorative brochures since 1969. Fellow enthusiast John Mawson started painstakingly to prepare a detailed history of Bournemouth Corporation Transport in the early 1960s but was beaten by the imminent closure of the trolleybus system and a lack of support from his publishers. Only the first volume actually appeared, in 1967, but I have benefited from free access to the second volume's incomplete manuscripts and John's intimate knowledge of the peak years of trolleybus operation.

The staff of the erstwhile Dorset County Council Library Service in Bournemouth, now Bournemouth Libraries, in particular Katharine Spackman (Assistant Reference Librarian, Local Studies), deserve my gratitude too. Very special thanks are also due to those at Southbourne Library, where the Transport Committee Minutes are held, especially Denise Bevans, Wanda Dennant and Caron Parrett who, in addition to their professional help, made me numerous cups of coffee.

Yellow Buses have also been most supportive. Here I must mention Ted Reid (Managing Director until September 1999); Chris Jepson (Engineering Director) and Roy Edgley (formerly Financial Director and now Managing Director) for their friendly, professional advice. It was Ted Reid who introduced me to Ian Cunningham, the last General Manager during the trolleybus era. Ian, still a committed believer in electric street traction, has welcomed me into his home and answered my most searching questions.

Finally, I wish to extend my thanks to all those in the trolleybus enthusiast community who have helped me to a greater or lesser extent in my labours, including members of the British Trolleybus Society (particularly Martin Nimmo); and the Bournemouth Passenger Transport Association. Thanks also to John Gillham for preparing the overhead wiring map and to the many photographers, sometimes unknown by name, who have provided me with suitable illustrations.

Bournemouth's pre-war standard trolleybus was the Sunbeam MS2, with bodywork by Park Royal or English Electric to the Corporation's own specification. This publicity view shows the first of the town's "production" trolleybuses, Park Royal-bodied 72 (AEL 400), posed at the junction of Southcote Road and St. Swithun's Road on 21st June 1934. Note the tramway reversing triangle in the roadway.
Bournemouth Transport Ltd.

Introduction

The end of the 1962 school summer term was just hours away. My classmates and I were discussing where each one of us were going to spend our holidays. Those having connections with H.M. Forces were off to Cyprus, Singapore and so on, whilst others with well-to-do parents were heading for Palma de Mallorca, still an exotic destination in that pre-package tour age. And me? Almost ashamedly, I admitted "A fortnight in Bournemouth".

Once at home I complained to my mother about the family's chosen holiday destination; it sounded so boring! She consoled me with a description of Bournemouth and together we studied the tourist guide; it didn't seem so bad after all. But what did the solid red lines on the town map denote? There were both motorbus and trolleybus routes in the town. I had already seen trolleybuses on occasional visits to Nottingham, in London and in various north eastern towns on a coach tour to Scotland. Now there was another incentive for the holiday.

We stayed at the Kildare Hotel on Bath Road, behind the Pier Approach Baths (now both demolished to provide a car park on potentially one of the finest sites in Bournemouth). There was overhead wiring outside the hotel, although I do not recall seeing any passing trolleybuses. The family made a number of trolleybus journeys during our stay, including a trip to Christchurch with its fascinating turntable terminus. On the last day of our holiday, I was allowed to repeat this trip alone and take a few trolleybus photographs – "Wasted film" my father said! And so a young schoolboy from the English East Midlands was "infected" with enthusiasm for Bournemouth's trolleybuses.

I started to collect information about the system and prepared some landscaped baseboards to represent the Square to Christchurch route by way of Tuckton Bridge, served by "Matchbox Toy" trolleybuses. Nails and cotton were used for the overhead equipment, whilst a cardboard Dairylea cheese box provided the Christchurch turntable. In those days the Bournemouth trolleybus system was a model of perfection. Spotlessly clean vehicles with precise destination displays and smartly turned-out crews glided throughout the town. Seated on the upper deck, one heard only the dewirement buzzer as the trolleybus passed beneath an overhead junction rather than the thunder of vibration from the trolleybooms experienced in other towns. And new vehicles were still being delivered, as evidenced by the fleet list which the Transport Department kindly sent me. My long-suffering parents recognised my interest in trolleybuses, particularly those of Bournemouth, and agreed to stays of varying duration in the town in 1964, 1966 and 1967, by which time I was considered old enough to travel there on my own. There were many more stays up to the time of final closure and I have remained a frequent visitor ever since.

My interest in this mode of transport has not wavered over the years and, although my career has given me the opportunity to explore systems all over the world, the trolleybuses of Bournemouth have always remained my particular favourites. Having lived in Switzerland for almost 25 years, my perceptions now differ from those of a UK resident. Inevitably I compare the wonderfully integrated, regular interval, high-quality urban and interurban public transport services found in Switzerland with those now prevailing in the UK. In Switzerland public transport ridership figures continue to grow, with operators putting service before profit, and the modernisation and expansion of environmentally-friendly trolleybus systems goes on. Accordingly it remains incomprehensible to me that the closure of the Bournemouth trolleybus system, now over thirty years ago and just six years after the last vehicles had been delivered, could ever have been allowed to happen. But then, I cannot identify with a society that appears to attach no importance to containing air pollution or protecting the environment, which identifies the private car and public transport with a new age "class structure", and which puts profit before public service. Certainly it was British political logic and the propaganda that trolleybuses were an outmoded form of transport which finally took Bournemouth's vehicles off the streets.

Over the last decade, the *Trolleybooks* Joint Publications Panel has published a number of definitive histories of British trolleybus systems. My enquiries as to when such a Bournemouth history might be published prompted the response that nothing was planned and why didn't I have a go myself. So here it is, my first – and probably last – book.

David Bowler
Pfungen, Switzerland
April 2001

For the benefit of non-enthusiasts the more obscure terms used in connection with trolleybuses, and in particular the trolleybus overhead line installations, are explained:

Bracket Arm A tubular steel support bolted to the traction pole at right angles, and projecting over the roadway, from which to suspend the running wire as an alternative to span wire. Usually employed where the length of span wire between traction poles would be unduly long, or along straight stretches on narrow roads to reduce the number of traction poles. Also referred to as single bracket arms to differentiate from gantries or double bracket arms, which were tubular supports joining two opposite traction poles.

Curve Segment A special curved fitting replacing several separate pull-offs in the running wire, which gave a smoother passage for the trolleyheads on sharp curves.

Frog The overhead 'points' where one line left or joined another, known as facing and trailing frogs respectively. Facing frogs were operated either by hand (the conductor leaving the vehicle and pulling the handle on an adjacent traction pole) or automatically by the trolleyheads of a vehicle energising a solenoid through a contact fitted to the overhead line a short distance before the frog. The setting of the frog would be changed by the trolleybus driver applying power as the trolleyheads passed beneath the contact. Trailing frogs, where one line converged with another, were spring-loaded.

Gantry Also known as a double bracket arm, this consisted of a tubular support joining two opposite traction poles, from which the running wires were suspended.

Pull-off An arrangement of span wires set out to support and align the running wires on bends under the correct tension, creating a curve consisting of a series of short straight sections.

Reversing Triangle (Reverser) An arrangement in the overhead line to turn vehicles by means of a three-point reversing procedure into and out of a side turning.

Rosette (Wall Plate) An anchor fitting, rag-bolted or otherwise fixed to the face of a building, used instead of a traction pole, to which span wire was attached.

Running Wires The conductor wires along which the trolleyhead ran or slid. These were usually 20ft above road level, the wire nearest the centre of the road being of positive polarity and that nearest the edge of the road negative polarity.

Section Insulator An overhead line assembly containing a short length of non-conductive material of the same profile as the running wire to break the route up into electrically isolated half-mile sections as required by law in the United Kingdom.

Span Wire The wire erected across the roadway (usually between opposite or diagonally opposite traction poles, but sometimes anchored to buildings) from which the running wires were suspended.

T-Poles A bamboo trolley retrieval pole with positive and negative power leads, which provided a connection between the overhead and the lowered trolleybooms for manoeuvring purposes.

Traction Pole A steel tubular pole used to support the overhead, usually about 31ft long, set 6ft into the roadside at a 5° rake away from the road and surrounded in concrete. There were four grades, light, medium, heavy and extra heavy, which were used according to prevailing circumstances.

Trolleybase The point at which the trolleybooms were attached to the vehicle body. The trolleybase included the large springs which provided the tension necessary to keep the trolleyheads in contact with the overhead line, together with sundry electrical accessories.

Trolleybooms The two booms (or poles) used as a means of connecting the trolleyheads with the running wires in order to draw current to propel the vehicle.

Trolleyhead	The device attached to the end of each trolleyboom as a means of collecting electrical current from the running wires. Early trolleyheads used a metallic trolley-wheel which rolled along the running wire. Later examples used a carbon slipper insert which slid rather than ran along the wire – this was quieter and enabled higher speeds to be obtained.
Twin line hanger	A spacer assembly designed to clamp the two running wires the correct distance apart (generally 2ft) when supported by span wire or bracket arm. The running wire itself was held by "ears" bolted to and insulated from the hanger assembly.
Turning Circle	An arrangement in the overhead line to turn vehicles back along the route by means of a U-turn.

The following abbreviations are used in the text:

AA	Anti-Attrition Metal Co.
AEC	Associated Equipment Company
ARP	Air Raid Precautions
ATS	Auxiliary Territorial Service
BCT	Bournemouth Corporation Transport/Tramways
BET	British Electric Traction Company
BICC	British Insulated Callenders Cables
BPTA	Bournemouth Passenger Transport Association
BTH	British Thomson-Houston
BTS	British Trolleybus Society
BUT	British United Traction
DC	Direct Current
FP	Feeder Pillar
H&D	Hants & Dorset Motor Services Ltd.
HCC	Hampshire County Council
LGOC	London General Omnibus Company
LSWR	London & South Western Railway
MCW	Metropolitan-Cammell-Weymann Ltd.
MEXE	Military Experimental Establishment
MoT	Ministry of Transport (known as the Ministry of War Transport between 1939 and 1945, and the Ministry of Transport & Civil Aviation between 1945 and 1959)
MP	Mains Pillar (used mainly in maps/appendices)
MPTA	Municipal Passenger Transport Association
NTA	National Trolleybus Association
pa	*per annum*
PDET	Poole & District Electric Traction Co.
PO	Post Office
PSV	Public Service Vehicle
REME	Royal Electrical and Mechanical Engineers
RTS	Reading Transport Society
SB	Switch Box
SEB	Southern Electricity Board
SR	Southern Railway
TGWU	Transport & General Workers Union
UK	United Kingdom

At various points in the text use has been made of a standard code (which will be familiar to enthusiasts) when referring to the type of body and seating capacity of a particular type of trolleybus. The code usually consists of two figures separated by an oblique stroke to indicate upper- and lower-deck seating capacity respectively. Letters are prefixed to indicate body type and suffixed to indicate doorway positions. The elements of this code used in connection with Bournemouth's trolleybuses are as follows:-

Prefix letter(s):	B : Single-deck bus
	H : Highbridge double-deck layout (i.e. with centre as opposed to side gangway in upper saloon)
Figures:	Indicate the number of seats in the upper and lower saloons respectively
Suffix letter(s):	C : Centre doorway position
	D : Dual-doorway vehicle; in the case of Bournemouth this was entry via an open rear platform and exit via a folding door at the front of the bus.
	R : Rear doorway position with open platform

For example, Sunbeam MS2s 72–83 (AEL 400–11) were H31/25D, i.e. highbridge bodywork with 31 seats upstairs, 25 downstairs and dual doorways.

Conversion Factors – Units and Currency

During the period in which the trolleybuses operated, Britain used Imperial units of measure and pre-decimal currency. These traditional units are used throughout this book. No conversions are provided in the text, both to save space and to avoid interrupting the flow of the narrative. The following table will be of use to readers wishing to convert to metric units and decimal currency.

Length:	1 inch = 25.4 cm
	1 foot = 12 inches = 30.5 cm
	1 yard = 3 feet = 91.4 cm
	1 chain = 22 yards = 20.1 metres
	1 furlong = 10 chains = 220 yds = 201 metres
	1 mile = 8 furlongs = 1.6 km
Area:	1 acre = 4840 sq. yards = 4046.86 sq. metres
Weight:	1 qtr (quarter) = 127 kg
	1 cwt (hundredweight) = 4 qtrs = 50.8 kg
	1 imperial ton = 20 cwt = 1.02 metric tonnes
Currency:	1d (penny) = 2.4p
	1s (shilling) = 12d = 5p
	£1 (pound) = 20s = 240d = 100p

CHAPTER ONE

Setting the scene

The physical geography of lowland Britain is dominated by a line of chalk hills running first south and then south-west from Flamborough Head in the north, through the Yorkshire and Lincolnshire Wolds, the East Anglian Heights, the Chilterns, the Berkshire Downs and Cranborne Chase. The easily erodable chalk layers then turn east, dipping almost into the vertical, making up the South Dorset coastline, the Isle of Purbeck, the Needles and the downs in the centre of the Isle of Wight. Tens of thousands of years ago, the soft chalk cliffs stretching from Durlston Head near Swanage to the Needles were breached by the waves of the English Channel, in the same manner as Lulworth Cove further west is being constantly enlarged to this day. The sea flooded into the valley running from west to east made by the present day rivers Avon, Corfe, Frome, Piddle and Stour, creating today's Poole Bay.

Folding westwards, chalk runs some 400 ft beneath the town of Bournemouth. Below the chalk lies the south-eastwards dipping London Clay and finally the sandy Bagshot Beds containing pockets of pipe clay, which come to the surface above the Bourne Stream at Branksome and once fed potteries there. The sour soil is made up of coarse sand which centuries of cultivation have turned grey and which will swallow both humus and rain in quantity. The gravelled uplands, covered by an urban blanket today, have been terraced by changing river levels, whilst the beds of dried-up streams are now the town's valleys and tree-lined chines, some still having traces of streams in them, the largest being the Bourne Valley. The Stour has also cut gravel terraces at Muscliffe and Tuckton but, where the river recedes from higher terrain, its alluvium has left the only fertile ground. A few farms and market gardens still exist here, the only area not yet completely covered with urban sprawl.

Bournemouth benefits from warm summers, the average temperature in July being 17°C, and a light average rainfall of 31ins. Seven miles of beach are particularly clean due to the phenomenon of a half-tide which follows each main tide, having made its way around the Isle of Wight and up the Solent. The beach has thinned somewhat since the construction of sea walls reduced its natural supply of sand but, in short, Bournemouth remains the perfect site for a seaside holiday resort.

In 1914, the Mayor wrote *"Bournemouth is a town unhampered by a past"*; yet Bournemouth does have a past. Iron Age man set up a trading post at Double Dykes and a harbour at Hengistbury; Neolithic man left a burial ground at Holdenhurst; and the Roman colonists left their spade marks in the clay too. The Danes landed nearby and Leland, the Tudor chronicler, mentioned "Bowurnemouth". The modern town was born at Holdenhurst, recorded in Domesday as "Holeest", but the sparse population ensured that the area remained popular for smuggling into the late 1700s. On the site of todays Square, a settlement sprang up around the first bridge across the Bourne Stream at Holdenhurst Bottom, the crossing still being known as Holdenhurst Bridge in 1856. The high ground between the Bourne Stream and Holdenhurst was named Littledown and, until the 1920s, it was grazed by sheep driven through Sheepwash to the west of Iford Bridge, and Broadway Lane was still a narrow track. Moordown, a mile south, was described in 1853 as *"a tract of heathland on which many poor families are settled"*.

The 1805 Enclosure Award provided the catalyst for the town's growth. Speculators invested in estates and extensive sites for later development. In 1810 Lewis Tregonwell was captivated by Bourne Chine, bought 8½ acres and built a new home, now part of the Royal Exeter Hotel. But it was Dr Granville who really influenced the development: in 1841 he made a brief visit and then went on to publish details of *"a perfect discovery among sea-nooks"* and *"a place suitable for the resort of the better classes"*.

The first guide book, in 1840, spoke of *"an air of tranquil repose"*. Sanatoria came, then residences, gardens and the ubiquitous pines, followed by hotels and businesses. By 1856 the population had reached some 7,000 and an Act of Parliament established a Board of Commissioners who controlled a semi-circular district radiating 1 mile from the Belle Vue, an early hotel situated on the site of the Pavilion. The Lansdowne – named after the circus in Bath, perhaps in the hope that Bournemouth would become as famous for its curative waters – was the point where the long climb of Old Christchurch Road was joined by the road which crossed the Bourne Stream near the Belle Vue Hotel. Tracks to Holdenhurst and Winton radiated from the junction. By

1882 Boscombe and part of Springbourne were in the Commissioner's District and the population had reached 17,000. In 1888 a Charter was granted and Bournemouth became an urban district of Hampshire. It became a Borough from 23rd July 1890, and County Borough from 1st April 1900. Gold and blue armorial bearings were received from the College of Arms in 1891. Throughout the period covered by this book Bournemouth remained a part of Hampshire but, from 1st April 1974, local government reorganisation saw the town – together with Christchurch – transferred to the neighbouring county, Dorset. Bournemouth became a Unitary Authority in 1997.

Between 1890 and 1900, Bournemouth acquired the rest of Boscombe, Malmesbury Park and Westbourne, reaching a population of almost 60,000 and growing to 67,000 by 1910. The town's administrative area grew in stages from the original 1140-acre Commissioner's District of 1856, as follows: 1876 Boscombe (503 acres); 1884 Boscombe and Westbourne (771 acres); 1895 Pokesdown, Southbourne, Tuckton and part of Winton (179 acres); 1901 Winton west of Wimborne Road (3,527 acres); 1914 Charminster and Strouden (793 acres); 1931 Ensbury, Kinson, Howe and Wallisdown (4,627 acres) and 1932 Hengistbury Head (357 acres).

By 1939, the Bournemouth Guide listed over 500 hotels and guest houses, with bed and breakfast from 21s weekly. In the luxury class, the Carlton, Miramar and Burlington Hotels offered hot and cold sea-water baths, whilst the Majestic had an indoor sea-water swimming pool. Later that year, some 40 hotels were requisitioned for military purposes. During the trolleybus era the population grew from 116,803 in 1931, to 144,451 in 1939, to 154,926 in 1951 and finally to 155,620 in 1961. Housing almost filled the heathland south of Kinson in the 1950s, yet today the town's deaths are double its births and 30% of the population is over retirement age – double the national average.

The railway linking Southampton and Dorchester opened in 1847 by way of Brockenhurst, Lymington Junction, Christchurch Road, Ringwood, West Moors, Wimborne, Wareham and Wool. Thus in 1859, James Bell, a grocer in Poole Road, started to operate a twice-daily horse omnibus service from the Bath Hotel, Bournemouth, to the LSWR Christchurch Road station (renamed Holmsley in 1888), 12 miles away, via Christchurch. A branch line was built from Ringwood to Christchurch via Hurn in 1862 and a bus linked Christchurch with Bournemouth. This line was extended across the River Stour into Bournemouth in 1870, initially ending at a station to the east of Holdenhurst Road with a further westwards extension to Bournemouth East (now named Bournemouth Central) on 20th July 1885. In 1888 the LSWR opened a direct line from Lymington Junction through Sway, New Milton and Hinton Admiral to Christchurch and the bus service, by now operated by Elliotts (of Royal Blue fame) lost its passengers from Holmsley to Bournemouth.

The first main line trains reached the town from the west, however. The Poole & Bournemouth Railway's end-on extension to the LSWR Broadstone Junction – Poole line reached Bournemouth West on 15th June 1874 and, from 20th July 1874, the Somerset & Dorset Railway from Bath (and hence the Midlands) also began working through to Bournemouth West. A link between East and West stations through Meyrick Park, mainly in a cutting, opened in 1884. Further stations opened in Pokesdown in 1886 and Boscombe in 1897, whilst a halt was in operation at Meyrick Park Bridge for Winton between 1906 and 1917.

In Bournemouth itself, a Francis Graham started horse bus operation from the West Station to the town centre in 1874, extended to East Station when it opened in 1885. The Hackney Carriage Inspector reported in 1897 that there were 97 licenced omnibuses in the town. By the end of the century there were three main companies licenced to operate within the Borough.

The Bournemouth, Boscombe and Westbourne Omnibus Ltd. (Messrs Mate and Peter) was registered on 15th March 1889, with offices at 4, Roumelia Terrace, Boscombe, and with depot and stables at Christchurch Road, Pokesdown. It operated the following services: Pokesdown – Boscombe – Bournemouth Square – County Gates, Westbourne; Richmond Park – Richmond Hill; Richmond Park – The Arcade; and Bournemouth Square – Winton. On 19th March 1889 they took over the operations of Henry Francis Beamish, who is known to have been operating Southbourne – Bournemouth services in 1872 at a return fare of 1s. In April 1889 they acquired Harry Laidlaw's two buses, running between Westbourne and Boscombe, for £120 and thirty £1 shares in the company. The buses are thought to have had a red livery, those used on Richmond Hill services being pulled by three horses. On 28th October 1901 the company amalgamated with the Bournemouth General Penny Omnibus, thus creating a sizeable undertaking by the standards of the day, with £12,000 authorised share capital. Operations ceased on 23rd July 1902, when the Corporation's Lansdowne – Warwick Road, Pokesdown tram service started.

An early 1890s view of a Bournemouth, Boscombe & Westbourne Omnibus Ltd. horse bus in Old Christchurch Road, passing the entrance to Bournemouth Arcade. Note the additional trace horse on the offside assisting up the gradient from the Square. *D. L. Chalk collection*

The Bournemouth General Penny Omnibus Co Ltd. (Messrs Horsey and Rolls) was founded on 5 January 1892, following the merger of several operators. The company had registered offices at 5 (later 6) Wootton Gardens, subsequently to become the tramways offices from 1920 to 1940, with stables in Stanley Road, Springbourne. They operated services Ashley Road, Boscombe – Holdenhurst Road – Bournemouth Square; Springbourne – Richmond Park – Bournemouth Square; Pokesdown – Boscombe – Bournemouth Square – County Gates, Westbourne. Following a merger with the Bournemouth, Boscombe and Westbourne Omnibus Ltd., the company was wound-up on 14 February 1902

The Boscombe Park, Pokesdown and Southbourne Omnibus Syndicate Ltd. (Messrs Welsman and Hinton), which operated Southbourne – Pokesdown – Bournemouth Square; Parkwood Road, Boscombe – Bournemouth Square – Seamoor Road, Westbourne, became a public company in January 1900, and changing its title to The Southbourne, Boscombe & Bournemouth Omnibus Co. Ltd.. It, too, was wound up, on 1st August 1902.

Horse buses did not run to any timetable and a rather lax licencing system resulted in agressive competition along the several parallel routes. In December 1898, the latter company suggested that a common timetable be agreed and the Corporation's Horse Committee appointed a full-time Omnibus Timekeeper in September 1899.

The first reference to the possibility of tramways in Bournemouth was in 1881, when the Provincial Tramways group proposed a line from Bournemouth Central Station to Poole but were unable to obtain operating powers. In 1897 the British Electric Traction Co. (BET) suggested a Bournemouth – Poole service but, following Bournemouth Town Council's objections, application was made only for that portion of the route outside the Borough, from County Gates (the other side of the Dorset/Hampshire border being Westbourne) through Upper Parkstone to Poole Station. A Light Railway Order was granted and work started on the 3ft 6ins gauge Poole & District Electric Traction Company (PDET) line, using the overhead trolley system of electric power collection, on 4th May 1900. Services commenced on 6th April 1901 at a through fare of 3d. A depot was built at Upper Parkstone. In 1899, the BET applied for an extension of their light railway through Bournemouth to Christchurch, prompting Bournemouth Corporation to apply for their own Tramways Act, primarily as a blocking measure. The following year Bournemouth Corporation went on to propose their own Lansdowne – Christchurch tramway.

More or less compromised into building their own tramways, a Bournemouth Council deputation visited Brussels and Paris in the summer of 1901 and returned recommending that the more expensive, but less obtrusive, underground conduit system of current collection be used in the town centre and overhead trolleys elsewhere. The Bournemouth Corporation Tramways Act, 1901, granted the Corporation powers to construct and operate tramways within the Borough, but with a two-year time-limit to commence construction. The powers would otherwise lapse and the BET would be granted authority to construct and work the tramways. That portion of the BET's Bournemouth – Christchurch application within the Bournemouth Borough boundaries was held in abeyance for two years. The 1901 Act also required that reciprocal through running powers be granted between the BET's Poole and Christchurch lines and the Corporation's town lines.

The Corporation soon realised that their proposed single-track and passing-loops line operating Westbourne – Bournemouth Square – Lansdowne – Boscombe –

Warwick Road, Pokesdown hardly offered a comprehensive public transport solution for the growing town. A revised scheme foresaw double-track on the originally-proposed route and additional single-track and passing-loop lines to Charminster along both Capstone Road and Charminster Road; to Springbourne along Holdenhurst Road; and to Winton along Wimborne Road. The Poole Hill – Lansdowne section of the "main line" was to be equipped with the conduit system. Elsewhere the overhead trolley method of current collection would be used.

Whilst these changes and improvements were being discussed, the BET decided to make a legal challenge. The resultant wrangling would have implications on the development of the trolleybus system some thirty years later and public transport in the area up to the present day. In 1902 they applied for an injunction restraining the Corporation from constructing the tramways as their powers had, in principle, already lapsed. They pointed out that no substantial progress had been made in implementing the Corporation's original scheme and that construction was unlikely to start within the stipulated two year period. Judgement was given in favour of the Corporation but, on 15th July 1902, the Court of Appeal overturned this decision and granted the injunction.

The Corporation decided to take the matter to the House of Lords but, at the last minute, the BET suggested that negotiations should take place to sell their tramway interests in Poole and Christchurch to Bournemouth Corporation. This was basically agreed to and an independent tribunal was appointed to decide the price. To complicate matters, in January 1903 the Poole Tramways Committee wrote to Bournemouth Corporation offering to purchase the PDET at the same price as Bournemouth Corporation had agreed to pay for the undertaking, with running powers to Bournemouth Square to be included in the agreement. In April, understanding between the local authorities was reached, namely that the Borough of Poole and Branksome Urban District Council would buy the PDET on the same terms as Bournemouth Corporation had agreed with the BET. It would then be leased to Bournemouth Corporation for thirty years and worked as a part of their tramway system. Bournemouth would pay Poole an annual fee which, with interest, would represent the whole of the capital borrowed by Poole to purchase the tramway and at the end of the thirty-year period Poole and Branksome would jointly own the light railway.

Arbitration to determine the price commenced on 27th May 1903; with adjournments and evidence from the tramway managers of Birmingham and Dublin. This continued until December 1904. The BET claimed £430,000, compared to Bournemouth Corporation's estimate of £60,000 – £70,000, representing their 35 years of tenure of Poole Light Railways, the anticipated advantage of through running, the traffic potential of the proposed Christchurch and Lower Parkstone extensions, their capital investments and estimated profits throughout the period of lease. The PDET, including the Upper Parkstone depot, together with the BET's rights in Bournemouth and Christchurch, were finally valued at £112,000. Bournemouth Corporation had to pay the legal costs, the whole transaction being completed on 22nd June 1905 at a total amount of £117,850.

In the meantime Bournemouth Corporation had started construction of their 3ft 6ins gauge tramways and sections were opened as soon as they were ready for traffic. The initial Lansdowne – Warwick Road, Pokesdown section, equipped on the overhead trolley system, together with the southern Southcote Road depot access line, opened on 23rd July 1902, followed by the Lansdowne – Holdenhurst Road – Ashley Road, Boscombe route and the northern depot access line on 16th October 1902. Services were extended to Westbourne on 18th December 1902, using the side-slot conduit lines for the first time, through the town centre and as far west as St. Michael's Church, Poole Hill. On 3rd July 1905, a link with the erstwhile PDET line at County Gates was installed. Additional depots were built at Moordown (enlarged in 1919) and Pokesdown, both surviving into the trolleybus era. As the Pokesdown line had by then been extended to Christchurch, through services between Poole and Christchurch were immediately introduced over the 11-mile route, with a running time of some 90 minutes. Bournemouth thereby became the first municipality to operate tramways in two other municipal areas.

Adjoining the main Southcote Road (or Central) Depot and Workshops, an electricity generating station was built. This initially had a capacity of 1,168 kW, supplied by four three-cylinder Bellis & Morcom triple-expansion engines coupled direct to British Thomson-Houston compound-wound generators and exhausting to condensers. Steam was raised by five Lancashire boilers supplied with coal by railway using a private siding off the LSWR main line at the rear of the property and taking water from an artesian well. Traction current at 550 volts DC was supplied to the lines in Bournemouth, whilst those in Christchurch and Poole were supplied from those towns' power stations. Two further turbines were added in 1926 and a third, following the tram to trolleybus conversion, in 1942-43.

Other tramway routes opened as follows:

- 22nd December 1902: Holdenhurst Road – Capstone Road – Charminster Road – Cemetery Junction – Bodorgan Road (top of Richmond Hill);

- 3rd January 1903: Holdenhurst Road (Central Station) – St. Paul's Road – Cemetery Junction;

- 17th January 1903: Cemetery Junction – Wimborne Road – Winton;

- 22nd January 1903: Winton – Moordown;

- 16th April 1903: Bodorgan Road (top of Richmond Hill) – Richmond Hill, Square;

- 17th October 1905: Warwick Road, Pokesdown – Southbourne – Christchurch Priory;

- 3rd August 1906: Branksome Station – Lower Parkstone – Poole Park.

Thus, Bournemouth's tramway system was now complete and, apart from the progressive doubling of the single-track with passing-loop sections and the premature abandonment of the conduit system of current collection, it remained little changed until 1929. The conduit system used in the town centre had soon proved unreliable and expensive in operation. For the sake of appearances, the conduit containing the positive and negative conductor rails was laid immediately below the offside running rail rather than centrally as on the London County Council Tramways network. Strengthened by underground yokes every 3ft 9ins, a concrete walled conduit some 2ft wide and 2ft deep lay beneath the road surface. The one-inch-wide offside running rail groove accommodated the tramcar's wheel flange and also served as a slot for the power collector's access to the conductor rails. Mechanical restraints required that the conduit be transferred to a central position at junctions and turnouts, although two Connett-patent side slot turnouts were installed at the Square in 1906. The conduit power collector, known as a "plough", was secured to a carrier beneath the centre of the tramcar and had to be wound up or down through a trap in the road surface at the end or beginning of the conduit section. The conduit required regular cleaning and constant drainage, whilst rubbish or metal objects touching the underground conductor rails frequently led to short circuits. By 1910 the Corporation was faced with renewals estimated at £4,000 and accordingly invited Mr A. L. C. Fell, Manager of the London County Council Tramways, to inspect the conduit section. He recommended their conversion to the overhead trolley system, bringing an estimated £3,000 pa economy in running costs. Conversion was carried out in early 1911 and, following a Board of Trade inspection, conduit operation in Bournemouth ceased on 12th May 1911, and the overhead trolley system was thus used throughout from the following day.

The tramway extension to Christchurch required the construction of a purpose-built reinforced concrete bridge at Tuckton over the River Stour, replacing a privately-owned narrow wooden structure. The new bridge was opened on 17th October 1905, tolls being levied on all traffic, including an additional ½d for all tram (and later trolleybus) passengers, receipted with a separate ticket. This practice continued until 1st December 1942.

The tramway system's early days were characterised by the lack of a professional tramways manager with overall responsibility for the undertaking. This probably led to the unnecessarily high operating costs in relation to similarly-sized systems, together with poor staff training and low standards of efficiency. This culminated in a runaway accident on 7th May 1908 with Brush open-top

Tramcar 15, on Brill 22E bogies, stops to load passengers at Boscombe Gardens, Christchurch Road, en route to County Gates. The style of destination box, the traction poles in the centre of the road (complete with Bournemouth coat of arms) and the passengers' dress, all suggest this to be an early view from the tramway era.

D. L. Chalk collection

bogie car 72 when descending Avenue Road from the Triangle to Bournemouth Square. The car derailed near Fairlight Glen and plunged over a wall into the garden of a private house below, killing seven passengers. The Board of Trade Enquiry identified faulty magnetic brakes, compounded by poor supervision, as the cause and exonerated the motorman. Shortly afterwards Mr J. B. Hamilton, Manager of Leeds City Tramways, was invited to prepare a report on the undertaking, leading in April 1909 to the combination of managerial responsibilities in a single position and the appointment of the undertaking's first General Manager, Mr Charles Hill, formerly of Birmingham Corporation Tramways. In 1911, Ignatius Mary[*] Bulfin, Bournemouth Corporation's Electrical Engineer, succeeded Mr Hill. He remained General Manager throughout the remaining tramway era in the town and the conversion to trolleybuses.

Throughout the life of the tramways, the following regular services and short-workings operated (refer to map at back of book):

- Poole Railway Station – Poole Park – Upper Parkstone – Branksome Station – County Gates – Square – Lansdowne – Boscombe – Pokesdown – Fisherman's Walk – Southbourne – Tuckton Bridge – Christchurch Priory (every 16 minutes).

- Upper Parkstone – Branksome Station – County Gates – Bournemouth – Lansdowne – Boscombe – Pokesdown – Fisherman's Walk – Southbourne (every 16 minutes).

- County Gates – Square – Lansdowne – Boscombe – Pokesdown – Fisherman's Walk (every 8 minutes).

- Poole Park – Lower Parkstone – Branksome Station – County Gates – Square (every 16 minutes).

- Bournemouth Square – Lansdowne – Holdenhurst Road – Ashley Road, Boscombe (every 8 minutes).

- Richmond Hill, Square (Albert Road) – Cemetery Junction – Wimborne Road – Alma Road, Winton – Peter's Hill – Moordown (every 8 minutes).

- Richmond Hill, Square (Albert Road) – Cemetery Junction – Wimborne Road – Alma Road, Winton – Peter's Hill (timetable unknown, presumed peak hours only).

- Richmond Hill, Square (Albert Road) – Cemetery Junction – Wimborne Road – Alma Road, Winton (timetable unknown, presumed peak hours only)

---

* The second forename *is* correct.

- Holdenhurst Road, Lansdowne – St. Paul's Road – Cemetery Junction – Wimborne Road – Alma Road, Winton – Peter's Hill (every 16 minutes).

- Holdenhurst Road, Lansdowne – St. Paul's Road – Cemetery Junction – Charminster Road – King's Road (timetable unknown, presumed peak hours only).

- Richmond Hill, Square (Albert Road) – Cemetery Junction – Charminster Road – King's Road – Capstone Road, Holdenhurst Road (every 16 minutes).

At its greatest extent Bournemouth Corporation Tramways operated a network of 21.95 route miles and 30 track miles. By 1922 the trams were carrying 24.27 million passengers per annum. At any one time there was a maximum of 131 double-deck open-top tramcars, of which 28 were mounted on four-wheel Peckham trucks and the remainder on Brill 22E bogies; one single-deck luxury saloon also mounted on Brill 22E bogie trucks; and a four-wheel works car. Some 17 open-top four-wheel cars were acquired with the takeover of the PDET fleet but, with the exception of three cars retained for permanent way maintenance purposes, these were withdrawn progressively in the period 1921–26 and replaced by additional bogie cars built to virtually the same design as those delivered 20 years earlier. However, all tramcars remained in stock until final closure. Apart from changed destination equipment and, in the case of the bogie cars, the addition of driver's vestibules, they remained unchanged in appearance throughout their entire operating lives.

Competing Hants & Dorset Motor Services Ltd motorbuses between Bournemouth and Poole along the route of the Lower Parkstone line, and the need to renew the permanent way, led to a decision to abandon this section on 5th January 1929. Although still operating at the peak of their efficiency, tramway operations were constrained by the number of single-track sections on the network, increasing road traffic and the need to extend lines (at considerable cost) into newly built-up areas. It is understood that the Corporation was not permitted to operate closed-top cars, as on many other 3ft 6ins gauge systems, and the necessity to run only open-top double-deck trams made the vehicles seem increasingly unattractive in a national anti-tramway environment. The expiry of the 30 year lease of the Poole Light Railways was beginning to loom on the horizon, whilst the ongoing need for track renewals and general modernisation "stacked the cards" increasingly against continued tramway operations in Bournemouth.

The first reference to railless electric street traction in Bournemouth has been found to be 1910, when the Tramways Committee instructed the then General Manager, Charles Hill, to keep himself informed of the progress being made with trackless cars with particular reference to the possible opening of a route between Boscombe and Boscombe Pier. On 26th June 1911, the newly appointed General Manager, Ignatius Bulfin, reported that the trackless trolley systems in Bradford and Leeds had opened just six days earlier. He suggested that it would be advisable to obtain trackless trolley operating powers and the Town Clerk was instructed to investigate the steps required to obtain them, which he duly presented at the Tramways and Parliamentary Committee Meeting on 24th November 1911. Mr Bulfin was then told to prepare a report, including suggested routes.

There was no immediate progress but at the Tramways and Parliamentary Committee Meeting on 24th May 1912 a letter from Mr C. J. Spencer, Secretary of the Municipal Tramways Association and Manager at Bradford, was read with respect to the trackless trolley vehicles content of the forthcoming Light Railways Bill. The Association had written to every MP asking them to vote in favour of the Bill and was now asking for Bournemouth Council's support. The Committee asked the Town Clerk to write to Bournemouth's MPs as suggested and instructed the General Manager to report on trackless trolley developments.

On 21st June 1912, Mr Bulfin briefed the Committee on his visit to the Municipal Tramways Association conference at Cardiff on 6th/7th June 1912, at which a paper entitled *The Relative Merits of Petrol Buses and Railless Trolley Vehicles*, by Mr Hatton, General Manager at Newcastle upon Tyne, had provoked discussion and mixed opinion as to which alternative was preferable. Mr J. R. Hamilton, General Manager at Leeds, operated and obviously favoured trackless trolleys. Overhead equipment cost £1,250 per mile, practically the same as at Bradford, working expenses averaged 4.01d per car mile and capital charges 1d per car mile, making a total cost of 5.01d per car mile. Mr C. J. Spencer, of Bradford, was not quite so sanguine, his working expenses being 6.6d per car mile and capital charges 1d per car mile, making a total of 7.6d per car mile, but the price of current was 1d per unit compared

to 0.43d in Leeds. Mr Luntley, of Wolverhampton, reported that the total running costs of his Albion petrol buses were 7.25d per car mile. Rotherham was reported as about to open a trackless trolley route incorporating several novel improvements and the Association looked forward to the results of their experience with interest.

Mr Bulfin gave a resumé of the presentation. Arguments in favour of trackless trolley cars had been that they used the same motors and gearing as electric tramcars and that the motive power was inexpensive; they were faster and more reliable than petrol buses; and motor maintenance was much cheaper than for petrol engines. However, if traffic did not develop on an experimental trackless trolley route, expensive infrastructure had to be scrapped. Other disadvantages were the additional initial cost of £1,250 per mile for overhead work and a lack of flexibility, in that trackless trolley vehicles could only work a suitably equipped route. Petrol buses needed no expensive fixed infrastructure, nor were they restricted to suitably equipped streets; in the event of one route not paying, the buses could be moved to another. Such buses cost about the same as trackless trolley vehicles; there was a good second-hand market value for modern motorbuses if it was found necessary to dispose of them; and their reliability had much improved in the previous five years. On the other hand, petrol bus engines were not as reliable as the electric motors of trackless trolleys, their average speed was lower, whilst repairs and maintenance probably cost more. The Association felt that no definite opinion could be given for another year.

With respect to Bournemouth, Mr Bulfin pointed out that the Board of Trade had a Bill for trackless trolleys before Parliament. If approved, the Board of Trade would be able to grant Orders, instead of prospective undertakings having to embark on the complicated and expensive procedures of a Parliamentary Bill, for trackless trolley operations. He anticipated that, by the time the Board of Trade proposals had become law, more reliable figures as to the advantages and economics of each system of traction would have become available.

On 11th October 1912, the Secretary of the Boscombe Progress Association wrote to the Tramways and Parliamentary Committee calling attention to *"the necessity of providing some suitable vehicle for passenger conveyance to and from the Boscombe seafront"* and suggesting a trackless car, to which the Town Clerk replied that the Council was not in a position to adopt the suggestion. The same request was repeated on 13th January 1913 and the General Manager was accordingly instructed, on 24th January 1913, to consider the matter. A local resident, Mr Langley Smith, wrote on 11th March 1913 about the same subject.

Mr Bulfin reported on 17th March 1913 on the relative merits of Trackless Trolleys and Petrol Omnibuses for use in Boscombe.

"On the suggested route for the system, namely, Boscombe Arcade to the Boscombe Pier, I have been in correspondence with those using the latest type of petrol-electric bus, and the opinion is that the gradients are such as almost to make it prohibitive for petrol buses to be used. This bears out our own experience with petrol and petrol-electric vehicles on the same route in past years.

"In regard to trackless trolleys, no such difficulty is entertained, as at the present time long grades of 1 in 15 are in daily use and in the present Session of Parliament a Bill is being promoted for a route, the grades on which are as high as 1 in 7. The brakes are capable of stopping the cars on a grade of 1 in 15 at a speed of 20 mph in a distance of 25 yards. The cost of the vehicles under either system is practically the same, £700 to £800, each capable of accommodating 28–30 passengers.

"In the event of the Committee agreeing to a system of public vehicles on this route, I would suggest that a larger scheme be adopted namely from Boscombe Arcade to Boscombe Pier and thence along the Under-cliff Drive to Bournemouth Pier and Bournemouth Pier Approach, with a terminus in the Square. Should such a scheme be approved, I recommend trackless trolleys with the use of trailers[*] on the seafront from Boscombe Pier to Bournemouth Pier Approach. The poles for the overhead equipment would be planted at the foot of the cliffs, thereby causing as little obstruction and unsightliness as possible, at the same time removed from storms and erosion. The poles could also be used for lighting on Undercliff Drive."

The estimated total cost for such a scheme was given as:

Promotion of Bill	£ 1,500
2½ miles overhead at £1,350 per mile	£ 3,125 *(sic)*
8 cars and 4 trailers	£ 7,600
Cables and connection	£ 1,000
Sundries	£ 375
Total	£13,600

---

[*] The mention of trailers is interesting. No British system ever used trailers, although they were already commonplace in Germany and Austria.

Mr Bulfin estimated working expenses at 6.75d per car mile and capital charges at 2.25d; receipts at 11.5d; giving a profit of 2.5d per car mile. Based on a five-minute service from 10.00 am to 10.00 pm, March to September inclusive, an estimated 150,000 miles pa would be operated, yielding an annual profit of £1,500. However, a 15-year loan would have to be incurred to finance the project.

Meanwhile, on 28th February 1913, a film and talk on trackless trolley vehicles was given at the Electric Theatre, in Commercial Road, Bournemouth, at which representatives of both Bournemouth and Poole Corporations were present, the evening being chaired by the Mayor of Poole. On the following day, 1st March 1913, the *Bournemouth Directory* included suggestions for a railless traction scheme for the Branksome Park, Canford Cliffs, Lilliput and Sandbanks area, as an extension of the Bournemouth Corporation tramway network was felt impracticable. Behind the scheme were Messrs Clough Smith, tramway and trolleybus overhead wiring contractors. The routes they proposed were:

1. County Gate – Sandbanks, via The Avenue, Western Road, Haven Road, Canford Cliffs Road, Flaghead Road, West Road and Banks Road

1A. From a junction with Haven Road along Ravine Road for 3.78 chains

2. Poole (Park Gates East), via Sandbanks Road and Lilliput Hill Road to a junction with West Road

2A. From Shore Road to West Road

A local company was subsequently formed to promote the scheme, which seems to have been known variously as The Poole, Sandbanks and Westbourne Electric Car Co Ltd; The Poole, Sandbanks and Westbourne Rail-less Traction Co; and The Sandbanks Railless Electric Car Co. Ltd.

Clough Smith were well known as designers, contractors and rolling-stock suppliers in relation to tramways and thus became involved with early trolleybus systems. These included the overhead wiring installations at Aberdare and Hove (1914 – both Cedes-Stoll[*] systems); vehicle suppliers for Teesside (1919, in association with Straker-Squire); and the complete installations at Chesterfield (1926) and Darlington (1927). Despite their Sandbanks endeavours, however, they never actually

---

[*] The Cedes-Stoll system used two closely-spaced trolley wires, the current being collected by a small four-wheeled carriage running on top of these wires and connected to the vehicle via a flexible cable.

operated a railless trolley car system themselves, although their overhead wiring activities with relation to trolleybuses continued until the 1960s.

At their meeting of 18th April 1913 the Town Clerk reported to the Tramways Committee that the matter of trackless trolley cars and petrol omnibuses had also been before the Beach Committee, who had recommended that a sub-committee be formed for full consideration, with a subsequent report to the Joint Tramways, Roads and Beach Committees. At the same Tramways Committee meeting a letter was read from a committee appointed to improve transport in the districts of Branksome Park, Canford Cliffs, Lilliput and Sandbanks, together with the district lying between Lilliput and Parks Gates East. Their Secretary asked for Bournemouth Council's co-operation and support in a proposed application for Parliamentary powers to construct a trackless trolley system in Poole from County Gates to The Haven (a hotel on the Sandbanks Spit, which led to the access road and the area in general being similarly named). This letter was referred to the newly-established special sub-committee.

The special sub-committee was appointed later in April 1913 and presented its report on the proposed Undercliff Drive Trackless Trolley route to the Tramways Committee Meeting on 23rd May 1913. They felt it inadvisable to proceed further until construction of the Undercliff Drive was complete. It was suggested that Bournemouth Council take no action on the Branksome Park proposals as the area was in Poole, Dorset, and outside their jurisdiction. They further suggested that the Town Clerk monitor the Council's interests during the progress of the proposed application for Parliamentary powers by the private promoter in Poole, which turned out to be the Poole, Sandbanks & Westbourne Rail-less Traction Co., supported by Clough, Smith & Co.. The Tramways Committee adopted these recommendations.

Mr Bulfin reported to the Tramways Committee Meeting of 20th June 1913 on his attendance at the Municipal Tramways Association, Managers' Section Meeting, on 5th/6th June 1913 in Sunderland.

"I took the opportunity of my visit to the North to inspect the different systems of trackless trolley at Bradford, Leeds and Keighley in order to see the latest developments and to test the ease of running and convenience to passengers on such a system after they have been running some considerable time. In each case I find that the original vehicles are being withdrawn and are to be superseded by vehicles of a stronger and more efficient type, the new designs being based on the experience gained from running the chain-driven original types. Bradford and Leeds have adopted the

RET system with chain and gear driven vehicles, the chain in each case being a weak point and a great source of trouble.

"The trackless trolleys in each of these towns ply over every class of road surface – wood paving, sett paving, tar macadam and ordinary granite and from the point of view of comfort to passengers, it becomes absolutely necessary that the roads traversed should be thoroughly well maintained. No trouble has been experienced in these systems, either with the trolleys or the motors.

"In Keighley, which has only just been opened, they are experimenting with the "Cedes-Stoll" system, in which there are no gears or chain-drive, the motors being in the hub of the rear wheels. The system, if it proves satisfactory in practice, should be the ideal one, but I have great doubts myself as to the practicality of the motors."

He concluded with reference to petrol vehicles both in bus and tramcar (London County Council and Morecambe) form.

On 28th October 1913 Bournemouth Council approved that application be made in the 1914 Parliamentary Session for powers to extend the tramways along Charminster Road, from the Capstone Road turn as far north as The Indian Hut at the junction with Hankinson Road. They also asked that the Tramways Committee consider the question of tramway extensions in general, together with the provision of alternative modes of transport as feeders to the tramways.

Also in 1913, local residents proposed that a tramway (or, failing Parliamentary approval, a trackless trolley route), be built between Wimborne Road, Moordown and Kings Road, via Charminster Road. Nothing further was heard about the tramway extension, but a notice in the *Daily Echo* appeared shortly afterwards stating the intention of The Bournemouth and District Railless Traction Co. to apply for a Bill in the next session of Parliament for the operation of trackless trolleys in that part of Bournemouth.

At the 19th December 1913 Tramways Committee Meeting a copy of the Bournemouth & District Railless Traction Co.'s Bill proposing *"a system of electrically propelled trolley vehicles"* along Charminster Road, Charminster Avenue and Malvern Road was presented. Fearing competition, the Tramways Committee recommended that the Bill be opposed. In the same meeting an application was made to the Board of Trade for a loan to operate motor omnibuses on routes between a) Alumhurst Road and Westbourne Arcade; b) Boscombe Arcade and Boscombe Pier; and c) Charminster Road (Queens Park Avenue) and Cemetery Junction.

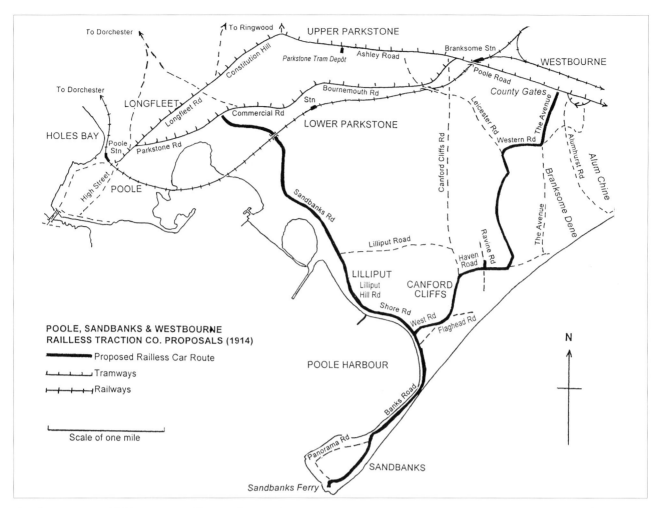

POOLE, SANDBANKS & WESTBOURNE
RAILLESS TRACTION CO. PROPOSALS (1914)

━━━━ Proposed Railless Car Route

└┴┴┴┘ Tramways

├┼┼┼┤ Railways

└─────────┘
Scale of one mile

N ↑

On 3rd January 1914, both the Poole, Sandbanks and Westbourne Rail-less Traction Co. and the Bournemouth District Railless Traction Co. formally deposited their Bills in the House of Commons. Both Bills were subsequently withdrawn.

The Poole, Sandbanks and Westbourne Rail-less Traction Co. (Clough Smith) had sought powers to construct and operate railless cars along three routes:

- County Gates – The Avenue – Western Road – Canford Cliffs – Haven Road – Shore Road, to the Haven Hotel at Sandbanks (a 6.56-mile-long line similar to the first section of the Branksome Park and Swanage Light Railway proposal of 1906)

- Poole Park East Gates (Parkstone tramway junction) – Sandbanks Road – Lilliput Hill Road – Shore Road – Sandbanks

- Ravine Road, Canford Cliffs to a depot at Westlands

Poole Council had already indicated that it was willing to grant all permissions, subject to Board of Trade approval, with the proviso *"that the company be prepared to sell the undertaking as a going concern after a period of 15 years"*. This could have made Poole a trolleybus operator in its own right by 1929, had the

scheme gone further, but the outbreak of the First World War in August 1914 finally sealed its fate and nothing was heard thereafter.

In February 1914, Clough, Smith & Co. Ltd. had written on behalf of the promoters of the Poole, Sandbanks and Westbourne Railless Traction Bill, to ask if Bournemouth Council would permit them to take their current supply from the tramway feeder cable in Parkstone Road. The Tramways Committee were obviously not in favour, whilst the Town Clerk reported that he had already lodged a Petition against the Bill. Later in the month, the Poole, Sandbanks and Westbourne Railless Traction Bill led to further discussion at a Tramways Committee Meeting and, following a meeting with the company, clauses for the protection of Bournemouth Corporation were incorporated in the draft Bill. Agreement was reached on 20th March 1914 and Bournemouth Corporation withdrew their Petition.

Following a meeting between a deputation from the promoters and the Council's Sub-Committee, the Bournemouth District Railless Traction Bill was withdrawn in February 1914. In September 1914 the promoters' solicitors wrote to ask why Bournemouth Corporation Tramways had withdrawn the Charminster Road motorbus service. The Council responded that there had been few passengers and that the service had been operated at a loss. Motorbus services later commenced between County Gates and Sandbanks in 1916, operated by an undertaking known as Bournemouth & District Motor Services Ltd., trading as the "Silver Fleet".

A seemingly unconnected public meeting, held in November 1914, suggested that trolleybuses should be used to extend public transport the short distance from the Queens Park Hotel (at the junction of Ashley Road with Holdenhurst Road) to the Queen's Park Golf Pavilion to serve the football ground. Nothing further was done until a trolleybus branch was constructed in 1934.

Trackless Cars Ltd. of Leeds demonstrated an advanced, front-wheel drive, dropped rear axle, double-deck trackless trolley vehicle on trade plates at the Tramways and Light Railways Congress held in Bournemouth on 22nd/23rd June 1922. The vehicle was fitted with a particularly ungainly body built by the Blackburn Aeroplane and Motor Co. Ltd. at their Olympia Works, Roundhay Road, Leeds. During its stay, the vehicle was housed at the tramways' Central Depot in Southcote Road. No additional trolley wires were erected, a skate for the return current trailing in the tram rails.

A leading article on railless electric traction published in the 15th June 1922 edition of *Tramway and Railway World* included illustrations of the vehicle in Bournemouth. After the Congress, it was taken to the London United Tramways' Fulwell Depot, where it was inspected by senior staff of the London & Suburban Traction Co. Ltd. (the holding company behind the London United Tramways, the Metropolitan Electric Tramways and the South Metropolitan Electric

Tramways). It was possibly demonstrated in Haydon's Road, Merton. It was subsequently sold, for a fraction of its actual cost, to Leeds Corporation. Here it was registered NW 5550 and given fleet number 513. It entered service in January 1924, only to be withdrawn by 1st January 1926 and scrapped a year later.

It was at this time the Royal Commission on Transport stated an opinion that:

"it will be to the advantage of the towns where they [the tramcars] *exist to get rid of them by degrees, and to substitute trackless trolley vehicles or motor omnibuses, as some authorities have done already. The substitution of the trackless trolley vehicles may ultimately prove to be the best solution in certain cases (or at all events it may form an economic transition from the tramcar to the motor omnibus), as already observed, the use of generating plant which supplied power for the trams can be continued, and the only serious cost involved consists in adapting the overhead equipment for trackless trolleys … and the provision of new vehicles."*

The topic of trackless trolley vehicles was not mentioned again in the Tramways Committee Minutes until 20th February 1925, when, in response to criticism of tramways and their apparent obsolescence, Mr Bulfin referred to the financial burden on tramway operators from which all road users benefited. Reference was made to the re-laying of the Poole line and possible trackless trolley vehicle substitution. Bournemouth's trams, he said, carried 60–70 passengers within an extreme width of 6ft 6ins. Trackless trolley vehicles and motor omnibuses, on the other hand, carried half that figure but were 12 inches wider, indicating that twice the number of vehicles would be required to carry the same number of passengers. Comfort required perfect road conditions and only small towns had given up their

The Trackless demonstrator at the Leeds works of the Blackburn Aeroplane & Motor Co. Ltd. in June 1922, being prepared for its journey to Bournemouth. It had a central entrance and staircase, with 34 seats in the upper and 30 in the lower saloon. The mainly transverse seating had sprung cushions and padded backrests. The stepped-frame chassis enabled all the traction equipment to be placed at the front and the body lower-set, reducing the height of the entry steps. The motors were placed on the fore-carriage, fore and aft of each axle, each wheel being driven by one of the two traction motors through a pinion on the motor spindle and an internal gear ring fixed to the wheel.
Blackburn Aeroplane & Motor Co. Ltd.

tramways, e.g. Chesterfield (3.5 million passengers yearly and 17 cars); Ipswich (5.5 million passengers and 36 cars); and Keighley (4 million passengers and 12 cars).

Mr Bulfin believed that the sole reason these towns had given up their tramways was because the track had worn out. Capital charge for renewing permanent way seemed so high that these undertakings had preferred to spend their money on new rolling stock as a *substitute* for the trams. If finance had been available to renew the permanent way, trams would undoubtedly have been retained. Although Birmingham, Bradford and Leeds operated trackless trolleys, they were in small numbers compared to the trams, e.g. Birmingham had 12 trackless trolleys compared to 658 tramcars; Bradford 19 compared to 250, and Leeds 14 compared to 362. None of these towns intended to scrap their tramways. He made the further point that the maximum permitted speed of trackless trolley vehicles was 12 mph whereas trams were allowed to travel at up to 20 mph. In his opinion trackless trolley vehicles were suitable for taking over a service which had been built up by motor omnibuses, but they required turning circles and regular attention to their steering. He added that since the end of the Great War, Bournemouth had spent £250,000 reconstructing its tramways, and quoted some interesting statistics:

- Bournemouth tramways, assessed on rails, cables, etc., paid almost £4,000 pa in rates, equal to a 1d rate.

- Road maintainance cost £15,000 pa, equal to a 4d rate.

- Annual capital charges on an outstanding amount in excess of £500,000 were £60,000, equal to a 1s 5d rate.

Bournemouth's tramways had never received financial support from the rates but, if they were abandoned, these charges would have to be met by the ratepayer.

	Trams	Motor Buses	Trackless Trolleys
Seats	70	30 – 40	30 – 40
Cost (£)	2,500–3,000	1,200–1,800	1,800–2,000
Life	20 years	5 years	5 – 10 years
Max speed	20 mph	12 mph	12 mph
Width	6ft 6ins	7ft 6ins	7ft 6ins – 7ft 10ins
Cost/mile	15.52d	12–18d	16.57d Aberdare
			17.49d Halifax
			17.65d Keighley
			12.15d Birmingham

Note that the table mentions trackless trolleys with a width of 7ft 10ins – even though road vehicles at that time were limited to a width of 7ft 6ins.

Mr Bulfin estimated that to convert the Poole tram routes to trackless trolley operation, entirely new overhead equipment, costing between £10,000 and £15,000, would be required, as the existing traction poles would be unable to take the additional strain. Some 30–35 vehicles would be needed to meet existing traffic demands, costing £60,000–£70,000. Road surface improvements would cost £25,000. The annual charge, of £6,930, on the Poole Light Railways would be payable until 1934. There was also no assurance that an application to Parliament for an Act or Order for the installation would be approved. In May 1925, the MoT sanctioned a 20-year loan of £30,000 for track reconstruction on the original Upper Parkstone portion of the Poole Corporation Light Railways, and work commenced in October 1925.

The Bournemouth and Poole Tramway Committees Joint Committee agreed on the future of the 2.09-mile-long Lower Parkstone tram route at their meeting on 18th March 1927. This line, which deviated from the main Christchurch – Bournemouth – Poole Station tram route some 60 yards west of Branksome Railway Station and rejoined the main line at Poole Park, had been constructed by Poole Corporation and worked by Bournemouth as part of the agreement covering any additional lines in the Borough of Poole following the takeover of the Poole and District Electric Traction Co. in 1905. Tramway services had started on 3rd August 1906 as already recorded. As Bournemouth Council was unable to obtain a Provisional Order to run motor buses outside their area, and Poole Corporation had no powers to run motor buses themselves, it was agreed that Poole should promote in the next Parliamentary session a Bill to operate motorbuses in their own right on any part of the route of the Poole & District Light Railway (except between Poole Terminus and Park Gates East, and within the County Borough of Bournemouth except with the consent of the Bournemouth Council). In the meantime the Lower Parkstone tram track was patched up to enable trams to continue operating safely until buses could be substituted. Towards the end of December, the MoT sanctioned a £20,000 loan for the proposed abandonment, road reinstatement and the purchase of replacing motor buses.

At their 12th March 1928 meeting, the Tramways Committee were advised that Poole Council planned to delegate the omnibus operating powers to Hants &

Dorset Motor Services Ltd. (who, therefore, attended to discuss possible arrangements in respect of any route where their bus services would be competitive). By mid-June 1928 certain concessions had been obtained in favour of Bournemouth Council. Trams stopped running along the Lower Parkstone line from 5th January 1929 and the removal of redundant tram track started at the end of that month.

Mr Bulfin briefed the Tramways Committee on 18th October 1929 about adding a clause to the proposed Borough Boundary Extension Bill for the provision of a trackless trolley system. At the same meeting the Committee approved the purchase of a small quantity of tram rail to be used for repairs only. Committee Members were taken by Corporation motorbus to Hastings and Maidstone to inspect the newly-inaugurated trackless trolley systems in those towns the following week. Whilst in Maidstone, and as a direct result of what they had seen, the Tramways Committee held a meeting at which it was unanimously agreed to recommend that powers be sought in the Boundary Extension Bill to run trackless trolleys on all existing tram routes in the Borough. Appropriate notices were subsequently posted on all routes in the Borough. This eventually became the Bournemouth Corporation Act, 1930, which also encompassed both motor bus operation and the necessary relationships with competing bus companies.

A report on a suggested scheme for operating express motor buses on routes paralleling the tram system was also presented. The decision provoked correspondence from ratepayers, to which the Town Clerk replied that there was (at least in December 1929), no proposal yet before Council to abolish the tramways or to establish a trolley vehicle system.

During the Tramways Committee Meeting on 10th March 1930, the Town Clerk submitted the Ministry of Transport's report on Part IV of the Bournemouth Corporation Bill (Tramways, Trolley Vehicles and Omnibuses) and referred to the petitions against this part of the Bill.

An independent advisor to Bournemouth County Borough Council, Mr A. R. Fearnley, General Manager of Sheffield Corporation Tramways, recommended the purchase of H&D's bus operations within Bournemouth, the areas to be added to the Borough, and between Bournemouth and Christchurch, if suitable terms could be arranged. Council representatives and Mr Fearnley negotiated with H&D and reached agreement on 24th March 1930 at a cost of £9,000 plus legal fees. This, it turned out, was well timed, as it was only a few months before the Road Traffic Act, 1930 – the Act which strictly regulated the operation of motorbus services for the next sixty years – reached the statute book.

The Bournemouth Corporation Act 1930, which received Royal Assent on 1st August 1930, amongst other things extended the Boundaries of the Borough of Bournemouth and empowered the Mayor, Aldermen and Burgesses of the Borough to run trolley vehicles and

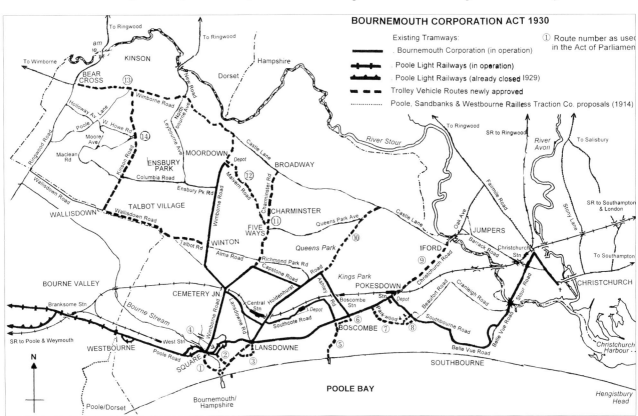

Sunbeam MS2 LJ 7701 operating on the experimental service to County Gates, photographed at the stop on the south side of the Square in 1933. Old Christchurch Road is visible in the background. The vehicles were not allocated fleet numbers during the period of hire. Note the destination blind "County Gates" and the passing tram. *Bournemouth Transport (D. L. Chalk collection)*

omnibuses within and beyond the borough and to abandon and discontinue the tramways of the Corporation. As a result, the County Boundary between Hampshire and Dorset was adjusted to include the parishes of Kinson and Holdenhurst in the Borough of Bournemouth, on the Hampshire side.

Under the provisions of the Act the estimated cost of the provision of trolley vehicles and motorbuses was as follows:

(a)	Provision of trolley vehicles	£300,000
(b)	Provision and adaption of electrical equipment and the construction of other works necessary for working such trolley vehicles	£157,000
(c)	Provision of omnibuses	£300,000
(d)	Erection and adaption of buildings for use by trolley vehicles and omnibuses	£ 80,000
(e)	Reconstruction of the roads upon which tramways to be removed and discontinued under this Act are situate	£ 63,000

Power was also given to work trolley vehicles along 14 new routes, the total authorised mileage being 30 (see Appendix L).

Another opportunity was offered to the Tramways Committee, together with Council members who wished to accompany them, to see a trackless trolley system in operation, with a visit to Wolverhampton on 27th/28th November 1930. The Council was cautious as to how best to replace the tramway system, which still had an outstanding debt of £311,000, so it was decided

Three-axle AEC 663T/English Electric trolleybus LJ 7702 seen at the loading island on the south side of the Square, having turned around the tramway waiting rooms. Note the service number (25) and destination "Holdenhurst Road". Note, too, the heavy trolley gantry and (just visible) the trolleybooms. The bonnet and dummy radiator were a short-lived fashion that made the vehicle look very much like the motorbus it was eventually to become. Further photos of this vehicle can be found in Appendix A. *A. B. Cross (G. Robbins collection)*

Two-axle AEC 661T/English Electric trolleybus LJ7703, also seen at loading island on the south side of the Square. It is just possible to make out the trolley gantry and booms. Further views of this vehicle can be found in Appendix A.
Bournemouth Transport (D. L. Chalk collection)

experimentally to convert a short section of tram route to trolleybus operation.

Only on 20th January 1933 was the trial route chosen, namely Bournemouth Square to County Gates, Westbourne, where the existing one-way traffic scheme around Seamoor Road already followed by the tramways provided a ready-made terminal loop. It also encompassed Commercial Road and Poole Hill, the steepest gradient on the tramway system, excluding Richmond Hill. The fact that all future overhead wiring work on the trolleybus system was carried out by the Transport Department itself indicates that they probably did the conversion for the trial route too.

Four different prototype trolleybuses were hired. They were garaged at the tramways' Central Depot in Southcote Road, which was reached by using one trolley arm on the tram (positive) wire and a trailing skate in the tram lines. As the trolleybus followed the alignment of the tram track it was accompanied by spectacular flashing as the skate made erratic electrical contact.

The experimental trolleybus fleet comprised a Sunbeam MS2 three-axle trolleybus with Weymann double-deck bodywork; an AEC 663T three-axle and an AEC 661T two-axle trolleybus, both with English Electric double-deck bodywork; and a Thornycroft two-axle trolleybus with Brush single-deck bodywork. They carried registration marks LJ 7701–4 respectively, these marks being issued at the start of the hire. The three double-deckers were delivered with conventional rear open platforms and finished in the then standard Bournemouth motorbus livery of primrose with two maroon bands. The single-deck Thornycroft, however, was originally blue which, coupled with its speed of up to 40 mph, earned itself the nickname *Bluebird*.

Perhaps having unwillingly given up their services within the extended County Borough of Bournemouth boundaries, H&D submitted an offer in January 1931 to

Few views exist of the two experimental AEC vehicles, and rear views are especially rare. This view shows LJ 7703, the two-axle AEC 661T, on the County Gates service in 1933. *S. E. Harrison (J. C. Gillham collection)*

Thornycroft trolleybus LJ 7704 – one of the only five trolleybuses ever built by this manufacturer – is seen here on the experimental County Gates route during 1933. This vehicle originally carried Hampshire registration CG 4313, but gained its Bournemouth registation before it entered service in the town. *S. E. Harrison (J. C. Gillham collection)*

purchase Bournemouth Corporation Transport, but were informed that the Council were not under any circumstances prepared to dispose of their undertaking to a company. From 22nd May 1931 the Tramways Committee was renamed the Transport Committee.

On Saturday, 13th May 1933, Bournemouth's experimental trolleybus system was inspected and approved by Colonel Woodhouse of the MoT, public service being inaugurated at 12 noon. The Sunbeam and the two-axle AEC started the service off, the Thornycroft single-decker following on 15th May 1933 and the three-axle AEC trolleybus on 23rd May 1933. There is no evidence, photographic or otherwise, that any of the vehicles carried fleet numbers during the experimental period; indeed, there was no reason to believe at this stage that these vehicles would be purchased should a trolleybus system be permanently established.

The fare from Bournemouth Square to Westbourne was 1d and, in connection with a self-printing ticket machine

which was introduced experimentally on the route from 27th February 1934, the service number 25 was used – although this was not yet displayed on the trolleybuses themselves. This suggests that the service number series 21 – 28, at least, had already been earmarked for trolleybus services.

The AEC 663T was on show at the Electrical Convention held in Bournemouth during the week commencing 12th June 1933. Also in June 1933, possibly in connection with the same event, London United Tramways 61, an experimental three-axle AEC 691T trolleybus with LGOC centre-entrance 74-seat bodywork, was loaned to the Corporation and operated on the experimental route.

Mr Bulfin reported to the Transport Committee meeting of 19th June 1933 on his initial and very positive experiences of operating trolleybuses and recommended that the vehicles be licensed for a further 3 months' service. Trolleybuses had at last arrived in Bournemouth!

London United 61 (AHX 801), an AEC 691T with LGOC bodywork, on demonstration on the experimental trolleybus route in June 1933. It is seen here at the eastern end of Seamoor Road, Westbourne at the top of Alum Chine Road.

M. P. M. Nimmo collection

<table>
<tr><td colspan="2">CHAPTER
THREE</td><td># Replacing the Trams</td></tr>
</table>

The trolleybus experiment proved a complete success, revenue covering both running and hire costs. Accordingly, on 22nd September 1933, the Transport Committee accepted Mr Bulfin's recommendations as follows;

(a) *That the policy to be adopted in connection with the transport of the town shall be the substitution of an Electric Trolley Bus system in place of the present tramways; such replacement to be undertaken as and when general circumstances and track renewals demand.*

(b) *After full consideration of the different routes, that the first to be taken in hand to be the Ashley and Holdenhurst Roads route to the Square.*

(c) *That the experimental service of Electric Trolley Buses from the Square to County Gates be made permanent and the necessary licences renewed.*

The full Council adopted these recommendations on 7th October 1933 and decided to replace the trams with trolleybuses over a three-year period.

A month later the Transport Committee instructed Mr Bulfin to arrange for the outright purchase of the four trolleybuses currently on hire and, in December 1933, they recommended that £7,345 be borrowed for this purpose under the provisions of Section 237 of the Bournemouth Corporation Act 1930. The individual purchase prices negotiated were: Sunbeam MS2 £2,000; AEC 663T £2,042; AEC 661T £1,853 and the Thornycroft £1,450. The vehicles were added to the department's fleet as numbers 68–71 respectively, 67 being until then the highest-numbered motorbus. The hire costs had been 3.921d per mile with receipts of 14.87d per mile. Some mileage statistics, unfortunately over widely different periods, were recorded on the 1¼ mile long experimental route:

Vehicle		Miles	Period
Sunbeam MS2	LJ 7701	244	13.05.33 – 02.06.33
AEC 663T	LJ 7702	3,300	23.05.33 – 07.07.33
AEC 661T	LJ 7703	34,000	13.05.33 – 30.07.34

Despite having re-laid and partially doubled the tram lines (in two stages, in 1914–15 and 1922), the Ashley Road and Holdenhurst Road route was the logical initial tram-to-trolleybus conversion as it passed the main access point to Central Depot, Southcote Road. In

November 1933 there was correspondence with the Ministry of Transport about plans for the route, and work started on preparing specifications and inviting tenders for twelve three-axle double-deck trolleybuses.

On 22nd December 1933, the tender of W. T. Glover & Co. Ltd., one of seven received, at £2,580 9s 4d, for the Ashley Road feeder cables, and that of the Sunbeam Motor Car Co. for twelve 56-seater three-axle double-deck trolleybuses at £2,135 each, were accepted. In the latter case, composite bodywork with separate rear entrance and front exit was stipulated. The bodywork order was shared equally between Park Royal and English Electric.

Preliminary arrangements for the start of the Square – Ashley Road trolleybus service also revealed recommendations that the tramway stopping points in Shelley Road, Grants Avenue, Shelbourne Road and at The Markets (Holdenhurst Road) be discontinued, and also the fare structure of the new trolleybus service as described in Appendix E.

At the Transport Committee meeting of 20th April 1934, the General Manager was instructed to prepare plans for the introduction of trolleybuses on the routes between a) Moordown and Bournemouth Square; b) Moordown and the Lansdowne; and c) Cemetery Junction and Castle Lane. This led to a Transport Committee Resolution at their May 1934 meeting that trolleybuses should replace trams on these routes and that tenders be invited at once, including 36 additional double-deck trolleybuses but excluding tram track removal, at an estimated cost of £123,493. On streets in which both trams and trolleybuses were expected to operate for any length of time, trolleybus wiring was to be hung between the tram wires and the kerb, using bracket arms instead of the tramway span wires wherever necessary.

Rather than seek an additional town centre terminus, it was felt that the turning circle at the Square, which had been provided for the experimental Westbourne route could be modified for use by trolleybuses from Moordown and Charminster Road (although, to provide trolleybus parking space, kerbside parking in Avenue Road might have to cease). The Superintendent of Police asked that the number of trolleybuses waiting at the

Sunbeam MS2 trolleybuses 72, 73 and four others, together with AEC 663T 69 at the rear, in Southcote Road on 21st June 1934 (the day before the Ashley Road extension opened). The generating station and cooling towers are visible at the rear. *Bournemouth Transport*

proposed Avenue Road stop at any one time be limited to five. In the event, the Richmond Hill trolleybuses were provided with their own circle of wiring independent of the "Main Road" routes. The question of the Moordown terminus was referred to a sub-committee and Mr Bulfin was instructed to advertise for the trolleybuses required.

The Transport Committee meeting of 19th June 1934, whilst rejecting a petition to retain the Grants Avenue stop, heard that the vehicles and overhead equipment for the Square – Ashley Road route had been inspected and passed by the MoT. Twelve Sunbeam MS2s (72–83) were delivered between 8th June and 27th July 1934.

The Parliamentary Secretary to the Minister of Transport, Lt. Col. C. M. Headlam, DSO, MP, provisionally accepted the invitation to attend the trolleybus inauguration ceremony. Invitations were also sent to the Municipal Tramways & Transport Association; the Incorporated Municipal Electrical Association; the Tram-

way, Light Railways & Transport Association; the Editors of the *Electrical Railway, Bus & Tram Journal; Transport World; Motor Transport;* the local press; and senior management of the Sunbeam Motor Car Co., Ltd., Park Royal Coachworks, English Electric and The British Thomson-Houston Co., Ltd.. The Mayor of Bournemouth invited guests to lunch at the Royal Bath Hotel to meet the Parliamentary Secretary to the Minister of Transport. Thereafter, guests were taken to the Town Hall to join those attending the inauguration ceremony.

Thus, on 22nd June 1934, the Westbourne – Bournemouth Square trolleybus service was extended under the new wiring to Ashley Road, Boscombe, and trams ceased operating along Holdenhurst Road except for depot access purposes. Two services were operated:

25 Square – Lansdowne – Central Station – Holdenhurst Road – Ashley Road, Boscombe

25A Westbourne – Square – Lansdowne – Central Station – Holdenhurst Road – Ashley Road, Boscombe

73 (AEL 401) heads west up Commercial Road towards Westbourne, decorated for the Ashley Road opening day, 22nd June 1934. The clock tower on top of the Square tramway passenger waiting room is visible to the rear of the trolleybus. Other decorated vehicles wait in Avenue Road.
D. L. Chalk collection

It is not known if service 25 started and terminated on the south side of the Square (at the stop previously used by the experimental service to Westbourne), or if Gervis (pronounced 'Jarvis') Place was used. The new portion of trolleybus route was 2.7 miles long and resulted in the withdrawal of twelve trams.

Like the trams before them, the trolleybuses followed separate routes between the Square and Horseshoe Common. Whilst the outbound wiring was along Old Christchurch Road, the inbound wiring turned south from Old Christchurch Road at Horseshoe Common into Fir Vale Road, reaching the Square via St. Peter's Road and Gervis Place. The route then continued to the Lansdowne and up Holdenhurst Road, with a junction opposite Central Station giving access to the Central Depot in Southcote Road. A reversing triangle was installed at Capstone Road. Further along Holdenhurst Road, the wiring turned south into Ashley Road towards Boscombe, where a terminal loop was constructed whereby the wiring turned east into Christchurch Road (paralleling the Lansdowne – Pokesdown tram route), then north into Portman Road and finally into Gladstone Road (two roads which had not previously been served by trams) before rejoining Ashley Road.

Central Depot was accessible both from Holdenhurst Road along Southcote Road and also from Boscombe, with wiring along Christchurch Road from Ashley Road as far as Palmerston Road, then up Palmerston Road and along St. Clement's Road to the eastern depot entrance. This paralleled the tramway access in both directions but was unusual in having a three-wire layout (two negative wires and one positive) along Southcote Road and a short section at the south end of Palmerston Road,

although conventional, single track wiring sufficed for the rest of Palmerston Road and all of St. Clement's Road. Scheduled trolleybuses did not serve these roads at any time in the life of the system, although passengers were carried on depot runs, stops being located in St. Clement's Road as well as on the motorbus route in Southcote Road.

Trolleybuses were high on the agenda of the 20th July 1934 Transport Committee meeting. Firstly, the General Manager was instructed to prepare plans for a) the Lansdowne – Southbourne – Christchurch tram route conversion; and b) for the introduction of trolleybuses along Christchurch Road between Pokesdown Station and Iford Bridge. Secondly, it was recommended that six more trolleybuses be ordered as a follow-on to the original Sunbeam contract. These were again Park Royal-bodied Sunbeam MS2 vehicles which became numbers 84–89. They were delivered in October 1934, bringing the trolleybus fleet up to 22.

Receipt of further correspondence regarding the deletion of the Grant's Avenue and Shelbourne Road tram stops led to their reinstatement until further considered by the Committee. However, the stops at Portchester Road and Windham Road, just north of Bournemouth Central Station on Holdenhurst Road, were discontinued and replaced with one at Ophir Road. Finally, the Roads Committee was asked for permission to erect a temporary queue barrier on the north side of the Square for passengers waiting for Ashley Road trolleybuses.

On 26th July 1934, the Committee inspected one of the new trolleybuses at Central Depot, Southcote Road and suggested some design modifications. Presumably these

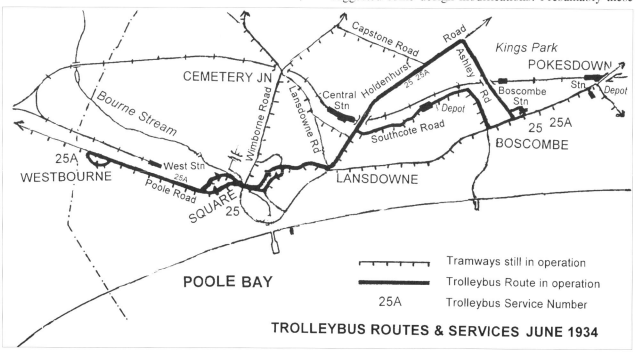

	Tramways still in operation
	Trolleybus Route in operation
25A	Trolleybus Service Number

TROLLEYBUS ROUTES & SERVICES JUNE 1934

were of a mainly superficial nature, the finer details of which have not survived.

The thirty-year lease of the tramway between County Gates and Poole Station through Upper Parkstone was now approaching expiry. By the early 1930s major track renewals and doubling were becoming urgently necessary; thus, in line with plans for the rest of their own tramway network, Bournemouth Corporation secured powers under a Provisional Order to substitute trolleybuses. On 1st August 1934, however, the Poole Town Clerk wrote to inform the Bournemouth Transport Committee that the Poole Transport Committee were unable to recommend that their Council should agree to the substitution of the existing tramways with trolleybuses. At the same time Hants and Dorset Motor Services (H&D) made an offer to take over the Poole tramways, pay off the outstanding loan and replace the trams with motorbuses. Somewhat daunted, Bournemouth Transport Committee instructed the Bournemouth Town Clerk, Mr H. Ashling, to find out Christchurch Council's views on a trolley vehicle service from Iford Bridge to Christchurch via Barrack Road.

H&D subsequently applied to the South Eastern Traffic Commissioners to operate replacement bus services in Poole, whereupon the Bournemouth Transport Committee authorised their Town Clerk and Mr Bulfin to oppose these applications. As a result the MoT wrote, at the end of September 1934, to invite Bournemouth Council to discussions about the proposed sale of Poole Council's light railway interests to H&D, and the Transport Committee recommended powers be sought for Bournemouth Corporation to operate transport services in the Borough of Poole.

In August 1934, the Town Clerk drew Mr Bulfin's attention to a number of legal points in connection with the planned Iford Bridge trolleybus extension. In his response, the General Manager interestingly asked that permission be sought for a trolleybus extension from Iford Bridge along Barrack Road and Stour Road to Christchurch with a turning circle in front of Christchurch Town Hall, which led to an informal contact with Wolverhampton Corporation Transport which was already operating trolleybuses in the areas of other local authorities e.g. Bilston, Coseley and Walsall.

The tramways terminated in Christchurch with two sidings in Church Street, an impossible terminal location for replacement trolleybuses. On 21st September 1934, following discussions, Christchurch Council gave their approval to the construction of a trolleybus turning circle

in Christchurch High Street outside the Town Hall when the tram service ceased. However, they did not agree to trolleybuses being extended from Iford Bridge along Barrack Road. Accordingly when, in October 1934, Christchurch Council requested a fare reduction on motorbus service 1 (Christchurch – Bournemouth) they were advised that this was impossible – although the introduction of trolleybuses would have permitted a substantial reduction!

On 3rd September 1934 the Transport Committee inspected the proposed Moordown terminus and recommended that application be made to the MoT to use "Old Wimborne Road", now Lawford Road, as part of a turning loop. They also considered the seven tenders received for the supply of 36 trolleybuses, of which the three lowest were:

Leyland Motors Ltd.	£72,360
English Electric Co.	£79,020
Sunbeam Motor Car Co.	£79,128

Mr Bulfin stressed the advantages of having a fleet of standard vehicles and equipment, whilst commenting on the electrical equipment offered by the tendering firms. Accordingly, on the next day the full Council accepted Sunbeam's tender for double-deck 56-seater trolleybuses, to be fitted with Park Royal bodywork with rear open-platform entrance and a folding front exit door.

The Transport Committee also adopted Mr Bulfin's recommendation that the extension of trolleybuses from a) the Square to the junction of Castle Lane West and Wimborne Road; and b) from the Lansdowne along Christchurch Road to Iford Bridge, be put in hand immediately the necessary approvals were obtained. Mr Bulfin reported that he was in negotiation in respect of a turning point at Iford Bridge. The following month, agreement was reached to purchase Council land on the north side of Christchurch Road on the Bournemouth side of Iford Bridge, between Bridle Crescent and the River Stour, for £2,250. The Committee also went on to seek authority for the purchase of a further 48 vehicles when required.

Subsequently, Sunbeam offered to supply the 48 additional trolleybuses as a "follow-on" to the existing order for a total cost of £101,304, some £4,200 less than the current contract, provided that the Council was prepared to accept delivery according to a mutually agreed programme over a nine-month period, commencing immediately following completion of the 36-vehicle contract. The Transport Committee were happy to accept this clause, which was aimed at retaining jobs at Sunbeam and Park Royal during the prevailing difficult economic climate.

A short branch, which also served the Dean Court football ground, opened on 20th October 1934. Where the trolleybuses turned south off Holdenhurst Road into Ashley Road and towards Boscombe, parallel wiring (but not a turnout frog) was installed for some distance to permit vehicles to continue the 350 yards north east along Holdenhurst Road as far as Littledown Avenue and the Queen's Park Golf Pavilion. Trolleybuses had to repole in Holdenhurst Road until a junction was installed at a later date. On 19th October 1934 (and again on 13th November 1934) instructions were issued to conductors that, on service 25 trolleybuses operating to Queen's Park Golf Pavilion, any passenger wishing to travel to the terminus should be allowed to do so without further charge; and also that passengers might be picked up at the same point again without additional charge. With police approval, the trolleybus waiting area at Queen's Park Golf Pavilion turning circle was moved to the other side of Holdenhurst Road sometime in the autumn of 1935.

Tenders for feeder cables, conduits, section boxes, etc., for the Iford Bridge extension were invited for submission by 25th October 1934. There were 17 replies, that of Messrs W. T. Glover & Co., Trafford Park, Manchester, at £14,774 6s 1d being accepted by the Council at their 30th October 1934 meeting, notwithstanding that Glover's past work had provoked a number of insurance claims relating to unprotected work, implements and unlit open manholes etc.. To minimise the number of lay-offs in the difficult economic climate, Mr Bulfin was able to arrange with Glover's that 63 seasonal conductors and cleaners not engaged in winter could be employed on cable-laying work for the expansion of the trolleybus system.

The Negotiating Sub-Committee met with Poole Council again on 7th November 1934. Poole Council requested an annual minimum amount in respect of the capitation fee in connection with the proposal to run trolleybuses instead of trams on the Upper Parkstone route. Bournemouth Transport Committee recommended that the Bournemouth offer be amended to include a guaranteed minimum of £3,500 pa but, at the end of the month, the Town Clerk reported that Poole Council had not responded to the revised offer, nor to their proposal that the MoT suggestion – to submit the matter to an independent expert – be taken up. On 21st December 1934 the Town Clerk reported that H&D had deposited the Poole Road Transport Bill for the operation of motor-bus services in that town. The Transport Committee therefore resolved that the Town Clerk should lodge an objection to this Bill and that H&D's applications to the South Eastern Traffic Commissioners also be opposed.

At their meeting on 22nd February 1935, the Transport Committee made a recommendation that the Corporation promote a Parliamentary Bill to operate trolleybuses in the Borough of Poole over the existing light railway route between County Gates and Poole Station, with installation of a reversing triangle proposed at Serpentine Road, just short of the railway crossing. Poole Town Council, however, retaliated by promoting a Bill seeking powers to acquire and abandon the tramways and replace them with motorbuses operated by H&D. The latter passed through the usual stages of Private Bill machinery, gaining Royal Assent on 2nd August 1935. Meanwhile, on 21st May 1935, the South Eastern Traffic Commissioners granted Poole's request and gave dispensation for services to commence prior to the Bill receiving Royal Assent. H&D motorbuses began to operate the day following the expiry of the tramway lease (7th June 1935), the company paying Poole Town

Sunbeam MS2 82, with English Electric bodywork built to a Park Royal design, heads a row of MS2s with both makes of bodywork in Holdenhurst Road at the opening of the Queen's Park Golf Pavilion branch, 20th October 1934.
G. O. P. Pearce
(D. L. Chalk collection)

Council £75,000 for the tramways and a contibution of £7,500 towards the cost of removing the rails.

The Bournemouth Corporation Act 1930 had authorised Bournemouth to make application to the MoT for a Provisional Order to run trolley vehicles *inter alia* in the Borough of Poole with the consent of the Corporation of Poole with the stipulation that this consent could not be unreasonably withheld. Bournemouth Corporation duly applied but objections were received from Poole Corporation, Dorset County Council and H&D.

As H&D's proposed Poole working agreement was not sanctioned by the MoT, they promoted a Parliamentary Bill to gain sanction to the agreement. To combat this, Bournemouth Corporation also promoted a Bill in the same tribunal and for the same purpose as the Provisional Order already applied for, leading to a post-ponement of the hearing of the Provisonal Order pending the hearing by the Parliamentary Committee of the petitions for the Bills. This led to protracted negotiations leading to the provisional agreement of May 1935:

a) Passengers picked up and set down within 150 yards of County Gates were also to be considered Corporation passengers; at all other points surrounding Bournemouth an imaginery line was drawn 440 yards outside the boundary and passengers picked up between this line and the actual boundary were also considered Corporation passengers unless a supplementary 1d fare was paid.

b) Corporation Inspectors could board H&D buses within the Corporation area and the 440 yard extension referred to above.

c) H&D would not introduce any fare concessions in addition to those already issued by the Corporation.

d) H&D vehicles travelling to/from the west would not stop in the Square without Corporation approval.

Noting plans to operate trolleybuses on Richmond Hill, the MoT instructed that vehicles must be equipped with coasting brakes to limit their downhill speed, and emergency run-back brakes to offer more safety when travelling uphill. The coasting brake was a specialised form of rheostatic braking (not to be confused with the rheostatic brake with which most trolleybuses were equipped) which limited the vehicle to a pre-set speed (8 mph in Bournemouth) when coasting down a gradient. The brake was independent of the power supply and, once selected, no further action was needed by the driver. The heat produced was dissipated throughout the descent rather than confining it to a period of heavy braking at the bottom of the hill. The run-back brake

prevented a trolleybus running backwards out of control on a gradient. A special contactor was energised and held open during normal running but, if there was a dewirement, power failure or voltage overload, the contactor closed and completed the braking circuit, limiting backward speed to 2 mph and giving the driver an opportunity to steer into the kerb or even chock the wheels. Under normal circumstances no action was required. If contact with the overhead line was maintained, however, on Bournemouth's vehicles it was necessary for the driver to switch off a circuit breaker manually to permit the run-back brake to operate – an important point in potentially a moment of panic !

Although the MoT later stipulated the use of a coasting brake for trolleybuses descending specified steep gradients in Bournemouth, Brighton, Hastings, Huddersfield and London, its earliest use of such regulatory power was in relation to the 1 in 8 (12.5%) gradient of Richmond Hill, Bournemouth.

The Council approved the purchase of British Thompson-Houston coasting and run-back brake equipment at a cost of £18 10s per vehicle and its attachment to the 84 trolleybuses then on order. On 21st December 1934, the Transport Committee approved Sunbeam's offer to supply and retrospectively install the additional equipment to those trolleybuses already in service for £25 per vehicle. Trolleybus operation on Richmond Hill began on 7th June 1935. In all, Bournemouth purchased 166 coasting brake-equipped trolleybuses (plus seven acquired secondhand many years later from Brighton and already so equipped), the maximum fleet thus equipped at any one time being 127.

On 31st December 1934 the Christchurch Town Clerk wrote to the Transport Committee with regard to the proposed turning circle in High Street, Christchurch and asked that an alternative site be considered. At the same time, the Christchurch Ratepayers' Association wrote to support any application to operate trolleybuses in their borough, as they were convinced that this would lead to lower fares both in and out of Christchurch Borough. The Boscombe Ratepayers Association, meanwhile, supported the Bournemouth Council in its promotion of a Bill to unify transport services in the Boroughs of Bournemouth, Poole and Christchurch, noting that the trolleybus was the recognised transport system of the future in Bournemouth's view. In January 1935, the Bournemouth Corporation (Trolley Vehicles) Provisional Order was duly deposited and all requisite notices served. The Town Clerk subsequently advised that six objections had been received.

The next stage in the system's development was the introduction of services to Iford. Trolleybus overhead wiring was erected paralleling the tram route along Christchurch Road between the Lansdowne and Palmerston Road, Boscombe, where the existing connection to the Central Depot in Southcote Road branched off, and eastwards as far as Pokesdown Station. Where the tram route swung south into Seabourne Road, the trolleybus wires continued down the hill through new housing developments in Christchurch Road, past the junction with Castle Lane East, where a turning circle was provided on the north side of Christchurch Road just before Iford Bridge. Trolleybuses did not directly replace a tram or motorbus route, although motorbus service 1 (Square – Purewell), which had commenced on 6th November 1930, also operated along Christchurch Road.

The inspection of the Lansdowne – Iford Bridge trolleybus route by Lt. Col. E Woodhouse was scheduled for Friday 22nd March 1935, commencing at the Lansdowne at 10.15 am. Subject to the line being passed for traffic, a formal opening was planned for 3.00 pm on Wednesday 27th March 1935, some three weeks earlier than originally planned.

Alderman F. B. Summerbee, Chairman of Bournemouth's Transport Committee, stated that the Corporation hoped to have the Square – Moordown route open by Whitsun 1935, with the Square – Castle Lane West and Lansdowne – Moordown routes open by the end of June 1935. Dealing with trolleybus fares he went on to say that, taking them as a whole, the average distance for a penny would work out at 1.06 miles, as against 0.98 miles on the tramways.

Mr Bulfin reported very satisfactory traffic returns for the Ashley Road – County Gates, Westbourne trolleybus service. From its inauguration on 22nd June 1934 until 20th September 1934 a quarter million more passengers had been carried than in the 1933 period of mixed trolleybus/tram operation. The period 20th September 1934 to 17th October 1934 showed an increase of 65,024 passengers over the number carried by trolleybuses and trams in the same period in 1933. Subsequent traffic returns showed continuing passenger growth.

Comparative traffic returns showed continuing passenger growth:

From 22nd June 1934 until	Trolleybus and tram	Trolleybus	Increase	Increase per week
21/11/34	3,298,801	2,848,555	450,346	20,470
12/12/34	3,647,009	3,105,188	541,821	21,672
16/01/35	4,266,866	3,562,592	704,274	23,476
13/03/35	5,178,618	4,246,627	931,991	24,526
15/05/35	6,272,461	5,145,899	1,126,562	23,969

During trolleybus driving training, drivers were paid only half their wages for the days (other than rest days) on which they received instruction, for it was essential that training was completed within seven weeks.

The Ministry of Transport Inspector's Report on the Lansdowne – Iford Bridge route, dated 28th March 1935, makes interesting reading:

"The new route, which is three miles in length, lies wholly within the Borough, and connects, at the Lansdowne, with the existing trolley vehicle route from the Square to Ashley Road, whence it follows Christchurch Road to a turning circle at Iford which has been constructed off the highway on land acquired by the Corporation. For about 2 miles from the Lansdowne the route follows the line of the existing tramway to Christchurch, which leaves it at Seabourne Road, Pokesdown. This tramway will continue in operation for the present. From Seabourne Road to the Iford terminus the route forms Route No. 9, authorised by the Bournemouth Corporation Act, 1930.

"The carriageway is of ample width throughout, and its surface, which is partly of wood blocks and partly of tar

Following withdrawal, the body of tram number 1, Bournemouth Corporation's sole single-deck passenger car, was placed at Iford Bridge trolleybus turning circle for use as a waiting room. This photo shows one of the Sunbeam MS2s, presumably in an official "posed" view as the offside destination indicator is set to "Reserved".

D. L. Chalk collection

Top: Sunbeam MS2 210 (ALJ 967) is seen here pulling out of Gervis Place at the Square on a service 23 working to Tuckton Bridge. It is wearing the latter-day livery, and has been fitted with flashing trafficators. Note the porcelain switchgear behind the driver (who is dressed in his summer drill jacket). This vehicle carried fleet number 93 until it was renumbered in 1958.
F. W. Ivey

Centre: This rear view of Sunbeam MS2 205 (formerly 84) was taken at the western end of Columbia Road. The trolleybus, on service 31, has just turned right out of Kinson Road and is heading towards Winton and the Square.
F. W. Ivey

Bottom: A venerable but spotless 212 (formerly 99) waits at the service 26 terminus at Castle Lane West, having just turned out of Lawford Road. Note the standard BCT-pattern passenger waiting shelter and the parallel wiring enabling vehicles from Broadway to overtake. *M. Eady*

Turning on the tight circle at Southbourne Cross Roads, 210 (ALJ 967, formerly numbered 93) is in its final state with built-in auxiliary destination display in the front between-decks panel and "segment" style flashing direction indicators. The 1935 Sunbeam MS2 is on a service 22 working to the Square. *M. Eady*

macadam, is in good condition. Lighting is by gas, the fittings being carried on the poles supporting the overhead work; the lamp brackets have been raised where necessary to give sufficient clearance for double-decked vehicles. There are no severe gradients, the steepest being one of 1 in 14 for a length of about 5 chains. The route crosses the Southern Railway near Pokesdown Station; I was informed that the Company have raised no objection to trolley vehicles crossing the bridge in question.

"The Iford turning circle is concrete surfaced and its dimensions are such that there is room for 1 or 2 trolley vehicles to stand there, without interference with those turning. A disused tramcar body has been adapted as a shelter for waiting passengers. The lighting of the turning circle appeared to be inadequate and the Transport Manager undertook to install extra lamps before operation over the route commences.

"On the section traversed by the tramway the overhead work is partly of span wire type; elsewhere double

brackets with poles on both sides of the road, are used. The latter form of construction is employed almost exclusively between Seabourne Road and the Iford terminus; none of the brackets exceeds 16ft in length. All new poles are of BS section, reinforced as a rule. The existing poles, of the heavy tubular section with un-welded joint which have been in use for many years, have been carefully examined and reinforced internally; they appear to be standing the additional load satisfactorily.

"The overhead contact wire is 4/0 grooved, mainly of copper, though some cadmium copper has been installed as an experiment. Triple insulation, positive to earth, is provided throughout. Current is supplied from the Corporation's tramway generating station, the positive and negative feeding points being as shown on plans 5, 6 and 7 which accompanied the Transport Manager's letter of 26th February 1935. Section switching arrangements comply with Requirements and all feeder pillars and poles carrying section switches are earthed to copper earth plates.

Sunbeam MS2 208 (ALJ 64, formerly numbered 88) is parked out of service at the Triangle, with its booms lowered. Behind is parked a Leyland Titan PD2 motorbus, while a post-war BUT 9641T trolleybus passes by in the background. *C. Aston*

"Guard wiring, of which there are a few spans near Pokesdown Station, is carried on full sized insulators and complies with Requirements. Elsewhere telephone crossings (which are few in number) are run in insulated wire, and hooks have been provided where a P.O. line runs alongside the route. The Post Office representative expressed his satisfaction with the arrangements which have been made.

"The proprietor of Hunt's Garage, Pokesdown, complained to me of the position of a pole outside his premises, which had been planted so close to the kerb that it was liable to damage the wings of cars drawn up to a petrol pump. As the presence of underground mains prevented this pole being set in the normal position, it was arranged on the spot that it should be re-sited at the back of the footpath, on the property belonging to the garage, span wire construction being substituted for double bracket at this point.

"The service over this route will be carried out by double-decked six-wheeled vehicles at intervals of about 8 minutes.

"At the request of the Transport Manager, I also inspected a short branch which has been made from the existing Holdenhurst Road – Ashley Road route, forming part of Route No. 10 authorised by the Bournemouth Corporation Act, 1930. This is about 350 yards in length and follows Holdenhurst Road, from Ashley Road as far as its junction with Littledown Avenue and Thistlebarrow Road, where a turning circle has been constructed. The carriageway width is ample and its surface, of the tarmac type, is in good condition. Span wire construction has been adopted, with triple insulation, the poles being of BS section, and the overhead contact wire 4/0 copper.

"This extension, and the intermediate turning point which it provides, will only be used occasionally, during daylight, to deal with traffic to and from football matches, etc., in Queen's Park [sic, the football ground being at Dean Court in Kings Park], to which it is adjacent. To avoid the necessity for facing points [and crossings] in the overhead work at the junction with the Ashley Road route, the contact wires leading to the extension have been run parallel over one span with those previously existing; it is the intention to transfer the trolley booms from one set of wires to the other during a stop at this point.

"Both on the Iford route and on the above-mentioned extension the work of equipment for trolley vehicle operation appeared to have been well carried out and I recommend that both be approved.

"No [Board of Trade] compulsory stops [for safety purposes] are recommended but Superintendent Deacon asked that request stops should not be fixed too close to traffic light signals, of which there are three sets on the Iford route. The Transport Manager agreed to fix such stops in consultation with the Police.

"I recommend the following speeds be authorised:

25 MPH

(1) in Christchurch Road between the Lansdowne and the Iford Terminus

(2) in Holdenhurst Road between Ashley Road and the Queen's Park turning circle.

5 MPH

(1) when passing below all overhead points and crossings

(2) when rounding all turning circles.

E. Woodhouse"

A through trolleybus service numbered 24A (Westbourne – Square – Lansdowne – Christchurch Road – Iford Bridge) was introduced at 3.00 pm on Monday, 25th March 1935, two days earlier than originally proposed. The Transport Department took this opportunity to introduce a new service numbering system whereby basic services carried a number whilst extensions and variations were given an alphabetical suffix. The trolleybus services now operated thus became as follows:

24 Square (Gervis Place) – Lansdowne – Christchurch Road – Boscombe – Iford

24A Westbourne – Square – Lansdowne – Christchurch Road – Boscombe – Iford

25 Square (Gervis Place) – Lansdowne – Central Station – Holdenhurst Road – Ashley Road, Boscombe

25A Westbourne – Square – Lansdowne – Central Station – Holdenhurst Road – Ashley Road, Boscombe

As far as Pokesdown Station the 24/24A trolleybuses paralleled the main Poole – Christchurch tram route, which continued to operate as before, although tram short workings to Boscombe ceased.

The 26th April 1935 Transport Committee meeting agreed to introduce a 1½d fare stage from Bournemouth Square to Boscombe Gardens on Service 24 and to a move of the existing bus stop at R. L. Stevenson Avenue, Westbourne, to Westbourne Arcade.

The Transport Committee interviewed the General Managers of the St. Helens, Blackpool and Burnley, Colne & Nelson undertakings, together with the Bournemouth Chief Assistant and Electrical Engineer, and on 3rd May 1935 appointed Mr Duncan Patterson Morrison from Hull as General Manager and Chief

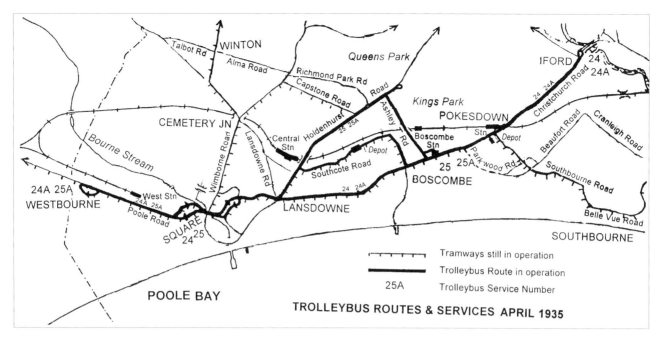

TROLLEYBUS ROUTES & SERVICES APRIL 1935

⊢─┬─┬─┤	Tramways still in operation
━━━━━	Trolleybus Route in operation
25A	Trolleybus Service Number

Engineer in succession to Mr Ignatius Bulfin, who retired having held the post since 1911. Mr Bulfin continued to live in Bournemouth until his death at the age of 80 in a Southbourne nursing home on 19th February 1954.

Mr Morrison had become General Manager and Engineer at Kingston upon Hull in 1931, having previously held the same position at Dundee. At the time of his appointment to Bournemouth he was 50 years old. He was a graduate of Durham University, where he had received a BSc in mechanical and civil engineering. After serving an apprenticeship, he became assistant engineer to Dick, Kerr and Co., Preston, then to Gateshead & District Tramways Co. of which his father, Mr William Morrison, was for many years General Manager. Later, Mr D. P. Morrison had become Chief Engineer and Assistant Manager to this company.

Later in the year, on 20th September 1935, Mr Wilfred Douglas Reakes, Area Traffic Superintendent of the United Automobile Services Ltd., Darlington, who was eventually to succeed Mr Morrison as General Manager, was appointed Traffic Superintendent.

Wooden "slip-boards" indicating the principal points en route, similar to those already in use on motorbuses, were mounted above the lower maroon band at lower saloon waist-rail level on the trolleybuses from the end of May 1935. Their use was discontinued later, when it was found that the vehicles so equipped exceeded the then maximum permissible width of 7ft 6ins. Also in May, notice was given to use part of the north side of Avenue Road above the Pleasure Gardens as a trolleybus parking space; and it was recommended that application be made again to Christchurch Corporation for consent

to extend the trolleybus route beyond Iford Bridge, along Barrack Road, to Stour Road, Christchurch.

Also, by May 1935, a provisional agreement had been formulated between Bournemouth Corporation and H&D, the key points of which were as follows:

1. H&D fares within the Corporation area could not be less than on Corporation services.

2. In line with the 1930s schedule agreement, the Corporation was to receive the revenue from all H&D passengers both taken up and set down on any one journey within the Corporation area less the cost of carrying such passengers. The Transport Department and H&D would serve the same stops in the Corporation area.

3. H&D passengers who were picked up outside the Corporation area and changed buses at the Square (including the H&D Bus Station) to continue their journeys and alight in the Corporation area were to be considered as passengers travelling totally within the Corporation area, both picked up and set down in the BCT area on the same journey as between the Square and the point where they were set down.

   Passengers who were picked up in the Corporation area and who changed buses at the Square to continue their journeys to points outside the Corporation area were to be considered as passengers both picked up and set down in the Corporation area on the same journey as between the points where they were picked up and the Square.

   The Square was deemed to be the commencing or terminal point (as the case may be) of all H&D services which entered or left Bournemouth.

4. H&D would pay £1,000 pa in quarterly payments.

In the short period between 7th and 28th June 1935, both trams and trolleybuses operated in service along Wimborne Road from Cemetery Junction to Moordown. Sunbeam MS2 98 (ALJ 972) is seen here passing tram 112 at Peter's Hill, Winton. Note how the tramway overhead wiring is suspended between the bracket arms. *D. L. Chalk collection*

5. H&D would not oppose any new routes for trolley vehicles or PSVs proposed by the Corporation within the Corporation area.

6. H&D would not apply for any new or additional routes within the Corporation area without the Corporation's consent.

7. The Corporation would not apply for any routes outside their area over which H&D were already operating without the company's consent.

8. H&D agreed to employ men displaced on the Poole Light Railways who could not be found employment by Bournemouth Corporation.

With Royal Assent being obtained for the Poole Road Transport Act, Bournemouth Corporation withdrew their application for a Provisional Order. Trams ceased running between Bournemouth Square and Poole Station on 8th June 1935, being replaced by H&D motorbuses operating from the Square Bus Station.

The withdrawal of the trams rendered 70 men surplus to requirements. Bournemouth Corporation Transport

submitted an initial list of 32 men, resident in Poole and employed for 15 years or less, to H&D suggesting their employment if satisfactory. A further list of 29 men in temporary employment was sent later.

On 7th June 1935, trolleybuses replaced trams between the Square and Moordown Depot via Richmond Hill and Wimborne Road, whilst on 28th June 1935 the connecting line between Cemetery Junction, Wimborne Road and Holdenhurst Road (Central Station) along St. Paul's Road and Lansdowne Road opened. The new trolleybus services were as follows:

26 Square – Richmond Hill – Cemetery Junction – Wimborne Road – Winton – Moordown

27 Square (Gervis Place) – Lansdowne – Central Station – St. Paul's Road – Cemetery Junction – Wimborne Road – Winton – Moordown

At Moordown, trolleybuses turned by driving into the depot forecourt and then reversing into Wimborne Road.

Sunbeam MS2 73 (AEL 401), built in 1934, and similar 134 (BEL 819) of 1935, seen passing tram 83 in Poole Road, Westbourne, during 1935. Note that the destination displays on the front and rear of these vehicles are of the original, short-lived layout (compare with photo on page 43)

D. L. Chalk collection

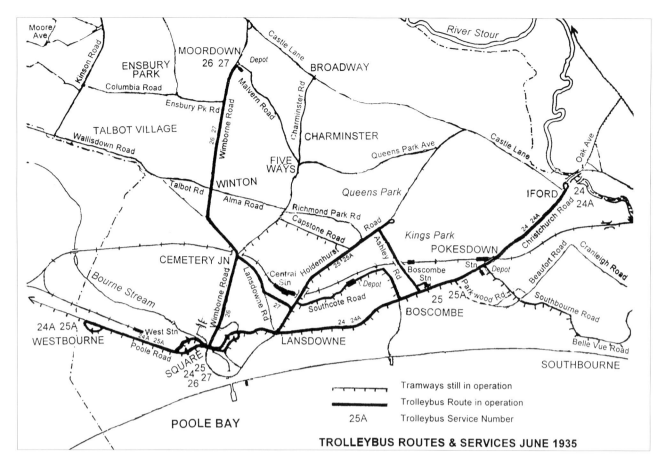

TROLLEYBUS ROUTES & SERVICES JUNE 1935

The trams had continued to Redhill Crescent, not more than one hundred yards beyond the depot, but to avoid unnecessarily complex overhead work, the tramway overhead wiring was cut back to the depot entrance for the three week period that both trams and trolleybuses operated along Wimborne Road. During the work to modify the overhead wiring at the junction of Waverley Road and Holdenhurst Road for trolleybus operation, a horse-drawn tower wagon toppled sideways as it was being manoeuvred, leaving the two linesmen hanging from the overhead. One fell and was slightly injured, while the other was brought down with a ladder.

In June 1935 the first batch of a new type of uniform was issued to staff, consisting of a double-breasted jacket with lapels in place of the tunic used until then.

The June 1935 Transport Committee Meeting recommended that the conversion of Pokesdown Station – Christchurch tram services for trolleybus operation should start in early September 1935 and, as a preliminary, a motorbus shuttle service began to operate on Monday 8th July 1935 between Pokesdown Station and Southbourne Cross Roads.

The *Bournemouth Echo* reported on 2nd July 1935 that:

"A start has been made with the work of constructing the overhead equipment for the trolleybus extension between
the Cemetery Junction and Castle Lane. The popularity of the trolleybus has been further demonstrated by the decision of Brighton Corporation to apply for powers to run trolleybuses in place of trams. The overhead tram wires have disappeared in Winton where the substituted wires for the trolleybuses are now in use. As in the bad old days of the tramcar a boy still has to operate a "points system" at Cemetery Junction, but they are now overhead and he now does it from a safer position on the pavement. The "narrow squeaks" that lad must have had while doing his job in the middle of a rushing stream of traffic must be "legion"."*

For the 1935 summer season, Southern Railway expresses were accelerated to bring Bournemouth within two hours of London, further encouraging tourism.

On 6th July 1935 the *Bournemouth Echo* published a letter from Bernard Curtis, of 87 Lansdowne Road:

"As a resident in the Lansdowne Road I wish to express my relief at the advent of the trolley-bus. The absence of the noisy trams has made my life now bearable. We find that the trolley-bus is the quietest of all the vehicles, much less noisy than the motorbus or an ordinary trade lorry. It seems to me that the trolley-bus is the very best mode of transit that can at present be devised; it is cooler, no heat from the engines (how the drivers of the motorbuses stand in this hot weather, I cannot imagine), no smell of petrol or fumes of the exhaust, the slight hiss

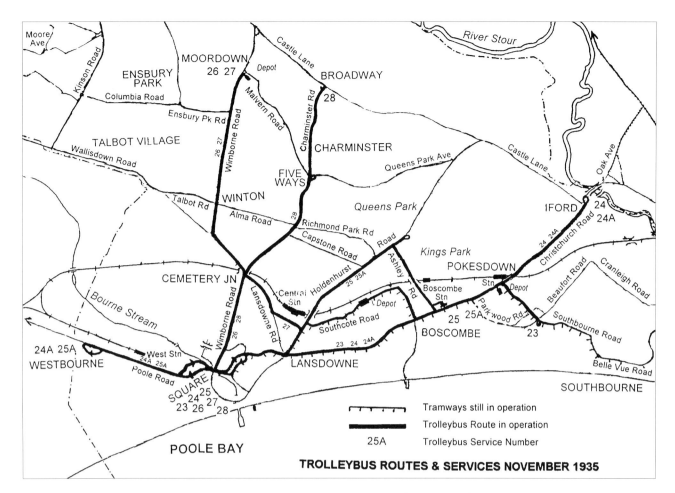

Tramways still in operation	
Trolleybus Route in operation	
25A	Trolleybus Service Number

TROLLEYBUS ROUTES & SERVICES NOVEMBER 1935

made overhead is not at all bothersome. When the tram lines, which are a menace to cyclists and a frequent cause of damage to motor tyres, are removed all will be well."

Mr Bulfin's Annual Report for the year ending 31st March 1935 contained a couple of interesting facts about the undertaking:

"The total output of current [from the Southcote Road generating station] amounted to 4,548,390 units, as compared with 4,362,110 units, some 186,280 more units than last year. This is due to increased trolleybus mileage being run. The coal consumed during the year was 5,629 tons, as against 5,335 tons last year. The total cost per unit, including all capital charges, worked out at 0.70d.

"In the year in question, on June 22nd, 1934, the trolleybus route from Ashley Road terminus (i.e. Christchurch Road) along Ashley Road, Holdenhurst Road to the Lansdowne and via Old Christchurch Road to the Square, was opened for traffic, the trams being taken off both the Holdenhurst Road and Ashley Road. On March 28th of this year the route from Iford Bridge to the Lansdowne was opened up for traffic, while on May 13th, 1933, the section from the Square to County Gates was opened up as a trolleybus route. The opening of these two routes, with the existing one, meant that a through service of trolleybuses was obtained between

Iford Bridge and County Gates, and between the Christchurch Road at its junction with Ashley Road, along Holdenhurst Road to County Gates, and, although it did not occur in the present financial year, a further section from Moordown to the Square was opened for traffic on June 7th. The receipts and running of these different systems have been very satisfactory."

In presenting his 24th and final Annual Report which recorded a deficit of £14,449 8s 4d after increased capital charges, income tax and the restoration of staff wages cut in the recession, and a fall in passenger numbers, Mr Bulfin had a valedictory message:

"During this period, not only has the Transport System not received any aid from the rates but they have contributed over £30,000 in relief on the rates. They have in the same period paid in rates to Bournemouth £83,182, to Poole £16,231, and to Christchurch £4,124. They have laid, maintained and kept in repair over one-third of the main road from Christchurch to Poole, and some miles of side routes in Bournemouth at an approximate cost of £18,000 per annum, and in this period they have run 55,885,657 miles, carried 632,490,720 passengers and taken in receipts £4,420,493. They have maintained a staff of over 700 and paid in wages in the period £1,895,360, and repaid capital to the extent of £710,150."

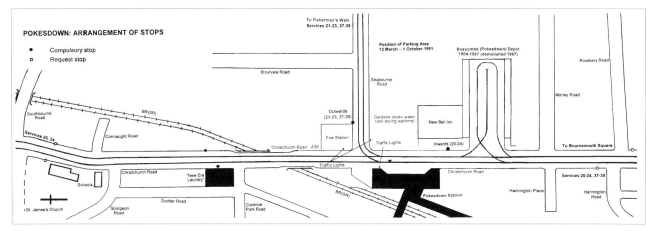

On 9th July 1935 the Negotiating Sub-Committee met Christchurch Corporation who were concerned about a pending BCT fare increase which included motorbus service 1 (Square – Iford – Christchurch) and who asked for the following concessions:

i)   the ordinary single fare between Christchurch Town Hall and Iford to be 2d with an intermediate 1d stage at Jumpers Road.

ii) the ordinary single fare between Christchurch Town Hall and Jumpers Corner to be 1½d.

iii) the ordinary single fare between Christchurch Town Hall and the Square to be 5½d.

iv) return tickets booked before 8.45 am to be available from any main fare stage along the route at the ordinary single fare.

Bournemouth's reply to the Christchurch Town Clerk was to the effect that, if Christchurch Council consented to and supported an application by Bournemouth

Corporation to run trolley vehicles along Barrack Road from Iford Bridge to Stour Road (and, if desired, along the continuation of Barrack Road to the High Street), Bournemouth Corporation would be prepared to grant more or less all the concessions requested. There was, however, a modification on the matter of return tickets booked before 8.45 am, as follows:

Christchurch Town Hall to Boscombe Arcade	4d
to Lansdowne	5d
to Bournemouth Square	6d
Jumpers to Boscombe Arcade	3d
to Lansdowne	4d
to Bournemouth Square	5d

The letter went on to suggest that the trolleybus service from Iford Bridge to Christchurch would be every eight minutes. It concluded by indicating that Bournemouth Council would be prepared to purchase property in Wick Lane and install a turntable and small depot there to house three vehicles, thus enabling the proposed turning circle at the Town Hall to be dispensed with.

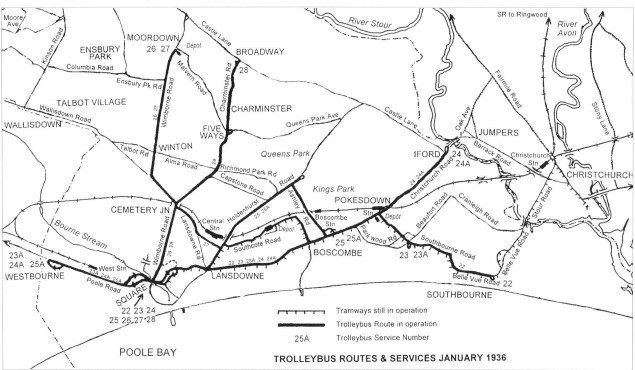

TROLLEYBUS ROUTES & SERVICES JANUARY 1936

Experimental Sunbeam MS2 LJ 7701, by this time numbered 68 and with changed lining on the front lower panels, seen at Littledown Avenue, Queens Park, followed by brand-new 98 in 1935. Note that both of these vehicles have had their destination boxes rebuilt to the new standard that was introduced with the delivery of the BEL-registered vehicles (126–149).

G. O. P. Pearce
(D. L. Chalk collection)

Christchurch Transport Committee could not agree to trolleybuses operating along Barrack Road. However a letter from a member of the public suggesting a turning point at Fisherman's Walk when the trolleybus service to Christchurch was introduced received a sympathetic hearing. Bournemouth's Transport Committee recommended that, subject to there being no objection from the MoT, a turning point should be installed there at once.

The *Bournemouth Echo* on 2nd August 1935 reported that a trolleybus had visited Christchurch High Street in the dead of night, using a single trolley arm on the tramway overhead wiring and a return skate in the rail, to test clearances.

During the year, London Transport loaned four trolleybus drivers from Fulwell Depot to train Bournemouth men. In the meantime, the overhead wiring teams worked north-wards from Cemetery Junction along Charminster Road but where the trams turned east into Capstone Road, the trolleybus wires continued along the full length of Charminster Road to its junction with Castle Lane West at the Broadway Hotel. From 23rd August 1935 motorbus service 4 was re-routed to run Kings Road – Capstone Road – Holdenhurst Road – Lansdowne (with a summer extension to Bournemouth Pier), instead of Broadway Hotel – Five Ways – Cemetery Junction – Square. The motorbus service thus covered those sections of the tram route not served by the new trolleybus service as follows:

28 Square – Richmond Hill – Wimborne Road – Cemetery Junction – Charminster Road – Five Ways – Broadway Hotel.

In September 1935 the MoT gave retrospective consent for the introduction of trolleybuses from Cemetery Junction, Wimbourne Road and Holdenhurst Road (Central Station) via St. Paul's Road and Lansdowne Road (services had started on 28th June 1935). Consent was given to the newly-completed Charminster Road extension from Cemetery Junction, Wimbourne Road and Castle Lane West, Broadway Hotel.

Although overhead construction along Charminster Road had been completed on 7th August 1935, road resurfacing between Alma Road and Castle Lane, and the correction of camber and elevations at road junctions before the route could be regarded as satisfactory, continued until 14th August 1935. Immediately thereafter, the invitation to the MoT Inspector, Major Wilson, was sent and the inspection took place on the afternoon of Thursday 22nd August 1935 in excellent weather. Major Wilson was accompanied by Police Superintendent W. Deacon, the recently-retired General Manager Ignatius Bulfin and his successor Duncan Morrison. The 1¾-mile extension included a turning circle at Five Ways, at the junction with Queens Park Avenue, and a terminal reversing triangle at Luckham Road. The warm, sunny weather saw joy-riders on the last open-top trams up Richmond Hill and Wimbourne Road to Capstone Road, which had paralleled the trolleybuses between the Square and Cemetery Junction since 7th June 1935.

Trolleybus services started first thing the next day, Friday 23rd August 1935, with capacity loads on the morning journeys, passengers being surprised at the new fares e.g. the Five Ways – Square return cost 2d, compared with 4½d return and 3d single on the motorbuses. Sadly the long-lasting excellent weather, with temperatures into the mid-eighties Fahrenheit, came to an end, the rain and additional terminating trolleybuses leading to severe traffic jams in the Square.

The passenger appeal of the new trolleybuses can be demonstrated with reference to the following traffic returns for service 26 (Square – Moordown) and service 27 (Square – Lansdowne – Moordown) compared to the 1934/35 tram figures:

From 07.06.35 until:	Trolleybus	Tram (1934–35)	Increase	Increase per week
17.07.35	685,051	481,566	203,485	33,914
17.09.35	2,021,247	1,505,171	516,076	36,863
09.10.35	2,496,330	1,873,685	622,645	34,591
13.11.35	3,007,250	2,267,410	739,840	32,167
11.12.35	3,401,059	2,558,813	842,246	31,194
15.01.36	3,914,890	2,959,257	955,633	29,864
15.04.36	5,171,719	3,884,200	1,287,519	28,611

The Roads Committee accepted responsibility for 41,502 square yards of road space where trolleybuses had replaced trams for an agreed payment of £15,540 15s:

> Square to Cemetery Junction
> Cemetery Junction to Moordown
> Charminster Road to Capstone Road
> Lansdowne to St. Paul's Road
> Capstone Road

Those portions of roadway occupied by tram lines (as defined in the Tramways Act, 1870) in Holdenhurst Road, from Central Station to the Queen's Park Hotel, and in Ashley Road, from the Queen's Park Hotel to Christchurch Road, Boscombe, were handed over to the Roads Committee on 10th January 1935. The Transport Committee contributed £4,326 towards the road reinstatement.

Attention now turned to the Pokesdown – Fisherman's Walk – Southbourne – Tuckton Bridge – Christchurch portion of the truncated mainline tram route between the Square and Christchurch. MoT inspection of the Pokesdown Station – Fisherman's Walk trolleybus extension took place on 20th November 1935 and, as planned, service commenced the next day. The new route was operated as follows:

23   Square (Gervis Place) – Lansdowne – Christchurch Road – Boscombe – Pokesdown – Fisherman's Walk.

The outward trolleybus stop for Fisherman's Walk was relocated outside the Fire Station, Pokesdown Station, whilst the inward one remained outside Boscombe depot as for the trams.

This trolleybus extension to Fisherman's Walk did not directly replace a short-working tram service on the Christchurch route but did lead to the 15-minute express motorbus service which had been operating Square – Southbourne – Christchurch (parallel to the trams) being cut back to run Fisherman's Walk – Christchurch only. When trolleybuses subsequently reached Southbourne Cross Roads, the short-working tram service to that point was withdrawn and the express motorbus service cut back further to run Southbourne – Christchurch only. Until then a 10-minute motorbus shuttle operated between Southbourne Cross Roads and Fisherman's Walk to connect with trolleybuses to the Square. A full 20-minute tram service between the Square and Christchurch continued to operate at the insistence of Christchurch Council until a through service of trolleybuses reached the town on 8th April 1936, whereupon the express motorbus service was also withdrawn completely.

MoT approval to operate trolleybuses between Fisherman's Walk and Southbourne Cross Roads was received in mid-December 1935 and the new services began operation on 23rd December 1935. Terminal loops were installed at Fisherman's Walk (Fisherman's Avenue) and at Southbourne Cross Roads (around the public conveniences in the junction of Southbourne Overcliff Drive and St. Catherine's Road). At Fisherman's Walk a trolleybus request stop was added at Grand Avenue, inward and outward, whilst the outward tram stop at Southbourne Cross Roads was moved further east along Belle Vue Road. The new service was:

22   Square (Gervis Place) – Lansdowne – Christchurch Road – Boscombe – Pokesdown – Fisherman's Walk – Southbourne Cross Roads.

Almost immediately, however, on 1st January 1936, trolleybus services to Boscombe and Southbourne were augmented by the introduction of:

22A Westbourne – Square – Lansdowne – Christchurch Road – Boscombe – Pokesdown – Fisherman's Walk – Southbourne Cross Roads.

23A Westbourne – Square – Lansdowne – Christchurch Road – Boscombe – Pokesdown – Fisherman's Walk.

The new General Manager was instrumental in the adoption of an improved destination layout on the undertaking's vehicles, and trolleybuses already in service were altered retrospectively. From November 1935, whenever a repaint took place the single-line final destination indicator boxes (with service number box immediately above at front and rear) were converted to a larger style which had been introduced with trolleybuses

An early view of Sunbeam MS2/
Park Royal 91 (ALJ 965) on service
21A at Christchurch Turntable.
G. O. P. Pearce
(D. L. Chalk collection)

126–149 then being delivered. All further deliveries were built to the new style by Park Royal. Screens now able to display four lines of destination information were incorporated into the front and rear between-deck panels of the earlier deliveries in a central position and the service number boxes moved to the right-hand (near) side of the new display at the front and to a position below the display immediately above the platform window on the nearside at the rear. The single-line tram-style ultimate destination boxes (which had ben salvaged from withdrawn trams), internally-mounted in the rear side windows of the lower deck saloon (both nearside and offside), were retained unchanged. The Transport Committee meeting on 24th April 1936 recommended that "cadmium amber lighting" be used to illuminate the destination blinds – but there is no record of this ever being done. More mundanely, work also started at this time on fitting heaters in the cabs of trolleybuses.

In January 1936 it was announced that the undertaking had recorded a deficit for the year ending 31st March 1935 of £5,999 15s 2d, which could not be met from reserves and was carried forward. Possibly seen as a way of increasing income to offset the deficit, the Lighting Committtee was asked for an annual payment of 2s for each lighting bracket attached to a trolleybus traction pole. As at 21st February 1936 there were 529 such attachments requiring a repaint every two years for a payment of 2s 6d each. The General Manager also reviewed operations with specific attention to surplus staff and petrol bus services. That same month the Transport Committee rejected an application to buy Boscombe Depot. Boscombe Depot continued to operate trams until April 1936, and was then used purely as a trolleybus store until it again came into use as an operating depot in 1940.

Having received a letter regarding overlapping fare stages on trolleybuses returning to the Central Depot, Southcote Road, 1d fares were introduced between Lansdowne and Central Depot via Southcote Road, and between Boscombe Arcade and Central Depot via Palmerston Rd.

On 21st February 1936, the Transport Committee rejected Ministry of Transport proposals for a new road layout at Cemetery Junction. Following a meeting between the Borough Engineer and General Manager they recommended, on 20th March 1936, that vehicle-actuated traffic lights be installed and that the trolleybus turning circle be removed to ease straight through running.

One months' notice was given in February 1936 to Christchurch (as required by Section 130 of the Bournemouth Corporation Act 1930) of intent to abandon the tramways operating in their Borough. To operate the replacement trolleybus services more vehicles had been delivered. Trolleybuses 90–125 entered service between 11th February and 18th June 1935; 126–149 between 8th August 1935 and 14th December 1935; and, finally, 150–173 between 17th December 1935 and 13th March 1936. All were Sunbeam MS2 three-axle vehicles with Park Royal H31/25D bodywork. The trolleybus fleet now comprised 106 vehicles, namely the four experimental vehicles (two AEC prototypes, the Thornycroft single decker and one Sunbeam MS2) and 102 Sunbeam MS2 three-axle standard-type 56-seat vehicles having rear entrance and front exit, twin staircases and driver operated folding doors at the front exit. This was to remain the largest single provincial fleet of trolleybuses of the same type in the country.

In September 1936 (and with standardisation in mind) the Weymann-bodied Sunbeam MS2 former demonstrator, by now numbered 68, was rebuilt with a front entrance, similar to that on the 1932 AEC Regent motorbuses, and fitted with a front staircase to match the standard trolleybuses. The non-standard AEC 663T three-axle and AEC 661T two-axle former demonstrators, numbered 69 and 70, were converted to petrol-engined motorbuses (in September–November 1936 and March–June 1936 respectively). Each vehicle required an AEC engine, gearbox, propellor shaft, radiator, exhaust pipe, silencer, 40 gallon fuel tank with Autovac equipment, brake gear including vacuum tank, Lockheed reservoir, new front springs to take the additional weight, lighting dynamo and a complete rewiring. The single-deck Thornycroft/Brush trolleybus, 71, was retained until 1943.

Pending complete reconstruction of Bournemouth Square (which was actually carried out in 1947), temporary measures for the coming summer season were discussed, including running all trolleybuses through to the Triangle with return via Avenue Road instead of turning at the Square. The Borough Engineer was asked to mark out suitable stops and, when approved, to add temporary queue barriers.

The Transport Committee Meeting on 27th March 1936 recommended that powers be sought to extend trolleybuses along Ensbury Park Road, from its junction with Wimborne Road to its junction with Boundary Road, Columbia Road and Redhill Drive, the construction of overhead to start immediately powers had been obtained.

The first reference to an alternative trolleybus terminus, in a pub yard off Church Street, Christchurch, adjacent to the tramways passenger waiting room, can be found in the Minutes of the Transport Committee meeting of 20th March 1936, when the lowest of five tenders for building work in the coach yard of the Dolphin Hotel, that of Bryant & Trowbridge, at £197 10s, was accepted. Of six tenders received for the supply and installation of a turntable, that of Sanderson Bros. Ltd., at £380, was also accepted. The MoT inspection of the Christchurch extension was scheduled for Wednesday 8th April 1936.

It had been apparent that additional current was needed for the summer season and, indeed, for the future in general. After negotiations with the Central Electricity Board and Bournemouth & Poole Electrical Supply Co. Ltd., the latter offered a ten-year agreement for DC traction current supply delivered at their substations at Electric House in Yelverton Road; Green Road, Winton; and Watcombe Road, Southbourne; for maximum loads of up to 500kW at point of supply. Charges under the ten-year agreement would be £4 10s for each kilowatt used in any half-hour in the months of January, February, November, December, plus a running charge of 0.3d per unit subject to price of coal and a service charge of £1,000 pa. Similar terms would apply at the company's Christchurch Substation (where existing agreements for agreed capacity of 400kW applied) if the total package was acceptable. The offer assumed the installation of mercury arc rectifiers at the substations, but no special provision for the handling of regenerative braking, with which all of Bournemouth's trolleybuses to date had been fitted.

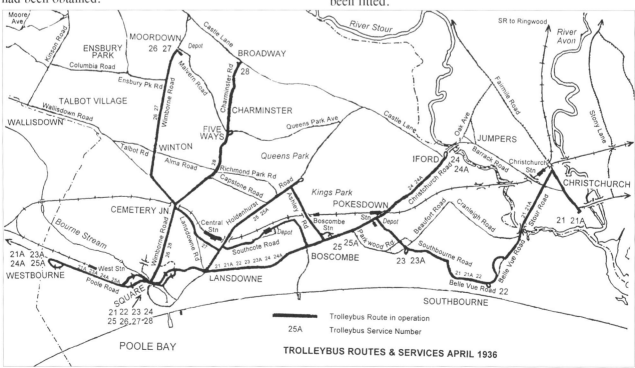

TROLLEYBUS ROUTES & SERVICES APRIL 1936

These arrangements were accepted, with capital expenditure to be borne by the Corporation, namely £3,500 for cables to connect to the supply paid out of the loan authorized by Section 237 of the Bournemouth Corporation Act 1930. The three substations and their equipment were provided and maintained by the company.

The last Bournemouth service tram, 108, left the Square at 2.15 pm on 8th April 1936 for Christchurch. On reaching Boscombe Depot it was joined by 115, bedecked with flags and special placards, carrying the Mayors of Bournemouth and Christchurch together with a group of civic officials. The two trams, picking up ordinary passengers *en route*, made their way to Tuckton Bridge, where a trolleybus was waiting to carry the civic party on to Christchurch terminus and back to Christchurch Town Hall for tea. The 10th April 1936 edition of the *Times & Directory* newspaper included the following article in its review of the trolleybus extension to Christchurch:

"The work of installing the overhead equipment for the extension of the trolleybus system from Southbourne Cross Roads to the Priory Town and the making of temporary arrangements for a terminus in the yard of the Dolphin Hotel, Church Street, Christchurch was pushed forward rapidly of late in order that the service might be in complete working for Easter. Only yesterday morning an Inspector of the Ministry of Transport inspected the extended route. He gave his permission for the trolley buses to be operated but an hour or so before the inaugural ceremony. The civic party disembarked from the tram at Tuckton Bridge where they boarded the first trolleybus on the extended route back to Christchurch. Before they left, the Mayor of Bournemouth declared open the section of the route from Southbourne Cross Roads to the Bridge and the Mayor of Christchurch that section from the Bridge to the Christchurch terminus.

"Ald. Summerbee handed to the Mayor of Christchurch (Councillor D. Galton) the first trolleybus ticket into Christchurch and to the Mayor of Bournemouth (Alderman H.G. Harris) the last tram ticket out of the Priory Town to Bournemouth. The trolleybuses were instituted in Bournemouth in June 1934 by Ald. Edgecombe, then Mayor. The trolleybus route from Southbourne Cross Roads to the Square (which for a few weeks ran only as far as Fisherman's Walk) had been in operation about 3 months. Taking the running costs of 10d per mile, the service had produced £2,222 over and above the running costs.

"The aggregate of trolleybus passengers from all services 1st April 1935 and 1st March 1936 had been 19,111,838 and yet there were people who said the trolleybuses were not popular. They were getting a return of 14.61d per car mile.

"In respect of the service opened that day it was intended to operate from Christchurch a 12-minute service but whether it would remain would depend on the support received. The new service would allow for a minimum saving of 11 minutes on the journey Bournemouth to Christchurch.

"On route 26 from Moordown to the Square from June 1935 to March 1936 with trolleybuses as compared with the same period the year previous with trams there had been an increase in the number of passengers of 597,829. The gross profit after allowing for the costs of running at 10d a mile for the trolleybuses was £6,768 against a gross profit on the trams of £2,799. Thus the trolleybus showed an increased profit of £3,969. The trolleybuses showed in addition a saving in running expenses of £909. Also on that route they had run 68,878 more miles, which meant that the public were getting a very much better service than before".

Two further trolleybus services were introduced as a result of the Christchurch extension:

21 Bournemouth Square (Gervis Place) – Lansdowne – Christchurch Road – Boscombe – Fisherman's Walk – Southbourne Cross Roads – Tuckton Bridge – Christchurch

21A Westbourne – Bournemouth Square – Lansdowne – Christchurch Road – Boscombe – Fisherman's Walk – Southbourne Cross Roads – Tuckton Bridge – Christchurch

Services 22 and 22A were suspended with effect from 8th April 1936, because the through-running trolleybuses to Christchurch along the same route offered sufficient capacity.

Trolleybus fares between Southbourne Cross Roads and Christchurch were held at the same level as those in use on motorbus service 2.

The new route featured a crossing of the River Stour over Tuckton Bridge, a reinforced concrete structure built in 1905 for the tramway extension to Christchurch. The overhead wiring on Tuckton Bridge was held by bracket gantries spanning the road, whilst the traction poles mounted in the deck of the bridge received extra support from metal buttresses across the footpath to the metal railings. Trolleybuses were prohibited from passing on the narrow bridge and were subject to a maximum speed limit of 10 mph. The Bournemouth Corporation Act, 1930 (paragraph 103), granted Christchurch Corporation the right to buy that part of the trolleybus system in their borough on the last day of 1955 or on the last day of every subsequent seventh year, if they so wished.

CHAPTER FOUR

The System Develops

The complete changeover from tramway to trolleybus operation, originally planned to take three years, was completed in just 22 months. Yet, despite having operated costly duplicate services during this period, the enormous growth in traffic promoted by the trolleybuses (passenger levels on service 26 increased by 31% in its first year of operation), albeit at lower fares, ensured a net profit of £10,000 on trolleybus operations in the financial year ending 31st March 1936 after paying all interest charges on capital expenditure. The trolleybuses were indeed a major success !

The Transport Committee Meeting of 19th June 1936 considered eight routes for trolleybus operation, as follows:

1. **Kinson – Wimborne Road:** from the junction of Columbia Road and Kinson Road, proceeding along Columbia Road and Ensbury Park Road to the junction of Ensbury Park Road and Wimborne Road.

2. **Ensbury Park Hotel – Ensbury:** from the junction of Ensbury Park Road and Redhill Drive, proceeding along Coombe Avenue, Leybourne Avenue, and Northbourne Avenue to the junction of Northbourne Avenue and Wimborne Road.

3. **Moordown – Iford:** from the junction of Wimborne Road and Castle Lane, south eastwards along Castle Lane to the junction of Castle Lane and Christchurch Road, Iford Bridge.

4. **Wimborne Road – Holdenhurst Road:** from the junction of Alma Road and Wimborne Road, proceeding along Alma Road and Richmond Park Road to the junction of Richmond Park Road and Holdenhurst Road.

5. **Tuckton Bridge – Seabourne Road:** from the junction of Tuckton Road and Stour Road, proceeding along Tuckton Road, Cranleigh Road, Beaufort Road and Beresford Road to its junction with Fisherman's Walk.

6. **Fisherman's Walk:** Parkwood Road, Southbourne Road terminal loop.

7. **Iford – Christchurch:** from the junction of Iford Lane and Christchurch Road, proceeding along Christchurch Road, Barrack Road, across Stour Road to the junction of Barrack Road and High Street, Christchurch.

8. **Bear Cross – Wallisdown:** from the junction of Wimborne Road and Ringwood Road, proceeding along Ringwood Road to the junction of Wallisdown Road and Ringwood Road, along Wallisdown Road to the junction of Wallisdown Road and Kinson Road.

It was resolved to apply for a Provisional Order in respect of Routes 1–6 and 8. Route 7 was referred to the full Transport Committee for review; this latter led to the Negotiating Sub-Committee being authorised to re-open negotiations with Christchurch Town Council.

Eventually, in early 1937, the following objections had been received to the Trolleybus Provisional Order:

- Barrack Road: Hampshire County Council, Christchurch Corporation, residents in the road.

- Wallisdown Road: Dorset County Council, Poole Corporation, H&D.

- Richmond Park Road: residents in the road and neighbouring roads.

- Ensbury Park Road: residents.

- Generally: Bournemouth and Poole Electricity Supply Co. Ltd..

Mr Morrison's first Annual Report for the undertaking, for the year ending 31st March 1936, showed a deficit of £21,307 despite the financial success of the trolleybuses. The following tram routes had been converted to trolleybus operation:

- Square – Moordown   7th June 1935

- Lansdowne – Moordown   28th June 1935

- Square – Charminster Road   23rd August 1935
(Castle Lane)

- Square – Fisherman's Walk   21st November 1935

- Fisherman's Walk – Southbourne   23rd Dec. 1935
Cross Roads

Mr Morrison considered that the financial results had been influenced by the almost complete tram to trolleybus change over, together with the following factors:

- the withdrawal of operations in Poole;

- service co-ordination with other operators, leading to a fall in motorbus fares;

- the introduction of trolleybuses at lower fares than on the trams;

while expenditure had increased due to:

- operation of duplicate services during the change-over;

- staff changes to suit the new conditions;

- the cost of staff retraining;

To recap, by mid-1936 the following trolleybus services were operated:

21 Square (Gervis Place) – Lansdowne – Christchurch Road – Boscombe – Fisherman's Walk – Southbourne Cross Roads – Tuckton Bridge – Christchurch

21A Westbourne – Square – Lansdowne – Christchurch Road – Boscombe – Fisherman's Walk – Southbourne Cross Roads – Tuckton Bridge – Christchurch

22 Square (Gervis Place) – Lansdowne – Christchurch Road – Boscombe – Fisherman's Walk – Southbourne Cross Roads

23 Square (Gervis Place) – Lansdowne – Christchurch Road – Boscombe – Fisherman's Walk

23A Westbourne – Square – Lansdowne – Christchurch Road – Boscombe – Fisherman's Walk

24 Square (Gervis Place) – Lansdowne – Christchurch Road – Boscombe – Iford

24A Westbourne – Square – Lansdowne – Christchurch Road – Boscombe – Iford

25 Square (Gervis Place) – Lansdowne – Central Station – Holdenhurst Road – Ashley Road, Boscombe

25A Westbourne – Square – Lansdowne – Central Station – Holdenhurst Road – Ashley Road, Boscombe

26 Square – Richmond Hill – Cemetery Junction – Wimborne Road – Winton – Moordown

27 Square (Gervis Place) – Lansdowne – Central Station – St. Paul's Road – Cemetery Junction – Wimborne Road – Winton – Moordown

28 Square – Richmond Hill – Cemetery Junction – Charminster Road – Five Ways – Broadway Hotel, Castle Lane

The Municipal Tramways and Transport Association again held their Annual Conference in Bournemouth in 1936, between 24th and 26th June and, as a background for participants, the 18th June 1936 issue of *Transport World* contained a review of the undertaking, concentrating on the "great success of the trolleybus". It was recorded that the tram-to-trolleybus conversion programme had been completed. The trolleybus network had reached 15½ route miles. A further 30 miles of conversion to trolleybuses was authorised, and the next extension would be of 1¾ miles from Wimborne Road along Ensbury Park Road, Coombe Avenue, Leybourne Avenue to Ensbury, where building development was taking place.

In the 51 weeks ending 27th May 1936, the number of passengers carried on the Square – Moordown service had increased from 4,417,452, when trams operated, to 5,805,830. A commensurate increase had been recorded on all converted routes. The changeover from trams had been fully justified both for technical reasons and public popularity. Motorbuses were seen as no more than trolleybus feeders.

Early problems with the overhead equipment had been overcome and, in an effort to speed up services, it was intended that the new routes would be equipped with non-fouling fittings to offer an extended test to slipper type collectors rather than the trolley wheels used hitherto. Negotiations were also under way with the appropriate authorities to rearrange stopping places to better suit the changed traffic conditions. Once this had been completed, overhead equipment, such as section insulators, would be relocated to the best positions to meet traffic conditions. A recommendation that all stopping places be set back 150ft from cross-roads or junctions, as well as a "staggering" of 300ft between stopping places for opposite directions, would be introduced as far as possible. Principal stops, it was decided, would be equipped with queuing barriers and yellow road markings. The Transport Department was also reportedly considering fitting at least a proportion of the fleet with emergency battery manoeuvering equipment, although this was never done.

On 24th July 1936, a sub-committee considered two alternative trolleybus routes to Bournemouth Pier and the Square from the Lansdowne, namely along Bath Road to the Square via the Pier Approach and Exeter Road, with a turning point at the Pier Approach; and along Bath Road and Westover Road to the Square. There was some disagreement and only the latter route was recommended, with construction to start as soon as possible. On 18th September 1936, the Transport Committee was advised that the Council had declined to adopt this resolution – but the Transport Committee

English Electric-bodied Sunbeam MS2 81 on service 24A (Iford – Westbourne) at the Square in September 1936. Note the short-lived wooden side destination boards, and also the fleet number above the coat of arms on the lower-deck side panels.
R. T. Wilson (D. L. Chalk collection)

once again recommended that installation be carried out as soon as possible, for economic reasons and to complete the system.

There is evidence that the public were keen to see a regular trolleybus service provided to the Queen's Park Golf Pavilion at Littledown Avenue, but the Transport Committee recommended that no change in the current arrangements were necessary.

Special destination boards "To and From the Tennis" were placed in trolleybuses travelling between Moordown and Winton and the Square and Lansdowne during the Bournemouth (Open) Lawn Tennis Tournament at Melville Park, which took place between 27th July and 8th August 1936.

To avoid corrosion, it was agreed to fit finials to the tops of traction poles and at bracket arm ends. In the same meeting it was recommended that tramway traction poles and overhead equipment remaining in Capstone Road be removed as soon as possible.

On 3rd July 1936 a special Transport Committee Meeting had instructed the General Manager to consider fare increases in the light of his Annual Report. This led to them proposing, on 9th October 1936, that the 1½d fares introduced on all services when trolleybus operations started be abolished and the previous tram fares reintroduced on the trolleybuses. On 26th November 1936, the General Manager's suggestions as set out in Appendix E were approved and submitted to the Transport Commissioners.

With effect from 25th January 1937, the Traffic Commissioners approved the revised fares excluding those between the Square and County Gates, which were still under discussion between Bournemouth and Poole Councils. As H&D were unable to adjust at such short notice, the fares were actually increased from 1st February 1937.

At the Transport Committee Meeting on 18th December 1936, Mr Morrison reported that plans for the Charminster Avenue extension were being prepared and would soon be submitted to the MoT, and that the Post Office Telephone and Telegraph Authorities had been informed.

Ancillary vehicles for the trolleybus fleet at that time comprised three tower wagons and one lorry. With tram-to-trolleybus route conversion complete, Mr Morrison recommended that two of the tower wagons be modernised by transferring their towers onto two Tilling-Stevens TS6 motorbus chassis. He also recommended sending the remaining tower wagon and lorry for scrap and the purchase of two suitable 25cwt chassis, one to be equipped with a tipping wagon body and the other with a telescopic tower. Tenders were invited and, by February 1937, the tender of Lee Motor Works (Bournemouth) Ltd. for a Bedford tipping wagon and a Bedford chassis for a tower wagon at a total cost of £440 8s 6d had been accepted and the work put in hand. Finally, two minor matters were dealt with at the same meeting:

- Taxicabs standing on the 28 stop at the entrance to the Central Gardens in the Square were deemed a problem.

- The Transport Committee instructed the General Manager to erect 25 traction poles in Bath Road and Westover Road in consultation with the Electrical and Public Lighting Engineer for use purely as lighting standards!

At their meeting on 11th January 1937 the Town Clerk reported to the Transport Committee on negotiations with H&D on the Council's application to operate trolleybuses along Wallisdown Road. H&D were making application to the Traffic Commissioners to operate motorbuses on a circular route through Wallisdown; and another service along Ringwood Road between Bear Cross and Upton. The Transport Committee resolved to oppose H&D running such services within the Bournemouth boundary, and advised the company of the terms whereby mutual running over Wallisdown Road between Kinson Road and Ringwood Road would be acceptable. Poole Council were again asked for their consent to Bournemouth Corporation motorbuses operating along those portions of Wallisdown Road within the Borough of Poole (the boundary between the two councils being on the north side of the road). The Transport Committee also agreed that the trolleybus service to Fisherman's Walk be extended to Southbourne Cross Roads from 9.30 am – 12.00 pm daily.

Ministry of Transport approval was given to the following extensions and turning points in January 1937:

- a new curve at the Lansdowne enabling vehicles to turn left out of Holdenhurst Road into Christchurch Road

- a turning point at the Lansdowne via Lansdowne Crescent island

- a turning point at Alma Road, Waterloo Road, and Crimea Road (Winton Banks)

- the turntable at Christchurch

- an extension from Moordown Depot to Castle Lane West via Wimborne Road, and single-line terminal loop in Lawford Road, Castle Lane West and Wimborne Road (Redhill).

Diagrams of the overhead wiring in Bournemouth Square and at the Lansdowne, and how they changed over the years, can be found in Appendix O.

Wiring was extended along Wimborne Road to the junction with Castle Lane, a turning loop being built northbound along Lawford Road, west along Castle Lane West and then back into Wimborne Road. The terminal arrangements were built with the authorised extension to Bear Cross in mind, a junction frog being placed in the outbound wiring which continued some distance north towards the junction between Wimborne Road and Castle Lane. Service 27 was extended under the new wiring from 11th March 1937. It was decided subsequently to operate the Lawford Road extension as part of service 26 instead and this took place with effect

from 15th April 1937. The new arrangements were therefore as follows:

26 Square – Richmond Hill – Cemetery Junction – Wimborne Road – Winton – Moordown – Lawford Road

27 Square (Gervis Place) – Lansdowne – Central Station – St. Paul's Road – Cemetery Junction – Wimborne Road – Winton – Moordown

Following MoT approval in January 1937 to the erection of overhead equipment in Charminster Avenue, work had proceeded apace, whilst the Borough Engineer hoped to have road resurfacing finished by the third week of April 1937. The Ministry advised that, due to other commitments, they were prepared to grant authority for the Corporation to operate trolleybuses on its own responsibility and subject to any requirements subsequently deemed necessary by the official inspection. With the completion of road resurfacing, the service commenced on 5th April 1937, thus:

29 Square – Richmond Hill – Cemetery Junction – Five Ways – Malvern Road

Meanwhile, on 19th February 1937, the Transport Committee recommended that construction should start on the route extension commencing in Talbot Road at its junction with Wimborne Road (commonly known as Winton Banks, because there was a branch of each of the major High Street banks on each corner), along Talbot Road and Wallisdown Road, to its junction with Kinson Road, East Howe. The island near the junction of Kinson Road with Columbia Road, East Howe, was deemed a more suitable location for the turning circle than that originally proposed at the Liberal Club. In November 1937, the Borough Engineer was able to acquire the land required for road widening at the junction of Kinson, Fernheath and Acres Roads and intimated that the Transport Committee should contribute £85, being half the estimated cost of carrying out the street works.

In April 1937, a petition with regard to radio interference allegedly caused by trolleybuses was investigated.

The Transport Committee recommended that the full Council's resolution of 30th October 1936 not to extend trolleybus wiring along Bath Road and Westover Road for a year be rescinded. An inbound service along these roads to the Square was urgently required to relieve congestion of inbound trolleybuses in Old Christchurch Road. Working fast, one-way inbound wiring from the Lansdowne, along Bath Road as far as the Royal Bath Hotel, and then along Westover Road past the Pavilion to a junction with the existing inbound wiring at Gervis

Place was brought into operation on Saturday 8th May 1937. Half of the journeys on the Ashley Road service and the "Main Road" group operating from the Lansdowne to the Square were thereafter re-routed along Bath Road and Westover Road. Special boards with white lettering on a red background were displayed in the nearside of the driver's cab windscreen indicating those vehicles traversing Bath and Westover Roads until vehicles were fitted with auxiliary destination screens at the top of the nearside driver's cab windscreen and immediately above the rear platform window. MoT authority was granted to operate trolleybuses on the Corporation's own reponsibility along Bath Road and Westover Road until the subsequent official inspection could be made.

The number of trolleybuses on service 27 running to the Square via Bath Road was soon questioned, and the General Manager carried out a census of the number of passengers on this service travelling to stops in Old Christchurch Road. By July 1937, the Transport Committee was able to recommend that the practice of running service 27 trolleybuses alternately over the two lines to the Square should continue.

On 19th February 1937 the Transport Committee had approved, at an estimated £300, the General Manager's designs for the decoration and illumination of a special trolleybus in connection with King George VI's Coronation and upon which premium fares would be charged. Decorations were proposed which could be fitted to any trolleybus, and it was suggested that subsequently the vehicle should be used on every suitable occasion, such as during conferences and carnivals. Consequently, trolleybus 152 was decorated and was used regularly on service 21 for the rest of the summer, double fares being charged.

In June 1937 the MoT approved the Bournemouth Corporation (Trolley Vehicles) Provisional Order, excluding Route 8 (Bear Cross – Wallisdown), which granted powers for a further ten miles of trolleybus routes:

1   Along Columbia Road and Ensbury Park Road, terminating therein at its junction with Wimborne Road, Moordown

2   From the junction of Ensbury Park Road and Redhill Drive, along Redhill Drive to and along Coombe Avenue, along Leybourne Avenue and Northbourne Avenue to Wimborne Road

3   Along Castle Lane from Lawford Road to Iford

4   Along Alma Road and Richmond Park Road from Wimborne Road to Holdenhurst Road

5   Fisherman's Walk to Tuckton Bridge via Cranleigh Road

6   Parkwood Road, Beresford Road terminal loop Fisherman's Walk

7   Iford Bridge to Stour Road, Christchurch via Barrack Road

The outbreak of the Second World War in 1939 necessitated several renewals of these powers. Authorised Route 1 of the 1937 Order was completed in April 1938, Route 2 in April 1939, Route 7 in July 1943, and Routes

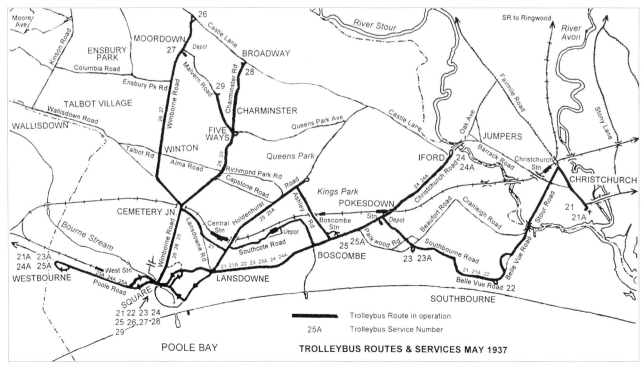

TROLLEYBUS ROUTES & SERVICES MAY 1937

Sunbeam MS2 152 (BRU 3) in Bournemouth Square during 1937, decorated for the Coronation of King George VI. Mr Morrison stands at the front, wearing a raincoat and trilby hat. Behind him can be seen the tramway passenger waiting room and the buildings in the apex between Old Christchurch Road and Gervis Place. Note the window-bills declaring double the normal fares payable on this bus.
D. L. Chalk collection

5 and 6 in August 1948. Routes 2 and 4 were never equipped for trolleybus operation at all.

Mr Morrison was able to report a gross surplus of £49,728 on the whole undertaking for the year ending 31st March 1937, an increase of £12,676. Income had decreased by £2,206 but working expenses had fallen by £14,882. After paying all capital charges there was a surplus of £14,058 19s 9d on trolleybus operations whereas motorbuses had lost £15,393 3s 9d. By financial wizardry, the final eight days of tramway operation in the Borough made a loss of £18,910 19s 11d, despite having operated just 4,460 miles!

Mr Morrison added that the undertaking was now feeling the full effect in capital charges of what had practically amounted to renewal of the majority of rolling stock and overhead equipment, as well as considerable investment in the underground feeder system. Total energy output from the generating station was 5,337,300 units compared to 6,021,470 in 1936, the reduced output being due to the introduction of three additional substations taking current from the grid at suitable places on the system. Coal consumption in the year fell from 7,286 to 6,734 tons. The total cost of electrical energy per unit including all capital charges was 0.71d. Service changes reduced the mileage run by 361,458 but the number of passengers carried had increased by 75,222. The National Joint Industrial Council, of which the Corporation were members, also increased wages scales, with drivers and conductors gaining 2s 6d per week and cleaners, labourers, etc.1s per week. Finally, the undertaking would have been £70 11s 4d worse off if it had not been for the introduction of uncollected fare boxes in August 1936.

A member of the public wrote to the Transport Committee in June 1937 asking if, when trolleybuses

A night-time view of illuminated Sunbeam MS2 152. The decorations included nearly 1,200 Mazda red, white and blue lamps, and various illuminated symbols supplied by British Thomson-Houston. Note the huge spotlights at the front, illuminating the borough coat of arms framed by a pair of Union flags. The crown at the front of the roof contained a rotating flasher, which gave a variety of changing effects.
D. R. H. Bowler collection

Illuminated trolleybus 152 is seen here on Coronation Day, 12th May 1937, at the traffic island on the northern side of the Square en route to Christchurch. In the background a service 26 or 30 trolleybus, bedecked with flags, pulls onto the Richmond Hill services loop at the junction with Bourne Avenue. *G. O. P. Pearce (Courtesy M. N. Pearce)*

replaced motorbus shuttle service 8 (Tuckton – Fisherman's Walk), a through service could be operated between Tuckton and the Square via Tuckton Road and Cranleigh Road. They had replied that favourable consideration would be given when the conversion was carried out, yet in September 1937 when a petition protesting against trolleybuses operating along Parkwood Road was received, they replied that there was no intention to operate such a service and it became a rarely-used terminal loop. The petition, however, may have been related to fears that plans for the alternative route between Christchurch Road and Seabourne Road, along the entire length of Parkwood Road avoiding Pokesdown Station, was being revived.

At their meeting on 23rd July 1937 the Transport Committee recommended that the installation of overhead equipment along Castle Lane from Wimborne Road to Charminster Road should commence as soon as powers were granted under the present Provisional Order. At the same meeting, permission was granted to

the 11th Troop, Bournemouth Boy Scouts, to use the barn at Iford turning circle as their headquarters as long as they kept it in repair. At about the same time, the Lighting Committee complained of the damage to street lamps by trolleybuses.

Presumably as an economy measure after it was found that there was over-provision of service, service 23A was withdrawn on 30th September 1937, while services 24A and 25 ceased to operate on 1st November 1937.

Christchurch Corporation would not agree to trolleybus operation along Barrack Road between Stour Road and High Street (Route 7 of the Bournemouth Corporation (Trolley Vehicles) Provisional Order) despite the offer of various incentives. On 15th November 1937 the Transport Committee visited an alternative route proposal made by Christchurch Corporation, but recommended that it be not accepted by the Council. The Provisional Order was amended accordingly, and the Barrack Road trolleybus service, when finally

Sunbeam MS2 76 (AEL 404) seen at the north side of the Square on service 27 to Moordown. Note the 'via' slip-board on the side, and 'Bobby's' in the background. *East Pennine Transport Group (R. Marshall collection)*

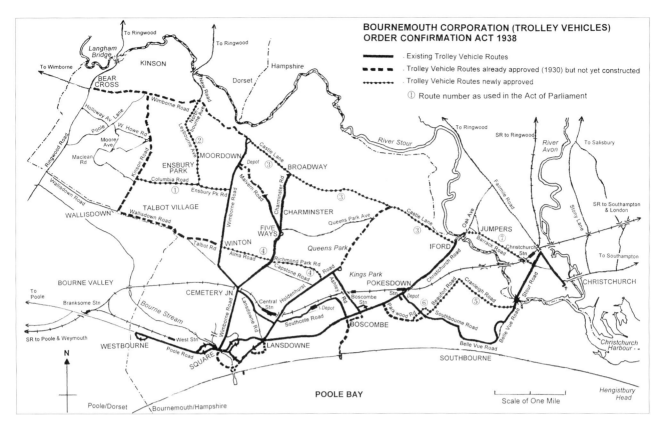

BOURNEMOUTH CORPORATION (TROLLEY VEHICLES)
ORDER CONFIRMATION ACT 1938

———————— . Existing Trolley Vehicle Routes
■ ■ ■ ■ . Trolley Vehicle Routes already approved (1930) but not yet constructed
· · · · · · · · . Trolley Vehicle Routes newly approved
① Route number as used in the Act of Parliament

introduced, had to operate via Christchurch Station under the existing wiring along Stour Road and Bargates.

Mr Morrison reported to the 28th January 1938 Transport Committee meeting that MoT approval had been received for trolleybus operation over certain routes, extensions and turning points, authorized by the Bournemouth Corporation Act, 1930, and recently inspected by a Ministry official, and in respect of which a provisional authority had been issued subject to that inspection. On 16th February 1938 the Bournemouth Corporation (Trolley Vehicles) Provisional Order Confirming Bill was read a second time in the House of Commons but a petition against the Order was made by Christchurch Corporation.

During March 1938 a complaint was received about the compulsory MoT stop on the inward journey at the top of Bath Hill (where the coasting brake was applied). The Transport Department investigated the conversion of the compulsory into a request stop although its position could not be altered. It remained signed "All Bus Stop" throughout the trolleybus era.

A meeting was held at this time between the Town Clerk, Poole Corporation and Hants & Dorset, leading to the introduction of joint services along Wallisdown Road. It was agreed that Bournemouth Corporation would seek no further powers to operate any form of transport in the Borough of Poole, excluding the then proposed Wallisdown Road service.

Sunbeam MS2 102 (ALJ 976), featuring the short-lived slip-boards and CEMETERY J^TN destination blind display, turns out of the Columbia Road turning circle at Wonderholme Parade into Columbia Road on 15th April 1938, the first day of operation of service 30.   *G. O. P. Pearce*
(D. L. Chalk collection)

The 22nd April 1938 Transport Committee meeting recommended that, subject to approval being obtained, work on the trolleybus extensions along Ensbury Park Road, Barrack Road, and Castle Lane (Charminster Road to Wimborne Road) should start as soon as possible.

The 1937 Provisional Order became the Bournemouth Corporation (Trolley Vehicles) Order Confirmation Act of 26th May 1938 and work started on Authorised Route 3, along Castle Lane from Lawford Road to Iford. Solely the north-westerly end of Castle Lane was wired, before priority was given to the Ensbury Park Road and Columbia Road route. In the meantime the Wallisdown extension had been completed and a turning circle built in front of a parade of shops (Wonderholme Parade) at the junction of Columbia Road and Kinson Road. Trolleybuses replaced motorbus service 9 (Winton – Wallisdown) on 15th April 1938 as service 30, as follows:

30 Square – Richmond Hill – Cemetery Junction – Winton – Talbot Road – Wallisdown – Columbia Road.

Trolleybuses operating this service were experimentally equipped with slipper trolley heads in place of wheel collectors as used hitherto.

The Minutes of the 22nd April 1938 Transport Committee Meeting made reference to the General Manager's Annual Report of 1937–38 as follows:

"Referring to trolleybus operation it will be seen that after meeting capital charges there is a surplus on the year's working of £14,407 15s 4d while on the motorbus side there is a deficit of £4,825 9s 9d. Total consumption of electrical energy was 7,093,600 units of which 5,233,360 units were generated at the Department's Southcote Road station at a cost of 0.81d. per unit including capital charges while the remaining 1,860,240 units were taken at the four substations from the Company at a cost of 0.78d. per unit. Compared with the previous year, the figures show a decrease of generation at the Department's station of 103,940 units while there was an increase of 470,710 units taken from the Company, the more economic distribution of energy being responsible for the adjustment.

"During the financial year under review the following extensions opened:

- *Five Ways – Malvern Road (service 29) 0.43 miles, constructed in the previous year but opened for service on 5th April 1937*

- *Bath and Westover Roads, 0.63 miles, opened 8th May 1937*

- *Talbot Road, Wallisdown, Kinson Road (service 30) 1.92 miles constructed and practically completed by 31st March 1938*

"Total mileage of trolleybus services was now 30.77 miles."

Mr Morrison added that 51 trolleybuses had been repainted during the year. The overhead equipment and underground feeder system were in satisfactory condition, whilst nine miles of trolleywire had been renewed. The carbon insert slipper shoe current collector system had proved successful and a complete changeover was planned, which would remove trolleywheel noise. Finally, the Transport Department were working closely with Post Office Engineering staff with respect to alleged radio interference.

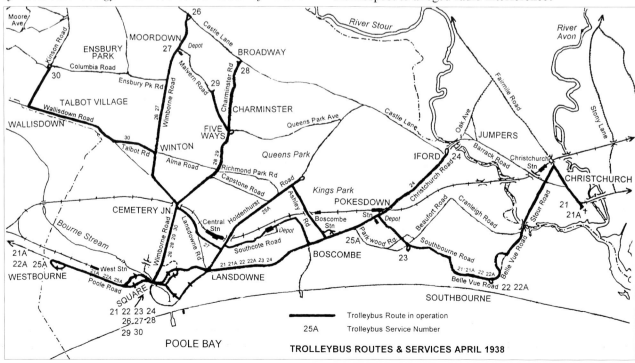

TROLLEYBUS ROUTES & SERVICES APRIL 1938

The General Manager reported on 27th June 1938 on a proposal to re-route some trolleybuses on the Christchurch – Bournemouth Square service via Ashley Road to provide a direct link from Southbourne and Fisherman's Walk to Central Station. Instead, he recommended that a link be introduced by extending every third vehicle on service 25 to Fisherman's Walk thus providing a vehicle every 15 minutes between Fisherman's Walk and Central Station. Thus, a new duplication service was introduced along Holdenhurst Road on 28th July 1938, namely:

25B Fisherman's Walk – Pokesdown – Ashley Road, Boscombe – Central Station – Lansdowne – Square – Westbourne.

In the same meeting a petition concerning the frequency of the Queen's Park trolleybus service was reviewed. The General Manager commented that a special summer season service from the Square to Queen's Park Golf Pavilion could be operated from 25th July 1938 and, if a demand was proved, one vehicle an hour on the Ashley Road service could be diverted to Queen's Park during the winter months. The timetable for service 25A was therefore drawn up in this manner.

By July 1938 the first war scares had begun to circulate. Mr Morrison asked for instructions as to staff wishing to receive Air Raid Precautions training.

Although no external advertising was displayed on the undertaking's vehicles, an offer for the sole right of placing external advertising was received but rejected.

The 30th September 1938 issue of *Passenger Transport Journal* reported that work on the new route along Castle Lane West, permitting the introduction of a circular trolleybus service (Square – Cemetery Junction – Winton – Moordown – Charminster – Cemetery Junction – Square), was almost complete following delays caused by armament work which had made it difficult to obtain the necessary junction castings. From 19th October 1938, Wimborne Road services to Lawford Road and Charminster Road services to the Broadway Hotel were linked along Castle Lane West, operating as two circular service with West Way as the nominal terminal point, as follows:

26A Square – Richmond Hill – Cemetery Junction – Wimborne Road – Winton – Moordown – Lawford Road – West Way

28A Square – Richmond Hill – Cemetery Junction – Charminster Road – Five Ways – Broadway Hotel, Castle Lane – West Way

As the continuation of the trolleybus route along the remainder of Castle Lane to the main Christchurch Road at Iford was then not expected for two years, it was proposed to introduce initially a route-developing motor bus service.

In September 1938 a suggestion to add the service number to the side destination indicators was rejected on cost grounds.

It was recommended that, on service 30, the fare between Cemetery Junction and Heathwood Road be 1d

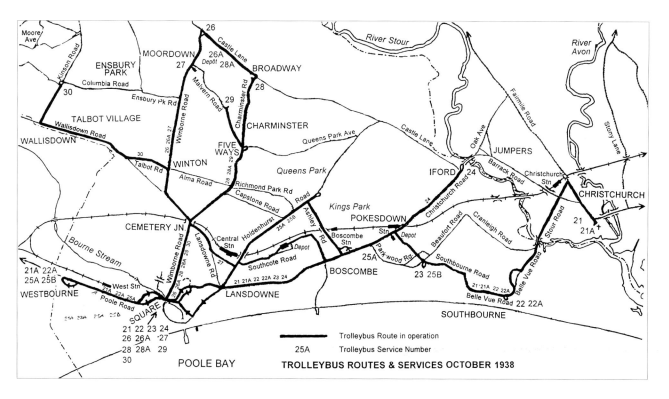

TROLLEYBUS ROUTES & SERVICES OCTOBER 1938

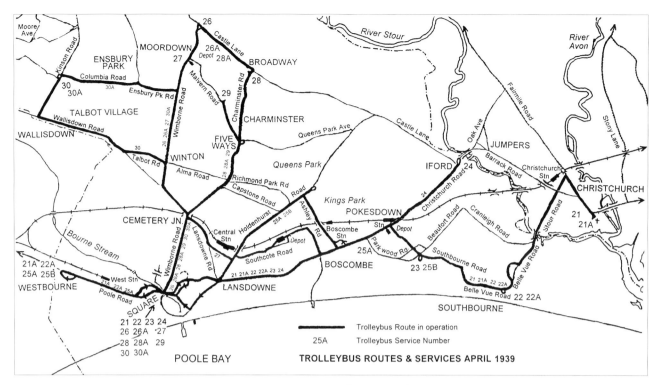

TROLLEYBUS ROUTES & SERVICES APRIL 1939

to correspond with the 1d fare between Cemetery Junction and Peter's Hill on services 26 and 27, and that 1½d fares be introduced between Castle Lane and King's Road (Service No. 28) and between Castle Lane Junction and Peter's Hill (Services 26 and 27). The suggestion that an additional fare stage Castle Lane to Dean Park Road on service 28 be introduced was rejected. The outward stop at Boscombe Crescent was moved towards the middle of the Crescent.

In April 1939, the MoT advised that they were unable to inspect the Ensbury Park Road trolleybus route at that time, but had no objection to it being brought into use prior to an inspection, subject to compliance with any requirements that may subsequently be made. Trolleybus services therefore commenced on 8th April 1939, when a circular operation with service 30 was introduced:

30A Square – Richmond Hill – Cemetery Junction – Winton – Moordown – Ensbury Park Road – Columbia Road.

Although the summer timetable map showed service 24 running as far as Stour Road, Christchurch, work had not commenced before the outbreak in September 1939 of the Second World War, which deferred effort on the extension until 1943. All other development of the trolleybus system, excluding the addition of emergency terminal points, ceased until the war was over.

Mr Morrison presented his Annual Report for 1938 to the Transport Committee meeting held on 23rd June 1939:

"After meeting capital charges there is a surplus on the year's working of £8,337 7s 5d whilst on the motor bus side there was also a surplus of £1,893 19s 6d. The capital charges attached to the abandoned tramway system were £8,910. After meeting this charge there remains a net surplus of £1,321 which I suggest should be transferred to the Renewals Account. Revenue was disappointing due to poor weather and the mounting crisis since September 1938.

"Extensions to trolleybus system:

- *Talbot Road, Wallisdown and Kinson Road, service 30, 1.94 miles, construction of route was almost completed in the previous year. Put into service 15th April 1938.*

- *Circular Services 26A and 28A, 0.64 miles, Castle Lane from Charminster Road to Wimborne Road. Constructed and put into service 19th October 1938.*

- *Ensbury Park and Columbia Roads, Circular Services 30 and 30A, 1.24 miles This route was constructed and partially completed by 31 March 1939.*

"Trolleybus route mileage now totals 33.35 miles.

"Two of the extensions referred to, which have been carried out during the year, have enabled the Department to operate the first two circular services which the Transport Committee had as their objective when trolleybus services were inaugurated in 1934.

"Fleet: The trolleybuses are now five years old but are in sound mechanical condition and compare favourably

in appearance with more modern types now available. 49 trolleybuses have been repainted and 18 miles of trolley wire renewed during the year. A complete changeover from wheel collector to slipper shoe collector had taken place at a high initial cost but it has proved a sound change. The irritating hissing noise of the wheel has been eliminated, while wear on the overhead line and fittings has been considerably reduced. The only cause for anxiety will be operation in severe damp frost but provision has been made for a special type of shoe to be fitted to remove ice from the overhead line. Overhead equipment of better design is now available and when renewals are carried out, every opportunity is taken to use the most modern types of fittings, while as far as possible we are replacing the heavy and perhaps objectionable-looking bracket arms by span wire construction.

"Generating Station: Major repairs have been necessary to the steam drums and superheaters of the B&W water tube boilers, while overhaul and certain replacements have been executed on the two turbines. It will be necessary to carry out extensive repairs to both the artesian well and the chimney stack".

In July 1939 a partition was placed across the Southbourne Cross Roads waiting room in connection with its use as an ARP Warden's post. By now it was clear to the nation at large that war was likely.

Two of Bournemouth's large fleet of Sunbeam MS2 trolleybuses, 130 (BEL 815) and 87 (ALJ 63), passing on the lower part of Richmond Hill. Note the disused tram track and, in the background, the Hants & Dorset Bus Station in Bournemouth Square. *Transport World*

At the time War was declared, on 3rd September 1939, the following trolleybus services were in operation:

21 Square (Gervis Place) – Lansdowne – Christchurch Road – Boscombe – Fisherman's Walk – Southbourne Cross Roads – Tuckton Bridge – Christchurch

21A Westbourne – Square (Gervis Place) – Lansdowne – Christchurch Road – Boscombe – Fisherman's Walk – Southbourne Cross Roads – Tuckton Bridge – Christchurch

22 Square (Gervis Place) – Lansdowne – Christchurch Road – Boscombe – Fisherman's Walk – Southbourne Cross Roads

22A Westbourne – Square (Gervis Place) – Lansdowne - Christchurch Road – Boscombe – Fisherman's Walk – Southbourne Cross Roads

23 Square (Gervis Place) – Lansdowne – Christchurch Road – Boscombe – Fisherman's Walk

24 Square (Gervis Place) – Lansdowne – Christchurch Road – Boscombe – Iford

25A Westbourne – Square – Lansdowne – Central Station – Holdenhurst Road – Ashley Road, Boscombe

25B Westbourne – Square – Lansdowne – Central Station – Ashley Road, Boscombe – Pokesdown – Fisherman's Walk

26 Square – Richmond Hill – Cemetery Junction – Wimborne Road – Winton – Moordown - Lawford Road

26A Square – Richmond Hill – Cemetery Junction – Wimborne Road – Winton – Moordown – Lawford Road – West Way

27 Square (Gervis Place) – Lansdowne – Central Station – St. Paul's Road – Cemetery Junction – Wimborne Road – Winton – Moordown

28 Square – Richmond Hill – Cemetery Junction – Charminster Road – Five Ways – Broadway Hotel, Castle Lane

28A Square – Richmond Hill – Cemetery Junction – Charminster Road – Five Ways – Broadway Hotel, Castle Lane – West Way

29 Square – Richmond Hill – Cemetery Junction – Five Ways – Malvern Road.

30 Square – Richmond Hill – Cemetery Junction – Winton – Talbot Road – Wallisdown – Columbia Road

30A Square – Richmond Hill – Cemetery Junction – Winton – Ensbury Park Road – Columbia Road

From 3rd September 1939, all the undertaking's vehicles were required to return to their depots by 8 pm (i.e. one hour after sunset), due to difficulties in maintaining services with many staff already having been "called-up" for military service and concerns about vehicles complying with blackout regulations. Lighting restrictions were severe. In addition to having masked headlamps, all saloon windows were painted with dark blue paint and only one internal lamp was retained in each saloon. Vehicle roofs were in due course painted chocolate brown as a kind of camouflage measure; from 1943, some motorbuses operated in grey undercoat or in brown with maroon bands, but all trolleybuses retained their primrose livery. The town being on the south coast, the legend "Bournemouth Corporation" along the maroon lower-deck waistband was also progressively removed on repaint as a security precaution. The last 3ft of each trolleyboom was painted white to assist in rewiring in blackout conditions and to enable the driver of the trolleybus behind to see the position of the trolleyheads of the vehicle in front. To avoid mass vehicle damage and destruction during air raids, some of the fleet was dispersed overnight in quiet side roads such as St. Clement's Road and Southcote Road, rather than parked in depot buildings.

Initially upon declaration of war, all cinemas, theatres and other places of entertainment were closed. No bands performed on the bandstands, the circus at the Winter Gardens was cancelled and the Concert Party on Boscombe Pier disbanded. The train service to and from London was reduced from 14 to six trains per day from 11th September 1939. Paintings were removed from the Russell-Cotes Art Gallery for safety and stored in the country. From the same date, Bournemouth Corporation motorbuses with suitably masked lighting maintained a skeleton service on the main motorbus and trolleybus routes after 8 pm; and from 18th September 1939 trolleybuses also operated a half-hourly service. The last departures from the Square and other main terminal points became 10 pm instead of 11.30 pm. However, the introduction of petrol rationing on Saturday, 23rd

September 1939 led to a reduction in motorbus services and the official finishing time for buses leaving Bournemouth Square on Sundays was brought forward to 10.15 pm from 28th October 1939. Accordingly Mr Morrison was asked to start work on construction of the Barrack Road trolleybus route (which passed the REME Barracks and the Military Experimental Establishment (MEXE) facilities) as soon as possible.

The Pavilion and cinemas had re-opened after a fortnight and, by the end of November 1939, audiences were up to pre-war levels. Last buses from the main termini were again revised, to 11 pm, from 13th November 1939. The crew mess room in the former tramway passenger waiting shelter in the middle of the Square, where a number of motorbus services still terminated, was enlarged at this time, although its external appearance remained unchanged. Four large air raid shelters had been constructed in the gardens opposite Palace Court Hotel just to the east of the Pavilion (they still exist under the rhododendrons, and are used to store Parks Department equipment).

To aid pedestrians and vehicles in the blackout, two horizontal white bands, one at eye level and the other about 1ft from the ground, were painted around some traction poles and trees on the pavement. A third band was added later. Kerbstones close to road junctions were painted white, whilst lines appeared across the road at pedestrian crossings, which until then had only been marked by square metal studs in the road surface. The blue paint on saloon windows was unpopular; it was gradually removed and window blinds were fitted to all buses. Some windows were covered with netting glued to the glass to reduce the risk of flying glass during air-raids while, as a government requirement, mudguards were painted white to aid visibility in the dark.

Until then some buses had been kept for daytime use only and did not have obscured windows, but this led to operational difficulties. By the end of October 1939, a country-wide system of interior and exterior lighting of passenger vehicles had been adopted to comply with blackout regulations.

Exceptionally, a population census took place on 29th September 1939, in order to register every civilian for an identity card. The number of Bournemouth residents recorded was 144,457, some 22,357 more than in 1938, due in part to a number of evacuees which had been brought to the town. Under normal circumstances the United Kingdom conducts a census every 10 years, the next one then being due (but not taken) in 1941.

From 9th October 1939, trolleybus service 26 was cut back from Lawford Road to Redhill Crescent, Moordown:

26 Square – Richmond Hill – Cemetery Junction – Wimbourne Road – Winton – Moordown.

Trolleybuses coming out of service from Boscombe to Central Depot, Southcote Road, were instructed to return via Portman Road, Ashley Road, Holdenhurst Road and Central Station rather than via Palmerston Road with effect from 7th December 1939, probably to avoid having to turn them in the depot yard in the blackout.

Wartime inflation had started and already there were increases in expenditure for the undertaking to absorb – variously tyres, coal, tickets, staff wages – in the present financial year. From 7th December 1939 a "war wage" of 4s per week was awarded to adult employees. Thus, the 31st January 1940 Transport Committee Meeting approved a proposal for revised fares which were introduced on 1st March 1940. They also recorded their appreciation of the traffic staff's effort in blackout con-

A Sunbeam MS2 turns east out of Kinson Road into Columbia Road in a rare wartime view. The roof and the upper-deck window surrounds have been repainted in chocolate as a precaution against being seen from the air. The lower-deck maroon band still displays the legend Bournemouth Corporation. On the left is the service 30 terminus in front of the shops of Wonderholme Parade. Note the white bands around the traction poles and street lamps and the white-painted kerbs, to allow them to be seen during the blackout. The man in the trilby hat is Mr Fred W. Harris, Overhead Superintendent.
W. R. Stride collection (courtesy E. Stride)

ditions. From 1st April 1940, the undertaking's headquarters moved from 6 Wootton Gardens to Southcote Road.

All piers around the British coastline were rendered unusable to any potential seaborne invader, and explosive charges were used to blow gaps in both Boscombe and Bournemouth Piers, whilst much of the decking was removed on what remained. Beaches became prohibited areas, mines were laid and various other defences were installed. Holiday-making virtually ceased and Bournemouth, as a seaside resort, suffered a severe decline in the volume of passenger traffic, particularly, of course, in summer. Accordingly, trolleybus services 21A, 22A and 25B ceased operation on 25th February 1940. On the other hand, evacuees had moved into the area. For example, Portsmouth Grammar School relocated to Clifton Road and Stourwood Road, Southbourne, whilst Taunton's School, Southampton, came to share with Bournemouth Grammar School for Boys.

One of the aspects of war on the Home Front was of individual towns and cities organising the raising of funds for the building of warplanes and warships. Permission was granted on 24th May 1940 for the Bournemouth War Savings Campaign Committee to erect an indicator on the shelter in the Square for the month of June.

The initial 'phoney war' period had developed into something far more serious in the late spring of 1940 with the German invasion of the Low Countries, then the ignominy of the evacuation of the British Expeditionary Force from Dunkirk as France, too, fell under German occupation.

In June 1940, the Military Authorities expressed their dissatisfaction with the dispersal of the municipal transport fleet at night and suggested that it be housed under cover in the depots. Mr Morrison reported that Boscombe (Pokesdown) Depot could no longer be used for this purpose due to the construction of an air raid shelter in the building. The ARP Committee was asked to find or construct an alternative shelter, so that the depot could once again be used to garage vehicles, although this was not done until later in the year. The artesian well at Southcote Road generating station was connected to the town's mains in case an auxiliary water supply was needed but, fortunately, it never had to be used.

The first enemy air-raid on Bournemouth took place just after midnight on 3rd July 1940. Properties were damaged and a house destroyed in Cellars Farm Road, Southbourne but without casualties. Later, in July 1940,

the Transport Department announced that if an air raid warning should sound in the evening and the "All Clear" not be given until after public transport would normally have ceased, buses would wait until after the "All Clear" and would take passengers home whatever the time. Drivers were instructed to halt their vehicles when the "Alert" sounded, and conductors to direct passengers to the nearest public shelters. In August 1940, revised regulations from the Ministry of Home Security permitted vehicular traffic to keep moving after an air raid warning (the so-called "Alert") had sounded. Traffic was only required to halt if an air raid was actually in progress in the vicinity. Trolleybuses were expected to proceed to the next public air raid shelter along their route with adequate accommodation and park in the vicinity. After the "All Clear", vehicles were required to wait for a reasonable period for the passengers to reboard before continuing their journey. The public appeared to favour this solution, which precluded traffic coming to a complete standstill during an "Alert".

A lamp, screened from above, was attached to various bus stop posts experimentally to enable waiting passengers to signal trolleybuses in the blackout instead of flashing torches at the driver and destroying his "night vision". However, the idea was not proceeded with.

Office and maintenance staff worked overtime to crew essential bus and trolleybus services, but the trolleybus fleet was not fully employed. At the end of July 1940 over a dozen trolleybuses, including three out of service with accident damage, were placed in store. A number of others were also withdrawn at the end of September 1940 for overhaul, but were replaced by some of those placed in store in July.

Elsewhere in Britain, transport undertakings in industrial towns were experiencing major growths in traffic demand, and Bournemouth's Transport Committee decided to offer some of the town's surplus trolleybuses to these towns on a rental basis. From autumn 1940 more than a dozen trolleybuses had been stored in Boscombe Depot. In October 1940, twelve Sunbeam MS2s (76, 84, 105, 107, 129, 130, 131, 132, 137, 156, 161 and 168) were loaned to Wolverhampton, the town in which they had been built, and 22 Bournemouth drivers and conductors were temporarily transferred to crew them. Five Bournemouth trolleybuses remained in Wolverhampton until 1946 and the remainder until 1948. In addition to the Wolverhampton hire, during the Transport Committee Meeting of 23rd August 1940 the General Manager was authorised to arrange the hire of a further 18 trolleybuses if required to do so. As part of an

Sunbeam MS2 130, operating in Wolverhampton, endeavours to confuse the enemy by retaining the *Bournemouth Corporation* legend and displaying service number 21A. Note that it retains its yellow roof. Wartime photographs of trolleybuses in service in Bournemouth are rare, probably because such activities would have aroused suspicion in the coastal town, with its heightened security measures. The novelty value of these buses under "foreign" wires, however, ensured that one or two views were captured for posterity!
National Tramway Museum

early wartime salvage drive, Wolverhampton Corporation also purchased a number of traction poles and items of overhead equipment deemed surplus to Bournemouth's needs.

Bournemouth did have some strategic value during the war, there being an assortment of government ministries, War Department offices, leave centres and munitions factories together with military hospitals scattered about the town. A considerable number of hotels were requisitioned, for example the Palace Court Hotel was used as accommodation for American troops, the Royal Bath Hotel was used variously as a Canadian billet and WAAF Officers Mess, whilst the Linden Hall was used by the Ministry of Agriculture. In view of the air raid risk, essential work was authorised in July 1940 to protect the roof lights of Central Depot, Southcote Road; Moordown and Boscombe Depots from damage.

From Monday 23rd September 1940, on the recommendation of the Municipal Passenger Transport Association, vehicles continued to operate during the period of air raid warnings until the time of the last bus.

Last buses were re-timed to leave the Square at 10.30 pm until 27th October 1940. The 18th October 1940 Transport Committee Meeting recommended that last buses from the main termini be cut back once again, to 10.15 pm, from 28th October 1940, with the exception of Saturdays when the last bus from the Square remained at 10.30 pm.

At 3.30 am on 16th November 1940, the Luftwaffe paid Bournemouth another visit. Six parachute mines were dropped, killing 53 people and damaging 2,321 properties.

In consultation with the Regional Transport Commissioner, an agreement was negotiated in November 1940 to loan the 18 remaining surplus trolleybuses (Sunbeam MS2s 72-75, 77-83, 85-87, 89, 117, 123 and 145) to London Transport. Accordingly, in December 1940, they were despatched for service in the east of London, based at Ilford Depot and operating exclusively on services 691 (Barking – Barkingside) and 693 (Barking – Chadwell Heath). These were the only Sunbeam trolleybuses to operate in London and some of

Another operator to receive Bournemouth trolleybuses on loan during the war was London Transport. English Electric-bodied Sunbeam MS2 79 (AEL 407) is seen here operating a southbound service 691 in Ley Street, Ilford. Note the air raid shelter indicator above the bus stop sign, and the absence of any traffic other than a solitary bicycle! *Omnibus Society (M. P. M. Nimmo collection)*

them, having suffered war damage, were repaired in London Transport's Charlton Works. London released them between November 1941 and September 1942, some returning to Bournemouth and others passing on to Newcastle upon Tyne Corporation, from where they were subsequently passed to either Llanelly & District or South Shields Corporation; some then went on to Walsall Corporation. All 18 vehicles had been returned to Bournemouth by August 1945. Prior to loan, each trolley-bus received an overhaul and its local equipment, e.g. destination blinds, run-back brake equipment and trolley-heads, was removed. The hire charge was around £25 per month. The loans appear to have been a voluntary move co-ordinated by the Ministry of War Transport.

The General Manager reported to the Transport Committee Meeting held on 2nd December 1940 that it was impossible to meet the current traffic situation with the number of staff available. He was therefore given permission to locate a supplier of female uniforms and engage conductresses. Mr Morrison added that the Department was trying to put additional services into operation where required.

In both 1940 and 1941 there was a revision of bus stops and several former request stops became compulsory, whilst others were abolished as a fuel economy. The first conductresses started work on 25th January 1941. Some were trained later as trolleybus drivers and the first of these took up her duties in April 1942.

The 24th January 1941 Transport Committee meeting agreed that any member of transport staff injured on duty as a result of enemy action would receive full wages for a period not exceeding 26 weeks, subject to the deduction of any allowance receivable under the Government's personal injury scheme. Also at about this

time, the Municipal Passenger Transport Association advised that application was being made for a further increase of 10s per week in wages on behalf of members of the TGWU.

Early in 1941 the undertaking's Transport Engineer, Mr W. Baxendale, gave notice of his appointment as Deputy General Manager with Wallasey Transport. The vacant position was immediately advertised. Seven applicants were invited for interview, including Mr F. J. Cunuder, of Hastings and two existing Bournemouth Corporation Transport employees. Following a special meeting on 28th February 1941, Mr H. W. Ashby, then Chief Engineer at Kingston upon Hull Corporation Transport, was recommended for appointment at a salary of £600 pa. He took up his appointment soon afterwards, remaining with the Bournemouth undertaking until his retirement in April 1944. It will be recalled that his new superior, Mr Morrison, had also come from Hull.

In February 1941 another proposal for external advertising on the vehicles, on this occasion from Henbest Publicity Service, was rejected.

Queue Positions were introduced in the Square and at the Lansdowne at the end of February 1941.

In February 1941, the Transport Committee discussed the case of a driver who had stopped his trolleybus during an "Alert" in frosty conditions which were causing *"terrific and continuous flashing of the overhead wires"*. He had been asked to stop by many of the passengers in case the flashing had been seen by enemy aircraft. Councillors were told that a departmental lorry (LJ 1608) equipped with trolley poles fitted with special ice cutters was used to disperse ice around trolleybus running wires when necessary. They were also informed

Walsall also received Bournemouth vehicles on loan. Sunbeam MS2 78 (AEL 406) is seen here at Bloxwich, with its crew posing for the camera.

Note the conductress – most British transport undertakings employed women in this role, to replace the male staff who were away at war. Note, too, the "Bournemouth Corporation" legend on the vehicle, and the white-painted front wing to make the trolleybus visible to pedestrians and other road users. This vehicle has received the chocolate-painted roof to reduce visibility from the air at night.

D. Vernon collection

that any flashes could not be seen from above and *"that the wheels of public transport must be kept turning"*.

Saloon lights with circular shades were fitted to the trolleybuses during the year, three downstairs and three upstairs, together with an additional three on each deck which were only used when there was no "Alert". On the platform there was also a shaded light, which acted as a spotlight, illuminating both the platform and the road and enabling passengers to board and alight safely. To help drivers in the blackout, oil lamps were placed at night on traffic islands.

On 21st March 1941, a meeting of the Transport Committee approved Mr Morrison's proposals that a further ½d increase be made to a number of 1d, 1½d and 2d fares, where the distance travelled exceeded the general average. The proposed increases affected about 25% of these fare values, no long-distance fares being involved. The necessary applications to implement this were therefore made to the MoT (in respect of trolleybuses) and the South Eastern Traffic Commissioners (in respect of motorbuses).

The TGWU asked that the war service allowance be based on the wage payable if employee had remained in civil employment on 1st April 1941, i.e. including war bonuses, and not as currently based on the date of his undertaking war service. In April 1941 the Industrial Court awarded an increase of 4s per week to the wages of transport employees.

During another air-raid, at around midnight on 10th/11th April 1941, four flats in Fern Bank, St. Stephen's Road, between Richmond Hill and the Town Hall, and F. W. Woolworth's store in Commercial Road near the Square, were destroyed and Richmond Hill Congregational church damaged. There were eight fatalities. On Saturday, 12th April 1941, a bomb was dropped immediately outside the premises of W. H. Smith, in the Square, blocking access eastwards up Old Christchurch Road. An overhead wiring link from Gervis Place into Old Christchurch Road, in front of the apex of buildings between these two thoroughfares, was immediately installed, enabling trolleybus services 21-24 and 27 to terminate in Gervis Place and to start their outward journey with an immediate turn to the right into Old Christchurch Road. Service 25 from Ashley Road, Boscombe was split in two, the eastern section also terminating at Gervis Place whilst the western section was presumably covered by motorbuses, as there was no longer an overhead wiring connection to enable trolleybuses from the west to turn back at the Square. These

terminal arrangements continued until gas and water main damage had been made good, but the emergency overhead wiring remained in place until May 1953, although in latter days a line of traffic bollards prevented trolleybuses from actually turning there.

In May 1941, the Ministry of Labour and National Service applied to the undertaking for the release for military service of three of the five electricians *(sic)* employed by the Transport Department. The General Manager was already operating with a skeleton staff and had so far refused to release them but notification had now been received that action would be taken to enforce compliance with the Ministry's application. The Transport Committee recommended that all possible steps be taken by the Council with a view to the retention of the men by the Corporation as, if the "call-up" came into effect, it would become impossible to operate trolleybuses. As a result, the Ministry of Labour notified the Transport Department that it had been re-classified as a "Protected" undertaking in connection with the revised Schedule of Reserved Occupations.

Also in May 1941, the TGWU approached the General Manager with the suggestion that canteen and travel facilities for conductresses should be available after late duties. Mr Morrison was asked to provide any reasonable facilities and see if these could be, in some way, co-ordinated with H&D. With reference to conductresses, and having investigated the availability of uniforms, it was decided to supply slacks and possibly light coats for summer use. A "forage" cap, similar to that used by the ATS, replaced the caps originally issued.

In the autumn of 1941, the local newspapers reported that the Transport Department wanted the thirty trolleybuses on loan to other undertakings returned, but that the prospects were remote. Although London would apparently soon be returning those motorbuses lent by other undertakings when rail services were in difficulty, there was no mention of returning Bournemouth's trolleybuses. In mid-October 1941, an arrangement was reached for the return of some of the trolleybuses from London and it was hoped that these would be back by 6th November 1941. A visit to Wolverhampton in connection with the trolleybuses and staff on loan there was also made. The trolleybuses on loan carried promotional advertising for Bournemouth.

During the summer of 1941, the departure time of the last trolleybuses from the Square was temporarily extended until 11 pm but, on the instructions of the Traffic Commissioners, it was brought forward again to

10.15 pm from 6th October 1941 and curtailed again to 9.30 pm from 17th November 1941.

The Department tried to reduce dust emissions from the generating station chimneys in Southcote Road caused by the enforced use of inferior quality coal. Until the war they had used nothing but the highest quality coal, paying as much as 12s per ton more than was usual in power station practice. The coal position had become progressively more difficult under wartime conditions. Supplies of high quality coal became limited and the only alternative offered by the Mines Department were screenings – practically coal-dust. It had proved impossible to burn the latter in Babcock & Wilcox boilers and, to raise steam satisfactorily in three of the Lancashire-type boilers, it was necessary to fit special turbine-type fire bars as well as installing a more modern form of forced draught. The cost of this additional installation was more than £1,000 and, at the same time, a 1,500kW Daniel Adamson/Mather & Platt turbo-generator was acquired from the blitzed Bristol tramways and installed at Southcote Road. The quality of coal continued to deteriorate, and it proved necessary to use a greater proportion of screenings. A dust extractor, again costing more than £1,000, was fitted to the base of the chimney flue in an effort to reduce the quantity of coal dust being emitted from the chimney. This did reduce the nuisance (50 – 70 cubic feet per day of dust was extracted) and the understanding of those neighbours who had complained was requested.

At the Transport Committee's request, the General Manager investigated the possibly of operation of outbound trolleybuses from Old Christchurch Road via Hinton Road, Gervis Place, Westover Road and Bath Road to the Lansdowne. They recommended that the necessary overhead equipment should be installed as soon as possible – but nothing further was heard.

Further bombing in the Old Christchurch Road area prompted the Corporation to install a rather tight emergency turning circle by Horseshoe Common, at the junction of Dean Park Road with Old Christchurch Road, where the Lansdowne – Square inbound wiring turned down Fir Vale Road. The overhead wiring was installed in late March or early April 1942 and was intended for use as a central terminal point for services from the east in the event of serious damage at the Square. Until 1947, the Lansdowne itself only offered turning facilities to vehicles coming from Holdenhurst Road, i.e. services 25 and 27.

In November 1941, the Beach and Pavilion Committee asked that trolleybus services be extended to 10.15 pm

to preserve some kind of social life, and it was decided that, until further notice, the current "autumn" services would continue to be operate, the last trolleybus leaving the Square at 10.15 pm.

On 19th December 1941 the Transport Committee approved the sale of the single-deck Thornycroft demonstrator trolleybus, 71, to South Shields Corporation for £300, although it only left Bournemouth (through a dealer, Derry & Co.) in 1943. It operated there until 1950, ending its days as a caravan on a South Shields amusement park.

As a general rule, most buses were running in service largely full for most of the day, and it became difficult to keep time. Conductors were under extreme pressure collecting fares. As a result, volunteer auxiliary conductors were engaged to take over the regular conductors' platform duties, including announcing stops, supervising loading and unloading, giving bell signals to the driver and generally aiding passengers. They were provided with blue and gold identifying armbands, and special insurance cover was arranged. At the same time, the increased number of passengers carried and excellent traffic returns permitted the redemption of all outstanding debts and loans on the former tramways from the Reserve Fund at the end of the 1941 financial year.

Inflationary pressure continued in 1942, with a wage award from the National Joint Industrial Council for all male employees of 4s per week from the first pay week in February, with corresponding increases for female and junior employees.

No. 21B Avenue Road, known as Fairlight Glen, was rented to provide canteen facilities at Bournemouth Square for staff during the war, at a rent of £78 pa.

Double summertime, in which the clocks were put forward to GMT plus 2 hours, was introduced on Easter Sunday 5th April 1942 in an effort to secure the maximum benefit from natural lighting and thereby reduce energy consumption. On the same date services were extended from 10.15 pm until 10.30 pm (11 pm on Saturdays), but were curtailed to 10.15 pm from 4th October 1942.

In May 1942 a delayed-action bomb, which had fallen only 30 yards from the War Memorial in the Central Pleasure Gardens, exploded after 72 hours. The public were advised to report any suspicious holes which might denote unexploded bombs below the surface. Enemy-occupied territory lay just 67 miles south of the town and "tip-and-run" raids were frequent. The Bourne Stream had been purposely dammed at the Square for use by the

Fire Brigade, creating a muddy pool in the Central Pleasure Gardens. Property was rented near Boscombe, (a shop at 934 Christchurch Road); Central, Southcote Road (a house at 25 Southcote Road, at a cost of £80 pa) and Moordown Depots (a shop) to accommodate fire watchers.

Appreciating that there was a national need for new buses and trolleybuses to carry vastly increased numbers of passengers, and to meet the need to replace war-damaged, commandeered and worn-out vehicles, the Ministry of Supply and the Ministry of War Transport had approved the manufacture of a strictly limited number of new vehicles per year which they allocated to undertakings who applied. Some double-deck "utility" trolleybuses were available under the 1943 build programme, and the Ministry of War Transport was prepared to allocate four such vehicles to Bournemouth. Mr Morrison suggested that the operators which had hired Bournemouth vehicles might consider the purchase of these new trolleybuses so that the hired trolleybuses could be returned. Resulting from these suggestions and negotiations with the Ministry of War Transport and London Transport, arrangements were made for the hire by Bournemouth Corporation Transport of six London ST-type double-deck motorbuses, primarily for use on service 8.

Despite having agreed to bury emergency water supply pipes below the road surface at the important trolleybus loading point of Winton Banks, these had been laid on the surface of the road and were considered to be a danger to passengers.

A Bournemouth driver transferred to Wolverhampton had written to the Transport Committee about the scale of sickness allowances and asked that Bournemouth employees might be allowed to return home, perhaps two at a time, for a month. The General Manager wrote to his opposite number at Wolverhampton Corporation Transport suggesting that they adopt the Bournemouth scale of sickness allowances for the transferees, and enquired whether it might be possible for the Bournemouth men to be returned either permanently or temporarily. In September 1942, the Ministry of Labour and National Service notified the Bournemouth undertaking that they would be carrying out a further review of the undertaking's staff with a view to "calling-up" more men for military service!

The temporary transfer of nine Bournemouth trolley-buses operating in London to Newcastle upon Tyne, which was awaiting delivery of utility vehicles, was approved in August 1942.

With effect from 4th October 1942, the time of the last trolleybuses from the Square and other main terminal points was brought forward again, to 10.15 pm (the last motorbuses left at 9.30 pm). From the same date, and on the recommendation of the Traffic Superintendent, some 34 stopping points on various motorbus and trolleybus routes were abandoned, the Ministry of War Transport having instructed that the number of bus stops must be reduced. In fact, the Regional Transport Commissioner wrote again in mid-November 1942 requesting further reductions in the number of stops.

Mr Morrison reported on the potential for extending trolleybus operation from Iford Bridge along Barrack Road into Christchurch, and was instructed to apply for permission from the Ministry of War Transport and to proceed with the work as soon as possible.

The undertaking was invited to a conference of local operators, hosted by the Regional Transport Commissioner on 10th November 1942, to address the subject of a general curtailment of transport services. Accordingly, from 15th November 1942, times of last journeys were once again adjusted, last trolleybuses leaving the Square and other terminal points at 9.30 pm on weekdays and 9 pm on Sundays (as did the motorbuses), and finally to 9 pm throughout the week from 6th December 1942. Also from 6th December 1942 Sunday morning services were withdrawn, the first buses operating at 1 pm.

The supplementary toll for trolleybus passengers crossing Tuckton Bridge was withdrawn concurrent with the abolition of pedestrian tolls from 1st December 1942. Vehicle tolls were not withdrawn until 1st October 1943.

The Acting Town Clerk applied to the Ministry of War Transport for an extension of the time for the implementation of the trolley vehicle services authorised by the Bournemouth Corporation (Trolley Vehicles) Order Confirmation Act, 1938, as the war moved into a critical phase. They were recommended to re-apply under the Special Enactments (Extension of Time) Act, 1940, for a three-year extension of the time for exercising the powers already granted to the Council by the 1938 Act. On 18th June 1943 the Transport Committee learned that this had indeed been granted by the Ministry of War Transport in respect of the Bourne-mouth Corporation (Trolley Vehicles) Order, 1937.

In February 1943, Bournemouth Council and Hants & Dorset agreed to continue their revenue co-ordination for a further three years, and then with an option to review at the end of each six months. At the same time the Transport Committee agreed to trolleybuses 78, 79 and 123, then on loan to Newcastle upon Tyne Corporation Transport, being passed on to nearby South Shields Corporation on loan.

As the four reciprocating generator sets used at Southcote Road power station for peak loads and emergency purposes required extensive overhaul, an order for new turbo-generator sets was placed.

Bell Punch advised that, from 1st April 1943, the price of pre-printed tickets would increase by 1d per thousand, but they agreed to renew the punch hire on the original terms and to supply fifty summer service punches free of charge if required!

Just before 1 pm on Sunday 23rd May 1943, a fine spring day, Bournemouth suffered a major air raid so sudden that, due to the enemy's low-level aproach, there was no time for an "Alert" to be given. Twelve Focke-Wulf 190 fighter-bombers accompanied by twelve Messerschmidt 109s roared over the cliffs at Southbourne and, during the next four minutes, 21 bombs exploded in ten areas, completely destroying 59 buildings and damaging 3,422 other properties. Later on, several unexploded bombs were found. People relaxing in the Central Pleasure Gardens were raked by machine gun fire. In total 77 civilians were killed and 196 injured, and there was a death toll of 131 of all nationalities amongst the military. Trolleybus Driver H. E. Rodgers was killed and Driver W. Sackley seriously injured. Fortunately this was the last air-raid on the town centre.

The Central Hotel, on Richmond Hill and Punshon Memorial Church next-door received direct hits, the hotel being destroyed and the church so seriously damaged that it had to be demolished and replaced with a new building in Exeter Road. Beales modern seven-storey department store on the corner of Hinton Road and Old Christchurch Road received a direct hit from a 500lb bomb and a ruptured gas main in the store caught fire, the blaze being finally contained at 5 pm but not before much of the building had collapsed. A raider shot down by a Spitfire crashed into a hotel in Grove Road, while the Metropole Hotel, Lansdowne – a billet for Canadian airmen – was hit by a 500lb bomb, causing walls and floors to collapse. The Shamrock & Rambler Coaches garage in Holdenhurst Road and Bobbys department store in the Square were also hit. Several trolleybuses suffered damaged panelling and blown-in windows, whilst others were raked with machine-gun fire.

Several roads in the town centre were closed for some time due to dangerous buildings. Until Cairns House in St Peter's Road was demolished, trolleybuses from the east could not traverse their normal route via Fir Vale Road, St. Peter's Road and Gervis Place to the Square and were turned at Horseshoe Common. During the afternoon of Saturday 29th May, rubble had been cleared sufficiently to permit the extension of trolleybuses back down Richmond Hill to the Square, whilst by 4 pm those from the east, which had been terminating at Horseshoe Common in the meantime, also reached the Square. The normal route was not resumed until 29th July 1943, however. Trolleybuses travelling from Central Depot, Southcote Road via Holdenhurst Road to Boscombe, which turned at the Lansdowne, could no longer do so until the Metropole Hotel had been demolished and the site levelled, and they too used Horsehoe Common. "Side-route" services terminated at the top of Richmond Hill and reversed by use of T-poles (the Bodorgan Road reversing triangle not being installed until 30th June 1945). At the beginning of June 1943, the Beales Corner stop of services 25 to Ashley Road, Boscombe and 27 to Moordown was temporarily moved some 50 yards north-east towards Horseshoe Common, presumably to permit demolition of damaged buildings in Old Christchurch Road.

Following the 23rd May 1943 "incident", the Transport Committee again recommended that a trolleybus over-head connection should be provided in Bath Road and Westover Road to permit a two-way service along these roads. They also recommended installation of a turning facility for trolleybuses at the top of Richmond Hill (the subsequent Bodorgan Road reversing triangle) and that the Town Clerk report with respect to certain other routes.

Having obtained the necessary authorities and, more importantly, the materials, the Barrack Road extension between Iford Bridge and Stour Road, Christchurch, past various military installations including MEXE, was constructed and the Ministry of War Transport raised no objection to services commencing on the Corporation's own responsibility before an official inspection. The route was inaugurated on 22nd July 1943, thus:

20 Square (Gervis Place) – Lansdowne – Christchurch
    Road – Boscombe – Iford – Jumpers – Christchurch

The frequency of service 21, which also operated between Christchurch and the Square but via Tuckton Bridge, Southbourne Cross Roads and Fisherman's Walk, was slightly reduced as a result, more trolleybuses from the Square terminating at Southbourne Cross Roads. From 8th November 1943, most

Bluebird, the only single-deck Thornycroft trolleybus ever built, gained fleet livery during the war. The vehicle, (71 (LJ 7704) is seen here in 1943 at Queens Park in what is probably an official photograph taken to promote its sale.   *D. L. Chalk collection*

trolleybuses terminating at Southbourne Cross Roads were extended to the west (Bournemouth) side of Tuckton Bridge, a reversing triangle having been installed opposite Wick Lane, operating as service 22:

22 Square (Gervis Place) – Lansdowne – Christchurch Road – Boscombe – Fisherman's Walk – Southbourne Cross Roads – Tuckton Bridge

The Transport Committee, at their 18th June 1943 meeting, recommended that the General Manager be authorised to commence overhead construction in Bath Road, the Pier Approach and Exeter Road to the Square. They also recommended an application to the Ministry of War Transport for authority to operate trolleybuses in Lansdowne Road from its junction with St. Paul's Road to the Lansdowne to give an emergency connection between the two existing trolleybus routes.

The National Joint Industrial Council recommended a further increase of 4s 6d per week from the first full pay period in July 1943, with proportionate increases for employees under the age of 21 years. A similar award of 4s per week was granted to those employees engaged in activities such as coach painting, body building, etc., from 19th July 1943.

By September 1943, work was under way to install the replacement turbo-generator set at Southcote Road power station. It proved necessary to dispose of two worn-out Bellis & Morcom reciprocating engines. Tenders for the purchase of engines had been received from three leading contractors and that of Messrs T. W. Ward, Ltd., of £187 accepted. An electric pump was also required for the turbo-generator set, and the General Manager recommended the purchase of a suitable pump, at an estimated cost of £390–£400.

Another official view of Thornycroft 71 (LJ 7704), evidently taken on the same occasion as the view shown above.   *D. L. Chalk collection*

In October 1943 plans to loan two trolleybuses to Llanelly were announced; these were to be 77 and 123.

In November 1943, the General Manager completed a Report on the supply of electricity to the undertaking. Technical considerations and the prevailing circumstances made it impractical to source all traction power needs from the Bournemouth & Poole Electrical Supply Company and, in the General Manager's opinion, proper use had been made of alternative supply sources. The Transport Committee thereupon asked the General Manager to prepare periodic statements of the quantities of electricity generated at the undertaking's own power station, the quantities purchased from the Company, and the costs involved, particularly with respect to the plant which was then being installed, aimed at achieving greater efficiency.

Transport services operated on Christmas Day, 1943, primarily for ARP purposes. It has not been possible during research for this book to determine whether services operated on Christmas Day before the war, or in previous wartime years.

The *Times & Directory* newspaper of 28th March 1944 carried a report that, to meet wartime conditions, the Council had given the Transport Department permission to experiment with plans to eliminate loading and unloading vehicles at islands in the Square, which had been under consideration since the introduction of trolleybuses. Work would start as soon as the necessary overhead fittings were obtained, it being the intention to construct queue bays in the vicinity of the Lower Gardens in Gervis Place where all buses from the east would unload and reload, then continue right around the Square

and on through Old Christchurch Road in the normal way. Thus, there would be no stop at the island opposite Burton's or on the outer side of the island near Bobbys. Trolleybuses for Moordown would continue straight round to Burton's Corner by the main road, instead of passing between the two adjacent islands; Westbourne buses would now load there instead. There would be no alteration to the loading of Ashley Road and Charminster services on the corner of the Public Gardens between Avenue Road and Bourne Avenue as there was a wide pavement with plenty of room for queueing.

There was also a plan to relieve the muddle at the Lansdowne, where all intending passengers waited in one queue for buses to Purewell, Christchurch, Iford, Boscombe and Southbourne. It was planned to form three queue positions at this location and to prevent queue changing when a bus approached. They were to be formed so that passengers moved in the opposite direction to that in which the bus was travelling.

On 21st April 1944, upon the retirement of Mr Ashby, Mr W. D. Reakes, AMInst.T, was appointed Deputy General Manager and Traffic Superintendent at a salary of £750 pa, rising by two annual increments of £50 to a maximum of £850 pa. He had joined BCT in 1935, and thus had seen virtually all of the replacement of trams by trolleybuses. Mr Reakes had received his early training with the Bristol Tramways & Carriage Co. Ltd., under Sidney Smith. He left in 1926 to join the United Automobile Services at Norwich as the District Manager's Assistant, and was in 1928 appointed Traffic Manager with East Midland Motor Services, returning to Norwich as District Manager the following year. At that time United and East Midland had shared a common

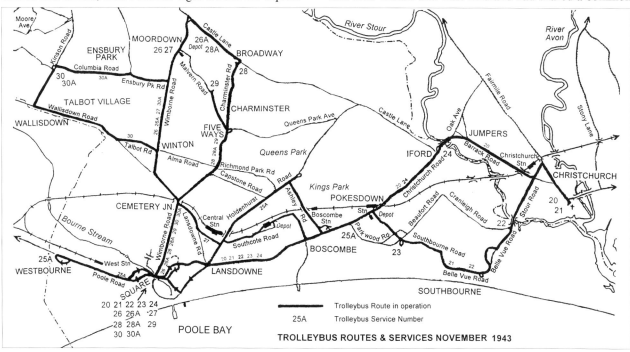

TROLLEYBUS ROUTES & SERVICES NOVEMBER 1943

Managing Director. When United centralised their activities in the north, he took over the Yorkshire area as District Manager and then the Durham District.

The National Joint Industrial Council had also released revised conditions of employment, namely an increase of 5s per week to adult males and pro rata increases to juniors and female employees, from 14th May 1944.

On 19th May 1944, the Transport Committee considered some comments made by the Chairman of the Bournemouth and Poole Electricity Supply Company Ltd., with respect to the renewal of plant at the Southcote Road generating station. The purchase had not been made without careful consideration, not least the wartime situation, during which it was particularly important to have an alternative to the "Grid" which was already heavily burdened and not immune to breakdown. The appropriate Government departments had approved and, indeed, urged the retention of every available power supply to relieve the load on the Grid and as a "stand-by", and the purchase of this plant received the approval of the Ministry of Supply, the Electricity Commissioners, the Ministry of War Transport and the Ministry of Fuel and Power. The Corporation had considered the ratepayers' and travelling public's best interests, whilst the Transport Committee were satisfied that the improved reliability of service and financial results demonstrated the wisdom of their policy. The electricity supply situation was under constant review and, should it be felt wise to take all or more power from the Grid in the future, the Committee would have no hesitation in so recommending to the Council.

Complaints had been received from persons wishing to travel from Winton to Bournemouth, after trolleybus services had ceased for the evening, that they had been being ignored by H&D buses travelling along the same route. H&D considered that, as the Corporation was running late buses for fire-watchers and night-shift workers, H&D were not permitted to pick up ordinary passengers.

In June 1944 Christchurch Council approved the proposed extension of trolleybus service 24 over Iford Bridge and around a single line turning loop along Oak Avenue and Stourvale Avenue (the actual terminal point) at Jumpers Corner, subject to the fares not exceeding those currently charged. Matters were delayed due to the non-availability of a junction for the overhead but, at 10 am on Monday, 7th August 1944, the Jumpers turning circle was pronounced ready for traffic. The rather tight Iford Bridge turning circle, together with its tramcar (No. 1) body waiting room, was retained for use by motorbus service 14 and short working trolleybuses. Trolleybus services operating along Christchurch Road beyond Pokesdown were amended to operate as follows:

20 Square (Gervis Place) – Lansdowne – Christchurch Road – Boscombe – Iford – Jumpers – Barrack Road – Christchurch.

24 Square (Gervis Place) – Lansdowne – Christchurch Road – Boscombe – Iford – Jumpers.

Iford Bridge residents soon complained of the in-frequency and unreliability of service 24, but the General Manager could only refer to staff shortages and make H&D aware regarding inward journeys from Iford.

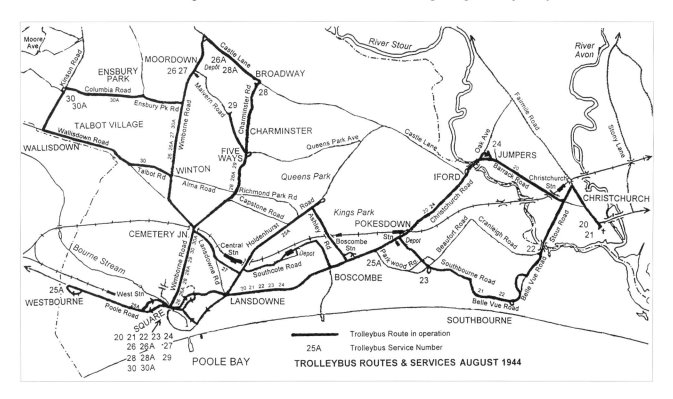

TROLLEYBUS ROUTES & SERVICES AUGUST 1944

In preparation for the D-Day landings in Normandy (6th June 1944), the area around Bournemouth, Poole Harbour and the Dorset coast was used as a major assembly point for equipment and troops. Security precautions made it necessary to ban pleasure visitors. The restriction on tourist visitors to Bournemouth was lifted on 12th July 1944 and on the August Bank Holiday Monday (at that time the first Monday in August) the town was crowded.

Continuing service cut-backs enforced on the undertaking for various reasons by Ministry of War Transport edict had led to long queues at key bus stops, particularly at peak periods. A Workers' Priority Travel Scheme, whereby key workers were issued with identifying permits giving them priority over other passengers queuing to board trolleybuses for their journeys to and from work, came into force on 6th September 1944. Over 20,000 priority passes (pink for men and buff for women) were issued to regular daily travellers who were dependent on public transport for their journeys to and from work, for use from 12.30 pm – 2.15 pm and 5.15 pm – 6.30 pm Monday – Friday and 12 pm – 1.30 pm Saturdays. Priority passengers queued on one side of the stop flag and boarded first, whilst non-priority passengers queued on the other side of the stop and only boarded after the priority queue had cleared. Stop signs indicated which side priority pass holders had to stand. Priority was also given to fire watchers, war workers on shift work, etc., on the last evening journey on each route and on Sunday morning services before 1 pm. Passes for school children were also approved on 24th November 1944 and came into effect shortly afterwards. The auxiliary conductors were responsible for enforcing the permit scheme, leaving the regular conductors free to get on with collecting fares on the full buses. All these Priority Pass arrangements were discontinued with effect from 20th October 1945.

Permission was sought from the Regional Traffic Commissioners to schedule the departure of last buses half an hour later, at 9.30 pm, during August and early September. This was granted and took effect from 5th August 1944. However, from 18th September 1944 to 5th November 1944, last buses were again curtailed to 9.00 pm but, with the main theatre of the war in Europe moving away from Britain's shores, they were thereupon extended to 10.30 pm and Sunday morning services reintroduced.

On the instructions of the Regional Transport Commissioner no ordinary services were operated on Christmas Day 1944.

At the end of March 1945, the erection of waiting shelters was authorised at the Square (for services 25, 28 and 29) and at Cemetery Junction a) at Lansdowne Road near the existing shelter; b) at Charminster Road (Cemetery side); c) at Wimborne Road (opposite side to St. Augustin's Church); and d) at Wimborne Road (opposite side of road to air-raid shelter).

The Emergency Committee of the National Joint Industrial Council considered that road passenger transport services should operate on VE (Victory in Europe) Day and for the two days thereafter and that employees should receive special rates of overtime pay. Victory in Europe was declared on 8th May 1945 and most of the trolleybuses were decorated with flags. Unfortunately, however, there was a serious breakdown of the turbo-generator shortly afterwards!

The Transport Committee Meeting on 22nd June 1945 recommended that a deputation be sent to the Ministry of Labour to express the Transport Department's urgent need for more staff to maintain (and, if possible, augment) the existing service.

The absence of overhead wiring in Stourvale Avenue suggests that this wartime view of Sunbeam MS2 113 on service 20 at Jumpers Corner was taken in spring 1944. Note the the masked headlights and the "via Iford" display in the windscreen. Note, too, the complete absence of any other traffic, white rings painted around each traction pole and the white-painted kerbside at the road junction in the background. On the right is a bus stop flag attached to the traction pole, and a rustic wooden shelter built by Twinns of Pokesdown and erected throughout the H&D area.   *G. O. P. Pearce*

The General Manager was instructed to take steps to have the air raid shelter in Boscombe Depot removed.

In July 1945 a sub-committee considered the General Manager's plan to improve accommodation at Central Depot, Southcote Road but recommended only temporary improvements until a scheme for the ultimate rebuilding and development of Central Depot and site had been completed. The same meeting confirmed that special overtime rates would apply on VJ (Victory in Japan) Day, 14th August 1945 and it was recommended that times of last services be extended to 10.30 pm as soon as practicable with representations to be made to the Ministry of Labour once again with regard to recruiting additional conductors.

Throughout the trolleybus era, tyres were supplied to the undertaking under a mileage agreement and the tender divided between well-known manufactures such as Dunlop, Goodyear and later Firestone. The manufacture of artificial rubber was in its infancy when the War broke out thus prices soared as demand increased, the sea journey from the natural rubber latex growing areas of South East Asia became increasingly dangerous and finally the plantations fell into the hands of the Japanese.

Date	Increase	Tyre cost (pence per vehicle mile
		0.24d
1st March 1940	5%	0.25d
1st January 1941	10%	0.275d
July 1941	7.50%	0.295d
1st January 1942	5%	0.31d
1st April 1942	12.50%	0.35d
July 1942	20%	0.42d
1st April 1943	9.50%	0.46d
1st January 1944	8.50%	0.50d
1st April 1944	16%	0.58d
1st July 1944	19%	0.69d
1st January 1945	14.50%	0.79d
1st April 1945	5%	0.83d
1st July 1945	10%	0.91d
1st October 1945	11%	1.01d
November 1945	9%	1.10d

Coal prices also fluctuated dramatically during the war; as tabulated in Appendix G.

WARTIME LOANS TO OTHER OPERATORS

LLANELLY

The start of production at Morris Motors' new Nuffield factory in Llethri Road, Felinfoel, in 1943, presented Llanelly District Traction with an immediate need for additional trolleybuses. Bournemouth 77 (which had recently returned from loan in Newcastle upon Tyne) and 123 (having spent 3 months in South Shields) were despatched to Llanelly. They were never fitted with local destination blinds and displayed service numbers only. The front exit doors were locked shut with a metal bar. The Bournemouth MS2s introduced carbon skid trolleyhead inserts to the Llanelly system. It is likely that one if not both trolleybuses arrived in Llanelly direct from the north-east, possibly for inspection or test purposes, and that they subsequently returned to Bournemouth for attention. After arrival in Llanelly, a change of bogie springs was needed due to damage sustained in Newcastle, and a Bournemouth engineer was on hand at Llanelly for a time after their introduction to put right any minor defects. They were used on all Llanelly routes without restriction and were highly thought-of by the drivers. Both trolleybuses are known to have suffered frontal damage during their stay in Llanelly. The hire cost of the Bournemouth trolleybuses was recorded in December 1944 as £840 12s 6d for the year end. They were returned to their home town on 29 June 1945, after a loan period of 18 months.

LONDON

In the early part of the war London Transport found itself short of all types of passenger vehicles, due to wartime losses and increased passenger demand. New vehicles were not available. All 18 trolleybuses loaned to London were based at Ilford Depot and used exclusively on local routes 691 Barkingside – Barking and 693 Chadwell Heath – Barking, which operated entirely in suburbia where the lower than normal seating capacity caused no hardship. Special destination blinds were made. These were the only Sunbeam trolleybuses ever to operate in service in London. 86 was repaired at Charlton following war damage. The Ilford staff nicknamed them "Yellow Perils", reportedly due to their doubtful braking performance. The Bournemouth vehicles carried Metropolitan Stage Carriage Licence plates on the open rear platform during their stay in London (number 77 carrying MSC plate 10946N). Half were released in November 1941 and the others in September 1942, as the SA class, intended for export to Durban and Johannesburg, South Africa, entered service with London Transport.

NEWCASTLE UPON TYNE

The remaining nine trolleybuses on loan to London Transport were released in September 1942, by which time sufficient AEC and Leyland vehicles of the SA class, intended for export to South Africa, had became available. They travelled direct to Newcastle upon Tyne. Both Bournemouth and the Newcastle upon Tyne Corporation Transport and Electricity Department operated a rear entrance, front exit policy at this time, and the loaned vehicles fitted in well with the local fleet. Four Bournemouth vehicles became surplus to requirements in March/April 1943 when Newcastle put into service six of the ten second-hand English Electric E11 trolleybuses dating from 1929-1932 which they had acquired from Bradford in October 1942. Three of the Bournemouth vehicles were passed to South Shields at the beginning of March 1943 and one (77) returned to Bournemouth in October 1943. The other five remained in Newcastle until May 1945.

The Bournemouth trolleybuses were used predominantly on the 4 group of services operating Denton – Westgate Road – Wallsend. One vehicle reportedly fell into the pits at Wingrove Depot.

SOUTH SHIELDS

Severe bombing of the town, home to many busy Tyneside shipyards, ensured that the 36 trolleybuses in the fleet (which by 1942 also included ex-Bournemouth Thornycroft LJ 7704, South Shields 236) were hard-pressed, although no route served the shipyards themselves.

A September 1941 air raid had seen three trolleybuses burnt out in the Market Place. A new trolleybus route Tyne Dock-Horsley Hill was built under 1939 Defence Regulations, increasing the demand for trolleybuses. It was opened by the ex-Bournemouth Thornycroft on 28 September 1942. Although official records state that only three Bournemouth MS2s (78, 79 and 123, despatched from Newcastle upon Tyne) were used in South Shields, there is some evidence that 77 also operated in the town in February – October 1943.

The Bournemouth MS2s worked on the Prince Edward Road services, Market – Fremantle Road or Marsden Bay (South Shields only introduced a service numbering system in 1950) which required five vehicles. It is known that in 1943 the service was maintained solely by

South Shields' Daimler CTM4 234 and Bournemouth vehicles, suggesting that four were on loan. But for this, 77 would have been idle in Newcastle upon Tyne for some 8 months – an unlikely situation in wartime. The Bournemouth trolleybuses were known as "Newcastle Trolleys" due to their livery and entrance/exit layout, despite the internal advertising panels being full of cards extolling the virtues of Bournemouth. Trolleybuses 78 and 79 stayed until May 1943, 77 apparantly until October 1943 and 123 remained until November 1943.

WALSALL

At the end of their stay in South Shields, Bournemouth 78 and 79 were despatched direct to Walsall for a further two years' service there. A number of motorbuses had been destroyed when an incendiary bomb hit the depot and the undertaking welcomed the opportunity of additional trolleybus capacity, not least as the Sunbeam MS2s were technically similar to 21 of its own fleet. The MS2s were based at Walsall's Birchills Depot and operated on service 30 (The Bridge – Leamore – Bloxwich), not venturing onto the Wolverhampton service, Walsall's only other trolleybus route at that time. Throughout their stay the Bournemouth vehicles had their front exit locked out of use. The delivery of new utility vehicles in June 1945 permitted their return to Bournemouth.

WOLVERHAMPTON

The news that ten new vehicles on order were unlikely to be delivered for a considerable period of time and wartime traffic growth in the industrial Black Country led Wolverhampton's Manager, Mr Charles Owen Silvers, to approach Bournemouth for the loan of 12 trolleybuses.

Not surprisingly, Wolverhampton also operated MS2s from the local Sunbeam works. The hire cost was £240 per each pa. Arrangements were made for Sunbeam to collect the trolleybuses from Bournemouth and tow them to Wolverhampton at the cost of £21 per vehicle. Mr Silvers also endeavoured to negotiate the hire of twenty Bournemouth drivers and twenty conductors to crew them, but only 23 staff in all were prepared to transfer. They were paid their normal wages plus 3s 6d per night subsistence and subsidized travel to their home town, but some soon returned due to their inability to find suitable accommodation and the lack of opportunities to visit Bournemouth. The transferred crews retained their dark blue uniforms with red piping.

The first ten, based at Park Lane Depot which had been built in 1938 to serve the town's northern routes, operated daily on service 13 (Pear Tree – Merry Hill) and from 1946 on cross-town service 12 (Pear Tree – Finchfield). They were used irregularly on all other Park Lane Depot services. Bournemouth 161 and 168 operated from Cleveland Road Depot on service 9 (Amos Lane – Jeffcock Road). When 161 returned to Bournemouth in 1946, 168 joined the others at Park Lane Depot. Very ocasionally, odd vehicles operated on other Cleveland Road workings for a day or two permitting easier supervision following repairs. Numbers 76 and 84 were renumbered 176 and 184 respectively to avoid confusion with vehicles having the same numbers in the native fleet.

The vehicles loaned to Wolverhampton operated in no other towns and, before being returned to Bournemouth, were given a full overhaul and repaint as the Black Country atmosphere and wartime lack of attention had made them shabby. Throughout their stay the MS2s had the front exit locked out of use and were fitted with wheel-type trolley heads.

Fleet Number	Registration Number	Loaned to	Date Delivered	Date Into Service	Date Withdrawn	Date Departed	Destination
72	AEL 400	London	21/12/40			01/09/42	Newcastle
		Newcastle	11/09/42	19/10/42	23/05/45	29/05/45	Bournemouth
73	AEL 401	London	13/12/40			01/09/42	Newcastle
		Newcastle	12/09/42	19/10/42	30/04/45	30/04/45	Bournemouth
74	AEL 402	London	23/12/40			11/11/41	Bournemouth
75	AEL 403	London	23/12/40			04/11/41	Bournemouth
76	AEL 404	Wolverhampton	04/09/40			27/10/48	Bournemouth
77	AEL 405	London	17/12/40			01/09/42	Newcastle
		Newcastle	17/09/42	19/10/42		05/02/43	South Shields
		South Shields	05/02/43			25/10/43	Llanelly
		Llanelly	28/12/43			29/06/45	Bournemouth
78	AEL 406	London	17/12/40			01/09/42	Newcastle
		Newcastle	28/09/42	02/12/42	26/02/43	02/03/43	South Shields
		South Shields	02/03/43			31/05/43	Walsall
		Walsall	01/06/43			22/08/45	Bournemouth
79	AEL 407	London	19/12/40			01/09/42	Newcastle
		Newcastle	22/09/42	19/10/42	26/02/43	02/03/43	South Shields
		South Shields	02/03/43			31/05/43	Walsall
		Walsall	01/06/43			17/07/45	Bournemouth
80	AEL 408	London	15/12/40			07/11/41	Bournemouth
81	AEL 409	London	19/12/40			11/11/41	Bournemouth
82	AEL 410	London	15/12/40			01/09/42	Newcastle
		Newcastle	03/10/42	04/12/42	12/05/45	30/04/45	Bournemouth
83	AEL 411	London	19/12/40			07/11/41	Bournemouth
84	ALJ 60	Wolverhampton	07/09/40			04/06/46	Bournemouth
85	ALJ 61	London	17/12/40			11/11/41	Bournemouth
86	ALJ 62	London	13/12/40			04/11/41	Bournemouth
87	ALJ 63	London	23/12/40			01/09/42	Newcastle
		Newcastle	27/09/42	19/10/42	12/05/45	12/05/45	Bournemouth
89	ALJ 65	London	23/12/40			07/11/41	Bournemouth
105	ALJ 979	Wolverhampton	09/09/40			08/06/46	Bournemouth
107	ALJ 981	Wolverhampton	13/09/40			29/06/48	Bournemouth
117	ALJ 991	London	21/12/40			04/11/41	Bournemouth
123	ALJ 997	London	13/12/40			01/09/42	Bournemouth
		Newcastle	06/10/42	02/12/42	22/01/43	01/03/43	South Shields
		South Shields	02/03/43			31/05/43	Llanelly
		Llanelly	28/12/43			29/06/45	Bournemouth
129	BEL 814	Wolverhampton	17/09/40			08/12/48	Bournemouth
130	BEL 815	Wolverhampton	20/09/40			20/07/48	Bournemouth
131	BEL 816	Wolverhampton	24/09/40			30/05/46	Bournemouth
132	BEL 817	Wolverhampton	27/09/40			06/07/48	Bournemouth
137	BEL 822	Wolverhampton	03/10/40			04/11/48	Bournemouth
145	BEL 830	London	17/12/40			01/09/42	Newcastle
		Newcastle	09/10/42	01/12/42	30/04/45	05/05/45	Bournemouth
156	BRU 7	Wolverhampton	16/10/40			23/05/46	Bournemouth
161	BRU 12	Wolverhampton	24/10/40			20/05/46	Bournemouth
168	BRU 19	Wolverhampton	10/10/40			27/07/48	Bournemouth

A Bournemouth Thanksgiving Week took place 13th – 20th October 1945 with savings as an aim, the Gardens and Square being illuminated. The end of the Second World War in 1945 saw the following trolleybus services operating:

20 Square – Lansdowne – Christchurch Road – Boscombe – Iford – Jumpers – Barrack Road – Christchurch

21 Square – Lansdowne – Christchurch Road – Boscombe – Fisherman's Walk – Southbourne Cross Roads – Tuckton Bridge – Christchurch

22 Square – Lansdowne – Christchurch Road – Boscombe – Fisherman's Walk – Southbourne Cross Roads – Tuckton Bridge

23 Square – Lansdowne – Christchurch Road – Boscombe – Fisherman's Walk

24 Square – Lansdowne – Christchurch Road – Boscombe – Iford – Jumpers

Sunbeam MS2 68 (LJ 7701), numerically Bournemouth's first trolleybus, stands at the 25 bus stop in Avenue Road, Bournemouth Square, shortly after the war. By this time, it had been rebuilt with a front exit to bring it into line with the layout of the 102 subsequent MS2s. *R. F. Mack*

25A Westbourne – Square – Lansdowne – Central Station – Holdenhurst Road – Ashley Road, Boscombe

26 Square – Richmond Hill – Cemetery Junction – Wimborne Road – Winton – Moordown – Lawford Road

26A Square – Richmond Hill – Cemetery Junction – Wimborne Road – Winton – Moordown – Lawford Road – West Way

27 Square – Lansdowne – Central Station – St. Paul's Road – Cemetery Junction – Wimborne Road – Winton – Moordown

28 Square – Richmond Hill – Cemetery Junction – Charminster Road – Five Ways – Broadway Hotel, Castle Lane

28A Square – Richmond Hill – Cemetery Junction – Charminster Road – Five Ways – Broadway Hotel, Castle Lane – West Way

29 Square – Richmond Hill – Cemetery Junction – Five Ways – Malvern Road.

30 Square – Richmond Hill – Cemetery Junction – Winton – Talbot Road – Wallisdown – Columbia Road

30A Square – Richmond Hill – Cemetery Junction – Winton – Moordown – Ensbury Park Road – Columbia Road

Following discussions with the police, the Arcade (Gervis Place) stop was replaced by one in St. Peter's Road, about thirty yards before its junction with Hinton Road, in October 1945. In December 1945 it was agreed that the stop west of the pedestrian crossing in Gervis Place be moved to a new position once this was available, and that the westbound service 25A Square stop be moved to the west side of the Square outside Bobbys department store.

Towards the end of 1945, Nelly Shelley, one of the first conductresses, was awarded the British Empire Medal *"for the efficient manner in which she had carried out her duties in the Transport Undertaking during the War"*. The award *"reflected great credit on the employees of the undertaking"*.

Evening services were extended to about 10.30 pm from 5th November 1945 and a skeleton service re-introduced on Sunday mornings from 11th November 1945. No trolleybuses operated on Christmas Day 1945 or, indeed, on any other Christmas Day thereafter, although it remained necessary for some employees to be on duty at the generating station.

Also in November 1945, a Transport Committee sub-committee visited two potential sites for a proposed depot in Castle Lane and asked Mr Reakes (in the absence of Mr Morrison, who was ill) to make further enquiries. Having considered the option of extending Moordown Depot by acquiring land at the rear and side, the proposal to construct a completely new depot and staff recreation ground on a ten-acre site on the Corporation's Strouden Farm, just off Castle Lane, was approved on 18th January 1946.

At their meeting on 21st December 1945, the Transport Committee made a recommendation that work should start as soon as possible on an extension of the trolleybus system from the Royal Bath Hotel to the Square via Bath Road, the Pier and Exeter Road, as already approved by the Council. The Highways & Works Committee were asked to develop a trial roundabout at the Lansdowne. In June 1946 Mr Morrison stated that the Lansdowne roundabout proposals created no overhead wiring difficulties and added that the police had no objections.

It was recommended that, as soon as alternative arrangements could be made, the parking of out-of-service trolleybuses in Gervis Place and Avenue Road cease, and that the Highways and Works Committee permit the use of St. Peter's Road car park or vacant land in Fir Vale Road instead. Suitable parking west of the Square was also required.

A generating station breakdown had led to an exceptional maximum electricity demand on 10th November 1945 but, in the circumstances, the Bournemouth and Poole Electricity Supply Co. agreed not to increase the maximum demand charge. The stoker gear for the Lancashire boilers at the Southcote Road generating station was considered life-expired and in need of urgent replacement. On 22nd March 1946 the Committee recommended that two sets, at £220 each, be purchased from Messrs J. Proctor, Ltd..

Despite inflation, there was a record surplus of £84,932 on the Undertaking's 1945–46 operations and some £30,000 was contributed to the rate fund. A further proposal for external vehicle advertising from Henbest Publicity Services Ltd. was rejected.

Rather than buy a new overhead tower wagon, it was decided on 11th January 1945 to recondition the chassis

of one of the six AEC Regent 661 petrol-engined motorbuses bought that month from Huddersfield Corporation, mount extendible towers and purchase appropriate bodywork from an outside firm at a cost of £500 – £600. Thus, tower wagon 10 (VH 6218) in the Overhead Department fleet, entered service on 1st February 1947. To prepare Bournemouth for its post-war holidaymakers some traction poles were repainted at about this time.

In March 1946 the Bournemouth and Poole Electricity Supply Co. were granted permission to attach street lighting equipment to overhead equipment and traction poles in Christchurch whilst, in April 1946, they were authorised to attach lighting cables to traction poles at Iford Bridge, Barrack Road Railway Bridge, and Stour Road, Christchurch.

In advance of a scheme to redevelop the Square it was decided at a meeting of the Transport Committee on 23rd March 1946 that stopping places be revised thus:

- Gervis Place: from the junction of Gervis Place with Old Christchurch Road eastwards to Westover Road, the stops to be a) services 21, 22 and 23; b) services 20 and 24; and c) service 27.

- Opposite the west island in the Square but beyond the pedestrian crossing, to be the location of the stop for service 25A (to Westbourne).

- Avenue Road, from the existing service 25A stop, westwards to Fairlight Glen or possibly Avenue Road car park, the stops to be a) service 25A (to Boscombe); b) services 26 and 26A; c) services 30 and 30A; and d) services 28 and 29.

Responding to a letter from the MoT regarding the Bournemouth Corporation (Trolley Vehicles) (Extension of Time) Order 1943, the meeting of the Transport Committee on 26th April 1946 recommended that further application be made under the Special Enactments (Extension of Time) Act 1940 to provide an extension of time for the introduction of trolleybus services on Routes Nos. 2, 4, 5, 6 and 8 and part of Route 3 authorised in Section 3 of the Bournemouth Corporation (Trolley Vehicles) Order 1937. This was done, ministerial approval for a further three-year extension being granted in September 1946. At the same time a request from a Mr J. Millson to use the Old Barn, Iford Bridge, for band practices was refused as the building was still used to store overhead equipment.

No sooner was the £2,000 bill for the overhaul and repair of the No. 2 Allen Turbo Set settled than the

General Manager reported that the No. 1 Set also needed a thorough overhaul. This was estimated to cost about £1,500 and Messrs W. H. Allen were once again recommended for the work.

Having received the Regional Transport Commissioner's permission, weekday and Sunday services returned to pre-war standards with effect from 6th May 1946, with the last trolleybuses from the Square being re-scheduled to 11.30 pm. On the same date, the outer terminal arrangements for trolleybus services 26 and 27 were rearranged (service 26 having been cut back from Lawford Road to Moordown on 9th October 1939) so that operation became:

26 Square – Richmond Hill – Cemetery Junction – Wimborne Road – Winton – Moordown

26A Square – Richmond Hill – Cemetery Junction – Wimborne Road – Winton – Moordown – Lawford Road – West Way

27 Square – Lansdowne – Central Station – St. Paul's Road – Cemetery Junction – Wimborne Road – Winton – Moordown – Lawford Road

The 24th May 1946 meeting of the Transport Committee studied the architects' (Messrs Jackson and Greenen) plan for the proposed new depot in Castle Lane. Although their remit had been to prepare reports and plans for extensions and alterations to various depots, Jackson and Greenen felt that the best solution would be to transfer all repair activities to Castle Lane, thereby relieving the shortage of space in the other depots.

As passenger figures continued to increase, Mr Morrison was instructed at the same meeting to report on the undertaking's requirements for new trolleybuses to meet future developments, bearing in mind the time lag between order and delivery. The Committee also considered an impending Order prohibiting standing passengers on buses and recommended that the General Manager press for a relaxation in the interests of the travelling public. They suggested that notices be displayed urging the public to avoid travelling during the peak periods of 11.45 am – 2.15 pm and 4.45 pm – 6.30 pm.

Several letters had been received from the public by the Transport Committee during May 1946 suggesting improved services, including a Square – Cemetery Junction shuttle service which the General Manager countered with plans for a service between the top of Richmond Hill and Winton Banks, but neither was ever introduced. A sub-committee considered a Moordown – Bear Cross trolleybus extension, which would permit a through service Square – Bear Cross. A further suggestion was that some service 22 schedules should be extended to and turn at Tuckton Bridge, instead of Southbourne Cross Roads. Mr Morrison stated that the position would improve when motorbus service 8 was converted to trolleybus operation but, in the meantime, some peak hour journeys would be extended to Tuckton Bridge.

A Bell Punch "Ultimate" Ticket Machine was demonstrated on the Ashley Road – Westbourne route during the Public Transport Association conference, which took place between 28th and 30th May 1946.

In March 1946, Mr Morrison had been instructed by the Transport Committee to convert motorbus service 8 (Fisherman's Walk – Cranleigh Road – Tuckton Bridge) to trolleybus operation as soon as possible. This was reiterated at the Transport Committee meeting on 21st June 1946 which, having considered his proposals for trolleybus route extensions, recommended that they be carried out in the sequence shown below and that the Highways and Works Committee evaluate any road improvements necessary:

1) Fisherman's Walk – Cranleigh Road – Tuckton Bridge (motorbus service 8)

2) Malvern Road extension to Moordown Depot

3) Holdenhurst Road and Castle Lane (from Charminster Road to Queen's Park)

4) Leybourne Avenue, Coombe Avenue to Wimborne Road

5) Wimborne Road, between Moordown and Bear Cross

6) Kinson Road from the junction with Columbia Road to the Dolphin Hotel, Kinson (on the south side of Wimborne Road between Kinson Road and Poole Lane)

7) Alma Road and Richmond Park Road

At the 21st June Transport Committee Meeting, Mr Morrison also presented his minimum needs to increase and modernise the undertaking's trolleybus fleet, namely 24 three-axle double-deck front-exit trolleybuses, and 30 double-deck and 15 single-deck motorbuses. He added that it was unlikely that the trolleybuses would be delivered in less than 2 – 3 years. Subject to the necessary consents, in September 1946 the Transport Committee recommended that the trolleybuses be to the newly-permitted 8ft width rather than the usual 7ft 6ins width.

On 19th July 1946 the Transport Committee received a deputation from the Southbourne Ratepayer's

Association, which pointed out that residents east of Southbourne Cross Roads, particularly in the Broadway district, found it difficult to board vehicles heading towards Bournemouth. In particular, service 21 trolleybuses were already full to capacity. It was also suggested that the Tuckton Bridge – Square service be improved between 12 noon and 7.00 pm. The Committee regretted that a lack of platform staff made this impossible to implement, but hoped that the situation would improve when motorbus service 8 was converted to trolleybus operation. The increasing number of passengers required more supervisory staff. Accordingly three Regulators were promoted to Inspector and seven Drivers promoted to Regulators.

In spite of all the tribulations during the war regarding the times of last departures on trolleybus and motorbus services, there was now a reduced number of late evening passengers, which made it possible to conserve fuel supplies by cutting back all services from a daily 11.30 pm finish to 11.00 pm on weekdays and to 10.00 pm on Sundays from 1st December 1946.

Plans to move the westbound service 25A trolleybus stop from its position by the Lower Pleasure Gardens to the west side of the Square at the lower end of Commercial Road were deferred until the Square re-development. The proposal to build a Transport Department traffic office at the Square above the Central Pleasure Gardens was approved by the Parks and Town Planning Department but, by late November 1946, the scheme had been amended to a much smaller, temporary structure.

Use of the Brassey Road reversing triangle, which was actually in Victoria Park Road opposite Brassey Road, ceased on 5th September 1946 due to increasing road traffic. It was replaced by one at Redhill Crecent, almost opposite Moordown Depot. Prior to this, trolleybuses terminating at Moordown Depot had done so by driving into the depot forecourt and then reversing out into Wimborne Road. Brassey Road triangle was dismantled on 29th May 1948. Also in September 1946, the police recommended that in general bus stops just before traffic lights be moved a short distance past the lights.

The 20th September 1946 Transport Committee meeting deferred consideration of a suggested Boscombe – Westbourne through service until the planned Lansdowne and Square roundabouts were completed. In October 1946, the General Manager made the unusual observation that, when vehicle trials at the new Lansdowne roundabout were carried out, it might be found that, rather than automatic frogs, *hand-operated*

frogs controlled from the centre of the roundabout would improve traffic movement. Meanwhile, the MoT approved a trolleybus extension along Lansdowne Road from its junction with St. Paul's Road to the Lansdowne for the purpose of connecting trolley vehicle routes, under the provisions of the Bournemouth Corporation Act, 1930.

The 18th October 1946 Transport Committee meeting considered Christchurch Council's proposals to build a new road across the Pit Site, Christchurch, from Bargates to Barrack Road, and to introduce a one-way system from the traffic lights by the Fountain Inn in a clockwise direction round the triangle formed by Barrack Road, the new road and Bargates, subject to trolleybuses conforming with the one-way traffic system. This was approved subject to Bournemouth Corporation not being responsible for the cost of overhead wiring changes. Hampshire County Council responded in February 1947 that they considered that trolleybus services would greatly benefit from the planned one-way system and that it was reasonable to ask the Corporation to make a contribution towards the estimated £550 cost of changing the overhead. Bournemouth Corporation then enquired what proportion the County Council would be prepared to contribute!

From 29th October 1946 return tickets ceased to be issued on Sundays.

TUCKTON BRIDGE REVERSING TRIANGLE

First Layout, 8th November 1943 – ca. December 1946

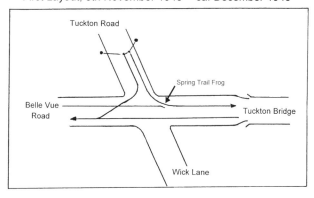

Second Layout, ca. December 1946 – 5th October 1947

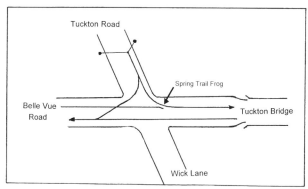

The Transport Committee meeting on 20th December 1946 recommended that a stop be provided near the junction of Seamoor Road with Alumhurst Road, Westbourne, and that this stop and the County Gates fare stage be regarded as the common terminus for service 25A.

It was also agreed to improve the layout of the Tuckton Bridge reversing triangle, which had been in use since 8th November 1943, opposite the junction of Wick Lane with Belle Vue Road, to avoid having to re-pole trolley-buses. This would have involved the installation of a frog on the "siding" in Tuckton Road, but it is not known if this alteration was ever carried out. The difficult reversing arrangements at this already busy junction were solved when, from 5th October 1947, all trolleybuses terminating at Tuckton Bridge were extended westwards along Tuckton Road to a turning circle at the junction of Carbery Avenue and Cranleigh Road.

Analysis of the reduced late evening services showed:

Date	Traffic receipts after 10.30 pm
Monday 02.12.46 (first day of curtailment)	8.22d per vehicle mile
Wednesday 04.12.46	10.09d per vehicle mile
Saturday 07.12.46	15.25d per vehicle mile

Operating costs, on the other hand, were then 18.56d per vehicle mile (excluding overhead expenditure).

A deputation from the Transport and General Workers Union was received on 22nd November 1946. As 99% of Transport Undertaking's employees were trade unionists, and as it was felt unreasonable that all employees profited from the benefits obtained by organised negotiation, they asked for the Council's help in respect of the remaining 1% of employees. A joint discussion with the non-trade unionists was agreed to.

On 22nd November 1946 the MoT authorised the equipment of Routes 5 and 6 (motorbus service 8) for trolleybuses. It was agreed to proceed as and when materials became available. The Ministry wrote again on 19th December 1946 to confirm that they had no objection to the equipping for trolleybus operation of Routes 1, 2 and 4 authorised by Bournemouth Corporation (Trolley Vehicles) Act and Order, 1930 and 1937, construction of which had been delayed due to wartime conditions. They also consented to the operation of trolleybuses (without passengers) along Hinton Road from its junction with Old Christchurch Road to its junction with Gervis Place.

In January 1947 the inward trolleybus service 25A stop near the school in Gladstone Road was reinstated.

At their meeting on 24th January 1947 the Transport Committee recommended that a second tower wagon be constructed by adapting the chassis of an ex-Huddersfield Corporation AEC Regent petrol-engined 661 motorbus and adding an extending tower thereon. The shortening of the chassis, by Lee Motors Ltd. of Bournemouth, was estimated to cost £425 and the cost of the tower equipment (to be fitted by the Transport Department) was estimated at £780. Tower wagon 12 (VH 6217) subsequently entered service on 1st November 1948.

The use of an auxiliary oil-burning plant and other boiler equipment was investigated. Mr Morrison was unable to obtain a quotation for the installation of such equipment at Southcote Road Generating Station, however, and the 24th January 1947 Transport Committee Meeting was forced to recommend that the existing boiler be reconditioned. It was felt that the first and second rings of both furnaces on the No. 1 Lancashire boiler should be renewed at an estimated cost of £1,000. The Transport Committee also approved the reblading of the 1,500kW turbine at the generating station at a cost of about £1,500.

Initial plans for the Lansdowne roundabout overhead wiring layout included frogs for access to and from Lansdowne Road, perhaps to offer alternative terminal arrangements for "Side Route" trolleybuses, but may also have been related to the earlier idea of a Square – Cemetery Junction shuttle service. However, no trolleybuses ever operated in the southern end of Lansdowne Road, and they retained their route along St. Paul's Road, passing close to Bournemouth Central Station. The Department's *Instructions to Trolleybus Drivers* dated 22nd January 1947 referred to frogs and some yards of overhead wiring extending into Lansdowne Road, but that this appears to have been removed shortly thereafter to avoid dewirements. Prior to the construction of the roundabout, there was an anti-clockwise turning circle at the very end of Lansdowne Road, in front of the Post Office, for turning service 27 short workings and for vehicles coming out of Central Depot, Southcote Road, to take up eastbound duties on service 25. (The development of the overhead wiring at the Lansdowne over the years is shown in Appendix O).

The Lansdowne was closed to traffic from Saturday evening, 25th January, until Monday morning, 27th January 1947, for the necessary road layout changes and trolleybus overhead installation. Work started at midnight, and it took just 3½ hours to cut down the old wiring and connect the new layout, which had been constructed during the previous weeks above the existing wiring. Four tower wagons were used, but the clear weather soon became atrocious. The *Bournemouth Echo* on 27th January 1947 reported: *"Snow began to fall. Soon, the rattle of shackles and the swish of falling wires broke the silence as the workmen commenced the big task of disconnecting the old trolleybus wires and connecting up the new overhead gear that encircled the central roundabout."* All road traffic to and from the Square was diverted via Stafford Road, Oxford Road, St. Pauls Road and St. Swithun's Road, or via Bath Road and Gervis Road East. A shuttle service of motorbuses was operated to and from the Square via Bath Road or Madeira Road, and trolleybuses from the east (services 20–25 and 27) reversed short of the Lansdowne at Christchurch Road/Gervis Road or at Holdenhurst Road/St. Swithun's Road using T-poles. A motorbus shuttle service operated from the Lansdowne to the Square and Westbourne via the diversions mentioned above.

Only one third of the kerbing was in place by the Monday morning, when trolleybuses started to use the roundabout. The *Bournemouth Echo* reported some dewirements at the Holdenhurst Road frog but no major hold-ups resulted.

In March 1947 the pre-war bus stop in Charminster Road near Acland Road, Charminster was reinstated.

On 28th February 1947 the *Bournemouth Echo* reported that *"Preparatory work now being done in the Square affords by the positions in which the kerbstones are being laid and new traction poles erected an indication of the route traffic will take on the southern side to make the journey round the new central island on a 30-foot carriageway"*.

Before construction of the the Square roundabout started, a single pair of wires was erected in Hinton Road enabling trolleybuses to leave Old Christchurch Road just after the Arcade and join the westbound wiring leading out of St. Peters Road into Gervis Place (the development of the overhead wiring at the Square over the years is shown in Appendix O). On Sunday, 30th March 1947 the new overhead layout at the Square roundabout came into operation. The terminal arrangements in Gervis Place for trolleybuses on services 20–24 and 27 were changed, the existing long loop in the overhead wiring being modified to become three individual loops. That nearest the Square served as

a terminus for services 21, 22 and 23 (via Fisherman's Walk), the middle loop served services 20 and 24 (via Iford), and that nearest to Westover Road was used by service 27 and for spare vehicles. A fourth passing loop was added in 1953 further west, where Gervis Place and Old Christchurch Road join the Square, to serve as a terminus for service 27. The Richmond Hill services, which had terminated on the west side of the Square, between Avenue Road and Bourne Avenue, were extended up Commercial Road to the Triangle, inbound vehicles offloading their passengers either at Richmond Hill (Albert Road) or immediately outside Woolworths. Outbound vehicles picked up in Avenue Road between the Fairlight Glen enquiry office and the Square. Three passing loops were added to the single-track overhead, that nearest Fairlight Glen serving services 28, 28A and 29 (via Charminster Road); the middle loop serving services 30 and 30A (via Winton); whilst that nearest the Square served services 26 and 26A (via Winton). The Triangle was now considered the official terminus of the "Side Routes", although most departures waited five or more minutes in Avenue Road before continuing to their suburban termini. Passengers were carried between the Square and the Triangle at an additional fare of ½d. "Double track" overhead wiring was erected westbound up Commercial Road between the Square and the Triangle, coming into use on Sunday, 6th April 1947. The tramway passenger shelter in the middle of the Square was demolished, leaving the shelter clock as a free-standing clock tower. Motorbus services terminating there were removed to Bourne Avenue or the extreme western end of Gervis Place.

With the extension of all "Side Route" trolleybus services (except the 27) from the Square to the Triangle, operations on this part of the network thus became:

26   Triangle – Square – Richmond Hill – Cemetery Junction – Wimborne Road – Winton – Moordown

26A Triangle – Square – Richmond Hill – Cemetery Junction – Wimborne Road – Winton – Moordown – Lawford Road – West Way

27   Square (Gervis Place) – Lansdowne – Central Station – St. Paul's Road – Cemetery Junction – Wimborne Road – Winton – Moordown – Lawford Road

28   Triangle – Square – Richmond Hill – Cemetery Junction – Charminster Road – Five Ways – Broadway Hotel, Castle Lane

28A Triangle – Square – Richmond Hill – Cemetery Junction – Charminster Road – Five Ways – Broadway Hotel, Castle Lane – West Way

29 Triangle – Square – Richmond Hill – Cemetery Junction – Five Ways – Malvern Road

30 Triangle – Square – Richmond Hill – Cemetery Junction – Winton – Talbot Road – Wallisdown – Columbia Road

30A Triangle – Square – Richmond Hill – Cemetery Junction – Winton – Moordown – Ensbury Park Road – Columbia Road

In November 1946, the Town Clerk had been instructed to investigate options for a proposed parking place for spare vehicles at the Triangle. He reported in February 1947 on the terms upon which the Durrant Estate would sell part of the grassed area at the Triangle and tenders were invited for the construction of a parking place. That of £982 from F. S. Loader was accepted.

At the end of financial year 1946–47 the Transport Committee contributed £50,000 to the rates.

On 10th April 1947 a 20-minute through service between Southbourne and Westbourne was re-introduced by extending some journeys on services 21, 22 and 23 beyond the Square to Westbourne showing service numbers 21A, 22A and 23A respectively, these services having been suspended on or around the outbreak of war. Services 23 and 23A were irregular peak-hours only journeys to Fisherman's Walk. The changed pattern of services serving the Southbourne and Tuckton Bridge areas was accordingly:

21 Square (Gervis Place) – Lansdowne – Christchurch Road – Boscombe – Fisherman's Walk – Southbourne Cross Roads – Tuckton Bridge – Christchurch

21A Westbourne – Square – Lansdowne – Christchurch Road – Boscombe – Fisherman's Walk – Southbourne Cross Roads – Tuckton Bridge – Christchurch

22 Square (Gervis Place) – Lansdowne – Christchurch Road – Boscombe – Fisherman's Walk – Southbourne Cross Roads – Tuckton Bridge

22A Westbourne – Square – Lansdowne – Christchurch Road – Boscombe – Fisherman's Walk – Southbourne Cross Roads – Tuckton Bridge

23 Square (Gervis Place) – Lansdowne – Christchurch Road – Boscombe – Fisherman's Walk

23A Westbourne – Square – Lansdowne – Christchurch Road – Boscombe – Fisherman's Walk

During the summer months of 1947, Sunday evening services were extended to 10.30 pm from Easter Sunday and to 11.00 pm from Whit Sunday (instead of 10.00 pm). Some service 22 journeys were extended across Tuckton Bridge and along Stour Road to its junction with Barrack Road, Christchurch. Here they turned left and headed along Barrack Road to Jumpers and Iford displaying 24A, and vice versa. The service was shown as operating daily every few minutes 10.00 am – 5.00 pm.

The police asked when trolleybuses would be extended to Bournemouth Pier, stressing the importance of this to the new traffic system at the Square. They were advised that this would be carried out as soon as possible following the completion of the motorbus service 8 conversion to trolleybuses, subject to equipment being available. However, by late June 1947, no overhead equipment had been erected in Beaufort Road or Cranleigh Road due to a shortage of traction poles. The unsatisfactory reversing

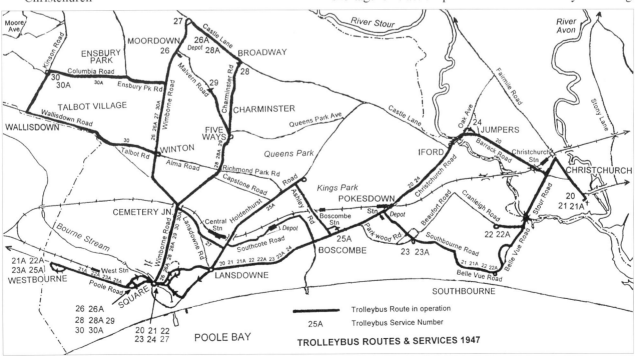

TROLLEYBUS ROUTES & SERVICES 1947

triangle turning arrangements at Tuckton Bridge provoked the suggestion that terminating trolleybuses be extended along Tuckton Road from its junction with Belle Vue Road to its junction with Carbery Avenue, the traffic island then at the junction of Cranleigh Road with Carbery Avenue offering a suitable turning circle. The Committee approved this, with slight adjustments to stops. At 4.30 pm on 5th October 1947, the first service trolleybus travelled up Tuckton Road from Tuckton Bridge and turned at the new Carbery Avenue turning circle. All vehicles previously terminating at Tuckton Bridge were extended thus, as construction of a new three-way road junction at the junction of Tuckton Road with Belle Vue Road had caused the reversing triangle to be removed.

At Christchurch Council's request the inward stops at the junction of Barrack Road with Avenue Road and Portfield Road opposite MEXE were re-positioned in May 1947.

The department was represented at the 19th September 1947 Transport Committee Meeting by Mr Reakes, the Deputy General Manager, as Mr Morrison was seriously ill. He reported that the replacement of the display "County Gates" by "Westbourne" in side destination boxes was under way. Trolleybuses never reached County Gates, this being on the rejected Poole extension, some one hundred yards beyond the terminus. Further consideration was given to winter services and, effective 12th October 1947, Sunday services terminated at 10.30 pm instead of 11.00 pm.

It was anticipated that the abolition of petrol rationing would result in greatly increased passenger traffic and lead to a further strain on existing services, which were already working under the difficulties of a shortage of vehicles and supplies. It was decided that the department would concentrate on maintaining existing services, with relief vehicles being operated wherever possible.

Also, in November 1947, the Transport Committee agreed to buy stoker gear costing £265 from Messrs J. Proctor, Ltd.. They also recommended the purchase of 24 three-axle double-deck front-exit trolleybuses. These went out to tender in December 1947 with a deadline for return of tenders of 1st March 1948.

On 11th September 1947 an empty trolleybus rolled away in High Street, Christchurch, and mounted a traffic island, demolishing the "keep left" bollard, before a Mr E. Hiscock jumped into the cab and pulled on the hand-brake. The driver later admitted that, having driven off the turntable, he had left the trolleybus unattended without placing a scotch under the wheels as instructed.

The undertaking introduced the 44-hour week, following its sanction by the National Joint Industrial Council effective 29th December 1947. This led to clerical staff helping as auxiliary Drivers and Conductors, a situation which continued into the 1960s during the summer season. The award covered a guaranteed week for platform staff, hours of work, overtime and holidays, the undertaking's increased costs being estimated at a minimum of £25,000 pa.

The new year found the department plagued with additional expenditure on the generating station. On 13th January 1948 a meeting took place between the new Area Electricity Board and transport undertakings in the Southern Area. It was disclosed that the Board intended to take over BCT's Generating Station as a part of the nationalisation of the electricity industry. Electricity "load-shedding" during the extreme winter normally did not effect the trolleybuses. Repairs to the turbo-generator diaphragms were made. The General Manager reported as to purchase of a phase changer in order to install three-phase machines and was instructed to obtain quotations. Repairs to the ash conveyor were needed but could be carried out by the department's own staff at cost of £150 – £200. A turbine overhaul and new shunt coils were required, one coil being faulty. It was suggested that a complete replacement set be bought at a cost of about £216.

The National Joint Industrial Council recommended advances from first full pay period following 11th March 1948:

> To adult male employees: 7s 6d per week
> To women: a proportional participation in that above.
> Youngsters: 3s – 4s 6d according to age

The following maximum rates were therefore achievable within 18 months:

	Group I	Group II
Drivers	107s 6d	105s
Conductors	103s 6d	101s 6d

The additional cost to the undertaking for the financial year ending 1st April 1949 was estimated as about £20,000 – £25,000.

On 24th March 1948 the Transport Committee considered the tenders received for the supply of new trolleybuses. Subject to the MoT approving the operation of 8ft wide vehicles, the Committee recommended acceptance of the British United Traction Co., Ltd. (BUT) tender for the supply of 24 chassis, with Crompton Parkinson electrical equipment, at £62,856.

Sunbeam MS2 79 (AEL 407) seen on 15th June 1948, parked out of service, with booms lowered, at the Triangle parking area. This was one of the six vehicles bodied by English Electric, to Bournemouth's standard Park Royal design. Note the chocolate roof, the fleet number on the maroon waistband and the elegantly-written legal lettering.
A. B. Cross

One lower tender was received. The recommended bodywork tender was from Metropolitan-Cammell-Weyman, Ltd. (MCW), to supply 24 all-metal bodies at £75,000. Should width permission not be granted, BUT would supply 24 chassis to a width of 7ft 6ins, with Crompton Parkinson electrical equipment, at a cost of £62,136, while MCW would supply 7 ft 6 ins wide, all-metal bodywork at a cost of £73,800. In addition, spare parts for the proposed new trolleybuses were approved:

a)   supply of electrical spares Crompton Parkinson (8ft or 7ft 6ins wide trolleybuses) £2,264 17s 0d.

b)   supply of chassis spares by BUT at £2,005 9s 0d.

Sanction was therefore sought for a loan of £142,726 to cover vehicles and spares, this to be met from three sources, namely an MoT loan of £30,621 for vehicles; a loan of £58,105 under the Bournemouth Corporation Act 1930, Section 237 (1); and a loan of £54,000 under the Bournemouth Corporation (Trolley Vehicles) Order Confirmation Act 1938. Over nine months later, on 8th January 1949, formal approval was given for the operation of 8ft wide trolley vehicles on services 24 and 25A, which subsequently became a general approval covering all routes on the system.

In April 1948, H&D suggested a new co-ordination agreement whereby the Company would pay the Corporation an annual sum to be agreed, based on the experience gained over recent years. This was referred to the Negotiating Sub-Committee.

The Standing Passengers Order, 1948, permitted the carriage (with restrictions) of up to eight standing passengers on trolleybuses, effective from 10th May 1948. A census was taken between 11th and 18th May 1948 at the Triangle and Avenue Road stops due to the prohibition on the carrying of standing passengers up

Richmond Hill. Only during the evening peaks were a substantial number of passengers left behind at the Avenue Road stop and, in very few cases during the week under review, was a trolleybus already full when reaching Avenue Road. The census showed that at peak periods the waiting time was not more than ten minutes. It was accordingly recommended that the Avenue Road stops be given priority for the provision of passenger waiting shelters.

On 15th May 1948, a single pair of trolley wires was erected at the Triangle parking area which had been in use by motorbuses since the beginning of the month. Trolleybuses commenced using the stand from 23rd May 1948, instead of running empty to/from Central Depot, Southcote Road, after the morning rush hour and prior to the evening peak. There was space for twelve vehicles.

No doubt influenced by the proposals for a new depot in Castle Lane, the 23rd July 1948 Transport Committee meeting recommended that the Strouden Park trolleybus route extension should have priority and requested a report from the General Manager as to suggested turning points. The Borough Engineer confirmed that a service road near the Strouden Park shopping centre would be suitable for use by trolleybuses, although this was never followed-up. The introduction of trolleybuses on the Strouden Park extension was accordingly recommended.

A request from Messrs Frank Mason & Co. Ltd., for advertising on bus shelters and, once again, on the exterior of the undertaking's buses, was rejected.

Material shortages had delayed the erection of overhead equipment on the extension from Fisherman's Walk, along Beaufort Road and Cranleigh Road, Southbourne, to Tuckton Bridge but, on 16th August 1948, trolleybuses replaced motorbus service 8. Trolleybuses on the replacement service to and from the Square

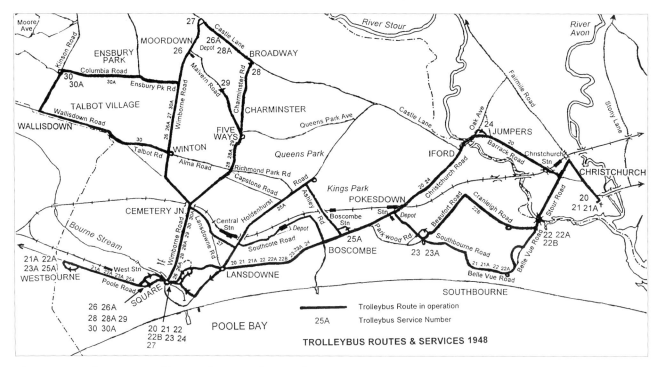

TROLLEYBUS ROUTES & SERVICES 1948

displayed service number 22B, which was linked with services 22 and 22A to offer a circular route. Carbery Avenue turning circle was therefore only used on a regular basis as the Tuckton Bridge trolleybus terminus during the period 5th October 1947 until 16th August 1948. Trolleybuses serving the Southbourne and Tuckton areas now operated as follows:

21 Square (Gervis Place) – Lansdowne – Christchurch Road – Boscombe – Fisherman's Walk – Southbourne Cross Roads – Tuckton Bridge – Christchurch

21A Westbourne – Square – Lansdowne – Christchurch Road – Boscombe – Fisherman's Walk – Southbourne Cross Roads – Tuckton Bridge – Christchurch

22 Square (Gervis Place) – Lansdowne – Christchurch Road – Boscombe – Fisherman's Walk – Southbourne Cross Roads – Tuckton Bridge

22A Westbourne – Square – Lansdowne – Christchurch Road – Boscombe – Fisherman's Walk – Southbourne Cross Roads – Tuckton Bridge

22B Square (Gervis Place) – Lansdowne – Christchurch Road – Boscombe – Fisherman's Walk – Beaufort Road – Cranleigh Road – Tuckton Bridge

23 Square (Gervis Place) Lansdowne – Christchurch Road – Boscombe – Fisherman's Walk

23A Westbourne – Square – Lansdowne – Christchurch Road – Boscombe – Fisherman's Walk

Following requests from the public, the 22nd October 1948 Transport Committee meeting discussed and made a recommendation that a through trolleybus service between the Square and Tuckton Bridge via Beaufort Road and Cranleigh Road should be re-introduced after 8.00 pm for a period of one month, and that loading figures should be recorded. This census rather surprisingly showed that no demand existed and the through service after 8 pm was discontinued, being replaced by a Fisherman's Walk – Tuckton Bridge shuttle service. However, in general, ever increasing passenger loads led to notices being displayed in trolleybuses from the end of September 1948 encouraging young persons to give up their seats to older passengers.

On 3rd October 1948 services 21A, 22A and 23A, which had been through-worked to Westbourne, were withdrawn and, from the following day, service 22B was extended in their place.

The September 1948 quotation of about £290 from W. H. Allen for overhaul and repair of the turbine rotor, etc., was accepted but the original quotation for a phase changer proved to be for unsuitable equipment. An alternative offer from the Westinghouse Brake & Signal Co. costing £189 4s was thus approved. Messrs Green & Son Ltd. supplied a replacement for the worn out economiser at the generating station for £3,521, with the department carrying out the installation at an estimated cost of £400, both costs being met from the renewal fund.

After several months of ill health the General Manager, Mr D. P. Morrison, died on 1st November 1948, aged 63. He had seen the number of passengers carried by the undertaking as a whole increase from 19,111,838 pa when he was appointed in 1935, to 60 million in 1947. It was Mr Morrison who had devised the "wee red boxes" (honesty boxes placed on each deck) which were then yielding £300 pa in uncollected fares.

Mr Wilfred Douglas Reakes, then Deputy General Manager and Traffic Superintendent and who had taken on much of Mr Morrison's work during his illness, was appointed General Manager at a salary of £1,350 pa, rising by annual increments of £50 to a maximum of £1,500 pa, plus travelling allowance for a private car.

On 10th December 1948 the last trolleybus on loan to Wolverhampton (129) returned to Bournemouth, while the use of Auxiliary Conductors in Bournemouth ceased on 31st December 1948.

At the suggestion of Southbourne Ratepayers Association, inward and outward request stops at the junction of Tuckton Road with Bellevue Road became compulsory stops at the end of December 1948.

On 21st November 1948, Col C. A. Langley carried out a number of MoT inspections, namely:

a) A preliminary inspection as to the suitability of Castle Lane from Charminster Road to Christchurch Road for trolleybuses. This line was subsequently constructed, opening on 15th October 1951.

b) A preliminary inspection of a proposed three-way overhead line at the junction of Tuckton Road with Bellevue Road, Southbourne, to permit a turn from Tuckton Road into Belle Vue Road towards Christchurch and also in the reverse direction. Permission was granted and, after erection of the new wiring, approved on 15th December 1950.

c) Retrospective inspection of the one-way Hinton Road (The Quadrant) connecting line between Old Christchurch Road and Gervis Place, originally authorised in the Bournemouth Corporation Act 1930, and in service, on the Corporation's own responsibility, since 1st August 1946. Official approval was granted on 19th December 1946.

Col Langley went on to suggest that the traction poles on Tuckton Bridge be painted with black and white rings to a height of six feet to aid visibility.

The District Valuer had made a valuation for the Committee's appropriation of 7.567 acres of land from the Highways and Works Committee and 9.72 acres of land from the Housing Committee for the proposed Castle Lane Depot. Following receipt of a letter from the MoT suggesting that the planned extension of the trolleybus overhead line along Castle Lane be re-considered due to the state of the nation's economy, it

was recommended that further consideration should be deferred until the result of a meeting with the Ministry about the planned depot was known. In the meantime, the proposed overhead line extension was changed from first to second priority. Suffficient equipment was available for the extension along Bath Road to the Pier Approach and onwards along Exeter Road to the Square. Thus, on 21st January 1949, the Transport Committee recommended that this extension, which had already received Council approval, should become the first priority and that the MoT should be approached for approval of the extension and of a turning circle at the Pier. For this extension, application was made for sanction to exercise borrowing powers conferred by the Bournemouth Corporation Act, 1930 for trolley vehicle equipment to the amount of £7,500.

The 18th February 1949 Transport Committee Meeting agreed to the erection of passenger waiting shelters at stops at Fisherman's Walk. Thus, in March 1949, a further twelve shelters were ordered from Light Steelwork Ltd. at a cost of about £2,400. The Stourfield School stop at the junction of Cranleigh Road with Beaufort Road was moved about ten yards along Cranleigh Road for safety reasons and barriers erected.

Special "To and from the Tennis" auxiliary indicators were displayed on trolleybuses passing Talbot Avenue for the period of the Lawn Tennis (Hard Court) Championship of Great Britain in April 1949.

H&D submitted a timetable for their proposed re-introduced services along Wallisdown Road to which the Transport Committee raised no objections. The timetable replaced that in the Second Schedule to the Agreement between the Company and the Bournemouth and Poole Corporations dated 5th July 1939.

At the end of April 1949 the service 25A stop in the Square was moved back some 20 feet whilst the alighting point for "Side Route" trolleybuses was moved a short distance up Commercial Road past the pedestrian crossing.

Immediately after the war, published plans had included the routes to Bear Cross (authorised under the 1930 Act) as well as the extension from Malvern Road to Moordown but no more was to be heard of either of them. However, application to the MoT for a further extension of time in respect of those trolley vehicle routes authorised by Section 3 of the Provisional Order of 1937, but which had not yet been introduced, was made in December 1948. The MoT consented in May 1949 to an extension of time for a further period of three

Sunbeam MS2 139 on summer service 30A at Bournemouth Pier, followed by a full-fronted Leyland Titan motorbus. Both vehicles are on layover, the crews leaning on the railings having a chat and a smoke. Note the "Columbia Road" slipboard in the windscreen of the trolleybus. *BTS Library*

years for the start of trolleybus operation on Routes 2 and 4 and part of Route 3. Until 1955, periodic renewal was made of the powers to construct routes along Richmond Park Road and Alma Road and from the Ensbury Park Hotel to Kinson (Wimborne Road) via Coombe Avenue, Leybourne Avenue and Northbourne Avenue.

The Transport Committee meeting on 20th May 1949 approved the construction of the new Castle Lane Depot and thus gave up the idea of acquiring land to extend Moordown Depot. It was recommended that the opening of the Castle Lane (Mallard Road) Depot and the inauguration of the Strouden Park trolleybus route extension should coincide. On 18th July 1949 motorbus service 31 commenced operation three times a day between Strouden Park (junction of Castle Lane East with Holdenhurst Road) and the Square via Charminster Road.

As the result of a petition, the same Transport Committee meeting agreed to reinstate the request stop at St. James' Church, Pokesdown, deleted during the war. It was also agreed with the Highways and Works Committee that, if road widening for the Bournemouth Pier trolleybus extension could not be completed before mid-July 1949, then work should not start until after September. The estimated cost of the first portion of the extension was £4,500 and the total £7,500.

An invitation to tender for the Castle Lane site clearance appeared in the press on 5th August 1949, while the highest tender for the purchase and removal of a 320-tube cast iron Green's economiser and related site clearance at the Generating Station, Southcote Road – that of George Cohen Sons and Co. Ltd. at £80 – was accepted.

At the 24th June 1949 Transport Committee meeting, Mr Reakes reported on the anticipated electrical distribution needs for the planned Castle Lane Depot and trolleybus route. It was estimated that rectifier equipment, additional switchgear at the existing Southern Electricity Board (SEB) substation at the junction of Castle Lane with Holdenhurst Road and the laying of a 0.5 sq. ins armoured cable from that substation to the junction of Castle Lane with Charminster Road, the total cost of which was estimated at £16,000. The SEB had quoted approximately £3,000 for a 500kW, rectifier with an eleven-month delivery time.

The start of site works for Castle Lane Depot was delayed when Trevor Construction withdrew their tender. The next lowest tender of £16,392 8s 7d, from Messrs Grounds & Newton, Ltd., was therefore accepted and, on 29th August 1949, the Transport Committee requested the Finance Committee to approve an estimated £151,216 for the first section of the scheme, which included road works, garage overhead and ancillary equipment. The following month it was recommended that the widening and reconstruction of part of Mallard Road for access purposes, at an estimated cost of £2,885, also be included in the cost of the new depot. By October 1949, fourteen tenders had been received for the construction of the new maintenance works and depot buildings. The lowest, from Messrs James Drewitt & Son Limited for £97,948, was accepted subject to Finance Committee and MoT approval, and satisfactory sureties being submitted.

In September 1949 the MoT approved the Bournemouth Pier trolleybus route extension (along Bath Road, Pier Approach and Exeter Road). Rather belatedly, the Highways and Works Committee requested that no services ran down Bath Road between Westover Road and Pier Approach until after road widening, but the Transport Committee would not agree, as the Council had already sanctioned the introduction of services and the MoT had also approved trolleybus operation over the road in its present state.

In September 1949 the Department received a letter of complaint about grit and smoke emissions from Southcote Road Generating Station, and the Transport Committee received a memo from the Health (General) Sub-Committee on the same matter. Mr Reakes acknowledged difficulties with the grit extractor and wrote to the coal suppliers for better coal in an effort to achieve improvements. In June 1949 a child had drowned in the reservoir under one of the cooling towers at Southcote Road.

On 23rd September 1949 the Transport Committee granted permission for street lights to be fixed on certain traction poles requested by the Borough Engineer.

In October 1949 an offer was received from Wolverhampton Corporation to sell a quantity of spare parts for Sunbeam trolleybuses for £450.

In November 1949 the suggestion that each stop be named was rejected on cost grounds.

Plans for a reversing triangle at the junction of Castle Lane East with Holdenhurst Road, then foreseen as terminus of the Strouden Park extension rather than Iford, were considered unsuitable by both the MoT and the police. The Borough Engineer suggested that a piece of land in the Meyrick Estate to the north east of the junction could be purchased for use as a turning circle, which could be constructed using direct labour at an estimated cost of £500. This was indeed subsequently built and was brought into use on 23rd May 1953, although the through trolleybus service to Iford opened on 15th October 1951.

The police suggested that the stop situated about thirty feet up Commercial Road from the Square, used by trolleybus services 26, 28, 29, 30 and 30A, be discontinued for safety reasons. As a compromise, early in 1950 the stop was relocated between the pedestrian crossing opposite Bobbys store and that at the bottom of Commercial Road.

It was reported at the Transport Committee meeting on 18th November 1949 that two passenger waiting shelters had been erected in Avenue Road for trolleybus services 28, 29, 30 and 30A; that work on a similar shelter for service 26 was about to commence; and that the proposed site of the shelter for trolleybus service 25 had been found to be immediately opposite the emergency vehicular access to the Central Pleasure Gardens. By the following Transport Committee meeting, on 23rd December 1949, it had been decided to move this latter entrance some thirty feet nearer the Square, although an additional sump for emergency use would have to be installed in the gardens near the taxi-drivers' shelter in

Bourne Avenue. This work was at the joint expense of the Fire Brigade and Transport Department and cost £156.

Yet more expense was being incurred at Southcote Road Generating Station. The turbo-generator velocity wheel needed re-blading, and a new guide-ring was required. The manufacturers, Messrs D. Adamson & Co. Ltd., submitted quotations of £687 and £320 respectively, which were accepted. However, an emergency Transport Committee Meeting was convened on 11th January 1950 to consider further repairs to the turbo-generator. In March 1950 an estimate of £126 from Messrs V.G. Morris Ltd. was accepted for repairs to the Generating Station chimney.

The immediate post-war period was greatly influenced by the Labour Government's policy of nationalising major industries and utilities, including public transport. The Area Managers' Committee of the MPTA wrote to the Transport Committee about the proposed Northern Passenger Transport Area nationalisation asking local authorities to examine the scheme and give their views with respect to their own area. It was recommended that the Council protest strongly against any suggestion that Bournemouth Corporation Transport be nationalised. Any enquiry should be open to the public and to the press. The Council supported the policy of the National Union of Ratepayers' Associations and Local Government League passed at their November 1949 conference:

"This Conference having considered the published scheme of the Transport Commission for the transfer of Road Passenger Transport to the said Commission, expresses its opinion that such proposals are contrary to the public interest. It further expresses its determination to resist any proposals involving the confiscation of valuable Municipal assets, and the complete abolition of local control regarding fares, provision of services, finance and administration of a service so essential to the welfare and convenience of the community".

As part of the south west branch of the Omnibus Passengers' Protection Association, an Action Committee was formed on 3rd March 1950 to retain local control of transport in the town. In an address, Alderman Langton, Chairman of the Transport Committee, hinted that an un-nationalised transport system in Bournemouth might still be able to avoid an increase in fares, and retain the penny fare. *"We can do it by other adjustments. Our bus service is the poor man's Rolls-Royce"*, he added.

In connection with the pending celebration of the Golden Jubilee of Bournemouth receiving County Borough status, Mr Reakes had estimated the cost of illuminating and decorating two trolleybuses at £1,600. This was considered too costly and was not proceeded with.

Amongst other items in connection with Castle Lane Depot, the Transport Committee meeting of 24th February 1950 recommended acceptance of the SEB's tender of £17,397 for feeder cables, including their installation and jointing for the Castle Lane trolleybus scheme. It was estimated that overhead equipment, including switching pillars and panels, would cost £15,899.

By now twelve trolleybuses required a thorough bodywork overhaul and, as the result of an inspection by Weymanns, this was estimated to cost about £284 per vehicle.

In March 1950, the MoT wrote to the undertaking approving the scheme for equipping Castle Lane between its junction with Charminster Road and that with Holdenhurst Road for trolleybus operation under the provisions of Section 3 of the Bournemouth Corporation (Trolley Vehicle) Order Confirmation Act, 1938. Faced with terminal point difficulties at Strouden Park, the Transport Committee recommended at their meeting on 24th March 1950 that application be made immediately for the equipment of Castle Lane East between Holdenhurst Road and Christchurch Road, Iford for trolleybus operation.

In early March 1950, the overhead wiring was completed from the junction of Bath Road and Westover Road (outside the Royal Bath Hotel) down to Pier Approach, with a passing loop in Bath Road at the side of the indoor baths. At the Hotel's request, traction poles outside the Hotel were painted white to match the building's colour, whilst poles painted white were also provided in Bath Road and Pier Approach to Bournemouth Pier itself. Turning facilities were provided around an island of gardens at the Pier. The wiring returned up Bath Road to the Royal Bath Hotel and under new eastbound wiring to the Lansdowne, while a single pair of wires continued from a frog in front of the Pier kiosks northbound up Exeter Road to the Square, wiring in the opposite direction never being installed. The MoT inspection took place during April 1950, the Inspector congratulating the Department on the standard of workmanship.

On trial runs, trolleybuses had reached the Pier on 14th March 1950. According to an interview which Alderman Langton gave to the *Bournemouth Echo*, published on 4th April 1950, the Transport Committee had still not decided which service(s) would operate to the Pier at Easter. Regular services to and from the Pier operated from Good Friday 7th April to Easter Monday 10th April 1950, then ceased until the 1950 summer timetable came into effect between 27th May and 1st October. During that time, extra journeys were made to and from the Pier on five services, each at 20 minute intervals, thus:

23 Bournemouth Pier – Lansdowne – Christchurch Road – Boscombe – Fisherman's Walk

24 Bournemouth Pier – Lansdowne – Christchurch Road – Boscombe – Iford

25 Bournemouth Pier – Lansdowne – Central Station – Holdenhurst Road – Queens Park Golf Pavilion (only)

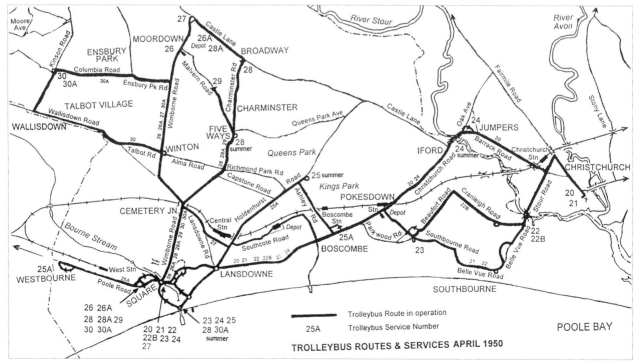

TROLLEYBUS ROUTES & SERVICES APRIL 1950

28 Bournemouth Pier – Lansdowne – Cemetery Junction – Charminster Road – Five Ways (only)

30A Bournemouth Pier – Lansdowne – Cemetery Junction – Winton – Moordown – Ensbury Park Road – Columbia Road

Despite gales, scudding clouds and showers, Good Friday 1950 brought Bournemouth the heaviest Easter tourist invasion since the war, with 50,000 visitors – and with 13,000 deck-chairs being occupied by lunch-time! There were half-mile-long traffic jams at the Lansdowne and the Square. Immediately after Easter, work started on repairing the breach in Bournemouth Pier, which had been made as a security measure early in the War.

It has proved impossible to establish during research for this book in which periods regular trolleybus services operated northbound along Exeter Road from the Pier to the Square; however, photographs exist, taken in 1950, 1953 and 1954, showing trolleybuses on services 23 and 35 loading at the western side of Pier Approach, having already passed the turnout frog for routing along Exeter Road. In addition to providing a source of additional traffic, it should not be forgotten that the Pier was also foreseen as an alternative town centre terminus, capable of reducing the number of trolleybuses at the Square and thus requiring direct routing along Bath Road, to and from the Lansdowne. Although the published timetables

offer no solution to this mystery, provision was made in the 1950 and 1951 fare tables for trolleybuses returning to Charminster or Winton via Richmond Hill. Even the 1956 tables still included fares for trolleybus services from Bournemouth Pier to Fisherman's Walk via the Square and Old Christchurch Road.

From 27th May 1950, service 22B was cut back from Westbourne to operate between the Square and Tuckton Bridge only, leaving only service 25A running to and from Westbourne.

Bournemouth Trades Council considered that turning trolleybuses at Redhill Crescent, Moordown Post Office, had become dangerous. The alternative of extending all Moordown-terminating trolleybuses to Lawford Road would have proved uneconomic. Mr Reakes therefore investigated using the inside of Moordown Depot instead. On 14th August 1950, Redhill Crescent reversing triangle was locked out of use and replaced by a newly erected anti-clockwise turning loop at Moordown Depot, across the entrance to the paint shop, through an opening constructed in the side wall of the main shed and back out of the front of the depot into Wimborne Road. The Redhill Crescent reverser was dismantled on 11th November 1950, although it was later reinstated, coming back into use on 26th July 1953.

Sunbeam MS2 121 leaves Bournemouth Pier for Iford on a service 24 working, passing by the service 28 (Five Ways) and 30A (Columbia Road) stops on the western side of the Pier Approach. Another, unidentified MS2, also still sporting a chocolate-painted roof, follows 121 around the terminal loop. The dull weather and the fashion of the pedestrians' warm clothing suggest that this composite photograph was taken at Easter 1950, when trolleybuses first reached the Pier for the first time.   *Southern Newspapers plc*

Delivery of the new BUT 9641T trolleybuses was taken at Weymann's works at Addlestone, Surrey, the Transport Department being responsible for towing to Bournemouth. This task was frequently delegated to Deputy Chief Inspector Bill Biddlecombe, using Thornycroft LJ 1608, a Departmental ancillary vehicle converted from bus 44. Here, we see the Thornycroft towing trolleybus 205 (KLJ 339) in the final stages of its delivery run to Bournemouth. *BTS Library*

In May 1950, the Transport Committee agreed to pay increased costs of £36 2s 0d due to rises in labour rates and materials in respect of the first two BUT 9641T chassis. The first of the BUTs to arrive was 203 (KLJ 337) on 8th July 1950, entering Central Depot, Southcote Road via Boscombe and Palmerston Road. The last, 218 (KLJ 352), arrived on 6th December 1950, bringing the trolleybus fleet up to its maximum of 127 vehicles. Because of a shortage of space, an area of open land in Seabourne Road adjacent to Boscombe Depot was wired so that trolleybuses could be parked there at night until Castle Lane Depot was completed. Before entering service, 203 was used for driver familiarisation, these vehicles being longer and wider than the existing members of the fleet. For this purpose, 203 was fitted with a particularly large **RESERVED** notice in the main destination box. Before being delivered to Bournemouth, 212 was an exhibit on Weymann's stand at the Commercial Motor Transport Exhibition, held at London's Earls Court between 22nd and 30th September 1950.

The first eleven vehicles delivered (200 – 210) entered traffic on service 25A (Westbourne – Ashley Road) from 1st October 1950. Eight more followed on 1st November 1950 and the final five on 1st January 1951. When all 24 new trolleybuses were in traffic first priority was given to using them on service 25A, then service 24 and then the "Side Routes" 26–32.

One of the BUTs reportedly turned on its side at the junction of Wimborne Road with Stoke Wood Road in snow in the early 1950s. Whilst 212 is recorded as having had an accident on 18th December 1950 (being returned to Weymann from 5th February 1951 to 11th April 1951, and not returning to service until 1st August 1951), the identity of the overturned casualty or indeed a photograph of the event has eluded the author during research for this book. It is possible, therefore, that the incident was less dramatic, and that the story grew in the telling – for instance, it may simply have skidded sideways across the road!

In September 1950, BUT notified a further increase of £147 4s 0d to the chassis cost due to additional equipment and price increases amounting to £664 4s 0d. In December 1950, Weymann also notified price adjustments caused by alterations and amendments to the original design and increased costs for certain equipment. The Transport Committee were thus obliged to accept increased costs of £4,315 for the 24 all-metal trolleybus bodies. Mr Reakes commented that the cost of a trolleybus was now 2½ times that of a pre-war one.

The Transport Committee meeting on 21st April 1950 deferred consideration of the site of a proposed sub-station near Bournemouth Pavilion for the supply of additional power required for the trolleybus system. In fact, this sub-station was never built.

In May 1950 the MoT approved a scheme to equip Castle Lane East, from Holdenhurst Road to Christchurch Road, Iford, for trolleybus operation. The estimated cost of the extension was £6,634 10s 3d and the Finance Committee were asked to apply for the necessary loan sanction. A suggestion the following month that the trolleybus overhead could be further extended along Holdenhurst Road, from Queen's Park to Castle Lane East, was considered premature.

The Transport Department recorded a deficit in the financial year 1949–50, despite carrying what turned out to be its maximum number of passengers, and anticipated a deficit for the financial year 1950–51. The 103 trolleybuses in service at the time earned £339,210 in revenue, covered almost 4 million miles and carried 44.2 million passengers. No part of the trolleybus network had less than a 15-minute service and the majority had a trolleybus every five minutes. Having considered the General Manager's report, the Transport Committee meeting of 21st July 1950 recommended that application be made for a general fares revision based on a mileage rate. The Deputy Town Clerk appeared at a public enquiry into the proposals on 23rd November 1950 and reported to the Transport Committee the next day on the Chairman of the Licensing Authority's remarks on rate relief from Transport Department profits. The Chairman had felt that every opportunity should be taken to build up a reasonable reserve to meet contingencies and, once such a reserve had been accumulated, the Licensing Authority would require an undertaking from the Corporation that no further rate relief from Transport Department profits would be made without the Licensing Authority and the MoT being consulted. The Finance Committee recommended that this undertaking be given.

The traction supply cable over Tuckton Bridge developed faults in August 1950 and was replaced at a cost of £375.

By September 1950 the Department's 30 cwt crane was considered life-expired and a Jones "Super 20" crane mounted on a Leyland SQ2 chassis (TF 447) was hired from Brighton Corporation Transport to plant traction poles along Castle Lane. As there was an option to buy the crane, the Transport Committee recommended that an offer of £500 (including £50 hire charge) be made. This was accepted and the crane, built in 1929, was used until September 1962 before being remounted on a Guy 'Arab' FD former bus chassis (FRU 224) in December 1962.

The SEB advised that the existing traction current tariffs would apply at the proposed new intake point at the Holdenhurst Road sub-station, subject to an annual service charge of £500. They added that the entire matter of traction supplies was subject to early review.

Confronted with a continued lack of suitable overnight parking accommodation following the BUT 9641T deliveries (Hurn Airport had already been considered), the Transport Department in October 1950 asked the Baths and Health Committees (subject to approval by the Planning Department) if a parcel of land near the junction of Seabourne Road with Christchurch Road, Pokesdown, adjacent to Boscombe Depot, could be used for overnight storage of 16 trolleybuses between 10.30 pm and 08.30 am, until Castle Lane Depot was commissioned. The land, which had been occupied by a military strong point, cottages making up the British Restaurant and advertisement hoardings, was reserved for a new public baths and health centre. The suggestion was approved, subject to there being no new entry from Christchurch Road and that the plot was cleared of rubbish daily before 08.30 am. The parking space was wired for trolleybuses and used from 12th March 1951 to 1st October 1951, the wiring being dismantled in spring 1952.

In October 1950 H&D wrote giving notice to terminate the existing co-ordination agreement effective 30th June 1951. Further information was requested by the Transport Committee.

The Boscombe Labour Party asked that earlier through service 25 trolleybuses be introduced to Westbourne (many of the first journeys terminated at the Square). In addition, they requested that a special workers' service

BUT 9641T 209 (KLJ 343) seen at Southcote Road Depot on the first day of BUT operation, 1st October 1950. W. R. (Bill) Stride, Depot Inspector, who joined the department in 1915 as a tram driver, is standing in uniform on the right. Note the **POKESDOWN** destination used for Boscombe (Pokesdown) depot runs.
E. Stride collection

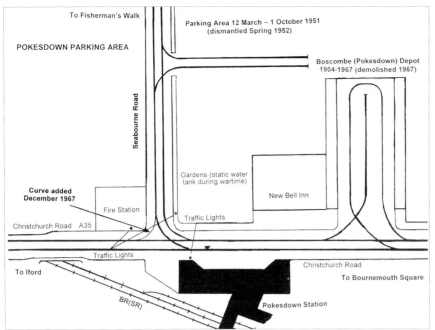

as a tower wagon by the Overhead Department, were offered for sale. A single tender, from Sherwood Car Sales, of Parkstone, at £150 per vehicle, was received and accepted.

The Licensing Authority and the MoT granted increases in trolleybus fares with effect from 1st March 1951.

The summer extension of trolleybus services to Bournemouth Pier had not developed the traffic hoped for in Summer 1950. Accordingly, for the 1951 season, only certain journeys on services 23, 24 and 27 were rerouted from the Square. The diverted services again operated from Good Friday to Easter Monday and then during the summer season from 4th June to 30th September 1951. Service 22B was again extended to Westbourne, from 18th June until 14th October 1951.

be introduced on Christmas Day. On the latter point, at least, no action was taken.

In order to ensure sufficient space for longer-distance passengers, it was suggested that either minimum fares be introduced on trolleybuses travelling to Christchurch, or express buses be operated, as trolleybuses loading in Gervis Place filled up with passengers travelling just as far as Boscombe or the Lansdowne. Another alternative would have been to extend more trolleybuses from Iford to Christchurch, but Alderman Langton stated that Christchurch turntable was already operating at full capacity, handling a trolleybus every five minutes.

At the end of October 1950, eleven motorbuses, including the two converted trolleybuses (69 and 70), together with the last 1925-vintage Tilling Stevens TS6 petrol-electric vehicle (RU 2013) which had been used

The 20th April 1951 Transport Committee meeting also authorised the Department to strip 18 trolleybuses and to use the salvaged electrical equipment, etc., as spares, with the bodies being scrapped. The department's scrap copper trolley wire was sold to Thomas Bolton and Sons Ltd. at the controlled price.

Traction poles in the Square and the Lansdowne were decorated in 1951 for the Festival of Britain.

With effect from 11th June 1951, the 48-hour week was reintroduced for traffic staff in place of the normal 44-hour week due to an acute shortage of personnel.

Sunbeam MS2 159 (BRU 10) at Avenue Road in 1950, with chocolate roof but primrose upper-deck window surrounds. The building in the background is Fairlight Glen, the BCT lost property and enquiry office. *A. B. Cross*
(M. P. M. Nimmo collection)

On 20th July 1951 it was announced that there had been a deficit in the 1950–51 financial year due to a reduction in the number of passenger carried and increases in operating costs. Mr Reakes was instructed to recommend further route and service economies, and a new increased fares structure. His recommendations were presented on 18th September 1951 and adopted immediately for effectiveness as soon as possible.

During the late summer of 1951 there was considerable correspondence with the MoT. The revised Trolley Vehicle Byelaws submitted on 3rd April received Ministerial approval, with effect from 1st August, whilst on 27th August use of the Castle Lane East trolleybus extension was approved pending official inspection, which actually took place on 21st November. Then, on 21st September, the Transport Committee decided to apply for an Order for a further extension of time in respect of those trolley vehicle routes authorised by Section 3 of the Order of 1937 and included in the Trolley Vehicle (Extension of Time) Order 1949 but which had not yet been put into operation.

On 15th October 1951, what proved to be Bournemouth's final trolleybus route extension, along Castle Lane from the Broadway Hotel, past the Mallard Road entrance to the Castle Lane depot site, to Christchurch Road, Iford, came into operation. As a result, motorbus services 14 and 31 were replaced by two circular trolleybus services, as follows:

31   Triangle – Square – Richmond Hill – Cemetery Junction – Charminster Road – Five Ways – Broadway Hotel – Castle Lane – Strouden Park – Iford – Boscombe – Christchurch Road – Lansdowne – Square – Triangle (clockwise only)

32   Triangle – Square – Lansdowne – Christchurch Road – Boscombe – Iford – Strouden Park – Castle Lane – Broadway Hotel – Five Ways – Charminster Road – Cemetery Junction – Richmond Hill – Square – Triangle (anti-clockwise only)

A petition suggesting improvements to service 30 was received. As the Transport Committee was in agreement with the suggestions, a copy of the General Manager's report was sent to the initiators.

In September 1951, tenders were invited for a new coal elevator plant for the generating station, at a cost of £500. In addition, from 1st October that year increased coal prices put extra costs of £5,945 pa on the undertaking and influenced the SEB's charges for traction power under the sliding scale.

On 18th January 1952, the General Manager advised the Transport Committee that a small number of passenger waiting shelters had been delivered and submitted a list of proposed sites for their erection.

Early in 1952, a petition was received asking that the Strouden Park trolleybus service along Castle Lane should operate to and from the Square via Moordown, rather than the existing route via Charminster Road. The department therefore carried out a census, over the period 14th January – 7th February 1952, which showed that only about 5% of passengers changed buses at the Broadway Hotel on to services going to Moordown. In any case, the existing routing and timetable had been prepared in consultation with the Strouden Park Local Government Association and there was accordingly no change.

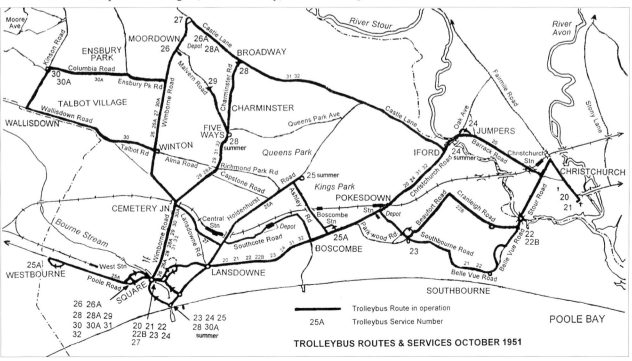

TROLLEYBUS ROUTES & SERVICES OCTOBER 1951

A flood of increased operating costs and the financial position of the undertaking provoked the Transport Committee on 21st March 1952 to authorise another application for a general fares revision as soon as possible. For this reason there was, sadly, no special celebration of the undertaking's Golden Jubilee on 23rd July 1952.

May 1952 saw the first scrapping of the older trolleybuses, the remains of the eighteen vehicles that had previously been stripped for spares being sold to James Thompson & Co., Cardiff.

Certain journeys on trolleybus services 23, 24 and 30A were operated to the Pier for the 1952 summer season.

On 23rd May 1952 the Transport Committee instructed that a conveyance be taken on the land purchased from Hampshire County Council for Iford turning circle in 1935 and Stamp Duty of £45 paid.

On 16th May 1952 the MoT consented to a further three-year extension for the commencement of Routes 2 (Junction Redhill Drive with Ensbury Park Road along Redhill Drive to and along Coombe Avenue, along Leybourne Avenue and Northbourne Avenue to Wimborne Road) and 4 (along Alma and Richmond Park Roads from Wimborne Road to Holdenhurst Road) contained in the Bournemouth Corporation (Trolley Vehicles) Order, 1937. The Transport Committee asked Mr Reakes for an estimate of the cost of equipping these routes.

In June 1952, a general review of trolleybus stops near pedestrian crossings took place, and the Highways Sub-Committee and Transport Sub-Committee recommended that:

i) the stop at Westbourne Lloyds Bank be moved 20 feet eastwards

ii) the pedestrian crossing at Brassey Road/Victoria Park Road/Wimborne Road be removed

iii) the stop outside the Richmond Hotel, Charminster Road, be moved nine feet south and part of the passenger waiting shelter there be dismantled to make this possible

Apart from ii), the recommendations were carried out.

On 19th May 1952 it was learned that increased labour rates and material charges had again raised the costs of the 24 BUT 9641Ts by £866 3s 0d. The Transport Committee accepted the increase and asked that the Finance Committee provide additional loan sanction.

In July 1952, an application to display external advertising on the department's vehicles was yet again rejected, in spite of the undertaking's financial position. One of the generating station cooling towers had been damaged in a recent gale and the quotation of Messrs J Carey & Co. (Steeplejacks) of £147 15s 0d for the repair was accepted.

The South Eastern Traffic Area Licensing Authority appointed Deputy Chief Inspector W. Biddlecombe as Driving Test Examiner for motorbus and trolley vehicle drivers in September 1952.

Bournemouth Chamber of Trade complained of television interference allegedly caused by trolleybuses. Mr Reakes stated that the matter was under discussion with the MPTA and the Joint Electricity Distribution and Collection Committee whose findings would be reported in due course. On 24th October 1952, permission to span private telephone lines above the trolleybus wires in Columbia Road was refused.

The 21st November 1952 Transport Committee meeting decided that the undertaking's financial position ruled out decorating vehicles for the pending Coronation of Queen Elizabeth II on 2nd June 1953. Although the Licensing Authority's decision was still pending it was agreed that, if approved, the new fare scale would be introduced on 1st December 1952.

The *Times & Directory* recorded in their 28th November 1952 issue that:

"From next Monday the one penny fare will go on all motor and trolleybus routes. The daily return ticket will be replaced by five- or six-day weekly ticket of which a million and half have already been printed. Each day's return journey will cost about one and one-third times the single fare based on the new fares. That is the same proportion as the daily return. These tickets will be issued on Mondays and Tuesdays only before 8.45 am; on each remaining day of the week the first journey must be commenced before the same hour.

"Bournemouth has been one of the last towns in the country to retain the one penny fare. The new minimum will be 1½d for 1,500 yards instead of 1d for 1,200 yards. A number of fare stages have been abolished mainly where stages are too close together. Another change is the abolition of ½d changes in fares higher than 2d. Special factory bus passengers will be charged one and a half times the single fare for a return instead of one and a third as now. Children's tickets will be reckoned to the nearest 1d instead of the nearest ½d".

BUT 9641T/Weymann 254 (KLJ 354) waits in Gervis Place for departure time on service 24 to Jumpers.

D. R. H. Bowler collection

The new fares were calculated to the nearest penny above e.g. half of a 5d fare was considered 3d. Although halfpenny fares i.e. 1½d, 2½d, 3½d, 4½d, 5½d, 6½d, 7½d, 8½d disappeared, halfpenny fare units were retained outside the Corporation area, in H&D territory on motorbus services 1 and 19 for a few more years, whilst a special 1½d ticket existed in the Ultimate ticket machine range between 1953 and 1956 for use as a schoolchildren's return. The *Times & Directory* newspaper reported:

"When the South Eastern Traffic Commissioners heard

the Corporation's application last month it was stated that the transport accounts would be down £52,000 by next March if it was not granted. A year's extra revenue from increased fares from 58 million passengers would yield £66,161 (sic) (£46,000 from trolleybuses, £19,200 from motorbuses) it was then said. Since the last application for fare increases in November 1950, ordinary wages have gone up 17.2%, skilled workers' wages 21.2%, coal 24%, petrol 49% and diesel fuel 48%. But since the present fare increase applications went in there had been another wage increase which averages about 7s per week. Thus even with the benefit of the new fares the undertaking will still be £18,000 in the red a year".

The post-war standard passenger waiting shelter, exemplified by the outbound stop in Holdenhurst Road, the Lansdowne. W. D. Reakes is seen standing next to Sunbeam MS2 164 (BRU 15). Note, too, the yellow bus stop flags and the contemporary fashions.

Bournemouth Transport

At the beginning of 1953 the following year-round trolleybus services were being operated:

20 Square (Gervis Place) – Lansdowne – Christchurch Road – Boscombe – Iford – Jumpers – Barrack Road – Christchurch (5½ miles)

21 Square (Gervis Place) – Lansdowne – Christchurch Road – Boscombe – Fisherman's Walk – Southbourne Cross Roads – Tuckton Bridge – Christchurch (6 miles)

22 Square (Gervis Place) – Lansdowne – Christchurch Road – Boscombe – Fisherman's Walk – Southbourne Cross Roads – Tuckton Bridge (5 miles)

22B Square (Gervis Place) – Lansdowne – Christchurch Road – Boscombe – Fisherman's Walk – Beaufort Road – Cranleigh Road – Tuckton Bridge (5 miles)

23 Square (Gervis Place) – Lansdowne – Christchurch Road – Boscombe – Fisherman's Walk (an unadvertised rush-hour service) (3 miles)

24 Square (Gervis Place) – Lansdowne – Christchurch Road – Boscombe – Iford – Jumpers (4 miles)

25 Westbourne – Square – Lansdowne – Central Station – Holdenhurst Road – Queen's Park Golf Pavilion (2½ miles)

25A Westbourne – Square – Lansdowne – Central Station – Holdenhurst Road – Ashley Road, Boscombe (3 miles)

26 Triangle – Square – Richmond Hill – Cemetery Junction – Wimborne Road – Winton – Moordown (3 miles)

26A Triangle – Square – Richmond Hill – Cemetery Junction – Wimborne Road – Winton – Moordown – Lawford Road – West Way (4 miles)

27 Square (Gervis Place) – Lansdowne – Central Station – St. Paul's Road – Cemetery Junction – Wimborne Road – Winton – Moordown – Lawford Road (4 miles)

28 Triangle – Square – Richmond Hill – Cemetery Junction – Charminster Road – Five Ways – Broadway Hotel, Castle Lane (3miles)

28A Triangle – Square – Richmond Hill – Cemetery Junction – Charminster Road – Five Ways – Broadway Hotel, Castle Lane – West Way (3½ miles)

29 Triangle – Square – Richmond Hill – Cemetery Junction – Five Ways – Malvern Road (2½ miles)

30 Triangle – Square – Richmond Hill – Cemetery Junction – Winton – Talbot Road – Wallisdown – Columbia Road (3½ miles)

30A Triangle – Square – Richmond Hill – Cemetery Junction – Winton – Moordown – Ensbury Park Road – Columbia Road (3½ miles)

31 Triangle – Square – Richmond Hill – Cemetery Junction – Charminster Road – Five Ways – Broadway Hotel – Castle Lane – Strouden Park – Iford – Boscombe – Christchurch Road – Lansdowne – Square – Triangle (clockwise) (9½ miles)

32 Triangle – Square – Lansdowne – Christchurch Road – Boscombe – Iford – Strouden Park – Castle Lane – Broadway Hotel – Five Ways – Charminster Road – Cemetery Junction – Richmond Hill – Square – Triangle (anti-clockwise) (9½ miles)

Having agreed in principle to close down the generating station adjoining Central Depot, Southcote Road, negotiations started with the SEB to take over the supply of traction power completely, and an electrical consultant was engaged to act for the Council in the disposal of machinery. Bournemouth and Glasgow (at Pinkston) were the last two municipal transport undertakings in the UK to generate their own electricity. Power cost economies, in the form of special tariffs, were sought whilst in the meantime tenders for a further year's coal supply were invited. Negotiations also took place with the SEB about their use of one of the Department's underground cable ducts between the Lansdowne and Cotlands Road.

In February 1953 it was suggested that a trolleybus service between Iford and Moordown Depot be introduced, but no action was taken. A traction pole outside Beale's store in Old Christchurch Road was removed, at the shop's expense, and a rosette attached to the building.

The Transport Committee accepted an offer from Elton Illuminated Civic Maps Co. to supply, install and maintain without charge for four years, three illuminated system maps and timetables. These replaced those already in place at the Square, Gervis Place and at the entrance to Bournemouth Pier.

On 12th March 1953 experiments started with two Bell Punch "Ultimate" ticket issuing machines (instead of the traditional Bell Punch system using a ticket-rack and punch). As a result, it was decided to standardize on the "Ultimate" system, leading to savings of £550 or more after the first year, the changeover being completed by 22nd March 1954. Instead of the standard five-denomination machines, Bournemouth used mainly six-denomination machines (360 machines), apart from 36 standard machines used during the summer peak period. Initially they held 1d, 1½d, 2d, 3d, 4d and 5d tickets but when the 1½d fare was abolished, a 7d was introduced. By using a combination of tickets, up to 16 fare values could be accommodated. The five-denomination machines did not contain 1½d tickets.

From 30th March 1953, trolleybus service 27 was curtailed to the Lansdowne in the evenings and, from 28th June 1953, the Square terminus of service 27 was moved from the eastern to the western end of Gervis Place, using a stop previously used by motorbus services 3 and 3A. Services 3 and 27 now shared this stop, while motorbus service 3A now used service 27's former stop. An additional passing loop in the overhead wiring was installed here on 3rd May 1953, at the same time as the wartime emergency link from Gervis Place directly into Old Christchurch Road (avoiding a circumnavigation of the Square) was removed.

Construction of a new turning circle at the junction of Holdenhurst Road and Castle Lane, Strouden Park (where the Cooper Dean roundabout was later built) commenced on 20th March 1953. On 23rd May 1953, service 33 was introduced between Winton Banks and the new turning circle, a tar-and-chippings track through

the gorse bushes. An MoT Inspection of the installation took place on 24th July 1953. Throughout the summer, services 31, 32 and 33 provided two journeys an hour each way through Strouden Park and a third was added by means of a short working of service 31 between the Square and the new turning circle, as follows:

31 Triangle – Square – Richmond Hill – Cemetery Junction – Charminster Road – Five Ways – Broadway Hotel – Castle Lane – Strouden Park – Iford – Boscombe – Christchurch Road – Lansdowne – Square – Triangle (clockwise)

32 Triangle – Square – Lansdowne – Christchurch Road – Boscombe – Iford – Strouden Park – Castle Lane – Broadway Hotel – Five Ways – Charminster Road – Cemetery Junction – Richmond Hill – Square – Triangle (anti-clockwise)

33 Winton Banks – Moordown – Lawford Road – Broadway Hotel – Castle Lane – Strouden Park (Holdenhurst Road)

The future of Moordown Depot was discussed at the 24th April 1953 Transport Committee Meeting, when it was agreed that the premises would be vacated and tenders issued for its sale or lease by the end of July 1953. The Committee also discussed the employment of students as temporary conductors in the summer period.

Only two trolleybus services reached Bournemouth Pier in summer 1953: services 23 from Fisherman's Walk and 30A from Columbia Road. These operated as required, the public timetable simply including a note in the appropriate positions that "a frequent service of buses" would operate to the Pier.

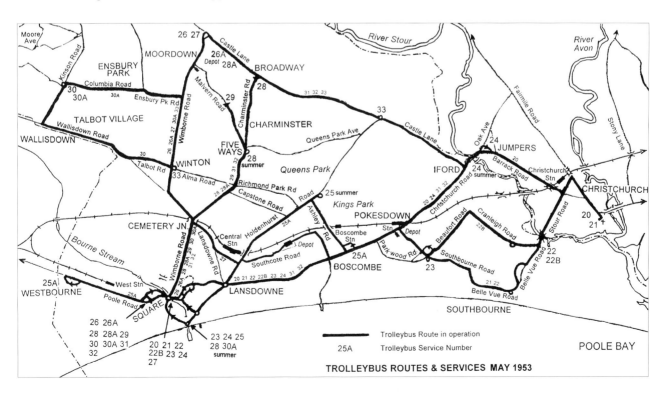

TROLLEYBUS ROUTES & SERVICES MAY 1953

The Coronation Festivities for HM Queen Elizabeth II led to services operating until midnight on 2nd June 1953, and until 11 pm on all other weekdays in the period 30th May – 6th June 1953 inclusive. Traction poles in Christchurch, Old Christchurch and Wimborne Roads were decorated for the occasion with flags and bunting.

Having studied the General Manager's report on the future use of Central Depot, Southcote Road, the Transport Committee, at their meeting of 19th June 1953, felt that the premises would be too small for use as an express coach park. They had no objection to the raising of a Territorial Army sub-unit when Castle Lane Depot opened.

In July 1953, six pre-war Sunbeam trolleybuses were sold for scrap to Messrs James Thompson and Company (Cardiff) Ltd for £300.

From 5th July 1953 the last buses on Sundays were re-scheduled to leave the Square at 11 pm instead of 11.30 pm.

Following an official opening by the Mayor (Councillor H. P. E. Mears, OBE, JP) on 23rd July 1953, the new £500,000 Castle Lane Depot came into use the next day and Moordown Depot, together with its turnround loop, ceased to be used. By 26th July 1953 Moordown was officially vacated and, having considered three tenders and rejected a request that the deadline be extended, the premises were leased, from 1st August 1954, to Post Office Telephones for 21 years as a vehicle depot, at an annual rent of £1,900 (in fact, they continued to use this building until it was demolished in 1984). The Redhill Crescent reversing triangle was reinstated but only used on a regular basis for a short time as, from 26th September 1953, trolleybus services 26 and 27 were extended to Lawford Road, thus:

26 Triangle – Square – Richmond Hill – Cemetery Junction – Wimborne Road – Winton – Moordown – Lawford Road

27 Square (Gervis Place) – Lansdowne – Central Station – St. Paul's Road – Cemetery Junction – Wimborne Road – Winton – Moordown – Lawford Road

The reversing triangle was last used by vehicles in normal service (on service 34) on 25th March 1956, but it remained intact until the withdrawal of trolleybuses to Moordown on 25th September 1966.

Service 32 was withdrawn on 12th October 1953, and services 31 and 33 were reduced to an hourly frequency, the 31 ceasing to operate as a circular route (although

trolleybuses continued from, or reached, Iford as service 24) as follows:

31 Triangle – Square – Richmond Hill – Cemetery Junction – Charminster Road – Five Ways – Broadway Hotel – Castle Lane – Strouden Park – Iford

33 Triangle – Square – Richmond Hill – Cemetery Junction – Wimborne Road – Winton – Moordown – Lawford Road – Broadway Hotel – Castle Lane – Strouden Park – Iford

The *Times and Directory* for 7th August 1953 carried the following report:

"The April 1953 report of the Consulting Transport Engineer on power supply for Corporation Trolleybuses, together with the General Manager's report dated 21st July 1953 were submitted to the Transport Committee at the end of July. They recommended that an alternative source of power should be implemented.

"Last February the council agreed to discontinue the use and dispose of the Southcote Road generating station. It was decided to approach an electrical consultant with a view to negotiating with the Southern Electricity Board for supply of electric power. Councillor O. E. Ellum (Conservative) warned that this investment needed careful consideration because many towns were discarding their trolleybuses in favour of diesel driven vehicles. In 1932 – 33 it had been argued in favour of trolleybuses that the Corporation had its own generating station. They had a good service from the trolleybuses but they had found great difficulty in making things pay. In 1936 there was a loss of £25,000, in 1937 a deficit of £26,604 (sic, these figures are not substantiated by the Department's records). During the war they did very well and transport made a profit. Other towns were making profits with motor buses. Now in 1953 the Borough Treasurer had stated they were going to lose £35,000 on transport. They would be entirely in the hands of the Southern Electricity Board.

"The Transport Committee Chairman, Alderman A. Langton, said that this was all part of the long going trolley versus motor bus arguments which Mr Ellum had been preaching 23 years ago in Southbourne. Any sensible interpretation of the consultant's report would prove without doubt that what was proposed was going to put the undertaking in a very much better position within 18 months. Transport finance would benefit from about £14,000 (a conservative figure as only £2,000 had been included for the disposal of the generating station plant)".

The 23rd October 1953 Transport Committee Meeting recommended that the Finance Committee apply to borrow £42,450 for the new buildings and equipment required for an alternative power supply to the existing distribution board. The consultant was awarded fees representing 5% of all capital expenditure on the traction power supply conversion (excluding buildings) plus the amount raised by the disposal of redundant power station plant and equipment.

The 4th November 1953 *Bournemouth Echo* noted *"Ald. Langton told the Council that Bournemouth Corporation are losing £1,000 per month by continuing to operate the Southcote Road generating station for trolleybus power. The Finance Committee considered that the application to borrow £44,325 for an alternative electricity source, including £1,875 consultant's fee, was excessive".*

Meanwhile, the Parks and Pleasure Grounds Committee had recommended that the proposed Iddesleigh Road Substation in Wimborne Road Cemetery be set back and the Parks Superintendent made responsible for removal of trees. Consent was given by the Ministry of Housing and Local Government in mid-April 1954 for the appropriation for transport purposes of 0.0235 acres of land in the cemetery. Pokesdown Substation was also constructed in Boscombe Depot at the same time, reducing the depot's capacity from 16 vehicles to 12.

In December 1953 negotiations started with the SEB about the rent for those portions of the substation buildings which they needed. The Board's request that the portion of land to be leased for 99 years for the proposed substation behind Central Depot, Southcote Road, be slightly enlarged was granted.

On 16th January 1954 the Ministry of Transport and Civil Aviation approved the Council's proposals for an alternative trolleybus power supply. Five tenders had been received for the electrical work at the proposed substation, that of the Hackbridge and Hewittic Electric Co. Ltd. at £41,135 for electrical equipment (12-phase working) plus £7,198 19s 0d for cables being accepted, and loan sanctions requested. In the meantime essential maintenance work at the generating station had to continue, the superheater tubes (£220) and the cooling towers being repaired. Indeed, repairs to the No. 2 Turbine Set at the generating station were made in September 1953.

By 1st January 1954 the fleet had fallen to 103 trolleybuses:

Sunbeam MS2: 80–93, 95–97, 99–101, 105, 106, 109,
111, 112, 114–119, 121–123, 125,
127–132, 134–150, 152–168, 170–173
(Total 79)

BUT 9641T: 200–223   (Total 24)

of which the following 86 vehicles were licenced for service:

Sunbeam MS2: 80–83, 85–89, 91, 93, 95–97, 99, 100,
105, 106, 109, 111, 112, 115–118,
121, 122, 125, 127, 128, 130–132,
134–138, 140–142, 144–146, 148, 149,
150, 152–154, 157, 158, 160, 162,
164–166, 168, 170–173   (Total 62)

BUT 9641T: 200–223   (Total 24)

The 17 unlicenced vehicles were all stored at Castle Lane Depot.

At the end of February 1954, having considered an anticipated deficit for the year 1954/55, an application was made to the Licensing Authorities for a 2d minimum fare on all services, an increase of 1d per day in the cost of weekly tickets where the daily rate was 3d and by 2d per day in all other cases, and a general service reduction after 7.30 pm during the winter months. The Transport Committee also instructed the General Manager to investigate the introduction of reduced rate books of tickets, but this does not appear to have been followed-up. Approval for the fare increases was granted and the changes took place on 13th December 1954, the minimum fare becoming 2d, although the 1d and 1½d values were retained for children's fares.

The 19th March 1954 Transport Committee meeting recommended no further action regarding sale or lease of land at Central Depot, Southcote Road, until the cooling towers had been dismantled. With regard to the power supply, the *Bournemouth Echo* reported that *"The changeover to power from the grid will be completed by the end of September 1955. When the Corporation decided in February 1954 to apply to the Ministry of Transport for sanction to borrow £50,702 to effect the changeover it was said that electrical equipment would cost £41,135, cables £7,198 and a consultants fee of 5% on £47,500 but that the alternative supply would save £14,000 pa. The current will come from the grid through eight substations, three – which Bournemouth Corporation have built at Southcote Road, Iddesleigh Road, and Pokesdown (inside Boscombe Depot) – and the remainder belonging to the Southern Electricity Board at Green Road, Winton; Electric House; Southbourne; Holdenhurst Road and Christchurch".*

In January 1953, the Christchurch Town Clerk had asked for the undertaking's support of the Hampshire County Council application to the MoT for the replacement of the Pit Site traffic lights at the junction of Barrack Road with Bargates and Christchurch High Street, by a roundabout. Should this be approved, BCT would be asked to relocate the stopping place in Christchurch High Street to a suitable point in Bargates. Bournemouth Council had no objection to the proposed roundabout, on the understanding that, in adopting the scheme, Hampshire County Council reimbursed them their expenses and that their existing operating and turning rights in Christchurch were retained.

Based on a letter from the Ministry of Transport and Civil Aviation, it was recommended on 23rd July 1954 that, again subject to HCC absorbing the cost and to appropriate safeguards in respect of BCT's interests, an application for trolleybus operating powers be made for roads in the vicinity of Fountain Corner, Christchurch, as required by the County Council and the Christchurch Borough Council for their proposed scheme. At the beginning of September 1954 HCC asked if Bournemouth Corporation would be prepared to bear the cost of obtaining the necessary Provisional Order for trolleybus operation around the roundabout. This was refused and, on 14th September 1954, the County Council agreed to accept these costs.

Christchurch Corporation started work on the construction of the Pit Site roundabout in the summer of 1954, together with the related short one-way system at what later became (in 1958) the western end of the Christchurch By-Pass on the then main Bournemouth – Southampton A35 road. When Bournemouth Corporation was notified of the expected date of completion, in order that the trolleybus overhead wiring could be modified to comply with the new road arrangements, it was realised that the necessary Parliamentary

Powers would not be granted in time. From 13th November 1954, all traffic *except the trolleybuses* began to use the new one-way system around what was subsequently to be the southern half of the roundabout. The trolleybuses continued to operate over their original course, those proceeding westbound actuating traffic lights by means of a contact skate on the overhead wire. The enactment of the Bournemouth Corporation (Trolley Vehicles) Order Confirmation Act, 1955, approved the erection of 9.1 chains of diverted overhead wiring and trolleybuses started to comply with the route taken by all other traffic with effect from 28th August 1955.

The Highways and Works Committee were of the opinion that their roads were being damaged by heavy vehicles and asked for their views to be considered by the Transport Committee in the future whenever deciding to buy new trolley vehicles.

On 17th May 1954 the police suggested that the inward service 30A stop in Columbia Road at the junction with Ensbury Road and Boundary Road be moved a short distance to the west.

In July 1954, trolleybus 147 was recorded as having been rebuilt in the bodyshop and 90 stripped for rebuilding. Also in 1954, 97 and 129 were rebuilt

Summer operation of trolleybuses on services 23 and 30A commenced on 5th June 1954, using the same arrangements as used in 1953, namely from Bournemouth Pier on an "as required" basis via Bath Road in both directions, but now with their own separate service numbers:

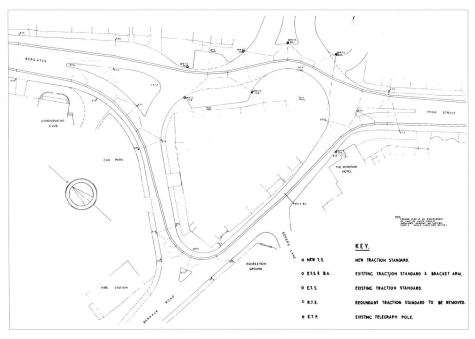

Mr William Pearce, Superintendent Overhead Linesman, and his three overhead gangs worked from very detailed plans showing the precise position of each pole, span wire and hanger. Here is their plan of the revised "Pit Site" at Christchurch.

This illustration has been substantially reduced in size. The key has been enlarged for clarity.

Sunbeam MS2 130 shows full steering lock at the Fisherman's Avenue turning circle, Fisherman's Walk, the summer season terminus of service 35, on 10th June 1954.   *G. O. P. Pearce*

34 Bournemouth Pier – Lansdowne – Cemetery Junction – Winton – Moordown – Ensbury Park Road – Columbia Road (previously service 30A)

35 Bournemouth Pier – Lansdowne – Christchurch Road – Boscombe – Fisherman's Walk (previously service 23)

By mutual agreement with the Transport & General Workers Union the 48-hour week was introduced from 7th June 1954 in an effort to cope with staff shortages.

Severe traffic congestion in the 1954 summer season caused considerable service dislocation and the Transport Committee placed on record their appreciation of Inspection and Platform Staff's work.

The Bournemouth Trades Council wrote on 12th June 1954 suggesting that trolleybuses should not turn at Redhill Crecent, although the reversing triangle had only been used occasionally since 26th September 1953.

The Transport Committee, at their meeting on 18th June 1954, recommended that two-section passenger waiting shelters already in stock be erected at Westbourne, Lloyds Bank (services 25, 25A), and Brassey Road, inward (services 30A, 34). However, the suggestion from Bournemouth Trades Council that a shelter should be erected at the Parkwood Road, outward, stop in Christchurch Road (services 20–24, 35) was rejected. At the same time, Southbourne Ratepayer's Association was informed that a bus shelter could not currently be provided at Southbourne Cross Roads (outward stop). Likewise, a proposal that a special 22B school service should be introduced was rejected, due to the relatively small number of schoolchildren who would use the

1935 Sunbeam MS2 116, still with chocolate-painted roof, waits at the Bournemouth Pier passing loop stop, in front of the Pavilion, in 1954. Note the **ENTRANCE** and **EXIT** signs above the lower saloon windows, immediately to the left and right (respectively) of the platform and front doors. Note, too, the auxiliary in-town "via" indicator in the nearside windscreen.   *R. Marshall (D. L. Chalk collection)*

service. The opinion of the Highways and Works Committee on the construction of a lay-by at the Tuckton Road service 22B terminus was sought.

Contrary to Section 15 of the Bournemouth Corporation Act, 1901, as extended by Section 99 of the Bournemouth Corporation Act, 1930, a Mr Nigel Ponsford was prosecuted on 13th June 1954 for wilfully interfering with trolleybus frog operating equipment. Subsequently, on 31st October 1954, the police reported a similar interference, but on this occasion a warning was given.

In June 1954 the revised tender from the Hackbridge and Hewittic Electric Co. Ltd. for equipment at the proposed substations, based on the electrical consultant's suggestions and thereby saving £2,100, were accepted. Two tenders were received for the construction of the Iddesleigh Road and Boscombe (Pokesdown) Depot substations, that of Messrs Cooper and Rowe (Contractors) Ltd. at £3,795 being accepted. The Finance Committee were asked to apply for a loan sanction for this amount and the estimated cost of the Central Depot, Southcote Road, substation. In October 1954, the sole tender received, that from Messrs Willis Bros. & Jackson Ltd. for the substation at Central Depot, Southcote Road, for £3,060, was accepted.

At their 22nd October 1954 meeting the Transport Committee learned that Christchurch had decided not to exercise their powers to purchase that portion of the trolleybus network in the Borough in 1955. However Christchurch Council's request that a preferential fare be introduced within their area was rejected.

At lunchtime on Monday 31st October 1954, a trolley wire broke in Holdenhurst Road near the Lansdowne, causing short hold-ups.

The SEB's proposals of 12th July 1954 for the supply of traction current, subject to an excess maximum demand tariff of £2 12s 6d per kilowatt, instead of £2 17s 6d, from March to October inclusive, were accepted. Regenerative equipment required at the substations at an estimated £573 18s 0d (not subject to tender) was ordered. In mid-March 1955 it was agreed that, subject to Ministry of Housing and Local Government approval, 0.178 acres of land at Central Depot, Southcote Road, be leased to the SEB for 99 years at a rent of £100 pa. Due to continuing delays in arranging the alternative power supply, however, the Corporation's coal suppliers were asked in March 1955 if they would extend the coal contract on a weekly basis as from 30th June 1955.

Tenders were invited to explore the potential of additional revenue from external advertising on buses, and two replies had been received by mid-March 1955. At the meeting of the Transport Committee on 22nd April 1955, further consideration was deferred for three months pending the receipt of more information from the tenderers as to the nature of the planned advertisements. However at their 22nd July 1955 meeting it was decided not to proceed with the idea.

In June 1953 the Highways and Works Committee had been advised that Iford Barn near the turning circle, which had been used variously in the past for storing overhead equipment and as a scout hut, was no longer required by the Transport Department. Efforts to find an alternative use for the building commenced in January 1954. Following a meeting with the Finance, Parks, Town Planning and Transport Committees on 1st December 1954, the Town Clerk suggested that no decision be taken about Iford Barn and the surrounding land until plans to build a roundabout at the junction of Castle Lane East and Christchurch Road had been finalised. In August 1955 the Transport Committee raised no objections to the roundabout's construction, on the understanding that the cost of altering the trolleybus overhead equipment was borne by the Highways and Works Department and with the recommendation that bus lay-bys be provided. Iford Barn was then demolished.

On Whit Sunday, 20th May 1956, the southern half of the Iford roundabout at the junction of Castle Lane East, Iford Lane and Christchurch Road came into use, and Boscombe-bound trolleybuses started following the new road layout. The eastbound (or northerly) side of the roundabout came into use on 2nd December 1956. The proposal to erect a complete circle of trolleybus overhead was rejected by the MoT and a crossing in the eastbound Pokesdown to Jumpers wiring by the westbound Castle Lane wiring had been recommended instead. There were auto frogs in the eastbound Castle Lane East wiring for turns to Jumpers or on to the roundabout, and in the westbound wiring on the roundabout itself for turns into Castle Lane or along Christchurch Road towards Boscombe.

The Ministry of Transport and Civil Aviation gave their final approval to the overhead installations at the Iford and Pit Site, Christchurch, roundabouts in September 1957. Only on 2nd July 1965, however, was a frog giving access from Christchurch Road eastbound wiring direct into Castle Lane installed, to handle the increased number of depot runs to Castle Lane Depot after the closure of Central Depot, Southcote Road. Prior to this date a

BUT 9641T/Weymann 220 (later renumbered 254) in Holdenhurst Road at Bournemouth Central Station on service 25A on 10th July 1955, heading towards Westbourne.   *J. C. Gillham (D. L. Chalk collection)*

trolleybus travelling east along Christchurch Road had to circle Iford roundabout, with the conductor operating the auto frog available to vehicles leaving Castle Lane by hand to gain access to the westbound Castle Lane wiring.

At the beginning of 1955 there were 103 trolleybuses in the fleet, but with 87 licenced for service – an increase of one over the previous year.

Application was made to the Ministry of Transport and Civil Aviation in January 1955 for a further extension of time in respect of the routes authorised by Section 3 of the Order of 1937 scheduled by the Bournemouth Corporation (Trolley Vehicles) Order Confirmation Act, 1938 but which had not yet been put into operation. Consent was given on 17th May 1955.

On 21st January 1955, it was agreed that those parts of the substation buildings at Iddesleigh Road and Boscombe Depot required by the SEB should be leased to them for 21 years on terms to be settled by the District Valuer. In the interim, the General Manager was to arrange for repairs to No. 1 Cooling Tower at the generating station, which had been damaged in a recent storm.

As an experiment, and following discussions with the police, the Arcade stop in Old Christchurch Road, between the Square and Dalkeith Steps, ceased to be used except for trolleybuses on services 25 and 25A, as it had become a cause of obstruction due to heavy traffic. The first stop after leaving the Square thus became Horseshoe Common. The stop in the Square at the bottom of Commercial Road outside Woolworths for services operating from Richmond Hill was also experimentally discontinued. Both of these changes

became permanent in July 1955. Stops in Boscombe also became more widely spaced. Possibly as a result of the foregoing experiments, consideration of a renewal of the overhead equipment in the Square was deferred.

The two MPs representing Bournemouth West, and Bournemouth East and Christchurch were asked to make representations for a reconsideration of the "no standing" rule in buses, whilst the Council's views were also brought to the attention of the MPTA.

A depot warning sign was erected on a traction pole on the west side of the junction between Castle Lane and Mallard Road during 1955. At the request of the Highway & Works Committee a feeder pillar at Cemetery Junction was moved circa 1955, half the cost being absorbed by the Transport Committee.

Continuing staff shortages in the summer months saw the 48-hour week reintroduced for traffic staff, with effect from 21st March 1955. Until the end of the trolleybuses in Bournemouth, the employment of university students as temporary conductors in high summer became a regular feature of operations, the annual contingent from Ireland proving particularly keen to supplement their income by working double shifts and on rest days! Some even slept on trolleybuses in the depot between late and early shifts. However, a request for a contribution towards their travelling expenses to and from Bournemouth was refused. In 1956, following representations from the TGWU, a special payment of 1s per day was made to conductors accompanying trainees, leading to additional costs of around £75 pa.

At their meeting on 22nd April 1955, the Transport Committee was advised that the Ministry of Transport and

Civil Aviation had authorised the Bournemouth Corporation (Trolley Vehicles) Provisional Order for the one-way system and roundabout at the Pit Site, Christchurch, and that the confirming Bill had been introduced and read a first time in the House of Commons. Royal Assent was subsequently given, on 27th July 1955.

At the same meeting the Finance Committee was asked to grant £560 for the erection of two-section passenger waiting shelters during the financial year at the following locations in sequence: Columbia Road, Ensbury Park Hotel (outward services); corner of Richmond Park and Charminster Roads (outward services); junction of Richmond Park and Holdenhurst Roads (outward services); junction of Castle Lane and Lawford Road (inward services); Wimborne Road, top of Peter's Hill (inward services); and Wimborne Road at Moordown Depot (two shelters for inward services). The resiting of the traction pole on the Grand Hotel forecourt in Fir Vale Road just south of Horseshoe Common, at the hotel's expense, was also approved, subject to an annual acknowledgement of 1s pa. It was here, where Fir Vale Road joined St. Peter's Road, that Bournemouth's sole pair of curve segments were installed in the overhead wiring shortly afterwards as an experiment.

Until 1955, Sunbeam MS2 repaints still featured the chocolate roofs that they had acquired soon after the outbreak of war in 1939, although the BUT 9641Ts were delivered with primrose roofs. BUT 207 received an experimental chocolate roof in 1954 but this was not deemed a success and, thereafter, all trolleybus repaints (including the pre-war Sunbeams) featured primrose roofs.

At its meeting on 20th May 1955, the Chairman of the Transport Committee, Ald. Langton, referred to the impending retirement of Aldermen Playdon and Summerbee and thanked them both for their long service to the Transport and Tramways Committees. Both had been active on various Committees since the late 1920s. Ald. Arthur Langton himself finally resigned from the position of Chairman in June 1957 due to ill health. He had become a member of the then Tramways Committee in 1930 and was appointed Chairman of the present Transport Committee in 1936. He served for many years on various national and regional bodies associated with municipal transport and during the period 1946 – 53, sat as Traffic Commissioner and, as a member of the Licensing Authority for PSVs for the South-Eastern Traffic Area. Arthur Langton had a regrettably short retirement; he died on 3rd October 1958.

In July 1955, the following trolleybuses were listed as being in store at Castle Lane Depot: 80, 88, 137, 144, 158, 159, 163, 167, 201, 207, 209, 212, 215, 218, 220, 222.

In view of the undertaking's financial position, the 22nd July 1955 Transport Committee Meeting recommended an application to increase the fares.

Lightning struck the overhead wiring near Central Station at 7.05 pm on 12th August 1955, putting the central area out of action until 8.50 pm. Arcing caused a fire on the main switchboard at Southcote Road.

The Transport Committee recommended in August 1955 that the negative feeder pillar and a traction pole at Tuckton Bridge be re-sited at an estimated cost of £92 3s 7d.

In September 1955, the undertaking stopped generating its own traction power. Thereafter, the entire supply came from the SEB. On 21st October 1955 the Transport Committee invited tenders for the purchase of the generating station equipment. Having considered two quotations for the demolition of the former generating station cooling towers, the 21st December 1955 Transport Committee Meeting accepted that of Messrs James Drewitt & Son Ltd. at £372 and, having considered eight tenders for the generating station equipment, that from Messrs George Cohen, Sons & Co. Ltd. for £5,770 was accepted. The final costs of the electricity substations at Iddesleigh, Southcote Road and Boscombe Depot had proved lower than the contract figures.

Having received six identical tyre mileage contract tenders, the Transport Committee decided on 18th November 1955 to bring the matter to the attention of the Association of Municipal Corporations with the request that they pass this to the Monopolies Commission. On 21st December 1955, however, they agreed to the following allocation for the supply of tyres on a mileage basis for two years ending 31st December 1957:

- Dunlop Rubber Co. Ltd. – 40%

- Goodyear Tyre and Rubber Co. Ltd. – 40%

- Firestone Tyre and Rubber Co. Ltd. – 10%

- India Tyre and Rubber Co. Ltd. – 10%

The Town Clerk reported to the 20th January 1956 Transport Committee meeting that the subject of tyre mileage contracts had been considered by the Monopolies and Restrictive Practices Commission, who felt that the arrangements were not against the public interest.

A rare view of BUT 9641T 207 (KLJ 341) showing the chocolate-painted roof which it carried for a short time in 1954. The vehicle is seen in the Triangle parking area.
R. Butler, courtesy C. Aston

A suggestion that a trolleybus or motorbus should be illuminated for the 1956 summer season was referred to the Publicity Committee who, limiting their consideration to trolleybuses only, decided on no further action.

A two-section shelter from stock was erected at Holdenhurst Road outside Dean's Nurseries (services 25 and 25A) whilst six further two-section shelters were purchased from the existing suppliers at an estimated cost of £500.

A new service numbering system for both motorbus and trolleybus services was introduced from 1st March 1956, which eliminated the A and B suffixes. Service 22B (Square – Cranleigh Road – Tuckton Bridge) was re-numbered 23, the previous service 23 (Square – Fisherman's Walk) having disappeared as a regular daily service in 1935 (when trolleybuses were extended on to Tuckton Bridge via Southbourne or, from 1948, via Cranleigh Road) although the service number had been retained for peak hour extras. From now on, vehicles terminating at Fisherman's Walk were supposed to display 37, although a blank often sufficed. Service 25A was renumbered 25. Since 1952, service number 25 had been used to denote trolleybuses terminating at Queen's Park Golf Pavilion but, by 1956, only occasional journeys were being operated thus; almost all journeys were now 25As, which simply dropped the "A" suffix. Services 26A, 27, 28A, 29, 30A, 31, 34 and 35 were renumbered 27, 34, 29, 35, 31, 32, 36 and 38 respectively. Services 28 (which had ceased to operate regularly circa 1946), 30 and 33 were not changed.

Trolleybus services thus became (with former numbers shown in brackets):

20 Square (Gervis Place) – Lansdowne – Christchurch Road – Boscombe – Iford – Jumpers – Barrack Road – Christchurch

21 Square (Gervis Place) – Lansdowne – Christchurch Road – Boscombe – Fisherman's Walk – Southbourne Cross Roads – Tuckton Bridge – Christchurch

22 Square (Gervis Place) – Lansdowne – Christchurch Road – Boscombe – Fisherman's Walk – Southbourne Cross Roads – Tuckton Bridge

23 Square (Gervis Place) – Lansdowne – Christchurch Road – Boscombe – Fisherman's Walk – Beaufort Road – Cranleigh Road – Tuckton Bridge (22B)

24 Square (Gervis Place) – Lansdowne – Christchurch Road – Boscombe – Iford – Jumpers

25 Westbourne – Square – Lansdowne – Central Station – Holdenhurst Road – Ashley Road, Boscombe (25A)

26 Triangle – Square – Richmond Hill – Cemetery Junction – Wimborne Road – Winton – Moordown – Lawford Road

27 Triangle – Square – Richmond Hill – Cemetery Junction – Wimborne Road – Winton – Moordown – Lawford Road – West Way (26A)

28 Triangle – Square – Richmond Hill – Cemetery Junction – Charminster Road – Five Ways – Broadway Hotel, Castle Lane

29 Triangle – Square – Richmond Hill – Cemetery Junction – Charminster Road – Five Ways – Broadway Hotel, Castle Lane – West Way (28A)

30 Triangle – Square – Richmond Hill – Cemetery Junction – Winton – Talbot Road – Wallisdown – Columbia Road

31 Triangle – Square – Richmond Hill – Cemetery Junction – Winton – Moordown – Ensbury Park Road – Columbia Road (30A)

32 Triangle – Square – Richmond Hill – Cemetery Junction – Charminster Road – Five Ways – Broadway Hotel – Castle Lane – Strouden Park – Iford (31)

33 Triangle – Square – Richmond Hill – Cemetery Junction – Wimborne Road – Winton – Moordown – Lawford Road – Broadway Hotel – Castle Lane – Strouden Park – Iford

34 Square (Gervis Place) – Lansdowne – Central Station – St. Paul's Road – Cemetery Junction – Wimborne Road – Winton – Moordown – Lawford Road (27)

35 Triangle – Square – Richmond Hill – Cemetery Junction – Five Ways – Malvern Road (29)

36 Lansdowne – Central Station – St. Paul's Road – Cemetery Junction – Wimborne Road – Winton – Moordown – Ensbury Park Road – Columbia Road (peak hours only, extended to/from Bournemouth Pier in summer) (34)

37 Square – Lansdowne – Christchurch Road – Boscombe – Fisherman's Walk (peak hours only) (23)

38 Bournemouth Pier – Lansdowne – Boscombe – Fisherman's Walk (summer only) (35)

Less than a month later, on 26th March 1956, service 34 was extended beyond Lawford Road to West Way, replacing the 27, and continuing back to the Square and the Triangle as a circular operation paired with service 29. Except for the period 22nd July – 25th September 1956, when service 27 again provided the paired service, the 34 and 29 remained paired with one another until 1963.

29 Triangle – Square – Richmond Hill – Cemetery Junction – Charminster Road – Five Ways – Broadway Hotel, Castle Lane – West Way

34 Square (Gervis Place) – Lansdowne – Central Station – St. Paul's Road – Cemetery Junction – Wimborne Road – Winton – Moordown – Lawford Road – West Way

Service 26 continued to terminate at Lawford Road but service number 27 thereafter disappeared from public timetables, although it continued to be used by trolleybuses continuing beyond West Way to Castle Lane Depot.

It seems that at the same time the frequency of services 29 and 34 was reduced, and a petition protesting against these reductions was presented. Having considered the traffic receipts, the Transport Committee rejected the petition at their meeting of 22nd June 1956.

Reference to what proved to be the UK's last production trolleybus design first appeared in the Minutes of the Transport Committee's meeting of 24th June 1955. The Committee agreed that the 79 remaining pre-war trolley vehicles, some over 20 years old, would have to be

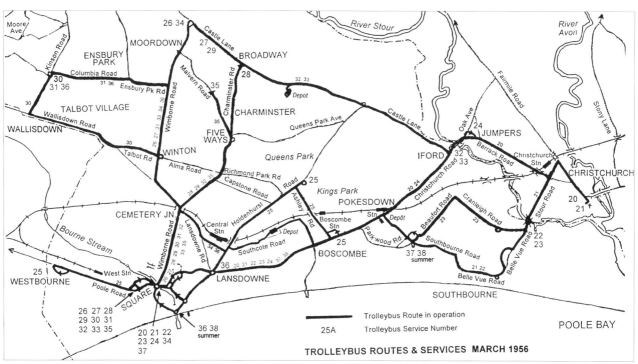

TROLLEYBUS ROUTES & SERVICES MARCH 1956

BUT 9641T/Weymann 204 (KLJ 338) seen on service 33 at the junction of Strouden Park with Holdenhurst Road on 15th June 1956. Note the "To and From the Cricket" display. *J. C. Gillham*

replaced over the next few years. They recommended that tenders be invited for twenty two-axle trolleybuses seating 60 or 61 passengers for delivery in 1957 and that the subject of further purchases and the most suitable time scale be considered at a later date. The full Council withdrew the item for further consideration by the Transport Committee on 5th July 1955. Subsequently, on 23rd March 1956, the Transport Committee again recommended that tenders be invited for the supply of twenty two-axle trolleybuses to replace vehicles dating from 1934/35, and that the Finance Committee be asked to apply for an appropriate loan sanction.

Easter operation of trolleybuses to Bournemouth Pier on service 38 took place for the last time in 1956. Thereafter extensions, on an irregular basis, were limited to the high summer season.

Notification of an increase in the maximum demand charge was received from the SEB on 20th April 1956. The Licensing Authority approved the Corporation's application for increased fares and made positive comments as to preparation and presentation.

In May 1956 proposals to erect street lighting attachments to 87 traction poles in Kinson Road and Castle Lane and to remove 13 existing attachments were approved with the usual conditions. Later in the year, at their meeting of 19th October 1956, the Transport Committee gave consent to the attachment of street lamps to traction poles in Charminster Road. Future *ad-hoc* requests for temporary or permanent direction sign attachments were delegated to the General Manager.

The Christchurch and District Model Parliament suggested in June 1956 that all trolleybuses terminate at

the junction of Bargates and Barrack Road rather than continue along High Street and Church Street to the turntable. No action was taken.

At about this time, Hampshire County Council suggested that a lay-by should be built at Jumpers on the south side of the road for inbound services 20 and 24. This was agreed, provided that the County Council paid the cost of the necessary alterations to the overhead equipment and for repositioning the existing shelter.

Passenger waiting shelters were erected opposite St. Augustin's Church in Wimborne Road, inward, i.e. on the Square side of Cemetery Junction (for services 26 and 28); at Tuckton Bridge outside Bridge House, outward (for service 21); and Strouden Park, inward, opposite the Hotel (for services 32 and 33). On the Education Committee's advice, a two-section shelter was erected at the junction of Cranleigh and Beaufort Roads, at a cost of £150. In an ongoing effort to improve passenger facilities, two further two-section shelters were ordered at an estimated total cost of £200.

The March 1956 service renumbering scheme had allocated 36 for seasonal services between Bournemouth Pier and Columbia Road via the Lansdowne, Cemetery Junction, Winton and Ensbury Park Road (the former 34) but this was not re-introduced for summer 1956. Thus, from 17th September 1956, the "winter season" version of the service was reintroduced at peak hours only:

36 Lansdowne – Central Station – St. Paul's Road – Cemetery Junction – Winton – Moordown – Ensbury Park Road – Columbia Road

The winter 1956 timetable also introduced a number of service reductions, including the withdrawal of trolleybus services 20 and 24 after the 7 pm departures from the Square. To compensate, the evening operation of limited-stop motorbus service 1 to Somerford, which paralleled the trolleybus route throughout but for a short length of Barrack Road, Christchurch, was diverted along Stour Road to serve Christchurch Station and Bargates, operating as a normal service observing all stops en route. Alternate winter evening service 1 journeys had been following this route since the introduction of the winter 1955 timetable.

There had been £438 0s 2d excessive expenditure above the loan sanction on electrical equipment for substations and it was recommended to the Finance Committee that this amount be met from revenue.

The 23rd November 1956 Transport Committee Meeting considered letters from the Regional Transport Commissioner and the MPTA regarding oil shortages due to the Suez Crisis. Although diesel fuel was not rationed, there were shortages and some motorbus service reductions, but this did not lead to any improvement of trolleybus frequencies or services. Petrol for private use was rationed for six months. Having considered a letter from Bradford's General Manager, the Town Clerk wrote to the Government expressing the Corporation's wish that every encouragement be given to the general use of electric road passenger transport.

The undertaking's finances based on the Borough Treasurer's half-yearly statement, and some pending wage awards, combined with reduced passenger loadings after 7 pm, led to a recommendation that service frequencies should be reduced immediately, subject to the Traffic Commissioners consent. Having considered a

reduced timetable on motorbus service 2, the full Council requested a report on the undertaking's economic position. On 21st December 1956 the Transport Committee considered a letter requesting increased frequencies on trolleybus services 28, 29 and 34 but rejected it due to the decline in passenger traffic. Following a further financial statement by the Borough Treasurer and the General Manager, an immediate fare increase under the Hydrocarbon Oil Duties (Temporary Increase) Act 1956 was deferred one month whilst ways in which the undertaking's additional costs could be met were investigated.

From 31st December 1956, trolleybus service 34 was cut back from the Square to the Lansdowne (as had been the case on winter evenings since 30th March 1953), but continued to operated a circular route with the 29, returning to the Square via Charminster Road, the nominal terminal point remaining West Way. Service 30 was curtailed to operate between Columbia Road and Talbot Road Junction (Winton Banks) using the Alma Road loop, except in the morning and evening peak hours when vehicles continued to operate to and from the Triangle. The Columbia Road – Wallisdown – Talbot Village route still operated in conjunction with service 31, and few vehicles on service 30 actually "shuttled" between Columbia Road turning circle and Winton Banks. Through transfer tickets were available for passengers to change at Winton Banks. This became a permanent feature of the winter timetable until 1959 – 60, when the curtailment was introduced on a year round basis.

A proposal to run trolleybuses from the top of Richmond Hill around a one-way terminal loop via Braidley Road and past the Town Hall, to Bourne

A rear view of Sunbeam MS2 157 (BRU 8) in front of Bobbys, on the south side of Bournemouth Square on 15th June 1956. This service 34 journey to West Way apparently operates "To and From the Cricket" at Dean Park.   *J. C. Gillham*

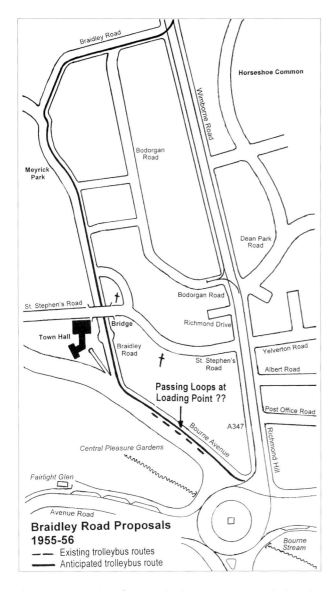

**Braidley Road Proposals
1955-56**
- – – Existing trolleybus routes
- ––––– Anticipated trolleybus route

(Map labels:) Braidley Road · Horseshoe Common · Wimborne Road · Bodorgan Road · Meyrick Park · Dean Park Road · St. Stephen's Road · Bodorgan Road · Richmond Drive · Bridge · Town Hall · Braidley Road · St. Stephen's Road · Yelverton Road · Albert Road · Passing Loops at Loading Point ?? · Post Office Road · A347 · Bourne Avenue · Richmond Hill · Central Pleasure Gardens · Fairlight Glen · Avenue Road · Bourne Stream

Avenue and the Square had been approved by the Transport Committee on 21st January 1955. However, they felt at that time that steps to obtain the requisite Parliamentary Powers should not be taken in isolation and that they should be included in a future Bill. The intent – to offer an alternative town centre terminus for Richmond Hill trolleybuses and a route to the Square less susceptible to congestion or icy winter conditions – would have required the road surface to be lowered under St. Stephen's Road Bridge. In November 1956, matters relating to the running of trolleybuses along Braidley Road and Bourne Avenue were deferred for a month.

On 21st December 1956, the Transport Committee reconsidered the suggested rerouting of "Side Route" trolleybuses down Braidley Road and then east along Bourne Avenue, avoiding the descent of Richmond Hill, and the Borough Engineer reported on pending proposals by other Committees concerning traffic routes. The report of a meeting held between representatives of the Transport and Highways and Works Committees was

adopted in February 1957 and, following discussions with the MoT Divisional Road Engineer, the Braidley Road scheme was dropped.

The Transport Committee's recommendation of 18th February 1955 with respect to equipping Braidley Road for trolleybus operation was therefore rescinded in April 1957, when it was recommended that the General Sub-Committee should consider a suggested alternative route for trolley vehicles proceding down Richmond Hill. However, on 24th May 1957 the Sub-Committee deferred consideration until their next meeting. In retrospect it would appear that the cost of bridge and/or road reconstruction was too high, bearing in mind that the concept of the one-way terminal loop was intended purely to avoid traffic congestion and would have attracted no additional passenger revenue.

By September 1956, six tenders had been received for twenty, two-axle trolleybuses and, at their Meeting of 23rd November 1956, the Transport Committee recommended that the following be accepted:

i) for 20 trolleybus chassis with electrical equipment: The Sunbeam Trolley Bus Company Limited (with electrical equipment by Crompton Parkinson Limited) at £3,642 each. (A lower tender had been received but did not comply with the specification).

ii) for 20 trolleybus bodies (Bournemouth design): Metropolitan-Cammell-Weymann Limited at £3,442 each. (Two lower tenders were received for bus bodies).

The Finance Committee's application for loan sanction of £141,680 was granted in February 1957 and, following negotiation with Sunbeam, the requirement to provide a surety for due performance of the contract was waived. The *Bournemouth Echo* later reported, on 16th April 1957, *"An £80,000 order for twenty, 62-seater trolleybuses has has been placed with the Sunbeam Trolley Bus Co. Ltd., an associate company of Guy Motors. It is for 20 double-deckers to replace an equivalent number of Sunbeams supplied by the Woilverhampton company in 1935, when the Bournemouth tramway system was replaced by 103 Sunbeam trolleybuses. The old vehicles have carried millions of passengers during their 22 years of service and many of them will continue operating until the original fleet is completely replaced. Chassis for the new Sunbeams will be of two-axle type with MCW 30ft bodies and Crompton-Parkinson electrical traction equipment."*

On 19th July 1957 the Transport Committee recommended that tenders be invited for ten more trolleybuses for delivery in 1959, to replace vehicles purchased in 1935.

The winter of 1956/57 saw the delicencing of Sunbeam MS2s 80-82, 84, 111, 114, 121, 127, 128, 138, 148, 153, 168 and BUT 9641Ts 200-211, 213, 214, 218, 221-223. Six of the MS2s were stripped of useful parts prior to sale for scrap: 80-82, 111, 127-128

As an economy measure, the number of borough coats of arms displayed on each trolleybus was reduced from six to two, those on the front, rear and lower-deck side panels no longer being applied. On the pre-war vehicles the fleet number replaced the coat of arms at the front and rear, instead of being applied to the lower-deck maroon band. The BUTs had previously carried their front fleet number above the offside headlight and that at the rear between the maroon band and the coat of arms.

By early 1957 the condition of Boscombe Depot was giving concern. Blocked drainpipes and defective glazing were allowing the ingress of rain, and there were fears that it could percolate into the substation. The economics of retaining the premises as an operational depot were therefore investigated. At that time one man was employed on ticket box and cash receipt duties, whilst three cleaners and one chargehand cleaner were allocated for night cleaning work. In case of closure, Mr T. Marsden, Deputy General Manager and Engineer, felt that three or four positions could be economised, saving £1,500 pa. The difficulty of operating a running depot so close to the Central Depot, Southcote Road, but without a unified control, together with the nightly changeover of twelve vehicles and building maintenance costs were also remarked upon. The savings would be minimal but, operationally, the closure was recommended. Mr W. J. Guy, Traffic Superintendent, reported that complete closure and the additional dead mileage involved until schedules were revised would increase wages by £13 6s 2d per week and mileage (ex-Central Depot, Southcote Road) by 417 miles per week.

In March 1957 Mr Reakes asked for quotations for providing doors to Boscombe Depot so that it could be closed up when required, but it was found that the entrance-widening carried out in 1938 limited this to shutter type doors. The next draft timetable, effective from 2nd June 1957, was prepared as if the depot was closed, with nine trolleybus duties transferred to the Central Depot, Southcote Road, and five to Castle Lane Depot. These proposals would have resulted in having to operate an additional 331.66 non-revenue miles and incur an additional £12 7s 6d in wages per week. Thus,

on 14th May 1957, the Transport Committee decided to take no action for twelve months.

The year commencing 1st April 1957 saw increased charges for bulk electricity supplies, involving an estimated annual increased cost of £1,164 and £1,848 for the year commencing 1st April 1958.

An application was made in May 1957 for a further extension of time in respect of those trolley vehicle routes authorised by Section 3 of the Order of 1937, scheduled in the Bournemouth Corporation (Trolley Vehicles) Order Confirmation Act 1938, but which had not yet been put into operation. This extension was granted on 8th November 1957.

As no other corporation department required the former Southcote Road generating station site, tenders were invited for a 21-year lease of the property. The Hotpoint Electrical Appliance Co. Ltd. expressed interest in twelve months' rental, but withdrew from the negotiations in July 1957.

By August 1957, five more pre-war trolleybuses (83, 114, 138, 148 and 153) were noted stripped and awaiting sale for scrap, in addition to the six previously mentioned and still awaiting disposal.

As in past years, it was foreseen that a number of the BUT 9641Ts, which were heavy in power consumption, would be temporarily taken out of service at the end of September 1957 and put in store for the winter. They would be replaced during this period by some or all of nine more economical Sunbeam MS2s which had been stored delicenced through the summer, namely trolleybuses 85, 129, 143, 147, 155, 158, 167, 171, 172.

At a special meeting held on 23rd August 1957 the Transport Committee considered the General Manager's report on the financial effects of a recent wage award (£30,072) and increased costs for materials and services (£9,228). Based on the existing fare scale, it was estimated that these additional expenses would result in a deficit of £9,806 in the current financial year, and of £30,971 in the financial year ending March 1959. These figures applied to the undertaking as a whole and not to the profitable trolleybus operations. Immediate application to the Traffic Commissioners for increased fares was therefore recommended, but later deferred until the 1958/59 estimates had been considered. This was perhaps just as well because, shortly afterwards, another wage award, of £1,716 pa, was announced by the National Joint Council for Craftsmen in Municipal Passenger Transport Undertakings.

In September 1957 Littledown Estate residents requested an improved frequency of service 25 from Queen's Park Golf Pavilion during the winter months. This was refused, but an application was made to the South Eastern Area Traffic Commissioners to divert motorbus service 18 (Throop to Boscombe) along William Road and Thistlebarrow Road instead of via Holdenhurst Road. This came into effect from 2nd December 1957.

The existing contract with the Sunbeam and MCW for 20 trolleybuses was extended in September 1957 to include an additional ten vehicles, at an estimated cost of £7,110 each, without calling for tenders. It was estimated that the cost would be an additional £30 per vehicle in respect of electrical equipment. Additional loan sanction was applied for. Under the existing contract, Sunbeam were not required to provide sureties, and no additional guarantee was required from MCW provided that their existing contract guarantee was extended to cover the extra vehicles.

In late 1957, a passenger waiting shelter was erected at Fisherman's Walk.

Alderman J. W. Moore, CBE, retired from the Council at this time, having been a member of the Transport Committee since 1934.

In mid-November Messrs George & Harding commenced repairs to defective brickwork in the gable end of Boscombe Depot. Shortly thereafter, a trolleybus reversing out of the depot dewired damaging a window at 928 Christchurch Road opposite.

Having considered a Report regarding the resiting of various bus stops on Poole Hill, in Westover Road, Old Christchurch Road and Westbourne, the Transport Committee made certain recommendations which were subsequently not proceeded with. However, subject to the approval of the Highways and Works Committee, authority was given to move the inward stop in Columbia Road (near its junction with Kinson Road) a short distance to the east. The inward stop in Charminster Road, at its junction with Acland Road, was resited in early 1958 to the junction with Hankinson Road, whilst the inward stop opposite the junction with Maxwell Road was deleted. At around this time, a passenger waiting shelter was erected outside Pokesdown Fire Station, Seabourne Road, for trolleybus services 21–23, 37 and 38, and permission was granted to Christchurch Corporation to hang flower baskets on fifteen traction poles in High Street, Christchurch.

In February 1958, the SEB announced plans to withdraw their staff from the substations at Christchurch and Electric House, Bournemouth, and indicated that it would be necessary to install automatic switching apparatus in them. Mr Reakes therefore inspected redundant automatic switchgear from Leeds Corporation's tramways and this was purchased for £400.

In the early 1950s, Mr Reakes had successfully introduced both double- and single-deck open-top motorbus services along the coast, and a circular coach tour of the town and environs. Eager to build on this principle, but with a minimum investment, the idea of operating a circular tour with open-top trolleybuses converted from vehicles which would otherwise be disposed of as life-expired was floated. The main proponent was probably Tom Marsden, the Deputy General Manager and Engineer. Following preliminary discussions with the MoT, exploratory work started on 1936 Sunbeam MS2 160 in September 1957. The 22nd November 1957 Transport Committee meeting authorised the conversion of two trolleybuses to open-top for use during the summer on a circular tour of the town. The same meeting gave authority to dispose of ten trolleybuses purchased in 1934/35. Having considered four offers the highest, that of James Thompson & Co. (Cardiff) Ltd., at £550, was accepted on 21st February 1958. Local newspapers announced on 4th December 1957 that two trolleybuses were to be converted to open-top for the next summer season.

The rebuilding of 160 as a prototype open-topper was completed by April 1958. Following a Ministry of Transport and Civil Aviation inspection on 17th April 1958, the new design was authorised for use and presented to the press the next day. It was made available for inspection in the Pavilion forecourt on 27th May 1958, the day of the Annual Council Meeting. The front staircase and exit were removed from the 1936 trolleybus and the upper-deck structure above the base of the windows cut away, although the upper-deck body walls were retained and increased in height. The trolley gantry remained in place with a small section of "roof" supporting the trolley gear, whilst the trolley retaining hooks were located on a matching single hoop at the rear. Seating capacity was increased to 69 (40 upstairs and 29 on the lower deck). Trolleybus 157, of the same batch, was ready in May 1958. In the meantime, the conversion of a third trolleybus was authorised and 112, of 1935, was selected, being completed in July 1958. The three open-top trolleybuses were renumbered: 157 (BRU 8), 160 (BRU 11) and 112 (ALJ 986) becoming 200–202, thus inaugurating a new fleet numbering series.

On Whit Saturday, 24th May 1958 the open-top trolleybus circular tour, taking one hour, was introduced operating in a clockwise direction only and with no service stops, using the two rebuilt vehicles available for service at that time:

39 Bournemouth Pier – Exeter Road – Square – Richmond Hill – Cemetery Junction – Charminster Road – Five Ways – Broadway Hotel – Castle Lane – Strouden Park – Iford – Jumpers – Barrack Road – Stour Road, Christchurch – Tuckton Bridge – Southbourne Cross Roads – Fisherman's Walk – Boscombe – Christchurch Road – Lansdowne – Bath Road – Bournemouth Pier

Following completion of the third conversion, the non-stop circular tour became a scheduled service from 7th July 1958, picking-up and setting-down passengers *en route*. This was an attempt to maximise revenue by carrying short-distance passengers in the invariably empty lower saloon, whilst those making the complete circular trip travelled upstairs. It was also a palliative to tour passengers who complained of delays behind service trolleybuses loading or unloading at stops. No further mention was made of the proponent's 1957 comment that the 22-year-old trolleybuses would be able to cope with a tour as this avoided the bodywork stresses of frequent starts and stops! However, persistent staff shortages meant that seasonal services were the first to be curtailed and, even during periods of fine weather, the 39 often operated only on Sundays.

Meanwhile, the silver jubilee of trolleybus operation in the town did not go unrecorded. The *Bournemouth Times* of 16th May 1958 published a *Tribute to a Trolley*. *"It was exactly 25 years on Tuesday that trolleybuses were introduced. Ten of which have just been sold to James Thompson (Cardiff) Ltd. for £550*

cost £2,100 each at the time. Two of the 1936 Sunbeams will be converted to two open-toppers this summer. The Corporation have ordered 30 trolleybuses, twenty for delivery this year and 10 next. The 20 complete vehicles will cost £142,000 and the 10 £71,000".

Road repairs in Church Street, Christchurch, carried out between 12th and 18th May 1958, prevented trolleybuses reaching the turntable. The opportunity was therefore taken to give the turntable its first major overhaul since installation in 1936. Initially, trolleybuses made a three-point turn at the top of Wick Lane using T-poles but later in the week the overhead wiring at the "Pit Site" roundabout was linked to provide a temporary terminal loop, whilst a motorbus shuttle operated to and from Church Street.

The 20th June 1958 Transport Committee Meeting recommended to the General Purposes Committee that powers be sought to operate trolleybus services in the newly-developed West Howe area, and that the General Manager report upon the proposed routes at the next meeting. However, on 18th July 1958 these proposals were rescinded, as the General Manager's report suggested that a cheaper and less cumbersome way of seeking powers for extending the trolleybus system (other than by separate application for each individual route) could be made in a more general Parliamentary Bill which the Corporation was then promoting.

At the same meeting another proposal to introduce external advertising on vehicles was rejected. Another review as to the use or development of the Castle Lane and Southcote Road accommodation, including possible centralisation of the depot and ancillary facilities, was recommended in twelve months time.

English Electric-bodied Sunbeam MS2 82 (AEL 410) enters Gervis Place with its destination blinds already set for its next round trip to Christchurch. St. Peter's Church is in the background, and the entrance to Bournemouth Arcade is immediately behind the trolleybus (in line with the pedestrian crossing).
R. Butler (courtesy C. Aston)

OPEN-TOP MISCELLANY

Three of the Sunbeam MS2s were converted to open-top format in 1958, for use during the resort's holiday season. These were 157 (BRU 8), 160 (BRU 11) and 112 (ALJ 986), renumbered 200 – 202 respectively in their new roles.

Top: 200 seen at Bournemouth Pier Approach Baths during its first summer of service in its new O40/29R layout.
D. R. H. Bowler collection

Centre: The Strouden Park turning circle consisted of a tar-and-chippings roadway through the gorse bushes at the junction of Holdenhurst Road with Castle Lane. Open-topper 202 (BRU 11) is seen at this location on an enthusiasts' tour on 3rd June 1962.
J. C. Gillham

Bottom: An atmospheric view of 200 (BRU 8) heading eastwards along Bath Road. Note the fine avenue of trees and the total absence of traffic!
F. M. Kingston (BTS Library collection)

In the evening of 28th July 1958, the Department's Guy Arab breakdown tender, FRU 180, arrived at Castle Lane Depot from the Weymann factory at Addlestone, Surrey, with the first Sunbeam MF2B, 258, on tow. The 31st July 1958 *Bournemouth Echo* recorded that *"Transport officials anticipate that the new buses will use less electricity. Those now in service use just over 3 units* (sic) *per day. The Corporation fleet is now 103. The fleet will not be increased, for as the new ones come in the old ones will be replaced. The vehicles are considerably lighter than their predecessors weighing 8 tons 19 cwt as opposed to 10 tons 6 cwt. The first one, which arrived at the beginning of the week, is expected to be in service at the weekend. Drivers are currently getting used to the front overhang"*. Two points of note are that the unladen weight of 10 tons 6 cwt referred to the BUT 9641Ts, not the Sunbeam MS2s which were being replaced, and the fact that the first two MF2Bs, 258 and 259, actually went into service on service 25 on Saturday 2nd August 1958.

A complete Sunbeam MF2B, 260, and the chassis of 272 were exhibits at the Commercial Motor Show, held at Earls Court, London, between 26th September and 4th October 1958.

An explosion in an underground cable duct in Foxholes Road was recorded on 19th September 1958 as *"being dealt with by the insurance company"*. Cables did not always follow the trolleybus route (which in this case was in Belle Vue Road). Some of the cables between

Pokesdown and Christchurch were from the tramway era, being simply laid in wooden troughing which was then filled with a compound, rather than conventional armoured cables in earthenware ducts. They were thus more susceptible to water penetration and easily damaged by excavation work. Similarly, a fault occurred on the mains at Stour Road, Christchurch, on 16th February 1960.

From 22nd September 1958, trolleybus service 33 (Square – Moordown – Iford) ceased to operate, although a few morning specials still followed the route as part of the service 32 timetable, but displaying 33. To compensate for the withdrawn through service, connections at the Broadway Hotel with circular services 29 and 34 which operated to Lawford Road, Moordown and Winton were advertised. On 6th October 1958, trolleybus service 32, by now the sole service operating through Strouden Park, was extended from Iford to Jumpers Corner, thus:

32 Triangle – Square – Richmond Hill – Cemetery Junction – Charminster Road – Five Ways – Broadway Hotel – Castle Lane – Strouden Park – Iford – Jumpers

Trolleybuses operating on service 32 normally returned to the Square on service 24 (through Pokesdown and Boscombe), and vice versa.

Although a deputation from the Transport and General Workers Union had asked that the reintroduction of the 44-hour week be postponed and that the existing

The first Sunbeam MF2B, 258 (WRU 258), loads at the Commercial Road stop in Bournemouth Square on service 25 to Westbourne during August 1958. Note the ventilator in the upper-deck dome, which typified the first five deliveries, and the primrose-painted driver's rear view mirrors. In the background, behind the coach circumnavigating the Square roundabout, can be seem the Lower Pleasure Gardens and the domed roof of the Pavilion.
D. L. Chalk collection

BUT 9641T 242 (KLJ 342) stops at the Queens Park Hotel, Ashley Road, Springbourne in August 1958. It is followed by newly-delivered Sunbeam MF2B 258, both vehicles heading towards Boscombe.
D. L. Chalk collection

seasonal 48-hour week be continued until Christmas, this was rejected. The 44-hour week was reintroduced on 13th October 1958. A wage award of the National Joint Industrial Council for the Road Passenger Transport Industry was granted, with effect from 27th October 1958, whilst the National Joint Council for Craftsmen in Municipal Passenger Transport Undertakings had awarded a 2d per hour increase to craftsmen effective 23rd July 1958. Together the estimated annual additional costs to the Department were £20,000.

A further 20 Sunbeam MS2 trolleybuses were advertised for sale in November 1958, three tenders being received. The highest bid, that of £1,200, from Messrs Scource and Son, was accepted.

Following discussions with the police, the Boscombe Library stop and the Boscombe Arcade stop – both in Christchurch Road between Heathcote Road and Sea Road on the inward journey – were deleted and temporarily replaced by a single stop outside the Public

Library. This was the principal stop in Boscombe, and the name Boscombe Arcade was retained. Outwards there had always been just one stop, but with separate boarding points for services 20, 24 and 21–23, 37, 38, the next stop being Ashley Road. At about this time, a passenger waiting shelter was erected at the inbound service 25 stop in Holdenhurst Road near its junction with Curzon Road.

The 19th December 1958 Transport Committee Meeting received a report from Mr Reakes on the possible purchase of secondhand trolleybuses from Brighton, and instructed him to make an offer for six vehicles. On 7th January 1959, the *Bournemouth Echo* recorded that *"Bournemouth Council is selling 20 of its old trolleybuses for £1,200 and buying six 8-year old ones from Brighton. The (old) buses cost £2,216 each in 1934–35 and have covered 700,000 miles since they were bought. Northern towns like Bradford, Huddersfield, Newcastle and South Shields are still building up trolleybus fleets"*. An alternative offer for

Guy Arab FD breakdown lorry FRU 180 (formerly motorbus 33) pulls out of Lewes Road Depot, Brighton with an ex-Brighton Corporation BUT 9611T trolleybus on tow in 1959. Note that the lorry is working under trade plates 094 EL. *Surfleet*
(D. L. Chalk collection)

the purchase of seven Brighton vehicles was recommended at the 23th January 1959 meeting. The reason for the increase from six to seven vehicles is unknown but, at the time the transaction took place, all but one of the other post-war Brighton Corporation vehicles on the market at this time had already been sold to other operators.

The *Bournemouth Echo* of 4th June 1959 reported that the first two ex-Brighton vehicles (293 and 294) had entered service at the beginning of the month, going on to write: *"Experienced passengers will miss the second exit on the seven Brighton trolleybuses. They are 26 ft long, 7ft 6ins wide and seat 56 passengers. They have undergone an extensive face-lift in the Corporation's workshops. First the colour had to be changed from red to yellow. Indicator boards (sic) also had to be altered. It is not yet known when all seven Brighton buses will be on Bournemouth's roads. They will replace a number of old trolleybuses which are expected to run until after the summer".*

The ex-Brighton BUT 9611T two-axle vehicles, four from the Corporation and three from the Brighton, Hove & District Omnibus Company, were the smallest trolleybuses in the post-war Bournemouth fleet. Their lack of a front staircase and exit ensured that they were normally limited to rush hour operation on the "Side Routes", particularly services 26, 28 and 35. Certain councillors and members of the press commented adversely on the purchase of Brighton's "cast offs", particularly as they had come from a rival seaside resort. They were, however, the fastest trolleybuses on the system!

Still on the subject of new rolling stock, the 20th February 1959 Transport Committee meeting approved an increase in the cost of the first batch of twenty Sunbeam MF2B trolleybuses (258–277), amounting to £5 8s 3d per chassis and, on 22nd May 1959, accepted MCW's final account, which included increased costs per body of £66 16s 0d for labour and £31 13s 6d for material. At their meeting on 14th July 1959, they approved a price adjustment on the second batch of ten Sunbeam MF2B chassis (278–287) amounting to about £30 per chassis. Crompton Parkinson were granted permission to advertise that they were responsible for the electrical installations in the new trolleybuses. Subsequently, on 8th December 1959, the General Manager reported a price adjustment of £179 each to the cost of ten trolleybus bodies delivered by MCW in 1959.

It was further recommended that the existing contracts with Sunbeam and MCW be extended again to include a further, third, batch of ten trolleybuses (to become 295–304) without calling for a new tender. Mr Reakes was asked to submit proposals, together with estimates of the likely cost, for a different body design featuring interior adjustments and a platform-type staircase. The next meeting considered his report, but the idea was dropped. The 10th November 1959 Transport Committee meeting thus recommended that the existing contracts with Sunbeam and MCW be further extended to include ten more trolleybuses, at a cost of £7,546 for each vehicle (compared to £5,571 for motorbuses ordered at same time) for delivery in 1961. The Finance Committee was asked to apply for loan sanctions.

Meanwhile, in January 1959, closure of Boscombe (Pokesdown) Depot was again considered but, once more, no action was taken. There were problems with the offices

Former Brighton Corporation BUT 9611T/Weymann HUF 45, in its new guise as Bournemouth 288, rounds the Lansdowne, terminus of the weekday peak hours-only service 36 to Columbia Road, on 16th May 1960. The Municipal College and Library in the apex of Christchurch Road and Meyrick Road is visible in the background on the right.

D. L. Chalk collection

In the northern suburbs and the fertile valley of the River Stour, 293 (formerly 392 in the Brighton, Hove & District fleet) waits under the Luckham Road reverser (Castle Lane West/Broadway Hotel/ Charminster Road).
BTS Library

being left unattended (with a gas ring left burning) – and a disproportionately high telephone bill!

The SEB announced that traction supply charges would increase from 1st April 1959, involving an estimated annual increased cost of £500.

In March 1959 it was recommended that the stop outside the Information Bureau, Westover Road, be abolished and an alternative position for the service 25 stop in Gervis Place be investigated. Following evaluation, it was decided on 14th July 1959 to delete the former and install a new one midway between the Information Bureau stop and that at the Pavilion.

Lightning struck the overhead wires in Castle Lane on 22nd May 1959, damaging the mercury arc rectifier in Holdenhurst substation. The equipment, covered by insurance, was replaced.

On 24th June 1959 a small roundabout came into operation at the western end of Talbot Road where it joined Talbot Avenue. No frogs were installed in the overhead wiring, only a slewing being required.

With the Summer timetable, commencing on 29th June 1959, circular open-top trolleybus service 39 was modified to operate anti-clockwise to avoid duplicating the circular motorbus tour of the town (service 15), namely:

39 Bournemouth Pier – Bath Road – Lansdowne – Christchurch Road – Boscombe – Fisherman's Walk – Southbourne Cross Roads – Tuckton Bridge – Stour Road, Christchurch – Barrack Road – Jumpers – Iford – Strouden Park – Castle Lane – Broadway Hotel – Five Ways – Charminster Road – Cemetery Junction – St. Paul's Road – Lansdowne – Bath Road – Bournemouth Pier

The lack of southbound wiring in Exeter Road prevented operation via the Square, although it was no doubt felt that the routing along Lansdowne and St. Paul's Roads, close to Bournemouth Central Station, might increase the service's popularity. This provided an example of a rare left turn from Charminster Road into St. Paul's

The old and the new: pre-war Sunbeam MS2 205 (ALJ 60) dating from 1934 is seen here in Avenue Road in company with a brand-new Sunbeam MF2B. *R. Saward (courtesy A. B. Cross)*

Road at Cemetery Junction. In retrospect, Mr Cunningham attributed the lack of success of the open-top trolleybuses with the general public to a certain fear of dirt from the trolleyheads (in fact they were located behind the passenger seating) or even trolley equipment itself falling on the upper-deck passengers. In the season, the population of Bournemouth almost doubled and this brought major pressures on the undertaking. The seasonal coastal open-top motorbus service 12 and the motorbus circular tour had excellent loadings in comparison to those of the 39 and, logically, it was the open-top trolley-bus circular service which was cut first when there was a shortage of crews. This compounded the problems of making the service attractive and the thought of a totally silent open-top journey never really "took-off".

From 1st July 1959, postmen on duty became entitled to travel free on the corporation transport network in return for a £615 annual payment by the Postmaster General.

In September 1959 tenders were invited for the disposal of a further twenty pre-war Sunbeam MS2 trolleybuses. There were three responses. The highest, once again that from Messrs Scource and Son at £1,550 (to include seven motorbuses as well) was accepted.

Trolleybus service 20 was experimentally extended from the Square to Westbourne, in company with service 25, from 14th September 1959, but it reverted to its previous town centre terminus from 13th November 1960.

The undertaking was increasingly troubled by summer traffic congestion, leading to delays and lost revenue. At a joint meeting of the Transport and the Highways Sub-Committees in April 1960 it was suggested that additional "No Waiting" signs be erected near the Square; and a discussion took place with regard to improvements to traffic flows at the Lansdowne, the delays caused by three sets of traffic lights between Boscombe Crescent and Parkwood Road, and traffic hold-ups at the lights at the junction of Alma Road and Wimborne Road. Unilateral waiting signs were fixed on various traction poles within the County Borough. A suggestion that trolleybuses proceeding down Richmond Hill should be able to turn east into Old Christchurch Road at the Square and then make their way back to Richmond Hill by way of Post Office Road or Yelverton Road instead of continuing to the Triangle was also on the agenda.

Instead, a new overhead wiring layout was installed from the stops in Avenue Road, across the Square to the base of Richmond Hill, giving a clear run for trolleybuses proceeding up the hill and eliminating the

operation of the frog at the junction of Bourne Avenue with the Square (outside Burton's premises). Trolleybuses leaving the easternmost 25 stop crossed those on the Richmond Hill services and followed the innermost wiring around the north side of the Square roundabout, whereas all other "Side Route" services followed the parallel outer wiring which gave a junction-free approach to the hill. The overhead work was completed with the removal of the switch frog at the foot of Richmond Hill on 29th May 1960. The Transport Committee had also proposed additional wiring from the bottom of Richmond Hill to a point at the start of Commercial Road, which would have eliminated the frog outside Bobbys in Bournemouth Square, but this was never carried out. The estimated cost for both these changes was £1,736.

A second, parallel, eastbound overhead line in Old Christchurch Road was brought into operation on 12th March 1960 from outside Trinity Church, just east of Dean Park Road, and into Holdenhurst Road, eliminating the need for operation of the frog outside the public conveniences at the Lansdowne (the frog, however, was retained for service 34 turning purposes). The new wiring continued around the outer, north side of the Lansdowne roundabout and gave service 25 trolleybuses a clear run into Holdenhurst Road, where a trailing frog linked up with the original northbound overhead wiring immediately after the Lansdowne stop. Service 34 trolley-buses waiting at their Lansdowne stop did so on the inner overhead wiring, which, due to the frequency of service 25 (every 6–7 minutes in peak hours) occasionally led to delays. It was recommended that the position of the frog for vehicles going down Bath Road be altered and that the overhead equipment for those going down Old Christchurch Road be realigned, but it is not known if this was ever carried out. The estimated cost was £958.

Early 1960 saw passenger waiting shelters erected at the bus stops on both sides of Barrack Road at its junction with Avenue Road, Christchurch, and – at the request of the Education Committee – on the north-west side of Charminster Road at the junction of East Way (Court Road).

The undertaking's quarterly insurance records for 1st April 1960 show the following trolleybus statistics:

- Insured and available for service (total 63)

Sunbeam MS2:	206, 209, 211, 215, 217, 218, 219, 221, 224, 225, 226, 228, 230, 231, 233
BUT 9641T:	234, 247–257

The rear, nearside view of Sunbeam MF2B 287 (YLJ 287) is seen here turning out of the eastern side of the Triangle, terminus of the Richmond Hill "Side Route" services, into Avenue Road on 3rd June 1962. Note the contradictory blind display, perhaps indicating that this service 31 departure to Columbia Road was subsequently routing through to Winton Banks (service 30) via Wallisdown. *J. C. Gillham*

| Sunbeam MF2B: | 258–278, 280–287 |
| BUT 9611T: | 288–294 |

- Not insured (total 27)

Sunbeam MS2:	205, 207, 208, 210, 212, 213, 214, 216, 222, 229, 232
Sunbeam O/T:	200, 201, 202
BUT 9641T:	235–246
Sunbeam MF2B:	279

Reflecting the need for additional rolling stock in commission at the height of the summer season (but also the high operating costs of the BUT 9641Ts), by 1st July 1960 the situation was:

- Insured and available for service (total 82)

Sunbeam MS2:	205, 206, 208, 209, 211, 213–215, 217–219, 221, 224–226, 228, 230, 231, 233
Sunbeam O/T:	201, 202
BUT 9641T:	234–257
Sunbeam MF2B:	258–287
BUT 9611T:	288–294

- Not insured (total 8)

| Sunbeam MS2: | 207, 210, 212, 216, 222, 229, 232 |
| Sunbeam O/T | 200 |

- Ancillary vehicles (in both April and July):

Bedford 2-ton Overhead Department tower wagon 3 (DEL 37).

AEC Regent 661 Overhead Department tower wagons 10 (VH 6218) and 12 (VH 6217).

During 1960, the department increased the seating capacity of thirty Leyland Titan PD2 motorbuses dating from 1950 from 48 to 58 by removing their front staircases. The frames for the extra seats came from withdrawn Sunbeam MS2 trolleybuses.

Wage awards of the National Joint Council for Craftsmen in Municipal Passenger Transport Undertakings and the National Joint Industrial Council for the Road Passenger Transport Industry involved further costs to the undertaking of £35,000 pa. The working week was reduced from 44 to 42 hours on 6th June 1960 provoking another fare review and further economies.

Apart from open-top circular service 39, the only other trolleybus service to Bournemouth Pier in the 1960 summer season was the 38, which operated from 4th July until 11th September between the Pier and Christchurch, via Fisherman's Walk, Southbourne Cross Roads and Tuckton Bridge. Alternate departures from Christchurch operated to Bournemouth Pier (as service 38) and to Bournemouth Square (as service 21).

At their 14th June 1960 meeting (and subject to the cost being borne by the Highways and Works Committee) the Transport Committee raised no objection to the proposals to resite traction poles situated close to pedestrian crossings at the junction of Wimborne Road and Victoria Park Road and at the junction of Charminster Road and Kings Road. The 20th September 1960 meeting of the Transport Committee recommended deletion of the outward stop in Wimborne Road near St. Augustin's Church and the inward stop in Charminster Road between Wellington Road and the railway bridge.

On 12th July 1960 it was decided that there should be no general revision of fares, but that the matter should be reconsidered when preparing the undertaking's 1961/62 estimates.

Following weekend dismantling work from 22nd October 1960 onwards, the remains of Cemetery Junction turning circle, accessible only by trolleybuses travelling south from Charminster Road or Wimborne Road, was removed on the night of 19th/20th November 1960. It had hardly been used since Moordown Depot's closure in July 1953 – the last trolleybus on service 29 (as it then was) from Malvern Road at night terminated at Cemetery Junction and then headed up Wimborne Road to Moordown.

Having considered the Finance Committee's comments about the Central Depot and Generating Station, Southcote Road, the General Manager had been asked to prepare estimates for the provision of additional accommodation at Castle Lane. On 12th July 1960, the Borough Architect reported on the likely cost and further consideration was deferred. In October 1960, approval was given to the erection of a single-storey administration block at Castle Lane Depot to accommodate all office staff at a cost not exceeding £37,000; an extension of the garage at an estimated cost of £46,000; construction of hard standing at an estimated £3,500; and the consequent demolition of two empty farm cottages (remaining from the days when the site was a Corporation-owned farm for horses pulling municipal wagons) at an estimated cost of £300.

Boscombe (Pokesdown) Depot was still required by the Transport Department, although the Civil Defence were eager to use it for their vehicles, and enquiries were made as to the provision of doors and general improvements. Mr Reakes wrote to the Borough Architect on 30th November 1960 suggesting a meeting at the depot. He felt that, apart from a repaint and tidy-up of the mess room, little more than repairs to the leaky roof were necessary. The depot had functioned without doors throughout the trolleybus era (and it is thought that it *never* had them) and he was reluctant to fit them now at a cost of around £1,000!

On Friday, 30th December 1960, the Transport Committee visited Boscombe Depot and, having considered the Borough Architect's report, they recommended roof-light repairs using asbestos; brickwork repairs and re-pointing; redecoration of roof trusses; removal of weeds and renewing the tarmac in the entrance forecourt; and patching of the ground floor area, all estimated at £525 and to be debited to the Reserve Fund. A further £50 was allocated for whitewashing the walls, to be carried out by the Transport Department themselves and to be charged to the Revenue Account. All the work had to be completed within the current financial year. It is worth quoting a few statistics regarding Boscombe Depot at this time:

Number of trolleybuses parked during day: none

Number of trolleybuses parked after services ceased: 10

Number of men:
    cleaners   1 all night
    maintenance supervisor   1 for 2 hrs
                                    (checking trolleyheads)
    platform staff   40
    (plus an unknown number of conductors paying-in who were in the depot at night or paid in during the day).

Cost of maintenance:	£ 2 19s 6d per week
Cost of cleaning:	£11 12s 2d per week
Cost of electric light (2,425W):	£68 8s 7d pa
Cost of water:	£19 15s 0d pa
Cost of heating – coke:	£36 0s 0d pa
Cost of heating – gas:	£20 13s 9d per annum

Cost of building repairs/painting   £ 500 in previous 5 yrs

Rates were levied on the undertaking and not on individual buildings.

Fisherman's Walk, Southbourne, Cranleigh Road, Christchurch and Jumpers were noted as being points served by trolleybuses from the depot when taking up service on their morning routes.

The Committee also visited the sites of a suggested lay-by in Castle Lane West, at Bournemouth School for Girls, and the bus stops and lay-by suggested at Dean's Nurseries, Holdenhurst Road. The stop outside the nurseries was resited in February 1961 to a point between Egerton Road and St. Ledger's Road, but the provision of lay-bys was not recommended.

The Transport Committee had, on 11th October 1960, recommended application for a further extension of time in respect of those trolley vehicle routes which had been authorised but not yet constructed. Accordingly, on 9th December 1960, the Town Clerk applied to the MoT to extend once more, for a period of three years, the time as limited by Section 4 of the Bournemouth Corporation (Trolley Vehicles) Order, 1937, as confirmed by the Bournemouth Corporation (Trolley Vehicles) Order Confirmation Act, 1938 (as extended in 1943 and 1946) and the consents of the MoT dated 14th May 1949, 16th May 1952, 17th May 1955, and 8th November 1957, for the commencement of the use of trolley vehicles along routes 2 and 4 authorised by Section 3 of the said order of 1937. Further details can be found in Appendix L.

These two extensions were now estimated to cost £22,400, an increase of 10% since last renewing the powers in 1957. BCT gave the following reasons for not having already implemented these powers since then:

- Completion of the making-up of Northbourne Avenue had only recently taken place

- Routes 2 and 4 were intended to form a link between Kinson, East and West Howe and other parts of the Borough but the exact position of Route 2 had remained unclear until the substantial housing development already underway in that part of the town was complete.

- It would have been necessary to retain a costly, parallel trolleybus and motorbus service along Alma Road during a time of financial difficulties.

Objections were received from almost fifty residents in Leybourne Avenue and Coombe Avenue, complaining about what they perceived as road overcrowding that would result from the introduction of trolleybuses, and the detrimental visual impact of the overhead equipment. The Town Clerk responded, stating that the roads were already licensed for 30ft long, 8ft wide buses; that traction poles would not spoil the area's visual amenities as they would in part be combined with street lighting standards; and that *the use of trolleybuses rather than diesel buses would eliminate noise and fumes*. Formal Ministerial consent for a further extension of time was given on 1st May 1961.

On 30th January 1961 a minimum fare was introduced on service 32 between 4.30 pm and 6.30 pm.

At this time, further passenger waiting shelters were erected, at Barrack Road (Manor Road/Stour Road, alias White Hart Hotel) inward (service 20); and at Kimberley Road inward (service 23). The outward stop in Belle Vue Road at the approach to Tuckton Bridge was also resited, a distance of about twenty yards towards the bridge, in early 1961. The Southbourne Ratepayer's Association's request for a service to Christchurch via Cranleigh Road was turned down at a Transport Committee Meeting on 14th February 1961.

On 18th March 1961 a roundabout was brought into use at the junction of Talbot Avenue with Wimborne Road, about a quarter of a mile south of Winton Banks,

although the only overhead work necessary was a slewing of the wires.

Fares had remained unchanged since March 1956, but by early 1962 a deficit of £23,934 was forecast. It was therefore agreed to consider a revision of fares, once the result of a pending wage claim by the National Joint Industrial Council for the Road Passenger Transport Industry was known. Meanwhile, the SEB increased their charges effective 1st April 1961 involving an additional £915 pa. It soon became known that wage awards had been made at national level to bus crews, costing £20,000 in a full year, and to workshop craftsmen costing £1,500 in a full year, which would lead to a loss by the undertaking of £48,000 in the present financial year. A fares increase was accordingly recommended by the Transport Committee, together with the possibility of new fare stages.

The Transport Department was represented at the "Welcome to Citizenship" Exhibition which opened at the Town Hall on 24th April 1961. Their stand included an auto frog assembly, a crossover assembly, sections of trolley wire and various overhead fittings.

Mr Reakes presented a report at the Transport Committee Meeting on 8th May 1961, recommending the introduction of additional fare stages. A first result was the Committee's agreement on 13th June 1961 to a new fare stage on service 25 at the British Legion in Ashley Road.

The South Eastern Traffic Commissioners granted the Corporation's request for increased fares, with effect from 11th July 1961. The Corporation were unable to agree to the request from the Christchurch Town Clerk that different fares should apply within that town. The arrangements for postmen travelling on duty were renewed, with a 9% increase in the charge and subject to review in twelve months time. Meanwhile, the reversing triangle at Court Road, Charminster, was cut down on 9th May 1961. It had been little used, mainly by infrequent school specials serving Bournemouth Grammar School and Summerbee Infants and Junior School on East Way, and was no great distance from Five Ways turning circle or the reversing triangle at Luckham Road.

Trolleybus services 38 and 39 again served Bournemouth Pier from 12th June 1961 but, during that summer, the 38 operated to Carbery Avenue via Fisherman's Walk, Beaufort Road and Cranleigh Road, instead of to and from Christchurch via Southbourne Cross Roads as in 1960. There was a continuing shortage of platform

In July 1961 a Sunbeam MF2B chassis is towed into the Castle Lane Depot by Guy Arab breakdown lorry FRU 180 after the fire at Weymann's. *D. L. Chalk*

staff during the 1961 summer season; this was unrelated and probably could not have been foreseen.

The Highways and Works Committee were informed that it was impossible to reduce the number of trolleybuses using Bournemouth Square.

The inward bus stop and passenger waiting shelter in Wimborne Road at its junction with Talbot Avenue was repositioned in June 1961.

Fire in the trimming shop at Weymann's, Addlestone, in early July 1961 had damaged three of the nine MF2B chassis already delivered by Sunbeam for bodying. On 6th July, Mr G. Chesson, Weymann's Contract Manager, wrote to confirm that *"One chassis would appear to be a complete write-off, the second has sustained considerable damage and the third, although showing no sign of damage, was in fact adjacent to the fire and for this reason must be considered suspect, and will require thorough checking before it is considered fit for operation"*. Mr Reakes reported in October 1961 that, as a result of the fire, delivery of the new trolleybuses would be delayed and could only commence in July 1962.

All three damaged chassis had to be taken back to Sunbeam's Wolverhampton works for repair. In view of the costs involved, it was recommended at the Transport Committee Meeting of 14th November 1961 that the destroyed chassis should not be replaced, and Weymann were informed that only nine bodies were now required. Mr Reakes reported that an increase in the cost of the new chassis had amounted to £145 14s 5d each but pointed out that, due to savings made on trolleybases, jacks and batteries for the entire batch, the cost of each chassis was still about £21 below the tender price.

The other six chassis on Weymann's premises at the time of the fire, two of which carried partially-completed bodies, were delivered to and stored at Castle Lane until Weymann's factory had been repaired sufficiently to permit normal coachbuilding to be resumed. They were returned to Weymann's between April and June 1962. The tenth chassis, which had still been at Wolverhampton at the time of the fire, was brought direct to Bournemouth for storage.

In July 1961 an offer was made to Brighton Corporation, which had recently abandoned its trolley-bus system, for a quantity of surplus overhead equipment in anticipation of the Holdenhurst Road extension.

Douglas Reakes was due to retire on 1st December 1961 but he was asked to extend his contract until 28th February 1962. Applications were invited for the post of General Manager on a scale of £2,640 pa rising by annual increments of £75 to £3,015 pa. Some 31 applications were received, and six candidates selected for interview. On 10th November 1961 the Transport Committee appointed Mr Ronald Cox, then Engineer and General Manager of Rochdale Corporation Transport, to the position with effect from 1st March 1962 at a salary of £3,015 pa. Mr Cox had previously been Assistant Rolling Stock Engineer, Bradford Corporation, and therefore had much trolleybus experience. Indeed, he had written an article on trolleybus starting and notching curves, which had been published in the March 1943 edition of *The Transport World*.

The highest of four tenders received for the disposal of redundant vehicles, that of Messrs W. J. Stevens and Sons, for the purchase of seven trolleybuses, three Leyland motorbuses and two old vans at an overall price of £600 was accepted on 14th November 1961.

Structural defects at Castle Lane Depot were discovered and, without prejudice to any financial liability between the Corporation and other parties, the work of temporary shoring at the depot was carried out by Messrs James Drewitt & Sons Ltd. at an estimated cost of £250. In November 1961 the Borough Engineer was authorised to order rubber packing for the repairs. Subject to approval of estimates, Drewitts were authorised to proceed with the necessary repairs on a cost-plus basis without the undertaking advertising for tenders. The cost was paid from the Reserve Fund. At the 15th December 1961 Transport Committee meeting, the Consulting Engineers reported that the Castle Lane Depot structure had behaved much as expected and the Borough Engineer was instructed to arrange for periodic inspections by the Consulting Engineers. The estimated cost of repairs to be carried out by Messrs Drewitt was £871.

The Borough Architect had inspected Boscombe Depot again in September 1961, reporting that brickwork and pointing were now in generally good condition, the slate roof fair, internal damp stains were due to the solid brickwork, the steel window frames and the rainwater pipes were corroded and the oak window cills were showing signs of decay. Subsequently, the full Council recommended that the depot be transferred to the Civil Defence, but the Transport Committee replied that they were unable to give it up because closure would involve running dead mileage of 15,250 miles pa at a cost of £1,500. Additionally, a special bus would have to be provided for the 20–30 staff living in the Castle Lane area before the early shift and after the late shift. Those conductors on early shift who lived in the Pokesdown area and paid-in there when going off-duty would be required to travel to Castle Lane or Central (Southcote Road) Depots to pay-in and time would have to be allowed for this. The likely cost for these two latter points was unknown. In January 1962 a letter was received regarding the possibility of car parking in Boscombe Depot between 9 am and 6 pm, but the response was deferred for two months. The Transport Committee rejected a renewed request received in May 1962 to permit parking there.

In reply to the Christchurch Civic Trust and Local Authority, the Council offered to co-operate in their street improvements and decorations but could not remove trolleybuses from the streets.

In early 1962 a passenger waiting shelter was erected at Christchurch Road, Boscombe Gardens (inward), following consultation with the Borough Architect as to the design.

The underground cables on Pokesdown railway bridge were damaged on 8th February 1962.

The Transport Committee, at their 13th February 1962 meeting, expressed their appreciation for 26 years of service to Mr Douglas Reakes on his retirement. He had been appointed Traffic Superintendent in 1935, becoming Deputy General Manager in 1944 and General Manager on 7th December 1948. An enthusiast of the trolleybus, he had become well-known throughout the industry.

With effect from 1st April 1962 the new SEB standard tariff was applied to the undertaking, involving an estimated increased annual cost of £600. From the same date revised meter rentals were charged, leading to an annual saving of £120. Also in April 1962, a five-day week was introduced for the undertaking's administrative staff.

The department's quarterly insurance records for 1st April 1962 showed the following trolleybus statistics:

- Insured and available for service (total 68)

Sunbeam MS2:	205–208, 210, 211, 215, 219, 221, 224, 232
BUT 9641T:	234–240, 244–257
Sunbeam MF2B:	258–278, 280–287
BUT 9611T:	288–294

- Not insured (total 15)

Sunbeam MS2:	212–214, 216, 222, 229, 230, 233
Sunbeam open-top:	200, 201, 202
BUT 9641T:	241–243
Sunbeam MF2B:	279

There was now an acute shortage of platform staff leading to summer season service cuts. Reflecting the need for additional rolling stock in the height of the summer season, but also the reduced winter use of the BUT 9641Ts, by 1st July 1962 the situation was as follows:

- Insured and available for service (total 80)

Sunbeam MS2:	205–208, 210–216, 219, 221, 224, 232, 233
Sunbeam open-top:	200, 201, 202
BUT 9641T:	234–257
Sunbeam MF2B:	258–287
BUT 9611T:	288–294

- Available for service but not insured (nil)

Sunbeam MS2s 222, 229, 232 had been withdrawn in the meantime

Breakdown lorry FRU 180 pulls away from Weymann's works at Addlestone, Surrey during late August 1962, towing Sunbeam MF2B 303 (303 LJ). This was numerically the last Bournemouth trolleybus, although it was actually the third of the batch of nine to be delivered.

D. L. Chalk collection

- Ancillary vehicles (in both April and July):

    Bedford 2-ton Overhead Department tower wagon 3 (DEL 37)

    AEC Regent 661 Overhead Department tower wagons 10 (VH6218) and 12 (VH6217)

    Guy Arab FD with Jones "Super 20" crane FRU 224

On 10th April 1962, the Transport Committee considered a report on the nine new Sunbeam MF2B trolleybuses and accepted the recommendations of the new General Manager, Mr Cox, that the nine Sunbeam MF2Bs on order be fitted with fluorescent lighting and lighter internal decor using modern finishing materials *"in the Rochdale style"*, at an estimated additional cost of £2,215 11s 6d. In a letter to the department's insurance brokers (Messrs A. R. Stenhouse & Partners (London) Ltd.) dated 12th April 1962, Mr Cox advised that Sunbeam MF2B chassis numbers TFD 80195–197 and TFD 80200–204 were then at Castle Lane until Weymanns could fit the bodies. TFD 80201 was apparently missing its Master Controller. TFD 80198 was at Sunbeam prior to despatch direct to Weymanns. By 19th June 1962 only TFD 80200–201 and TFD 80204 were still at Castle Lane.

In May 1962 the Transport Committee agreed to the provision of a bus lay-by in Castle Lane West near its junction with Lawford Road, provided it was at no cost to the undertaking. The original Iford turning circle, between Bridle Crescent and Iford Bridge, largely made redundant by the construction of the roundabout at the junction of Castle Lane East and Christchurch Road in 1956, had been removed on 19th/20th May 1961.

Starting in July 1962 an addition "To and From Athletic Centre", referring to Kings Park south of Dean Court Football Stadium, began to be added to the auxiliary blinds. This was presumably only used for outward journeys on service 25 trolleybuses, the usual display being necessary on the inward journey because of the choice of route via Bath Road or Old Christchurch Road.

Just £150 had been allocated to the undertaking's Diamond Jubilee celebrations on 23rd July 1962. On that day Councillor Alban Adams, Bournemouth's Mayor, drove 296, the first of the nine final Sunbeam MF2B trolleybuses, accompanied by Alderman Deric Scott (Chairman of the Transport Committee), representatives of MCW, Sunbeam (by then owned by Jaguar Cars) and Mr Ronald Cox, General Manager. The Mayor commented that the town was immensely proud of its Transport Undertaking and said *"the new trolleybuses will certainly enhance our fleet"*. The *Bournemouth Echo* recorded that in 1961 the department had carried 42 million passengers some 4.5 million miles and had taken £770,000 in revenue. Out of a fleet of 180 vehicles there were 90 trolleybuses. Other events included the publication of a commemorative brochure, prepared by Mr W. P. Ransom, Commercial Assistant to the General Manager since 1951, and special decorations on some vehicles.

Mr Ransom retired on 31st July 1962 after 47 years of service, interrupted only by military service during the First World War. It was Mr Ransom who ensured the careful retention of the undertaking's historical records and who prepared the basis for the excellent public relations exercises of latter years.

At their meeting on 18th September 1962 the Transport Committee approved the extension of the existing trolleybus route from Queen's Park Golf Pavilion, along Holdenhurst Road to Castle Lane, Cooper Dean, Strouden Park, subject to statutory consent. Mr Cox was authorised to make the necessary arrangements for the work to be carried out in the 1963/64 financial year. They went on to invite tenders for the disposal of a further nine Sunbeam MS2 trolleybuses and, having considered three tenders at the 10th November 1962 meeting, the highest received, that of Messrs Scource, at £46 each, was accepted.

Also in September 1962 the amended scheme for an administrative block at Castle Lane Depot was approved, subject to the Finance Committee and the Town Planning and Buildings Committee's approval, at an estimated cost of £45,000 (plus architect's fees of £5,300).

What proved to be Bournemouth's last new trolleybus, Sunbeam MF2B 301, was delivered on 12th October 1962. Its delivery marked a sea change in local transport policy. The MF2Bs reportedly gave more maintenance problems per vehicle than any other type of Bournemouth trolleybus. The underfloor contactors proved to be susceptible to damp and water ingress, the 24-volt lighting generator gave problems and there were excessive half-shaft failures. It was felt that this last weakness was probably due to an influx of Guy motorbus engineers into the Sunbeam design team, who simply did not appreciate the stresses involved in trolleybus acceleration.

The removal of traction poles in Victoria Park Road, which had supported the former Brassey Road reversing triangle off Wimborne Road, Moordown, until 29th May 1948, was approved, subject to no cost being borne by the Council.

Consignments of unused overhead wiring equipment and traction poles were purchased from the erstwhile Brighton and Ipswich trolleybus systems, for use in construction of the Holdenhurst Road route extension. Until October 1962 these plans, together with the Boscombe (Gladstone and Haviland Roads) – Winton via Richmond Park Road, Alma Road, Coombe Avenue and Leybourne Road extension, remained active. Further proposals, never submitted for parliamentary approval, covered the route of motorbus service 7 in the Kinson area, from the junction of Columbia Road with Kinson Road (trolleybus services 30 and 31) along Fernheath Road, Maclean Road, Moore Avenue, West Howe Road to Francis Avenue, or along Poole Lane and Holloway Avenue to Bear Cross.

At the end of October 1962, approval was given to the move of the inward bus stop in Poole Road near its junction with Seamoor Road (western junction) a short distance to the east.

An accumulated deficit of almost £40,000 at the end of March 1956 had been turned into reserves of double that figure by early 1962 but, having considered the undertaking's financial position, the Transport Committee recommended on 10th November 1962 that an application for fare increases be made to the Traffic Commissioners.

Southbourne Ratepayer's Association again asked that the Cranleigh Road trolleybus service be extended to Christchurch, and Mr Cox was asked to report.

Reportedly disappointed at having failed to secure promotion to General Manager upon the retirement of Douglas Reakes, the Deputy Transport Manager and Engineer, Tom Marsden, resigned in December 1962 having secured the position of General Manager at Barrow-in-Furness. Applications for his successor were invited at the prevailing salary within the scale of £1,825 pa. rising to £2,085 pa.

At the end of 1962 the entrance to the bus park at the Triangle was widened at an estimated cost of £40 to enable two additional trolleybuses to be parked there.

On 19th/20th December 1962, the wiring at Strouden Park turning circle, through the gorse bushes at the junction of Holdenhurst Road with Castle Lane, was cut down and the site disappeared beneath works for a new roundabout. Temporarily, trolleybuses passed through the centre of the "island" whilst other traffic followed the normal circuitous course. From 18th December 1962, those peak hour trolleybuses terminating there, together with a single Sunday afternoon service, were extended to Iford for turning purposes.

The winter of 1962/63 proved particularly hard, and Bournemouth's trolleybus services were totally suspended on 30th December 1962 for the first time in their history, due to ice formation on the overhead wiring, leading to poor contact and jerky operation on the ice-covered roads. Bodorgan Road reversing triangle was reportedly used during periods when icy weather conditions made it impossible for trolleybuses to negotiate Richmond Hill safely.

At their first meeting of 1963, the Transport Committee instructed Mr Cox to submit a report on future trolleybus policy, including their involvement in any fleet replacement scheme. The Borough Engineer was asked to prepare a scheme for Stage II of the Castle Lane Depot development relating to the area between the workshops and the trolleybus depot.

There were 19 applications to fill the position of Deputy General Manager and Engineer, vacated by Mr Marsden, and five applicants were selected for interview. With effect from 4th March 1963, Ian Cunningham, Assistant Rolling Stock Engineer, Edinburgh Corporation Transport, was appointed at a salary of £1,825 pa on the scale £1,825 – £2,085 pa.

The application to increase fares was granted by the South Eastern Traffic Commissioners, with effect from 21st February 1963.

On 13th February 1963, the Transport Committee approved payment, under the terms of the contract, of an additional £160 per vehicle in respect of the nine new trolleybuses that had been delivered during 1962.

Mr Cox presented his report on the future of trolleybus operation and suggestions on fleet replacement on 19th March 1963. It indicated that British-built trolleybuses were virtually impossible to obtain except at bespoke prices, if at all. Most other British trolleybus operators had already announced a policy of trolleybus replacement, whilst spare parts and items of overhead line equipment were becoming increasingly difficult to obtain. Nonetheless, several professional observers consider that Mr Cox's report was unnecessarily pessimistic, in view of the excellent state of the undertaking's overhead line installations and its fleet of 39 ultra-modern Sunbeam MF2Bs with an expected 25-year operating life ahead of them. The Transport Committee had little alternative but to recommended that:

i)   no further purchases of trolleybuses be made;

ii) General Manager to report annually on the condition and suitability for continued operation of the then existing trolleybuses;

iii) That as groups of trolleybuses age, and their condition becomes uneconomic to operate, the General Manager be requested to report as to the routes which can best continue to be served by the remaining and decreasing trolleybus fleet;

iv) That the council resolve to discontinue the use of trolley vehicles as from a date in the future to be determined, when the then remaining fleet has been reduced to such an extent as to make its continuance uneconomic;

v)   subject to the approval of the next Finance Committee, tenders be invited for vehicle replacement for the next three years, namely thirty double-deck motorbuses at the rate of ten per year for spring delivery in 1964, 1965 and 1966.

1950 BUT 9641T 255 (KLJ 355) turns out of the Square to start the 1-in-8 ascent of Richmond Hill to Castle Lane West, Broadway Hotel and West Way. Note the postman just about to drop off the rear (entrance) platform to return to his office.

D. R. H. Bowler collection

With respect to the proposed trolleybus extension from Queen's Park, along Holdenhurst Road to Castle Lane, a further report was requested.

Having considered reports in March 1963 from the Highways and Works Committee and the General Manager on the cost of diverting trolleybus overhead at the junctions of Littledown Road with Lansdowne Road and St. Paul's Road to accommodate the planned Town Centre By-Pass (now Wessex Way), the Transport Committee instructed Mr Cox to replace trolleybus services 34 and 36 with motorbuses when work started. In this connection, Mr Cox recommended in May 1963 that, in view of planned road widening along that part of Holdenhurst Road between Littledown Avenue and Castle Lane, foreseen as a continuation of the town centre by-pass, no trolleybus route extension should now be made.

On 22nd March 1963 the full Bournemouth Council decided that no further trolleybuses would be purchased and that a progressive run-down would commence as vehicles aged and the fleet contracted in size, eventually leading to route closures. It was estimated that operations would continue for another 10–15 years, bearing in mind that the latest MF2Bs had a foreseen service life of 22 years, indicating final closure in 1978. History was to prove that this estimate was over-optimistic.

On 22nd March 1963 the *Bournemouth Times* recorded:

"Trolleybuses cost more than diesel buses due to increased charges for electric current, overhead wiring and cause traffic obstruction. So, after 30 years, these 10-ton transports which so impressed the residents with their silence after the trams, are to be dispensed with by a progressive run-down of the 90 which remain of the original 103-strong fleet. It is believed that criticism of the trolleys is related to congestion in the main thoroughfares and a transformer breakdown which resulted in the centre around the Square being cluttered up with inert trolleys during a peak period, finally decided the Transport Committee.

"Mr Ronald Cox was reportedly embarrassed when the Traffic Commissioners asked him the age of the buses (some are 30 years old) when the Corporation was seeking to raise fares in February. Unhappily for Mr Cox he had been saddled with 9 new trolleys, ordered before his arrival last year. Cash price of these would have been around £75,000. They are being bought on a 14-year loan and the final cost per vehicle will be about double the price of an excellent make of diesel double-decker recently demonstrated to the Corporation. The undertaking is in fact still paying for trolleys it bought 6 years ago and will be doing so until 1975, by which time, undoubtedly, the vehicles will have disappeared from the roads. The whole trolley set-up has been an expensive one. Some people think that the Council took

the wrong turning when Southcote Road power generating station came to the end of its life a few years back. That, they say, would have been an opportune time to scrap the trolleys. Instead the Council borrowed £60,000 for buildings and equipment for a switch-over of the trolleys to the Grid. And the greater part of this loan was for 20 years. Now, not surprisingly, the cost of electric current is more than it cost the Corporation to generate it, and the price is always increasing.

"In the financial year ending March last year, the trolleys cost 39.92d per mile or 3.41d per passenger. The diesel buses cost 35.84d per mile or 4.73d per passenger. Trolley revenue was £389,558 and diesels £361,006. There is not, in these figures, any real indication that in working costs alone trolleys are still cheaper. For the trolleys still hold the most remunerative routes and take more money for lower mileages than do the diesels. Diesels ran more than a quarter of a million miles more than the trolleys in that year. Trolleys carried 24,557,919 passengers against 17,749,495 carried by the diesels.

"There are obvious advantages in the use of diesels – fewer hold ups, no packing in columns, nose to tail resulting from the inability of one trolley to overtake another, quicker "taking" of roundabouts and corners, and better pace-keeping with traffic generally. The town's present traffic conditions demand that the trolleys should go. Only the older residents will mourn their passing. They will complain about fumes and noise. But the increase in these nuisances contributed by diesels can be no more than slight in face of the growing number of vehicles on all roads. And how pleasantly different the town will look with all those ugly standards and overhead wires cleared away".

On the same day the *Bournemouth Echo* reported:

"The undertaking has had to cope with the twin problems of rising costs and dwindling passengers. The new trolleybuses bought in 1958 cost in the region of £7,000 each (in 1934 they were £2,135 each) which will give some idea of how costs have gone up and the drop of 14 million passengers carried by the trolleybuses comparing the figures for 1953 with those for 1962 certainly calls for no comment.

"As a form of urban transport in the UK the trolleybus has fallen out of favour; local councils see them – as indeed has been suggested in Bournemouth – as causes of road congestion and managements plead that motorbuses are far more flexible in operation, although the vast majority of the travelling public who use them have great affection for the trolleybus. Whatever the decision of Bournemouth, the town can be very proud of what has been achieved in providing a silent, swift, safe and smokeless service".

On 21st April 1963, eastbound trolleybuses operating along Castle Lane started to circumnavigate the new

Cooper Dean roundabout at the top of Holdenhurst Road, Strouden Park. Westbound vehicles ceased to use the narrow track through the middle of the roundabout on 18th May 1963. The peak hour terminating services which had been temporarily extended to Iford were cut back to the new roundabout on 27th May 1963, the wiring on the east side of the roundabout being equipped with an auto frog. Additional wiring to make a complete circle around the roundabout, with the foreseen Holdenhurst Road extension in mind, was added later, as planned. Frogs were included for westbound trolleybuses to turn and return to Iford, but were not connected up until 12th July 1963, and no services from Iford were scheduled to turn here.

At the end of May 1963 the westbound bus stop adjacent to Iford roundabout was moved 82ft to the south-west.

In an effort to increase capacity and achieve operating economies with the BUT 9641T fleet, work started in September 1962 on removing the front staircase of 234. This was deemed a success and conversion of the entire BUT 9641T fleet, one after the other, commenced. The rebuilding involved the removal of the front staircase (although the front exit doors were retained) and the fitting of seat frames from recently-scrapped Sunbeam MS2s. Flashing trafficators were fitted at the sides and rear. Strip bell-pushes were fitted and the original Alhambrinal ceiling linings were removed to reveal the

Cooper Dean Roundabout Construction 1963

1. Original layout (until 19/20 December 1962)

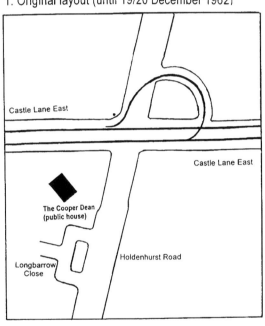

2. First stage of construction

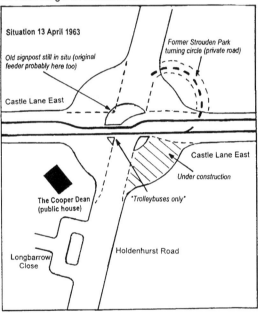

3. Second stage of construction

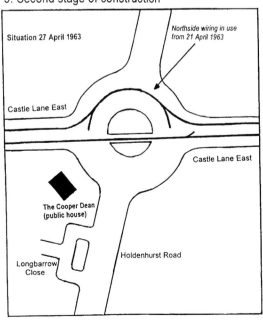

4. Completed roundabout (from 18 May 1963)

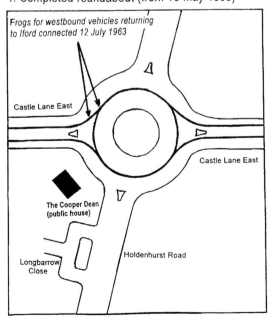

Rebuilt BUT 9641T 242 (KLJ 342), which operated the final service 25 from Westbourne, is seen here in Ashley Road, Boscombe earlier on 12th September 1965. Note the window behind the driver, in place of the panel which had previously covered the front staircase.

D. L. Chalk collection

metal above. Each rebuilt vehicle was put into operation on the heavily-used service 25 as soon as it became available. The rebuild programme ceased in June 1963 after ten vehicles (234 – 243) had been converted, in view of the decision to run down trolleybus operations.

The environmentally-minded Health and Watch Committee questioned the wisdom of withdrawing pollution-free trolleybuses and replacing them with fume-producing diesel buses. The Transport Committee replied that they had always maintained their vehicles to the highest possible level and that they did not anticipate any difficulties as a result of the introduction of diesel buses in the place of trolleybuses!

In spring 1963 wage awards (£21,525 pa) and increased employer's National Insurance contributions (£3,000) placed a further burden on the undertaking.

Plans to extend service 23 from Tuckton Bridge to Christchurch during the ensuing winter were not carried out, but a review was promised when a scheme for a roundabout at Tuckton was completed. The erection of traction poles on the Bournemouth side of Tuckton Bridge, at the junction of Tuckton Road with Belle Vue Road, commenced in May 1963, prior to the construction of a roundabout there. Following an overnight operation by the overhead gang, a complete circle of wiring was brought into use on Sunday 30th June 1963, enabling trolleybuses on services 22 and 23 to turn back at the roundabout, although normally through-routing made this unnecessary. The new wiring had been erected over the top of the old during the preceding weeks and, after the last trolleybus had passed on the Saturday evening, the latter was cut down and the new joined up, being completed in time for the first

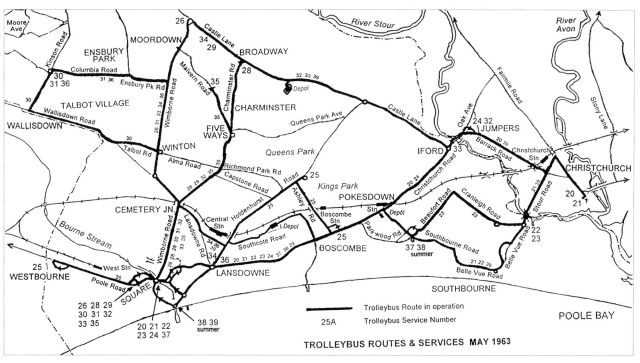

TROLLEYBUS ROUTES & SERVICES MAY 1963

vehicles on the Sunday morning. Sunbeam MS2 212, operating on a Reading Transport Society tour on 7th July 1963, was the first trolleybus to use the new wiring running from Tuckton Bridge into Tuckton Road.

In July 1963 an additional stop was introduced in Beresford Road on the inward journey of trolleybus service 23.

The 1963 summer timetable operated from 27th May until 29th September, trolleybus circular service 39 being run using open-top MS2s 200 and 202, with 201 stored delicensed at Castle Lane Depot. Closed-top MS2s 208, 210, 212, 213, were in service, with 205, 206, 214, 215, 216, 224 also stored delicensed at Castle Lane.

The SEB's standard tariff increased on 30th April 1963 involving additional expenditure of £700 pa.

In November 1963, the surrounds of Christchurch turntable was closed for resurfacing. Vehicles turned in Church Street by means of T-poles and battery-powered extension wires attached to the anchored-down trolleybooms. The overhead in Christchurch Road each side of Iford roundabout was temporarily slewed to one side to permit road works and one-way traffic which were expected to last most of the winter.

By the middle of the 1963 summer season, all the remaining MS2s except 224 (which had been withdrawn with an electrical fault in 1962 and which was never reinstated) were reported as licensed, many operating on all-day duties. Open-top 201, which retained its older blue- shaded fleet numbers, was also back in service.

In September 1963, orders were placed for 20 Leyland and 10 Daimler rear-engined double-deck motorbuses with MCW bodies for trolleybus replacement purposes.

Tenders were invited for the sale of five of the remaining Sunbeam MS2 trolleybuses, whilst the General Manager was authorised to negotiate with the Reading Transport Society (RTS) for the sale for preservation of an additional vehicle. The 20th September 1963 edition of the *Bournemouth Echo* recorded that 212 had been selected, and interviewed the Society's Chairman, Mr M. J. C. Dare. Closed-top Sunbeam MS2s 205, 208, 210, 212, 214 and 224 were withdrawn at the end of September 1963 and, with the exception of 212, were towed away by Scource & Son (Breakers) of Weymouth in early November 1963. On Saturday 16th November 1963, with the press in attendance, 212 was officially handed over to the Society. The afternoon was spent operating on the Castle Lane Depot circuit with enthusiasts on board. At 6.15 am on the Sunday, 212 left Bournemouth behind departmental lorry FRU 180 for Reading, reaching its new home at 11 am. The remaining MS2s, namely 206, 213, 215 and 216, together with the three open-top vehicles, were held in store for possible use in 1964, although continuing staff shortages made it unlikely that services 38 or 39 would operate. Rumours circulated that the open-top MS2s would be operated on service 21, making the Bournemouth Pier wiring prematurely redundant.

Following rumours in the summer that work would shortly commence on the town centre by-pass, the end of the summer timetable on Sunday 29th September 1963 saw the first trolleybus route closure. Trolleybus

Maintenance work under way on the Christchurch Turntable in Dolphin Yard in November 1963. In the background, a Sunbeam MF2B on service 20 is being turned by means of T-poles.
Bournemouth Evening Echo (D. L. Chalk collection)

service 34 (Lansdowne – Cemetery Junction – Moordown – West Way) was replaced by motorbuses the next day, operating a clockwise route Square – Lansdowne – Moordown – Charminster – Strouden Park – Holdenhurst Road – Lansdowne – Square, with service 33 operating anti-clockwise. Peak-hour trolleybus services 33 (Triangle – Square – Winton – Moordown – Cooper Dean – Iford) and 36 (Lansdowne – Winton – Ensbury Park – Columbia Road) were withdrawn on Saturday, 28th September 1963. As service 34 trolleybuses had continued back to the Square down Charminster Road as service 29 and vice-versa, the 29 was now linked with a reinstated service 27 operating via Moordown, Winton and Cemetery Junction to and from the Triangle. From Monday, 30th September 1963, all scheduled eastbound journeys on service 25 continued to Ashley Road, Boscombe, leaving the Queen's Park branch served by motorbuses only, although trolleybus football specials continued to turn at Queen's Park.

The Mains Department started removing feeder cables in St. Paul's Road on 16th December 1963 but, despite the promised early removal of the overhead to permit work on another new roundabout in St. Paul's Road at Littledown Road, the redundant wiring from Cemetery Junction along Lansdowne Road and St. Paul's Road to Holdenhurst Road remained intact for depot runs until 30th December 1963. All the overhead and traction poles in St.Paul's Road and Lansdowne Road were removed by February 1964, except for the last 30 yards at the Cemetery Junction end which was retained for feeder purposes. The Mains Department altered the switching to feed the section from an alternative feeder pillar in order that the remaining wiring in Lansdowne

Road, and redundant frogs and crossings at Cemetery Junction, could also be removed. By mid-October 1964 the Mains Department had completed their work at the top of Lansdowne Road, and the remaining service 34 wiring and junction work at Cemetery Junction had been cut down.

The predicted date for final abandonment of trolleybuses in Bournemouth was now given as 1973.

Having considered the General Manager's report, a new electrical supply agreement was made with the SEB based on the Board's draft. The figures in the table on the following page are based on details from a SEB letter dated 4th September 1963.

At the end of October 1963, in a continuing effort to improve passenger facilities, eight experimental stainless steel bus stop columns were purchased at £23 2s 8d each and placed in the town centre, whilst proposals to erect illuminated signs at other town centre stops were approved. Around the same time, a bus shelter was erected at the inward stop in Belle Vue Road near Tuckton Roundabout, and another at the Holdenhurst Road (Lansdowne) inward stop.

The first Transport Committee Meeting of 1964 considered falling revenue and the effects of the 1963 wage awards. Mr Cox was instructed to submit a report on a revision of the existing fares structure, which led to an application being made to the Traffic Commissioners to increase certain fares. They granted a general increase effective 27th June 1964; transfer fares were abolished and the issue of weekly tickets was limited to journeys where

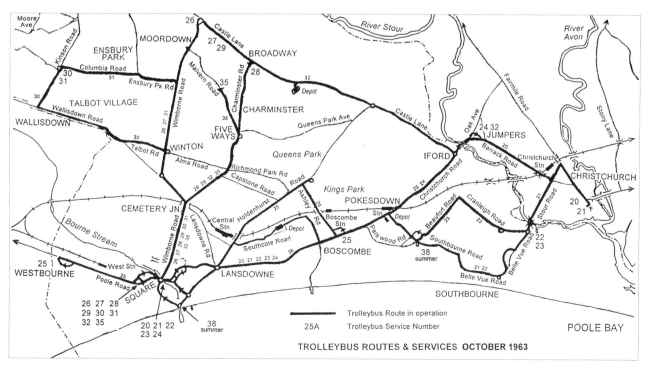

TROLLEYBUS ROUTES & SERVICES OCTOBER 1963

Traction units and maximum demands for the month ending 1 September 1963

Substation	Units	Maximum demand	Simultaneous maximum demand (5.00 pm, 2nd & 22nd August 1963)	
Electric House	77,580	330KVA at 5.00 pm, 01.08.63	260	190
Winton	50,740	200KVA at 8.00 am, 06.08.63	150	150
Southbourne	68,750	200KVA at 5.30 pm, 01.08.63 & 5.30 pm, 13.08.63	175	180
Christchurch	50,430	175KVA at 5.30 pm, 23.08.63	125	125
Holdenhurst	48,840	180KVA at 5.30 pm, 01.08.63 & 7.30 am, 16.08.63	125	140
Pokesdown	74,080	235KVA at 7.30 am, 30.07.63 & 5.00 pm, 01.08.63	200	210
Iddesleigh Rd	88,400	280KVA at 5.00 pm, 02.08.63 & 5.00 pm, 22.08.63	280	280
Southcote	332,500	1,020KVA at 5.00 pm, 22.08.63	980	1,020
TOTAL	**791,320**		2,295	2,295

the single fare was 7d or more. The minimum adult fare increased to 3d, and that for children to 2d. Questioned on travel concessions for Old Age Pensioners, the Transport Committee were informed that this was illegal.

In February 1964, the Highways and Works Committee advised that they did not wish to use any disused traction poles for street lighting purposes and the General Manager was authorised to dispose of any no longer required on the best possible terms. An annual charge of £1 per pole applied to the few retained, and these were gradually replaced by conventional lighting standards.

Also in February, the four remaining closed-top Sunbeam MS2 trolleybuses 206, 213, 215, 216 were advertised for sale and, having considered 11 tenders for a mixture of motorbuses, trolleybuses and a van, the highest, from a Mr N. Stanley, of Poole, at £75 each, was accepted. By 4th April 1964, 215 had been collected but the rest were still at Mallard Road one week later. The final two closed-top MS2s, 206 and 216, were finally removed for scrapping in early July 1964.

The 1964 summer timetable was operated as follows:

- 16th May 1964 – 7th June 1964: Bournemouth Pier and duplicate services as required.

- 8th June 1964 – 13th September 1964: full summer service.

- 14th September 1964 – 4th October 1964: Bournemouth Pier and duplicate services as required.

Meanwhile, the department's quarterly insurance records for 1st April 1964 showed the following trolleybus statistics:

- Insured and available for service (total 70)
  Sunbeam MS2:   all withdrawn
  BUT 9641T: 234–257
  Sunbeam MF2B: 258–287, 295–303
  BUT 9611T: 288–294

- Not insured (total 3)
  Sunbeam open-top: 200, 201, 202

By 1st July 1964, in high summer, the situation was:

- Insured and available for service (total 72)
  Sunbeam open-top: 200, 201
  BUT 9641T: 234–257
  Sunbeam MF2B: 258–287, 295–303
  BUT 9611T: 288–294

- Available for service but not insured (total 1)
  Sunbeam open-top: 202

- Ancillary vehicles (both in April and July 1964)
  DEL 37   Bedford Tower Wagon
  VH6217/8   AEC Tower Wagons
  FRU 224   Guy Arab mobile crane

Traffic signs authorising the parking of cars without lights began to be added on traction poles carrying street lamps in selected roads.

At this time, the Transport Committee received much correspondence expressing regret at the decision to discontinue trolleybuses and operate diesel buses.

Top: In 1950, Bournemouth Corporation took delivery of 24 BUT 9641T trolleybuses fitted with Weymann bodywork. This view shows trolleybus 255 (KLJ 355) pulling out of St. Paul's Road into Lansdowne Road near Central Station. This whole area has since disappeared underneath the Inner Relief Road (Wessex Way), the travel interchange and other, associated works. The dent in the front panel is most untypical of Bournemouth's buses and trolleybuses, and no doubt was swiftly rectified!   *F. W. Ivey*

Centre: This offside view of 240 shows how ten of the type were rebuilt in 1962/63, the front staircase having been removed and glazing fitted in place of the erstwhile stairway panel. The trolleybus is seen waiting in Seamoor Road, Westbourne, before heading back to Boscombe on service 25. According to the auxiliary display, there must have been a circus in town.   *M. Eady*

Bottom: BUT 9641T 252 (KLJ 352) leaves the Triangle on service 28 to Castle Lane (Broadway Hotel) in the early 1960s. An assortment of BUTs, Sunbeam MF2Bs and motor-buses are gathered in the parking area.   *D. R. H. Bowler*

Top: In 1959, Bournemouth bought seven secondhand BUT 9611T trolleybuses from Brighton. 289 (HUF 46) was formerly 46 in the Brighton Corporation fleet. It is seen here displaying a blue "via Old Christchurch Road" auxiliary screen, waiting in Seabourne Road, Fisherman's Walk on a peak-hour service 37 working.
M. Eady

Centre: 294 (DNJ 994) was one of the three BUT 9611Ts that once formed part of the company-owned Brighton, Hove & District (BH&D) fleet. It is seen here at the top of Richmond Hill, heading towards the Square (in spite of its destination!). Note the reversing triangle at Bodorgan Road in the background. *F. W. Ivey*

Bottom: 293 (DNJ 993), another ex-BH&D vehicle, waits at the junction of Lawford Road with Castle Lane West, Moordown, terminus of service 26. *F. W. Ivey*

Open-top trolleybus circular service 39 was not reintroduced with the summer 1964 timetable, perhaps due to the removal of the Cemetery Junction – Lansdowne overhead wiring. The open-top MS2s 200 and 201 (BRU 8 and BRU 11) were relicensed from 1st June 1964 but, apart from an enthusiast's tour using 200 on Sunday 14th June 1964, they did not enter service until 1st July 1964 and then only irregularly, on the 38 (Bournemouth Pier – Carbery Avenue). 202 was not relicensed. Service 38 required three vehicles, the third being a Sunbeam MF2B. The service was reduced to a 40-minute frequency after 7 pm. Thereafter, the relieved vehicle operated specials between the Square and Fisherman's Walk (in principle this was service 37, although it was no longer advertised as such) – an unusual working for an open-top trolleybus if the closed-top one was not used! A continued shortage of seasonal staff led to the premature withdrawal of service 38, which operated for the last time on Monday, 23rd August 1964, this effectively being the end of normal scheduled services to Bournemouth Pier. For much of the short season only an hourly service had been operated, instead of the scheduled 20-minute service. All three open-top trolleybuses were retained in the fleet until September 1965, but solely 202 was used after the end of the 1964 summer season – and then only on enthusiasts' tours.

In March 1964 it had been announced that, subject to confirmation by Edinburgh Council, Ronald Cox had been appointed Manager of that City's transport undertaking. The vacancy so created in Bournemouth was advertised at a salary of £3,130 pa raising by annual increments of £90 to £3,400 pa and ultimately to £3,490 pa. The *Bournemouth Echo* recorded in their 10th July 1964 edition: *"Ronald Cox said goodbye at a supper given in his honour at the Castle Lane bus depot canteen on 9th July 1964. At Edinburgh Mr Cox, who is 48, will have charge of a fleet of 720 buses (4 times the size of the Bournemouth fleet) which raises about £14.5 million in revenue compared with Bournemouth's figure of about £800,000. The salary at Edinburgh was advertised at £4,240 rising to £4,600; that at Bournemouth was £3,125 pa. A native of St. Helens, he joined the Corporation Transport Department there in 1935 and in 1948 was appointed Traffic Superintendent at Salford City Transport. Before coming to Bournemouth he was Transport Manager at Rochdale for 8 years."*

Questioned in 1998 as to Ronald Cox being responsible for the trolleybus closure decision, Ian Cunningham was emphatic that this was not the case. Cox was then a "live wire" in the industry and, although eager to change things at Bournemouth after a long period of conservative and admittedly pro-trolleybus management, he was not anti-trolleybus as such. During the first 15 months of his tenure he had sent out his deputy to secure quotations for new trolleybuses, although it had proved almost impossible to obtain offers from British manufacturers or they quoted grossly inflated prices. The "pros" and "cons" of motorbus compared to trolleybus operation were tabulated; acceleration, longevity, quietness and smoothness still speaking for the trolleybus, although the cost of providing and maintaining the power supply (including switchgear, underground feeder cables and ducts, and the overhead wiring) were quantified as a disadvantage. The introduction of a diesel fuel rebate and the frequency and cost of modifying the overhead layout and feeders to cater for roadworks helped tip the balance against the trolleybus. Throughout Britain trolleybuses were already on the way out, although Bournemouth was in the fortunate position of having modern rolling stock and a good quantity of overhead spares, partly acquired second-hand from other operators. Nevertheless, it was his report which recommended closure to the Transport Committee and he could have easily made a better case for trolleybus retention.

Having received 29 applications for the position and selected six for interview on 20th May 1964, the Transport Committee chose Mr Ian Cunningham, BSc, AMI MechE, then Deputy General Manager of the undertaking, as the new General Manager at a salary of £3,130 pa. Mr Cunningham had been Deputy since March 1963 and was previously Assistant Rolling Stock Engineer in Edinburgh, having had responsibility for their tram fleet from 1950 to 1956. At the time of his promotion he was aged 39, married with a son and daughter, and lived in Southbourne. In 1998 he recalled how, at Transport Committee Meetings, even the General Manager could not join in the discussions unless invited to speak which, in the author's opinion, says much about the abilities of amateur, local politicians in making far-reaching decisions about public transport! Fortunately, Mr Cunningham had a cordial relationship with Alderman Deric Scott, Chairman of the Transport Committee until 7th May 1964, and an unofficial discussion about the agenda often took place before each Meeting. The Transport Committee themselves could only make recommendations to the full Council and not make decisions.

The position of Deputy Manager was then advertised; the 23 applications received were reduced to a short-list of seven candidates, who were interviewed on 1st July 1964. With effect from 21st July, Mr Stuart Hindle, AM InstT, then Traffic Superintendent, was appointed Deputy General Manager.

The position of a number of bus stops was changed: the service 25 terminus in Portman Road was moved to the boundary line of St. George's Methodist Church, the service 23 stop in Tuckton Road near Saxonbury Road was moved about thirty yards eastwards and the stop between Iford Lane and Riverside Lane, again service 23, deleted.

The overhead wiring layout at the junction of The Grove and Barrack Road was altered on Sunday 26th July 1964 due to the completion of a short portion of dual carriageway in Barrack Road, Jumpers Corner. The Overhead Department worked from 11.30 pm on the Saturday until 8.00 am on the Sunday to complete the task, using all three tower wagons and lorry 304 LJ (the registration number originally reserved for the tenth and final Sunbeam MF2B).

Due to a continuing strike at the MCW finishing shop, the date of delivery of trolleybus-replacement motorbuses still remained uncertain at the end of June 1964. Indeed, only in late October did the Department learn that delivery of ten trolleybus-replacement Leyland Atlanteans could be expected in November 1964.

From November 1963, the County Borough coat of arms on the front of the Sunbeam MF2Bs had been reintroduced on all trolleybuses, commencing with re-painted BUT 9641T 248 and, by mid-1964, at least one BUT 9641T had been fitted with a blue enamelled badge bearing the coat of arms (similar to those on the replacement motorbuses) in place of the maker's name plate.

At 7.10 am on 30th September 1964, a lorry skidded in Holdenhurst Road, bringing down a traction pole and about fifty feet of wiring, disrupting service 25. By 8 am the Overhead Department had erected a new pole, adjusted the wiring and removed the old one!

The fleet had now been reduced to 70 trolleybuses, all of which were licensed for the winter season, although a maximum of 60 were needed to operate services. No further route closures had been announced, although there were rumours of the impending withdrawal of services 20 and 24. The trolleybus fleet now consisted of:

200–202	Sunbeam MS2/Park Royal O69R open-top (withdrawn but still in stock)
234–243	BUT 9641T/Weymann H68D (rebuilt without front staircase)
244–257	BUT 9641T/Weymann H56D
258–287	Sunbeam MF2B/Weymann H63D
288–294	BUT 9611T/Weymann H56R (ex-Brighton)
295–303	Sunbeam MF2B/Weymann H63D

The ex-Brighton BUT 9611Ts could be found operating on service 25 and on the evening peak services along Christchurch Road. It was already evident that they would be the first to be withdrawn, 293 having had no repaint since entering service in Bournemouth in March 1959. By 20th February 1965, 288 (ex-Brighton) was parked in the open at Castle Lane Depot, presumed withdrawn.

From 25th October 1964, Sunday morning schedules on trolleybus services 21, 22 and 23 were revised. Short workings on service 23 operating via Cranleigh Road between Fishermans Walk and Tuckton Bridge only ceased, journeys being extended to the Square. The Parkwood Road – Southbourne Road turning circle became redundant, although it remained intact and was used subsequently as part of the abortive one-way system at Fishermans Walk, introduced on 12th November 1967 and abandoned three months later on 12th February 1968.

Two Sunbeam MF2Bs emerged from the paint shop in autumn 1964 with experimental interior colour schemes, 263 being painted in coffee and 264 in grey.

At their 20th October 1964 meeting, the Transport Committee authorised the sale to the National Trolleybus Association (NTA) of one of the three open-top trolleybuses which would become available in Spring 1965 at the then tendered price. In November 1964 the *Bournemouth Echo* announced that *"the world's only open-decked trolleybuses are for sale. They operated for the last time in Summer 1964 and will be on the market next spring"*. One was reportedly to go to Plumtree Station, near Nottingham, where the NTA planned a museum. It was decided that service 38 would not operate in 1965, confirming the end of scheduled service trolleybus operation to Bournemouth Pier, although private hire trolleybuses operated there in October 1964, March 1965 and July 1965 at least, as well as occasional school specials to the Winter Gardens in Exeter Road.

The bus stops at Talbot Road, Winton Banks, were re-arranged in September 1964 and, in October 1964, the stop outside 289 Holdenhurst Road was removed.

The Mayor, Alderman Harry Mears, was concerned how the trolleybus replacement motorbuses with their front entrance overhang would be able to negotiate corners but added that *"Trolleys are completely out of date"*.

Having received further correspondence from the Highways and Works Committee, the Transport

Committee confirmed an earlier decision that a £5 charge would be made for each traction pole used for street lighting purposes.

A fatal accident occurred between a trolleybus and an elderly lady cyclist on 8th December 1964, at the junction of Talbot and Sedgley Roads, Winton. A verdict of accidental death was returned at the inquest into what was the first such fatality in the system's history.

On 2nd February 1965 the full Council approved the Transport Committee's recommendations to cut costs by reducing services. Trolleybus services were extensively affected as follows:

20 Square (Gervis Place) – Lansdowne – Christchurch Road – Boscombe – Iford – Jumpers – Barrack Road – Christchurch: to be withdrawn on winter Sundays.

24 Square (Gervis Place) – Lansdowne – Christchurch Road – Boscombe – Iford – Jumpers: to be reduced to a 30-minute frequency on winter Sundays.

25 Westbourne – Square – Lansdowne – Central Station – Holdenhurst Road – Ashley Road, Boscombe: basic service to be reduced to 12 minutes but with additional trolleybuses operating at certain times between Square and Queens Park giving a 6-minute service on the common section of route.

26 Triangle – Square – Richmond Hill – Cemetery Junction – Wimborne Road – Winton – Moordown – Lawford Road: to be withdrawn.

28 Triangle – Square – Richmond Hill – Cemetery Junction – Charminster Road – Five Ways – Broadway Hotel, Castle Lane: to be withdrawn at certain times of the day.

30 Triangle – Square – Richmond Hill – Cemetery Junction – Winton – Talbot Road – Wallisdown – Columbia Road: to be withdrawn.

31 Triangle – Square – Richmond Hill – Cemetery Junction – Winton – Ensbury Park Road – Columbia Road: to operate only every 30 minutes during the evenings and on Sundays.

35 Triangle – Square – Richmond Hill – Cemetery Junction – Charminster Road – Five Ways – Malvern Road: (the least frequent of all trolleybus services, having an hourly frequency) to be withdrawn.

The General Manager was authorised re-route of any existing services required on the withdrawal of trolleybus service 30 between Wallisdown and Winton Banks.

These cuts were designed to avoid a deficit at the end of 1965. The possibility of another fare increase, the last having been made on 2nd June 1964, was also considered. No immediate decision was taken as to the withdrawal of services 26, 30 and 35.

At the same meeting, the Council also resolved to replace trolleybuses by motorbuses *"as soon as possible"*, with a programme of fleet replacement for the years 1966–69. This was the first intimation of an expedited programme which would see seven-year-old trolleybuses withdrawn for scrapping.

With effect from 8th February 1965, a wage award by the National Joint Industrial Council for the Road Passenger Transport Industry led to additional costs of £5,000 for the remainder of the financial year and £33,000 in a full year. Improved conditions were still under discussion.

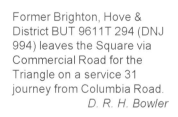

Former Brighton, Hove & District BUT 9611T 294 (DNJ 994) leaves the Square via Commercial Road for the Triangle on a service 31 journey from Columbia Road.
D. R. H. Bowler

The 1965 summer timetable operated as follows:

- 5th – 6th June: duplicate services as required.

- 7th June – 12th September: full summer service.

- 13th – 26th September: duplicate services as required.

The Council discussed a complaint from residents in the Lawford Road and Castle Lane West area about reduced bus services, specifically the 26, but adhered to their decision stressing that there had been no reduction in services during peak periods. The possibility of re-routing some motorbuses via Richmond Hill, instead of the Lansdowne, to Bournemouth Square was investigated.

A Public Enquiry into the proposed closure of Bournemouth West Station was held at the Town Hall on 27th April 1965. Mr Cunningham attended in order to indicate any service changes that would be needed should the closure take place. The last train on the original Ringwood – Hurn – Christchurch branch line route to Bournemouth had run before the war, on 28th September 1935. In 1964 services between Bournemouth and Salisbury via Wimborne, West Moors and Fordingbridge, together with those on the "old road" from West Moors through Ringwood to Lymington Junction, ceased. On 4th October 1965, Boscombe and Bournemouth West stations were closed.

Apparently, at about this time the MPTA received an enquiry from Portugal for the purchase of a complete trolleybus system, and Mr Cunningham was instructed to find out more. The author's researches have unfortunately brought no more information to light.

Trolleybus services were affected by the undertaking's worsening economics and, from Monday 5th April 1965, service 20 was withdrawn entirely on Winter Sundays and service 24 operations reduced to half-hourly, the service to Iford being reduced from six vehicles an hour to two in a single stroke. Christchurch Borough Council complained but, in view of the alternative services available, Bournemouth's Council adhered to their previous decision.

Trolleybus services 26 and 28 were reduced to weekday peak-hour and occasional Sunday journeys, whilst service 35 was withdrawn entirely after operation on Sunday 4th April 1965, and the Five Ways, Charminster – Malvern Road, Moordown route closed. Opened on 12th April 1937, the Malvern Road service was originally numbered 29, becoming the 35 on 1st March 1956. The final Sunday service consisted of departures from the Triangle hourly from 2.13 pm to 6.13 pm, with corresponding hourly departures from Malvern Road from 2.40 pm to 6.40 pm. The final vehicle to leave Malvern Road, at just after 6.40 pm on 4th April 1965, was Sunbeam MF2B 279. Other vehicles operating the four final journeys were 281, 300, 280 and 276 in that sequence. No replacement motorbus service was introduced, and bus stop signs were removed the next day. The overhead wiring, however, was only cut down in July/August 1966. To retain a 15-minute service on Sundays along Charminster Road, service 32 was strengthened during the afternoon, terminating at Iford instead of Jumpers Corner. Trolleybus service 30 ceased to run after 6 pm daily and on Sunday mornings, whilst service 31 was reduced to a half-hourly service on Sundays and after 7 pm during the week.

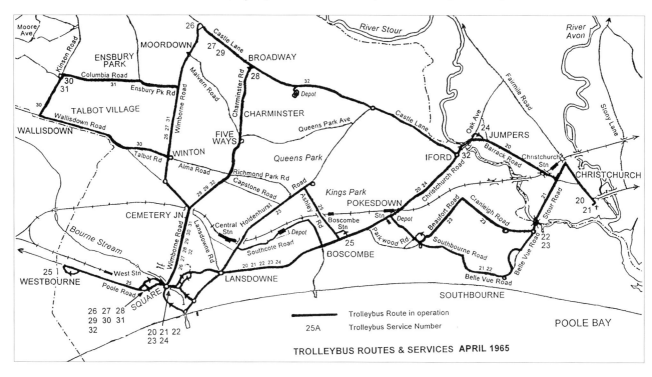

TROLLEYBUS ROUTES & SERVICES APRIL 1965

Yet another application to increase fares was made to the Traffic Commissioners in March 1965. The Public Hearing took place on 7th April 1965; the new fares were approved, and took effect on 15th April 1965.

Following discussions with TGWU representatives, it was agreed on 20th April 1965 that the carriage of standing passengers at off-peak periods (but at no other time) would be permitted as follows:

- **Monday-Friday:** 7 am – 9 am; 12 pm – 2 pm; 4 pm – 6.30 pm; last bus on each service.

- **Saturday:** 12 pm – 6.30 pm; 9 am – 6.30 pm (during Summer Season); last bus on each service.

- **Sunday:** last bus on each service.

A proposal to introduce the 24-hour clock in the undertaking was not accepted.

The undertaking's administrative staff moved from 99 – 101 Southcote Road to new offices to the west of the Castle Lane workshops and stores on 26th April 1965, the official opening, together with that of the second motorbus garage, being made by the Mayor on 7th May 1965. The legal lettering at the base of each vehicle's nearside panels was changed to show "Mallard Road" as the Transport Department's Head Office. The traction poles around the depot loop were repainted at this time, with several still standing in 1998!

A complete timetable for trolleybus replacement was announced in May 1965:

- **Summer 1965:** trolleybus service 25 and the six remaining ex-Brighton BUT 9611T vehicles to be withdrawn and replaced by ten Daimler Fleetline motorbuses.

- **Summer 1966:** all "Side Road" trolleybus services using Richmond Hill (26–32) and the 24 BUT 9641T vehicles built in 1950 to be withdrawn and replaced by 20 new rear-engined, front-entrance motorbuses.

- **Summers 1967–1969:** all "Main Road" (Christchurch Road) trolleybus service (20–24) and the 39 Sunbeam MF2Bs to be withdrawn and replaced by 30 new rear-engined, front-entrance motorbuses.

On 7th June 1965, Central Depot, Southcote Road was vacated and taken over as a base for the Corporation's refuse vehicles (still remaining in use 35 years later, albeit with one entrance closed-up). Following the closure, it was at this stage unclear if, after the planned

1966 trolleybus route closures, access to Castle Lane Depot would be retained along Castle Lane East, or whether this would be up Richmond Hill and along Charminster Road. The former, shorter and less-obtrusive access route proved to be the case.

All trolleybus repaints now featured small black stock numerals, instead of the plain gold Gill Sans used from about 1960 and the larger blue shaded gold transfers used previously in the post-war period. At this time all three types of fleet numbers could be seen on the trolleybuses, including some vehicles which carried two types as a result of accident damage repairs. Sunbeam MF2Bs 258–287 were at this time in the course of having their front and rear staircases painted grey instead of dark brown.

No scheduled service trolleybuses reached Bournemouth Pier during the 1965 summer season, as neither the open-top trolleybuses nor service 38 were operating (the route as far as Fisherman's Walk being covered by open-top Daimler Fleetline motorbuses on a new service 16).

Open-top MS2 202, which had last been used in September 1963, was relicensed for the period May–August 1965 but solely for use on two enthusiast's tours, namely on Sunday, 23rd May by the Bournemouth Railway Club; and on Sunday, 4th July by the National Trolleybus Association. The latter was hailed as the last open-top trolleybus tour in the world and was joined by Ian Cunningham, the General Manager. Disused open-top MS2s 200 and 201 were reportedly in poor condition by this time, and had lost many of their seats.

On 10th May 1965 the service 25 timetable, which had only been introduced on 5th April, was revised, whilst special journeys between the Square and Queen's Park in connection with football matches ceased. A 7-/8-minute frequency between Westbourne and Boscombe was reintroduced until 6.30 pm, after which a 15-minute service operated. The Sunday service was unchanged.

The Transport Committee Meeting of 25th May 1965 discussed further fare increases and service economies, Mr Cunningham being instructed to submit more information about the 5d fare between Ensbury Park Hotel and Winton Banks. The winter frequency of service 24 was left in the hands of the Chairman in consultation with the General Manager. The same meeting considered a petition by Charminster residents concerning the withdrawal of trolleybus service 35, and asking for a report thereon. This report was provided by the 29th June 1965 meeting, at which the Committee

In this scene, BUT 9641T trolleybus 246 (KLJ 346) is seen in Holdenhurst Road on service 25 – the usual haunt of this type of vehicle during the 1960s.

F. W. York (BTS Library)

recommended no action; the full Council, however, referred the matter back again for further consideration.

On Sunday, 30th May 1965, the RTS made another of their annual tours, this time using BUT 9611Ts 292 (ex-Brighton Hove & District Omnibus Company) and 290 (ex-Brighton Corporation). This enthusiasts' tour was the last to visit Central Depot, Southcote Road.

The withdrawal of ex-Brighton BUT 9611Ts continued, with 291 in May 1965 following rear-end damage, and 289, 290 and 292 in July 1965. They were stored outside at Castle Lane Depot ready for disposal, together with 288 and the open-toppers 200 and 201, leaving just 293 and 294 of the ex-Brighton fleet recorded as still in service in August 1965. The entire ex-Brighton fleet and all three open-toppers were offered for sale. The highest tender, of £76 for the ex-Brighton trolleybuses and £101 for the three open-toppers was received from Colbro Ltd. (Dealers), Leeds. Open-top MS2 202, however, passed to the NTA for preservation.

In June 1965, a turnout and a trailing frog were inserted in the Iford roundabout overhead to enable trolleybuses coming from the Boscombe direction to turn directly into Castle Lane East for Castle Lane Depot without having to circle the roundabout. It was brought into use on 2nd July 1965. By August 1965 the overhead wiring at the former Central Depot and in St. Clement's Road, the access route from Boscombe, had been dismantled. The hand-operated turnout frog at the junction of Stour and Barrack Roads, Christchurch, for trolleybuses travelling from Castle Lane Depot to take up service and wishing to turn south towards Tuckton, was converted into an auto frog from 2nd August 1965. Due to the laying of a trunk sewer to the new Holdenhurst disposal works, the Cooper Dean feeder had to be relocated two poles further east from the roundabout about this time, cables

being strung from the original feeder pillar between the traction poles along the north side of the road.

The *Bournemouth Echo* noted, on 9th September 1965, that *"On Sunday the last trolleybus will operate on what was the first trolleybus route in Bournemouth. This will be the first visible indication of the change of policy which will lead to the eventual disappearance of the trolleybuses from the streets of Bournemouth by 1970. The 33 and 34 circular services around Strouden Park have been operated by motorbuses for quite some time now and the first section of overhead wire along St. Paul's Road on the old 34 route has been taken down. With the change to motorbuses on the 25, wires will be taken down Triangle – County Gates and all along Holdenhurst Road and Ashley Road.*

"The next step will be in 12 months' time when the services using Richmond Hill change from trolley to motor. Target date for the withdrawal for all the remaining trolleybus services is 1968. The death knell for the trolley was in 1963 when Bournemouth Town Council at their April meeting decided to do away with them in 5–10 years".

Planned major road works at the western end of Holdenhurst Road, together with the closure of Central Depot a few months previously, led to trolleybus service 25 (Westbourne – Square – Holdenhurst Road – Ashley Road, Boscombe) being selected as the next candidate for withdrawal. This service had been operated entirely from Central Depot until its closure. Motorbuses took over with the introduction of the winter timetable on 13th September 1965.

The end of the ex-Brighton BUT 9611Ts in August 1965 and the withdrawal of trolleybuses from service 25 on Sunday 12th September 1965 signalled the completion of

Stage 2 of the withdrawal programme. The last service 25 journey was operated by BUT 9641T 242, which left Westbourne in wet weather at 11.21 pm with just three people on board. Trolleybuses in operation on the route during its last day were 235, 238, 242–244, 276. Thereafter ten BUT 9641Ts (245, 247–250, 252, 254–57) were delicensed, leaving only 244, 246, 251, 253 still in service (all in unrebuilt form, with two staircases).

Further trolleybus service cuts coincided with the introduction of the Winter 1965/66 timetable on 13th September 1965. Service 24 disappeared entirely apart from Monday – Friday peak-hour workings and Sunday afternoons (2.30 pm – 6.30 pm), in place of service 20 which did not operate at all on Winter Sundays. During the week service 20 was increased to operate every 20 minutes.

On 14th September 1965 the Transport Committee agreed to altered timings for services 20 and 24, to give an evenly distributed service along Christchurch Road but, despite public pressure to reintroduce service 35 along Charminster Avenue, for which the wiring remained intact, no action was taken. Only in October 1965 did they agree to retain, for an experimental six-month period, a weekday 35 motorbus service at 8.40 am to Bournemouth Square, returning at 5.45 pm.

The last of the wiring on the approach roads to the former Central Depot, Southcote Road, was removed by early September 1965. On the nights of 13th/14th September 1965, the frogs and crossing at the junction of Palmerston Road and Christchurch Road were removed. During October 1965 the traction poles in Southcote, Palmerston and St. Clements Roads were

removed, nearly 100 poles being removed in a fortnight, working just three hours every morning. The former depot exit into St. Clements Road was sealed off, and the footpath extended across it.

In October 1965 a report into the replacement of the Ultimate ticket system was instigated. In the same month, the Highways and Works committee had white lines painted on the road at Southbourne Grove to indicate possible traffic islands. Mr Cunningham felt that they would make bus operation impossible, however, and the idea was abandoned.

A letter dated 15th October 1965 from Federation of Municipal Passenger Transport Employers stated that, subject to completion of current negotiations with the appropriate National Joint Councils, the 40-hour week would be introduced for craftsmen from 1st November 1965 and for drivers, semi-skilled and unskilled employees from 3rd January 1966. The cost to the undertaking was estimated as £5,000 in the current financial year and £19,000 in a full year.

On 30th October 1965, work commenced on the removal of the overhead wiring between Westbourne and the Triangle, i.e. in Poole Road and Seamoor Road, continuing through November whilst, in December 1965, those traction poles not retained for lighting purposes were burned off about 6ins below ground level. This was complicated by some of the older, ex-tramway traction poles having been filled with concrete reinforcing. Many were sold to a firm of contractors near Portsmouth for use in sea defence work. The frog in Commercial Road outside Woolworths was taken out

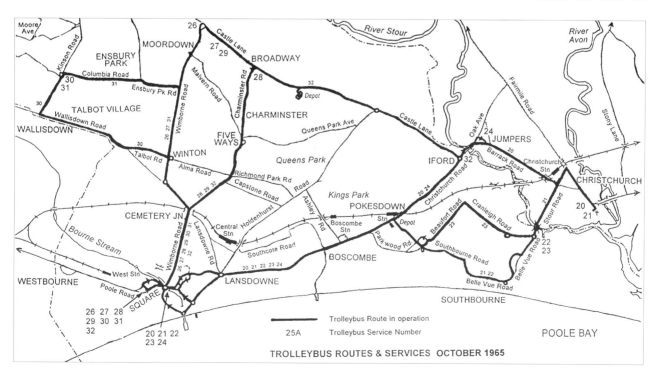

TROLLEYBUS ROUTES & SERVICES OCTOBER 1965

on the night of 30th/31st October 1965. The switch frog at Trinity Church, Old Christchurch Road, for eastbound 25 trolleybuses had gone by 21st November 1965. At Portman Road, Boscombe; outside Woolworths in the Square; and at Trinity Church, Old Christchurch Road, pieces of wire replacing the frogs were joined by two end fittings bolted together instead of the usual mid-span splices. Just before Christmas, all section boxes and feeder cables were removed along Ashley Road and Holdenhurst Road. After the holiday, work started on removing the running wire and, within a few weeks, the section from Queens Park Hotel to the former Roxy Cinema in Cleveland Road had been cut down to prepare for road widening.

From 6th January 1966, the Overhead Department was reorganised and, for the first time since trolleybus operation commenced, no overhead crew was on duty at night. Removal of overhead equipment from defunct routes was therefore now limited to day-time, normally Friday mornings (as two crews were on duty together) or, for more complicated work, Sunday mornings when there was, in those days, little road traffic.

Queen's Park junction and the Golf Pavilion branch were cut down by mid-January 1966. The route was tied off between the end of Ashley Road ("White House" switch box) and Cleveland Road feeder by 22nd January 1966. Removal of wiring was started, working outwards from the Lansdowne. By mid-March 1966, all wiring and traction poles had been removed from Holdenhurst Road, including the Central Station junction but excluding the section between the Lansdowne and the Station, whilst half a mile in Ashley Road, up to but not including the railway bridge, had gone.

The 27th January 1966 Transport Committee meeting recommended a further application for increased fares, subject to a maximum increase of 1d except on Summer holiday services. In order to limit the increases, further departmental economies were proposed, including service changes and more one-man-operated vehicles. A completely new route structure, based on main routes and feeder services with transfer ticket facilities, was proposed. On 1st April 1966, the Traffic Commissioners approved the proposals, and the increased fares were brought into operation on 8th April 1966.

A short history of the trolleybus system appeared in the February 1966 edition of *The Hampshire Magazine*, in which Ian Cunningham was quoted as saying that the main reason for the abandonment of trolleybus operation was the increasing cost of, and difficulty in obtaining, vehicles and spare parts. The undertaking had been

making its own spares for quite some time, initially for the Sunbeam MS2s and later for the MF2Bs, as well as overhead parts. It should be noted that the Deputy Chief Inspector was the undertaking's senior supervisor. The Mayor's chauffeur was, *ex officio*, the Chief Inspector – although having little, if anything, to do with bus operations!

The annual acknowledgement fee for attachments to traction poles was increased to £1 1s 0d but, in view of the pending final abandonment, no new applications for the addition of direction signs were accepted.

From 6th March 1966, falling patronage provoked a further reduction in Sunday services. The "Main Road" trolleybus services (21–23) and the 31 were cut to half-hourly, and the Richmond Hill services (27–29 and 32) were reduced to hourly, with service 28 extended to Mallard Road Depot (and, from 1 pm to 7 pm, further east to the Cooper Dean Hotel). Service 24 was reduced to weekday peak-hour only operation, and service 26, by now just a single advertised weekday journey, disappeared altogether, being regarded as a short-working of service 27. The half-hourly Sunday trolleybus service 30 was replaced by motorbuses.

Having considered Mr Cunningham's report of 31st December 1965, tenders were invited for internal and external advertising on Corporation buses, effective 1st August 1966 when the existing (internal) advertising contract was due to expire. Advertising was also to be permitted around ten bus shelters but not in the timetables.

The Transport Committee recommended at their 15th March 1966 meeting that, having considered four tenders for exterior advertising on Corporation buses, the highest from Howards Publicity Ltd. (£10,660 pa for five years plus 5% for the sixth and seventh year) be accepted as from 1st August 1966. Included in this sum was £3,496 6s 0d plus 5% for interior advertising. However, the full Council rejected this recommendation on 12th April 1966 and tenders were reinvited for internal and external advertising on double-deck buses for periods of 3, 5 and 7 years. The existing contract with Messrs Frank Mason in respect of internal advertisements was extended for three months from 1st August 1966. In July 1966 they considered four revised tenders; the highest again came from Howards Publicity (£11,162 1s 6d pa for three years commencing 1st November 1966), and this was accepted. Thus the Council at last agreed to external advertising on the Transport Department's vehicles. Until this time, Bournemouth, Huddersfield and the Teesside Railless Traction Board had been the only latter-day trolleybus operators not to display external advertising.

It was suggested that the passenger waiting room at the trolleybus turntable off Church Street, Christchurch, be closed and, if permitted, tenders be invited for the right to use the building as a shop. Back in September 1962, in response to a letter, the Council had not been prepared to dispose of the waiting room.

From Saturday, 16th April 1966, weekday trolleybus service 30 ceased to run and was replaced by diversions of the half-hourly motorbus service 7 (Boscombe – Kinson via Turbary Park Avenue). Trolleybus service 31 was revised between 9 am and 7 pm accordingly. The withdrawal of service 30 did not lead to any wiring being made redundant, as some trolleybuses running into and out of service from Columbia Road continued to travel by way of Kinson Road, Wallisdown Road and Talbot Road to Winton Banks. Trolleybuses 236 (a BUT 9641T which had had its front staircase removed in 1962) and 273 (a seven-year-old Sunbeam MF2B) were withdrawn. At about this time it was announced that no further trolleybus repaints would take place; 281, the last, left the paintshop in August 1966.

An RTS Tour on Sunday, 12th June 1966, used BUT 9641Ts 239 (single staircase) and 244 (unrebuilt), participants changing at the half-way point, Castle Lane. This tour was accordingly able to traverse the route of the erstwhile service 30 through Wallisdown, in addition to little-used sections of overhead in Southbourne and Bournemouth town centre.

Importantly, it was agreed with the Highways and Works Committee on 19th April 1966 that all bus stops in the Borough be made "No Waiting" areas.

Augmented services operated during the summer of 1966 between 13th June and 11th September.

With the introduction of the summer timetable on 13th June 1966, service 20 was reintroduced on Sundays with a 20-minute frequency (compared with every 30 minutes in 1965) but there was, of course, no longer a service 24 as far as Iford on Sundays. The terminal loop at Jumpers Corner was nevertheless still in use on Sunday mornings until about 1 pm for short workings on service 20. Non-scheduled mid-day "peak hour" and Saturday trolley-buses were noted at the rarely used Southbourne Cross Roads and Five Ways, Charminster, turning circles. Only the latter had vehicles timetabled to turn there and then only on Sunday mornings.

The trolleybus network by this time had contracted to:

20 Square (Gervis Place) – Lansdowne – Christchurch Road – Boscombe – Iford – Jumpers – Barrack Road – Christchurch

21 Square (Gervis Place) – Lansdowne – Christchurch Road – Boscombe – Fisherman's Walk – Southbourne Cross Roads – Tuckton Bridge – Christchurch

22 Square (Gervis Place) – Lansdowne – Christchurch Road – Boscombe – Fisherman's Walk – Southbourne Cross Roads – Tuckton Bridge

23 Square (Gervis Place) – Lansdowne – Christchurch Road – Boscombe – Fisherman's Walk – Beaufort Road – Cranleigh Road – Tuckton Bridge

24 Square (Gervis Place) – Lansdowne – Christchurch Road – Boscombe – Iford – Jumpers

27 Triangle – Square – Richmond Hill – Cemetery Junction – Wimborne Road – Winton – Moordown – Lawford Road

28 Triangle – Square – Richmond Hill – Cemetery Junction – Charminster Road – Five Ways – Broadway Hotel, Castle Lane

29 Triangle – Square – Richmond Hill – Cemetery Junction – Charminster Road – Five Ways – Broadway Hotel, Castle Lane – Lawford Road

31 Triangle – Square – Richmond Hill – Cemetery Junction – Winton – Ensbury Park Road – Columbia Road

32 Triangle – Square – Richmond Hill – Cemetery Junction – Charminster Road – Five Ways – Broadway Hotel – Castle Lane – Strouden Park – Iford

By April 1966, the erstwhile service 25 wiring had almost completely vanished, apart from a few short stretches in Ashley Road, Boscombe, and in Holdenhurst Road, near the Lansdowne. The last portions in Ashley Road were removed on 24th April 1966, with the remains of the Holdenhurst Road equipment on 8th May 1966. It was expected that all traction poles and redundant wiring would have been removed by the end of May 1966. Redundant frogs and crossings at the Lansdowne and the junctions of Ashley Road, Christchurch Road and Portman Road, Boscombe, i.e. the former service 25 passing loop, remained in place for the time being as it was not considered worthwhile to pay overtime to overhead crews to work at night to remove them. By July 1966 only 400 yards of overhead wiring remained between Central Station and the Lansdowne and all the wiring had gone from Ashley, Portman and Gladstone Roads.

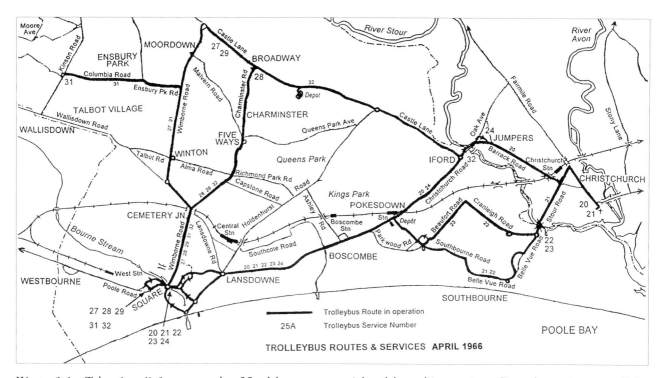

TROLLEYBUS ROUTES & SERVICES **APRIL 1966**

West of the Triangle, all former service 25 wiring was down, with the exception of one trailing frog in Avenue Road where the eastbound line from Westbourne had joined that from the Triangle and the parking area there.

In May 1966 a traction feeder cable in Belle Vue Road was damaged: the offer of Messrs Bedford & Co. to pay half the cost i.e. £82 9s 0d, for the repairs was accepted.

Road works at the top of Richmond Hill suggested that the Bodorgan Road triangle might have to be removed early but this did not take place.

Mr Cunningham now submitted proposals for changes to the Richmond Hill services upon withdrawal of trolleybus operation, which was scheduled to take place in September 1966. Subject to the Traffic Commissioners' approval, his proposals to withdraw trolleybus services along Wimborne Road were agreed by the Transport Committee, provided that transfer tickets were introduced on that part of the route previously served by motorbus services 6 and 10 and for which there would be no through bus to the Square under the proposed new arrangements.

During July and August 1966 the Overhead Department concentrated on the removal of overhead installations from former service 35. Apart from a short stretch of plain wiring mid-way along Charminster Avenue, all the wiring, including Five Ways junction and the Malvern Road reversing triangle, was down by 22nd July 1966, although the traction poles remained *in situ*.

During the early summer, the overhead wiring was realigned and about half a dozen traction poles were repositioned due to road works at the Tuckton and Cooper Dean roundabouts. On 22nd August 1966 work started on major alterations to the overhead wiring in Castle Lane East, as the approach road to Holdenhurst Road roundabout was converted to dual carriageway, requiring the planting of 20 new traction poles. It was announced that Castle Lane East would provide the trolleybus access route to Castle Lane Depot from 26th September 1966, although service trolleybuses would cease to operate along this route with effect from the previous day.

The meeting of the Transport Committee on 15th August 1966 to discuss the forthcoming winter timetable was attended by the TGWU, who objected to the Wimborne Road service changes, running times and one-man-operation. As a palliative, the Committee offered to schedule an additional bus and amend the timetable accordingly up to 7pm each day in an effort to ensure that one-man-operation according to the new schedules could be introduced for a six-month trial.

Tenders were invited for the disposal of 24 BUT 9641T and ten Sunbeam MF2B trolleybuses, and the supply of eight single-deck motorbuses in the year 1967/68, and 20 double-deckers in the year 1968/69, to complete the trolleybus conversion programme.

At this time, BUT 9641Ts 236, 246, 247, 248, 249, 250, 252, 254, 255, 256 and 257 were at Castle Lane Depot awaiting sale for scrap. By arrangement, open-top MS2 202, now owned by the National Trolleybus Association, was also still garaged at Castle Lane. On the positive side Sunbeam MF2B 273, which had been withdrawn upon closure of service 30, was reinstated into the running fleet.

This was an era of considerable inflation, and the Association of Municipal Corporations drew attention to the prices and incomes standstill (which included bus fares) which the government had imposed. These measures also affected a wage award for platform staff and semi-skilled workers by the National Joint Industrial Council which had been agreed in July. The Council would honour the agreement in due course, but in the meantime the national wage award of July 1966 affecting craftsmen employed in Municipal Passenger Transport Undertakings was "frozen" under the Government's Prices and Incomes Policy, whilst an incentive bonus scheme was also put on "hold". No action could be taken either on a suggested experiment that only two fares, namely 3d and 6d, be charged. Having considered a letter from H&D, the charge for carrying folding pushchairs was abolished.

The Council had asked that old age pensioner's concessionary fares (with a five years' residential qualification) be introduced. In November 1966, a joint report was submitted as to the cost of alternative schemes. The Transport Committee felt that the simplest solution would be to introduce concessions to all persons of pensionable age having a Social Security Book, subject to the following:

i)   the cost of operating any concession scheme be reimbursed from the General Rate Fund;

ii) July/August excluded;

iii) facilities only available:

     Monday to Friday 09.30 am – 12.00 noon,
     2.00 pm – 4.00 pm, 7.00 pm – 10.00 pm

     Sunday all day;

iv) concession passes to be issued at a charge of 2s;

v)   retrospective payment should be made, taking into account any increase or decrease in the overall passenger figures and financial receipts after the first year of the operation together with such information as can be obtained from physical checks on the extent of concessionary travel during the year;

vi) that the appropriate Standing Orders be observed concerning the necessity for proposed additional expenditure of this nature to be further considered by the Finance Committee.

Numerically the last Bournemouth trolleybus, Sunbeam MF2B 303 takes on passengers from 276, an MF2B from the previous batch, at Jumpers Corner. The junction with Stour Vale Road – where 276 had lost a trolleyhead in the frog – is visible in the background. Note the simpler, unshaded gold fleet numerals on 303, and the Hants & Dorset Bristol Lodekka in Stourvale Avenue on the left of the picture.
D. R. H. Bowler

The trolleybus "Side Routes" traversing Richmond Hill (shrunken by now to services 27, 28, 29, 31 and 32) were scheduled for closure on 11th September 1966, but were given a fortnight's stay of execution due to delays in the delivery of replacement motorbuses. The summer timetable was extended accordingly. An enthusiasts' tour using two BUT 9641Ts, single-staircase 234 and unrebuilt 246, one of the four still retaining their original twin staircases, visited all the remaining "Side Routes" and the Wallisdown line which had closed to service vehicles on 16th April 1966. The itinerary made 246 the last trolleybus to use the reversing triangles at Bodorgan Road (top of Richmond Hill) and at Redhill Crescent, Moordown. A foggy Sunday, 25th September 1966, proved to be the final day of "Side Route" trolleybus operations. The Bournemouth Railway Club had hastily organised a further "farewell" tour, using BUT 9641T 246. On this occasion 246 became the last trolleybus to turn at Five Ways, Charminster, and also visited Bournemouth Pier, traversing the rarely used Exeter Road line between the Pier and Bournemouth Square. The *Bournemouth Evening Echo* contained an article in its 14th October 1966 edition headed "Enthusiasts sought to preserve old trolleybus".

Last vehicles were:

- last through journey on 27 (forming 29), 10 pm from Triangle: 261

- last through journey on 29 (forming 27), 10.18 pm from Triangle: 282

- last 28 to Broadway Hotel (Luckham Road reverser), 7.13 pm from Triangle: 286

- last 31 to Columbia Road, 11 pm from Triangle: 282

- last 32 full-working to Iford, 10.33 pm from Triangle: 299

- last 32 short-working to Cooper Dean Hotel, 10.53 pm from Triangle: 283

- last working of all from Triangle, 11.07 pm to Lawford Road, Broadway and Mallard Road Depot via service 27 (but showing 26): 279

- last vehicle into Castle Lane Depot was 282 (off service 31) arriving at 11.36 pm

All the remaining BUT 9641Ts (234, 235, 237–244, 246, 251 and 253) were withdrawn for scrapping, and ten of the initial 1958 batch of Sunbeam MF2Bs (258–267) were also withdrawn from service, potentially for sale but *de facto* to provide spare parts for the remaining fleet as supplies started to dry-up. They were advertised for sale and parked in two lines in the open at Castle Lane Depot.

The 18th October 1966 Transport Committee meeting considered five tenders received for disposal of the BUT 9641Ts and accepted those from a Mr R. Higgins, of Christchurch, for the purchase for preservation of 246 for £103, and Wombwell Diesel Co. Ltd. for the other 23 at £75 each for breaking. Mr Higgins was unable to find a suitable storage site and 246 rejoined its sisters heading for the scrapyard but, at the eleventh hour, it was acquired by Mr R. Cromwell of the NTA for preservation. Wombwell Diesels started collecting the vehicles in December 1966, the first vehicle to leave having had its roof removed to avoid any difficulties

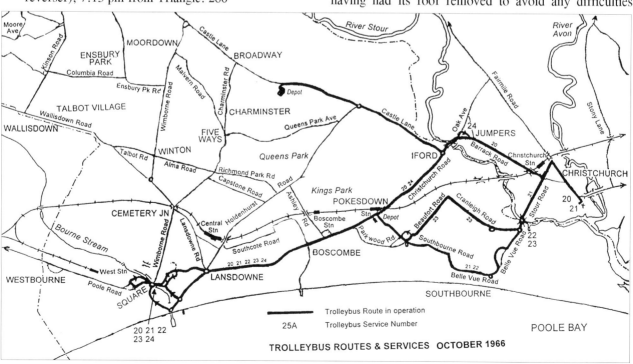

TROLLEYBUS ROUTES & SERVICES OCTOBER 1966

with low bridges *en route*. The scrapmen then tried to move the vehicles intact but, after 244 had become wedged under Fisherton Street railway bridge, Salisbury, on 11th December 1966, the trolley gear and gantry of the remaining vehicles were removed at Bournemouth before towing. 250 also moved north on 11th December 1966. On 14th December 1966, 236 and 242 were collected, 251 and 254 on 15th and 17th December 1966 respectively. As at 18th December 1966, 234, 235, 237–240, 243, 245, 247–249, 252, 253, 225–257 remained to be collected but all had left by the end of January 1967.

It was formally decided to retain the ten withdrawn Sunbeam MF2Bs (258–257) stored in Castle Lane Depot yard (except for 258, which was retained under cover), where they were gradually stripped of useful parts.

The decimated system, with only the Christchurch Road services 20, 21, 22, 23 and the occasional peak-hour 24 remaining, was now operated entirely by two-axle Sunbeam MF2Bs. The fleet now consisted of 29 trolleybuses, although the maximum schedule required just 18:

268–277 (WRU 268–WRU 277) H35/28D of 1958
278–287 (YLJ 278–YLJ 287)   H35/28D of 1959
295–303 (295 LJ–303 LJ)   H37/28D of 1962

There were only limited changes to the routes followed by the replacement motorbus services, the 31 being extended to Moore Avenue to provide a circular working with service 3, and services 6, 9, 33 and 34 being amended somewhat to follow more closely the erstwhile trolleybus routes.

The running wires disappeared from Richmond Hill itself during the first week after closure, due to a

pressing need to start work on a new roundabout at the top (an early stage in the construction of the town centre by-pass, now known as Wessex Way). The west side connecting link at Cooper Dean roundabout (Castle Lane/Holdenhurst Road) was removed on 23rd September 1966 in connection with road widening in Castle Lane, where new poles and span wires were being erected westbound. The trailing and facing frogs remained *in situ* until March 1967. It was accordingly no longer possible to travel all around the roundabout.

Iddesleigh Road substation and its equipment was now redundant. The building was offered to both the Highways and Works Committee and the Parks Committee, it being noted that part of the building was leased to the SEB until 1976.

Removal of wiring along Wimborne Road now commenced with the "straight" stretches being cut down on Friday mornings, and more complex parts on Sunday mornings, Cemetery Junction being dealt with on Sunday, 30th October 1966. By 10th November, the last of the traction poles in Charminster Avenue had been removed. Also in November 1966, the wiring inside Castle Lane Depot was reduced from three lanes to two.

On 22nd November 1966, permission was granted for the NTA to operate their preserved Portsmouth trolleybus, 313, on the remaining system in spring 1967, at a charge of 6½d per mile for traction current, subject to a satisfactory legal position and appropriate insurance cover. The decision to permit "foreign" trolleybus operation was encouraged by Ian Cunningham, who saw the opportunity to create much goodwill in making Bournemouth a haven of electric street traction!

During the final two years of the Bournemouth's trolleybus system numerous enthusiasts' tours took place. Most of these involved the use of native vehicles hired from the undertaking, but some used privately-owned trolleybuses that formerly ran in other British towns. This view shows Portsmouth 313 (ERV 938), a 1951 BUT 9611T with Burlingham bodywork. It is seen here on an NTA tour on 30th April 1967, laying over at the Triangle during the participants' lunch break . Native MF2B 282 is parked alongside as the "standby" vehicle, and a BCT Bedford OB coach is visible behind.
D. Barrow

The first trolleybus (273) to display external advertising appeared on 11th December 1966, long after the first motorbuses had received such adornments.

On 4th December 1966, the Overhead Department managed to remove all wiring in Charminster Road, from Cemetery Junction to Five Ways, in just four hours. They then continued to the Broadway Hotel, where some of the junction was removed, and cut down the Five Ways complex and the Luckham Road reverser. Span wires and hangers remained from Five Ways northwards. By 5th December 1966, wiring had been removed from the foot of Richmond Hill along Wimborne Road, up to but excluding the complex Winton Banks junction. All frogs remained at the Square. Anchor wires had been attached to the overhead at Lawford Road at the point where the projected Bear Cross line was to have branched off.

The Overhead Department concentrated on removing as much valuable copper overhead wiring as possible in order that it could be sold within the 1966/67 financial year. By early January 1967, Charminster Road was completely clear, and during the rest of that month Castle Lane West from Broadway to Lawford Road was removed. From the beginning of the year both overhead gangs worked most Sunday mornings and, on 22nd January 1967, they removed the complex Winton Banks "umbrella". From 6 am – 11.30 am the two gangs removed five facing frogs, five trailing frogs and three crossings, a total of 13 line assemblies which had been concentrated in a distance of just 30 yards. On the next two Sundays the northbound wires from Winton Banks to Ensbury Park Road junction were removed, as were the southbound set from Redhill Crescent to Ensbury Park Road junction.

By 4th February 1967 both ends of Lawford Road had been dismantled. Both wires had been cut down between Lawford Road and Broadway Hotel (inclusive), and at Ensbury Park Road junction, Redhill Crescent and Broadway Hotel, all that was left of the junctions were the parts of the frogs and crossovers which had formed the main lines. The Wallisdown – Columbia Road route was intact, as was the Winton Banks loop, but both were anchored off and neither were connected to anything in particular. Wiring from Broadway Hotel to Castle Lane Depot was intact, and the ex-Iford depot entry frog seemed to be still set for the straight.

In the meantime, work was proceeding on re-aligning the depot wiring between Cooper Dean and Mallard Road. New traction poles and span wires were erected in Castle Lane between the Cooper Dean roundabout (Holdenhurst Road/Castle Lane) and Strouden Park in preparation for road widening. Some new hangers were attached but, elsewhere, adjustable hangers were used to support the existing wiring in order that it could be slewed over when necessary. Re-alignment for trolleybuses heading east towards Iford took place on the night of Saturday/Sunday 11th/12th March 1967, whilst that for vehicles travelling towards Mallard Road took place in three stages; in the afternoon of 23rd March 1967, on the night of 25th/26th March 1967 and in the morning of 31st March 1967. This involved the first night work for some 15 months.

Another wage increase was implemented from 16th January 1967. The increase to the undertaking represented £3,500 for the remainder of the current financial year and £17,450 in a full year. Craftsmen benefitted from a previously-agreed increase from 26th December 1966. It was estimated to cost the Undertaking £500 for the remainder of the current financial year and £2,000 in a full year.

It was in November 1966 that the Transport Committee first heard about the Southbourne Traffic Plan, proposing the prohibition of all traffic, except buses, on a small section of Southbourne Grove, and the provision of traffic and pedestrian operated signals. A three-month experiment was proposed, with the potential of a further three months, during which period the Council would consider a further extension or permanency. Formal plans were announced in February 1967 for a one-way traffic scheme at Fisherman's Walk (starting 1st July 1967) banning vehicles entirely from one part of Southbourne Grove, except for "public service trolley vehicles" and motorbuses run in conjunction with them, and for an unrelated roundabout at the top of Bath Hill, Grove Road junction.

In March 1967 an application to use the trolleybus portion of Castle Lane depot for a television relay of the Billy Graham "All Britain Crusade" was rejected.

The MoT wrote advising that the Government White Paper provisions for a prices and incomes standstill would end in June 1967, but that it remained important that rises in bus fares should be avoided.

On 21st February 1967 the brewers Strong & Co. of Romsey Ltd., gave notice to terminate the tenancy of the yard at the Dolphin Hotel, Christchurch, in which the trolleybus turntable was situated, with effect from 30th April 1970. The agreement was subsequently extended until 10th June 1973, the turntable being used by the replacing motorbuses.

By early March 1967 all wiring (including spans) had been removed from Richmond Hill, Wimborne Road, Lawford Road, Charminster Road, and Castle Lane from Wimborne Road to Charminster Road. The frogs and wires had also gone from the junction of Columbia Road and Kinson Road. The only traction poles to be removed (in late May) were on Richmond Hill and in Wimborne Road up to Cemetery Junction, whilst a few had gone in Charminster Road.

On Saturday, 11th March 1967, preserved ex-Portsmouth BUT 313, which had last run on 27th July 1963 to close the Portsmouth system, arrived at Castle Lane Depot towed by ex-Rotherham tower wagon CET 440. Following a trial the next day, including a visit to rarely-used Horseshoe Common turning circle, it operated an enthusiasts' tour on Sunday, 30th April 1967, lasting eight hours and including virtually all the surviving wiring, including that within Boscombe Depot.

On 14th March 1967 it was decided that 185 Setright "Shortrange" self-printing ticket machines and 24 electric drives be purchased at a cost of £12,012 with delivery commencing in September 1967. The hire of Bell Punch "Ultimate" machines would be discontinued. No change in the sale of weekly return tickets was proposed, but the General Manager was asked to investigate the introduction of monthly returns, together with alternative proposals as to the method and place of sale of such tickets. Despite the department's financial position, and the possibility of further losses in 1967/68, no fare increases were proposed. A sales promotion exercise was planned with a further review in six months' time.

Having considered the General Manager's further report, the Transport Committee, at their 30th May 1967 meeting, authorised the introduction of 50-journey tickets valid for three months at a 20% discount for single fares of 9d or over, sold at Transport Department premises or through the post, and 12-journey tickets valid for two weeks at a $16^2/_3\%$ discount for single fares of 9d. or over, sold only on Transport Department premises. This package was introduced on 4th September 1967, replacing weekly tickets.

In April 1967 Sunbeam MF2Bs 270–272, 277, 279, 295–298, 300, 302 were fitted with Whiteways Cyder between-decks advertising panels. 269, 282, 283 (near-side) and 272, 276, 283, 284, 296 (offside) now carried advertisements for Watneys Red Barrel. Acriflex took space on 270 (offside) and 280 (nearside).

During the night of 13th–14th May 1967, two of the overhead loops at the stops in Gervis Place were combined by removing a facing frog and a trail frog, creating a single loop for services 20–24. The frog was set for all trolleybuses to enter the loop, so that only vehicles proceeding straight through Gervis Place needed to have the frog handle pulled.

A power failure from 11.45 to 12.45 pm on Friday 26th May 1967 immobilised trolleybuses and cut off electricity to all other users.

On 18 May 1967 a private tour, organised by Graham Teasdill, curator of the Russell-Cotes Art Gallery and

Sunbeam MF2B 285 (YLJ 285) stands in Beresford Road, under the revised Fisherman's Walk wiring for the abortive traffic management scheme, en route for Bournemouth Square on a peak-hour extra. Note that the vehicle carries adverts – in this case for Watney's Red Barrel beer. *D. R. H. Bowler*

Sunbeam MF2B 299, one of the 1962 batch, heads towards the Square across Tuckton Bridge. Note the gantry method of overhead suspension used at this point on the system, and the warning sign attached to the traction pole.   *D. R. H. Bowler*

Museum, using preserved open-top Sunbeam MS2 202, operated Bournemouth Pier – Exeter Road – Square – Triangle – Square – Old Christchurch Road – Gervis Place – Square – Old Christchurch Road – Lansdowne – Bath Road – Bournemouth Pier for the South Eastern Federation of Museums and Art Galleries. The vehicle was loaned by the NTA and driven by Mr P. H. Lepine-Smith.

A fatal accident occurred in Seabourne Road on 5th June 1967 involving a trolleybus, a motor cycle and a pedestrian. The front of the trolleybus had to be jacked up to release the motor cyclist.

The guard wires on many sections of the Wallisdown route where telephone wires crossed the trolleybus wires were removed in May/June 1967. On Sunday morning, 2nd July 1967, the running wires at Wallisdown Cross Roads were removed with about 100 yards each along Kinson Road and Wallisdown Road. Span wires were removed the following Friday. On Fridays 21st and 28th July 1967, the negative running wire was removed from Winton along Talbot Road and part of Wallisdown Road. Unlike most previous running wire removal, instead of being cut off at each side of every mechanical ear, the wire was first unscrewed from all the ears and then removed in one long section, presumably for reuse. In July 1967 work was resumed in burning off redundant traction standards in Charminster Road.

During August 1967 further traction poles were burned off in Charminster Road, and more sections of negative running wire cut down in the Wallisdown area along Kinson Road, Columbia Road, part of Wallisdown Road, and part of Ensbury Park Road. Another minor alteration in August 1967 was the replacement of two

traction poles at the junction of Tuckton Road with Southbourne Road, because the original poles were blocking a driveway and a road respectively, in new housing and flat development at that corner.

The winter timetable came into operation on 4th September 1967. Trolleybuses services were as in the preceding winter, i.e. no service 20 or 24 trolleybuses operated on Sundays.

It was recommended to the Town Planning and Buildings Committee that advertising be permitted on 25 bus shelters and, having considered the three tenders received, the highest, that from Messrs Frank Mason and Co. was accepted.

At the beginning of September 1967 work commenced on overhead alterations at Fisherman's Walk in preparation for the new one-way system. During the night of Saturday/Sunday 9th/10th September 1967 additional trailing frogs were inserted outside the Ravenscourt Hotel at the junction of Southbourne Road with Beaufort Road on the outward journey after leaving Fisherman's Walk, and on the corner of New Park Road/Beresford Road just before Fisherman's Walk on the inward journey. A third facing frog was added on Wednesday 13th September 1967 in Southbourne Road itself, on the single-line turning wire, shortly after the crossover in the "main line". From 10th September 1967, the section of single line wiring along Parkwood Road and Southbourne Road was electrically isolated by inserting a breaker at each end of the section. This enabled essential work to be carried out on this section, which eventually became one-way in the opposite direction to that then used.

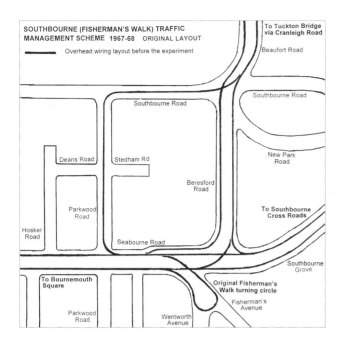

SOUTHBOURNE (FISHERMAN'S WALK) TRAFFIC
MANAGEMENT SCHEME 1967-68   ORIGINAL LAYOUT

—————— Overhead wiring layout before the experiment

SOUTHBOURNE (FISHERMAN'S WALK) TRAFFIC
MANAGEMENT SCHEME 1967-68   AMENDED LAYOUT

—————— Overhead wiring layout before the experiment
············ New overhead wiring
+—+—+—+ Redundant wiring

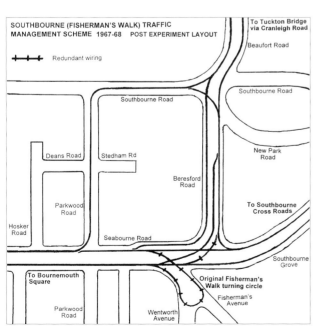

SOUTHBOURNE (FISHERMAN'S WALK) TRAFFIC
MANAGEMENT SCHEME 1967-68   POST EXPERIMENT LAYOUT

+—+—+—+ Redundant wiring

By 7th October 1967 the entire overhead wiring arrangement was in place:

a) a new curve was put in from Seabourne Road leading into Parkwood Road, together with associated frog;

b) new curves were put in from Seabourne Road to Beaufort Road and Beresford Road, for services 23 and 21/22 respectively;

c) new curves were put in from Beresford Road into Seabourne Road for trolleybuses to turn both left and right (as trolleybuses heading for Pokesdown would pass to the right of the existing traffic island).

Although part of the new system had been brought into service on Thursday 5th October 1967 enabling trolley-buses from Bournemouth Square to turn using Parkwood Road, Southbourne Road and Beresford Road instead of the circle at the top of Fisherman's Walk itself (which was disconnected), the complete work was only tested on Sunday 15th October 1967. As the scheme was envisaged for an initial six-month experimental period, the majority of the disused overhead wiring was left intact unused or strung above that actually in use, whilst only two small lengths of wiring were removed.

At about 6.30 pm on Wednesday 18th October 1967 a gas main burst at the junction of Parkwood Road and Seabourne Road, and workmen found a hole twenty feet deep under the road. All trolleybus services were immediately withdrawn and replaced by motorbuses using alternative routes. The entire trolleybus fleet was housed at Castle Lane Depot for the first time ever, whilst the replacement motorbuses were based temporarily at Boscombe. All trolleybuses were off the road until Friday 27th October 1967, except for two vehicles per day which operated morning rush hour journeys on service 20 and returned to Castle Lane in the tea time peak on service 23 by using the new wiring. When full trolleybus operation resumed on 27th October 1967 vehicles immediately started to use the new wiring, although its introduction had only been planned for 12th November 1967. No trolleybuses at all operated on Sunday 22nd October 1967, when a tour on 202 had to be cancelled.

On the 16th October 1967 the Transport Committee, having considered the report on the introduction of a concessionary fares scheme at off-peak periods, recommended that no action be taken thereon, but that the Council be reminded of the recently introduced multi-journey ticket system.

At the same October meeting, the Transport Committee learned that trolleybus abandonment would be completed during 1968. Mr Cunningham was authorised to make suitable commemorative arrangements provided that they were at no cost to the undertaking. The closure events were very much of his own initiative, and proved profitable!

From mid-October 1967, the Overhead Department resumed burning off redundant traction poles in Charminster Road, and removing wires in the Wallisdown area at Columbia Road and Ensbury Park. The last traction pole in Charminster Road was burned off on Wednesday 22nd November 1967. On Fridays, 27th October, 3rd November and 10th November 1967, wiring was removed from Ensbury Park Road, followed on 17th November by that in Kinson Road. On the morning of Sunday, 19th November, all running and span wires were cut down by the Ensbury Park Hotel and for about 100 yards along Columbia Road. More wiring along Columbia Road was removed on Friday, 24th November 1967. Traction poles in Alma Road, Winton Banks, were burned off on 23rd November and, on the next day, the Overhead Department started removing most of the remaining wiring in the Wallisdown area.

At the 21st November 1967 Transport Committee meeting, it was resolved that the Highways & Works Committee's comments on the former Moordown Depot (namely that the Transport Department should be credited with the value of the depot and surrounding property) be referred to Finance Committee. The General Manager reported that he was proposing to discontinue use of Boscombe (Pokesdown) Depot at the earliest opportunity.

On 27th November 1967, the Highways & Works Committee received a deputation of Southbourne traders, complaining that the Traffic Management Scheme had led to heavy losses in trade, insufficient shoppers' parking and increased vehicle speeds. They suggested that unilateral waiting (instead of "No Waiting") and a one-way system for Southbourne Road and Seabourne Road be introduced, and it was requested that the current scheme be suspended until May 1968. On 6th December 1967, the Highways & Works Committee agreed that a special full Council meeting that same day should request the MoT to vary the experiment until the end of December 1967, so as to permit parking on one side of parts of Southbourne Road and Seabourne Road.

The electricity generating station with its prominent chimney at the former Central Depot, Southcote Road, was demolished in late 1967 and, on 1st December, work started on the new roundabout at the top of Bath Hill.

The *Bournemouth Echo* carried the following report in its issue of 30th December 1967:

"Pokesdown Depot, the town's last link with the tram era, will close on 31st December 1967. To mark the occasion a preserved trolleybus (246) bought about a year ago by Mr Richard Cromwell of the National Trolleybus Association will make a tour. It will be visiting Pokesdown Depot throughout the day and when it makes the final departure from there at about 4 pm there will be a ceremony in which a ribbon will be put across the entrance to symbolise the closure."

Pokesdown Depot (officially always known as Boscombe Depot) closed on 31st December 1967 with a special ceremony just after 4 pm. Vehicles always reversed out of the depot into Christchurch Road under the guidance of an inspector; the last vehicle to operate in and out of the depot was preserved BUT 9641T, 246. The closure led to new overhead being erected to enable in-bound trolleybuses to turn left from Christchurch Road into Seabourne Road, outside Pokesdown Fire Station. The left-hand facing frog in Christchurch Road was inserted on the night of 5th/6th December, and the trail frog in Seabourne Road on 12th/13th December. Twin-line hangers were inserted in existing span-wires on 14th December, and the running wire was strung up on the night of 16th/17th December 1967. A trial run took place on Friday 29th December. The twelve trolleybuses which had terminated at Boscombe Depot each night (vehicles were never allocated to specific depots) operated out of Castle Lane Depot as from 1st January 1968.

At this stage, trolleybuses continued to operate on the following services:

20 Square (Gervis Place) – Lansdowne – Christchurch Road – Boscombe – Iford – Jumpers – Barrack Road – Christchurch

21 Square (Gervis Place) – Lansdowne – Christchurch Road – Boscombe – Fisherman's Walk – Southbourne Cross Roads – Tuckton Bridge – Christchurch

22 Square (Gervis Place) – Lansdowne – Christchurch Road – Boscombe – Fisherman's Walk – Southbourne Cross Roads – Tuckton Bridge

23 Square (Gervis Place) – Lansdowne – Christchurch Road – Boscombe – Fisherman's Walk – Beaufort Road – Cranleigh Road – Tuckton Bridge

24 Square (Gervis Place) – Lansdowne – Christchurch Road – Boscombe – Iford – Jumpers

There were, however, still some unusal operations; for instance, two journeys per day turned at Fisherman's Walk (2.42 pm and 5.13 pm) and there was a weekdays-only turn at Carbery Avenue from Pokesdown at 8.28 am.

Having reviewed five schemes for yet another fare increase, the Transport Committee informed the Council that an anticipated loss of £64,000 in the forthcoming financial year could not have been foreseen when the last increases were implemented in April 1966. To prevent the undertaking from becoming a charge on the rates, they recommended an application for increases to cover the loss and additional running costs which would be incurred on the conclusion of the then pending wage negotiations. Altered fare stages and fare levels were envisaged. In due course the application was approved, resulting in a completely new fare structure, based on fare stages of approximately 0.45 miles being introduced with effect from 15th June 1968. Although the Traffic Commissioners did not consider the application unreasonable, they "would need to be convinced that the Corporation had implemented far-reaching improvements with regard to one-man operation of its double-deck fleet" in the case of future applications. Fifty two double-deck motorbuses were suitable for one-man operation. The Commissioners conceded that £70,000 of additional revenue was needed. Even with these increases, it was anticipated that there would be a deficiency of £11,000 by 31st March 1969, reducing the undertaking's reserves to just £32,000.

On 2nd January 1968, the full Council revoked the County Borough of Bournemouth (Various Roads, Southbourne) (No. 1) Experimental Traffic Order 1967. Motorbuses were substituted for trolleybuses on Sunday 11th February 1968 while workmen removed the temporary traffic signs and kerbstones which had created the pedestrian precinct. From 12th February 1968, trolleybuses reverted to the routes which had been in operation prior to 12th November 1967, with the exception of trolleybuses turning at Fisherman's Walk. These continued to use the Parkwood Road turning circle in the clockwise direction. The turning circle to the south of Seabourne Road, at the top of Fisherman's Walk, was declared permanently out of use. Sunbeam MF2B 275 was recorded as being the last to use the amended wiring in the Southbourne area, on 10th February 1968.

In January 1968, the erstwhile service 25 passing loop in Christchurch Road, Boscombe, together with the frogs leading to and from Boscombe Depot, were taken out, resulting in an uninterrupted run from the Lansdowne to Pokesdown junction. All that now remained of the wiring peculiar to service 25 was a frog at the Triangle and frogs at the Lansdowne (the redundant facing frog for service 25 at the Lansdowne roundabout was subsequently removed on Sunday 26th May 1968). The last wiring in Wallisdown was removed on 19th February 1968. On 1st March 1968, the positive, and on 8th March 1968 the negative, running wire was cut down in Castle Lane West outwards from Broadway to Mallard Road. Dismantling of span wire on this stretch started on 12th March and, by 15th March 1968, all had gone. In the period 25th–28th March 1968 traction poles in Wimborne Road, Winton and Moordown, were burned off.

Based on the District Valuer's reports, the former Moordown and Boscombe Depots were appropriated to the General Rate Fund in the sums of £38,000 and £23,250 respectively.

At lunchtime on 16th April 1968, a service 23 trolleybus dewired at a trailing frog at Fisherman's Walk, causing a 30 minute power failure. At one time 16 trolleybuses were caught on either side of the section and, to restore the scheduled service, one vehicle was turned at Southbourne, two at Fisherman's Walk and two were terminated short at Jumpers, displaying service 24, instead of continuing to Christchurch as service 20.

Trolleybus 286 re-entered service on 9th May 1968 after a 39-day "rest" for no known reason. 274, which had been involved in an accident on 8th December 1967, was under repair, although a repaint was not planned. "Whiteways Devon Cyder" advertisements were now displayed by 13 vehicles, namely 268, 271, 273, 277, 280, 282, 283, 285, 286, 295, 296, 301 and 302.

Even at this late stage there were occasions when it was necessary to erect new traction poles: one at the Bath Hill (top)/Grove Road roundabout site at Easter 1968; one in Castle Lane, Strouden Park, in May 1968 to permit the construction of an access road to a new shopping centre (The Hampshire Centre); one at Stour Road in June 1968, where a new road was built; and poles in Charminster Avenue, on the former 35 service. Four poles in Christchurch Road were also repainted for street lighting purposes. On the other hand, redundant poles in Kinson Road, Wallisdown, were burned off in May 1968 to facilitate pavement resurfacing, while in mid-July work resumed in burning off traction poles in Wimborne Road at Moordown.

The 1968 summer timetable came into operation on 2nd June, and the weekday morning trolleybus short working to Carbery Avenue (referred to above) ceased, although vehicles continued to turn there on Sundays at 12.30 pm and 2.15 pm. It became noticeable that more motorbuses were running as extras on trolleybus routes.

In an article which appeared in the 15th June 1968 issue of *The Bournemouth Times*, Leslie Amos wrote:

"The fleet of trolleybuses was doomed by the nationalisation of public transport. The town council, expecting to have its buses taken over, transferred financial reserves to the rate fund and created a debt in the building of Castle Lane Depot for the government of the day to take over. But Bournemouth was left holding its transport undertaking and a crippling loan liability. The electrical generating station was the worse for wear after the war and with reserve funds long spent by the ratepayers and the repayments on Castle Lane Depot already taking the cream off the fares receipts, the council had again to cut itself a huge chunk of humble pie. Following a lightning strike at the power station arrangements were made to take current from the electricity board and soon Bournemouth and the other towns which were also no longer generating their own power had their former cheapest-running trolleybuses costing more than motorbuses.

"And as town after town got rid of its trolleys, the manufacturers cut down production and raised prices. Then spares became short and expensive, and overhead wires and other gear also became special-supply equipment with matching price tags. 17 years ago Bournemouth had 127 trolleybuses. It dropped the fleet to 93 when facing up to the problem of the old power station, then bought 20 brand new replacements between July 1958 and January 1959, to make the fleet 113. In 1959 it bought 7 which Brighton had redundant and 10 more new ones at the end of 1959. In fact 9 new trolleys were delivered between August and September 1962. Now presumably the fleet of trolleys is the 19 bought since September 1959. And after 10 of them have done 9 years service and the rest 6 years – built to last 20 years at least, they say – these, too, will be towed away for breaking up.

"Only the Boscombe – Southbourne – Tuckton areas still enjoy the trolleys. The people there have had the luck of the last of the silent, smokeless, gasless, most civilised of conveyances for a few years longer than most of us. Very soon they too must close their windows and, if they travel by bus, take the bruises suffered by the initiates of the rough ride".

On 2nd July 1968 a contract with MCW for the supply of 17 double-deck bus bodies during 1968 was terminated by mutual agreement, and a substitute agreed with Walter Alexander & Co. (Coachbuilders) Ltd. for delivery in December 1968/January 1969. This provided a "stay of execution" for the remaining trolleybuses, and

it was announced that trolleybus operations would continue until spring 1969. The *Bournemouth Echo* asked on 23rd August 1968 if one trolleybus route could be kept as a tourist attraction, and drew a comparison with Blackpool electric trams and Douglas horse trams.

The winter timetable, effective from 8th September 1968, included various historical snippets and depicted Sunbeam MF2B 270 on the cover, with the statement *"Last Trolleybus Year – the trolleybuses will be replaced by motorbuses in 1969"*. Service 20–24 timings were specifically titled *"Trolleybus Service"*.

At about 9.30 am on 14th September 1968, Sunbeam MF2B 275 suffered electrical damage at Pokesdown due to a nearby lightning strike and was withdrawn from service, thus providing replacement half-shafts for 276, which was reinstated after a period in storage. Following an accident, 279 received the front panels from withdrawn 258. In the period 15th–17th October 1968, six of the nine vehicles (272, 275, 277, 280, 281, 283, 295, 300 and 301) which had retained their triangular Sunbeam maker's badge had them removed. The Corporation had previously sold the badges to enthusiasts at the princely sum of 2s 6d each (the author has one – and the official receipt!).

The 17th September 1968 Transport Committee Meeting authorised the General Manager to handle an application for the purchase of five redundant trolleybuses without advertising for tenders. The application presumably came from the Teesside Railless Traction Board, which was then seeking a similar number of vehicles but which had already committed itself to purchase five of Reading's front-entrance Sunbeam F4As. It is known that Reading Council put Teesside under pressure to honour their contract, and Bournemouth heard no more.

The last redundant traction poles in Wimborne Road were burned off on 18th September 1968. Those in Lawford Road were removed on 4th October 1968 with those in Castle Lane West between Mallard Road and Wimborne Road coming next.

In November 1968, trolleybuses 269 and 281 (the last to be repainted) were withdrawn due to the lack of replacement half-shafts, whilst 302 was withdrawn with a burnt-out traction motor.

The *Bournemouth Times* of 28th December 1968 recorded that *"Bournemouth trolleybuses were expected to go off the road for all time in September 1968 but were reprieved due to the late delivery of diesel buses to replace them. They will finally enter Mallard Road Depot next spring and electric current over the last 12 miles of wiring Square – Christchurch will be switched off. Thousands of people are sad at the end of the era of silent, fumeless, smooth-running electric cars. The Corporation is arranging a decent "funeral". There will be a final parade on the last-run day, special tickets to become souvenirs for passengers, and some sort of civic "requiem"".*

Mr Peter Lepine-Smith, a serious enthusiast who operated a ⅓-scale model of a Reading trolleybus in his Great Bookham, Surrey, garden, was permitted to work as a driver on middle/late shifts for five weeks

On 19th January 1969, preserved Sunbeam MS2 212 was towed from its storage in Walsall to Reading and, on 25th January 1969, onwards to Bournemouth, with the intention of it operating tours in February 1969 over the remains of its home system.

Looking back, Ian Cunningham was adamant that there was never a conscious decision to cut back on vehicle maintenance and no short-cuts were taken; indeed, he was proud that there was never a serious accident or fatality which could be attributed to poor maintenance or technical inadequacy. Nonetheless, by now maintenance of the remaining 25 trolleybuses (268, 270–274, 276–280, 282–287, 295–301, 303) had become minimal, many vehicles having defective destination blind illumination and dewirement indicators. An overview of the fleet indicated:

- 268 unused (reason unknown)

- 271, 278, 286, 296 remained respectable

- 271, 279, 280, 282, 286, 295, 296, 300, 301, 303 in the best mechanical order

- 271, 296 were noted for their rapid acceleration

- 273 had an exceptionally leaky windscreen

- 274, 296 were sluggish

- 280, 282, 300 were speedy

- 280 the only trolleybus retaining olive green lining (with a black appearance)

- 287, 297 suffering from worn shock absorbers

- 297 noted for various hues of primrose due to accident repairs

- 298 the only member of the final batch to have been repainted (in 1966)

The last of the redundant traction poles in Castle Lane West, between Mallard Road and Lawford Road, was removed on 7th January 1969. From 8th January, the Overhead Department was busy, almost daily, removing traction poles in the Wallisdown area. Talbot Road and Wallisdown Road were cleared by the end of January, and it was expected that Columbia Road and Ensbury Park Road would be cleared by early March 1969.

In March 1969 an offer of £250 from the SEB was accepted for equipment in the Carbery Substation.

On 26th March 1969, road resurfacing in Christchurch High Street led to "wrong-wire working", with in-bound trolleybuses leaving the turntable and returning to Bournemouth Square using the outbound wiring.

The end was, indeed, approaching. On 3rd April 1969, workshop staff decorated MF2B 278 with special side boards around the upper deck side, and coloured lights borrowed from Blackpool's tramways. The vehicle operated in normal service throughout the Last Trolleybus Week, making an impressive sight in the evenings.

The Last Trolleybus Week (14th–19th April 1969) featured a trolleybus-operated special service from Bournemouth Pier to Castle Lane Depot via Boscombe, Christchurch Road, Iford and Castle Lane East (outbound via Exeter Road, the Square and Old Christchurch Road, and inbound via Bath Road). Departing from a separately signed stop outside the Pier Approach Baths (starting point of service 39 in better days), trolleybuses operated an hourly service leaving Bournemouth Pier at 30 minutes past the hour (except 1.30 pm) between 10.30 am and 4.30 pm, and leaving Castle Lane on the hour between 10 am and 4 pm (except 1 pm). Passengers could board or alight at any stop *en route*, the single fare being 1s 6d adults and 9d children. Destinations displayed were (outbound) "via Lansdowne Castle Lane Depot" and (inbound) "Bournemouth Pier via Lansdowne", in both cases with the via blind reading "To and From Show".

In the depot canteen, a free exhibition of trolleybus memorabilia, photographs and models had been assembled, which included extracts from Council Minutes, tenders for trolleybuses and large photographs of every type of vehicle operated, as well as one of a wartime loan in Wolverhampton. Scale drawings of 202 and 216 were on show, together with a number of models, including two MF2Bs (one of which is still proudly displayed in the office of the Managing Director, Bournemouth Transport) and a larger model of a 1950 BUT 9641T chassis, with a portion of the lower deck

During the final week of trollybus operation in Bournemouth (14th–19th April 1969) Sunbeam MF2B 278 operated in normal service decked with suitable illuminated decoractions. Here, 278 waits in Gervis Place for departure to Tuckton Bridge on service 22.
Bournemouth Times
(D. L. Chalk collection)

bodywork mounted, which had been loaned by MCW. There was also an "00" scale model tower wagon.

A collection of different types of ticket issuing machines was also displayed, together with souvenir tickets, including examples for the 1937 and 1953 Coronations, sundry relevant brochures and a complete series of timetables. There was also a display of overhead wiring and underground equipment, including sections of feeder cable, a complete frog, a section box, power station units and vehicle mounted items, including the control gear of an MF2B and a sectionalised demonstration BTH motor. Three preserved trolleybuses – open-top Sunbeam MS2 202, closed-top Sunbeam MS2 212 and BUT 9641T 246 – were parked outside the canteen from Monday until Friday. Bobbys department store in Bournemouth Square had a special display in their ladies' fashions window, and announcements were made on several local news or current affairs bulletins on radio and television.

On Monday 14th April 1969 trouble was experienced with the switch frog at the Square for Commercial Road, and the tower wagon was in attendance all morning. The frog was permanently fixed for Old Christchurch Road on the last day, so that trolleybuses could no longer access the Triangle or Avenue Road.

Saturday 19th April 1969 was the last day of normal service, and it became necessary to operate duplicates on the special service to the Castle Lane Depot Exhibition. Sunbeam MF2B 271 was the last normal service trolleybus to leave Bournemouth Square for Castle Lane Depot. Operating as the 11.25 pm service 20 to Iford

only, it left the Square ten minutes late at 11.35 pm, having accommodated the large queue which had accumulated at Gervis Place to board it. The penultimate departure was the delayed 11.10 pm service 23 to Tuckton Bridge operated by 286. Determined to be the last scheduled trolleybus to operate in Bournemouth, the driver used the Carbery Avenue turning circle as a delaying tactic before operating via Stour Road, Barrack Road, Iford (with a dewirement at the roundabout) and Castle Lane East to Castle Lane Depot which was reached some ten minutes after 271. There was a considerable police presence to deter souvenir collectors.

The final day, Sunday, 20th April 1969, dawned clear but bitterly cold. The first enthusiasts' tour of the day to take to the streets was the Reading Transport Society's Sunbeam MS2, 212, with Driver A. Hayward of 44 years' service at the controls, which departed from Castle Lane at 8.05 am. 212 had the system to herself for one hour. Open-top MS2 202 (Driver P. Lepine-Smith) and BUT 246 (driven by former Deputy Chief Inspector W. Biddlecombe) set out at 9 am, whilst a special quarter-hourly tour was operated by the Corporation for the general public between Bournemouth Pier and Christchurch, from 10 am until 1 pm, outbound via the service 20 route and inbound via that of service 21, at a special return fare of 3s (children 1s 6d). Vehicles did not pick up after leaving the Pier, and business was brisk.

Vehicles in the closure procession were given black identification letters on a white card, which were displayed in the lower nearside corner of the windscreen. From 1 pm trolleybuses began to make their way down to the Pier and were parked in alphabetical order, with chocks under the wheels, between the Royal Bath Hotel roundabout and the Pier Approach Baths. The identification letters were carried by:

A: 301 B: 298 C: 297 D: 303 E: 278 F: 285 G: 202
H: 246 J: 212 K: 295 L: 273 M: 274 N: 279
P: 283 Q: 280 R: 282 S: 284

By 2 pm a considerable crowd had assembled, and the Mayor of Bournemouth despatched the trolleybuses, which travelled up Exeter Road at some distance apart and not exceeding 20 mph to avoid overloading the power supply. The author was in the cab of J (212) which still managed to blow out a circuit breaker on the initial ascent from the Pier! Trolleybuses P–S departed at 2.20 pm, followed by K–N, F–J and finally A–E serenaded by the local Air Training Corps band. The Mayor and the Transport Committee travelled in 301, which was accompanied for the first part of the journey by local celebrity Ken Bailey (who later achieved fame in a Yellow Buses advertising campaign), dressed in a red long tailed coat, Union Flag waistcoat and top hat, and riding a bicycle. The first three groups of trolley-buses operated via the Square – Lansdowne – Boscombe – Pokesdown – Fishermans Walk – Tuckton Bridge – Stour Road (Christchurch) junction – Iford – Jumpers – Castle Lane East – Castle Lane Depot. The passengers had to alight at the depot entrance, where a crowd had assembled. With the exception of F–J, which were lined up across the front of the depot building to show the various stages in the fleet's development, all the vehicles were marshalled under cover.

Trolleybuses A–E followed the same route to Stour Road (Christchurch) junction under police escort, and then proceeded past Christchurch Railway Station to the terminus. C and D waited outside Christchurch Town Hall whilst E was on the turntable and A and B waited in Bargates, moving forward to the terminus one after the other under the direction of an Inspector. Once off the turntable B–E waited in Bargates until rejoined by A (301), which had been turned by the Mayor of Bournemouth. The convoy then reformed and returned to Stour Road junction before running along Barrack Road to Jumpers, Iford, Castle Lane East and Castle Lane Depot, where they were met by the Air Training Corps band and a large crowd of well-wishers.

Trolleybus E disembarked its passengers at the depot entrance and was held temporarily on the loop running through the bus wash whilst B, C and D travelled with passengers to the rear of the depot and were immediately depoled just beyond the canteen. Trolleybus A with passengers still on board followed, and the Mayor took the controls for a circuit of the depot wiring. E was then reversed out of the bus wash and followed A around, parking outside the canteen. There followed a handover ceremony for the 17 Leyland Atlantean/Alexander-bodied replacement motorbuses.

After the final procession on 20th April 1969, most of the vehicles were left outside the depot but they were all moved inside under their own power on Monday, 21st April 1969, in the forlorn hope of sale to another operator. The last to be driven in was 278, which was moved from the bodyshop into the main garage after the removal of its illuminations on Tuesday, 22nd April 1969.

The 21st April 1969 edition of the *Bournemouth Echo* carried the following report:

"One of the drivers in yesterday's procession was 65-year old William Biddlecombe who, in May 1933,

Preserved Sunbeam MS2 212 (ALJ 973) crosses Tuckton Bridge heading east towards Christchurch on a tour by its owners, the Reading Transport Society, on the morning of the final day, 20th April 1969. The vehicle is now owned by the British Trolleybus Society (successor to the RTS) and carries its original fleet number, 99.
D. R. H. Bowler

drove LJ 7701 on the opening of the first experimental route. Until last year he was Deputy Chief Inspector and Driving Instructor/Examiner of the Corporation Transport Department. In the 33 years up to his retirement he was responsible for training 1,671 trolley drivers.

"Today work will start on removing the 40 miles of overhead wires that still exist.

"Because of the difficulty in obtaining spares – one of the reasons for the death of the trolleys – the Corporation have been using 10 trolleys as spare parts donors to keep the trolley fleet alive. Apart from the difficulty in obtaining spares, the trolleys have proved uneconomic to run. New road schemes, the high cost of wiring, and the increase of privately owned cars have also contributed to the downfall of the trolley.

"In the year ending 31st March 1937 Bournemouth's trolleys carried 26,324,803 passengers. 10 years later this soared to 42,735,741. But the figures for 1957 were the beginning of the end for the trolleys: they carried 29,086,555 passengers".

The *Bournemouth Echo*'s 26th April 1969 edition continued: *"Bournemouth Passenger Transport Association is negotiating for the purchase of 301, the last trolleybus built for use in the UK. A spokesman said that the fate of 301 and the other trolleybuses still at Mallard Road would be decided within four weeks pending the results of an experiment with one of Bournemouth's trolleys in Walsall to see if it was suitable for their requirements. Walsall were reportedly interested in purchasing the entire fleet but had yet to make an offer".*

The General Manager reported to the Transport Committee on 6th May 1969 about the final day of trolleybus operation. The Committee thanked Mr Cunningham and his staff for the arrangements, Mr D. Chalk for the preparation of the souvenir booklet and Mr G. Teasdill, the Curator of the Bournemouth Museums, for his assistance with the exhibition of trolleybus relics. A trolleybus was offered to the Montagu Motor Museum on permanent loan and Mr Cunningham was authorised to invite tenders for the purchase of the remainder of the fleet.

Prematurely withdrawn 269, 270 and 281 were stored in the open with 258–267 on abandonment. The final withdrawal dates for the rest of the fleet were:

19th April 1969: 268, 271, 272, 276, 277, 286, 287, 296, 299

20th April 1969: 273, 274, 278, 279, 280, 282, 283, 284, 285, 295, 297, 296, 301, 303

A four-page leaflet advertising the MF2Bs, accompanied by a personal letter from Ian Cunningham, was sent to all known trolleybus operators worldwide, based on their entries in the *Little Red Book,* but produced no replies. There had been informal contact with both Reading and Teesside but nothing transpired, whilst the mounting of the MCW bodies on motorbus chassis had also been considered but was discounted due to the necessity of one-man- operation. A Bradford newspaper suggested that Bradford should buy Bournemouth's bargain fleet for £150 – £250 per vehicle.

Ian Cunningham confirmed that the conversion of the Sunbeam MF2B fleet to one-man operation was never considered at Bournemouth, although Walsall's Manager, Mr Edgely Cox, reportedly planned this in his prototype conversion of 300 into a bimodal diesel/trolleybus.

In the first two weeks after abandonment, the Overhead Department started anchoring-off various sections ready for cutting down. All the running wires in Beaufort Road, and some in Castle Lane, were unscrewed from the ears to facilitate the easy removal of ¼-mile lengths for sale to the Teesside Railless Traction Board. On 23rd April 1969, wiring was removed in Mallard Road from the depot entrance to Castle Lane, to permit the removal of a single traction pole which was in the way of road construction, whilst in Pokesdown a pole was removed to provide access to the forecourt of a new filling station.

Reading had reportedly received an offer of just £20,000 for the dismantling its trolleybus overhead network for its scrap value. Ian Cunningham felt that it would be more remunerative for the undertaking's own Overhead Department to carry out the task, and there was no great rush as copper prices were increasing! The three overhead gangs and their Superintendent, Bill Pearce, were mainly long-service employees close to retirement age, and who would be unlikely to obtain alternative employment in the event of redundancy. It was thus agreed that the remaining overhead installation would be dismantled by the Transport Department's staff and tenders be subsequently invited for the disposal of redundant substation equipment, overhead line materials and underground supply cables. Ian Cunningham studied the *Financial Times* in order to sell the scrap copper running wire at the right moment: over a seven-year period £250,000 was raised from the sale of redundant trolleybus equipment and, at the same time, the undertaking had proved its social responsibility. This went a long way to meeting the costs of the replacement motorbuses, and no additional cost was put on the

THE LAST DAY
20th April 1969

Top: The Last Trolleybus procession assembles at Bournemouth Pier Approach. The Royal Bath Hotel and Hants & Dorset's coach garage are the two white buildings in the left-hand background. *Evening Echo*

Centre: Trolleybuses A–E (301, 298, 297, 303, 278 respectively) of the final closure procession wait in High Street, Christchurch, opposite the town hall, with their police escort. Note the tower of Christchurch Priory in the background.
R. Adams
(D. L. Chalk collection)

Bottom: Sunbeam MF2B 301 – the last trolleybus to enter service in Britain – was also the last to operate in Bournemouth. Here, it is seen at Bournemouth Pier during the final procession, amid a sea of spectators, and wearing the final style of fleet number. It is followed by local personality Ken Bailey on his bicycle, dressed in red tails, top hat and Union Flag waistcoat. *Evening Echo*

local ratepayers, all in an era when municipal transport undertakings were expected to make neither a profit nor a loss, but always to "break-even" in their operations. As no better offers were expected, the sales of 600 and 200 traction poles respectively, and three miles of overhead wiring, to preservation societies without inviting tenders was agreed. The Finance Committee was charged with disposing of the Transport Department's substations and substation sites on the most satisfactory terms.

On 25 July 1969 the Works and Transportation (General) Sub-Committee considered eleven tenders for redundant trolleybuses, and accepted those of the Transport Museum Society of Ireland for one trolleybus (299) at £200; Bournemouth Passenger Transport Association for 301 at £150; and the tender of Wombwell Diesels Co. Ltd. for the purchase of the remaining 36 vehicles (258–287, 295, 296, 298, 300, 302, 303) for £150 each. No response had been received from the Montagu Motor Museum, and the offer to loan a vehicle was accordingly withdrawn. Sunbeam MF2B 297 was offered on permanent loan to the Russell-Cotes Art Gallery and Museum, with authority to loan it to the Portsmouth Transport Museum, on the condition that the vehicle was displayed indoors.

Wombwell Diesels started towing away the Sunbeam MF2Bs as follows:

11th August	270, 281	13th August	264, 269
15th August	258, 267	18th August	265, 266
29th August	261, 262	2nd September	285
3rd September	259, 260	5th September	263, 275, 278

In March 1998 Ian Cunningham reminisced to the author about the trolleybuses and stressed how it was the major road works in the centre of Bournemouth, specifically today's Wessex Way, which had influenced their premature withdrawal. It was felt impractical to make frequent overhead changes, re-route underground services and resite deeply-embedded traction poles around the underpass excavations beneath the current roundabouts at the top of Richmond Hill and on St. Paul's Road. When challenged as to the ability of foreign operators to cope with similar upheavals, he pointed out that such temporary solutions were expensive and no grants would have been forthcoming, all costs having to be met from revenue.

Although motorbuses permitted more flexible scheduling, direct comparison showed the trolleybus to be no more expensive to operate than motorbuses on heavily-trafficked, profitable routes. It should also be remembered that, by the 1960s, motorbus operations benefited from fuel tax rebates whereas the nationalised electricity boards were not prepared to offer any further discounts on supplies used for DC traction current, making it subsequently easy for motorbuses to earn the same revenue at less cost. In retrospect, had Bournemouth continued to operate trolleybuses, Mr Cunningham would have seriously considered equipping them with traction batteries to permit easier rerouting around diversions or road works, and unscheduled turning manoeuvres. Despite an occasional complaint of trolleybooms dewiring, for example at the top of Fir Vale Road (a location for which a complete solution was never found), and crashing through first floor windows, or dirt falling from the trolley heads onto cars behind, damaging their paintwork, the people of Bournemouth did not want to lose their "Silent Service" and he remained convinced that electric traction, perhaps including trolleybuses on reserved track, could survive even in post-deregulation Britain.

A sad scene at Castle Lane Depot on 26th April 1969, six days after the final run. Nearest the camera is 275, with 260, 262 and two unidentified vehicles behind. 264 is hidden from the camera, and 269 is in the distance with its back to the camera.   *J. C. Gillham*

Life after Death

Since 1969 there have been several projects to establish an operating museum for preserved Bournemouth trolleybuses, or British trolleybuses in general, in the immediate Bournemouth area. To date, all have failed.

Following the successful rescue attempt of a representative collection of vehicles from the fleet in the years leading up to the system closure and immediately thereafter, attention turned towards preserved trolleybus operation. Although the Transport Department had disposed of redundant overhead equipment to both the National Trolleybus Association (NTA) and the Reading Transport Society (RTS) for their museum projects, these were not specifically aimed at the Bournemouth vehicles. Some fifty traction poles were stored from 1972 until 15th June 1973 at Castle Lane Depot for the NTA's museum scheme at Matchams Park near Ringwood, Hampshire, when they were moved to the proposed museum site. The Bournemouth Passenger Transport Association were also involved in this project, which was later abandoned.

At a subsequent date, the BPTA purchased 46 traction poles in Talbot Road from the Lighting Department for use in another museum project, this time at Muscliffe Farm, but this project was also abandoned.

In the early 1990s, a project to operate preserved trolleybuses on a one-way circular route in the town centre, commencing at the Square, south along Exeter Road to the Pier, up Bath Road as far as the Royal Bath Hotel roundabout then west along Westover Road and Gervis Place back to the Square, almost became reality. In a report prepared by consultants Merz & McLellan and quoted in the *Evening Echo* of 27th March 1991 and 3rd April 1991, it was stated that such a route, potentially with extensions to a proposed retail development at the Triangle or east to the Travel Interchange, would be entirely feasible and environmentally welcome. A number of local Councillors led by Mike Peters, who had had the opportunity to see preserved Bournemouth trolleybuses in operation at the Black Country Museum, lobbied for the project. There seemed to be support from the local authority, which envisaged a tourist attraction similar to Blackpool's trams, and from Bournemouth Transport Ltd., by now trading as Yellow Buses Bournemouth,

subject to the trolleybuses not running in competition with their own scheduled services. Having agreed on the route and legal requirements, Bournemouth Borough Council's Borough Engineer and Surveyor's Department put out the provision of trolleybus equipment and trolleybus operations to tender in November 1992, attracting six expressions of interest which developed into three responses.

On 2nd February 1993, the Borough Engineer and Surveyor gave details of the proposed Bournemouth Town Centre Heritage Trolleybus Route to the Policy & Resources Committee. Tenders had been received from Bournemouth Heritage Transport, (i.e. the BPTA); the Electrical Trolley Vehicle Co. Ltd. in association with Peter Brett Associates (i.e. Mr Mike Russell a trolleybus enthusiast and operator of Reading Mainline Buses); and Bournemouth Transport Ltd. (i.e. Yellow Buses). Except for the BPTA, the tenderers had requested exemption from "Local Service" under the Transport Act 1985 for what was considered a unique tourist venture.

The lowest tender received, at no cost whatsoever or alternately with payment of 5% of gross revenue to the Council (if lawful), was presumably from Bournemouth Heritage Transport. They offered to provide at least one vehicle, and a more frequent peak service when trolleybuses would run after 10pm. Theme events using other operators' vehicles were also foreseen. Stops were proposed on Exeter Road (opposite the Bournemouth International Centre and outside the old bus station); on Bath Road (opposite Bath Road South Car Park) and Gervis Place (outside the Pavilion, the layover timing point). They planned to use their own preserved vehicles (including an open-top trolleybus) which would be garaged and maintained at the former Southcote Road Depot. The proposed fare structure was £1.00 adult, 40p children, 60p OAPs, subject to periodic review and valid all day. The tenderer would extend the service to Westbourne or Boscombe if it was commercially attractive to both parties.

The Electrical Trolley Vehicle Co. Ltd. tender was in the sum of £276,001.04 (including a provisional £142,110.50 for equipment, administration and Order-making procedures) covering setting up the system. These figures would have been reduced if possible

Department of Transport sponsorship for a demonstration trolleybus project was forthcoming. Operations would have been self-financing and at no cost to the Council. The Borough Engineer and Surveyor commented that the provisional figures would have to be confirmed to avoid invalidating this offer.

They proposed to use five different vehicles, including open-top trolleybuses and one modified for disabled users, on a rotating basis, with special events when other vehicles might be operated. The tenderer requested permission to use the route for test and demonstration purposes to pursue trolleybus research, subject to no adverse effect on services. Stops were proposed at Gervis Place (timing point); Exeter Road near Exeter Crescent; Bath Road opposite the Bournemouth International Centre (timing point) and opposite Bath Road South Car Park; and Westover Road outside Pavilion. The service would run a 15-minute frequency to 11pm during the peak season, with one-person-operation in the low season. The proposed fare structure was 70p adults and 40p children for the round trip, with 40p adults and 20p children for point-to-point, subject to periodic revision.

Bournemouth Transport Ltd. tendered £2,040,000, qualified by a link to the Retail Price Index (RPI) and requiring the Council to commit £290,000 in year 1, £175,000 in year 2 and £1,575,000, payable monthly in arrears, for years 3 to 11. They planned to hire preserved vehicles and would operate a ten-minute frequency May to mid-June and mid-September to May, with a five-minute frequency mid-June to mid-September. The proposed fare structure was 50p (year 2), adjusted by RPI for years 3–11. Stops at Gervis Place (near Old Christchurch Road); Exeter Road, (near Exeter Crescent); Exeter Road (opposite the Bournemouth International Centre); Bath Road (opposite Bath Road South Car Park); and Westover Road (between the Pavilion and the Tourist Office) were suggested.

The Borough Engineer and Surveyor drew attention to the recent legislative changes affecting the Order-making procedure for setting up a trolleybus system, for which there was no precedent. Any statutory objections, perhaps provoked by Council proposals to make points on the route Conservation Areas, might lead to a Public Enquiry, thereby delaying the procedure. He went on to note that reports on the financial standing of two of the tenderers was still outstanding but that, in principle, the nil tender (No.2) offered the most attractive proposition, subject to appropriate financial and insurance cover being provided. On this basis, authority was sought to proceed with the project as quickly as possible.

In late April 1993 the Council advised all tenderers that it had been decided not to proceed with the project. It is understood that this decision was taken as a result of their interpretation of the 1992 change in the official approval process whereby a Ministerial Order instead of a Private Bill sufficed for trolley vehicle installations. Although intended as a cheaper and less cumbersome procedure, promotion of the Order for the Bournemouth Heritage Trolley Bus Route would have been a test case, with no clear financial precedent. Under these circumstances the Council got "cold feet", whilst a local election shortly afterwards bringing a different party into the majority and voting Mr Peters out of office led to the project's final collapse.

Disappointed local enthusiasts then planned restoring the circuit of overhead wiring around the Castle Lane Depot premises for trolleybus demonstration purposes. This would have been modelled on the access circuit used during the trolleybus era, aided by the continued existence of a number of wall-mounted rosettes and traction poles. There were reportedly objections from neighbouring residents fearing increased noise in the immediate depot area and damaged property from flying trolley heads. At this time the BPTA became somehow involved in the Routemaster Bournemouth operation of crew-operated motorbuses on key services, in direct competition with Yellow Buses, and the author believes that this situation contributed to a break down in discussions.

Until the end of September 1998 the BPTA collection of preserved Bournemouth trolleybuses and motorbuses, together with its operating fleet of "Vintage Yellow Buses" from Bournemouth, Portsmouth and the immediate area, was housed under cover but not on display at the Bournemouth Hurn Airport, which became base of Christchurch Buses, the "low cost" contract arm of Yellow Buses in the post-deregulation environment. Selected representatives, including some trolleybuses, have since been moved, together with the operating base of Christchurch Buses, to the former Norton's timber yard in West Quay Road, Poole. There is reportedly sufficient space for the preserved vehicles to be put on public display at a later date.

The following Bournemouth trolleybuses have been preserved:

Sunbeam MS2 151 (BRU 2) or 169 (BRU 20)

An unidentified but decapitated MS2 has been identified in South Wales and could be a future restoration project.

Sunbeam MS2 202 (112) ALJ 986

In November 1970 open-top MS2 202, owned by the NTA, was removed from Castle Lane Depot due to a lack of space and was taken to Bournemouth (Hurn) Airport for open-air storage. Since then 202 has been stored variously at Hurn or Castle Lane. During its stay at Castle Lane, restoration work was carried out to the upper-deck seating, internal walls and trolley gantry. Coinciding with the move of the BPTA collection from Hurn to Poole, 202 was moved to premises near Maidenhead, Berkshire, where it is undergoing further restoration, including a major overhaul of its braking system. The NTA ran 202 at the Black Country Museum, Dudley in 2000 and plan to return it to Bournemouth in 2001.

Sunbeam MS2 212 (99) ALJ973

212 was withdrawn together with the remaining pre-war closed-top trolleybuses, after several years of summer-only use, on 29th September 1963 following 28½ years of service. In anticipation of the demise of the MS2s, the RTS had hired 212 for a tour of the system on 7th July 1963. At about the same time the Society had begun negotiations with the Transport Department for its purchase for preservation. Although 210 was a possible candidate, 212 was chosen as it appeared to be in the best structural condition and because it had been repainted in 1959. A price of £67 was agreed (including the towing cost and a set of "slave" tyres). The trolleybus was formally handed over on 16th November 1963 to the Society's Secretary at a ceremony reported by the local press at Castle Lane Depot, during which 212 made several circuits of the depot wiring. The following day 212 made the 5½ hour journey, on tow behind Bournemouth Corporation's Guy Arab breakdown lorry and subsequently towing tender FRU 180, to its new home at Smith's Coaches garage in Reading. A tarpaulin was slung across the open back platform and the trolley booms de-tensioned.

On 19th July 1964, 212 attended the Bean Car Club's rally at Bracknell, where it won second prize for being the prettiest vehicle!

In March 1965, Mr R. Edgley Cox, General Manager and Engineer, Walsall Corporation Transport, and Vice-President of the Reading Transport Society, granted permission for 212 to be stored under cover at Walsall's Birchills Depot. 212 arrived there on 28th March 1965.

As the final trolleybus abandonment loomed closer in Bournemouth, arrangements were made for 212 to return to the South Coast to perform enthusiasts' tours. Walsall Corporation kindly prepared 212 for the tow south, in two stages again via Reading on 19th January 1969 and 25th January 1969, and loaned a set of new tyres. Once back at Castle Lane, RTS members cleaned the trolleybus internally and externally, made minor body repairs and touched-up the paintwork. 212 was tested, taxed as "private" and insured by the Maypine Trolleybus Company (an enthusiast organisation) ready for three special tours of the remnants of the Bournemouth system on 16th February 1969 (separate morning and afternoon RTS tours) and 23rd February 1969 (BPTA). A trial run was also made during the late afternoon of 15th February 1969. These were the first preserved trolleybus tours operated by the RTS.

On 20th April 1969 and taxed as "Hackney", 212 left Castle Lane Depot at 8.15 am for its final tour of the system before making its way to Bournemouth Pier (Bath Road) to take its place in the closure procession with RTS members on board and the author in the driver's cab.

In December 1969, 212 was moved to the RTS's new museum venture at Sandtoft in North Lincolnshire, where it has consistently been stored under cover. Some test runs were made around the demonstration circuit in July 1978, but 212 has never operated at the Sandtoft Transport Centre in passenger-carrying service. In 1979, the trolleybus was repanelled where necessary, the destination indicator boxes rebuilt to late 1930s standards and flatted down or stripped. The body's wooden structure proved to be in excellent condition. It was July 1982 before 212 entered Sandtoft's workshops for a full repaint in the original 1935 lined-out livery, to reappear with its pre-war fleet number 99. Electrical tests were carried out in the hope of bringing the vehicle up to operating standards, but these showed a major fault in the main cabling, probably due to the rubber insulation breaking down. Re-cabling was carried out at the ill-fated Transperience transport museum in Bradford in December 1996, but 99 was then found to have a defective traction motor. A suitable replacement motor was located in the first quarter of 1998. Once sufficient funds are available, final signwriting, interior redecoration, rejuvenation of the leather seats and the refitting of glass louvres above the side windows and upper-deck front windows will be carried out in order that 99 can return to passenger-carrying duties at Sandtoft Transport Centre.

BUT 9641T 246 (212) KLJ 346

In the winter of 1974/75 246 was repainted into 1950s livery, after a period of storage outside in Weybridge between April/May 1969 and October 1971. It was then stored at Bournemouth (Hurn) Airport until undercover storage became available at Castle Lane in May 1973. 246 has been stored variously at Hurn or Castle Lane ever since, and is currently at the Christchurch Buses premises West Quay Road, Poole, looking rather weary.

Sunbeam MF2B 286 YLJ 286

The last service trolleybus, now owned by the London Trolleybus Preservation Society and operating at the East of England Transport Museum, Carlton Colville near Lowestoft.

Sunbeam MF2B 297 297 LJ

On 23rd/24th July 1977 Sunbeam MF2B 297 operated with a generator trailer loaned by London-based enthusiasts around Castle Lane Depot's perimeter road in connection with the 75th anniversary celebrations of Bournemouth Transport. Other preserved Bournemouth trolleybuses made battery powered trips during the first six months of 1977. In June 1989, 297 operated on test at the Black Country Museum, Dudley, prior to a July 1989 appearance at the Sandtoft Transport Centre before returning to Dudley for their fortnight-long "Trolleydays" event later in the month. In a more adventurous excursion, 297 ran under power between Westbourne and the (post-trolleybus) St. Michael's roundabout on Saturday 28th September 1991, again using the generator

trailer. It made a number of round trips and, towards the end of the afternoon, ventured into Branksome, well off the former trolleybus route. 297 has been stored variously at Hurn, Castle Lane and at the Christchurch Buses premises at West Quay Road, Poole.

In June 1999, the Czech town of Usti-nad-Labem, in northern Bohemia, celebrated its public transport centenary. Enthusiasts from all over Europe, together with their preserved vehicles, were invited to participate and the BPTA resolved to send 297 to operate in the event. Professional hauliers were engaged to take 297, on suspended tow, to Usti-nad-Labem by way of a "high vehicle" route – but with instructions to halt and check bridges with restricted clearance. Unfortunately, the trolleybus struck a bridge in Luxembourg at speed, which devastated the roof as far back as the trolley gantry. The hauliers returned immediately to the UK and accepted full responsibility for the accident. Repairs to the bodywork were completed by May 2000 and the trolley gantry will be replaced.

Sunbeam MF2B 299 299 LJ

This vehicle is stored in the open at the Irish Transport Museum, near Dublin, in a derelict condition.

Sunbeam MF2B 301 301 LJ

In 1976 the last trolleybus to be delivered to Bournemouth, 301, received a complete external repaint and was exhibited locally. It is currently on loan to the Museum of Land Transport, Leyland, Lancashire.

Sunbeam MF2B 297 seen in service at the Black Country Museum, Dudley, in July 1992. While trolleybuses no longer operate in public service in Bournemouth – or anywhere else in Britain – they can still be seen and experienced at a handful of museums.   *T. Bowler*

68   LJ 7701   **Delivered 1933**

Chassis: Sunbeam MS2 three-axle manufactured by Sunbeam Motor Car Co. Ltd., Moorfield Works, Wolverhampton.
Motor: British Thomson-Houston Co. Ltd. Type 201 (80 nhp), compound-wound.
Electrical equipment: British Thomson-Houston type 101 scissors-type controller, 12 notches (1–6, resistance; 7, full power; 8–12, field weakening).
Dewirement indicators: 2 orange line-lights and buzzer.
Body: Weymann's Motor Bodies (1925) Ltd., Station Road, Addlestone, Surrey. H32/28R.
Length: 27 ft 6 ins   *Width* 7 ft 6 ins   *Unladen weight:* 7 tons 19 cwt 3 qtrs 17 lbs (as delivered)

Fleet Number	Registration Number	Chassis Number	Body Number	Date of Delivery	Date into Service	Date of Withdrawal	Date of Disposal	Initial Disposal
68	LJ 7701	12007	C560	10.05.33	15.05.33	. .51	.05.52	James Thompson, Cardiff

Delivered on 10th May 1933 as one of the four experimental vehicles. Participated in the official opening ceremony of 13th May 1933 and, together with the AEC 661T (70), entered service that same day on the Bournemouth Square – Westbourne trial route.

Brakes: Regenerative on power pedal. Rheostatic and Lockheed vacuum-assisted hydraulic on brake pedal. Reavill vacuum exhauster.

Bodywork: Composite six-bay construction with timber-framing in English oak and roof structure in best white ash. Conventional rear, semi-vestibuled open platform. The trolley gantry was constructed of three externally-mounted steel channels carried down to the top of the lower-deck pillars of bays 2 and 3, which linked at upper-deck floor level with a horizontal steel channel running along each side from above the driver's cab to the middle of the rear platform. External panelling was in 18G aluminium, the shaped panels being in 20G steel, an additional skin being evident at the rear of the upper deck. The internal roof skin was in plywood with Alhambrinal ceilings. The internal side panels were in brown rexine-covered plywood. Both decks were fitted with oak-slatted floors. The driver's cab was equipped with a single offside hinged door, an offside opening windscreen and sliding signalling windows on both sides. A small rectangular driver's rear-view mirror was mounted externally on the front offside cab pillar only.

Widney Stuart "Aero" pattern half-drop windows were fitted to bays 1, 3, 5 (both sides) of the upper-deck and bays 2–4 (both sides) of the lower deck. The front upper-deck windows were fixed. The rear elevation was particularly upright, and the upper-deck window/emergency exit was centrally divided. All windows were surrounded internally by varnished wood frames. A non-standard length window with normal glazing was fitted at the rear of the offside saloon showing the staircase behind. Originally the bodywork above the saloon side windows and those at the front of the upper-deck were equipped with metal louvres, those between the trolley gantry (bays 2 and 3) being at about 20° to the sides of the vehicle. Flettner Extractor ventilators were fitted to the roof.

Destination equipment: the original destination equipment was a single-line final-destination indicator box at front (centred above the driver's windscreen) and rear (centred above the rear platform window). Above the front and rear boxes was a square service number indicator centred above the final-destination screen. There was no side indicator box above the rear entrance platform.

During the September 1936 reconstruction the destination and service number indicator boxes were combined into a single rectangular aperture centrally situated on the primrose between decks panel, glazed completely and roller blind equipment installed upon which up to four

Sunbeam MS2 LJ 7701 seen in Wolverhampton prior to delivery to Bournemouth for trials. Note the original curved trolleybooms and the primrose rear dome. With the success of the trials, the vehicle was acquired and became number 68 in the Bournemouth fleet. LJ 7701 proved to be the basic prototype for 102 similar Sunbeam MS2s.
Surfleet Transport Photos/ D. L. Chalk collection

lines of intermediate and final destination points could be displayed. A separate square service number indicator box was added to the nearside at the front and to the offside at the rear.

Lighting: External lighting comprised two headlights mounted on plinths on the front panel. No front sidelights (these were added later on the lower maroon band). There was a single rear light mounted in the offside corner just below the yellow band and to the offside of the rear platform window. A red triangular power-brakes warning sign and light was mounted on the offside of the rear panel immediately above the registration number plate. Open reflector-type interior lights were provided in each saloon. Lighting from motor generator.

Seating: Based on Accles & Pollock painted tubular steel frames with chromium-plated corner and built-in torpedo-shaped grab adjacent to the aisle. Squabs and backs were upholstered in Connolly Brothers brown hide (pleated squabs and plain backs) with brown scratchproof rexine leather-cloth seat-backs. The driver's seat was in brown hide.

Internal Livery: Cream scratchproof rexine leathercloth-covered ceilings with varnished/polished wooden mouldings. Side panels covered in brown-grained scratchproof rexine leathercloth. Brown paint to staircases and seat frames. All handrails and stanchions covered in black Doverite.

External Livery: All over primrose, with off-white roof (except rear dome), trolley gantry and rear retaining hooks, two maroon bands (below windows of each deck) and one yellow band (above lower-deck windows); mouldings below roof line, to all coloured bands and to bottom of lower panels all edged in olive green; lower and upper-deck panels lined in ¼ ins width and each window in ⅛ ins width red lining; black mudguards and lifeguard rails; maroon wheels; black legal lettering/ownership details at bottom of nearside lower panel of bay 2, seating capacity to bottom of lower panels of front and rear elevations (nearside and offside respectively). The Bournemouth coat of arms was carried on both sides of the lower deck immediately below the third side pillar, also front and rear lower deck panels with additional small coat of arms positioned centrally on yellow band of rear elevation. Once in Corporation ownership the position of the side coat of arms was moved backwards to centrally on bay 3, with an additional transfer on the upper-deck side panels. 5" gold sans serif upper-case lettering **BOURNEMOUTH CORPORATION** to each side on lower deck maroon band (originally affixed immediately behind the driver's cab and running to the front of the rear bogie, and subsequently moved further to the rear, running between the front of bay 2 and the middle of the rear bogie). Following reconstruction with a front exit, 1" upper-case lettering in red reading **EXIT ONLY** and **ENTRANCE** (nearside) and **EMERGENCY**

EXIT (rear). By the end of the war the **EXIT ONLY** and **ENTRANCE** lettering was applied above the bay 2 and bay 6 lower-deck nearside windows, with an arrow pointing forwards and backwards respectively.

The white roof was painted primrose at an early date. The yellow between-decks band and the red lining were also removed during the late 1930s. At the beginning of the war the legend **BOURNEMOUTH CORPORATION** was removed from the lower maroon band as a security precaution and the roof repainted chocolate, this colour being retained until final withdrawal.

Upon purchase, plain gold fleet numerals were applied at the front in the bottom nearside corner of the front panel below the nearside headlight and at the rear. These were replaced in the late 1930s with larger ornate gold numbers having heavy blue shading applied to the lower deck maroon band centrally positioned under the drivers cab windscreen necessitating the removal of the triangular Sunbeam maker's badge and at the rear on the primrose lower panel below the platform window.

The trolleybus was originally on hire from Sunbeam at a cost of 3d per mile but was purchased in November 1933 for £2,000 and allocated the Bournemouth fleet number 68. The Sunbeam MS2/Park Royal combination was selected as being the most appropriate for Bournemouth's needs.

Subsequent alterations: Coasting brake (8 mph) and run-back brake (2 mph) added in 1935. Bodywork changes included reconstruction in September 1936 with a forward-descending front staircase and a front exit equipped with a two-leaf folding door manually operated from the driver's cab by means of a slide-handle, immediately above the nearside bulkhead window, coupled to an interlock to break the controller circuit thus preventing the trolleybus from starting off with the door open. To open the door, the driver flipped over the safety catch and pulled the slide towards him. To accommodate the front staircase, seats in both the upper and lower saloons were staggered, thus the lower deck had a four-person bench seat over the rear bogie on the offside and a five-person bench seat on the nearside, thereby reducing the seating to 56 (H31/25D). This increased the unladen weight to 8 tons, 7cwt, 1qtr, 14 lbs. At a later date half-drop windows with glass louvres above were fitted to the front of the upper deck and diffused glass added to the offside lower-deck windows backing onto the front and rear staircases. A larger rectangular driver's rear view mirror replaced that mounted externally on the front offside cab pillar and a matching mirror was added to the front nearside pillar.

Disposal: 68 went to James Thompson & Co. (Cardiff) Ltd., Dumballs Road, Cardiff, breakers, in May 1952.

---

69   LJ 7702 Delivered 1933

Chassis: AEC-EEC 663T three-axle manufactured by Associated Equipment Co. Ltd.,Windmill Hill, Southall, Middlesex.
Motor: English Electric Co. Ltd. Type DK 130/2F, series-wound, augmented field, non-regenerative
Electrical equipment: English Electric D.701B controller.
Body: English Electric Co Ltd., Preston. H32/28R

Length: 26 ft 9 ins	*Width:* 7 ft 6 ins	*Unladen weight:* 8 tons 3 cwt 0 qtrs 0 lbs (as delivered)
Wheelbase: 16 ft 6 ins	*Turning Circle:* 59 ft 3 ins	*Tyres:* 36 x 8 to all wheels

Fleet Number	Registration Number	Chassis Number	Body Number	Date of Delivery	Date into Service	Date of Withdrawal	Date of Disposal	Initial Disposal
69	LJ 7702	663T.003		20.05.33	23.05.33	.09.36	.12.50	Sherwood Car Sales, Poole

There are indications that AEC-EEC 663T.003 was one of three prototypes built at Southall and Preston between April and September 1930, and that this vehicle was demonstrated in Nottingham during summer 1930 as their 26 (HX 1460). The original English Electric full-fronted body proved structurally weak and was thereafter rebuilt into, or scrapped and replaced by, a half-cab design. The third prototype, 663T.002, was rebuilt into 663T.070 and became one of Birmingham's five AEC trolleybuses.

LJ 7702 was delivered on 20th May 1933 as the last of the four experimental vehicles to arrive, equipped with a half-cab, bonnet and

dummy motorbus-style radiator (similar to the Nottinghamshire & Derbyshire Traction Company's AEC 661Ts) which was mounted particularly high. The vehicle entered service on the Bournemouth Square – Westbourne trial route on 23rd May 1933.

The maximum section of the frame was 11⅛ ins deep and included a "kick up" over the front and rear axles, the frame level under load being 1 ft 10½ ins. All cross-members were of tubular construction to eliminate distortion. Roller-bearing front axle with worm-and-nut steering. Chrome-vanadium spring steel torque blade carried in centrally-mounted cast brackets on each of the axle casings. The rear

Top: The first batch of Sunbeam MF2B trolleybuses is represented by 262 (WRU 262), seen here at the Triangle awaiting departure on service 32. The first five MF2Bs were easily distinguished from later deliveries by the ventilator in the front roof dome.
D. R. H. Bowler

Centre: Towards the end of their lives, Bournemouth trolleybuses began to carry advertisements. 300 is seen here on Sunday 28th May 1967 reversing out of Boscombe (Pokesdown) depot into Christchurch Road, carrying advertising for Whiteways Devon Cyder. *G. Teasdill*

Bottom: Sunbeam MF2B 297 (297 LJ) seen shortly after delivery, as evidenced byt he primrose-painted rear-view mirrors. It is seen here turning out of Castle Lane West into Wimborne Road, Moordown, on a service 26 working. Note the cherry red paintwork around the driver's cab.   *F.W.Ivey*

Top: Sunbeam MF2B 280 (YLJ 280) at Bournemouth Pier on service 38, with a throng of tourists in the background, and assorted motor-buses on the hill. *J. M. Llewellyn*

Centre: Sunbeam MS2 open-top conversion 200 (BRU 8) at the junction of Southcote Road and St. Swithun's Road, *en route* to the Central Depot. Note the three-wire overhead and the traditional architecture of the houses in the background. The traction pole on the right has a cast base featuring the borough coat of arms. *F. W. Ivey*

Bottom: A selection of tickets as used on Bournemoutn's trolleybuses:

Bell Punch 1d pre-war child ticket, with geographical fare stages.

Bell Punch 2d and 3½d postwar tickets with numbered fare stages.

Bell Punch 1½d Hants & Dorset ticket with BCT overprint.

Bell Punch "Ultimate" tickets, as used from the mid-1950s: a string of three 3d values.

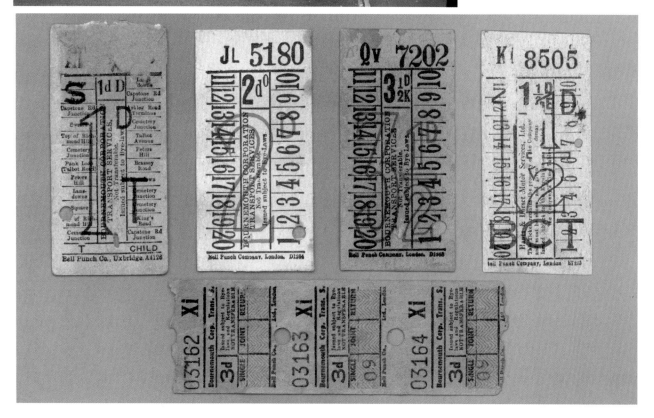

AEC 663T three-axle trolleybus LJ 7702 is seen here loading at Bournemouth Square in May 1933, on the experimental service to County Gates, Westbourne. The vehicle was given fleet number 69 upon acquisition by the Corporation.

*Bournemouth Transport Ltd
(from D. L. Chalk collection)*

axle bogie was supported by two springs carried in the centre by two chairs swinging in GM bushes in the bogie brackets, which were riveted to the frame and further stiffened by a 4" tubular cross-member brazed in the brackets to resist torsion. The 3" diameter rear axles were made from a one-piece 100-ton nickel steel forging, mounted on adjustable taper roller bearings and carrying the worm gear in separate casings. The motor drove through a Spicer coupling on both rear axles.

Track:	Front Axle: 6 ft 5³/₈ ins	Rear Axle: 6 ft 2³/₄ ins

Gear Ratio: 9¹/₃ : 1
Centre between two rear axles: 4 ft
Chassis Weight: 4 tons 4 cwt

Brakes: Rheostatic; Lockheed compressed air-actuated hydraulic, activated by the brake pedal and operating on all six wheels. A small motor-driven compressor supplied air to a reservoir at 100 lbs/sq. inch, controlled through a Westinghouse valve operated by the foot pedal. Automatic adjustment was provided on the rear wheels. The mechanical handbrake operated on a separate set of shoes in the rear brake drums.

Bodywork: Six-bay composite construction with rear open platform. The front of the top-deck featured a curvaceous, almost bulbous roof line with V-shaped half-drop windows and a semi-piano front between-decks panel which overhung the driver's cab. On the lower deck bays 2 and 4, and on the upper deck bays 1, 3 and 5 were equipped with half drop windows, having glazed louvres above. The upper deck rear emergency exit/window was divided centrally into two panes. An elongated side "blank" extending above bays 1–3 of the upper deck hid

the trolley gantry from view. Metal trolleyboom retaining hooks were mounted at the rear. The driver's cab had a single front-hinged door on the offside (with bonnet on the nearside), the window being horizontally divided and the lower portion equipped with a sliding signalling window. The upper portion of the driver's windscreen could be opened.

Destination Equipment: There was a single-line final-destination indicator box at the front, with a square service number box situated centrally above.

Lighting: Headlights were mounted in motor bus style, the nearside one on the nearside mudguard and the offside one on the driver's cab front panel. The sidelights were mounted on stems at the base of the nearside and offside cab corner pillars.

Internal Livery: Unknown.

External Livery: All over primrose including the front and rear domes; off-white roof extending from bays 1–6, including the trolley gantry; a maroon band below the windows of each deck (covering the top of the semi-piano front on the between-decks front panel) and one yellow band (above lower-deck windows). The upper-deck maroon band was broader than that on the lower-deck. No Bournemouth Corporation insignia was originally carried. The lower-deck and between-decks primrose panels were lined. Black trolleyboom retaining hooks, wheels, mudguards and lifeguard rails. Black ³/₄-inch-high copperplate-style legal lettering/ ownership details at bottom of offside lower panel of bay 1, seating

The AEC 663T, 69 (LJ 7702) after conversion to a motor-bus. This is a wartime view, showing the vehicle with headlamp covers and white mudguards – but still showing "Bournemouth Corporation" on the side. Note that the glass louvres above the opening windows were deeper towards the centre of the pane.

*A. B. Cross
(from G. Robbins collection)*

capacity to bottom of lower panels of front and rear elevations (nearside and offside respectively).

Later, the Bournemouth coat of arms was added on both sides, upper and lower deck, bay 3, also rear lower deck panels with additional small coat of arms positioned centrally on yellow band of rear elevation. The narrowness of the lower-deck maroon band prevented the legend **BOURNEMOUTH CORPORATION** being added to the sides. Following the 1934 reconstruction with front exit and staircase, 1" upper-case lettering in red reading **EXIT ONLY** and **ENTRANCE** (nearside) and **EMERGENCY EXIT** (rear). By the end of the war the **EXIT ONLY** and **ENTRANCE** lettering was applied above the bay 2 and bay 6 lower-deck nearside windows, with arrows pointing forwards and backwards respectively. The final livery style saw this information applied to the lower maroon band in white lettering behind the front exit and in front of the rear entrance.

The white roof was repainted primrose at an early date, to be replaced with chocolate during and after the war. The primrose roof was never reinstated. The yellow between-decks band and the red lining were removed during the vehicle's 1936 reconstruction and the legend **BOURNEMOUTH CORPORATION** applied above the lower-deck windows. Once in Corporation ownership, plain gold fleet numerals were carried on the sides between the maroon lower deck band and the coat of arms and at the rear below the platform windows. These were replaced from the late 1930s by larger ornate gold numbers with heavy blue shading.

The trolleybus was originally on hire from AEC at a cost of 3d per mile,

but was purchased in November 1933 for £2,042 and allocated the Bournemouth fleet number 69.

Subsequent Alterations: Following the decision to place major orders for Sunbeam MS2s the two AECs became non-standard and in 1934 (commencing on 8th October 1934) 69 was rebuilt with separate front staircase and a front exit equipped with a two-leaf folding door manually operated from the driver's cab by means of a slide-handle, immediately above the nearside bulkhead window, coupled to an interlock to break the controller circuit, thus preventing the trolleybus from starting off with the door open. To open the door, the driver flipped over the safety catch and pulled the slide towards him. This rebuild reduced the seating capacity to 52 (H28/24D).

From September to November 1936 the vehicle was converted to a motorbus by removing the electrical control equipment, replacing the front suspension and substituting an AEC six-cylinder petrol engine, "crash" gearbox and working radiator and bonnet with a rebuilt half-cab. It re-entered service on 10th November 1936. Its unladen weight in this form was reduced to 7 tons 17 cwt.

Disposal: 69 was stored at Christchurch Generating Station yard from 27th September 1950 and sold to Sherwood Car Sales, Ringwood Road, Parkstone, Dorset, dealer, on 24th December 1950. Re-sold to Southend-on-Sea Corporation in early 1951, who converted it (and a former AEC-EEC demonstrator of the same type, chassis number 663T.001) into a mobile toilet. Both vehicles were disposed of in early 1967. 69 went to Kirby, Rochford, Essex, breakers, in May 1967.

---

70   LJ 7703   Delivered 1933

Chassis: AEC-EEC 661T two-axle manufactured by Associated Equipment Co. Ltd.,Windmill Hill, Southall, Middlesex.
Motor: English Electric Co. Ltd. Type EE 403A (80 hp)
Electrical equipment: English Electric D487B controller.
Body: English Electric Co. Ltd., Preston, H26/24R
Length: 25 ft 8 ins   *Width:* 7 ft 6 ins   *Unladen weight:* 6 tons 0 cwt 8 qtrs (as delivered).
Wheelbase: 16 ft 3 ins   *Turning Circle:* 57 ft 8 ins   *Tyres:* 36 x 8 (front) 36 x 9 (rear)

Fleet Number	Registration Number	Chassis Number	Body Number	Date of Delivery	Date into Service	Date of Withdrawal	Date of Disposal	Initial Disposal
70	LJ 7703	661T.007		11.05.33	13.05.33	.03.36	.12.50	Sherwood Car Sales, Poole

Delivered on 11th May 1933 as one of the four experimental vehicles. It was equipped with a half-cab, bonnet and short dummy motorbus-style radiator (similar to the Nottinghamshire & Derbyshire Traction Company's AEC 661Ts) which was mounted particularly high. It participated in the official opening ceremony of 13th May 1933 and, together with Sunbeam MS2 LJ 7701, entered service that same day on the Bournemouth Square – Westbourne trial route.

The maximum section of the frame was 11 ins deep and included a "kick up" over the front and rear axles, the frame level under load being 1 ft 10½ ins. All cross-members were of tubular construction to eliminate distortion. Roller-bearing front axle with worm-and-nut steering. The fully floating rear axle was made from a one-piece nickel steel forging, carrying the worm gear in a separate casing. Hydraulic shock absorbers.

Track: Front Axle: 6 ft 5⅜ ins   Rear Axle: 6 ft 2¾ ins
Gear Ratio: 9⅓ : 1
Centre between two rear axles: 4 ft
Chassis Weight: 4 tons 4 cwt

Brakes: Rheostatic; Lockheed compressed air-actuated hydraulic, activated by the brake pedal and operating on all wheels, controlled through a Westinghouse valve operated by the foot pedal. Automatic adjustment was provided on the rear wheels. The mechanical handbrake operated on single shoes in the rear brake drums.

Bodywork: Six-bay composite construction with rear open platform. The front of the top-deck featured a curvaceous, almost bulbous, roof line with V-shaped fixed windows and a semi-piano-front between

decks panel which overhung the driver's cab. On the lower deck, bays 2 and 4, and on the upper deck bays 1, 3 and 5, were equipped with half-drop windows, having glazed louvres above. The glass louvres were deeper towards the centre of the pane. The upper deck rear emergency exit/window was divided centrally into two panes. An elongated side "blank" extending above bays 1-3 of the upper deck hid the trolley gantry from view. Metal trolleyboom retaining hooks were mounted at the rear. The driver's cab had a single front-hinged door on the offside (with bonnet on the nearside), the window being horizontally divided and the lower portion equipped with a sliding signalling window. The upper portion of the driver's windscreen could be opened.

Destination Equipment: There was a single-line final destination indicator box at the front, with a square service number box situated centrally above.

Lighting: Headlights were mounted in motorbus style, the nearside one on the nearside mudguard and the offside one on the driver's cab front panel. The sidelights were mounted on stems at the base of the nearside and offside cab corner pillars.

Internal Livery: Unknown

External Livery: As per 69.

The trolleybus was originally on hire from AEC at a cost of 3d per mile but was purchased in November 1933 for £1,853 and allocated the Bournemouth fleet number 70.

AEC 661T LJ 7703 looked very similar to its three-axle sister LJ 7702 (see page 169), but was shorter and had only two axles. It is seen here descending the western side of the Triangle *en route* to the Square. This vehicle subsequently gained the number 70 in the Bournemouth fleet.   *Bournemouth Transport Ltd. (from D. L. Chalk collection)*

Subsequent Alterations: Following the decision to place major orders for Sunbeam MS2s the two AECs became non-standard and, in 1934 (commencing on 11th October), 70 was rebuilt with separate front staircase and front exit equipped with a two-leaf folding door manually operated from the driver's cab by means of a slide-handle, immediately above the nearside bulkhead window, coupled to an interlock to break the controller circuit thus preventing the trolleybus from starting off with the door open. To open the door, the driver flipped over the safety catch and pulled the slide towards him. This rebuild reduced the seating capacity to 46 (H24/22D).

From March to June 1936 the vehicle was converted to a motorbus by removing the electrical control equipment, replacing the front suspension and substituting an AEC six-cylinder petrol engine, "crash" gearbox and working radiator and bonnet with a rebuilt half-cab. In its motorbus form the unladen weight became 6 tons 14 cwt. The bus re-entered service on 1st July 1936.

Disposal: 70 was stored at Christchurch Generating Station yard from 2nd August 1950 and sold to Sherwood Car Sales, Ringwood Road, Parkstone, Dorset, dealer, on 24th December 1950. Later used as a mobile toilet in Bristol.

Like its larger sister, the AEC 661T, 70 (LJ 7703) was also converted to a motorbus. It is seen here at Bournemouth Pier Approach. *A. B. Cross (from G. Robbins collection*

Chassis: Two-axle type manufactured by John I. Thornycroft Co. Ltd., Basingstoke, Hampshire.
Motor: Believed to be a compound-wound motor by Brush Electrical Engineering Co. Ltd., Loughborough., although it is unclear whether Brush
             were still manufacturing motors at that time.
Electrical equipment: British Thomson-Houston Co. Ltd., Rugby.
Body: Single-deck with combined centre entrance and exit built by Brush Electrical Engineering Co. Ltd., Loughborough, B32C.
Length: 26 ft 0 ins   *Width:* 7 ft 6 ins   *Unladen weight:* 5 tons 19 cwt 3 qtrs

Fleet Number	Registration Number	Chassis Number	Body Number	Date of Delivery	Date into Service	Date of Withdrawal	Date of Disposal	Initial Disposal
71	LJ 7704	BD10269		11.05.33	15.05.33	. .41	.01.42	Derry & Co.

The established steam- and motorbus manufacturer Thornycroft never seriously entered the trolleybus market. In the period 1922–33 they built five trolleybus chassis, that supplied to Bournemouth for demonstration purposes being the last but one and the only single-deck Thornycroft trolleybus to enter regular service in Britain. The vehicle was delivered by rail to Bournemouth on 11th May 1933 as the third of the four experimental vehicles to arrive, and entered service on the Bournemouth Square – Westbourne trial route on 15th May 1933. The original Hampshire registration mark, CG 4313, was replaced with the Bournemouth County Borough mark LJ 7704 prior to entering service.

The trolleybus was originally on hire from Brush at a cost of 3d per mile, but was purchased in November 1933 for £1,450 and allocated the Bournemouth fleet number 71. Following the decision to standardize on Sunbeam MS2s, *Bluebird* became very much an "odd man out".

Brakes: Regenerative on power pedal.

Bodywork: Of six-bay composite construction with oval rear window and centre entrance and exit, the bodywork narrowed in the driver's cab area to give pronounced front wheel mud-guards. On the nearside, bays 1 and 4, and on the offside, bays 1,2, 4 and 5, were originally equipped with half-drop windows. Metal louvres were affixed above the side windows and rounded rear panes. The centre entrance/exit was equipped with a forwards-sliding hand-operated door. The trolley gantry, comprised of two uprights, was mounted above the first saloon window and equipped with side "blanks". Metal trolleyboom retaining hooks were mounted at the rear, and a bamboo trolley retriever pole hung from three hooks along the roofline of the nearside between bays 2–5.

The front panel below the driver's windscreen had a centrally-mounted, blank "radiator" outline which initially carried the manufacturer's symbol and later the Bournemouth coat of arms, and a circular access hole for towing purposes. The driver's cab had front-hinged doors on both sides, the window on the offside being horizontally divided and the lower portion equipped with a sliding signalling window. The offside driver's windscreen had a chromium-plated frame and the upper portion could be opened.

A single vertical handrail at the top of the entrance and exit steps towards the front of the vehicle was chromium covered. A second, curved handrail to the rear of the steps was covered in Doverite. There were three bell-pushes, on the nearside at the tops of the 2nd, 4th and 5th window pillars. The saloon floor was covered with linoleum and included two small access hatches on the nearside and a longer hatch along the aisle.

Destination Equipment: A single-line final destination indicator box with external illumination at the front, mounted centrally on the pronounced roof "peak" over the windscreen, but none at the rear.

Lighting: In addition to rather prominent chromed headlights, large and somewhat dated sidelights were mounted on stems at the base of the nearside and offside cab corner pillars. Internally there were eight circular lamps with diffused glass covers and chromium-plated surrounds.

Seating: Based on metal frames with "wrap around" backs and torpedo-shaped grab handles on top of the seats adjacent to the aisle. Seats were staggered to give more space around the centre entrance and exit. There were 11 forward-facing double seats, of which one each side was behind the rear axle and three on the near side were in front of the centre entrance and exit. Bench seats above the rear axle accommodated three on the offside and two on the nearside, whilst there was a five-person bench seat across the vehicle at the rear. Squabs and backs were upholstered in leather (plain seats and pleated backs), with leathercloth seat-backs including a cigarette stubber on the forwards-facing seats. The driver's seat was similarly upholstered. A used-ticket box was attached to the rear of the nearside double seat immediately in front of the centre entrance and exit.

Internal Livery: Cream ceilings with varnished/polished window surrounds and window pillars where they continued into the ceiling. Side panels covered in dark leathercloth.

External Livery: The demonstrator was painted in a two-tone blue livery with dark blue lower panels, pale blue window surrounds and roof, separated by a white band. The dark blue panels had a single gold line immediately below the central white band and carried the legend "Brush – Thornycroft" in gold-block lettering below the first two side windows on the near and offsides of the saloon. The front wheels had black-painted wheel-nut protectors and hub covers with a "T".

The blue livery was initially retained, but with the "Brush – Thornycroft" lettering removed. 71 was out of service from 24th November 1934 until 23rd December 1936, during which time the motor was returned to Brush for overhaul, and the vehicle was repainted in standard Bournemouth primrose livery. A single maroon band, carrying gold lettering **BOURNEMOUTH CORPORATION**, shaded in blue along the sides, and narrowing above the "radiator" outline apex, replaced the white band. Bournemouth coats of arms were carried on the side and front panels. No provision was made for the display of a service number.

Disposal: 71 was sold to Derry & Co., dealers, on 14th January 1942 and passed to South Shields Corporation Transport, where it was also the only single-deck trolleybus on the system, as their fleet number 236. Due to wartime conditions it entered service in South Shields in primrose livery with the maroon bands repainted blue. Withdrawn from service in 1950, it had become a caravan in a local amusement park by August 1953.

These three official photographs show the Thornycroft with its original Hampshire registration mark, CG 4313, prior to delivery in May 1933. The location has not been identified; it does not appear to be anywhere in Bournemouth, and might well be somewhere in Basingstoke, in which town the Thornycroft factory was situated.

After trials, the vehicle was acquired by Bournemouth Corporation, to become its only single-deck trolleybus. It ran in its original two-tone blue livery for some 18 months, gaining it the nickname *Bluebird*. The trolleywheels and bamboo retriever pole (above the side windows) are clearly visible in the central photo.

The interior view is taken from the rear of the vehicle. Note the manner in which the internal lamps were angled to throw light over the central entrance/exit, and the excellent forward view through the cab.

All photos from D. L. Chalk collection

Chassis: Sunbeam type MS2 three-axle manufactured by Sunbeam Motor Car Co. Ltd., Moorfield Works, Wolverhampton.
Motor: British Thomson-Houston Co. Ltd., Type 201BW compound-wound (80 nhp).
Electrical equipment: British Thomson-Houston type 101 scissors-type controller, 12 notches (1–6, resistance; 7, full power; 8–12, field weakening).
Dewirement indicators: 2 orange line-lights and buzzer.
Body: 72–77   Park Royal Vehicles Ltd., H31/25D
             78–83   English Electric H31/25D to Park Royal design
             84–89   Park Royal Vehicles Ltd., H31/25D
Length: 28 ft 7¾ ins   *Width:* 7 ft 6 ins   *Height:* 15 ft 7½ ins (laden, measured over trolley-hooks)
Wheelbase: 17 ft 0 ins (from front axle to centre of rear bogie), giving a turning circle of 59 ft.   *Tyres:* 36 x 8 (postwar 9.00 x 20.00) to all wheels.
Unladen weight: 72-83 : 8 tons 7 cwt 2 qtrs   84-89 : 8 tons 12 cwts 0 qtrs

Original Fleet No.	New Fleet No.	Registration Number	Chassis Number	Body Number	Date of Delivery	Date into Service	Date of Withdrawal	Date of Disposal	Initial Disposal
72		AEL 400	12031	3477	08.06.34	13.06.34	.03.53	.07.53	James Thompson, Cardiff
73		AEL 401	12032	3478	13.06.34	22.06.34	.03.53	.07.53	James Thompson, Cardiff
74		AEL 402	12034	3479	15.06.34	22.06.34	.12.51	.05.52	James Thompson, Cardiff
75		AEL 403	12036	3480	17.06.34	22.06.34	.12.52	.07.53	James Thompson, Cardiff
76		AEL 404	12038	3481	20.06.34	22.06.34	.12.52	.07.53	James Thompson, Cardiff
77		AEL 405	12037	3482	20.06.34	22.06.34	.12.52	.07.53	James Thompson, Cardiff
78		AEL 406	12030		14.06.34	22.06.34	.12.51	.05.52	James Thompson, Cardiff
79		AEL 407	12033		01.07.34	04.07.34	.09.52	.07.53	James Thompson, Cardiff
80		AEL 408	12035		03.07.34	05.07.34	.12.54	.03.58	James Thompson, Cardiff
81		AEL 409	12039		20.07.34	22.07.34	.03.55	.03.58	James Thompson, Cardiff
82		AEL 410	12040		22.07.34	24.07.34	.03.55	.03.58	James Thompson, Cardiff
83		AEL 411	12041		24.07.34	28.07.34	.01.57	.03.58	James Thompson, Cardiff
84	205	ALJ 60	12047	3611	02.10.34	03.10.34	.09.63	.10.63	Scource, Weymouth
85	206	ALJ 61	12048	3612	18.10.34	22.10.34	.09.63	.03.64	N. Stanley, Parkstone
86	207	ALJ 62	12049	3613	07.10.34	09.10.34	.10.62	.01.63	Scource, Weymouth
87		ALJ 63	12050	3614	09.10.34	12.10.34	.12.58	.01.59	Scource, Weymouth
88	208	ALJ 64	12051	3615	11.10.34	13.10.34	.09.63	.10.63	Scource, Weymouth
89		ALJ 65	12052	3616	13.10.34	20.10.34	.10.57	.01.59	Scource, Weymouth

Brakes: Regenerative braking for conventional stopping, the driver releasing the power pedal until speed was reduced to about 10 mph and bringing the trolleybus to a halt with the Lockheed vacuum-assisted hydraulic footbrake (operating on all wheels). Mechanical handbrake to all rear wheels. Electrical coasting brake (8 mph) selected at master controller and emergency electrical run-back brakes (2 mph) added in 1935.

As the footbrake had a purely hydraulic action, it was possible for a driver to draw power to change automatic frogs by depressing the power and brake pedals together thus avoiding the tiring and potentially dangerous arrangement of pulling hard on the handbrake lever whilst taking power and steering at the same time. This was necessary on trolleybuses equipped with electric braking on the footbrake pedal, where engaging the electric brake cut off the power pedal circuits.

Electrics: There was no traction battery equipment, but a facility was provided for the fitment of a "skate" to allow current return via the tramway track. Initially, trolley-wheels were fitted; these were replaced by Anti Attrition Metal Co. OB type slipper heads with carbon inserts from 1938.

Bodywork: Composite six-bay construction, with timber-framing in English oak and the roof structure in best white ash. The trolley gantry was constructed of three externally-mounted steel channels carried down to the top of the lower-deck pillars of bays 2 and 3, which linked at upper-deck floor level with a horizontal steel channel running along each side from the front of the trolleybus to immediately above the rear entrance platform. External panelling was in 18G aluminium, the shaped panels being in 20G steel. The roof of the lower saloon was pine boards, covered with cotton duck roofing canvas laid in thick white lead paint and having a further floor covering of pine boards, the space between the two decks being ventilated. The upper saloon roof was of 18G aluminium, the upper side painted and enamelled white. The internal side panels were in brown rexine-covered plywood. Both decks were fitted with oak-slatted floors.

The vehicles featured twin staircases with a conventional rear, semi-vestibuled open platform entrance and a front exit equipped with a two-leaf folding door manually operated from the driver's cab by means of a slide-handle, immediately above the nearside bulkhead window, coupled to an interlock to break the controller circuit, thus preventing the trolleybus from starting off with the door open. To open the door, the driver flipped over the safety catch and pulled the slide towards him. The rear staircase was forward ascending, with a shelf and supporting pedestal below, and that at the front of the vehicle forward descending.

Widney Stuart "Aero" pattern half-drop windows were fitted in bays 2, 3, 5, 6 (both sides) of the upper-deck, bays 2-4 (both sides) of the lower-deck and at the front upper-deck windows, all being surrounded internally by varnished wood frames. The upper-deck front windows on at least 72-77 were fixed, whereas 78-83 featured small ventilators across the top of each pane. The upper-deck side windows immediately above the driver's cab on 84-89 had a small non-opening triangular pane followed by a half-drop window using a ²/₃-size pane of glass. Originally the saloon side windows in bays 1–6 were equipped with internal spring roller blinds. All saloon side windows and those at the front of the upper-deck were equipped with glazed louvres in chromium-plated frames. The driver's cab was equipped with an offside opening windscreen and single offside front hinged door with sliding signalling window. A round driver's rear view mirror was mounted externally on the front offside cab pillar only, there originally being none on the nearside. There were four Flettner Extractor ventilators on the roof and four side ventilators above the bay 2–4 (both sides) lower-deck windows, mounted towards the rear of each bay. All three axles featured chromium-plated hub caps.

There were four bell-pushes on each deck and a single one on the rear platform. Card advertisements could be displayed internally in wooden retaining channels immediately above the side windows and between the lighting installations. In addition to the vertical handrails in the lower saloon, two ceiling-mounted handrails extended above the gangway with sliding leather-hung grab handles towards the rear. Horizontal grab-rails were fitted at the upper-deck front and rear windows. Used-ticket boxes were fitted on the rear panel at the top of the front staircase, immediately below the nearside cab rear window by the front exit and on the rear platform. A bamboo trolley retrieval pole was carried 9 ins to the nearside of the centre line under the chassis.

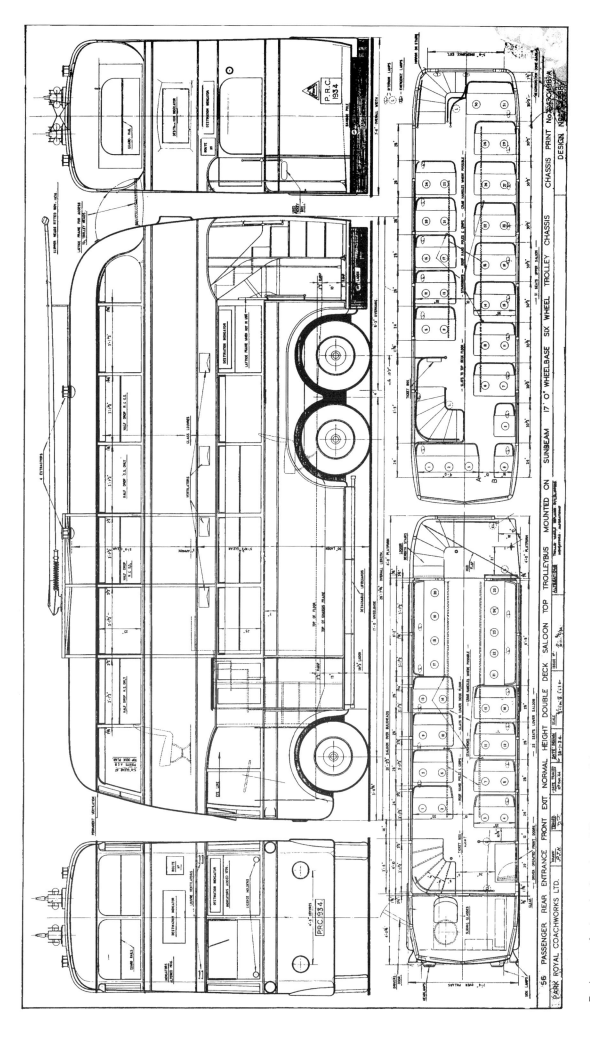

Body manufacturer's drawing of Bournemouth's pre-war standard trolleybus, the Sunbeam MF2B, as envisaged in 1934. There are one or two discrepancies between this drawing and the vehicles "as built": the trolleygear and seats are shown for indication purposes only, while on the front elevation the destination aperture is too shallow, a the sidelights are too far apart and there is a spurious licence holder in the offside windscreen.

Park Royal Coachworks Ltd.

Destination equipment: Originally a single-line final-destination indicator box was fitted at front (centred above the driver's windscreen and flush with the between-decks panelling) and rear (incorporated into a rectangular box with an arched top centred above the rear platform window but projecting from the between-decks primrose panelling due to the curve of the bodywork). Above the front and rear boxes was a square service number indicator centred above the final-destination screen. Additional single-line final-destination indicator boxes were mounted inside the lower saloon at the top of the bay 6 side window on both sides (behind the longitudinal seat). Wooden "tramcar-style" slip-boards showing principal *en route* points in black on a white background could be mounted externally above the lower maroon band at lower saloon window level and running from halfway along bay 3 to halfway along bay 5 on both sides.

Lighting: External lighting was by two headlights mounted on plinths on the front panel, two front sidelights on the lower maroon band and a single rear light mounted in the offside corner just below the yellow band, to the offside of the rear platform window. A red triangular power brakes light was mounted on the offside of the rear panel immediately above the registration number plate. Lighting circuits were supplied from a motor generator charging a 24 volt lead-acid battery, with open reflector-type interior lights being provided in each saloon.

Seating: Dunlop fillings based on Accles & Pollock painted tubular light-alloy steel frames with adjustable legs, chromium-plated corner and built-in torpedo-shaped grab facility adjacent to the aisle. Squabs and backs were upholstered in Connolly Brothers brown hide leather (pleated squabs and plain backs) with brown scratchproof rexine leathercloth seat-backs. Due to the position of the offside front staircase, seats in both the upper and lower saloons were staggered, which gave more space for moving along the gangways. Accordingly, the lower deck had a four-person bench seat over the rear bogie on the offside and a five-person bench seat on the nearside. The upper saloon had a 3+1 arrangement forward of the front staircase, a single seat on the nearside in the second row and a double seat on the nearside at the rear adjacent to the rear staircase. The driver's seat was in brown hide leather.

Internal Livery: Cream scratchproof rexine leathercloth ceilings with mahogany mouldings. Side panels covered in brown-grained scratchproof

rexine leather-cloth. Brown paint to staircases and seat frames. All handrails and stanchions covered in black Doverite. Cab area painted yellow.

External Livery: All over primrose, with off-white roof (except rear dome), trolley gantry and rear retaining hooks, two maroon bands (below windows of each deck) and one yellow band (above lower-deck windows); mouldings below roof line, to all coloured bands and to bottom of lower panels all edged in olive green; lower and upper-deck panels lined in ¼ ins width and each window in ⅛ ins width red lining; black mudguards and lifeguard rails; maroon wheels; black ¾ ins high legal lettering-ownership details at bottom of nearside lower panel of bay 2 and offside lower panel of bay 1, seating capacity at bottom of rear lower panels (nearside). Coat of arms on both sides, upper and lower decks, bay 3, also front and rear lower deck panels with additional small coat of arms positioned centrally on yellow band of rear elevation. 5 ins high gold sans serif upper-case lettering **BOURNEMOUTH CORPORATION** to each side on lower deck maroon band. 1 ins high upper-case lettering in red reading **EXIT ONLY** and **ENTRANCE** (nearside) and **EMERGENCY EXIT** (rear). By the end of the war the **EXIT ONLY** and **ENTRANCE** lettering was applied above the bay 2 and bay 6 lower-deck nearside windows with an arrow pointing forwards and backwards respectively. The final livery style saw this information applied to the lower maroon band in white lettering behind the front exit and in front of the rear entrance.

The white roofs proved impractical and were painted primrose at an early date. The yellow between-decks band and the red lining were also removed during the late 1930s. At the beginning of the war roofs were painted chocolate and most (but not all) vehicles had **BOURNEMOUTH CORPORATION** removed from the lower maroon band as a security precaution. The chocolate roofs were retained until about 1955 when primrose was reintroduced.

Originally plain gold fleet numerals were carried at the front in the lower nearside corner of the front panel below the nearside headlight and in the lower offside corner to the right of registration plate at the rear. These were replaced from the late 1930s by larger gold numbers with heavy blue shading, applied to the lower deck maroon band centrally positioned under the drivers cab windscreen (necessitating the removal of the triangular Sunbeam maker's badge), on the lower deck

Sunbeam MS2 85, one of the Park Royal-bodied examples delivered in 1934, photographed prior to entering service in October that year. Note the small triangular upper-deck side window above the cab and the over-optimistic destination *Poole Park* on the offside blind (visible through the lower saloon windows). *Surfleet/M. P. M. Nimmo Collection*

The upper deck of one of the standard Sunbeam MS2 trolleybuses, looking towards the rear. Note the single seat on the nearside, opposite the stairwell, and the moulded grab rails on the seat frames.
Bournemouth Transport Ltd.

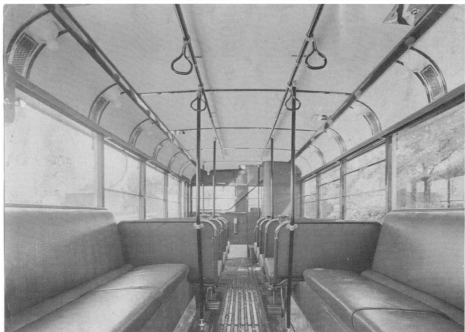

The lower deck of a Sunbeam MS2, looking towards the front of the vehicle. Note the naked light bulbs, the grab-handles for standing passengers, the decorative ventilation grilles and the extensive use of polished mahogany mouldings in the cream rexine-covered ceiling.
Bournemouth Transport Ltd.

Sunbeam MS2 81, with bodywork by English Electric, is seen here in the western side of the Square on 23rd August 1953 on a service 22B journey. *A. B. Cross*

side panels, bay 3, between the maroon band and the coat of arms, and at the rear on the primrose lower panel below the platform window. Immediately after the war, additional fleet numbers were affixed to the sides on the lower deck maroon bands mounted centrally in bay 3.

The final livery style saw the coat of arms on the front panel removed and replaced by slightly smaller blue-shaded gold stock numerals, again centrally located.

Subsequent alterations: In 1935 this first batch of MS2s were fitted with electrical coasting and run-back brakes as required by an MoT instruction related to trolleybus operation on Richmond Hill. As a "follow-on" to similar work being carried out on the second batch then being delivered, Sunbeam fitted this equipment retrospectively to the first batch at a charge of £25 per vehicle. The vehicle had to be brought to a definite stop at the top of a hill and, by selecting the "brake" position on the master controller (or reverser as it was known in Bournemouth), the driver could limit the descending trolleybus' speed to about 8 mph. The vehicle had to be stopped again at the bottom of the hill to disengage the coasting brake. The run-back brake was for emergencies only and, in the event of a complete brake and power failure when ascending any hill, the driver placed one circuit breaker in the "off" position which then limited the run-back speed to about 2 mph.

From 1938, the panel incorporating the destination and service number indicators into the rear rectangular box was glazed completely and roller blind equipment installed, upon which up to four lines of intermediate points and the final destination could be displayed. A separate square service number indicator box and a single line in-town "via" indicator were added immediately above the platform rear window, with the number box to the nearside. A matching rectangular intermediate and final destination indicator, with a square service number indicator box on the nearside, replaced the original equipment at the front at the same time. An additional "tramcar-style" wooden cased single-line indicator box was added at the top of the nearside driver's cab windscreen primarily to indicate the alternative in-town route options between the Lansdowne and Bournemouth Square (i.e. Bath Road and Old Christchurch Road), but also short-workings and journeys via special events. Post-war, the front rectangular *en route* points and final destination indicator were moved up to edge against the maroon band at the top of the between-decks panel, and a single-line in-town "via" indicator added immediately below, the separate box in the driver's cab windscreen being removed.

Bodywork changes included the panelling over of the diffused glass lower-deck window behind the front (exit) staircase, the merging of the first upper-deck side windows above the driver's cab into a single fixed pane and the replacement of the fixed glazing in the front upper-deck windows with half-drop windows. The glass louvres above the front windows were replaced with metal rainshields, but those above the main side windows and the rear upper-deck side window were retained until at least 1953 (from photographic evidence). The round driver's offside rear view mirror was replaced with a larger rectangular mirror, and a matching external mirror was mounted on the nearside front cab pillar. Semaphore arm illuminated traffic indicators were fitted to the pillar at the rear of the driver's cab.

73 was used prior to 22nd June 1934 for driver training purposes.

86 and 87 were reconditioned by Reading & Co. Ltd., London Road, Hilsea, Portsmouth: 86 between 1st August and 17th October 1950, and 87 between 2nd June 1950 and 31st August 1950.

All of this class, except 88, as the oldest trolleybuses in the fleet, were loaned to other operators during the Second World War, apparently deliberately retaining the **BOURNEMOUTH CORPORATION** legend on the lower maroon band. 84, 85, 86 and 88 survived long enough to be renumbered in 1959/60 in the 1958 scheme.

Disposals: 72, 73, 75, 76, 77, 79 to James Thompson & Co. (Cardiff) Ltd., Dumballs Road, Cardiff, breakers, in July 1953

74, 78 to James Thompson & Co. (Cardiff) Ltd., breakers, in May 1952

80, 81, 82, 83 to James Thompson & Co. (Cardiff) Ltd., breakers, in March 1958 (at £55 each plus £2 each for reinstating the handbrake for towing).

87, 89 to Scource & Sons, Putton Lane, Chickerell, Weymouth, breakers, in January 1959.

207 to Scource & Sons, breakers, in January 1963.

205, 208 to Scource & Sons, breakers, in October 1963 (at £46 each), the front number plate of 205 being retained for a local resident.

206 to N. Stanley, Alder Road, Poole, breakers, in March 1964.

---

90 – 173 (ALJ 964 - 999, BEL 811 - 834, BRU 1 - 24)   Delivered 1935/36

Chassis: Sunbeam MS2 three-axle.
Motor: British Thomson-Houston Co. Ltd., Type 201BW compound-wound (80 nhp).
Electrical equipment: British Thomson-Houston type 101 scissors-type controller, 12 notches (1–6, resistance; 7, full power; 8–12, field weakening).
Dewirement indicators: 2 orange line-lights and buzzer.
Body: Park Royal Coachworks Ltd., H31/25D
Length: 28 ft 7¾ ins   *Width* 7 ft 6 ins   *Unladen weight:* 8 tons 12 cwt 0 qtrs
Height: 15 ft 7¾ ins when laden, measured over trolley-hooks.
Wheelbase: 17 ft 0 ins (from front axle to centre of rear bogie), giving a turning circle of 59 ft.   *Tyres:* 36 x 8 (postwar 9.00 x 20.00) to all wheels.

Original Fleet No.	New Fleet No.	Registration Number	Chassis Number	Body Number	Date of Delivery	Date into Service	Date of Withdrawal	Date of Disposal	Initial Disposal
90	209	ALJ 964	12053	3627	11.02.35	25.03.35	.09.60	.12.61	W. J. Stevens, Gloucester
91		ALJ 965	12054	3628	13.02.35	23.03.35	.08.58	.01.59	Scource, Weymouth
92		ALJ 966	12055	3629	15.02.35	25.03.35	.10.58	.01.59	Scource, Weymouth
93	210	ALJ 967	12056	3630	18.02.35	25.03.35	.09.63	.10.63	Scource, Weymouth
94		ALJ 968	12057	3631	20.02.35	25.03.35	.12.51	.05.52	James Thompson, Cardiff
95		ALJ 969	12058	3632	22.02.35	25.03.35	.07.59	.12.59	Scource, Weymouth
96		ALJ 970	12065	3633	25.02.35	25.03.35	.10.59	.12.59	Scource, Weymouth
97	211	ALJ 971	12066	3634	27.02.35	25.03.35	.10.62	.01.63	Scource, Weymouth
98		ALJ 972	12067	3635	01.03.35	25.03.35	.12.51	.05.52	James Thompson, Cardiff
99	212	ALJ 973	12068	3636	04.03.35	25.03.35	.09.63	.11.63	Reading Transport Society
100		ALJ 974	12069	3637	06.03.35	17.04.35	.09.59	.12.59	Scource, Weymouth
101	213	ALJ 975	12070	3638	08.03.35	17.04.35	.09.63	.03.64	N. Stanley, Parkstone
102		ALJ 976	12071	3639	11.03.35	28.03.35	.12.51	.05.52	James Thompson, Cardiff
103		ALJ 977	12072	3640	13.03.35	25.03.35	.12.51	.05.52	James Thompson, Cardiff
104		ALJ 978	12073	3641	15.03.35	25.03.35	.12.51	.05.52	James Thompson, Cardiff

Original Fleet No.	New Fleet No.	Registration Number	Chassis Number	Body Number	Date of Delivery	Date into Service	Date of Withdrawal	Date of Disposal	Initial Disposal
105	214	ALJ 979	12074	3642	18.03.35	06.06.35	.09.63	.10.63	Scource, Weymouth
106	215	ALJ 980	12075	3643	20.03.35	06.06.35	.09.63	.03.64	N. Stanley, Parkstone
107		ALJ 981	12076	3644	20.03.35	06.06.35	.12.51	.05.52	James Thompson, Cardiff
108		ALJ 982	12077	3645	25.03.35	06.06.35	.12.51	.05.52	James Thompson, Cardiff
109		ALJ 983	12078	3646	27.03.35	07.06.35	.12.57	.01.59	Scource, Weymouth
110		ALJ 984	12079	3647	29.03.35	07.06.35	.12.51	.05.52	James Thompson, Cardiff
111		ALJ 985	12080	3648	01.04.35	07.06.35	.12.55	.03.58	James Thompson, Cardiff
112	202	ALJ 986	12081	3649	03.04.35	06.06.35	04.07.65	.11.65	National Trolleybus Association
113		ALJ 987	12082	3650	05.04.35	06.06.35	.12.51	.05.52	James Thompson, Cardiff
114		ALJ 988	12083	3651	08.04.35	07.06.35	.09.56	.03.58	James Thompson, Cardiff
115		ALJ 989	12084	3652	11.04.35	03.07.35	.09.59	.10.59	Scource, Weymouth
116		ALJ 990	12085	3653	26.04.35	02.07.35	.09.59	.12.59	Scource, Weymouth
117	216	ALJ 991	12086	3654	29.04.35	04.07.35	.09.63	.03.64	N. Stanley, Parkstone
118		ALJ 992	12087	3655	01.05.35	02.07.35	.12.58	.02.59	Scource, Weymouth
119	217	ALJ 993	12088	3656	03.05.35	04.07.35	.09.60	.12.61	W. J. Stevens, Gloucester
120		ALJ 994	12089	3657	08.05.35	03.07.35	.12.51	.05.52	James Thompson, Cardiff
121	218	ALJ 995	12090	3658	13.05.35	07.07.35	.09.60	.12.61	W. J. Stevens, Gloucester
122		ALJ 996	12091	3659	15.05.35	07.07.35	by 21.05.59	.12.59	Scource, Weymouth
123		ALJ 997	12092	3660	17.05.35	07.07.35	.11.58	.01.59	Scource, Weymouth
124		ALJ 998	12093	3661	20.05.35	07.07.35	.12.51	.05.52	James Thompson, Cardiff
125		ALJ 999	12094	3662	18.06.35	07.07.35	.09.59	.12.59	Scource, Weymouth
126		BEL 811	12095	3664	08.08.35	10.08.35	.12.51	.05.52	James Thompson, Cardiff
127		BEL 812	12096	3665	10.08.35	14.08.35	.12.55	.03.58	James Thompson, Cardiff
128		BEL 813	12097	3666	13.08.35	17.08.35	.12.55	.03.58	James Thompson, Cardiff
129	219	BEL 814	12098	3667	15.08.35	18.08.35	.10.62	.01.63	Scource, Weymouth
130	220 *	BEL 815	12099	3668	17.08.35	22.08.35	.09.58	.12.59	Scource, Weymouth
131	221	BEL 816	12100	3669	20.08.35	24.08.35	.10.62	.01.63	Scource, Weymouth
132	222	BEL 817	12101	3670	22.08.35	04.09.35	.10.59	.01.63	Scource, Weymouth
133		BEL 818	12102	3671	26.08.35	04.09.35	.12.51	.05.52	James Thompson, Cardiff
134		BEL 819	12103	3672	28.08.35	04.09.35	.08.58	.01.59	Scource, Weymouth
135		BEL 820	12104	3673	30.08.35	06.09.35	.11.58	.12.59	Scource, Weymouth
136		BEL 821	12105	3674	03.09.35	10.09.35	.07.59	.12.59	Scource, Weymouth
137	223 *	BEL 822	12106	3675	05.09.35	14.09.35	.09.59	.12.59	Scource, Weymouth
138		BEL 823	12107	3676	15.10.35	01.06.36	.09.56	.03.58	James Thompson, Cardiff
139		BEL 824	12108	3677	17.10.35	01.06.36	.08.59	.12.59	Scource, Weymouth
140		BEL 825	12109	3678	19.10.35	01.06.36	.12.58	.11.59	Scource, Weymouth
141	224	BEL 826	12110	3679	22.10.35	01.06.36	.09.62	.10.63	Scource, Weymouth
142		BEL 827	12111	3680	24.10.35	01.06.36	.11.58	.10.59	Scource, Weymouth
143		BEL 828	12112	3681	05.12.35	01.06.36	.07.59	.12.59	Scource, Weymouth
144	225	BEL 829	12113	3682	26.10.35	01.06.36	.09.60	.12.61	W. J. Stevens, Gloucester
145		BEL 830	12114	3683	04.12.35	01.06.36	.12.58	.02.59	Scource, Weymouth
146		BEL 831	12115	3684	07.12.35	01.06.36	.08.58	.02.59	Scource, Weymouth
147	226	BEL 832	12116	3685	09.12.35	01.06.36	.09.60	.12.61	W. J. Stevens, Gloucester
148		BEL 833	12117	3686	11.12.35	01.06.36	.09.56	.03.58	James Thompson, Cardiff
149		BEL 834	12118	3687	14.12.35	01.06.36	.09.59	.10.59	Scource, Weymouth
150		BRU 1	12119	3688	17.12.35	09.04.36	.08.57	.01.59	Scource, Weymouth
151		BRU 2	12120	3689	19.12.35	08.04.36	.12.51	.05.52	James Thompson, Cardiff
152	227 *	BRU 3	12121	3690	21.12.35	07.04.36	.12.58	.01.59	Scource, Weymouth
153		BRU 4	12122	3691	07.01.36	09.04.36	.09.56	.01.59	Scource, Weymouth
154		BRU 5	12123	3692	08.01.36	09.04.36	.09.57	.01.59	Scource, Weymouth
155		BRU 6	12124	3693	10.01.36	08.04.36	.11.58	.01.59	Scource, Weymouth
156		BRU 7	12125	3694	13.01.36	09.04.36	.09.59	.10.59	Scource, Weymouth
157	200	BRU 8	12126	3695	20.01.36	09.04.36	23.08.64	.11.65	Colbro, Rothwell
158		BRU 9	12127	3696	22.01.36	09.04.36	.11.58	.01.59	Scource, Weymouth
159	228	BRU 10	12128	3697	24.01.36	09.04.36	.09.60	.12.61	W. J. Stevens, Gloucester
160	201	BRU 11	12129	3698	25.01.36	01.06.36	23.08.64	.11.65	Colbro, Rothwell
161		BRU 12	12130	3699	27.01.36	01.06.36	.09.59	.10.59	Scource, Weymouth
162	229	BRU 13	12131	3700	14.02.36	01.06.36	.10.59	.01.63	Scource, Weymouth
163	230 *	BRU 14	12132	3701	22.02.36	01.06.36	.09.60	.01.63	Scource, Weymouth
164		BRU 15	12133	3702	15.02.36	01.06.36	.09.57	.01.59	Scource, Weymouth
165		BRU 16	12134	3703	18.02.36	01.06.36	.01.59	.12.59	Scource, Weymouth
166		BRU 17	12135	3704	20.02.36	01.06.36	.09.57	.01.59	Scource, Weymouth
167	231	BRU 18	12136	3705	25.02.36	01.06.36	.09.60	.12.61	W. J. Stevens, Gloucester
168	232	BRU 19	12137	3706	27.02.36	01.06.36	.10.62	.01.63	Scource, Weymouth
169		BRU 20	12138	3707	29.02.36	01.06.36	.12.51	.05.52	James Thompson, Cardiff
170	233	BRU 21	12139	3708	04.03.36	01.06.36	.10.62	.01.63	Scource, Weymouth
171		BRU 22	12140	3709	06.03.36	02.06.36	.08.59	.10.59	Scource, Weymouth
172		BRU 23	12141	3710	11.03.36	01.06.36	.08.59	.10.59	Scource, Weymouth
173		BRU 24	12142	3711	13.03.36	01.06.36	.08.57	.01.59	Scource, Weymouth

* Note that 130, 137, 152 were allocated new fleet numbers 220, 223, 227 respectively in the 1958 renumbering scheme, but were withdrawn before their new numbers were applied.

Brakes: Regenerative and vacuum-assisted hydraulic as 72–89.

Before trams were replaced on the "Side Routes" traversing Richmond Hill by trolleybuses on 7th June 1935, the Ministry of Transport instructed that additional equipment be installed to limit the speed of trolleybuses travelling downhill (the coasting brake) and to prevent them running backwards in case of a power failure when ascending the hill (the run-back brake). Sunbeam fitted this equipment to vehicles on order at an additional charge of £18 10s per vehicle, and for £25 to those that had already been delivered. The General Manager added Poole Hill and Bath Road Hill to the Ministry's single Richmond Hill specification. The vehicle had to be brought to a definite stop at the top of a hill and by selecting the "brake" position on the controller (or reverser as it was known in Bournemouth) the driver could limit the descending trolleybus's speed to about 8 mph. The vehicle had to be stopped again at the bottom of the hill to and the "forward" position reselected.

The run-back brake was for emergencies only and in the event of a complete brake and power failure when ascending any hill, the driver placed one circuit breaker in the "off" position which then limited the run-back speed to about 2mph.

Electrics: see 72–89.

Bodywork: Composite six-bay construction with timber framing in English oak and roof structure in best white ash. The trolley gantry was constructed of three externally mounted steel channels, carried down to the top of the lower-deck pillars of bays 2 and 3, which linked at upper-deck floor level with a horizontal steel channel running along each side from bays 1 to 7. External panelling was in 18G aluminium, the shaped panels being in 20G steel. The internal roof skin was in plywood with Alhambrinal ceilings.

All other details as for 72–89 except:

The Widney Stuart "Aero" pattern half-drop windows to bays 1–6 (both sides) of the upper-deck, bays 2–4 (both sides) of the lower-deck and to the front upper-deck windows were surrounded internally by varnished wood frames. Half-drop windows were fitted to the front of the upper-deck. Originally the saloon side windows in bays 1–6 were equipped with internal spring roller blinds. All saloon side windows and those at the front of the upper-deck were equipped with glazed louvres in chromium-plated frames.

The superior internal specifications included chromium-plated trimmings to some fittings and glazed louvres in chromium-plated frames to both decks and at the front of the upper deck.

The original Park Royal specification included an 8-day clock in the lower saloon, but these were not actually fitted. There was also provision for a clock in the cab, but it is not known if these were fitted and removed later.

Destination equipment: The first deliveries of the second batch of MS2s featured the single-line final destination and square service number indicator boxes, as used on 72–89. Commencing with the BEL-registered deliveries (126–149), rectangular indicator boxes were fitted at front (centred above the driver's windscreen, flush with, and in the middle of the between-decks primrose panelling) and rear (centred above the rear platform window, in the middle of the between-decks primrose panelling but projecting therefrom, due to the curve of the bodywork, with a slightly arched top) upon which up to four lines of intermediate points and the final destination could be displayed. There was a separate square service number indicator box mounted to the nearside of the front indicator box, and at the rear immediately above the platform rear window, again on the nearside. Additional single-line final-destination indicator boxes were mounted inside the lower saloon at the top of the bay 6 side window on both sides (above the longitudinal seat). Wooden tramcar-style slip-boards showing principal intermediate points in black on a white background could be mounted externally above the lower maroon band at lower saloon window level and running from halfway along bay 3 to halfway along bay 5 on both sides.

Lighting: see 72–83.

Seating: Based on Accles & Pollock painted tubular steel frames, with chromium-plated corner and built-in torpedo-shaped grab adjacent to the aisle. All other details as for 72–89.

Delivery: The tender of the Sunbeam Motor Car Co. Ltd. at £79,128 for 36 trolleybuses was accepted by Bournemouth Town Council on 4th September 1934 and, although there were two lower tenders, the Transport Committee in making their recommendation took heed of Mr Bulfin's advice *"on the advantages of having uniform vehicles and equipment throughout the undertaking"*. A month later another order, the fifth within 12 months, was placed for a further 48 trolleybuses. This brought the total number of Sunbeam vehicles already supplied or on order up to 103 which was at that time the largest trolleybus fleet of one manufacture to be purchased by a British municipality.

By special arrangement with Sunbeam the two orders (90–173) were delivered consecutively at a rate of one or two vehicles per week between February 1935 and March 1936, thus ensuring continuity of work on the production line. Between the placing of the orders and the start of production, the Sunbeam Motor Car Co. Ltd. formed a subsidiary company, Sunbeam Commercial Vehicles Ltd., to manufacture trolleybuses and heavy commercial vehicles.

The first ten vehicles of the batch, 90–99, entered service together on 25th March 1935, opening the new route 24 (Bournemouth Square – Iford Bridge) and its westward extension 24A (Westbourne – Bournemouth Square – Iford Bridge).

Chassis 12132T (later to carry trolleybus 163) and complete trolleybus 145 (BEL 830) were exhibits at the 12th Commercial Motor Transport

Sunbeam MS2/Park Royal 134, an example from the second major order delivered in 1935/36. Note the "tramcar-style" slipboards showing the principal points en route

I. Blee collection

Rebuilt Sunbeam MS2 201 at the western end of Central Depot, Southcote Road, on 3rd June 1962. Note the bamboo trolley retriever pole; this was carried in a tube beneath the vehicle (visible beneath the seating capacity information at the bottom of the lower rear panel) when not in use. *J. C. Gillham*

Exhibition held at Olympia, London, 7th – 16th November 1935. Photographs taken *prior* to the Exhibition show BEL 830 carrying the fleet number 143.

Internal Livery: Cream scratchproof rexine leathercloth-covered ceilings with varnished/polished wooden mouldings. Other details as 72–89. Cab area painted brown.

External Livery: As 72–89.

Subsequent alterations: The first deliveries were retrospectively fitted with the electrical coasting and run-back brakes fitted as standard to later vehicles (see "Brakes", above).

From 1937 an additional "tramcar-style" wooden cased single-line indicator box was added at the top of the nearside driver's cab windscreen to indicate the alternative in-town route options between the Lansdowne and Bournemouth Square (i.e. Bath Road and Old Christchurch Road), but also short-workings and journeys via special events. A similar single line in-town "via" indicator was added immediately above the platform rear window to the offside of the rear square service number box. Post-war, the front rectangular intermediate and final destination indicator was moved up to edge against the maroon band at the top of the between-decks panel, and a single-line auxiliary indicator added immediately below, the separate box in the driver's cab windscreen being removed.

Bodywork changes included the panelling-over of the diffused glass lower-deck window behind the front (exit) staircase, the replacement of the half-drop front upper-deck windows with fixed glazing (other side windows) and the disappearance of the glass louvres above the side and front windows in favour of metal rainshields. Semaphore arm illuminated traffic indicators were fitted at the front of the driver's cab side pillar upon which the door was hinged being subsequently replaced from the late 1950s by flashing "orange segment" shaped trafficators mounted on the lower maroon band.

On 10th December 1935, 113 (ALJ 987) was fitted with a vacuum operated G. D. Peters front exit door, and it is believed that other MS2s were also subsequently so fitted.

The following vehicles were reconditioned by Reading & Co. Ltd., London Road, Hilsea, Portsmouth:

92:    29th August 1950 – 20th October 1950
96:    13th June 1950 – 28th September 1950
106:   28th September 1950 – 7th December 1950
112:   31st August 1950 – 6th November 1950
135:   17th October 1950 – 1st January 1951
136:   2nd September 1950 – 23rd November 1950

139:   1st June 1950 – 1st August 1950
148:   12th June 1950 – 29th August 1950
167:   20th October 1950 – 9th January 1951
173:   6th November 1950 – 7th February 1951

The following vehicles were rebuilt as open-top trolleybuses by the Transport Department:

112:   entered service July 1958 renumbered as 202
157:   entered service May 1958 renumbered as 200
160:   entered service on trial 18th April 1958 (as 160); renumbered as 201 by 24th May 1958

On 4th December 1957, a press announcement advised that two trolleybuses (and six motorbuses) would be converted to open-top in time for the 1958 summer season. Trolleybus 160 was taken as a prototype for the conversion and, in the period September 1957 – April 1958, the front staircase and exit door were removed (and replaced by standard near and offside glazed panels), and seating added in the space thereby created, increasing the passenger capacity from 56 to 69 (O40/29R). The roof and upper-deck window area were removed entirely, whilst the upper-deck side panels were increased in height and a curved ellipse added to the front panels above the destination indicator boxes. The trolley gantry was retained, and a matching, externally mounted steel channel, linked to the horizontal between-decks steel channel, was added at the rear of bay 7 to support the trolleyboom retaining hooks. The vertical channels, trolley gantry (sides and top) and trolleybases were painted aluminium. The maroon band and beading below the former upper-deck windows were removed. The internal upper-deck side panels, which had no lining panels behind bay 1, the insides of the vertical channels supporting the trolley gantry and trolleyboom retaining hook arch, and the underside of the small roof section supporting the trolleybases were painted cream. The floor was waterproofed and painted brown, a longitudinal rain water outlet being added behind the horizontal steel channel along both sides. Metal anti-slip ridging was added to the floor. There was no lighting on the open upper deck. Varnished slatted wooden seats replaced the previous leather seats on the upper-deck, the original tubular metal frames being retained. Internally there was little change, but for the addition of two forward-facing double seats which had formerly been on the upper-deck. The original dull brown interior finish was replaced with cream and white paintwork, including in the driver's cab. The rear staircase floor area was painted light grey, and the panels cream. The additional comment **CIRCULAR SERVICE** was added in white letters on a red background to the blind in the single line auxiliary indicator, whilst – on at least 112 (202) – the service number 39 was printed in white on a pale green background. The prototype, 160, was presented to the public on 18th April 1958; following an MoT inspection the day before. The second conversion was ready for service in May in time for the introduction of the circular tour, service 39, on 24th May 1958. The rebuilt open-top trolleybuses introduced a new fleet numbering system whereby fleet and registration numbers coincided as far as possible.

181

Disposals: 94, 98, 102, 103, 104, 107, 108, 110, 113, 120, 124, 126, 133, 151, 169 to James Thompson & Co. (Cardiff) Ltd., Dumballs Road, Cardiff, breakers, in May 1952

111, 114, 127, 128, 138, 148 to James Thompson & Co. (Cardiff) Ltd., breakers, in March 1958 (at £55 each plus £2 each for reinstating the handbrake for towing).

91, 92, 109, 118, 123, 134, 140, 145, 146, 150, 152, 153, 154, 155, 158, 164, 166, 173 to Scource & Sons, Putton Lane, Chickerell, Weymouth, breakers, in January 1959

95, 96, 100, 115, 116, 122, 125, 130, 135, 136, 137, 139, 142, 143, 149, 156, 161, 165, 171, 172 to Scource & Sons, breakers, in December 1959 (at £70 each).

209, 217, 218, 225, 226, 228, 231 to W. J. Stevens & Sons, 59 Alvin Street, Gloucester, breakers, in December 1961 (for £600, together with three Leyland motorbuses and two vans).

211, 219, 221, 222, 229, 230, 232, 233 to Scource & Sons, breakers, in January 1963 (at £46 each)

210, 214, 224 to Scource & Sons, breakers, in October 1963 (at £46 each)

213, 215, 216 to N. Stanley, Alder Road, Poole, breakers, in March 1964 (at £75 each)

200, 201 to Colbro Ltd., Jaw Bone Works, Rothwell Haigh, Leeds, dealers, in November 1965 (at £101 each)

212 to the Reading Transport Society for preservation on 17th November 1963 (at £67, inclusive of towing costs and a set of "slave" tyres)

202 to the National Trolleybus Association for preservation in December 1965 (at £101).

---

200 – 223 (KLJ 334 – KLJ 357)   Delivered 1950

Chassis: BUT 9641T three-axle manufactured by the British United Traction Co. Ltd., Hanover House, Hanover Square, London W1 at the AEC works, Southall, Middlesex.

Motor: Crompton Parkinson Ltd., Chelmsford, Essex, Type C422 light compound-wound, air-filtered, 120 nhp. The traction motor was offset to the left hand side, as was the underslung worm drive on the two fully-floating rear axles and transmission from the motor to these drives was by a "split" propeller shaft.

Electrical equipment: Allen West Co. Ltd., Brighton, 13 notches. Control equipment mounted alongside and underneath the driver's seat.

Dewirement indicator: single Urcol line-light and buzzer.

Body: Weymann H31/25D.

Length: 30 ft   *Width:* 8 ft 0 ins   *Unladen weight:* 10 tons 6 cwt 0 qtrs   *Laden weight:* 14 tons 10 cwt

Wheelbase: 18 ft 5ins with a rear bogie wheelbase of 4ft giving a turning circle on either lock of 63 ft.

Original Fleet No.	New Fleet No.	Registration Number	Chassis Number	Body Number	Date of Delivery	Date into Service	Date of Withdrawal	Date of Disposal	Initial Disposal
200	234	KLJ 334	9641T.426	M4300	23.08.50	01.10.50	25.09.66	.12.66	Wombwell Diesels, Wombwell
201	235	KLJ 335	9641T.427	M4298	23.07.50	01.10.50	25.09.66	.12.66	Wombwell Diesels, Wombwell
202	236	KLJ 336	9641T.428	M4295	21.07.50	01.10.50	.04.66	.12.66	Wombwell Diesels, Wombwell
203	237	KLJ 337	9641T.429	M4294	08.07.50	01.10.50	25.09.66	.12.66	Wombwell Diesels, Wombwell
204	238	KLJ 338	9641T.430	M4301	25.08.50	01.10.50	25.09.66	.12.66	Wombwell Diesels, Wombwell
205	239	KLJ 339	9641T.431	M4296	25.07.50	01.10.50	25.09.66	.12.66	Wombwell Diesels, Wombwell
206	240	KLJ 340	9641T.432	M4297	21.08.50	01.10.50	25.09.66	.12.66	Wombwell Diesels, Wombwell
207	241	KLJ 341	9641T.433	M4299	28.07.50	01.10.50	25.09.66	.12.66	Wombwell Diesels, Wombwell
208	242	KLJ 342	9641T.434	M4302	30.08.50	01.10.50	25.09.66	.12.66	Wombwell Diesels, Wombwell
209	243	KLJ 343	9641T.435	M4303	07.09.50	01.10.50	25.09.66	.12.66	Wombwell Diesels, Wombwell
210	244	KLJ 344	9641T.436	M4304	12.09.50	01.10.50	25.09.66	.12.66	Wombwell Diesels, Wombwell
211	245	KLJ 345	9641T.437	M4305	14.09.50	01.11.50	.09.65	.12.66	Wombwell Diesels, Wombwell
212	246	KLJ 346	9641T.438	M4306	19.10.50	01.11.50	25.09.66	.01.67	Wombwell Diesels, Wombwell
213	247	KLJ 347	9641T.439	M4308	25.09.50	01.11.50	.09.65	.12.66	Wombwell Diesels, Wombwell
214	248	KLJ 348	9641T.440	M4307	22.09.50	01.11.50	.09.65	.12.66	Wombwell Diesels, Wombwell
215	249	KLJ 349	9641T.441	M4313	06.10.50	01.11.50	.09.65	.12.66	Wombwell Diesels, Wombwell
216	250	KLJ 350	9641T.442	M4309	04.10.50	11.11.50	.09.65	.12.66	Wombwell Diesels, Wombwell
217	251	KLJ 351	9641T.443	M4312	13.10.50	01.11.50	25.09.66	.12.66	Wombwell Diesels, Wombwell
218	252	KLJ 352	9641T.444	M4314	06.12.50	01.01.51	. .65	.12.66	Wombwell Diesels, Wombwell
219	253	KLJ 353	9641T.445	M4311	10.10.50	01.11.50	25.09.66	.12.66	Wombwell Diesels, Wombwell
220	254	KLJ 354	9641T.446	M4317	14.11.50	01.01.51	.09.65	.12.66	Wombwell Diesels, Wombwell
221	255	KLJ 355	9641T.447	M4310	26.10.50	01.01.51	.09.65	.12.66	Wombwell Diesels, Wombwell
222	256	KLJ 356	9641T.448	M4315	08.11.50	01.01.51	.09.65	.12.66	Wombwell Diesels, Wombwell
223	257	KLJ 357	9641T.449	M4316	10.11.50	01.01.51	.09.65	.12.66	Wombwell Diesels, Wombwell

Brakes: Westinghouse compressed air, hand, 2-stage rheostatic, coasting and run-back brakes. Rheostatic braking was used down to 4 mph, further pressure on the brake pedal at this speed bringing the compressed air brake into use. The rear bogie carried four cylinders, instead of the customary two, mounted on the axles in order to eliminate the effects of spring deflection on the brake linkage. The area of brake linings was 810 sq. in. for the footbrake and 648 sq. in. for the handbrake. The coasting brake limited speed to 7 mph on 1 in 9 gradient, and the emergency run-back brake restricted speed to less than ½ mph. To absorb vibration, the traction motor and the air compressor were mounted on rubber supports. The rear bogie design incorporated radius arms to transmit the axle torque reaction directly to the frame, thus equalizing the axle loading and providing greater acceleration

without wheelspin, and smoother and more efficient braking. A mechanical pump provided automatic lubrication to 40 points on the chassis.

The BUT 9641Ts were inspected by the MoT on 21st November 1951. The roads were slippery at the time and Col. C. A. Langley found it difficult to get satisfactory brake tests with the Tapley recorder. He noted that the rheostatic/air brake on the first vehicle was not as powerful as it should have been and, from a speed of 30 mph, the Tapley recordings varied from 45% to 55%; the handbrake however gave 25%. On the second vehicle the power brake was satisfactory and gave a reading of 61%, but the maximum recordings with the handbrake was only 15%. Recordings of 60% with the power brake and 25% with the handbrake should have been obtainable with new vehicles, and Col. Langley considered that the brakes on the BUTs should be adjusted so as to give these minimum readings.

Electrics: Brecknell Willis & Co. Ltd. trolley collector gear with BICC Edinburgh type slipper heads using renewable carbon inserts, supplied with radio interference suppression to meet MoT requirements. The 15 ft long trolley booms, when restrained by the retaining hooks, extended 1 ft 3 ins beyond the rearmost part of the bodywork. The "controlled rheostatic" electrical equipment incorporated a resiliently mounted, self-ventilating, floodproof Crompton Parkinson traction motor, type C422, with a one-hour rating of 120 hp at 550 volts, drawing 185 amps. Access to the brush gear and commutator was through large openings at the top and bottom of the frame, protected in service by screened air inlets and commutator inspection covers. The main Allen West control gear was of unit construction. It featured the assembly of all electrical control items on one insulating base, mounted by the driver's seat, on the cab bulkhead. Provision was made for battery manoeuvering equipment, should this eventually be required. The main resistance, mounted in the chassis frame, had stainless steel grids and spot welding throughout to prevent rust and corrosion. The lightweight shunt resistance was of non-corrodible resistance material having a negligible temperature coefficient. Protection from severe overload was given by two main circuit breakers situated in the driver's cab. The 13 steps in the electrical control equipment comprised 9 resistance (1–9), a full power (10) and 3 weak field (11–13) notches. In notch 11 the shunt field was cut out, and in 12 and 13 the field-weakening resistors cut in. Oldham batteries supplied a 24-volt power source for auxiliaries such as the dewirement indicators, trafficators, windscreen wipers and lighting. Twelve of the vehicles had Metropolitan-Vickers/CAV motor generator sets, and the other twelve Metropolitan-Vickers/Simms sets.

Bodywork: All metal six-bay highbridge construction with integral trolley gantry. The body pillars were secured to the cross members with self-lubricating bushes and stainless steel pins to relieve the body of strains caused by chassis distortion.

The vehicles featured twin staircases with a conventional rear, semi-vestibuled open platform entrance and a front exit equipped with a G. D. Peters air-operated two-leaf folding door, controlled from the driver's cab by means of a lever coupled to an interlock to break the controller circuit, thus preventing the trolleybus from starting off with the doors open. The rear staircase was forward ascending, and that at the front of the vehicle forward descending.

The front exit was equipped with a glazed vestibule panel. There were three steps. Sliding openers were fitted to the tops of the side windows in in bays 1–5 (nearside) and 2–5 (offside) of the upper-deck and bays 2–4 (both sides) of the lower-deck. The front upper-deck windows had bottom-hinged, "pull-in" opening top hopper ventilators, surmounted by metal rainshields and two horizontal inlet ducts linked through concealed trunking to extractor ventilators. Smaller inlet ducts were installed above the driver's cab windscreens. Large single pane rear upper-deck window/emergency exit. The windows were all surrounded internally by varnished wood frames. The driver's cab was equipped with two opening windscreens having chromium plated frames, windscreen wipers and adjustable sun visor on both sides, and front-hinged doors equipped with sliding signalling windows on both the nearside and offside. There were two glazed panels in the bulkhead behind the driver, that on the offside being smaller due to the presence of the staircase. The control handle for controlling the front exit door was mounted at driver's shoulder height on the pillar between these two panels. Rectangular driver's rear view mirrors were mounted externally towards the top of the front cab pillars.

There were used ticket boxes on the rear panel at the top of the front staircase, immediately below the nearside bulkhead window by the front

The Weymann official photographer snapped 203 before delivery to Bournemouth on 8th July 1950. Note the original livery style featuring olive green lining to the panels above the lower-deck windows, the rear coat of arms and the illuminated semaphore-arm traffic indicators. Destination blinds have yet to be fitted.

C. K. Bowers/D. L. Chalk collection

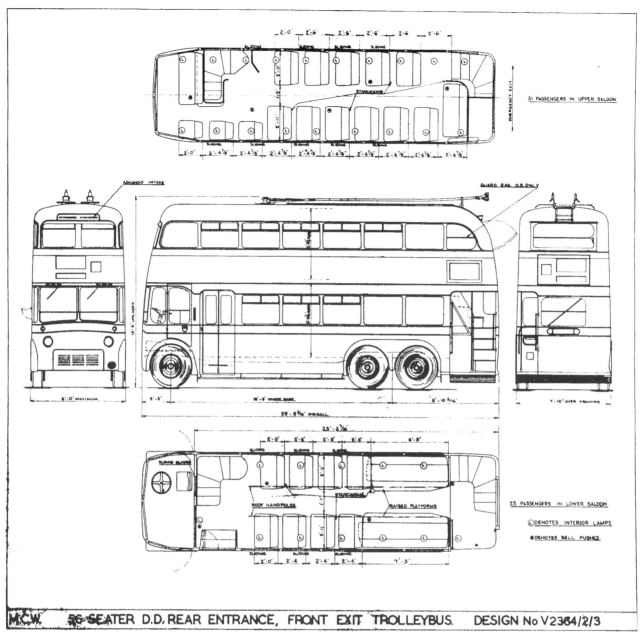

M.C.W. 56-SEATER D.D. REAR ENTRANCE, FRONT EXIT TROLLEYBUS. DESIGN No V2364/2/3

Body manufacturer's drawing of the bodywork fitted to the Bournemouth BUT 9641T trolleybuses, 24 of which joined the fleet during 1950.

Metropolitan-Cammell-Weymann

exit and below the nearside vestibule window on the rear open platform. Internal advertisement frames were mounted on the panel behind the front offside bench seat visible half way down the front exit staircase. Fluted front removable panel (three horizontal columns of vanes). The bodywork featured Weymann characteristics of the period such as the gently curving front and rear elevations, a rounded roof, flared out skirting panels to sides and rear, low-set front headlamps and curved upper corners to the rear platform window. A bamboo trolley retrieval pole was carried centrally under the chassis. The conductor had a locker on the rear platform under the stairs.

Destination equipment: Rectangular off-centre indicator box capable of displaying up to four lines of *en route* points and the final destination, with single-line in-town "via" indicator immediately below, and a separate square service number indicator box to the nearside at front and rear. A further rectangular indicator box, repeating up to four lines of *en route* points and the final destination, was fitted immediately above the rear open-platform entrance.

Some, if not all, of the vehicles were fitted later with a wooden fold-down flap indicating when the "minimum fare" used on services 20 and 32 was in operation. This was mounted on hinges immediately above the rear open platform entrance.

Lighting: External lighting was by two low-set headlights on the front panel, two front side lights on the lower maroon band, and combined rear lights and brake lights mounted to left and right of the illuminated rear glass registration number plate built into the lower maroon band immediately below the rear platform window. Red reflectors were fitted towards the base of the rear panel above the outward curve of the skirting in 1954. A spot light was fitted below the nearside headlight. Lighting circuits were supplied from a motor generator (Metropolitan Vickers/Sims or Metropolitan Vickers/CAV), with square diffused glasses being provided to the interior lights in each saloon. Semaphore arm illuminated traffic indicators were fitted to the side pillars immediately to the rear of the driver's cab doors.

Seating: Based on painted tubular steel frames with chromium-plated top and built-in "orange segment" shaped grab facility adjacent to the aisle. Squabs and backs were upholstered in patterned moquette with brown hide tops and sides to the backs, and Dunlopillo cushions with scratchproof patterned seat-backs. Due to the position of the offside front staircase, seats in both the upper and lower saloons were staggered which gave more space for moving along the gangways. Accordingly the lower deck had a four-person bench seat over the rear bogie on the offside and a five-person bench seat on the nearside. The upper saloon had three rows of single seats on the front nearside and a bench seat for

three passengers on the offside immediately in front of the front exit staircase well. At the rear of the upper saloon, a bench seat above the open platform could accommodate three passengers. The other double seats were staggered, there being five on the offside and six on the nearside. The driver's seat (plain squab and pleated back) was in brown hide.

Internal Livery: Ceilings and coves were covered with cream coloured Alhambrinal panels with maroon and primrose insets, and varnished/polished wooden mouldings. Side panels below the waist rail were brown Alhambrinal. Brown paint to staircases and seat frames. Handrails and stanchions were chromed steel or covered in black Doverite. Cab area painted primrose.

The saloon floors were covered in brown linoleum with brown painted metal, anti-slip transverse strips in the upper deck gangway at the rear and the top of the entrance staircase.

External Livery: All over primrose, with two maroon bands (below windows of each deck), the lower maroon band being arched to the centre of the driver's cab windscreen. The mouldings above and below the horizontal panel immediately above the lower deck windows (which were originally yellow on the pre-war trolleybuses), and those edging the maroon bands, were olive green on these vehicles. Mudguards and lifeguard rails were black and wheels maroon. Legal lettering/ownership details were painted at the base of the nearside lower panel of bay 2, with the seating capacity being indicated at the base of the rear lower panel, on the near side at platform height, in black ¾ ins high lettering.

The Bournemouth coat of arms was displayed on both sides, upper and lower decks, bay 3, also centrally on the front and rear lower deck panels. Red upper-case **EXIT ONLY** and **ENTRANCE** lettering was applied above the bay 2 and bay 6 lower-deck nearside windows, with an arrow pointing forwards and backwards respectively. The final livery style saw this information applied to the lower maroon band in white lettering behind the front exit at in front of the rear entrance. The upper-deck rear emergency exit was indicated by 1 ins high red upper-case lettering. Gold numerals with heavy blue shading were carried on the front panel between the offside headlight and sidelight, and centrally mounted on the primrose lower panel below the rear platform window between the illuminated registration number and the coat of arms. The subsequent livery style saw the olive green mouldings above the lower deck windows painted primrose; the coat of arms on the front and rear panels and the lower deck side panels removed; and the fleet numbers replaced by slightly smaller blue-shaded gold stock numerals, again centrally located. These were finally replaced by unshaded plain gold Gill Sans numerals.

Subsequent alterations: The semaphore arm illuminated traffic indicators fitted on the side pillars immediately to the rear of the driver's cab doors were replaced by flashing "orange segment" shaped trafficators mounted immediately above the lower maroon band.

234–243 had their front staircase removed, and their seating increased to H39/29D by adding two double seats on the offside of the lower saloon and replacing the original three rows of single seats on the nearside of the upper saloon, with three rows of double seats and the front offside bench seat and staircase with four rows of double seats. The slightly larger seat pitch on the offside of both saloons facilitated this alteration. One vehicle, probably 234, was stripped of all the original seating and fitted with noticeably narrower re-trimmed seating removed from withdrawn Sunbeam MS2s. This provided a float of standard BUT 9641T Deans "Dapta" seats for the subsequent rebuilds. Most vehicles retained their bell-push buttons, although one or two benefitted from strip bell-pushes. Most rebuilt vehicles additionally gained rear flashing trafficator globes mounted on the lower-deck maroon band below the rear platform window. The rebuilding increased the unladen weight to 10 tons 9 cwt 2 quarters.

On 13th November 1962, the new General Manager, Ronald Cox, wrote to Col W. P. Reed, MoT, advising him of the alterations being carried out to all 24 (sic) of the BUT 9641Ts, involving the removal of the front staircase and increasing the seating capacity from 56 to 68 seats. The spacing of the new seats conformed with the then current PSV regulations, and all work was to be carried out is in accordance with the current MoT regulations (i.e. The Trolley Vehicles Memorandum). Satisfactory tilt test had been carried out at London Transport's Aldenham works. Referring to their 1951 figures, the MoT queried the braking. Tapley readings were taken that same month, unloaded at 20mph, and recorded handbrake 34%, footbrake 57.5%. Loaded, the figures were: footbrake 49%, handbrake 24%. The MoT would have preferred higher results, and commented that they would be relying on the department's workshops to ensure that these figures were maintained. The staircases of rebuilt BUT 9641Ts were repainted dove grey in a similar manner to Sunbeam MF2Bs 259-287.

Dates of rebuilding:

234	September 1962	235	October 1962
236, 237, 238	December 1962	239	January 1963
240	February 1963	241	March 1963
242	April 1963	243	May 1963

Notes: The 24 Weymann bodies on the BUT 9641Ts were part of a larger order encompassing 30 Leyland PD2/3 motorbuses 224–253, the largest single bodywork order placed by the department. Delivery brought the trolleybus fleet up to its maximum level of 127 vehicles, beyond the undercover storage capabilities of the undertaking: 18 Sunbeam MS2s were withdrawn and stored at the Castle Lane Depot site until being sold for scrap in May 1952.

203 was used from 24th July 1950 for driver training.

212 was exhibited on the Weymann stand at the 15th International Commercial Motor Transport Exhibition at Earls Court, London, 22nd – 30th September 1950.

212 returned to Weymann from 5th February – 11th April 1951 following a collision with 141 on 18th December 1950 and re-entered service on 1st August 1951. It also suffered rear-end damage in Boscombe in July 1960. It is rumoured that these repairs used the rear portion of a Leyland TD5/Weymann motorbus. 212 was considered the fastest trolleybus on the system and was reputedly the first trolleybus to enter the then new Castle Lane Depot.

200–223 were all renumbered to 234–257 between June 1958 and February 1959.

207 was painted with a chocolate roof 1954.

Disposal: 234–257 all sold to Wombwell Diesels Co. Ltd., breakers, in December 1966 (at £75 each).

246 was initially reserved for a Mr R. Higgins, Christchurch, for preservation but when the sale fell through it joined the batch sold to Wombwell Diesels, being subsequently purchased from the breakers by Mr Richard Cromwell, Effingham, Surrey, for preservation in December 1966 (at £125).

246 was initially stored at Castle Lane Depot and used on a number of enthusiasts' tours, including the closure procession on 20th April 1969. It was transferred to storage at Epsom, Surrey, on 15th June 1969 and then to Weybridge in Spring 1970, being used on an enthusiasts' tour of the Cardiff system on 7th September 1969. In August 1971, 246 was sold to the BPTA for £400 and transferred to storage at Bournemouth (Hurn) Airport on 12th September 1971. Since then it has been stored variously at Castle Lane Depot, Hurn Airport and Poole.

Chassis: Sunbeam MF2B two-axle "transit" type, manufactured by Sunbeam Trolleybus Co. Ltd., Fallings Park, Wolverhampton; type primarily foreseen for export markets.
Motor: Crompton Parkinson Ltd., Chelmsford, Essex. Type C423 (95 nhp), light compound-wound.
Electrical equipment: Allen West and Company Ltd., Brighton, incorporating automatic acceleration with 13 power notches, (1–10, resistance; 11, full power; 12–13, field weakening) and two stage rheostatic braking. An auxiliary generator/dynamo charged the battery when the traction motor was running; the battery supplying power for the control systems and lighting.
Dewirement indicators: green line-light and buzzer.
Body: Weymann all-metal double deck highbridge construction with twin staircases, rear open platform entrance and separate front exit with air-operated folding doors placed forward of the leading axle.
Seating: 258/259 and 261–269 : H34/28D   260 and 270–287 : H35/28D
Length: 30 ft   *Width:* 7 ft 11¾ ins   *Unladen weight:* 8 tons 19 cwts 2 qtrs
Height over trolleybase: 15 ft 7 ins   *Wheelbase:*   15 ft 10 ins, giving a turning circle of 58 ft (65 ft over the full body)

Fleet Number	Registration Number	Chassis Number	Body Number	Date of Delivery	Date into Service	Date of Withdrawal	Date of Disposal	Initial Disposal
258	WRU 258	STB80157	M8233	28.07.58	02.08.58	25.09.66	15.08.69	Wombwell Diesels, Wombwell
259	WRU 259	STB80158	M8234	29.07.58	02.08.58	25.09.66	03.09.69	Wombwell Diesels, Wombwell
260	WRU 260	STB80159	M8235	13.10.58	01.11.58	25.09.66	03.09.69	Wombwell Diesels, Wombwell
261	WRU 261	STB80160	M8237	05.08.58	07.08.58	25.09.66	29.08.69	Wombwell Diesels, Wombwell
262	WRU 262	STB80161	M8236	01.08.58	02.08.58	25.09.66	29.08.69	Wombwell Diesels, Wombwell
263	WRU 263	STB80162	M8238	07.08.58	01.09.58	25.09.66	05.09.69	Wombwell Diesels, Wombwell
264	WRU 264	STB80163	M8239	11.08.58	01.09.58	25.09.66	13.08.69	Wombwell Diesels, Wombwell
265	WRU 265	STB80164	M8240	29.08.58	01.10.58	25.09.66	18.08.69	Wombwell Diesels, Wombwell
266	WRU 266	STB80165	M8241	03.09.58	01.10.58	25.09.66	18.08.69	Wombwell Diesels, Wombwell
267	WRU 267	STB80166	M8242	09.09.58	01.11.58	25.09.66	15.08.69	Wombwell Diesels, Wombwell
268	WRU 268	STB80167	M8244	18.09.58	01.12.58	19.04.68	14.10.69	Wombwell Diesels, Wombwell
269	WRU 269	STB80168	M8243	15.09.58	01.12.58	30.11.68	13.08.69	Wombwell Diesels, Wombwell
270	WRU 270	STB80169	M8245	08.10.58	01.01.59	28.02.69	11.08.69	Wombwell Diesels, Wombwell
271	WRU 271	STB80170	M8246	16.10.58	01.01.59	19.04.69	17.09.69	Wombwell Diesels, Wombwell
272	WRU 272	STB80171	M8251	15.12.58	01.02.59	19.04.69	11.09.69	Wombwell Diesels, Wombwell
273	WRU 273	STB80172	M8247	04.11.58	01.01.59	20.04.69	09.09.69	Wombwell Diesels, Wombwell
274	WRU 274	STB80173	M8248	13.11.58	01.01.59	20.04.69	09.09.69	Wombwell Diesels, Wombwell
275	WRU 275	STB80174	M8250	03.12.58	01.02.59	14.09.68	05.09.69	Wombwell Diesels, Wombwell
276	WRU 276	STB80175	M8249	25.11.58	01.02.59	19.04.69	01.10.69	Wombwell Diesels, Wombwell
277	WRU 277	STB80176	M8252	07.01.59	01.02.59	19.04.69	11.09.69	Wombwell Diesels, Wombwell
278	YLJ 278	STB80177	M8582	15.09.59	01.11.59	20.04.69	05.09.69	Wombwell Diesels, Wombwell
279	YLJ 279	STB80178	M8583	21.09.59	01.10.59	20.04.69	11.09.69	Wombwell Diesels, Wombwell
280	YLJ 280	STB80179	M8580	07.09.59	01.10.59	20.04.69	25.09.69	Wombwell Diesels, Wombwell
281	YLJ 281	STB80180	M8577	07.08.59	01.09.59	30.11.69	11.08.69	Wombwell Diesels, Wombwell
282	YLJ 282	STB80181	M8578	27.08.59	01.09.59	20.04.69	16.09.69	Wombwell Diesels, Wombwell
283	YLJ 283	STB80182	M8575	21.07.59	01.08.59	20.04.69	23.09.69	Wombwell Diesels, Wombwell
284	YLJ 284	STB80183	M8581	12.09.59	01.11.59	20.04.69	23.09.69	Wombwell Diesels, Wombwell
285	YLJ 285	STB80184	M8579	02.09.59	01.10.59	20.04.69	02.09.69	Wombwell Diesels, Wombwell
286	YLJ 286	STB80185	M8574	16.07.59	01.08.59	19.04.69	16.11.72	Wombwell Diesels, Wombwell
287	YLJ 287	STB80186	M8576	23.07.59	01.08.59	19.04.69	16.09.69	Wombwell Diesels, Wombwell

Chassis: The frame was built of high tensile steel channel side-members with pressed-steel centre cross-members and other tubular cross-members for torsional rigidity, the whole assembly being bolted together. I-section carbon alloy steel front axle with 16½ ins diameter front brake drums having liners 4 ins wide and ½ ins thick. The rear axle had an underslung worm driven unit with fully floating axle shafts, the casing being a one-piece alloy steel drop forging. The hardened steel worm had 8½ ins centres and an axle ratio of 10.33 to 1.

Conventional suspension used semi-elliptic 4 ins wide Silico Manganese leaf-type springs, 54 ins long at the front and 62 ins at the rear. The individual leaves were shot peened for fatigue resistance, fitted with anti-roll clips and supplemented by overload rubber buffers. Telescopic shock absorbers were fitted to both axles. A 24-point Tecalemit belt-driven lubricator provided automatic chassis lubrication. Normal ventilated disc type wheels were equipped with 11.00 x 20 14-ply tyres at the front and 10.00 x 20 12-ply at the rear. The 21 ins diameter driver's wheel with a ratio of 5½ turns lock to lock connected with cam and double roller type steering gear mounted in a cast-iron casing on the chassis frame.

Brakes: Coasting, runback (equipment type CT/MP.2.) rheostatic and Westinghouse air brakes. The foot braking system was operated by Westinghouse air-pressure equipment with separate cylinders for each wheel, the air compressor delivering 4.8 cu ft actual swept volume per minute driven by a ¾ hp electric motor. A pull-on handbrake was linked

to the rear shoes. The rear brake drums were made of Chromidium iron alloy, manufactured by the Midland Motor Cylinder Co. Ltd., and had a diameter of 16¼ ins with brake linings 6½ ins wide and ½ ins thick. Two notches of rheostatic braking down to about 3 mph were available before the air brakes came into operation.

Electrics: Brecknell Willis & Co. Ltd. trolley bases, Accles & Pollock trolleybooms, slipper-type trolley collector gear equipped with Anti-Attrition OB type heads and renewable carbon inserts with radio interference suppression to meet Ministry of Transport requirements. The 16 ft long, lightweight trolley booms, insulated at the sockets by means of Bakelite sleeves, allowed 15 ft deviation to either side of the overhead line. When restrained by the retaining hooks, the trolley head centres extended only 6 ins beyond the rearmost portion of the bodywork. To control the vertical movement of the trolleybooms a hydraulic damping device was fitted, and a brake restricted the swing of the poles in case of dewirement. There was a concealed trolley gantry above bay 2.

The "controlled rheostatic" non-regenerative electrical equipment incorporated a resiliently mounted, self-ventilating, floodproof Crompton Parkinson C423 traction motor with a one-hour rating of 95 hp at 550 volts. Arranged for rheostatic braking, the motor was supported on four rubber anti-vibration mountings and could be easily removed from the chassis for overhaul. The drive to the rear axle was by a short tubular shaft with Hardy Spicer universal joints at each end. A

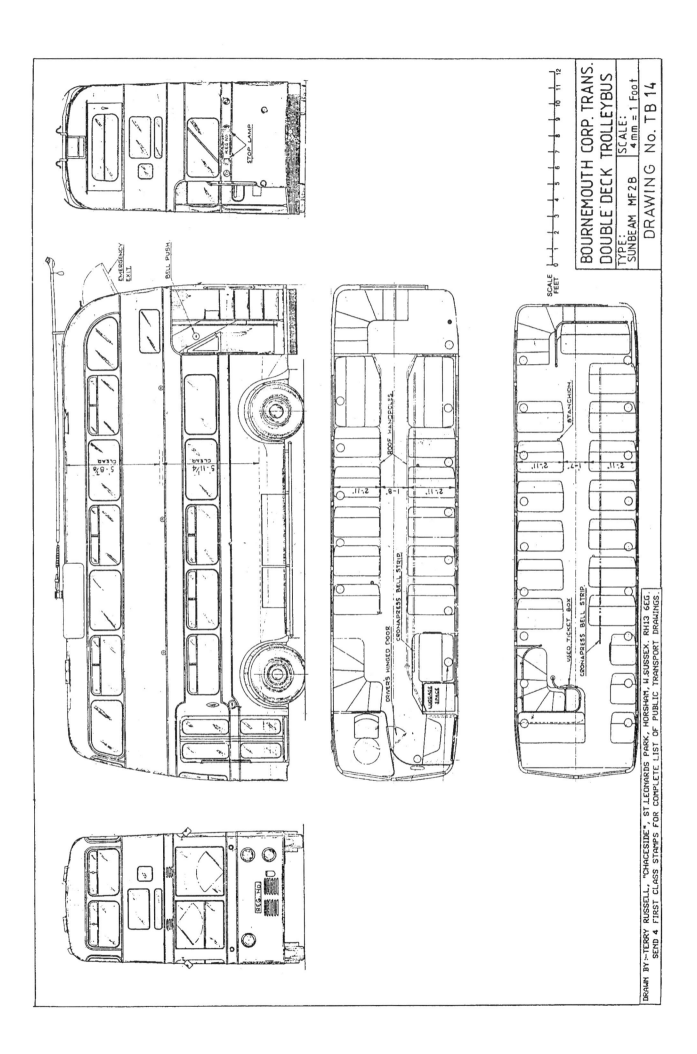

BOURNEMOUTH CORP. TRANS.
DOUBLE DECK TROLLEYBUS.
TYPE:
SUNBEAM MF2B
SCALE:
4 mm = 1 Foot
DRAWING No. TB 14

SCALE FEET 0 1 2 3 4 5 6 7 8 9 10 11 12

EMERGENCY EXIT
BELL PUSH
STOP LAMP

5.8⅜ CLEAR
5.11¼ CLEAR

ROOF HANDPOLES
DRIVER'S HINGED DOOR
CRONAPRESS BELL STRIP
2.11.
1-8.
2.11.
LUGGAGE SPACE

STANCHION
USED TICKET BOX
CRONAPRESS BELL STRIP
2.11.
1.7.
2.11.

REG. NO.

DRAWN BY:- TERRY RUSSELL, "CHACESIDE", ST LEONARDS PARK, HORSHAM, W. SUSSEX. RH13 6EG.
SEND 4 FIRST CLASS STAMPS FOR COMPLETE LIST OF PUBLIC TRANSPORT DRAWINGS.

187

24-volt CAV overhung auxiliary generator (basically a version of the standard motorbus dynamo directly coupled to the back of the traction motor) was fitted, together with control board and Crompton Parkinson batteries. The auxiliary generator/dynamo turned with the armature, and was thus independent of the overhead power supply i.e. it operated when the trolleybus was on tow or coasting. Allen West control gear was used, with the master controller and reverser placed beneath the driver's seat. The main resistors were mounted between the chassis side-members, fully shielded against splashing from the road, with a further steel and asbestos shield mounted over them to protect the body from undue heat. The contactor panel was mounted in a waterproof steel case on the side of the chassis frame. Pre-adjusted automatic acceleration and coasting and run-back brakes were provided. Shielded R.P. resistors were mounted between the frame side members. Nonetheless, water ingress to the underfloor contactors and failure of the lighting generator proved recurrent operational problems.

The automatic acceleration device was an entirely electro-mechanical, compact unit located in the position normally used by the over-current relay. The master controller was driven through a pre-compressed spring incorporated in the drive. An eddy-current drag unit was driven from the master controller, thus delaying the controller so that the spring was wound up if the speed of power pedal depression exceeded a certain rate. Provided this rate was not exceeded, the controller remained under the driver's direct control and the trolleybus could be driven in a similar manner to one equipped with normal equipment. A ratchet allowed the master controller to be returned instantaneously to the "off" position.

The drag unit consisted of an eddy-current disc rotating in a magnetic field. This field was created by a coil connected across the main motor series field, so that the drag field strength varied according to the current being taken by the motor, and regulated the speed of progression of the controller according to grade and load conditions. A resistance was incorporated in series with the drag coil. Part of this resistance was provided with accessible tappings, enabling the operator to pre-set the acceleration rate required by changing one connection. Up to four tappings could be provided for selected acceleration rates on the level.

The drag coil series resistance was cut out until the B.1. contactor closed by means of an interlock on this contactor. This reduced the rate of controller progression over the first three notches, ensuring smooth, uniform acceleration under all conditions. A current limit relay in the main motor circuit cut out the drag coil series resistance when the accelerating current exceeded a pre-determined figure and reduced the rate of controller progression to a crawl until the current had fallen to a safe figure.

The drag device did not come into action until the first notch had been obtained, so that there was no delay in obtaining power. When the trolleybus was travelling at speed and the pedal was rapidly depressed to its full extent, such as after a section insulator, controller progression from the "off" position to the last notch took place in less than 1 second. The drag unit construction was robust; the ½ in pinions driving the eddy drag disc ran in ball-bearings, whilst the ratchet was also ½ in wide and made from lubricant-free materials. The parts were intended to have the same life-expectancy as the vehicle. The entire unit was totally enclosed and required no maintenance, excluding lubrication at each major vehicle overhaul.

Bodywork: All-metal five-bay construction with twin staircases, rear open platform entrance and separate front exit with air-operated two-leaf folding doors placed forward of the leading axle. The body was based on the Weymann "Aurora" design, but with a heavyweight ancestry similar to the main frames used on the BUT 9641Ts. A standard MCW centrally-mounted rectangular ventilator in the upper-deck front dome was fitted to the early deliveries, 258–262. Both the upper and lower portions of the folding doors were glazed. The rear staircase was forward ascending and that at the front of the vehicle forward descending. There were three single seats on the front nearside of the upper saloon, and a triple bench (originally a double bench on 258, 259, 261–269) on the offside immediately in front of the front exit staircase well. The third single seat from the front (opposite the staircase) was equipped with an armrest on the gangway side. Rectangular driver's rear view mirrors were mounted on the front offside and nearside front pillars.

Channel steel floor bearers were connected to the tubular steel lower saloon pillars (which had timber inserts) by means of steel brackets, the upper-saloon pillars being of aluminium alloy section. The saloon floors were of ¾ ins tongue and groove softwood covered in brown linoleum, with conventional Pyramid floor treading. Structural lining panels were provided in both saloons, and alloy roof hoopsticks and purlins used. The carlines supporting the upper deck floor were of flanged steel channel section, connected to the pillars by means of fabricated brackets. The exterior panelling was 18-gauge aluminium, with the exception of the front and rear domes which was in 16-gauge, and the lower offside rear corner panel which was glass fibre. The panels were butt-jointed and covered with alloy mouldings, secured to the timber inserts by wood screws. The front exit door (forward of the front axle) was of the Deans "Glider" pattern, air-operated via a separate air reservoir supplied by a Westinghouse compressor. An interlock to break the controller circuit prevented the trolleybus from moving with the doors open.

Hand rails and sockets were Doverite-covered and insulated from the metal structure. The rear entrance and front exit staircases were of wooden construction, covered in brown linoleum and with Lite Steel treads. Fluted aluminium treads were added between the seats. A Desmo staircase mirror on each staircase enabled the conductor to watch the upper deck.

Three pairs of single slide Rawling's "Streamlight" windows in polished aluminium frames were fitted to bays 1, 3, 5 (both sides) of the upper deck, and bays 1-3 (nearside) and bays 2-4 (offside) of the lower deck. Auster "pull-in" opening windows were fitted at the front of the upper deck. Direct Claytonrite rubber glazing as used in Weymann's "Orion" bodies, instead of steel pans, was used for the saloon windows. The upper-deck rear emergency window featured a lightweight walkway, looking like a small aluminium step-ladder, manufactured by Deans to provide easy access to the trolley gear. The driver's cab was equipped with an offside opening windscreen and a fixed nearside screen manufactured by British Steel Frames Ltd., both with electric demisters and wipers (the wipers being top mounted on the offside and bottom mounted on the nearside). The second offside cab window was equipped with a Rawlings double sliding light, the lower light forming a driver's signalling window.

The front exit staircase backed on to the driver's cab, which had a draught screen incorporating a single curved window facing the passenger gangway behind the driver's left shoulder and a waist-high front-hinged door on the nearside in the style of a one-person-operated bus of the period. There was no external cab door. The driver was provided with an adjustable Chapman 32 H.B. seat with brown Vynide and Rexine covered Dunlopillo cushion and squab.

Cronapress strip bell-pushes were added to the ceilings of both saloons, with an additional bell push placed in the rear staircase stringer for use by the conductor when standing on the rear entrance platform. Card advertisements could be displayed internally in retaining channels immediately above the side windows and between the lighting installations, and in display cases on the front staircase and on the offside rear bulkhead of the lower saloon. Used-ticket boxes were fitted on the rear panel at the top of the front staircase, immediately below the nearside cab windscreen by the front exit and on the rear platform. A bamboo trolley retrieval pole was carried centrally under the chassis.

Destination equipment: Rectangular off-centre indicator box capable of displaying up to four lines of *en route* points and the final destination, with single-line in-town "via" indicator immediately below and a separate square service number indicator box to the nearside at front and rear. A further rectangular indicator box, repeating up to four lines of *en route* points and the final destination, was fitted immediately above the rear open platform entrance. The destination equipment gearing was manufactured by Equipment & Engineering Co..

A wooden fold-down flap indicating when the "minimum fare" used on services 20 and 32 was in operation was mounted on hinges immediately above the rear open platform entrance.

Lighting: Externally there were two headlights mounted on slight protrusions to accommodate the curved near and offside of the front panel, two sidelights mounted similarly on the lower maroon band and two combined BMAC rear lights and reflectors mounted $2/3$ of the way down the rear lower deck panel. That on the nearside was fitted in a separate plinth at the base of the rear platform window nearside pillar, which also provided the base for a rear passenger grab rail. A spotlight was fitted below the nearside headlight. All lights were of the Simms flush type and controlled by a Simms 6.B.100 switchboard. A Simms flasher unit controlled flashing "orange segment" shaped trafficators mounted immediately above the lower maroon band between the front exit doors and the lower deck bay 1 side windows on the nearside, and behind the driver's cab signalling window on the offside. Circular CAV 556 units were fitted on the lower maroon band at the rear. Internal exposed-bulb tungsten lighting was fitted in both saloons, the rear platform entrance and destination boxes.

Seating: Deans "Dapta" lightweight frames painted brown with stainless steel top rail. Dunlopillo cushions and polyether squabs covered in brown coloured Vynide and Rexine, both seat and squab being fully fluted. In the lower saloon, a bench seat having space for two passengers was fitted on the nearside behind the front exit door over the front wheel arch. At the rear, bench seats over the rear wheel arch on both the near and offsides accommodated three passengers each. There were also five rows of front-facing double seats. The upper saloon had three rows of single seats on the front nearside and a bench seat for three passengers on the offside immediately in front of the front exit staircase

well. At the rear of the upper saloon, a bench seat above the open platform could both accommodate two passengers on 258, 259, 261–269 and three passengers on 260, 270–287. A larger rear bench seat for three passengers was fitted to 258, 259, 261–269 in October 1958. There were seven rows of front-facing double seats on the nearside and six on the offside.

Internal Livery: The side panels inside the body were lined in brown Rexine leathercloth, with the ceilings cellulosed in broken white. Window cappings were stove-enamelled in a gold metallic colour. Brown paint was used for the front and rear staircases, lower saloon front bulkheads, the driver's cab and the seat frames. All handrails and stanchions were covered in black Doverite.

External Livery: All over primrose, with two maroon bands (below windows of each deck). The driver's rear view mirrors were also painted primrose. The lower maroon band curved down from the height of the side windows to that of the front windscreen immediately behind the front exit on the nearside and the driver's cab signalling window on the offside. The moulded edging to the maroon bands was olive green. Mudguards and lifeguard rails were black and wheels maroon. Trolley gear (apart from white "spats" and aluminium heads), the roof-mounted catwalk and retaining hooks were black. Dockers paint was used throughout. Legal lettering/ownership details were painted at the base of the nearside lower panel of bay 2 immediately behind the front axle with the seating capacity being indicated at the base of the rear lower panels on the near side below the platform rear window in black $3/4$ ins high letters.

The Bournemouth coat of arms was displayed on both sides of the upper decks, bay 3, and centrally on the front lower deck primrose panels. The transfer was larger and squarer than in the past. White lettering applied to the lower nearside maroon band behind the front exit and in front of the rear entrance indicated **EXIT ONLY** and **ENTRANCE** respectively. The upper-deck rear emergency exit was indicated by 1 ins high red upper-case lettering centrally above the window. Blue-shaded gold stock numerals were carried in the lower offside corner of the front panel below the offside headlight and centrally mounted on the primrose lower panel below the rear platform window.

Subsequent alterations: 258, 259, 261–269 were reseated October 1958 to HR35/28D by replacing the upper saloon rear double bench seat above the open platform with a larger bench seat for three passengers.

Scheduled maintenance saw many of the earlier deliveries repainted externally to the same standards as the second batch of MF2Bs (295–303), but this work came to an end in early 1964 with the decision to run down the system. A handful of trolleybuses, including 269, 278, 279, 286, benefitted from a repaint in the then current livery style in 1966.

Plain gold Gill Sans stock numerals gradually replaced the more traditional shaded version from 1963 and, from 1966 and often as a result of accident damage, several of these trolleybuses received plain black stock numerals. These were mounted slightly higher than the gold numerals at the front, below the offside headlight and lower on the primrose lower panel below the rear platform window (to accommodate an advertisement). From September 1967, exterior advertising was carried on the upper-deck side panels (obliterating the Bournemouth coat of arms) and below the rear platform window. Additional coats of arms were accordingly added to the lower-deck side panels, centred on bay 3. From 1966 onwards, the triangular Sunbeam manufacturer's plate was removed from the front lower maroon band.

All vehicles had the upper and lower saloon metallic gold window surrounds repainted in clonquite (light primrose) and some had their staircases and cabs repainted in dove grey (varying treatments) in an effort to brighten their interiors. As an experiment, one of the low-numbered vehicles appeared in 1962 with a light peppermint green ceiling on one deck and light salmon pink on the other.

The primrose driver's external rear view mirrors were repainted black during routine maintenance.

Notes: The 19th International Commercial Motor Transport Exhibition held at Earls Court, London, 26th September 1958 – 4th October 1958,

Sunbeam MF2B 263 is seen here at the Luckham Road reverser on 7th August 1959, ready to return to the Square on service 28. Note the ends of the wires in the background.   *J. S. King*

featured 260 (bodied and complete) and the chassis of 272 on the Sunbeam Stand (stand 63). 260 was fitted with a non-standard pressed registration number plate for the exhibition and retained this until withdrawal. 278–287 were originally allocated registration marks WRU 278–287. These ten trolleybuses were ordered while 258–277 were under construction and the thirty chassis were produced as one batch. The chassis of 278–285 were delivered to Mallard Road Depot for storage on the following dates:

278	18th March 1958	279	10th February 1959
280	16th December 1958	281	7th January 1959
282	3rd February 1959	283	7th February 1959
284	26th February 1959	285	10th March 1959

The chassis were delivered by BCT to Weymann's on 29th, 30th, 31st May and 3rd, 10th, 19th, 23rd, 25th June 1959 respectively.

Disposals: 258–287 all sold to Wombwell Diesels Co. Ltd., breakers, August 1969 for £150 each (258–267 having been withdrawn on 25th September 1966 and stored and cannibalised in the open at the rear of the Castle Lane Workshops). 286 was sold by Wombwell Diesels the same month to the London Trolleybus Preservation Society. Initially stored at Castle Lane Depot, 286 was transferred to the East Anglia Transport Museum, Carlton Colville, on 16th November 1972, where it has been restored to working order.

---

288 - 294 (HUF 45 – 48, DNJ 992 – 994)   **Delivered 1959**

Chassis: BUT 9611T two-axle. Fully-floating rear axle with conventional propellor shaft transmission.
Motor: Crompton Parkinson Ltd., Chelmsford, Essex, Type C422 light compound-wound, 120 hp.
Electrical equipment: Allen West & Co. Ltd., Brighton, 13 accelerating notches, ("*1st notch weak field; 2–10 series resistance notches; 11 opens shunt field circuit; 12–13 series field diverter notches*" Crompton Parkinson & Allen West manual 1947) without automatic acceleration. Control equipment mounted at the front of the chassis and to the left of the driver's seat.
Traction batteries: The low voltage system was fed by a 24-volt overhung CAV D.13 TB generator.
Body: Weymann highbridge double-deck metal-framed five bay construction with conventional rear, semi-vestibuled open platform combined entrance and exit. Seating H30/26R.
Length: 26 ft 0 ins   *Width:* 7ft 6 ins   *Wheelbase:* 16 ft 4ins giving a turning circle on either lock of 59 ft.
Weight: 7 tons 6 qtrs on delivery to Brighton; Bournemouth recorded 8 tons 10 cwts

Fleet Number	Registration Number	Chassis Number	Body Number	Brighton Fleet & Fleet No.	Date into Service (Brighton)	Date of Delivery to B'mth	Date into Service (B'mth)	Date of Withdrawal	Date of Disposal	Initial Disposal
288	HUF 45	9611T.027	M3399	45 (BCT)	.05.48	28.02.59	02.11.59	28.02.65	.11.65	Colbro, Rothwell
289	HUF 46	9611T.028	M3398	46 (BCT)	.05.48	24.02.59	01.10.59	31.07.65	.11.65	Colbro, Rothwell
290	HUF 47	9611T.029	M3396	47 (BCT)	.06.48	21.02.59	01.12.59	31.07.65	.11.65	Colbro, Rothwell
291	HUF 48	9611T.030	M3397	48 (BCT)	.06.48	19.02.59	01.01.60	30.05.65	.11.65	Colbro, Rothwell
292	DNJ 992	9611T.047	M7075	391 (BH&D)	.03.48	10.03.59	02.11.59	31.07.65	.11.65	Colbro, Rothwell
293	DNJ 993	9611T.048	M7076	392 (BH&D)	.03.48	04.03.59	01.06.59	31.08.65	.11.65	Colbro, Rothwell
294	DNJ 994	9611T.049	M7077	393 (BH&D)	.03.48	07.03.59	01.06.59	31.08.65	.11.65	Colbro, Rothwell

Purchased from Brighton Corporation Transport (their 45–48, becoming Bournemouth 288–291) and Brighton, Hove & District (their 391–393, originally 6391–6393, becoming Bournemouth's 292–294) these were the only second-hand trolleybuses to be operated by Bournemouth.

The Corporation vehicles had been delivered to Brighton in March and April 1948, entering service in May and June 1948. The three BH&D vehicles, the company's only post-war trolleybuses, had entered service in March 1948 and had been used primarily on the Brighton system's 41 and 42 Queens Park circular services, and the 43, 43A and 44 services to Race Hill and Black Rock, operating out of the company's Whitehawk garage. They were identical in most external respects to

Brighton Corporation's 45–52. Between 1955–58 the BH&D vehicles, delivered as 6391–6393, were renumbered 391–393.

The post-war Corporation trolleybuses were withdrawn from service in December 1958, and the BH&D vehicles in early February 1959, although the first Brighton route withdrawals (41,42, 43, 43A and 48) only took place on 24th March 1959. In February 1959, Bournemouth purchased four of Brighton Corporation's eight post-war trolleybuses, the others (49–50) going to Bradford (becoming their 802–303) and (51–52) to Maidstone (where they retained the numbers 51–52), and all three BH&D post-war vehicles. Brighton Corporation's maintenance records give some further information about their vehicles at the time of sale:

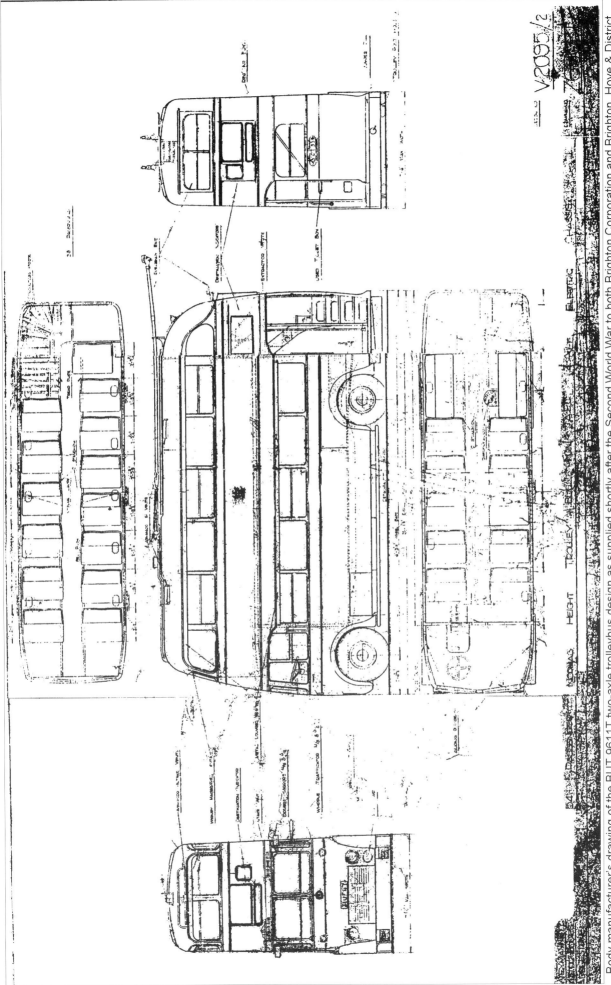

Body manufacturer's drawing of the BUT 9611T two-axle trolleybus design as supplied shortly after the Second World War to both Brighton Corporation and Brighton, Hove & District. Seven of these vehicles were acquired second-hand by Bournemouth in 1959.

Metropolitan-Cammell-Weymann

Former Brighton Corporation BUT 9611T 290 (HUF 47) displays its rebuilt rear destination box whilst on learner duties at Castle Lane Depot.   *M. J. C. Dare.*

Fleet numbers:	45 (288)	46 (289)	47 (290)	48 (291)
Mileage:	280,000	291,000	316,000	310,000
Last painted:	1957	1957	1955	1956
Overhauled:	Partial 1953	Partial 1954	Partial 1957	Partial 1957

Brakes: Two-stage rheostatic series dynamic and Westinghouse air brakes, with coasting brake set for 14 mph and run-back brake set for 1 mph (both on 1 in 9 gradient). Hand brake.

Electrics: Brecknell Willis & Co. Ltd. trolley collector gear with Anti Attrition OB type slipper heads using renewable carbon inserts were supplied with radio interference suppression to meet MoT requirements. The 15 ft long trolley booms, when restrained by the retaining hooks, extended 2 ft 3 ins beyond the rear-most part of the bodywork.

The "controlled rheostatic" Crompton Parkinson traction motor, type C422, with a one-hour rating of 120 hp at 550 volts, were incapable of regeneration.

Bodywork: Metal-framed body of five-bay highbridge construction. Conventional rear, semi-vestibuled open platform. Half-drop Widney

"Aero" windows were fitted to bays 1, 3, 5 of the upper-deck and bays 1, 3 of the lower-deck on both sides. The front upper-deck windows had bottoms hinged opening top hopper ventilators. The rear upper-deck window/emergency exit was centrally divided with a grab handle and pronounced "step" end to the roof-mounted trolley access planks. Metal rainshields were fitted above all side windows and the front upper-deck windows. Both nearside and offside driver's cab windscreens opened. Opening cab door on offside only, with curved rearward top corner (matching nearside) and sliding signalling window. Originally equipped with front and rear destination boxes of a two-blind rectangular type with ultimate destination box, that at the front being flush with the between-decks panel but that at the rear projecting beyond the curve of the body. A large single-blind rectangular side destination box was mounted over doorway. Used ticket box below the nearside vestibule window on the platform. Fluted front removable panel. The bodywork featured Weymann characteristics of the period such as the gently curving front and rear elevations, a rounded roof, flared out skirting panels to sides and rear, low-set front headlamps and curved tops to the rear platform window. Lighting was from an auxiliary generator. A bamboo trolley retrieval pole was carried centrally under the chassis. The ex-Brighton trolleybuses were virtually smaller, two-axle, versions of Bournemouth's own BUT 9641Ts (200–223).

Former Brighton, Hove & District BUT 9611T/Weymann 294 (DNJ 994) waits for entry into service at Central Depot, Southcote Road on 22nd May 1959.   *D. L. Chalk.*

Delivered with chromed front wheel rings and spot lights, the spot lamps were removed prior to 1956. In 1954, Brighton Corporation Transport increased the seating capacity of their 45–48 (and 49–52) from the original H30/24R to H30/26R. The BH&D vehicles had been delivered with this seating capacity. Rear reflectors were added in 1954.

Internal Livery: Brighton Corporation's internal livery featured dark green lower panels, except platform and stairs which were red, varnished wood window frames and Alhambrinal coverings to the ceilings. Moquette-covered tubular framed seats. Black plastic covered stanchions and grab rails. BH&D vehicles had an identical colour scheme except that the ceilings were painted white instead of being covered with Alhambrinal.

External Livery: Red lower deck and between deck panels, cream lower and upper deck window surrounds and roof. Black wings. Brighton Corporation vehicles had red wheels, BH&D black. Vehicles of both operators carried the fleet name **Brighton Hove & District Transport**.

Alterations upon purchase: Standard Bournemouth three-aperture destination, in-town "via" screen and service number equipment were added at front and rear, that at the rear being mounted within the existing, protruding destination box panel. The side destination box was retained. Flashing "orange segment" shaped trafficators mounted immediately above the lower deck maroon band on the pillar separating the driver's cab and bay 1 of the lower deck saloon, and globes mounted on the lower deck maroon band below the rear platform window, replaced the semaphore arm indicators used in Brighton. The illuminated registration number, incorporating brake lights on each side

immediately below the rear platform window, was retained. A spotlight was reinstated below the nearside headlamp.

The coasting brake was reset for 8 mph and the battery traction equipment was removed, reducing the unladen weight to 8 tons 7 cwt. Bournemouth-pattern dewirement indicators and buzzer were fitted. Horizontal metal rods about 2 ft long were added at the outer base of each trolley retaining hook to ease the task of stowing the trolley booms.

Livery changes: Upon delivery to Bournemouth, all vehicles were repainted in the then current Bournemouth Corporation Transport livery of all over primrose with two maroon bands edged in olive green below the windows of each deck, black mudguards and lifeguard rail; and maroon wheels (including the front wheel rings). Blue-shaded gold fleet numbers were applied on the cab front between the maroon band and the registration plate, and centrally on the primrose panel below the rear platform window. The Bournemouth coat of arms was carried on the upper deck side panels centrally mounted in bay 3. Black ¾ ins high legal lettering and ownership details were carried at the bottom of the nearside panel. Seating capacity information was displayed in the same style in the lower nearside corner of the panel below the rear platform window between the nearside rear reflector and the chrome bottom to the flared skirting.

Internal changes: Grab rails, the length of the lower deck ceiling, were installed. The advertising panels above the windows in the cab bulkhead were removed and replaced by additional glazing.

Disposal: 288–294 to Colbro (Dealer), Rothwell, Yorkshire, in November 1965 (at £76 each) for scrap.

---

295 - 303 (295 – 303 LJ)   **Delivered 1962**

Chassis: Sunbeam MF2B.
Motor: Crompton Parkinson Ltd., Chelmsford, Essex, type C423, 95 nhp, light compound-wound.
Electrical equipment: Allan West, incorporating automatic acceleration with 13 power notches, (1–10, resistance; 11, full power; 12–13, field weakening) and two stage rheostatic braking. An auxiliary generator/ dynamo charged the battery when the traction motor was running; the battery supplying power for the control systems and lighting.
Dewirement indicators: Green line-light and buzzer
Body: Weymann all-metal double deck highbridge construction with twin staircases, rear open platform entrance and separate front exit with air-operated folding doors placed forward of the leading axle.
Seating: H37/28D.
Length: 30 ft   *Width:* 7 ft 11¾ ins   *Unladen weight:* 8 tons 19 cwts 2 qtrs
Height over trolleybase: 15 ft 7 ins   *Wheelbase:* 15 ft 10 ins, giving a turning circle of 58 ft (65 ft over the full body)

Fleet Number	Registration Number	Chassis Number	Body Number	Date of Delivery	Date into Service	Date of Withdrawal	Date of Disposal	Initial Disposal
295	295 LJ	TFD80195	M9524	26.09.62	01.10.62	20.04.69	17.09.69	Wombwell Diesels, Wombwell
296	296 LJ	TFD80196	M9518	16.07.62	17.07.62	19.04.69	23.09.69	Wombwell Diesels, Wombwell
297	297 LJ	TFD80197	M9519	18.08.62	01.09.62	20.04.69	. .72	Bournemouth Passenger Transport Assn
298	298 LJ	TFD80198	M9522	17.09.62	03.10.62	20.04.69	09.10.69	Wombwell Diesels, Wombwell
—	—	TFD80199	M9517	—	—	—	—	Destroyed in fire at Weymann's prior to delivery.
299	299 LJ	TFD80200	M9523	24.09.62	01.10.62	19.04.69	10.12.71	Tramway Museum Society of Ireland
300	300 LJ	TFD80201	M9521	31.08.62	01.09.62	15.01.69	26.01.69	Loaned to Walsall Corporation Transport
301	301 LJ	TFD80202	M9516	12.10.62	01.11.62	20.04.69	.08.69	Bournemouth Passenger Transport Assn
302	302 LJ	TFD80203	M9525	05.10.62	01.11.62	06.02.69	07.10.69	Wombwell Diesels, Wombwell
303	303 LJ	TFD80204	M9520	24.08.62	01.09.62	20.04.69	01.10.69	Wombwell Diesels, Wombwell

The final batch of MF2B trolleybuses conformed in general dimensions and chassis details with the earlier batches purchased by the department in 1958 and 1959. There were a number of changes to the internal decor, seat covering and lighting, giving a brighter interior finish, which was to become the standard for future Bournemouth Corporation Transport motorbus orders well into the 1980s.

Chassis: see 258–287.

Brakes: Coasting, hand, run-back (equipment type CT/MP.2.), rheostatic and Westinghouse air brakes — see 258–287.

Electrics: see 258–287.

Bodywork: see 258–287, except a modification to the front exit stairhead in relation to the earlier MF2B deliveries permitted the replacement of the three single seats on the front nearside of the upper saloon with double seats, although the very front offside seat was thereby reduced from a triple to a double bench, increasing the seating capacity to 65 (37 upper saloon, 28 lower saloon). The second and third row of nearside seats were narrower than normal, and the third row (opposite the staircase) and equipped with an armrest on the gangway side.

The saloon floors were of ¾ ins tongue-and-groove softwood covered in brown linoleum. The rear entrance and front exit staircases, fabricated from 20-gauge steel, were fitted with light steel Pneustrip treads and nosings with the centre gangway in both saloons covered in brown Multislat Treadmaster.

The draught screen behind the driver's left shoulder incorporated two glazed panels: a curved one facing the passenger gangway and a second, flat pane facing the staircase.

The driver was provided with an adjustable Chapman 32 H.B. seat with cherry red hide-covered Dunlopillo cushion and squab

Destination equipment: see 259–287.

Lighting: see 258–287, except internal Philips fluorescent lighting was fitted in both saloons, the rear platform entrance and destination boxes.

Seating: Deans "Dapta" lightweight frames painted cherry red with stainless steel top rail. Latex foam filled cushions and polyether squabs were trimmed in a cherry red Connolly hide, both seat and squab being fully fluted. The seat backs were "Yellow Snug" shade Warerite. Bench seats, each having space for four passengers each, were fitted on the nearside of the lower saloon over the wheel arches and on the nearside over the rear wheel arch. There were also four rows of front-facing double seats. The upper saloon had double seats throughout, but for the rear bench above the open platform which could accommodate three passengers.

Internal Livery: The saloon ceilings on both decks were finished in off-white plastic coated Darvic panels, the single-skin domes and lower saloon front bulkheads painted to match. The pressed aluminium window cappings were stove enamelled in a jonquil colour. Interior lining panels were covered with "Red Relief" Warerite, and a matching cherry red finishing line was added at cant rail level. Cherry red paint was also used for the front and rear staircases, the driver's cab and the seat frames. All handrails and stanchions were covered in black Doverite. The interior colour scheme had been developed by the newly-appointed General Manager, Ronald Cox, during his time at Rochdale and was closely related to that undertaking's specifications.

External Livery: All over primrose, with two maroon bands (below windows of each deck) the maroon being of a slightly darker shade that that previously used. Then as 258–287, except that the moulded edging to the maroon bands was bright Buckingham green. Docker Bros. Ltd. paint was used throughout. Plain gold Gill Sans fleet numbers were carried at the front in the lower offside corner of the front panel below the offside headlight and centrally mounted on the primrose lower panel below the rear platform window.

Subsquent alterations: see 258–287, except that most of this batch (280, 295, 296, 297, 299, 300, 301, 302, 303) never received a full external repaint.

Notes: These vehicles were scheduled for delivery in 1961 but were delayed by a fire at MCW's factory at the beginning of July 1961, in which chassis TFD80199 was destroyed, TFD80198 severely damaged and TFD 80201, due to its proximity to the fire and water damage, considered suspect. Three chassis had not left Sunbeam at the time of the fire. The two damaged chassis were returned to Sunbeam for repair and eventually eight out of the nine remaining chassis were stored at Castle Lane Depot, two with the lower-deck framing mounted. They were towed back to MCW between April and June 1962. Body M9517 was never built, £3,932 16s 8d being the insurance valuation. The registration 304 LJ, which was rendered surplus by the fire, was subsequently allocated to a departmental van, as described in the table on page 229.

These nine vehicles were the only trolleybuses in England, Scotland and Wales with "reversed" registration marks, and were the last trolleybuses to be built for scheduled service use in the UK. 301 was the last trolleybus to enter scheduled service in the UK and was the last trolleybus to operate in Bournemouth.

Disposals: 300 was loaned to Walsall Corporation Transport from 26th January 1969 for experimental rebuilding as a one-man-operated, bi-

Numerically the last Bournemouth trolleybus, Sunbeam MF2B 303 (303 LJ) waits for collection from Weymann's Addlestone works in August 1962.   *Weymann/D. L. Chalk collection.*

The layout of the Sunbeam MF2B chassis is shown in this official photograph of one of the Bournemouth examples. The master controller (known as the "reverser" in Bournemouth) is under the driver's seat. The main resistances are under the floor, within the chassis frame, as is the motor. The contactor cabinet and the batteries for auxiliary electrical equipment are mounted on the offside of the chassis frame. No traction batteries (for manoeuvring away from the wires) were fitted, in common with all trolleybuses delivered new to the operator. The comparative simplicity of a trolleybus is evident.
Crompton Parkinson
D. L. Chalk collection

modal diesel/trolleybus based on the design of the Walsall General Manager and Engineer Mr R. Edgley Cox. The vehicle was to feature a single front staircase, a widened (combined) front entrance and exit, increased seating capacity on both decks and a diesel engine at the rear of the vehicle in the space provided by the former open platform and rear staircase. 300 would have been a prototype for a possible purchase of the entire Bournemouth MF2B fleet, but Walsall's plans were given up when the corporation transport undertaking was merged into the West Midlands Passenger Transport Executive in October 1969.

295, 296, 298, 300, 302, 303 were sold to Wombwell Diesels Co. Ltd., breakers, in August 1969, for £150. They were collected on the following dates:

295	17th September 1969	296	23rd September 1969
298	9th October 1969	302	7th October 1969
303	1st October 1969		

300 was collected from Walsall in February 1970 and went to Hoyle, Wombwell, breaker, in July 1970.

297 was sold to the BPTA in December 1971, for £250 and has since been stored variously at Castle Lane Depot and Bournemouth Hurn Airport. The vehicle had been offered on free loan to the Montagu Motor Museum, Beaulieu; then to the Russell-Cotes Museum and Art Gallery, Bournemouth and finally to the Portsmouth Transport Museum, but none of these bodies were able to store it at the time it was offered to them. Fully restored to operating condition, 297 has run under power at the Black Country Museum and Sandtoft Transport Centre.

299 was sold to the Transport Museum Society of Ireland in August 1969 for £200. Towed away from Bournemouth 10th December 1971 to Birkenhead for shipment to Dublin, it arrived on the museum premises at Howth, County Dublin, on 24th June 1972 and remains there (1999) in a delapidated condition.

301 was sold to the BPTA in August 1969, for £150 and has since been stored variously at Castle Lane Depot and Bournemouth Hurn Airport. Fully restored to operating condition, 301 has run under power at the Black Country Museum and Sandtoft Transport Centre and is currently on loan to the Museum of Land Transport, Leyland, Lancashire.

One of Bournemouth's Sunbeam MF2B trolleybuses of the 295 – 303 batch, being fitted with its bodywork at Weymann's Addlestone, Surrey factory in 1962.
D. L. Chalk collection

Working Timetables

The following information relates to the situation existing circa 1963.

Known internally as Master Timetables or Running Timetables, just three tables sufficed for the entire trolleybus network, namely the Bournemouth Square – Christchurch services (20–24, 37, known as the "Main Road" group); those passing Cemetery Junction (26–36, known as the "Side Routes"); and, lastly, the Ashley Road service (25). Separate timetables were issued each Summer for seasonal services 38 and 39. The "Side Routes" Master Timetable included the actual service number to be displayed, due to the existence of "ghost" numbers 27, 33 and 36 for vehicles running to and from Castle Lane Depot or operating short-workings. The Master Timetables were duplicated on foolscap sheets (double foolscap for the "Main Road" and "Side Route" groups) and, in common with all the Transport Department's stationery relating to trolleybus operation, were printed in blue.

Letter	Central	C.Lane	Pokes.	To	For	To	Ser	Finish	At	Go to
A			5.31	Fishermans Walk	5.35	Square	37	Jumpers	11.08pm	Pokes
B	6.36			Fishermans Walk	6.51	Christchurch	21	Tuckton	11.08pm	Pokes
C	6.28			Jumpers	6.43	Christchurch	21	Square	11.20pm	Central
D			5.51	Fishermans Walk	5.55	Square	37	Square	8.46am	Park (E)
E	6.50			Fishermans Walk	7.05	Tuckton	22	Tuckton	11.20pm	Pokes
F			6.14	Jumpers	6.20	Square	24	Square	9.09am	Park (E)
G			7.00	Jumpers	7.05	Christchurch	20	Tuckton	11.32pm	Pokes
I	7.05			Cross Roads	6.45	Square	22	Square	11.24pm	Central
J			7.28	Fishermans Walk	7.32	Tuckton	22	Square	9.01am	Central
K	7.09			Square	7.20	Tuckton	23	Tuckton	10.46pm	Pokes
L			7.38	Fishermans Walk	7.42	Tuckton	22	C'church	11.16pm	Pokes
M			7.47	Fishermans Walk	7.51	Tuckton	22	C'church	11.06pm	Pokes
N	7.28			Square	7.39	Tuckton	23	Jumpers	10.48pm	Pokes
O			8.07	Fishermans Walk	8.11	Tuckton	22	C'church	10.51pm	Pokes
P			7.21	Cross Roads	7.30	Square	22	Tuckton	11.23pm	Pokes
R		7.32		Jumpers	7.40	Square	24	F. Walk	11.08pm	Pokes
S		7.50		Jumpers	7.58	Square	24	Square	11.05pm	Central
T				Jumpers (A)	8.33	Square	24	Tuckton	11.28pm	Pokes
W				Jumpers (B)	10.09	Square	24	Jumpers	10.58pm (D)	
X			6.37	Jumpers	6.43	Square	24	Iford	11.04pm (F)	
Y				Jumpers (B)	9.39	Square	25	West Way	11.18pm	C.Lane
Z	6.42			Lansdowne		(C)		Iford	10.34pm(F)	
				(A) off special duty						
				(B) off service 32						
				(C) to Cen.Stn, Fishermans Walk and Tuckton						
				(D) to ser. 32						
				(E) ? work tea-time special						
				(F) off ser. 32						

A summary of the "Main oad" routes. Note that the letters are not shown in time sequence. The requirement was for 22 trolleybuses, of which 4 were shared with "Side outes" (service 32). Ten trolleybuses departed from Boscombe (Pokesdown) in the morning, and 12 ran in to Pokesdown at the end of the day.

SUMMARY OF VEHICLES REQUIRED
Monday – Saturday

Depot:	Central	Boscombe	Mallard Rd	No. of vehicles
"Main Road"	8 *	10	2	20
"Side Routes"	–	–	26	26
Ashley Road	9 *	–	–	9
Service 38	3 +	–	–	3
Service 39 (open top)	2	–	–	2
Specials	7	–	–	7
Total vehicles	29	10	28	67 + +

* included one trolleybus after working an early morning special duty, which may have been one of the seven Specials listed below

\+ these three trolleybuses could all be allocated after having worked early morning specials

\+ + allowing for notes * and + the total could be reduced to 62 vehicles, the number of dedicated specials then being only two, but this did not include any specials starting from Castle Lane (details unknown). Total requirement on a full day was probably in the order of 70 trolleybuses

Table based on Summer 1963 timetables, when the system was at its maximum extent.

Master Timetables were read horizontally across the page, only the minutes past each hour being shown. Each journey was marked with a Bus Letter denoting the vehicle working it. The first trolleybus to run out of the depot on the "Main Road" services each morning was allocated Bus Letter A, each successive run-out receiving the next letter in the alphabet. By following the Bus Letter through the table, an individual vehicle's duties throughout the day could be seen. The trolleybuses themselves did not carry any physical indication of their Bus Letter unlike the "running numbers" used by other large operators.

The "Leave Depot" column contained a single-letter code for the respective depot: B for Boscombe (Pokesdown), C for Central i.e. Southcote Road, and MR for Castle Lane (Mallard Road). The former Moordown Depot used the code M. No code was used for service 25, as all vehicles used ran-out from Central Depot.

During the day, although trolleybuses operated different services within each Master Timetable, they rarely changed group. An exception involved the "Main Road" group, where two of the four buses each hour on service 24 were in fact "Side Route" vehicles which had worked along Castle Lane to Iford (Jumpers Corner) and which, having completed a return trip to Bournemouth Square, rejoined service 32.

A dash (–) next to the Bus Letter indicated that a service operating from the Lansdowne to Bournemouth Square ran via Bath Road. On the "Main Road" alternate trolleybuses passing through Boscombe, but not alternate vehicles on each individual service, took the Bath Road, Westover Road route. The same rule applied to the Holdenhurst Road services: alternate 25 and 34 (earlier 27) trolleybuses operated via Bath and Westover Roads. The lack of alternative eastbound wiring ensured that all trolleybuses on all services from Bournemouth Square to the Lansdowne operated via Old Christchurch Road. The alternative routes were not advertised in public timetables, although trolleybuses displayed the appropriate blue or red "in town" auxiliary screen at front and rear. Exceptionally, the October 1949 timetable showed all westbound 22B services operating via Bath and Westover Roads.

A continuous shortage of crews during the period that open-top service 39 operated led to its frequent cancellation, staff only being released for seasonal services when all normal services had been fully crewed, with motorbus coastal service 12 taking priority. A gap between the return of the 3.40 pm and the 7.20 pm departure enabled the crews to be used on other services and meal break reliefs.

Top Left: Service 39 Working Timetable

Bournemouth Corporation Transport

SERVICE 39   WEEKDAYS & SUNDAYS

SUMMER 1963

Route to be followed:

Bournemouth Pier via Bath Road to Lansdowne, Boscombe, Fisherman's Walk, Cross Roads, Tuckton Bridge, Stour Road, Barrack Road, Iford, Strouden Park, Castle Lane, Five Ways, Cemetery Junction, Lansdowne and Bath Road to Bournemouth Pier.

Bus Let	Lve. Dpot	Bmth Pier	Fish Walk	Crss Rds.	Tuck ton.	Stour Road	Ifrd Circ	Str- den.	Cast Lane	Five Ways	Lans down	Bmth Pier
A	1129	1140	1158	12.3	12.6	1210	1214	1219	1223	1227	1236	1240++
A	2.20	2.35	2.53	2.58	3.01	3.05	3.09	3.14	3.18	3.22	3.31	3.35
B	50	3.05	3.23	3.28	31	35	39	44	48	53	4.01	4.05+
A		40	58	4.03	4.06	4.10	4.14	4.19	4.23	4.27	36	40++
A		7.20	7.38	7.43	7.46	7.50	7.54	7.59	8.03	8.07	8.16	8.20
B		50	8.08	8.13	8.16	8.20	8.24	8.29	33	37	46	50
A		8.20	38	43	46	50	54	59	9.03	9.07	9.16	9.20++
B		50	9.08	9.13	9.16	9.20	9.24	9.29	33	37	46	50+

Top Right

Descriptive Captions

Top Left: Working timetable for the open-top circular trolleybus service, 39, summer 1963.

Top Right: Public timetable for the open-top trolleybus service, 39, summer 1958.

Right: Working timetable for trolleybus services 20, 21, 22, 23 and 24, commencing 27th May 1963. This page – one of several – shows the mid-morning weekday roster.

Below: Public timetable for trolleybus services 20 and 24, summer 1958. This page shows the weekday service between Christchurch and the Square, and the Sunday service in both directions.

Right: Services 20, 21, 22, 23 & 24

Bournemouth Corporation Transport   Comm. 27th May, 1963.

SERVICES 20, 21, 22, 23 & 24   WEEKDAYS   Page 2.

Bus Let	X'ch dep.	Tuck ton.	Cran Road	Crss Rds.	Fish Walk	Jump ers.	Squ- are.	Bus Let	Squ- ers.	Jump ers.	Fish Walk	Crss Rds.	Cran Road	Tuck ton.	X'ch arr.
E	–	8.10	8.14	–	8.20	–	8.39	E	8.43	–	9.02	9.07	–	9.10	–
A	–	–	–	–	–	8.18	41	A	48	9.11	–	–	–	–	9.19
B	–	8.10	16	–	8.20	25	44	B	53	–	12	17	–	21	27
D	–	15	–	–	–	23	46	++							
O	–	–	20	24	–	30	49	O	55	18	–	–	–	–	–
P	–	–	26	–	30	35	54	P	58	–	17	–	22	26	–
T	From Special					33	56	T	9.01	–	21	27	–	30	–
Z	–	30	34	–	40	–	59	Z	05	28	Then 32 service				
J	–	–	–	–	–	38	9.01	++							
G	–	30	36	–	40	45	04	G	11	–	31	37	–	40	46
L	–	–	–	–	–	45	08	L	16	–	36	–	42	46	–
F	–	–	40	44	–	50	09	++							
K	–	–	46	–	50	55	14	K	20	43	–	–	–	–	51
R	45	–	–	–	–	–	15	R	21	–	41	47	–	50	–
S	–	–	50	54	–	9.00	19	S	25	48	–	–	–	–	–
I	50	–	56	–	9.00	05	24	I	31	–	51	57	–	10.0	10.6
C	9.02	–	–	–	–	9.02	25	X	35	58	Then 32 Service				
X	9.02	–	–	–	–	–	09	C	36	–	56	–	10.2	06	–
N	–	9.06	–	–	10	15	34	N	41	–	10.1	10.7	–	10	–
E	–	–	10	14	–	21	42	E	48	1011	–	–	–	–	19
O	–	–	–	–	–	19	42	O	51	–	11	17	–	20	26
M	–	10	16	–	20	26	47	H	55	18	–	–	–	–	–
A	–	23	–	–	–	30	53	A	56	–	16	–	22	26	–
P	–	–	26	–	30	36	57	P	10.1	–	21	27	–	30	–
Y	–	–	–	–	–	39	10.2	Y	05	28	Then 32 Service				
T	–	30	34	–	41	–	02	T	11	–	31	37	–	40	46
B	–	30	36	–	40	46	07	B	16	–	36	–	42	46	–
S	–	–	–	–	–	49	12	S	20	43	–	–	–	–	51
L	–	–	46	–	50	56	17	L	21	–	41	47	–	50	–
R	–	–	50	54	–	10.1	22	R	25	48	–	–	–	–	–
G	–	50	56	–	10.0	06	27	G	31	–	51	57	–	11.0	11.6
K	57	–	–	–	–	–	27	Y	35	58	Then 32 Service.				
W	–	–	–	–	–	–	09	C	36	–	56	–	11.2	06	–
C	–	10.6	–	–	10	16	37	C	41	–	11.1	11.7	–	10	–
M	–	–	–	–	–	19	42	H	48	1111	–	–	–	–	19
N	–	–	10	14	–	21	42	N	51	–	11	17	–	20	26
I	1010	16	–	–	20	26	47	I	55	18	–	–	–	–	–
E	23	–	–	–	–	–	30	E	56	–	16	–	22	26	–

Below: Services 20 and 24 Public Timetable

20 / 24

Bournemouth Square—Boscombe—Jumpers Corner—Christchurch

Bournemouth Square—Boscombe—Jumpers Corner

WEEKDAYS (continued)

(Detailed departure/arrival columns for Christchurch, Jumpers Corner, Pokesdown (Station), Boscombe (Arcade), Lansdowne, Square (Gervis Place), with times throughout the day. SUNDAYS service shown. "Then at the following mins. past each hour." * Via Central Station.)

18

Destination/Service Number Displays

The hired trolleybuses used on the first experimental route (except single-deck Thornycroft LJ 7704) and the first Sunbeam MS2s had a single-line destination indicator with service number blind above at the front and rear. From spring 1935, wooden "tramcar-style" side destination boards were carried, showing up to four points *en route* in black lettering on a white background. They were mounted on both sides of the trolleybus, above the lower maroon band at lower saloon window level. Following some experiments, in March 1935 the Transport Committee agreed that the single-line destination boxes mounted inside the platform vestibule of the trams should be salvaged and placed in the trolleybuses at the top of the rearmost lower saloon window on each side.

Sunbeam MS2 145 (probably numbered as 143) appeared at the 1935 Commercial Motor Transport Exhibition with larger destination screens, and these were adopted as standard in November 1935, using a four-line display which accomodated short workings by the judicious placing of blank lines. The screens were approx. 15 x 31 ins and the lettering on the new blinds (which latterly were up to 40 ft long) was to a common height of $2^{7}/_{8}$ ins at $3^{3}/_{8}$ ins centres, but varied in width according to the length of the word concerned. However, photographs show that, at first, some destinations continued to be shown by means of a single large name; when trolleybuses started to operate on service 30 between Bournemouth Square and Columbia Road via Winton and Talbot Village, some blinds showed the single destination **WALLISDOWN** in large letters. The displaced single-line destination blinds were re-mounted in the ex-tramcar side destination boxes. The four line destination indicators superseded the slip-boards, which were found to be illegal because they extended the effective width of the trolleybus to more than the prevailing 7ft 6ins maximum, but the holders remained in place well into the 1940s.

The place names were printed on the blinds in groups: the Bournemouth Square – Christchurch via Southbourne route for example having three blank lines followed by

BOSCOMBE
FISHERMANS WALK
SOUTHBOURNE
TUCKTON BRIDGE
CHRISTCHURCH

A trolleybus operating from the Square to Christchurch would display:

FISHERMANS WALK
SOUTHBOURNE
TUCKTON BRIDGE
CHRISTCHURCH

whereas one going only as far as Southbourne Cross Roads would show one of the blank lines followed by:

BOSCOMBE
FISHERMANS WALK
SOUTHBOURNE

Judicious use of the blank lines before and after the place name groups permitted the display of any logical combination of *en route* points and final destination.

The post-war BUTs and Sunbeam MF2Bs did not have the single-line side indicator blinds but, unlike the Sunbeam MS2s, had a third main destination display on the nearside immediately above the rear entrance platform. The only legend borne by trolleybuses not on public service was **RESERVED**, although the MS2 side blinds also included **DEPOT ONLY** and **SPECIAL**. Motorbus blinds had reduced destination displays but all service numbers, so that they could work on trolleybus routes in an emergency. There were no special displays for the various terminal points in the town centre such as Gervis Place or the Triangle, only **BOURNEMOUTH SQUARE** or **SQUARE** being included on the blinds.

The service number boxes originally used on the pre-December 1935 Sunbeam MS2 deliveries were even smaller than those used latterly at the rear immediately above the platform rear window. They featured suitably-sized number blinds. Once the service number indicator box had been moved to the nearside of the front destination display and increased in size to 10 x 10 ins, $10^{3}/_{8}$ ins-wide blinds using 8-ins high numerals and 6-ins high alphabetical suffixes were used front and rear. On the MS2s, sans serif characters were used except for the number **1**. As the aperture at the rear was smaller than that at the front, the rear number display appeared as a rather tight fit.

There is photographic evidence that, once the rectangular displays were in use, the original Sunbeam MS2 destination blinds, whilst apparently using the same style of lettering throughout, certainly used a variety of sizes e.g. **RESERVED** or **WALLISDOWN**. Their service number blinds featured "tails" on the ends of each number in an unidentifiable style of script.

There were at least two batches of indicator blinds produced in circa 1954 and 1957 to re-equip those Sunbeam MS2s that remained in the fleet, and for the second-hand ex-Brighton BUT 9611Ts. The content of the destination blinds was similar to the 1958 Sunbeam MS2 blinds and included **BOURNEMOUTH SQUARE** rather than **SQUARE**. Only the first batch had service number blinds including **A** and **B** suffixes. The figure **2** had a swan neck, and the **3** was flat-topped. Similar style inserts were used to add the service number **24** to some early Sunbeam MF2B number blinds between **31** and **32**, and to add service numbers **36** – **38** to the original BUT 9641T blinds. Only very occasionally was this type of blind found in a Sunbeam MF2B, although a handful of BUTs gained them in later life.

The BUTs and Sunbeam MF2Bs used the same size of aperture and blinds but, apparently, a different style of characters, perhaps of Gill Sans script style, the service number blinds being identifiable by their "straight-necked" **2** and "round-topped" **3**.

It is important to point out that, during the trolleybus era, commercial blind manufacturers for provincial undertakings tended to use their own styles and not a particular style of character. Additions, exchanges and repairs meant that individual vehicles of the same type frequently contained different styles on a single blind.

The introduction of services along Bath and Westover Roads in 1937 brought with it the use of auxiliary (in-town "via") indicators to denote which of the two alternative routes to the Square the trolleybus was taking. Lettering on the auxiliary blinds was generally 4 ins high. The idea of a coloured blind (at first a board in the driver's cab window) was perpetuated from tramway days, when trams to Poole via Upper Parkstone carried a red destination board. The size of the lettering was in principle unimportant, the coloured background providing the identifying feature. The **VIA BRASSEY ROAD** display presumably distinguished trolleybuses going to Wallisdown via Ensbury Park, as opposed to **VIA TALBOT VILLAGE**, or to West Way via Moordown, as opposed to the post-war **VIA CHARMINSTER ROAD** and corresponding to the unused **VIA PETERS HILL** on the Sunbeam MF2B blinds. **ALBERT ROAD ONLY** was used by trolleybuses operating via Richmond Hill and destined for the Triangle parking area, following the deletion of the Commercial Road stop for "Side Route" services. Yellow-painted boards lettered in black were carried in the driver's cab windows of those earlier trolleybuses not equipped with this display on their blinds.

Indicators were normally changed for the next journey before reaching the actual terminus, so that the trolleybus was displaying its new destination as it arrived there. It became common practice to change destination indicators on vehicles proceeding to the Square once the Lansdowne had been reached. On service 32, which in Summer 1963 worked a circular route in conjunction with service 24, Bournemouth Square – Charminster – Iford – Bournemouth Square, it was officially laid down that vehicles on service 32 would change their service number indicators to **24** immediately before reaching Strouden Park and on service 24 the **32** indicator would be displayed from Boscombe. On other circular routings e.g. 22/23 and 29/34, the indicators were

---

Sunbeam MS2
Front and rear blinds (final style)

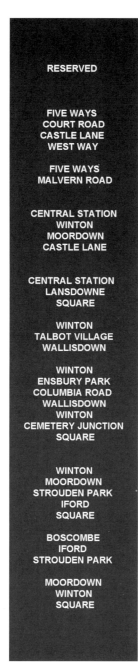

POKESDOWN *

LANSDOWNE
BOSCOMBE
IFORD
JUMPERS
CHRISTCHURCH

IFORD
BOSCOMBE
LANSDOWNE
SQUARE

BOSCOMBE
FISHERMANS WALK
SOUTHBOURNE
TUCKTON BRIDGE
CHRISTCHURCH

BOSCOMBE
FISHERMANS WALK
CRANLEIGH ROAD
TUCKTON BRIDGE
CARBERY AVENUE

FISHERMANS WALK
BOSCOMBE
LANSDOWNE
SQUARE
WESTBOURNE

CENTRAL STATION
QUEENS PARK
ASHLEY ROAD

CENTRAL STATION
SQUARE
WEST STATION
WESTBOURNE

BOURNEMOUTH PIER
VIA
LANSDOWNE
CASTLE LANE DEPOT

WINTON
MOORDOWN
CASTLE LANE
WEST WAY
CEMETERY JUNCTION
SQUARE

RESERVED

FIVE WAYS
COURT ROAD
CASTLE LANE
WEST WAY

FIVE WAYS
MALVERN ROAD

CENTRAL STATION
WINTON
MOORDOWN
CASTLE LANE

CENTRAL STATION
LANSDOWNE
SQUARE

WINTON
TALBOT VILLAGE
WALLISDOWN

WINTON
ENSBURY PARK
COLUMBIA ROAD
WALLISDOWN
WINTON
CEMETERY JUNCTION
SQUARE

WINTON
MOORDOWN
STROUDEN PARK
IFORD
SQUARE

BOSCOMBE
IFORD
STROUDEN PARK

MOORDOWN
WINTON
SQUARE

BUT 9611T and BUT 9641T
Front, platform and rear blinds

POKESDOWN *

STROUDEN PARK
IFORD

CEMETERY JUNCTION
BOURNEMOUTH SQUARE

LANSDOWNE
BOSCOMBE
IFORD
JUMPERS
CHRISTCHURCH

IFORD
BOSCOMBE
LANSDOWNE
SQUARE

BOSCOMBE
FISHERMANS WALK
SOUTHBOURNE
TUCKTON BRIDGE
CHRISTCHURCH

BOSCOMBE
FISHERMANS WALK
CRANLEIGH ROAD
TUCKTON BRIDGE
CARBERY AVENUE

FISHERMANS WALK
BOSCOMBE
LANSDOWNE
SQUARE
WESTBOURNE

BOURNEMOUTH SQUARE
CENTRAL STATION
QUEENS PARK
ASHLEY ROAD

CENTRAL STATION
SQUARE
WEST STATION
WESTBOURNE

BOURNEMOUTH PIER
VIA
LANSDOWNE
CASTLE LANE DEPOT

WINTON
MOORDOWN
CASTLE LANE
WEST WAY
CEMETERY JUNCTION
SQUARE

RESERVED

FIVE WAYS
COURT ROAD
CASTLE LANE
WEST WAY

FIVE WAYS
MALVERN ROAD

CENTRAL STATION
WINTON
MOORDOWN
CASTLE LANE

CENTRAL STATION
LANSDOWNE
SQUARE

WINTON
TALBOT VILLAGE
WALLISDOWN

WINTON
ENSBURY PARK
COLUMBIA ROAD
WALLISDOWN
WINTON
CEMETERY JUNCTION
SQUARE

WINTON
MOORDOWN
STROUDEN PARK
IFORD
SQUARE

BOSCOMBE
IFORD
STROUDEN PARK

MOORDOWN
WINTON

Notes:

* The maker's name, Norbury & Co., Statham Street, Pendlebury, appeared here.

Notes:

* The maker's name, Norbury & Co., Statham Street, Pendlebury, appeared here.

changed at the nominal terminus of the outward journey, although in all cases passengers could be conveyed through and this was indicated in the respective fare tables. Until the 1950s the conductor was responsible for changing the destination blinds in readiness for each trip, coming upstairs to open the access panels at the front for the purpose, but during the 1950s that the driver took charge of the front blinds, and new vehicles were equipped with handles in the cab roof.

The Sunbeam MF2Bs featured number blinds running from 20 to 42 with no **A** suffixes but the number **24** appeared twice, once after **23** and again after **31**, to accommodate the circular routings along Castle Lane. This facilitated a minimum of blind changing when services 24 and 32 interworked. The BUT 9641Ts brought with them a simplification in the coloured auxiliary (in-town "via") blinds, **VIA BATH AND WESTOVER ROADS** appearing on a red background,

Sunbeam MF2B
Front, platform and rear blinds

POKESDOWN *	WINTON MOORDOWN CASTLE LANE WEST WAY CEMETERY JUNCTION BOURNEMOUTH SQUARE
STROUDEN PARK IFORD	RESERVED
CEMETERY JUNCTION BOURNEMOUTH SQUARE	
LANSDOWNE BOSCOMBE IFORD JUMPERS CHRISTCHURCH	FIVE WAYS COURT ROAD CASTLE LANE WEST WAY
	FIVE WAYS MALVERN ROAD
IFORD BOSCOMBE LANSDOWNE BOURNEMOUTH SQUARE	CENTRAL STATION WINTON MOORDOWN CASTLE LANE
BOSCOMBE FISHERMANS WALK SOUTHBOURNE TUCKTON BRIDGE CHRISTCHURCH	CENTRAL STATION LANSDOWNE BOURNEMOUTH SQUARE
BOSCOMBE FISHERMANS WALK CRANLEIGH ROAD TUCKTON BRIDGE CARBERY AVENUE	WINTON TALBOT VILLAGE WALLISDOWN
	WINTON ENSBURY PARK COLUMBIA ROAD WALLISDOWN WINTON CEMETERY JUNCTION BOURNEMOUTH SQUARE
FISHERMANS WALK BOSCOMBE LANSDOWNE BOURNEMOUTH SQUARE WESTBOURNE	
	WINTON MOORDOWN STROUDEN PARK
BOURNEMOUTH SQUARE CENTRAL STATION QUEENS PARK ASHLEY ROAD	BOURNEMOUTH SQUARE
	BOSCOMBE IFORD STROUDEN PARK
CENTRAL STATION BOURNEMOUTH SQUARE WEST STATION WESTBOURNE	MOORDOWN WINTON
BOURNEMOUTH PIER VIA LANSDOWNE CASTLE LANE DEPOT	

Notes:

* The maker's name, Norbury & Co., Statham Street, Pendlebury, appeared here.

Open top Sunbeam MS2 200-202
These vehicles also had:

written in deep letters on 2 lines taking up the entire screen

Sunbeam MS2
Side destination screens (nearside and offside rear saloon windows)

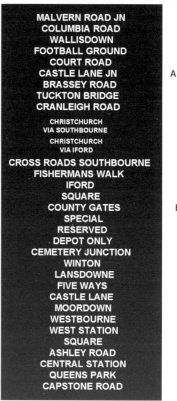

Notes:

A. Castle Lane Junction referred to Lawford Road

B. Blacked-out on the vehicle inspected (206), a move carried out in autumn 1947 (see main text).

Although the actual side destination boxes had been removed from the below staircase position on the trams, the blinds were not so old and probably originated from the single-line front and rear destination screens used on the trolleybuses between 1933 and 1935, as they did not reflect the routes opened after 1950.

VIA OLD CHRISTCHURCH ROAD on a blue background and all others on black. The MF2Bs retained solely **VIA BATH AND WESTOVER ROADS** on a coloured (red) background, all other displays being printed on black, but blind changes with the motorbus fleet ensured that a few vehicles still had blue **VIA OLD CHRISTCHURCH ROAD** blinds, in some cases only in one display. In general, less use was made of the auxiliary blinds on the trolleybuses than the motorbuses, those on the "Main Road" and Ashley Road services being restricted to the displays **VIA BATH AND WESTOVER ROADS** or **VIA OLD CHRISTCHURCH ROAD** while those on the "Side Routes" displayed a blank black screen (white on the Sunbeam MF2Bs). Special indications were used as appropriate.

Service number **39** was added to the three open-top MS2 conversions, whilst the main screen showed **CIRCULAR TOUR** in large letters, but when the service started to pick up and set down *en route* normal indications were used. On 202, the service number **39** was added on a length of pale green material used for the open-top motorbus coastal service.

Although there were detail differences over the years, typical blind displays for the three main types of trolleybus are shown in this Appendix.

Sunbeam MS2
Auxiliary blinds

Notes:

A   This display was on an additional piece of blind sewn in.

B   Open top MS2 202 (at least) had a dark red background to this display. This was possibly an older display intended for use on services 26A, 28A, 30 and 30A when they first commenced.

C   White letters on blue blind.

D   White letters on red blind.

E   White letters on green blind.

F   White letters on orange blind.

Sunbeam MF2B
Auxiliary blinds

Notes:

A.   White letters on red blind

Service Number Blinds

Sunbeam MS2	BUT 9611T/9641T	Sunbeam MF2B
20	20	20
24	24	21
24A	24A	22
21	21	23
21A	21A	24
22	22	25
23 (A)	22A	26
23A	22B	27
25	23	28
25A	23A	29
26	25	30
26A	25A	31
27	26	24
28A	26A	32
29	27	33
30	27A	34
30A	28	35
31	28A	36
24	29	37
32	30	38
33	30A	39
34	31	40 (C)
35	24	41 (C)
36	32	42 (C)
37	33	
38 (B)	34	
	35	
	36	
	37	
	38	

Notes:

A   An MS2 was recorded in March 1954 as having numbers **22A** and **22B** between **22** and **23**. After 30A, numbers **31 35** had been added, presumably in the mid-1950s. Only on to completely new blinds was **24** repeated after **31**. Originally such numbers as **22B**, **25B** and so on brought into use during the lifetime of the trolleybus were added by sewing on additional lengths, sometimes at the end of the blind and out of numerical sequence.

B   Open-top MS2s 200-202 also had the number **39** and in the case of 202 this was printed on a piece of green material.

C   Intended for any additional services.

Services and Service Alterations

The information in this Appendix was kindly supplied by David Chalk.

Service 20

22.07.43	Trolleybus service commenced Bournemouth Square to Christchurch via Old Christchurch Road, Lansdowne, Christchurch Road, Boscombe, Iford, Jumpers Corner, Barrack Road, Stour Road, Bargates and High Street. Alternate journeys inwards to Bournemouth Square operated via Bath Road and Westover Road or Old Christchurch Road
14.09.59	Extended from Bournemouth Square to Westbourne
14.11.60	Curtailed to Bournemouth Square
11.04.65	Sunday service withdrawn
13.06.65	Sunday service re-introduced and subsequently operated each summer only
19.04.69	Last day of operation by trolleybus

Service 21

08.04.36	Trolleybus service commenced Bournemouth Square to Christchurch via Old Christchurch Road, Lansdowne, Christchurch Road, Boscombe, Seaborne Road, Southbourne Grove, Southbourne Road, Belle Vue Road, Foxholes Road, Tuckton Bridge, Stour Road, Bargates and High Street
08.05.37	Alternate journeys inwards to Bournemouth Square diverted via Bath Road and Westover Road instead of Old Christchurch Road
18.10.67	Diverted outwards at Fisherman's Walk via Parkwood Road, Southbourne Road and Beresford Road instead of Seabourne Road
11.02.68	Fisherman's Walk diversion ceased
19.04.69	Last day of operation by trolleybus

Service 21A

08.04.36	Trolleybus service commenced Westbourne to Christchurch via Poole Road, Bournemouth Square, Old Christchurch Road, Lansdowne, Christchurch Road, Boscombe, Seaborne Road, Southbourne Grove, Southbourne Road, Belle Vue Road, Foxholes Road, Tuckton Bridge, Stour Road, Bargates and High Street
08.05.37	Alternate journeys inwards to Bournemouth Square diverted via Bath Road and Westover Road instead of Old Christchurch Road
25.02.40	Service suspended
10.04.47	Service re-introduced Westbourne to Tuckton Bridge via original route
03.10.48	Last day of operation

Service 22

23.12.35	Trolleybus service commenced Bournemouth Square to Southbourne Cross Roads via Old Christchurch Road, Lansdowne, Christchurch Road, Boscombe, Seaborne Road, Southbourne Grove and Southbourne Road
08.04.36	Service suspended
01.10.37	Service re-introduced, with alternate journeys inwards to Bournemouth Square diverted via Bath Road and Westover Road instead of Old Christchurch Road
04.10.48	Extended from Southbourne Cross Roads to Tuckton Bridge via Belle Vue Road and Foxholes Road
18.10.67	Diverted outwards at Fisherman's Walk via Parkwood Road, Southbourne Road and Beresford Road instead of Seabourne Road
11.02.68	Fisherman's Walk diversion ceased
19.04.69	Last day of operation by trolleybus

Service 22A

23.12.35	Trolleybus service commenced Westbourne to Southbourne Cross Roads via Poole Road, Bournemouth Square, Old Christchurch Road, Lansdowne, Christchurch Road, Boscombe, Seabourne Road, Southbourne Grove and Southbourne Road
08.04.36	Service suspended
01.10.37	Service re-introduced, with alternate journeys inwards to Bournemouth Square diverted via Bath Road and Westover Road instead of Old Christchurch Road
25.02.40	Service suspended
10.04.47	Service Westbourne and Southbourne Crossroads re-introduced
03.10.48	Last day of operation

Service 22B

16.08.48	Trolleybus service commenced Bournemouth Square to Tuckton Bridge via Old Christchurch Road, Lansdowne, Christchurch Road, Boscombe, Seabourne Road, Beresford Road, Beaufort Road, Cranleigh Road and Tuckton Road
04.10.48	Extended from Bournemouth Square to Westbourne via Poole Road
27.05.50	Curtailed to Bournemouth Square
01.03.56	Service renumbered 23 (ii)

Service 23 (i)

21.11.35	Trolleybus service commenced Bournemouth Square to Fisherman's Walk via Old Christchurch Road, Lansdowne, Christchurch Road, Boscombe and Seabourne Road
08.05.37	Alternate journeys inwards to Bournemouth Square diverted via Bath Road and Westover Road instead of Old Christchurch Road
01.10.37	Service reduced to peak hours only
07.04.50	Summer season supplementary service Bournemouth Pier to Fisherman's Walk via Exeter Road, Bournemouth Square, Old Christchurch Road (outwards), Lansdowne, Christchurch Road, Boscombe and Seabourne Road introduced. Inwards services operated from Lansdowne to Bournemouth Pier via Bath Road
12.04.50	Summer season supplementary service suspended
27.05.50	Summer season supplementary service reinstated
02.10.50	Summer season supplementary service suspended
23.03.51	Summer season supplementary service reinstated
28.03.51	Summer season supplementary service suspended
12.05.51	Summer season supplementary service reinstated
15.05.51	Summer season supplementary service suspended
04.06.51	Summer season supplementary service reinstated
01.10.51	Summer season supplementary service suspended
1952	Summer season supplementary service operated Good Friday – Easter Monday
31.05.52	Summer season supplementary service reinstated
29.09.52	Summer season supplementary service suspended
1953	Summer season supplementary service operated Good Friday – Easter Monday
23.05.53	Summer season supplementary service reinstated
21.09.53	Summer season supplementary service suspended and renumbered 35 (i)

Service 23 (ii)

01.03.56	Trolleybus service commenced Bournemouth Square to Tuckton Bridge via Old Christchurch Road, Lansdowne, Christchurch Road, Boscombe, Seabourne Road, Beresford Road, Beaufort Road, Cranleigh Road and Tuckton Road
18.10.67	Diverted outwards at Fisherman's Walk via Parkwood Road and Southbourne Road instead of Beresford Road
11.02.68	Fisherman's Walk diversion ceased
19.04.69	Last day of operation by trolleybus

Service 23A

01.01.36	Trolleybus service commenced Westbourne to Fisherman's Walk via Poole Road, Bournemouth Square, Old Christchurch Road, Lansdowne, Christchurch Road, Boscombe, Seabourne Road and Southbourne Road
08.05.37	Alternate journeys inwards to Bournemouth Square diverted via Bath Road and Westover Road instead of Old Christchurch Road
30.09.37	Last day of operation

Service 24

25.03.35	Trolleybus service commenced Westbourne to Iford Bridge via Poole Road, Bournemouth Square, Old Christchurch Road, Lansdowne, Christchurch Road, Boscombe and Iford
01.01.36	Curtailed to Bournemouth Square (and replaced by service 24A)
08.05.37	Alternate journeys inwards to Bournemouth Square diverted via Bath Road and Westover Road instead of Old Christchurch Road
07.08.44	Extended from Iford Bridge to Jumpers Corner, Stourvale Avenue
28.02.66	Reduced to weekday peak hours only operation
19.04.69	Last day of operation by trolleybus

Service 24A

01.01.36	Trolleybus service commenced Westbourne to Iford Bridge via Poole Road, Bournemouth Square, Old Christchurch Road, Lansdowne, Christchurch Road, Boscombe and Iford
08.05.37	Alternate journeys inwards to Bournemouth Square diverted via Bath Road and Westover Road instead of Old Christchurch Road
01.11.37	Service withdrawn

Service 25

13.05.33	Experimental (un-numbered) trolleybus service commenced Bournemouth Square to Westbourne via Poole Road
27.02.34	Service number 25 allocated, for use with a new design of ticket machine
22.06.34	Extended eastwards Bournemouth Square to Ashley Road, Boscombe, via Old Christchurch Road, Lansdowne, Holdenhurst Road and Ashley Road
22.10.34	Some journeys curtailed to Queen's Park Golf Pavilion, Holdenhurst Road
01.03.36	Curtailed to Bournemouth Square (journeys to Westbourne replaced by service 25A)
08.05.37	Alternate journeys inwards to Bournemouth Square diverted via Bath Road and Westover Road instead of Old Christchurch Road
01.11.37	Service Bournemouth Square to Ashley Road, Boscombe withdrawn
07.04.50	Summer season supplementary service 25 introduced, Bournemouth Pier to Queen's Park Golf Pavilion via Lansdowne and Holdenhurst Road
12.04.50	Service suspended
27.05.50	Summer season supplementary service 25 reinstated, Bournemouth Pier to Queen's Park Golf Pavilion via Lansdowne and Holdenhurst Road
01.10.50	Last day of operation
01.07.51	Service number 25 reintroduced for journeys to Queen's Park Golf Pavilion, Holdenhurst Road
01.03.56	Services 25 and 25A combined for all journeys Westbourne to Ashley Road, Boscombe, or Queen's Park Golf Pavilion, Holdenhurst Road, via Poole Road, Bournemouth Square, Old Christchurch Road, Lansdowne, Holdenhurst Road and Ashley Road (for journeys terminating at Boscombe). Alternate journeys inwards to Bournemouth Square operated via Bath Road and Westover Road instead of Old Christchurch Road
30.09.63	Journeys to Queen's Park Golf Pavilion, Holdenhurst Road, withdrawn
05.04.65	Journeys to Queen's Park Golf Pavilion, Holdenhurst Road, reinstated on weekdays only
08.05.65	Journeys to Queen's Park Golf Pavilion, Holdenhurst Road, withdrawn
12.09.65	Last day of operation by trolleybus

Service 25A

01.03.36	Trolleybus service commenced Westbourne to Ashley Road, Boscombe, via Old Christchurch Road, Lansdowne, Holdenhurst Road and Ashley Road
08.05.37	Alternate journeys inwards to Bournemouth Square diverted via Bath Road and Westover Road instead of Old Christchurch Road
25.02.40	Journeys to Queen's Park Golf Pavilion, Holdenhurst Road, suspended
01.11.48	Journeys to Queen's Park Golf Pavilion, Holdenhurst Road, reinstated
30.06.51	Service number 25A ceased to be used for journeys to Queen's Park Golf Pavilion, Holdenhurst Road
01.03.56	Services 25 and 25A combined as service 25

Service 25B

28.07.38	Trolleybus service commenced Westbourne to Fisherman's Walk via Poole Road, Bournemouth Square, Old Christchurch Road, Lansdowne, Holdenhurst Road, Ashley Road, Christchurch Road and Seabourne Road
08.05.37	Alternate journeys inwards to Bournemouth Square diverted via Bath Road and Westover Road instead of Old Christchurch Road
24.02.40	Last day of operation

Service 26

07.06.35	Trolleybus service commenced Bournemouth Square to Moordown Depot via Richmond Hill and Wimborne Road
15.04.37	Extended to Castle Lane West, Lawford Road via Wimborne Road
09.10.39	Curtailed to Moordown Depot
30.03.47	Town Centre terminus extended from Bournemouth Square to Triangle via Commercial Road westbound and Avenue Road eastbound
12.10.53	Re-extended to Castle Lane West, Lawford Road via Wimborne Road
05.04.65	Service reduced to Sunday mornings and weekday peak hours only
05.03.66	Last day of trolleybus operation

Service 26A

19.10.38	Trolleybus service commenced Bournemouth Square to West Way via Richmond Hill, Wimborne Road and Castle Lane West
30.03.47	Town Centre terminus extended from Bournemouth Square to Triangle via Commercial Road westbound and Avenue Road eastbound
01.03.56	Service 26A renumbered 27 (ii)

Service 27 (i)

28.06.35	Trolleybus service commenced Bournemouth Square to Moordown Depot via Old Christchurch Road, Lansdowne, St. Paul's Road, Lansdowne Road, Cemetery Junction and Wimborne Road
11.03.37	Extended to Lawford Road, junction with Castle Lane West
08.05.37	Alternate journeys inwards to Bournemouth Square diverted via Bath Road and Westover Road instead of Old Christchurch Road
15.04.37	Curtailed to Moordown Depot
06.05.46	Re-extended to Lawford Road, junction with Castle Lane West
01.03.56	Service 27 (i) renumbered 34

Service 27 (ii)

01.03.56	Trolleybus service commenced Triangle to West Way via Bournemouth Square, Richmond Hill, Wimborne Road and Castle Lane West
26.03.56	Service suspended
22.07.56	Service Triangle to West Way reinstated
17.09.56	Service suspended
30.09.63	Service reinstated and extended along Castle Lane West to Broadway
25.09.66	Last day of trolleybus operation

Service 28

23.08.35	Trolleybus service commenced Bournemouth Square to Broadway, Castle Lane, via Richmond Hill, Wimborne Road and Charminster Road
30.03.47	Town Centre terminus extended from Bournemouth Square to Triangle via Commercial Road westbound and Avenue Road eastbound
07.04.50	Some journeys extended to Bournemouth Pier and operated to Five Ways via Bath Road (inwards and outwards), Lansdowne, St. Pauls Road, Lansdowne Road and Charminster Road
12.04.50	Service Bournemouth Pier to Five Ways suspended
27.05.50	Service Bournemouth Pier to Five Ways reinstated
01.10.50	Last day of trolleybus operation Bournemouth Pier to Five Ways
25.09.66	Last day of trolleybus operation

Service 28A

19.10.38	Trolleybus service commenced Bournemouth Square to West Way via Richmond Hill, Wimborne Road, Charminster Road, Broadway and Castle Lane West
30.03.47	Town Centre terminus extended from Bournemouth Square to Triangle via Commercial Road westbound and Avenue Road eastbound
01.03.56	Service 28A renumbered 29

Service 29

01.03.56	Trolleybus service commenced Bournemouth Square to West Way via Richmond Hill, Wimborne Road, Charminster Road, Broadway and Castle Lane West
30.09.63	Extended along Castle Lane West to junction with Lawford Road
25.09.66	Last day of trolleybus operation

Service 29

05.04.37	Trolleybus service commenced Bournemouth Square to Malvern Road, junction with Charminster Avenue, via Richmond Hill, Wimborne Road, Charminster Road, Five Ways and Charminster Avenue
30.03.47	Town Centre terminus extended from Bournemouth Square to Triangle via Commercial Road westbound and Avenue Road eastbound
01.03.56	Service 29 renumbered 35

Service 30

15.04.38	Trolleybus service commenced Bournemouth Square to Columbia Road, junction with Kinson Road via Richmond Hill, Wimborne Road, Talbot Road, Wallisdown Road and Kinson Lane
30.03.47	Town Centre terminus extended from Bournemouth Square to Triangle via Commercial Road westbound and Avenue Road eastbound
31.12.56	Curtailed to Winton Banks, Alma Road, to Columbia Road via Talbot Road, Wallisdown Road and Kinson Lane, except at weekday peak hours when services continued to operate to/from Triangle via Bournemouth Square
15.07.57	All journeys re-extended to Triangle
15.09.57	Curtailed to Winton Banks, Alma Road, to Columbia Road via Talbot Road, Wallisdown Road and Kinson Lane, except at weekday peak hours when services continued to operate to/from Triangle via Bournemouth Square
14.07.58	All journeys re-extended to Triangle
21.09.58	Curtailed to Winton Banks, Alma Road, to Columbia Road via Talbot Road, Wallisdown Road and Kinson Lane, except at weekday peak hours when services continued to operate to/from Triangle via Bournemouth Square
13.07.59	All journeys re-extended to Triangle
13.09.59	Curtailed to Winton Banks, Alma Road, to Columbia Road via Talbot Road, Wallisdown Road and Kinson Lane except, at weekday peak hours when services continued to operate to/from Triangle via Bournemouth Square
06.03.66	Motorbuses took over Sunday service
16.04.66	Last day of trolleybus operation

Service 30A

08.04.39	Trolleybus service commenced Bournemouth Square to Columbia Road, junction with Kinson Road via Richmond Hill, Wimborne Road, Ensbury Park Road and Columbia Road
30.03.47	Town Centre terminus extended from Bournemouth Square to Triangle via Commercial Road westbound and Avenue Road eastbound
07.04.50	Summer season supplementary service introduced, Bournemouth Pier to Columbia Road, junction with Kinson Road via Bath Road (inwards and outwards), Lansdowne, St. Paul's Road, Lansdowne Road, Cemetery Junction, Wimborne Road, Ensbury Park Road and Columbia Road introduced
12.04.50	Summer season supplementary service suspended
27.05.50	Summer season supplementary service reinstated
02.10.50	Summer season supplementary service suspended
1952	Summer season supplementary service operated Good Friday – Easter Monday
31.05.52	Summer season supplementary service reinstated
29.09.52	Summer season supplementary service suspended
1953	Summer season supplementary service operated Good Friday – Easter Monday
23.05.53	Summer season supplementary service reinstated
21.09.53	Summer season supplementary service suspended and renumbered 34 (i)
01.03.56	Service 30A Bournemouth Square to Columbia Road numbered 31 (iii)

Service 31 (i)

15.10.51	Trolleybus service commenced Triangle to Bournemouth Square, clockwise, in conjunction with service 32 via Bournemouth Square, Richmond Hill, Wimborne Road, Charminster Road, Broadway, Castle Lane, Iford, Christchurch Road, Boscombe and Lansdowne
11.10.53	Last day of operation

Service 31 (ii)

12.10.53	Trolleybus service commenced Triangle to Iford via Bournemouth Square, Richmond Hill, Wimborne Road, Charminster Road Broadway and Castle Lane
01.03.56	Service 31 (ii) renumbered 32 (ii)

Service 31 (iii)

01.03.56	Trolleybus service commenced Triangle to Columbia Road, junction with Kinson Road, via Bournemouth Square, Richmond Hill, Wimborne Road, Ensbury Park Road and Columbia Road
25.09.66	Last day of trolleybus operation

Service 32 (i)

15.10.51	Trolleybus service commenced Bournemouth Square to Triangle, anti-clockwise, in conjunction with service 31 (i) via Lansdowne, Boscombe, Christchurch Road, Iford, Castle Lane, Broadway, Charminster Road, Wimborne Road, Richmond Hill and Bournemouth Square
11.10.53	Last day of operation

Service 32 (ii)

12.10.53	Trolleybus service commenced Triangle to Iford Bridge via Bournemouth Square, Richmond Hill, Wimborne Road, Charminster Road, Broadway and Castle Lane
06.10.56	Extended from Iford Bridge to Jumpers Corner, Stourvale Avenue
30.01.61	Minimum fare introduced, outwards on weekdays 4.30 pm – 6.30 pm
05.04.65	Curtailed to Iford Roundabout, junction with Castle Lane East
25.09.66	Last day of trolleybus operation

Service 33

23.05.53	Trolleybus service commenced Winton to Castle Lane East, junction with Holdenhurst Road, via Wimborne Road, Moordown and Castle Lane
12.10.53	Extended to Triangle and Iford via Bournemouth Square, Richmond Hill, Wimborne Road, Moordown and Castle Lane
22.09.58	Service reduced to operate at weekday peak hours only
28.09.63	Last day of operation

Service 34 (i)

05.06.54	Summer season supplementary trolleybus service commenced Bournemouth Pier to Columbia Road, junction with Kinson Road, via Bath Road (inwards and outwards), Lansdowne, St. Paul's Road, Lansdowne Road, Cemetery Junction, Wimborne Road, Ensbury Park Road and Columbia Road
20.09.54	Summer season supplementary service suspended
28.05.55	Summer season supplementary service reinstated
18.09.55	Last day of operation

Service 34 (ii)

01.03.56	Trolleybus service commenced Bournemouth Square to Lawford Road, junction with Castle Lane West via Old Christchurch Road, Lansdowne, St.Paul's Road, Lansdowne Road, Cemetery Junction and Wimborne Road with alternate journeys inwards to Bournemouth Square via Bath Road and Westover Road or Old Christchurch Road
26.03.56	Extended to West Way via Castle Lane West
17.09.56	Extended to Broadway via Castle Lane West
31.12.56	Curtailed at Lansdowne instead of Bournemouth Square
29.09.63	Last day of operation

Service 35 (i)

16.04.54	Summer season trolleybus service commenced Bournemouth Pier to Fisherman's Walk via Exeter Road, Bournemouth Square, Old Christchurch Road (outwards), Lansdowne, Christchurch Road, Boscombe and Seabourne Road. Inward journeys operated from Lansdowne to Bournemouth Pier via Bath Road
19.04.54	Summer season service suspended
05.06.54	Summer season service reinstated
20.09.54	Summer season service suspended
1955	Summer season service operated Good Friday – Easter Monday
28.05.55	Summer season service reinstated
19.09.55	Summer season service suspended and renumbered 38

Service 35 (ii)

01.03.56	Trolleybus service commenced Triangle to Malvern Road, junction with Charminster Avenue, via Avenue Road eastbound and Commercial Road westbound, Bournemouth Square, Richmond Hill, Wimborne Road, Charminster Road, Five Ways and Charminster Avenue
05.04.65	Service suspended. Last day of trolleybus operation

Service 36

17.09.56	Trolleybus service commenced Lansdowne to Columbia Road, junction with Kinson Road, via St. Paul's Road, Lansdowne Road, Cemetery Junction, Wimborne Road, Ensbury Park Road and Columbia Road
28.09.63	Last day of trolleybus operation

Service 37

21.11.35	Trolleybus service commenced Bournemouth Square to Fisherman's Walk via Old Christchurch Road, Lansdowne, Christchurch Road, Boscombe, Seabourne Road, peak hours only, with alternate journeys inwards to Bournemouth Square via Bath Road and Westover Road instead of Old Christchurch Road
30.09.63	Service 37 ceased to be advertised, although un-numbered peak hour extras Bournemouth Square to Fisherman's Walk continued to operate until 20th April 1969

Service 38

1956	Summer season trolleybus service operated Good Friday – Easter Monday, Bournemouth Pier to Fisherman's Walk via Exeter Road, Bournemouth Square, Old Christchurch Road (outwards), Lansdowne, Christchurch Road, Boscombe and Seabourne Road. Inward journeys operated from Lansdowne to Bournemouth Pier via Bath Road
19.05.56	Summer season service reinstated
17.09.56	Summer season service suspended
1957	Summer season service operated Good Friday – Easter Monday
03.06.57	Summer season service reinstated
16.09.57	Summer season service suspended
1958	Summer season service operated Good Friday – Easter Monday
24.05.58	Summer season service reinstated
22.09.58	Summer season service suspended
16.05.59	Summer season service reinstated
14.09.59	Summer season service suspended
04.07.60	Summer season service reinstated and extended to Christchurch via Southbourne Road, Belle Vue Road, Foxholes Road, Stour Road, Bargates and High Street
12.09.60	Summer season service suspended
12.06.61	Summer season service reinstated and curtailed to operate Bournemouth Pier to Carbery Avenue, Tuckton, via Exeter Road, Bournemouth Square, Old Christchurch Road (outwards), Lansdowne, Christchurch Road, Boscombe, Seabourne Road, Beresford Road, Beaufort Road and Cranleigh Road. Inwards services operated from Lansdowne to Bournemouth Pier via Bath Road
11.09.61	Summer season service suspended
09.06.62	Summer season service reinstated, operating outwards from Bournemouth Pier to the Lansdowne via Bath Road instead of via Exeter Road, Bournemouth Square and Old Christchurch Road
10.09.62	Summer season service suspended
27.05.63	Summer season service reinstated
30.09.63	Summer season service suspended
08.06.64	Summer season service reinstated using open-top trolleybuses
23.08.64	Last day of operation

Service 39

24.05.58	Summer season open-top trolleybus circular tour commenced, operating to/from Bournemouth Pier clockwise only via Exeter Road, Bournemouth Square, Richmond Hill, Wimborne Rd, Charminster Rd, Broadway, Castle Lane, Iford, Barrack Rd, Tuckton Bridge, Southbourne, Fisherman's Walk, Seabourne Rd, Boscombe, Christchurch Rd, Lansdowne and Bath Road, with no scheduled stops
07.07.58	Tour commenced operating as a circular service, picking up and setting down *en route*
22.09.58	Summer season service suspended
16.05.59	Summer season service reinstated
29.06.59	Summer season open-top trolleybus circular service re-routed to operate anti-clockwise to/from Bournemouth Pier via Bath Road, Lansdowne, Christchurch Road, Boscombe, Seabourne Road, Fisherman's Walk, Southbourne, Tuckton Bridge, Barrack Road, Iford, Castle Lane, Broadway, Charminster Road, Lansdowne Road, St. Paul's Road, Holdenhurst Road, Lansdowne and Bath Road
14.09.59	Summer season circular service suspended
04.06.60	Summer season circular service reinstated
12.09.60	Summer season circular service suspended
12.06.61	Summer season circular service reinstated
11.09.61	Summer season circular service suspended
09.06.62	Summer season circular service reinstated
10.09.62	Summer season circular service suspended
27.05.63	Summer season circular service reinstated
29.09.63	Last day of operation

Fares, Fare Tables and Tickets

FARES

The 20th April 1934 Transport Committee meeting recommended that new fares be charged on the Square – Ashley Road trolleybuses:

	Present tram fare	Proposed
Square to Lansdowne	1d	1d
Lansdowne to Capstone Road	1d	1d
Capstone Road to Ashley Road terminus	1d	1d
Square to Central Station	1½d	– *
* Stage to be extended to read:		
Square to Capstone Road	2d	1½d
Lansdowne to Queen's Park Corner	1½d	1½d
Central Station to Ashley Road terminus	1½d	1½d
Square to Capstone Road	2d	– *
* Stage to be extended to read:		
Square to Queen's Park Corner	2½d	2d
Lansdowne to Ashley Road terminus	2d	2d
Square to Ashley Rd terminus	3d	2½d

On 22nd February 1935, in preparation for the opening of the Lansdowne – Iford Bridge trolleybus route, the Transport Committee approved the following fare stages (shown with an asterisk) and stops:

Iford Post Office *	Square *
Exton Road	Bournemouth Arcade (Albert Rd)
Warnford Road	Horseshoe Common
Hambledon Road	Trinity Church
Harewood Avenue *	Stafford Road
Clarence Park Road	Lansdowne *
Pokesdown Station	St. Swithun's Road
Hannington Road	Derby Road
Parkwood Road *	Boscombe Gardens
Crabton Close Road	St. John's Church
Ashley Road	Boscombe Arcade *
Sea Road *	Ashley Road
St. John's Church	Crabton Close Road
Boscombe Gardens	Parkwood Road *
Derby Road	Hannington Road
St. Swithun's Road	New Era Laundry
Lansdowne *	Harewood Avenue *
Stafford Road	Hambledon Road
Trinity Church	Warnford Road
Grand Hotel	Exton Road
St. Peter's Church	Iford Post Office *
Square *	

They went on to consider fares and fare stages on all the proposed trolleybus services, recommending that the time up to which return fares may be issued be extended from 8.30 am to 8.45 am. Service numbers had clearly already been asigned.

24   Square – Iford via Christchurch Road

Ordinary Fares:–

Square and Lansdowne	1d
Lansdowne and Boscombe Arcade	1d
Boscombe Arcade and Harewood Avenue	1d
Harewood Avenue and Iford Bridge	1d
Lansdowne and Parkwood Road	1½d
Boscombe Arcade and Iford Bridge	1½d
Square and Boscombe Arcade	2d
Square and Parkwood Road	2½d
Lansdowne and Iford Bridge	2½d
Square and Iford Bridge	3½d

and vice versa

Workmen's Fares and Returns:–

	Workmen's	Returns
Square and Boscombe Arcade	1d	2d
Lansdowne and Harewood Avenue	1d	2d
Boscombe Arcade and Iford Bridge	1d	2d
Square and Harewood Avenue	1½d	3d
Lansdowne and Iford Bridge	1½d	3d
Square and Iford Bridge	2d	4d

and vice versa

Return Tickets at Reduced Fares:–

A Return Ticket was issued to any passenger on request boarding any trolleybus at any place at which the trolleybus should be, according to the timetable in force, before and including 8.45 am on any day, excepting Sundays, Christmas Day, Good Friday and Bank Holidays. Return Tickets were available for return journeys at any time on day of issue only, within the same stage only.

Fares:– 2d for any 1d workmen's stage
3d for any 1½d workmen's stage
4d for any 2d workmen's stage

Conditions:–

The tickets were not transferable.

The tickets were issued subject to the Corporation Bye-laws.

Through tickets were only issued and accepted on trolleybuses.

Return tickets, if mutilated, were not accepted on the return journey.

Workmen's Tickets:–

Workmen's hours: On weekdays but not on Sundays, Christmas Day, Good Friday or Bank Holidays, before 8 am; between 12 noon and 2 pm, Saturdays only; other days between 4.30 pm and 6 pm from 1st November to 28th February, and between 5 pm and 6.30 pm from 1st March to 31st October.

26   Square – Moordown via Wimborne Road

Ordinary Fares:–

Square and Cemetery Junction	1d
Top of Richmond Hill and Talbot Avenue	1d
Cemetery Junction and Peter's Hill	1d
Talbot Avenue and Brassey Road	1d
Peter's Hill and Moordown Post Office or Depot	1d
Brassey Road and Moordown (Castle Lane Jn.)	1d
Square and Peter's Hill	1½d
Cemetery Junction and Moordown PO or Depot	1½d
Talbot Avenue and Moordown (Castle Lane Jn.)	1½d
Square and Brassey Road	2d
Cemetery Junction and Moordown (Castle Lane)	2d
Square and Moordown Post Office or Depot	2½d
Square and Moordown (Castle Lane Jn.)	3d

and vice versa

Workmen's Fares and Returns:–

	Workmen's	Returns
Cemetery Jn and Moordown PO or Depot	1d	2d
Square and Brassey Road	1d	2d
Talbot Avenue and Moordown	1d	2d
(Castle Lane Junction)		
Square and Moordown PO or Depot	1½d	3d
Top of Richmond Hill and Moordown	1½d	3d
(Castle Lane)		
Square and Moordown	2d	4d
(Castle Lane Junction)		

and vice versa

28   Square – Castle Lane (Broadway Hotel) via Charminster Road

Ordinary Fares:–

Square and Cemetery Junction	1d
Top of Richmond Hill and King's Road	1d
Cemetery Junction and Five Ways	1d
King's Road and Court Road	1d
Five Ways and Castle Lane	1d
Square and King's Road	1½d
Top of Richmond Hill and Five Ways	1½d
Cemetery Junction and Castle Lane	1½d
Square and Court Road	2d
Square and Castle Lane	2½d

Special Transfer:–

King's Road and Holdenhurst Road Junction	1d

and vice versa

Workmen's Fares and Returns:–

	Workmen's	Returns
Square and Five Ways	1d	2d
Top of Richmond Hill and Court Road	1d	2d
Cemetery Junction and Castle Lane	1d	2d
Square and Castle Lane	1½d	3d

and vice versa

27   Lansdowne – Moordown via St. Paul's Rd and Wimborne Rd

Ordinary Fares:–

Lansdowne and Cemetery Junction	1d
Cemetery Junction and Peter's Hill	1d
Peter's Hill and Moordown Post Office or Depot	1d
Talbot Avenue and Brassey Road	1d
Holdenhurst Road Junction and Talbot Avenue	1d
Brassey Road and Moordown (Castle Lane Jn.)	1d
Lansdowne and Peter's Hill	1½d
Cemetery Junction and Moordown PO or Depot	1½d
Talbot Avenue and Moordown (Castle Lane Jn.)	1½d
Cemetery Junction and Moordown (Castle Lane)	2d
Lansdowne and Brassey Road	2d
Lansdowne and Moordown Post Office or Depot	2½d
Lansdowne and Moordown (Castle Lane Jn.)	3d

and vice versa

Workmen's Fares and Returns:–

	Workmen's	Returns
Lansdowne and Brassey Road	1d	2d
Cemetery Junction and Moordown PO or Depot	1d	2d
Talbot Avenue and Moordown (Castle Lane Jn.)	1d	2d

	Workmen's	Returns
Lansdowne and Moordown PO or Depot	1½d	3d
Holdenhurst Road Junction and Moordown (Castle Lane Junction)	2d	4d

and vice versa

Revised fares were proposed on 26th November 1936 and approved on 25th January 1937 (except County Gates – Square, which took effect on 1st February 1937):–

21, 22, 23   Square – Christchurch

Reintroduction of tram fares with the exception of the following:

	Tram	Present	Proposed
Boscombe Arcade – Christchurch	4½d	4d	4d
Lansdowne – Christchurch	5½d	5d	5d
Square – Christchurch	6½d	6d	6d
Surrey Road – Christchurch	7½d	7d	7d
County Gates – Christchurch	8d	7½d	7½d

Deletion of the following fare:–

Square – Boscombe Gdns	1½d	1½d	–

The Square – Christchurch trolleybus service fares could not be raised above those used on motorbus service 1 (Square – Purewell) due to the agreement between Bournemouth Corporation and Christchurch Council. Fares between those points which were common to both routes between the Square and Pokesdown Station were retained.

24   Square – Iford

Reintroduction of tram fares between Square and Pokesdown Station with the exception of the following which was to be deleted:–

	Tram	Present	Proposed
Square – Boscombe Gdns	1½d	1½d	–

The existing trolleybus fares between Pokesdown Station and Iford Bridge were to remain but the following through fares increased:–

Boscombe Arcade – Iford	–	1½d	2d
Lansdowne – Iford	–	2½d	3d

The following special fare was to be introduced:–

Portman Road – Iford	–	–	1½d

25, 25A   Westbourne (County Gates) – Ashley Road, Boscombe

Reintroduction of tram fares.

26   Square – Moordown via Richmond Hill

Reintroduction of tram fares and the deletion of the Richmond Hill fare stage.

27   Square – Moordown via Lansdowne

Reintroduction of tram fares between Lansdown and Moordown and the retention of the following present fares:–

Holdenhurst Road – Talbot Avenue	1d
Bournemouth Square – Cemetery Junction	1½d
Bournemouth Square – Winton Banks	2d

28   Square – Castle Lane

As trams had previously operated only as far as King's Road, the reinstatement of tram fares were proposed for this portion and the retention of the existing trolleybus fares between King's Road and Castle Lane.

Increase through fares as follows:–

	Tram	Present	Proposed
Square – Court Road	–	2d	2½d
Square – Castle Lane	–	2½d	3d
Cemetery – Castle Lane	–	1½d	2d

with the deletion of Richmond Hill fare stage.

FARE TABLES

The trolleybuses adopted a staged fares list, in principle 1d per stage of equal distance and ½d for a half stage, similar to that used on the tramways, but it was only with appearance of the May 1935 timetable that the first proper fare tables were issued. The express motorbus services paralleling the tram route had operated at premium fares, which had led to discrepancies as the trolleybuses were introduced. Also in May 1935, fares between any two points cost the same whether made by motorbus, tram or trolleybus. Fares were charged for a stage or portion of a stage. Thereafter, fare table booklets were issued in connection with each fare increase or major service revision, duplicated sheets being used for intermediate amendments.

BELL PUNCH TICKETS

Initially, trolleybus tickets were of the same Bell Punch geographical fare stage type as used on the trams. The conductor was equipped with a wooden rack holding pre-printed paper tickets, divided by value, under a spring and cancelling punch. The stages were printed along the edges of the ticket with the title "Bournemouth Corporation Transport Services" and other information in a central column. The cancelling punch was used by the conductor to make a small round hole against the fare stage, indicated by geographical name or number, where the passenger had started the journey whilst the fare paid indicated how far the passenger could travel. The Bell Punch recorded the number of holes punched on a secure register inside the machine whilst the small coloured circle of paper punched out of the ticket was retained in the machine (for accounting purposes if required). During the trolleybus era, the return journey on the greatly discounted return fares was handled by issuing an exchange ticket of the same value as the original one to avoid misuse. From early 1939 until 1942 a single universal exchange ticket was used, with fare values instead of stages printed down the sides, which was then punched to show the return ticket value to which it corresponded. On 10th July 1942, exchange tickets were discontinued as an economy measure and conductors used nippers which made a square hole in the originally issued return ticket. Normal return fares were abolished in 1952.

The tramway period ticket colours were retained but overprinted with the fare value and a "TB" suffix in green. Towards the end of the geographical-stage period (1939), oversized geographical 1½d (on tramway-standard pink paper) and 2½d (on motorbus-standard red paper) tickets appeared, including both motorbus and trolleybus stages. These lacked the overprinted "TB" suffix. In early 1939 there was a change to numerical-stage tickets, the "TB" overprint ceased and a single set of colours was used for both motorbus and trolleybus services. The first generation of numerical-stage tickets had stages 1–20 reading from top left to top right but this was reversed later, the stages reading from bottom right to bottom left. In general the tramway period colours were retained, but red was used for the 2½d and 3½d tickets in accordance with the above precedent. During the War, Bell Punch stopped supplying grey tickets and the grey 6d became primrose. There were certain colour changes in higher values, and some new high values were added.

Although experiments were carried out with ticket issuing machines during the 1930s, the Bell Punch remained the undertaking's standard until the "Ultimate" system was adopted in 1953. In the 1930s trials took place with both TIM and Verometer machines, the TIM being used on the experimental County Gates, Westbourne – Bournemouth Square trolleybus service from 27th February 1934. Similar trials using Gibson and "Ultimate" machines were carried out in 1952.

SERVICE 25

WESTBOURNE (1)

| | | | | | | | | SPECIAL FARE |
| Pavilion or Horseshoe Common – Westbourne : 4d. |

2	WEST STATION (2)
3	2	SQUARE (4)
5	3	2	LANSDOWNE (5)
5	4	3	2	CENTRAL STATION (6)
6	5	4	3	2	CAPSTONE ROAD (7)
7	6	5	3	3	2	QUEEN'S PARK CORNER (8)
7	6	5	4	3	2	2	GOLF PAVILION or KING'S PARK GATES (9)
8	7	6	5	4	3	2	2	ASHLEY ROAD and PORTMAN ROAD (10)

TRANSFER FARES			
JOURNEY	5-DAY	6-DAY	CHANGING AT
Maclean Road (7) – Lansdowne	5/6d	6/9d	Banks to 2,3,6,34
– Barracks	8/3d	10/–d	Boscombe to 1, 20
Columbia Road (7) – Lansdowne	4/9d	5/9d	Banks to 2,3,6,34
– Barracks	7/9d	9/3d	Boscombe to 1, 20
– Somerford	8/3d	10/–d	Boscombe to 1
Winton Banks (7) – Barracks	6/3d	7/6d	Boscombe to 1, 20
– Somerford	7/9d	9/3d	Boscombe to 1
King's Road (7) – Barracks	5/6d	6/9d	Boscombe to 1, 20
Central Station (25) – Pokesdown	4/3d	5/–d	Boscombe to 1,20-24
– Fisherman's Walk	4/3d	5/–d	Boscombe to 21,22,23
– Tuckton Corner	4/9d	5/9d	Boscombe to 21,22
– Cross Roads	5/6d	6/9d	Boscombe to 21,22
– Tuckton Bridge	6/3d	7/6d	Boscombe to 21,22,23
Broadway (28,29,32) – Lansdowne	4/3d	5/–d	Cemetery to 2,3,6,34
West Way (29) – Boscombe	4/9d	5/9d	King's Road to 7, 8
Columbia Road (30,31)– Lansdowne	4/9d	5/9d	Banks to 2,3,6,34
Wallisdown (30) – Lansdowne	4/9d	5/9d	Banks to 2,3,6,34
Talbot Village (30) – Lansdowne	4/3d	5/–d	Banks to 2,3,6,34
Howeth Road (31) – Lansdowne	4/9d	5/9d	Banks to 2,3,6,34
SERVICES 18, 33 to SERVICES 28, 29	As Ser. 32 P.21		Broadway
SERVICE 8 to SERVICE 2	As Ser. 6 P.7		Ensbury Park Hotel

Excerpt from the fare table of 11th July 1961, showing the table for service 25 (including a special 4d fare between Pavilion/Horseshoe Common and Westbourne), and a table of the various five- and six-day transfer fares.

Ticket colours and styles

a)   Pre-war:–

Title "Bournemouth Corporation Transport Services". Geographical or numerical fare stages. All printing in black.

Singles:–

Beige/buff with green value overprint	1d
Pink with blue value overprint	1½d
White with green value overprint	2d
Sage with blue value overprint	2½d
Orange with green value overprint	3d
Salmon with blue value overprint	3½d
Light blue with orange value overprint	4d
Yellow with orange value overprint	5d
Grey	6d
Lilac	7d
White/red	1d Parcel
Mauve	1d Dog
Pink	½d Tuckton Bridge Toll

b)   Post-war :–

Title "Bournemouth Corporation Transport Services". Numerical fare stages. All printing in black.

Singles:–

Beige/buff with green value overprint	1d
Pink with blue value overprint	1½d
White with green value overprint	2d
Orange with green value overprint	3d
Mauve with orange value overprint	4d
Yellow with orange value overprint	5d
Beige/buff with orange value overprint	6d
Purple with orange value overprint	7d
Pale brown with green value overprint	8d
Pale(r) brown with green value overprint	9d
Bright orange with green value overprint	10d
Pink with blue value overprint	11d
Pale purple with blue value overprint	1s
Light olive with orange value overprint	1s 2d
Beige/buff with blue value overprint	1s 3d

Returns:–

Beige/buff with orange value overprint	1½d school child only
Purple with orange value overprint	1½d school child only
Pale green with blue value overprint	2d blue "X" across ticket
Pink with green value overprint	3d
Beige with green value overprint	4d
White with black value overprint	6d orange "X" across ticket
Blue with orange value overprint	1s 3d
Pink with green value overprint	1s 9d
Beige/buff with orange value overprint	2s 6d blue stripe across ticket
Beige/buff overprinted "Parcel" or "Dog"	1d orange stripe across ticket
Beige/buff transfer pass (for return ticket holders)	No value
Pale blue black print	3s 4d combined road + river trip return
Purple black print	3s 9d combined road + river trip return
Beige/buff black print	1s 10d combined road + river trip child return
Orange black overprint	2s combined road + river trip child return
Pale green black	2s All day (except services 12, 14, 15)
Blue black	1s All day Child

Weekly returns (used until the end):

Orange with black print and orange value overprint	9d 3 days e.g. Christmas, Boxing Day
Purple with black print and green value overprint	3s 8d 4 days e.g. Bank Holiday
Pale green with black print and orange value overprint	1s 8d 5 days
Pink with black print and green value overprint	8s 6 days

ULTIMATE TICKETS

Following a successful trial with two machines in March 1953, the undertaking converted to the Bell Punch "Ultimate" system by 22nd March 1954, the entire stock of machines being hired from the manufacturers. The majority (360) of the "Ultimate" machines used in Bournemouth accommodated six, instead of the more customary five, fare denomination, pre-printed on rolls of 1,000, colour-coded, 1¼ ins square paper tickets. The blank tickets were printed in black with red wave effect over the Single, Joint and Return boxes and titled "Bournemouth Corp. Trans. S.".

Each ticket compartment on the "Ultimate" machine had its own operating lever which, when depressed, printed the fare stage number from 00 to 99 in one of three possible squares, Single, Joint and Return, in purple ink across the base of the ticket. When the lever was released, the ticket was ejected, torn off by the conductor and given to the passenger as a receipt for his fare paid. When a button below the operating lever was depressed in the same issuing operation a double length ticket of the required denomination was ejected, in which case the the fare stage number was printed in the Single, Joint or Return square of the first ticket only whilst a cancellation was made across the serial number of the second ticket.

The following ticket colours and denominations limited to a maximum of six at any one time, were used during the period that "Ultimate" ticket machines were used in Bournemouth:–

Colour	Type	Denomination	Period	Comment
Beige	Single	1d	1953-1964	
Pink	Single	1½d	1953-1956	
White	Single	2d	1953-1968	
Orange	Single	3d	1953-1968	
Purple	Single	4d	1953-1968	
Yellow	Single	5d	1953-1968	
Pink	Single	6d	1964-1968	
Pale green	Single	7d	1956-1968	
Green	Return	1s 9d	1953-1956	overprinted "return"
Pale green	Single	2s	1958-1964	overprinted "single"
Mauve	Single	2s 6d	1950-1964	
Green	Circular tour	3s	1964-1965	
Purple	Circular tour	3s 6d	1965-1968	

In order to make up additional fare values, "joint issues" of more than one ticket were made in a defined combination. This was originally as follows:

1d	single 1d ticket
2d	single 2d ticket
3d	single 3d ticket
4d	single 4d ticket
5d	single 5d ticket
6d	two 3d tickets
7d	single 7d ticket
8d	two 4d tickets
9d	one 7d ticket and two 1d tickets
10d	two 5d tickets
11d	one 7d and two 2d tickets joint issue
1s	one single and one double 4d tickets
1s 2d	two 7d tickets
1s 3d	one single and one double 5d tickets
1s 6d	three double 3d tickets
1s 9d	one single and one double 7d tickets

From 27th June 1964, the minimum adult fare became 3d and that of a child 2d, making the 1d compartment of the "Ultimate" ticket machine redundant. This was used for a new 6d ticket instead of a double 3d and all fares over 1s were thereafter made up from a double 6d ticket plus a second ticket of the necessary value.

The reason for a defined combination was purely statistical. A counter, recording only the number of double length issued made, was fitted to each of the six ticket compartments. As a double 1d ticket was only issued when a 9d fare was taken, the number of double 1d tickets issued represented the number of passengers travelling at that fare.

The undertaking offered a large number of transfer fares between points not linked by direct services at the beginning of the trolleybus era e.g. Iford Bridge to Fisherman's Walk. By the time the "Ultimate" machines were in use, these were basically limited to fares between points in Winton or Moordown and points beyond Strouden Park on service 32 (to compensate for the infrequent operation and subsequent withdrawal of Services 33 and 34), and points on the outer portions of services 23 (Fisherman's Walk-Tuckton Bridge) and 30 (Winton Banks – Columbia Road) which did not work their full length throughout the day.

As with the Bell Punch, it was necessary for the conductor to complete a waybill at specified "booking-up points". Those in operation on trolleybus services were as follows in November 1957:

20, 24
Square
Boscombe
Warnford Road
Jumpers Christchurch

21, 22, 23
Square
Boscombe
Fisherman's Walk
Seafield Road
Southbourne Cross Roads

25
Boscombe
Queen's Park
Lansdowne
Square
Westbourne

26
Triangle
Cemetery Junction
Brassey Road
Lawford Road

30
Triangle
Cemetery Junction
Boy's Home
Columbia Road

31
Triangle
Cemetery Junction
Brassey Road
Columbia Road

32
Triangle
Cemetery Junction
Five Ways
Castle Lane
Strouden Hotel
Iford

33
Triangle
Cemetery Junction
Brassey Road
Lawford Road
Castle Lane, Broadway
Strouden Hotel
Iford

28
Triangle
Cemetery Junction
Five Ways
Castle Lane, Broadway
West Way

29
Triangle
Cemetery Junction
Five Ways
Castle Lane, Broadway
West Way

34
Lansdowne
Cemetery Junction
Brassey Road
Lawford Road

When a vehicle operated a short-working, the terminal was considered the "booking-up point".

SETRIGHT "SPEED" TICKETS

Increasingly frequent fare increases and consequently changed denominations in the last few years of trolleybus operation encouraged the undertaking to evaluate a more flexible ticketing solution. In 1968, the Setright "Speed" machine was introduced. The Bournemouth machines added in purple ink the fare value, up to 19s 11d; the class of travel e.g. single, return, workman, etc.; stage boarded, from 00 to 99; serial number of the ticket; date of issue and machine identity, on to a pre-printed roll of buff paper. The conductor "dialled" his inputs on a superimposed boss on the top of the machine whilst the blank paper roll was held in a magazine beneath. The machines contained counters showing the total value of fares issued, in units of 1d and 1s, together with the total number of tickets sold. A statistical counter recorded the number of tickets sold at one predetermined value.

HANTS & DORSET/WILTS & DORSET

The Bournemouth Corporation Act, 1930, granted H & D the right to continue carrying local passengers within the Bournemouth area on their country services which paralleled urban trolleybus and motorbus services, but all revenue, less operating costs, passed to Bournemouth. The same conditions applied to Wilts & Dorset's Salisbury service 38 to and from Christchurch. A special issue of Bournemouth Corporation Bell Punch tickets using a colour system approximating to that used pre-1939 for Corporation motorbus tickets, cancelled latterly using the Setright Speed return ticket punch, was printed for use on a journey which could also be made by trolleybus.

Not all H & D services carried local passengers, in which case a wooden board showing "Not on service for Bournemouth Corporation passengers", lettered in white on a maroon background, was carried across the motorbus radiator.

The special ticket issued on the illuminated Coronation trolleybus, 152 (BRU 3) in the summer of 1937. Fares charged on this vehicle were double the normal rate. A selection of standard BCT tickets is shown in colour on page 168.

Depots

GENERAL

Vehicles were not allocated to or based at specific depots. A trolleybus starting from Moordown one morning could return to Central Depot, Southcote Road that evening and operate on any of the workings from there the next day. When the fleet was at its maximum extent it was impossible to store all the trolleybuses under cover.

CENTRAL DEPOT, SOUTHCOTE ROAD

The tramcar sheds at Southcote Road constituted just a portion of a complex which originally embraced a generating station, cooling towers, stores and workshops and, later, the Transport Department offices and motorbus garage. The original buildings were in brick, with stone facings and round-topped windows. The main car shed comprised six long "run-through" stabling roads in two bays, featuring roof lights and "Doric" arches at each end. Built onto the southern wall of the shed was a shorter two-road workshop. The depot came into use for the opening of the first tramway, Lansdowne – Pokesdown, on 23rd July 1902.

In 1926, an additional car shed was built to the south of the eastern end of the main depot with six short roads accessible from the west only. This later became a motorbus garage.

As the main operating depot and workshops, Central Depot, Southcote Road was able to accommodate a maximum of 54 trolleybuses by parking them in six rows of nine vehicles each, although official reports indicate that it was planned for just 36. Roller-shutter doors, possibly with "drawbridge" sections in the overhead wiring, were installed before tramway operations ceased, but fell into disuse. In latter years they tended to be shut solely on Christmas Day, when no trolleybus services operated.

The eastern entrance to Central Depot, Southcote Road, looking across Vale Road. Note the 3 ft 6 ins gauge tram track entry fan, including access towards the later motorbus garage (on the left of the main tram shed) which remained intact until final closure. Normal two-wire trolleybus overhead served this entrance from St. Clements Road. The railway goods yard is on the right, beyond the boundary fence.
J. C. Gillham

The western entrance to Central Depot, Southcote Road, clearly showing the three-wire overhead line leading into the north lye of the shed building. The Nissen hut on the left is part of the stores. Breakdown and towing tender FRU 180 stands outside the workshop and office buildings. Tram track is evident in the main shed entrances. *J. C. Gillham*

CENTRAL DEPOT, SOUTHCOTE ROAD

A   trolleybus garage (formerly tram shed)
B   motorbus garage (a roofed-over yard)
C   Overhead Department store
D   Overhead Department office and workshop
E   two-storey office block
F   Head Office building (99 Southcote Road)
G   power house - boiler room
H   power house – generator room
I   Mains Department office
J   railway siding
K   SEB substation (transformer and switch yard at rear)
L   BCT substation

M   garage
N   cable store
P   Dawson washing machine
Q   store
R   scrap metal compound
S   private houses and shops
T   workshops and offices, including Conductors', Inspectors' and Depot Foreman's Rooms; Canteen and recreation room above
U   position of former cooling towers

Depot layout immediately before its vacation on 6 June 1965

Courtesy: John Mawson (extract from an original plan prepared in 1965)

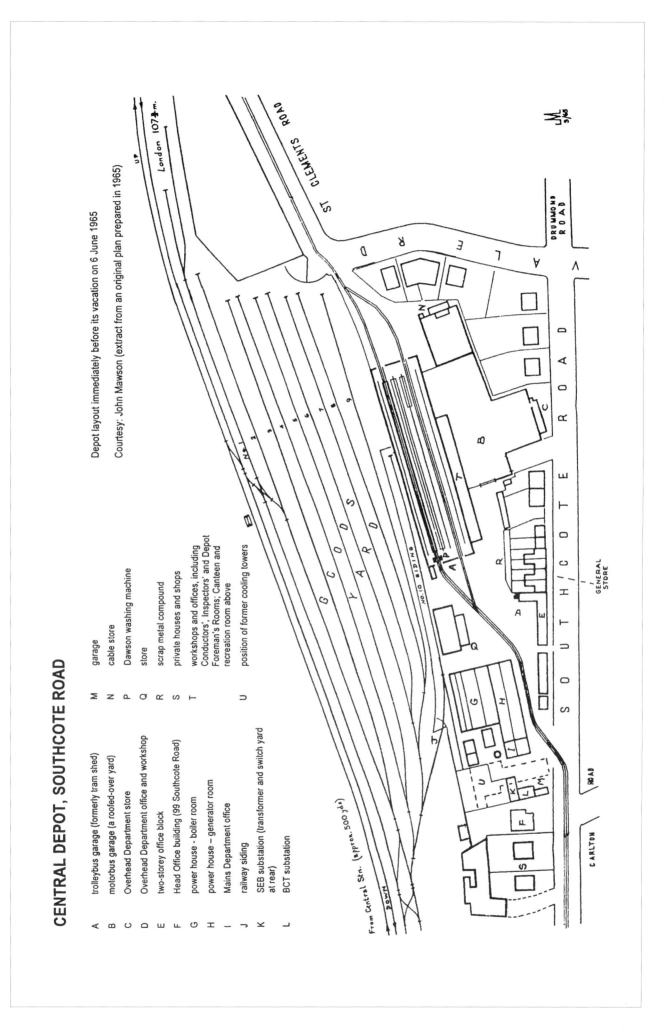

215

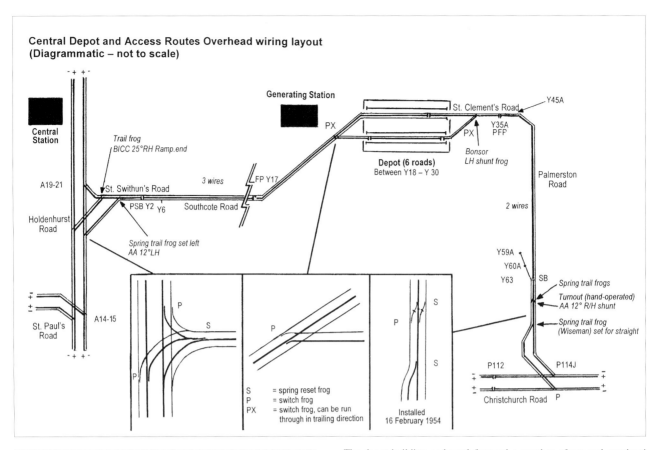

Central Depot and Access Routes Overhead wiring layout
(Diagrammatic – not to scale)

S = spring reset frog
P = switch frog
PX = switch frog, can be run
through in trailing direction

Installed
16 February 1954

Moordown Depot extension, viewed from Wimborne Road,
with (from right to left) the rears of Sunbeam MS2s 88,
145 and 122 identifable. The overhead wiring branching
off to the left made up part of the "through the depot"
turning circle.   *K. Baynton collection*

The depot building and yard featured a number of unusual overhead
wiring installations in conjunction with the three-wire layout along the
Southcote Road western access route. This layout probably dated back
to the period of time in the mid-1930s when both trams and trolleybuses
were using the access routes to get to and from the depot, with minimal
alterations being made once the tramways had been completely
abandoned. During the tramway era there were two short sections of
(single, positive) overhead wire on each side of the single through wire
in each of the two bays of the depot building. These four sections were
limited to the inside of the building, thereby giving each of the six
tramway sidings its own overhead wire while avoiding the use of frogs.
It would seem that these four single, positive overhead wires were left
in place following tramway abandonment, one each side of the through
trolleybus wiring in each bay of the building, for testing purposes.
Rewiring trolleybuses inside the depot building in the hours of darkness
must have been something of a nightmare!

On 26th April 1965, the Transport Department's headquarters moved to
new office accommodation at Castle Lane Depot and, on 7th June 1965,
Central Depot, Southcote Road was vacated, to be taken over by the
Sanitary Department as a base for its waste disposal vehicles. The main
shed was still intact in 2000, albeit with the eastern entrances sealed off.

MOORDOWN DEPOT

This depot, in the then northernmost suburbs of Bournemouth, was
opened in June 1906 to provide a practical operating base at the end of
the line for the "Side Route" trams which, in any case, could not easily
access Central Depot due to trackwork limitations. Constructed in brick,
it was built on a plot of land on Wimborne Road opposite the
present-day Barrie Road, just south of the Malvern Road/Redhill
Crescent crossroads. The car shed had two bays: the narrower one to the
north accommodated a three-road paintshop, whilst the wider second
bay had six roads accessed by two three-line fans. Trams entered and
left the building from the inbound line of the Moordown terminal loop.

The Moordown Depot property was extended twice prior to the
trolleybus era. In 1919 a small, shallower building with four shorter
roads, set back further from Wimborne Road, was added to the south
and angled from the original main shed. The side and end walls of this
building were built of brick, and were windowless but for a circular

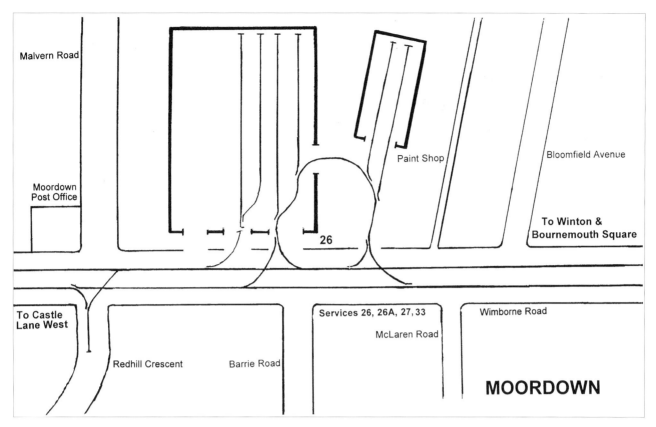

Malvern Road

Moordown
Post Office

Paint Shop

Bloomfield Avenue

**To Winton &
Bournemouth Square**

26

To Castle
Lane West

Redhill Crescent   Barrie Road

Services 26, 26A, 27, 33

McLaren Road

Wimborne Road

MOORDOWN

and angled from the original main shed. The side and end walls of this building were built of brick, and were windowless but for a circular window in the upper portion of the rear wall. The front entrance was left open, with vertical wooden planking extending to the apex of the roof. Old tram rails were used for the girder work. Later, in 1930, the original main shed was extended forwards to within about six feet of the footpath along Wimborne Road. It was equipped with a brick and stone "public building" front typical of the period, and roller-shutter doors, which were seldom used with the exception of those at the front of the paint shop.

On 28th June 1935, trams ceased using Moordown Depot after a three-week period of combined tram and trolleybus operation along Wimborne Road. Initially, trolleybuses turned into the depot forecourt and reversed into Wimborne Road for turning purposes but, from 5th September 1946, a reversing triangle came into use at Redhill Crescent, about 50 yards past the depot. Increasing road traffic led to use of the triangle being discontinued on 14th August 1950 and trolleybuses started to use a turning circle which had been erected in

the depot yard and through the south side wall of the original shed. The nominal capacity of this depot was 44 trolleybuses, achieved by parking eight rows of four vehicles in the main shed and a further four rows of three in the later separate extension (although up to seven vehicles were parked in the open when the fleet was at its maximum). Moordown served the "Side Routes" of the system, although no trolleybuses were actually based there.

An ex-driver recalls *"Moordown based crews were in many ways a breed of their own and we* [Central Depot crews] *didn't mix a lot. In fact if you had to take a bus into Moordown Depot for any reason and went into their canteen for a cup of tea, you were regarded with suspicion".*

From 24th July 1953, coinciding with the opening of Castle Lane Depot, the Moordown depot complex and turning circle ceased to be used, being vacated completely by 26th July 1953. The paintshop was used throughout the trolleybus period. It was then leased to the Post Office Telephones as a vehicle depot and subsequently demolished in 1984. A supermarket and associated car park has since been built on the site.

Moordown Depot, main building, showing the 1906 frontage, viewed from Barrie Road. The building visible in the background above the roof of the low building, on the right of the photo, is the extension.
K. Baynton

Open-top Sunbeam MS2 201 enters Boscombe (Pokesdown) Depot from the eastbound Christchurch Road wires. Note the hand-operated BICC 25° right-hand facing frog into the depot overhead line, and the substation on the eastern boundary wall. The junction with Seabourne Road is visible in the background. The New Bell Inn is immediately behind the trolleybus.

J. C. Gillham

BOSCOMBE (POKESDOWN) DEPOT

A brick building with stone facings in the same style as that in Southcote Road, the small Boscombe (Pokesdown) Depot was set back about 20 feet from the south side of Christchurch Road about 100 yards west of its junction with Seabourne Road and close to Pokesdown Station. The structure featured a single circular window centred above the entrance with matching circular embellishments and arches each side of the entrance, which was surmounted by a deep girder. Internal natural illumination was by roof lights supplemented by whitewashed walls. Entrance doors were apparently never fitted to the depot building. A small low-walled yard brought the property in line with the shops on the south side of Christchurch Road. The yard entrance was equipped with metal gates until removal during the wartime salvage drive.

The trams accessed the depot building by a trailing junction from the outbound line of the Pokesdown Station passing loop. There were four short terminal roads and a siding, the floor space taken up by this siding being built over in 1955 when a BCT-owned traction power substation was built alongside the eastern boundary wall. An office and crew mess-room, approached by wooden stairs, was added over the top of the substation. No other structural alterations were ever made to Boscombe Depot.

Trams were operated until services to Christchurch ceased on 8th April 1936 and, although equipped with trolleybus overhead wiring, the depot was initially only used for storage purposes, becoming a running depot in 1940. There were three lines of trolleybus overhead wiring inside the depot, which offered cramped overnight accommodation for up to 17 trolleybuses (but, once the substation had been added, capacity fell to 12 vehicles). The central overhead line was entered over a facing frog from the westbound Christchurch Road wiring. The other line entered from the eastbound wiring, made a tight loop at the rear of the building which could not be negotiated by trolleybuses and exited into a trail frog in the westbound Christchurch Road wiring. Trolleybuses entered the depot nose-in and had to reverse out into the main road under the guidance of an inspector. Boscombe (Pokesdown) never garaged motorbuses.

After closure, the depot was used as an indoor market for the sale of second-hand goods. It was demolished in the mid-1990s and the site has since been redeveloped as an apartment block.

A diagram of the overhead in this depot appears on page 92.

CASTLE LANE (MALLARD ROAD) DEPOT

On 13th March 1945 a Transport Sub-Committee recommended the compulsory purchase of property in Rose Gardens (numbers 5, 7, 9, 13, 15, 17), at the rear of Moordown Depot to permit an extension, increased maintenance facilities there and an alternative depot exit into Rose Gardens and Malvern Road. This would have enabled all vehicles in the fleet to be housed under cover. At that time, the proposal was simply to buy the necessary land and houses but not to demolish the buildings. The MoT pointed out that such a Compulsory Purchase Order would not be confirmed unless recommended on the grounds of public safety. The Finance (Negotiating) Sub-Committee was instructed to acquire numbers 5, 7, 9 Rose Gardens, together with the allotment ground at the rear, at an estimated cost of £2,500 each, and the rear of numbers 13, 15, 17 Rose Gardens at £1,500. Ultimately the houses at 13, 15, 17 would have been required. The initial plans for an extension to Moordown Depot were available in June 1948 and sent to Mr Lindsay Clegg, Town Clerk.

Plans for extended depot accommodation had been shelved in October 1939 due to the outbreak of war. The architects had visited London Transport's Chiswick works, various trolleybus depots and the Hants & Dorset Motor Services maintenance facilities at Southampton. In an effort to look ahead some 35 years, they anticipated that Bournemouth, Christchurch and Poole Boroughs might come under unified control, and that all transport services could be nationalised. Whatever the future might bring, Bournemouth would retain its prominent position and a much larger fleet of vehicles was anticipated. Their plans were based on the need to accommodate 240 vehicles, but they felt that 350 might be required to serve just Bournemouth and Christchurch in the not-too-distant future. Should Poole also be considered, the figure could reach 500. The alternative sites considered were Boscombe (Pokesdown), the Central Depot (Southcote Road), Moordown, and Strouden Farm, Castle Lane. The architects felt that the existing depots at Boscombe (Pokesdown) and Moordown should be closed, the Central Depot (Southcote Road) enlarged to accommodate 100 vehicles and a new depot off Castle Lane built for an additional 200.

In early 1945 the Transport Committee considered requirements for post-war developments and visited the Castle Lane area in November 1945, the Town Planning Committee favouring the Corporation Farm, Strouden Park site (measuring about 10 acres) for a new depot. Strouden Farm had been used to keep the horses used to haul municipal refuse carts, etc., mechanisation of which had been deferred due to the Second World War. An alternative site at Sheepwash, bordered by Castle Lane East and Riverside Avenue, was felt to be unsuitable. On 13th December 1945, Mr Morrison wrote to the Town Planning Committee that, in selecting the most suitable position for a new depot, the Transport Committee had services in the east of Bournemouth particularly in mind. He anticipated the following situation would result:

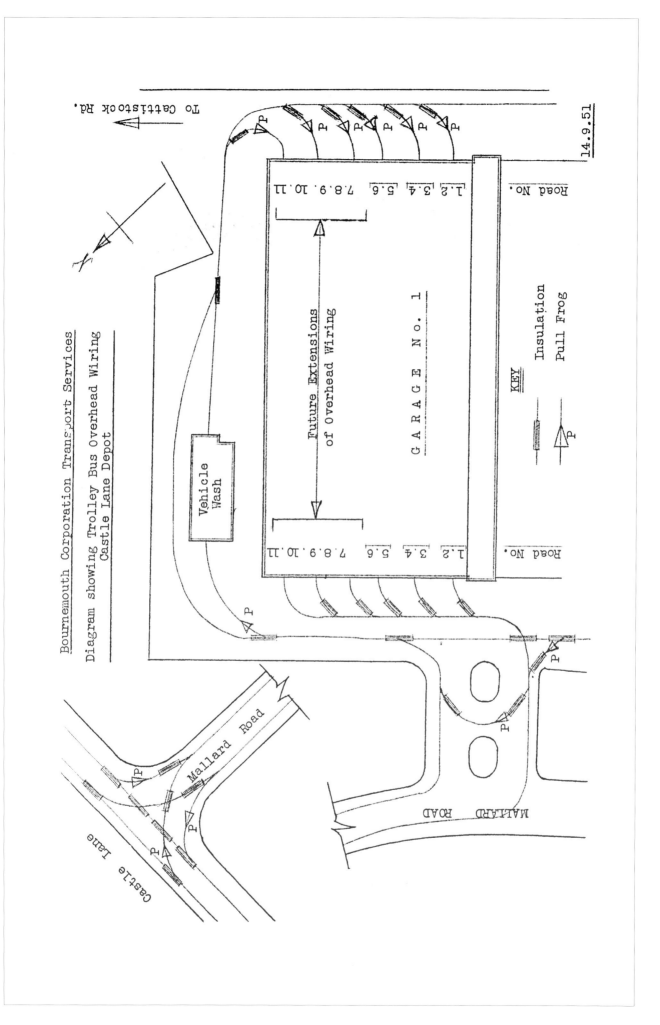

Bournemouth Corporation Transport Services

Diagram showing Trolley Bus Overhead Wiring
Castle Lane Depot

GARAGE No. 1

Future Extensions of Overhead Wiring

Vehicle Wash

Road No.   1.2 3.4 5.6 7.8.9.10.11

Road No.   1.2 3.4 5.6 7.8.9.10.11

To Cattistock Rd.

14.9.51

KEY

Insulation
Pull Frog

Mallard Road

MALLARD ROAD

Castle Lane

219

Boscombe (Pokesdown) depot: to be disposed of as soon as alternative accommodation available.

Castle Lane: a new depot to be built, housing and servicing vehicles in the eastern parts of the Borough.

Central Depot, Southcote Road: the existing depot, maintenance and workshop facilities to be retained as the undertaking's operational hub.

Moordown depot: to be retained and expanded as a running depot to cater for the northern parts of the Borough.

Sufficient land would be required off Castle Lane to initially accommodate 70 trolleybuses (or motorbuses). Ideally the depot building would be open at both ends to ease trolleybus operations and, in design and construction, free from obstructions such as roof columns i.e. a single-span building. Shell concrete construction was preferred, to economise in the use of steel (which would have been required in a framed structure and which was subject to supply restrictions). Provision for future extension was to be allowed for. There should be space for the long-planned staff recreational facilities.

The first plan showed an area of about 300 x 750 ft for an initial 300 x 100 ft depot on part of the Strouden Farm, and a surrounding housing development, fronting Strouden Lane and Broad Avenue. There was also an area intended for use as an open space. This was passed to Messrs Jackson & Greenen, Chartered Architects, Bournemouth, to prepare a scheme and to co-ordinate with Town Planning officials.

On 4th June 1946, the land was transferred to the Transport Committee at a figure agreed by the District Valuer. In May 1948, it was discovered that a space marked on an old map of the proposed site was in fact a house which had not been conveyanced to the Transport Department and which, accordingly, remained under the control of the Housing Committee!

Shortage of undercover garage accommodation prompted the examination of a temporary building at Beales, Old Christchurch Road, in September 1948, but the eaves height of 10ft 7ins was totally unsuitable for trolleybuses. At that time, Central Depot had parking space under reasonable conditions for 32 motorbuses, but was home for 40. The trolleybus garage, planned for 36 vehicles, was accommodating 45, whilst six departmental lorries were parked in the open. There was thus a lack of accommodation for 23 vehicles. At Moordown Depot, seven vehicles were regularly parked in the open and there were three others which needed to be moved from the new shed to ease congestion. At Boscombe there was reasonable space for 12 trolleybuses, but 17 were in fact garaged there.

Jackson & Greenen presented their plans and estimates on 30th October 1948, offering alternative methods of construction featuring reinforced concrete, an aluminium frame and a steel frame. Shell concrete construction (the second most expensive option) was recommended, consisting of an 81-vehicle garage (£47,238) and workshops (£116,833). In view of structural and wind pressure difficulties, any form of temporary building was not recommended. If instructed within a month, the architects felt that they could go to tender at the end of January 1949, allowing construction to commence in March and with the hope of some accommodation being available by end 1949.

There was much correspondence with the MoT and the Regional Traffic Commissioners with respect to securing approval, leading to a Mr Ralfs of the MoT, Southampton, visiting Bournemouth to inspect the situation. This resulted in a suggestion that the Castle Lane trolleybus extension (and thus access to any new depot on the site) be reconsidered in view of the nation's economy. However, by spring 1949, the construction of the new depot off Castle Lane had become formal policy and tenders were invited.

The start of site works for Castle Lane Depot was delayed when Trevor Construction withdrew their tender. The next lowest tender, of £16,392 8s 7d from Messrs Grounds & Newton, Ltd., was accepted and, on 29th August 1949, the Transport Committee requested the Finance Committee to approve an estimated £151,216 for the first section of the scheme, including road works, garage overhead and

ancillary equipment. In September, it was recommended that the widening and reconstruction of part of Mallard Road, at an estimated £2,885, also be included in the cost of the new depot. By October 1949, 14 tenders had been received for the new garage and workshop buildings. The lowest, from Messrs James Drewitt & Son Limited for £97,948, was accepted subject to Finance Committee and MoT approval, and to satisfactory sureties being submitted.

By 15th October 1951, the trolleybus route extension along Castle Lane was in operation, and access to the new depot was guaranteed. Construction work was well underway at the Castle Lane site, but not without the customary trials and tribulations related to any building project, large or small. Only a single garage, No. 1 (the only one to be equipped for trolleybuses), was constructed in this first phase of the development. It provided for 11 lines of nine vehicles, from Road 1 on the east to Road 11 on the west. Three pairs of trolleybus wires ran through the building serving Roads 6–11, so that 54 trolleybuses could be accommodated under the wires, plus any parked elsewhere out of reach of the overhead such as the open-top Sunbem MS2s in winter. Trolleybuses were parked according to type i.e. BUTs together on one road, Sunbeam MS2s on the next and so on.

On 24th July 1953 the new Castle Lane depot came into use, following the official opening by the Mayor, Councillor H. P. E. Mears, OBE, JP, the previous day. The Souvenir Brochure produced for the opening of the Mallard Road (Castle Lane) depot and workshop facilities recorded the following information [with the author's additions or explanations are shown in square brackets]:

"In 1946 Mr Morrison's proposal to build a new depot off Castle Lane was approved by the Transport Committee and full Council, and under his direction plans for the buildings were put in hand. The Government ban on capital expenditure in 1947 caused preparatory work to be deferred and it was ca. 12 months later that approval to go forward was received from the Ministry of Transport. There was a condition that the general construction must be such as to economise in the use of steel. So far the proposed buildings had been designed as steel framed with an estimated steel requirement of 634 tons but after research work it was finally decided to use a combination of reinforced and prestressed concrete, saving 416 tons of steel. The 24 acre Strouden Farm site had previously been used for the stabling and grazing of the Corporation's cart horses. The plans were prepared with a view to the work being carried out in sections spread over a number of years and to be readily extended with the growth of the fleet. The Maintenance Workshops so far constructed are capable of dealing with 240 buses but the plans have been prepared so that this section may eventually be enlarged to deal with up to 500 buses. James Drewitt & Son Ltd. were the building contractors and Phorpres bricks were used (600,000 common, 150,000 rustics, 150,000 Saxon facings).

"Description of the buildings

"Garage: 300ft long x 150ft wide offering a column-free covered space of 45,000 square feet. The 150ft span is the largest constructed in the UK with prestressed beams and shell roof. The roof consists of 9 reinforced concrete shells of 2½ins thickness, pressure sprayed on the "Gunite" system, with a span of 33ft, the intermediate beams are alike 10in wide and 5ft 6ins deep. The external beams are slightly larger. The beams were cast in-situ and post-tensioned by the Magnel-Blaton system. An extractable rubber core was used to form the ducts through which the completed cables were threaded.

"The wire used is 0.276 ins in diameter and during stressing was extended 7¾ins inducing a compressive force in the concrete of 507 tons. With the exception of the outside walls the building is constructed entirely of concrete thus eliminating all maintenance work which would be needed in a steel roofed building. An inspection pit with glazed tiles and fluorescent lighting is provided and at one section gallery pits are formed on either side for the easy inspection of electrical equipment of vehicles.

"Administration Block: constructed on the south-west side of the garage and designed to accommodate the second similar garage when required. It consists of workshops, tyre store, drying rooms,

One of the three open-top Sunbeam MS2s undergoing inspection over the eastern-most white-tiled pit at the Castle Lane (Mallard Road) workshops. *J. C. Gillham*

conductors' and inspectors' rooms, washing rooms and toilets, a first aid room, mess room and accompanying kitchen. A sprinkler system with 583 heads is provided. [In fact when No. 2 Garage was eventually opened in 1965, it was of a different construction from No. 1.]

"*Drive-through vehicle wash: designed for 2 vehicles one behind the other.* [A pair of trolley wires ran through the vehicle wash.] *Each vehicle as it passes through is vacuumed inside and all rubbish conveyed directly to an incinerator. The bus then moves forward to the second position where it is sprayed over with water from sparge pipes attached to side gantries, outside cleaning being completed with a brush.*

"*Workshop & maintenance works: a concrete building divided into maintenance, machine, body and stores sections. The maintenance block contains repair pits. There is a series of 10 pits connected to a master pit and 2 isolated pits. 2 pits are provided with hydraulic jacks to accommodate the various wheel bases of vehicles for the purpose of hoisting for the removal of wheels. The pits are lined with glazed tiles and equipped with fluorescent lighting. The machine block contains a machine shop, engine room, electrical shop, timber store, timber mill, smiths' shop, panel beaters' shop, tyre store and repair shop. Foundations were laid for a paint shop but this work was deferred for economic reasons. Ample storage space is provided for the needs of a large and growing undertaking. Just inside the main entrance on the south-west side of the building is a loading platform over which a travelling crane operates to convey heavy items to the first floor. Also on the first floor is a records room, paint store and clothing store.*

"*In general the roof consists of 45 half shells with north lights with the exception of the stores block which has a flat roof. Prestressing is also used here on the Freyssinet system whereby 4 cables are used in each shell, each cable containing 12 wires 0.20 ins in diameter encased in a plastic sheath and placed in position before the concrete was pressure sprayed. The wires in this case were extended 3¼ins to 3½ins in a length of 54 feet. Runways with travelling cranes are provided to carry heavy equipment to such parts of the building as required. Hot air heating is diffused through thermostatically controlled electric fans. Fire precautions similar to the garage comprise 734 automatic sprinkler heads.*

"*Canteen: a steel-framed building with brick infilling walls capable of seating 150. An up-to-date kitchen with spacious serving hatch provided with a tray sliding counter where meals can be provided on the cafeteria system. Provision is made for future developments such as an Assembly Hall, Sports Pavilion and a billiards and games room above the canteen.*

"*Boiler house: a mechanically-fed boiler is installed, this being sufficient to supply the needs of the workshops. There is space for a second boiler should the workshops be extended.*

"*Substation: A 2-section building, part containing the transformer and thus under the control of the Southern Electricity Board and from which the main cable is extended to supply the school on the adjoining site, and the other containing the Transport Department's main switches.* [Note that the substation did not supply traction current].

"*Garage lighting: angle type parabolic reflectors with 300 watt lamps mounted 22ft above the ground and spaced 27ft apart, the average illumination at ground level being 3–4½ lumens per sq ft.*

"*Pit lighting: the 300ft long pit is lit with 41, 4ft 40-watt Sieray fluorescent lamps in a staggered arrangement, the lamps being set 16ins below ground level providing ca. 20 lumens per sq ft. and providing good illumination to the underside of trolleybuses, minimal glare and visibility even when working immediately above the tube.*

"*Esavian shutter doors*

"*The entire site is surrounded by a concrete road with one-way trolleybus overhead wiring. There is a fire hydrant ring main with hydrants at convenient intervals*".

The trolleybus depot featured a white-tiled and illuminated access pit with removable metal gratings at floor surface level on one side to make wheel changes easier. It was kept particularly clean, aided by a large number of "home-made" racks, stands and tables for spare parts and replacement items.

The trolleybuses received intermediate servicing every 75,000 miles, and major overhauls every 150,000 miles, based on individual vehicle records. Except in the system's closing years, trolleybuses received an external repaint every three years, resulting in a very smart turnout. Electrical equipment required little maintenance apart from cleaning, lubrication, the checking of wiring and connections, and the renewal of worn contacts. Such items were covered on a time-interval rota system. Every seven weeks, each trolleybus was checked for electrical and mechanical faults, including adjustment of the traction motor brush pressure, motor generator sets, greasing of the control equipment and trolley heads, testing all high voltage cabling and checking the upward pressure of the trolley heads. This pressure had to be 30lbs at 21ft above the ground, and was checked by hanging a 21ft long bamboo trolley rewiring pole, with a 30lb weight attached to the end, to the trolleyhead. The spring tension was correct if the weight just touched the ground. The trolley pole itself was a steel tube, 15ft long and weighing 40lbs, extended by a further 3ft by the trolleybase itself.

Drivers wrote down any faults noted in service on vehicle report sheets, which were entered in a book by the night staff for attention the next day. No trolleybus was allowed to return to service until reported brake or steering faults had been rectified. Each month, all recorded faults were accumulated into a monthly defect report on squared paper which showed brake, dewirement and steering faults by date and vehicle, thus providing an easy way of tracing the cause of recurrent defects. Faults were shown as crosses in the appropriate squares, and their frequent repetition indicated a need to investigate their cause, e.g. poor driving skills, the overhead wiring, etc..

Coloured pins on a progressive mileage chart indicated the total mileage recorded by each vehicle and the dates at which intermediate service and major overhauls had been given or were due. Each vehicle's maintenance history was recorded in a Kardex file; major and minor repairs were shown in red and green ink respectively together with the chassis number and the dates of last overhaul, servicing, body overhaul and painting. Another Kardex file recorded to which trolleybus all the main removable chassis units were fitted, in order that their location could be quickly identified. A card index was also used to record the maintenance history of main units; on a separate card for each unit were entered details of work done, time spent on it, and material used.

The MoT required that a daily electrical leakage test be made, each vehicle being equipped with "test sockets" attached to half-a-dozen points into which a tester could be plugged. If leakage exceeded 3 milliamps the trolleybus was taken out of service. Trolleyheads were examined nightly and the carbon inserts changed when required, wear being greatest in icy and wet weather. The night foreman recorded E (examined), A (adjusted) or G (greased) as appropriate against the fleet number. In latter years, when the fleet had fallen to around 70 trolleybuses, the 3 depots were using between 6 and 12 carbon inserts per night, but this figure rose to about 20 in periods of wet weather. To ensure good electrical conductivity and smooth running, a cast iron slipper was fitted to the trolleyheads of special empty "ghost" trolleybuses, which operated throughout the night (see page 249), and the first service vehicles each morning, to clear ice and sleet from the running wires during periods of very frosty weather.

As each trolleybus ran into Castle Lane Depot after service, it passed through a carefully-isolated washing bay built alongside the east wall of the main garage before being parked under cover until next required for service.

The workshops themselves were accessible through wooden doors on the north side of the building leading directly on to 12 white-tiled pits, there being two spurs from the overhead wiring around the site. Ten of these pits continued into a sunken area, from which dismantled components could be hoisted and carried by runway through a degreasing plant into the units assembly and machine shop adjoining. This runway passed above a line of workbenches to an enclosed store of reconditioned parts, and components were issued direct for replacements without passing through the main stores. Current for the motor-driven machinery in the unit assembly and machine shop was taken from overhead busbars from which short leads could be dropped directly to the machines wherever they were placed.

Many worn parts were reconditioned for further service by welding, the worn surfaces being built up with new metal and machined to the original dimensions. This included the splined ends of half-shafts, differential casings, broken hub flanges and the hollow trunnion shafts that carried the rear springs of the BUT 9641T chassis. When the outer ends of these shafts were worn, the shaft was cut into halves which were then reversed and joined in the centre over a tight-fitting inner shaft. The new outer ends, when worn, were cut off and replaced by new additions, again using the same method of jointing. The amount of reconditioning work increased as it became difficult to obtain replacement spares from the manufacturers.

One of the workshop pits was divided by a broad central trench, extending to the pits on either side, to ease the work of dismantling heavy chassis components such as the offset Crompton Parkinson motors used in the BUT 9611Ts and 9641Ts. When a trolleybus was positioned over this pit, the front wheels were run across two steel channel girders that bridged the trench; the girders were then removed until needed again for the vehicle's departure. A mobile hydraulic jack was used to lower the components and take them away from the pit.

The workshops made up a number of assembly benches consisting of used lathe faceplates rotatably mounted on tramcar trolleybases cut down to a convenient height. Once a traction motor armature had been dismantled and removed, annular steel plates were bolted to the end flanges of the housing so that, when supported by these and engaged with free-running flanged wheels on one of the special assembly benches, the housing could be turned over to any suitable position for checking or repair.

In a letter to the Transport Committee, dated 6th December 1957, the General Manager revisited the subject of expanded and improved depot and workshop accommodation. He detailed the following alternative solutions:

Former Generating Station, Southcote Road: Consideration was given to retaining the whole or part of the then existing building but so many structural alterations would have been needed that the General Manager recommended the demolition of the shell and its replacement with a new structure.

To convert the former generating station into a workshop would have required much work to the front portion e.g. removal of pillars and switchboard platform, dismantling of the gantry and filling-in of pits. The rear, lower level, portion would have had to be built up to the height of the front portion. The chimney would have been demolished, thus providing hard core. The front and dividing walls, together with

Castle Lane (Mallard Road) depot, seen from the entrance to the site in Mallard Road. The vehicle visible in the depot is a motorbus.

J. C. Gillham

the low wall at the rear of the building bordering on the railway line would have had to be removed, leaving the side and rear walls. The heating of the 40ft high building would have proved costly.

A new steel-framed structure was planned for the Southcote Road site, having asbestos cement sheeting some 20ft high at the front, for maintenance pits and on the east side to provide paint and body shops and to allow sufficient space at the point where these two shops would join the engine shop for two storeys, having offices and stores on the first floor, and ablutions, toilet and heating boiler on the ground floor. The remainder of the building was foreseen as comprising machine, electrical, engine, panel beaters', welders' and smiths' shops, tyre stores and saw mills. This would need to be 15ft high. The construction would have provided 23,660 square feet of accommodation, compared to 34,250 at Castle Lane.

Central Depot, Southcote Road: By now this depot was deemed able to accommodate a maximum of 50 trolleybuses and 46 motorbuses, tightly packed. This was considered undesirable, for manoeuvering and fire risk reasons. The end of the leaseholds on 143, 145, 147, 149, 151 Southcote Road in 1964 would have provided an opportunity to extend the depot, offering accommodation for up to 36 more vehicles. The floor would have had to be supported on pillars due to the fall of the land at the rear of the houses, the existing garage floor being 10ft higher than the gardens at the rear of the then existing houses. Single-deck motorbuses could have been accommodated below the main garage, with ramped access from Vale Road. If the entire site under the houses was excavated to allow for a 12ft headroom, it would have proved possible to accommodate the entire single-deck fleet (then 23 motorbuses) and construct a two-floor depot accommodating about 155 vehicles. In 1957 BCT had 191 vehicles in their fleet, thus – even allowing for 14 trolleybuses kept at Boscombe (Pokesdown) Depot – 22 vehicles would still have had to be housed elsewhere.

Castle Lane (Mallard Road) Depot: An alternative suggested by Mr Reakes was to centralise everything under one roof at Castle Lane Depot, including the administrative offices, but excluding Boscombe (Pokesdown) Depot. A portion of land lying between the workshops and the existing garage could be treated with cement, offering sufficient accommodation in total for the undertaking's entire fleet. Half would be under cover and half on a hard-standing.

A rearrangement of the stores in the workshops could provide office accommodation for the entire administration and the offices at Central Depot, Southcote Road would be available for alternative use. The existing substation would have been retained.

Having deliberated for several years, it was decided in early 1962 to build a second garage of similar size to the initial structure at the Castle Lane site, limited to motorbuses, located to the west of the existing garage, enabling the entire fleet to be stabled at one place. At the same time, a new administrative block was constructed on the west side of the depot loop road, opposite the workshops and stores, to replace the "temporary" solution which had existed at Southcote Road since the move from Wootton Gardens on 1st April 1940. On 26th April 1965 the Transport Department headquarters relocated to Castle Lane, an official opening by the Mayor of the new offices and second garage taking place on 7th May 1965. The garage and office accommodation at Central Depot, Southcote Road was vacated completely by 7th June 1965.

In recent years, Yellow Buses have endeavoured to establish a more economic headquarters operation and move out of Castle Lane. Their plans were thwarted in 1999, when English Heritage recommended their Garage No.1 building for listing as of architectural significance due to the innovative single-span concrete roof. Garage No.1 now has Grade 2 listing from the Department of Culture, Media and Sport.

Trolleybuses neatly lined-up in Central Depot, Southcote Road. Sunbeam MS2s 206 (ALJ 61) and 221 (BEL 816) are at the front of the row. Numerous other MS2s are present, together with some BUT 9641Ts.

London Trolleybus Preservation Society

<table>
<tr><td>APPENDIX
G</td><td colspan="3">Power Supply and Generating Station</td></tr>
</table>

The Transport Department's own generating station, built in 1902 to supply power for both lighting and tramway traction current purposes, initially provided power to the majority of the trolleybus system. The generating station building was 150 ft wide, 100 ft deep and 40 ft high. It was constructed on two sections with a dividing wall. The front portion, which contained the generators, was not level throughout but had a number of pits accommodating ancillary equipment, whereas the rear portion was 6–8 ft lower and housed the boilers. There were also a number of auxiliary buildings, including the coal bunkers, electrical workshops, switchboard, offices, stores, toilets and bathrooms, cooling towers and chimney, making up an integral part of the Central Depot, Southcote Road facilities, situated between the main car shed and the head office building.

The original plant comprised four 3-crank Bellis and Morcom Triple Expansion engines, 450 bhp, having 12 ins, 18½ ins and 28ins x 12 ins cylinders, running at 360 rpm, taking steam at 175 psi and exhausting to condensers. Each engine was coupled direct to a multi-polar British Thomson-Houston compound wound generator with a constant potential of 550 volts DC. The condensing plant comprised two 2-crank Bellis and Morcom compound engines, having cylinders 5½ ins and 9 ins x 5 ins, running at 500 rpm, which were used to drive the condensing pumps. Five coal-fired Lancashire boilers provided the steam. The main Stather switchboard had seventeen panels, comprising six generator and one motor generator panel on the right-hand side, and seven feeder panels, two Board of Trade panels and one main panel on the left. The original capacity was 1,168 kW.

In 1926, two turbo-generators and associated Babcock & Wilcock boilers had been installed to replace the original reciprocating motors, necessitating the construction of a gantry to accommodate these sets. In 1942 a 1,500 kW Daniel Adamson/Mather & Platt turbo-generator set was added, requiring an extension to this gantry and an increase in the number of supporting pillars.

Coal was not only the prime cost factor in electricity generation, but also the leading industrial fuel, charges being set by national agreement. Throughout the trolleybus era, coal and coke were supplied by Messrs W. D. Barnett & Co. under contract, typical deliveries being Elliott Washed Beans, Seaborne Screenings and furnace coke. Looking back at the year ending 31st March 1935, Mr Bulfin recorded: *"The total output of current amounted to 4,548,390 units, as compared with 4,362,110 units, some 186,280 more units than last year. This is due to increased trolleybus mileage being run. The coal consumed during the year was 5,629 tons, as against 5,335 tons last year. The total cost per unit, including all capital charges, worked out at 0.70d".* Just one year later, coal prices had increased by over 10% or 2s per ton due to increasing industrial demand.

Wartime inflation, and dramatically increased demand, led to coal rationing, supply being co-ordinated by the Ministries of Mines, and Fuel and Power. Prices rocketed, whilst it became increasing difficult to obtain quality furnace fuels suitable for power generation, as public transport usage rose to unprecedented levels. In the closing months of the war and immediately thereafter (when the best grade coals were, as a priority, being exported to gain valuable foreign currency) it became problematical to get deliveries of *any* type of solid fuel in sufficient quantity. The fluctuations in the price of coal during the wartime period is shown in the table at the top of the next column.

Coal prices stabilised briefly in 1950 at 76s 1d per ton for Elliot Washed Beans and 74s 5¾d per ton for Seaborne Screenings, but then continued to rise inexorably until power generation at Southcote Road ceased.

It is not known how it was possible for Bournemouth Corporation Transport to continue generating its own electrical supply at

Date	Increase	Price per ton
		35s 11d
1st October 1939	6d	36s 5d
3rd November 1939	1s 4d	37s 9d
May 1940	2s 1d	39s 10d
1st November 1940	2s 9d	42s 7d
1st December 1940	11d	43s 6d
1st January 1941	8d	44s 2d
June 1941	10d	45s
19th July 1941	10d	45s 10d
1st July 1943	1s	46s 10d
1st February 1944	3s	49s 10d
1st August 1944	4s	53s 10d
1st April 1945	8d	54s 6d
1st May 1945	3s 6d	58s
11th February 1946	2d	58s 2d
1st July 1946	1s 3d	59s 5d
1st March 1948	3s 4d	62s 9d
19th July 1948	3s	65s 9d

Southcote Road following the nationalisation of the power industry in 1948. One can only surmise that Bournemouth, Glasgow (Pinkston) and various London Transport power stations (Greenwich; Lots Road, Chelsea; and Neasden) were allowed to continue as production was limited to DC power for traction purposes only. In the early post-war period, when capacity-related (rather than strike-related) load-shedding was a relatively common event, the Southern Electricity Board (SEB) was probably relieved not to have an additional peak-hour demand from the trolleybuses when their own domestic and industrial needs were at their height. In the early tramway days, Southcote Road had also supplied power for the first electric street lights, but this was discontinued as the requirement for traction purposes increased.

When operational, Southcote Road generating station consumed about 200 tons of coal per week in summer. This all arrived by train on the Transport Department's own siding (No. 10), which led off the railway goods yard on the south side of the main line about 500 yards east of Bournemouth Central Station.

In late August 1955, shortly before the generating station closed down, a lightning strike to the overhead wiring near Central Station managed to negotiate the various safety devices and reached the Southcote Road switchboard, setting it on fire and causing serious damage. The strike found a path to the Mather & Platt generator, which was destroyed. The incident took place at 7.05 pm and brought trolleybus services to a standstill in the central area for about two hours, until alternative supplies and temporary repairs could be effected. As the changeover to SEB supplies was about to take place, the generator was never repaired. Until then, the undertaking had generated about 60% of its traction power needs. On 6th September 1955, just after the changeover, the national supply failed, and the boilers were steamed-up and the turbo-generators turned for the last time, but SEB power was restored soon after power production re-started at Southcote Road.

Thereafter, current came into Southcote Road substation from the National Grid at 11,000 volts, having been stepped down from 33kV at the SEB's own substation immediately behind the Transport Department's building. Three-phase AC current came in at about 20 amps, varying according to demand, and passed through two heavy-duty circuit breakers, before reaching two transformers which reduced the voltage to that usable by the trolleybuses, nominally 565V DC. The actual voltage varied with demand, but was not allowed to reach 600 volts, being counterbalanced by subsequent transmission losses. The transformers produced a six-phase AC current, the two halves of the system being slightly out of phase so that in effect a 12-phase current resulted. This was fed to two pairs of Hewittic glass-bulb rectifiers, from

224

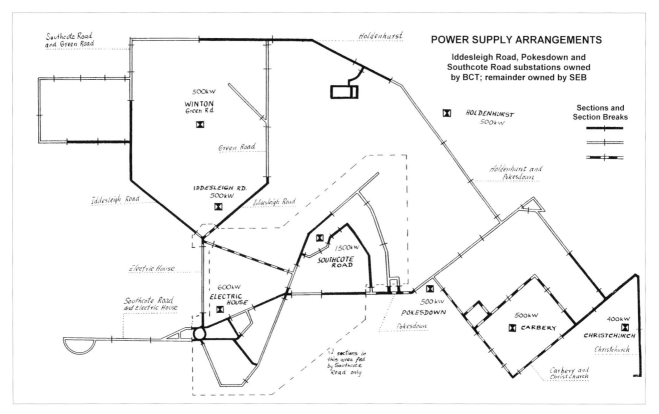

POWER SUPPLY ARRANGEMENTS

Iddesleigh Road, Pokesdown and
Southcote Road substations owned
by BCT; remainder owned by SEB

which the current emerged as an almost steady DC supply. A mercury arc rectifier functions according to the principle that mercury vapour can only conduct electricity in a single direction. AC is fed to the anodes of the octopus-like glass bulbs, and an arc was set up between the anodes and a pool of mercury in the bottom of the bulb. Incoming current, alternating at a frequency of 50 cycles a second (the standard frequency of the National Grid supply) flashed 50 times per second between the anodes and the mercury-covered cathodes, forming a virtually continuous arc. There were six arms on each bulb, each connected to a phase of the supply, and thus the output was close to being a continuous current. The windowless substation was filled with a ghostly greenish light, wavering slightly, the mercury bubbling constantly in the bulbs.

The traction current was taken from the rectifiers to the switchboard busbars (bars of solid copper running the length of the rear of the board, their heavy rectangular section offering virtually no resistance to the current and enabling connections to the various switches to be solidly bolted to them). From the busbars, 19 feeder cables went out to various parts of the system, each being connected to the busbars through a heavy-duty circuit breaker and isolating switch.

If the current exceeded a set value, its magnetic effect opened the automatic circuit breaker, preventing excessive current from entering a cable and damaging it. Current would be cut off by a broken trolley wire if the live ends made a good contact with earth; a dewired trolley head might create a short circuit across the insulators of a frog or crossover, etc.. The circuit breakers were equipped with time relays, which automatically restored current after a pre-set period. If the fault was still present, they reopened. If this cycle of events occurred three times, on the fourth occasion the circuit breakers stayed open and an alarm sounded in the Mains Superintendent's office. It was then necessary to locate the fault and isolate the feeder concerned until it was safe to restore current.

As a "fail safe" feature, each feeder cable was equipped with indicator lights which illuminated only when power was off. When it was necessary to switch off the current from a particular feeder, for example to inspect a broken wire, the automatic circuit breaker was made to function by pressing a switch and the isolating switch was then quickly opened before the restoring device on the breaker had time to operate. The isolating switches were of the "knife" pattern, which could not be opened when under load as this would have caused arcing which could potentially burn the entire switch out.

At the Corporation-owned substations at Iddesleigh Road and Boscombe (Pokesdown) Depot, red exterior warning lamps illuminated if a circuit breaker opened and stayed open. Drivers of passing trolleybuses were instructed to report any lamp seen illuminated.

The Sunbeam MS2 trolleybuses had regenerative braking, which fed current back into the overhead wires and subsequently to the sub-stations. This caused overload problems if no other vehicles were drawing current in the section at the time, and later trolleybus deliveries were equipped with rheostatic braking. As the overhead line was divided into sections connected at substations, it sufficed to install banks of ballast resistances in the Christchurch, Pokesdown and Southcote Road substations, with Allen West over-voltage relays to absorb any over-voltage (or, in other words, to simulate the presence of another trolleybus). If no current at all was being taken from the over-head, the arc within the mercury arc rectifier could die out. To prevent this, bleeder resistances between the positive and negative busbars of each substation ensured that current was always flowing. At Southcote Road the bleeder resistance was provided by two electric fire elements, connected in series, which also served to keep the substation warm and dry.

The overhead remained live 24 hours a day. At the substations there were metering devices to record the state of the system. Voltmeters and ammeters recorded the incoming current, and further meters recorded the output from the rectifiers. During the mid-1960s the maximum output from both pairs of rectifiers at Southcote Road was 600 volts at 500 amps, totalling 300 kW. Two recording meters in the circuit, at the point where the feeds from the rectifiers were connected to the busbars, traced a continuous graph on recording paper so that the maximum output at any given time could be seen. At the height of the morning rush hour, 8.45 am, output typically reached 1,850 amps. In the peak of the summer season, maximum system demand rose to 2,175 kW (July 1963) and 2,295 kW (August 1963). Demand was, of course, related to the size of the fleet, but in 1960, when the number of trolleybuses available for service averaged 63 in winter and 82 in summer, Mr W. D. Reakes, writing in *Electrical Review* gave the following figures: maximum winter system demand 2,000 kW; in summer 2,700 kW. Traction current consumption for an average week: winter 130,000 kW, summer 200,000 kW.

Meters in each of the eight substations recorded the amount of AC current consumed. The basis for payment was a contract with the SEB for the supply of current over a given period at a rate per unit based on

225

the quantity used. This special rate was based on the maximum demand figures taken from the abovementioned recording meters.

Nineteen feeder cables left Southcote Road substation for different parts of the central area. Two sections, Moordown and Westbourne, were fed jointly by Southcote Road and Green Road or Electric House substations respectively, whilst the ten sections making up the outlying parts of the system were fed by five other unattended substations independent of Southcote Road. The connections between the power supply feeder cables and the overhead wiring were installed in cast iron feeder pillars or switch boxes, every half-mile along the line of route and elsewhere as electrically necessary. Within each pillar, knife switches could be opened to interrupt the supply to the overhead or link sections as required. Fuses were also fitted in the cables leading to the overhead, although the automatic circuit breakers within the substations were the first line of defence against excessive current passing into the line. A further piece of equipment was the lightning arrester, a coil and spark gap, to "choke" the very high voltage current and impede its progress in the hope that it would find it easier to pass to earth. Each trolleybus was also equipped with a lightning arrester; on the Sunbeam MS2s the "choke" coil was wound into the positive cable and could be seen mounted over the centre pillar of the front windscreen, immediately next to the positive circuit breaker.

In each feeder pillar a card diagram showed the normal connections and position of each switch, in addition to showing to which cables the pillar was connected. Nine of these roadside boxes, known as Mains Pillars, were not connected to the overhead at all, but contained junctions between various mains, enabling the current supply to be varied. Twenty-three other switch boxes were connected to the overhead wiring only, and served to link a section with its neighbour. Six of these were smaller boxes containing just one or two knife switches and were often mounted on the traction poles themselves.

The boxes were kept securely locked. Originally, Inspectors and other officials were supplied with keys so that they could open the boxes in an emergency and cut off the current to a section, but at a later date their issue was restricted to employees of the Mains and Overhead Department, who better understood the implications of their actions.

The strategically important layout at Bournemouth Square could be supplied from any one of five feeder pillars or pole switch boxes, Albert Road, Bobbys (outside the department store on the Square which then bore that name), St. Peter's (the one normally used), Square Office or Yelverton Road. It could also be fed from the Lansdowne cables by closing the switches at the Royal Bath Hotel switch box or a combination of those in the Bobbys feeder pillar and the Bournemouth Pier switch box. In an emergency it would also have been practical to link the Square wiring to the Richmond Hill, Old Christchurch Road or Poole Hill sections.

EARTHING

The Bournemouth system was all-insulated, with the continuous negative wire earthed at a single point. This could be identified by the apparently continuous negative wire, devoid of the half mile gaps evident in the positive wire. In fact, the negative wire was broken by section insulators at Castle Lane, near Broadway Hotel (replaced latterly); Oak Avenue, Iford (installed when those at the Broadway Hotel were removed); Roslin Road, Winton; Rushton Crescent, near Cemetery Junction; the Triangle (a jumpered-over "breaker") and the White Hart Hotel, Christchurch. The negative insulators were inserted for line testing purposes and were normally bridged over by jumper cables, Meyrick Park Crescent being an exception. There was a complete network of negative return cables which brought the return current back to a busbar connected to electrodes buried in coke breeze in the Central Depot, Southcote Road yard where the entire system was earthed.

The negative return cables were connected to the overhead by means of pole-mounted switch boxes, although at six places (Broadway, Crantock Grove, East Way, Holdenhurst, Square Office and Yelverton Road) they were connected at positive feeder pillars from which six cables, instead of the usual four, led out to the overhead wiring. Each was identifiable by name. The negative return connections were usually adjacent to the positive feeders, and thus at approximately half mile intervals, but the two were normally given separate names e.g. the positive feeder at pole M98 was named Peter's Hill, whereas the negative at pole M99 was named Pine Road (for an explanation of pole and wiring route numbering, see Appendix I).

Neither the positive mains nor the negative returns always ran parallel to an actual trolleybus route, whilst there were even sections of overhead not connected to the underground network, where the overhead itself carried the return current. A mile-long section, Seabourne Road to Kimberley Road, was created in 1948 when the Cranleigh Road route opened. Where there was double-track overhead and thus two negative wires, these were cross-connected to equalise the current in them and reduce resist- ance to a minimum. The two negative wires were normally connected through the switch boxes, by which they were coupled to their under- ground return cables, but where there were no cables along the route, equalizers, consisting of short lengths of cable connected at either end to the negative wires and running along a convenient span wire (usually the one next to a half-mile section insulator) could be seen. In addition, Mallard Road switch box had both positive and negative switches connected to the outward line, to enable the depot wiring to be fed from Castle Lane in an emergency (the inward line had insulators in both wires with jumpers omitted). Under normal circumstances, the depot was fed by its own cables running along Cattistock Road to the east of the property from Cattistock mains pillar on Castle Lane, which was not connected to the overhead and which had both positive and negative cable connections. The negative feeder was removed well before 1969.

The power station, looking west, on 3rd June 1962. Note the cobbled yard, the decorative brickwork and the lamp suspended from the overhead span wire.

J. C. Gillham

High-voltage tests were made to check the insulation on all positive feeder and negative return cables periodically. Leakage from the positive system was checked every Friday night after the last trolleybus had run into the depot, and when any current passing was clearly leaking to earth. The MoT's 1936 Regulations for Bournemouth stipulated a maximum permissible leakage current of $^1/_{100}$ amp per mile of route, and required that operations had to cease if the fault could not be located and corrected within 24 hours.

No limit was placed on the number of trolleybuses which could operate on a given section at any one time but, if several vehicles were all starting away at the same time, the line voltage fell. The vehicles' controls were designed to function at half the normal line voltage, but problems developed if this fell below 400 volts. At times when few trolleybuses were operating, line voltage was accordingly high, and high speeds could be obtained.

SIZE OF CABLES

The nineteen feeder cables leaving the Southcote Road main switchboard were, from left to right:

Cable	Name	Size*	Comment/Note
1.	Southcote Road	0.183	
2.	St. Clement's Road	0.183	Including Central Depot
3.	Ashley Road	0.183	
4.	Holdenhurst Road	0.183	
5.	Winton	0.31	See Note A
6.	Cemetery	0.243	See Note A
7.	Lansdowne No.1	0.31	Fed Lansdowne (exclusive) to the Royal Bath Hotel Junction and Bournemouth Pier
8.	Cleveland Road	0.183	Fed part of the Ashley Road route. See Note B
9.	St. Peter's	0.31	Fed the Square. See Note C
10.	Lansdowne No.2	0.31	Fed Lansdowne (exclusive) to Derby Road
11.	Richmond Hill No.1	0.31	Fed Lansdowne (inclusive) to Trinity Church
12.	Richmond Hill No.2	0.31	Live cable to Beales mains pillar. See Note D
13.	Beales	0.31	Fed Albert Road to Trinity Church
14.	Poole Hill	0.31	Coupled to Grosvenor Road
15.	Grosvenor Road	0.243	Coupled to Poole Hill
16.	Meyrick Park Cres.	0.31	Part of a Southcote Road – Moordown and Winton link
17.	Charminster	0.5	See Note E
18.	Parkwood Rd 1 ins	0.5	Fed Boscombe Hill – Pokesdown substation
19.	Parkwood Rd ½ ins	1.00	Fed route "P" Palmerston Hotel- Warwick Road. See Note F

Notes:

* Cross-sectional area of copper conductor (sq. ins)

A Both cables were connected to the overhead at St. Paul's Road and Lansdowne Road to feed Route "O" but, beyond, were disconnected by normally open switches. The Cemetery Junction cable ended at St. Augustin's feeder pillar, where it was live but not connected to the line. The substation at Electric House fed the overhead up to this point, and the 0.243 sq. ins Cemetery cable was thus merely an alternative source of supply for emergency purposes. The rest of the 0.31 sq. ins Winton cable was again divided into two by an open switch in Ensbury mains pillar. The part from Cemetery Junction to Peter's Hill feeder pillar was fed from Iddesleigh Road substation which fed the overhead on this part of route "M". The final section of the cable was live and connected to a 0.5 sq. ins cable fed by both Green Road and Southcote Road substations.

B Coupled to the Ashley Road cable by virtue of the fact that they both fed the same overhead wire, adjacent half mile sections

being connected by normally closed switches at the White House pole switch box.

C The St. Peter's cable continued to Bobbys feeder pillar, where it was live but not normally connected to the overhead.

D Alternative supply for any section in an emergency.

E The part immediately connected to Southcote Road was coupled to Iddesleigh Road substation at Cemetery Junction, and served as an equaliser between the two substations. The next section was used to join Iddesleigh Road substation to the overhead at Alma Road. It divided again, the next section connecting Green Road substation to the line at Five Ways and Luckham Road feeder pillars. The final section was connected to Holdenhurst substation, and fed the Castle Lane route including Castle Lane Depot.

F Cables 18 and 19 were coupled to feed Boscombe Hill, and were then isolated by open switches. The third and final section of cable 19 was a connection to Carbery substation.

Each of the outgoing cables was connected to an ammeter which showed the current passing, the meters being of the centre zero type as, due to the inter-connections, some cables were feeding back current to the substation. For example, the cables which connected Southcote Road to sections also fed by other substations (such as Electric House, Green Road, Iddesleigh Road, etc.), fed current to Southcote Road when traffic in the sections concerned was light. On sections not connected to any other cables, it was possible to judge how many trolleybuses were moving in the section. At night the trolleybuses returned to depot, and the various meters reached zero indicating when the last trolleybus was "home".

The actual route of the cable runs, together with their cross-sections, was carefully mapped for both departmental use and to guide the public utilities in their excavating activities. Their position could also be identified from the unique style of manhole covers every few hundred yards along the pavement. These covers incorporated a rectangular metal grid ventilator (until it filled up with dirt and dust), making them very different from those used by the GPO or, latterly, the SEB. Cable runs were installed parallel to all the former tram routes, but did not always contain power supply cables. The Derby Road – Lansdowne and Bournemouth Square – Poole Hill via Avenue Road runs contained only telephone cables. Underground cables did not always follow the trolleybus routes; the Parkwood Road ½ ins cable ran from Southcote Road via Derby Road to Christchurch Road; the Cleveland Road and Ashley Road feeders ran via Cleveland and Tower Roads respectively, and at Southbourne the cables deviated via Tuckton and Seafield Roads whilst the trolleybuses ran along Belle Vue Road. The 1 ins Parkwood Road cable ran via Parkwood Road, hence its name, and did not go via Pokesdown (Boscombe) Depot and Seabourne Road.

Under normal conditions the overhead system was divided into 21 electrical sections, and was broken into 93 half-mile lengths of running wire plus the seasonal Bournemouth Pier section, Central Depot constituting three separate sections, the Mallard Road complex and its bus wash, all of which could also be isolated separately, making a total of 28 sections. The electrical sections were frequently linked. For example, the lines from Bournemouth Square (exclusive) to Westbourne formed one section fed by Electric House and Southcote Road substations, although the line could have been divided up into four sub-sections by the use of feeder pillar switching.

Dead ends in the feeder cables at Columbia Road and at the junction of Castle Lane East with Holdenhurst Road, together with the tied-off overhead line at Lawford Road, Redhill, gave evidence of planned extensions which never came to fruition. Before the Castle Lane/ Holdenhurst Road roundabout was built, there was a supplementary mid-section feeder to the overhead at Holdenhurst mains pillar, the intention being to link up with Route "Q" which would have had breakers at the junction. A live tail which would have gone off to Route "Q" was connected to Holdenhurst switch box, was left standing in isolation in the middle of the new roundabout, making it a mains pillar. As Route "F" eastward from this point was linked via the overhead to Pokesdown substation, the two substations were coupled.

INSTALLATION

As the trolleybuses started to replace the tramways, entirely new wiring was installed. The trams continued to use their own positive lines until final withdrawal, rather than share it with the new vehicles. Separate wiring was hung between the kerb and the tram overhead, enabling trolleybuses to "overtake" the slower trams. On occasions the trolleybus wires were hung from the tramway side bracket poles, whilst the tramway positive wire was rehung on short span wires running between the ends of opposite bracket arms. Much of the Bournemouth system was constructed with single-line hangers, as used on the tramways, but new material was used throughout.

Large scale route diagrams showing the proposed line, together with plans and profiles of the roads over which the trolleybuses would operate, were prepared to accompany the application for Parliamentary powers. Once granted, details of the individual pole positions, plans of junctions, etc., were drawn up. On the electrical side, requirements were prepared for the provision of section insulators, feeder cables, etc.. Actual construction commenced with the planting of traction poles in their appointed positions, after which the span wires would be placed in position and tightened up so as to pull the tops of the backwards-slanting poles slightly together. The span wires were immersed in Stockholm tar for one week before use, to provide a lifetime's corrosion protection. Before the span wires were slackened off, the hangers were inserted. A half mile cod line (a thin rope) would be attached to the span wires as if it were the first of the trolley wires. Its position represented the position of the negative wire of the first pair, and its location was carefully adjusted so that straight sections were really straight, and curved sections smoothly curved. The position of the negative wire for either the outbound or inbound pair of wires was then marked on each of the span wires, the procedure being repeated for the position of the second pair before the cod line was moved to the next half mile section. The span wires were then cut, a turnbuckle being used to keep the two parts of the span wire taunt during this operation, and the hangers placed in position. The trolley wire would then be run out and simply tied to each span wire alongside the hangers, the ends of each half-mile length being temporarily fastened to a suitable traction pole.

The linesmen then worked along the length, fitting the trolley wire to each hanger and screwing the ears up tight, riveting the ends of the screws over to prevent them working loose at any time. The half-mile section breakers were fitted, and the battered ends of the trolley wire which had been fastened to the traction poles were trimmed off. Usually a route was connected to an existing line at one or both ends, and the final connecting up could be done at the last moment after the route itself was complete, usually in a single overnight operation when traffic on the existing route had ceased. If the ends of the trolley wire which had been tied off to traction poles could not be made long enough to allow for trimming later, new undamaged lengths were spliced in or, alternately, the wire could be straightened by using special rollers to iron out any kinks.

When two lengths of trolley wire were ready to be joined, they were pulled together by the use of clamps and a screw tensioner, a dynamometer or heavy duty spring balance being used to adjust the tension in the wires to the correct figure of 2,000 lbs. This would indicate where the new wire should be cut. Both ends were then cleaned, straightened and joined, adjustments being made to the hangers along the whole line if any had been pulled slightly out of position by the tensioning. After a number of trial runs, the overhead wiring was ready for official inspection.

In the early days of operation, the majority of urban telephone wires were still hung in the air rather than installed underground, and guard wires were hung above the trolleybus overhead where telephone wires crossed the road to prevent a broken or sagging telephone wire being charged at trolleybus line voltage. The guard wires consisted of a second pair of thinner wires attached to span wires of the same material, the whole network being suspended about three feet above the trolley wires themselves. At intervals the guard wires were earthed through a connection to the negative trolley wire. Examples could be seen on traction pole Route "T" until the mid-1960s.

Protective netting hanging between the traction poles some 15–20 feet above the ground and parallel to the actual running wires immediately above the footpath was installed at points where dewirements were more frequent and where a swinging trolley pole could cause damage. Installations could be found until the end of trolleybus operation at the beginning of the eastbound overtaking wiring in Old Christchurch Road preceding Lansdowne roundabout and on the entry curves to Fir Vale Road travelling towards Bournemouth Square.

MAINTENANCE

The Overhead Department followed a scheduled maintenance programme, and each route was inspected on a regular basis. Occasional work such as layout alterations, the renewal of fittings and rewiring was done at night. Some worn parts of the overhead wiring equipment such as crossings, frogs and trolleyheads, were reconditioned by the department by building up using sifbronze. Maintenance work included an examination of all bracket poles, one pole being thoroughly overhauled each week, every bolt being inspected and the whole painted with protective paint. Working seven days a week in three eight-hour shifts until almost the end of the system, four gangs of linesmen carried out this work 24 hours per day, their whereabouts at any given time being shown on a special board at Central Depot. A "gang" consisted of a driver and two linesmen. When major installation or layout alterations were carried out, two or more gangs would operate between 10 pm Saturday and 6 am (or later) on Sundays.

Linesmen were despatched to the correct location for their duties by reference to the alpha-numeric code painted on each traction pole. Simple diagrams were drawn to complement instructions given for work at junctions or other points where there were many line fittings needing attention. Crossovers, frogs and insulators received an annual coat of Kalbitum paint; in addition automatic frogs were stripped down, cleaned and lubricated every three months. All renewals were recorded in a book, compiled from inspection reports, showing the condition of the entire system which had a single track length of 107 miles as at its maximum extent in Summer 1963. Also recorded were the particulars and times of emergency calls to remedy defects and the times that these were cleared.

Some statistics from 1963, provided by John Mawson, are of interest:

Line miles:	107
Route miles:	29
Turnouts:	92
of which, Auto Frogs:	27
Junctions:	80
Crossovers:	55
Section Insulators:	
AA:	36
BICC:	94
Traction Poles:	3237

The life of trolley wire was between thirteen and fifteen years. The totals for section insulators do not include insulator units incorporated into turnouts, junctions and crossovers.

An oddity was the turnout used by trolleybuses from Tuckton Bridge to turn at Carbery Avenue, which had its operating handle on the right-hand side of the road.

228

During the trolleybus era, the Overhead Department operated a number of tower wagons and ancillary vehicles, as shown in the table at the foot of this page.

SOUTHCOTE ROAD SPECIALITIES

At the Boscombe end of Palmerston Road (traction pole Route "Y") there was a unique arrangement whereby the four running wires making up the double junction with Christchurch Road, immediately past the Palmerston Hotel, were reduced to two (see map, page 216). The two positive wires divided at an ordinary spring reset trail frog which was normally set for the left-hand line. The northwards i.e. from Boscombe towards Central Depot, negative wire was tied-off at two traction poles provided for this purpose and a trolleybus proceeding towards the depot had to stop on the three-wire section for the booms to be transferred, the positive to the right-hand wire and the negative to the centre wire. In 1954 a crossover was made up from spare ramp-end fittings, enabling trolleybuses to run through without re-poling, but it was considered advisable for trolleybuses to come to a complete standstill at the junction, and thus the frogs at the Boscombe end of the crossover were hand-operated, although those at the Central Depot end were spring trail frogs enabling a trolleybus to run straight through towards Christchurch Road. Trolleybuses heading north towards the depot were thus running as if on the "wrong" set of wires. This required no special electrical switching arrangements on the vehicle or at the roadside as a trolleybus motor, being compound wound, rotates in the same direction as usual if the polarity of the supply is reversed (i.e. to reverse, *either* the direction of current through the field coils *or* through the armature – but not both – must be reversed). However a depot-bound trolleybus meeting one taking up service would have to hook down a trolley pole to enable the vehicles to pass.

At the other end of the same route, between Central Depot and Holdenhurst Road, there was another section of three-wire overhead (two negative either side of a single central positive). It was rumoured that this was a remnant from the last days of the trams, which avoided unnecessary overhead wiring reconstruction when both trolleybuses and trams were operating to and from Central Depot. At the junction with Holdenhurst Road, a spring reset frog led the positive trolley onto the left-hand line of the conventional "twin track" overhead layout.

This route was not used by scheduled trolleybus services, but passengers waiting at the motorbus stops could hail trolleybuses travelling to or from Central Depot.

FROGS

Although hand-operated frogs (points or switches in the overhead wiring) were installed throughout in the early days of the system, increasing trolleybus and other traffic, together with consideration of the conductor's workload encouraged BCT to look for other alternatives. Until then, the conductor had to leap from the rear platform and pull the handle attached to a convenient traction pole when the trolleybus needed to follow a "branch" line. This system was retained at little-used junctions throughout the life of the system e.g. Broadway Hotel to go between Charminster and Strouden Park in either direction, Five Ways turning circle, Lawford Road to head towards West Way, etc..

The first "auto frogs" came into use at the Lansdowne junction (eastbound) on 6th March 1936. By 5th May 1938 there was an auto frog at the foot of Richmond Hill, whilst another was installed at Pokesdown by 28th May 1939. The Overhead Department standardised on the Forest City automatic frog setter. This required a break in either the negative or, exceptionally in Bournemouth, positive wire and the installation of a transfer contact ahead of the frog with a restoring contact skate hung about half an inch above the positive wire just beyond the frog to return it to the normal route.

As the trolleybus approached the transfer contact, a driver wishing to take the "branch" line would keep his foot *on* the power pedal, simultaneously controlling the vehicle's speed with the hand brake, thereby drawing current from the positive wire and returning it to the negative through the motor. Passing under the transfer contact in the negative wire, current would return through the operating relay installed in a traction pole mounted box about 8 ft above the ground which then sent current to the operating solenoid further up the pole. This set the frog and lit a confirming signal lamp.

If the driver wished to remain on the "main" line, he would coast under the transfer contact with his foot *off* the power pedal, ensuring

Tower Wagons and Ancillary Vehicles

Fleet No	Reg No	Type	Into service	Withdrawn	Note
–	EL 2105	Tilling-Stevens TS3 petrol-electric tower wagon	Not known	June 1936	1
–	EL 2103	Tilling-Stevens TS3 petrol-electric tower wagon	August 1917	March 1937	2
–	EL 2106	Tilling-Stevens TS3 petrol-electric tower wagon	July 1933	January 1936	3
1	RU 2012	Tilling-Stevens TS6 petrol-electric tower wagon	January 1936	May 1945	4
2	RU 2013	Tilling-Stevens TS6 petrol-electric tower wagon	June 1936	October 1950	5
6	RU 2014	Tilling-Stevens TS6 petrol-electric tower wagon	May 1937	October 1948	6
3	DEL 37	Bedford 2-ton tower wagon with Rawlins tower	June 1937	December 1965	7
10	VH 6218	AEC Regent 661/Lee Motors tower wagon	February 1947	May 1967	8
12	VH 6217	AEC Regent 661/Lee Motors tower wagon	November 1948	Post 1969	8
–	TF 447	Leyland SQ2 crane	October 1950	September 1962	9
–	FRU 224	Guy Arab FD crane	December 1962	Post 1969	9, 10
–	304 LJ	Morris Commercial FG tipper	November 1962	Post 1969	11

Notes:

1   Converted from single deck motorbus rebuild dating from April 1915. After withdrawal, tower transferred to RU 2016.
2   Converted from open-top double deck motorbus dating from April 1914. After withdrawal, tower transferred to RU 2014
3   Converted from single deck motorbus rebuild dating from May 1915 and withdrawn in 1930. After withdrawal, tower transferred to RU 2012
4   Converted from single deck motorbus 13 dating from October 1925.
5   Converted from single deck motorbus 14 dating from October 1925.
6   Converted from single deck motorbus 15 dating from October 1925.
7   Purchased new. After 1948 mainly used for painting traction poles and accordingly given a green livery.
8   Ex-Huddersfield Corporation motorbuses, first registered in March 1934 and purchased by Bournemouth 11th January 1945. They were not used in public service in Bournemouth. Rebuilt with shortened chassis by Lee Motors and fitted with tower by the Transport Department. Originally in scarlet livery with maroon bands.
9   After withdrawal, crane transferred to FRU 224
10   Converted in March 1962 from a 1944 Utility double-deck motorbus, which had itself been converted to open-top format in June 1952.

Ashley Road shortly after the introduction of trolleybuses in the 1930s. A single line of tram track remains in the centre of the road. Note the section insulators, the tramway-style line hangers (in the shape of an inverted "U") and the span wire (with insulators) linking the traction poles on opposite sides of the street. Note, too, the charming period atmosphere of the corner shop, the bicycle and the Victorian housing – and the more modern buildings already encroaching into the background.

Stanford, Boscombe

that no current was sent into the setter. Bournemouth became particularly adept at installing the transfer contact and frog prior to a road junction where the vehicle's reduced speed passing beneath a frog might prove a disruption to other vehicles e.g. at Trinity Church, Old Christchurch Road, heading east towards the Lansdowne, and in Commercial Road heading west to the Triangle. This had a further advantage of ensuring that there was a reduced amount of complicated overhead immediately above busy road junctions or roundabouts, thereby reducing the risk of dewirements.

The skate used as a restoring contact with the Forest City machine had a contact strip held down by light springs. As the trolley head passed beneath, the strip was lifted, closing the sprung contact, which thus sent a current at line voltage back to the frog setter relay and restored the frog to normal. The same skates were used for signalling purposes i.e. in Christchurch High Street, to indicate that the turntable was occupied.

Both hand-operated and auto frogs were equipped with indicator lights, normally attached to the nearside traction pole immediately after the frog itself, which confirmed to the trolleybus driver that the frog switch tongues had moved to the required position both before and after the trolleyheads had passed beneath the frog. If the light went out before they had cleared the frog or if the light did not go out after the trolley-heads had cleared the frog, the driver would stop and send his conductor back to pull the frog manually or to pull the reset cord if the frog had not restored. Although BICC and Forest City offered their own indicator light systems, BCT developed their own simplified version. The indicator box had two separate lenses and lamps, but in many cases the second lens was blanked off. When the frog was set for the "main" line there was no indication; the other lamp, normally equipped with an orange lens, gave the "branch" line indication. Exceptionally both lamps illuminated to confirm the "branch" line had been set.

There appeared to be no system to the colours used in the indicator boxes, whether related to route or junction (left or right) frog used. The auto frog at Bournemouth Square proceeding from Gervis Place back into Old Christchurch Road had red and green lenses probably to distinguish its indication from that of the second auto frog controlling

the divergence of the Westbourne and Triangle lines, which had white lenses, a short way ahead. The signal indicator box at Westbourne acted as a headway regulator by displaying both a red and white light when an inbound trolleybus was on the section of Poole Road between the two ends of Seamoor Road.

Experimental installations of other types of auto frogs were made from time to time. The Webster and the Wiseman types both resembled the BICC product, which had small operating solenoids mounted on the frog itself. The Forest City setter exerted a pull of about 80 lbs, and worked a normal hand operated frog which could be operated or reset manually in case of failure. It is known that BCT investigated the driver-controlled radio operated frogs with which London Transport experimented in the Croydon and Sutton areas in the late 1940s.

Sprung trail or shunt frogs were used at reversing triangles, on the Columbia Road turning circle, in the Central Depot, Southcote Road, access route and in the Castle Lane Depot wiring.

There were reversing triangles at the following locations during the life of the system: Bodorgan Road, Brassey Road (removed to Redhill Crescent), Capstone Road, Court Road (used by occasional school specials), Luckham Road, Malvern Road, Redhill Crescent and Tuckton Bridge (replaced by a roundabout). By 1961 only four remained. The emergency installation at Bodorgan Road (top of Richmond Hill) had a switch frog in place of the normal spring trail frog at the entrance, thus providing an example of a facing frog being run through in the wrong direction. This triangle was used only when severe weather conditions made it unsafe for trolleybuses to use the hill. The triangle at Redhill Crescent, almost opposite the erstwhile Moordown Depot, also remained for emergency use. Those at Malvern Road and Luckham Road (just south of the Broadway Hotel/Castle Lane junction) were used for normal service trolleybuses.

At Columbia Road turning circle, a shunt frog was included in the layout as the BUT 9614Ts had some difficulties in swinging round in one go. This frog enabled trolleybuses to reverse back towards Fernheath Road for a second attempt.

A view of Christchurch looking north-east, with Stour Road straight ahead and Barrack Road running from left to right. This late 1960s view shows the detailed overhead layout at this junction, including frogs, insulators, span wires and all the other overhead fittings. Sunbeam MF2B 286 is disappearing into the distance on service 21. *J. C. Gillham*

The standard traction pole used on the Bournemouth system was a 31 foot heavy steel pole, $9\frac{5}{8}$ ins diameter at the base, tapering initially to $8\frac{5}{8}$ ins and then again to $7\frac{5}{8}$ ins at the top. They were manufactured by a variety of steel tube manufacturers e.g. Stewarts & Lloyds, and were not a specialist item. About $6\frac{1}{2}$ feet of the pole was buried in the ground. Longer e.g. 33 foot or 35 foot, and heavier poles were used on curves, junctions and turning circles to support the greater weight and sag of the overhead wiring, some being filled with concrete for further strengthening or to extend their lives.

Poles were planted or removed using the Transport Department's own crane. To remove a pole, a chain attached to the crane was secured to the top. A heavy cast iron collar was bolted around it near the base, and steel wedges driven in to secure the collar. Hydraulic jacks were then placed under the collar and, by the use of a hand pump, a single employee could force the pole up out of the ground. The crane could then lift the pole up completely and place it at the side of the road or onto a waiting lorry. Poles filled with concrete were more difficult to remove and, in many cases, were cut off at footpath level. The heavy cast-iron base featuring the Bournemouth Borough coat-of-arms was a relic of tramway days, intended to protect the traction pole from damage by other road vehicles. They were added and removed by lifting over the top of the pole, although in latter days a well-aimed sledge hammer sufficed for their final removal.

The traction poles, some 3,200 poles by Summer 1963 when the system was at its maximum extent, supporting the overhead wiring along each trolleybus route were individually identified by alpha-numeric code. Each route had a unique alphabetic code, and every traction pole was numbered consecutively along the line of route commencing at the Bournemouth Square "end". The purpose was to allow accurate identification of the location of any incident or of any work that needed to be done. Traction poles on the left hand side of the road (looking outwards from Bournemouth Square) received a white-painted alpha-numeric code e.g. B1, C70, whilst the counterpart on the right hand side received the same code plus an "A" suffix e.g. B1A, C70A. On sections having bracket arm traction poles or additional poles for bridles supporting pull-offs on the outside of bends, the alpha-numeric sequence continued but without the matching partner on the opposite side of the road. A similar coding system had been used in tramway days, the entire system being renumbered once the trolleybus network was well established.

Poles supporting crossovers, junctions and turnouts had "J" suffixes e.g. W86J. Turning circles and loops were distinguished by the addition of an "L" suffix to the normal route alpha-numeric code. The bracket arm traction poles along the left hand side of Oak Avenue and Stourvale Avenue making up the service 24 terminal loop at Jumper's Corner were accordingly coded I1L – I18L. The prefix "T" was used to denote the Christchurch turntable e.g. XT1.

There were exceptions in the vicinity of Bournemouth Square. The additional traction poles supporting the emergency turning circle at Horseshoe Common were given the same alpha-numeric codes as the adjacent poles on the main ("P") route plus a "Z" suffix. The circle was thus poled with P14Z, P31Z and P31ZA. The Hinton Road (The Quadrant) line, which enabled trolleybuses from Avenue Road or Bournemouth Pier to turn back into Gervis Place to take up service from there, was installed in August 1946 prior to the construction of the Bournemouth Square roundabout. It had only 2 or 3 poles and branched off Old Christchurch Road at P5, where the insulation at the frog also served as a section breaker, and thus had no jumper bridging the gap. The first pole on the loop was P6A, paired with P6 on the main line, then followed P6Z. The only other pole was "jointly" owned by route PL and carried the code P277AL, instead of P27ZAL, as presumably the painter left the bottom bar off the "Z".

The additional traction poles planted at roundabouts added to existing trolleybus routes upset the coding sytem. An "R" suffix was added rather than re-code the entire route e.g. at Iford the normal sequence between I43 and I46 was broken into by IR1 – IR20 inclusive. The major roundabouts at Bournemouth Square (some 40 poles) and the Lansdowne had their own coding using the letters "S" and "L" respectively. The Bodorgan Road reversing triangle at the top of Richmond Hill employed poles M10B - M10G to avoid interrupting the existing numbering sequence all the way to Moordown.

The pre-roundabout Strouden Park turning circle on Castle Lane was coded "FQ" instead of the more logical "FL" in preparation for the extension of wiring along Holdenhurst Road from Queen's Park to Castle Lane, Route "Q". On Route "H", the Fisherman's Walk loop also received the non-standard pole route coding "E", as "HL" had already been used for the Carbery Avenue turning circle. This code would have been used for the Boscombe via Parkwood Road route, authorised in the 1930 Act but never constructed.

Traction poles were painted leaf green, which weathered down to a paler, almost olive grey, shade over the years. Repainting took place at regular intervals, one route at a time, the work being recorded on a running list which the foreman painter entered when the work was complete. The finials were originally orange. Exceptionally, the poles immediately in front of the Royal Bath Hotel (Route "B") and in the vicinity of Bournemouth Pier (Route "R") were painted white. In 1962 the poles in High Street, Christchurch, between the Pit Site roundabout and just past the Town Hall (XR7 – X183 inclusive) were repainted grey to blend better with the character of the street. Also in the system's latter days, the traction poles in Westover Road immediately in front of the Pavilion (B25, B26) were painted black relieved in orange to make them less obtrusive when the illuminated fountains in the Pavilion forecourt were operating.

Before European standard street signs were introduced those traction poles supporting notices or traffic lights received yellow or black and white bands up to a height of about 10 feet. Poles A6A and A7A flanking the Central Fire Station on the south side of Holdenhurst Road were painted red from 6 – 11 feet above the ground as a warning to traffic. In the war, traction pole bases were painted white as an aid to black-out driving.

The narrow approach and sharp turn onto the Christchurch turntable, and the lack of space in the yard itself for more than one vehicle at a time, required the installation of a special signal to show approaching trolleybuses if the terminal was already occupied. A skate on the overhead at pole X188 illuminated lamps on poles X189 and X190 indicating that the turntable section was occupied. When the trolleybus turned out of the yard, a second overhead contact extinguished the signal lamps. The original plans for this signalling arrangement included a set of breakers and switch to cut off power to a short section of line, ensuring that no following trolleybus could reach the occupied turntable, but this was subsequently deemed "overkill".

A similar signal facility was installed at the stop preceding the junction of Poole Road and Seamoor Road, Westbourne, to prevent trolleybuses bunching up in Poole Road prior to returning to Bournemouth Square in the years that many services were extended to Westbourne. This signal was removed in early 1964.

Full details of the various traction pole routes are given in the following pages. Where it has proved possible to quote distances, these are based on average out/inwards distances calculated by BCT on 19th March 1959. On this date total route mileage was considered to be 29.04 miles, plus 1 mile of depot wiring. The use of David Chalk's records in the compilation of the this table is gratefully acknowledged.

Traction Pole Routes
Showing alpha coding and highest number reached on each route

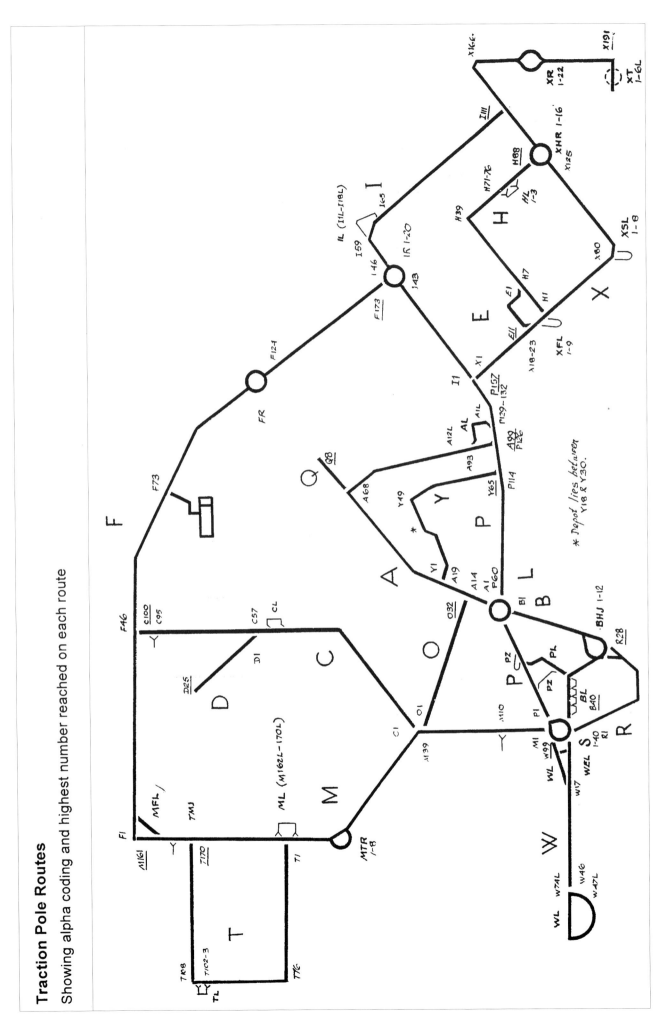

Letter	Route	Date
A	**Lansdowne -- Boscombe** via Holdenhurst Road, Ashley Road, one-way loop Portman Road, Christchurch Road Boscombe and Gladstone Road, reversing triangle at Capstone Road junction with Holdenhurst Road (1.98 miles)	Opened to traffic 22 June 1934
	Separate eastbound wiring introduced for services 25/25A along Old Christchurch Road, junction with Stafford Road (Trinity Church), across the Lansdowne and into Holdenhurst Road	18 March 1945
	Capstone Road reversing triangle removed	1946
	Separate wiring for services 25/25A in Old Christchurch Road and at Lansdowne removed and replaced by roundabout	27 January 1947
	Separate eastbound wiring reintroduced along Old Christchurch Road junction with Stafford Road (Trinity Church), across the Lansdowne and into Holdenhurst Road	12 March 1960
	Holdenhurst Road junction with St. Paul's Road: Facing frog and crossover removed Trailing frog removed	21 January 1964 23 January 1964
	Route A last used	12 September 1965
	Equipment removed	Dec. '65 to June '66
B	**Lansdowne – Bournemouth Square** one-way inbound via Bath Road, Westover Road, Gervis Place (0.64 miles)	Opened for traffic 8 May 1937
	Separate service 27 terminal loop in Gervis Place	30 March 1947
	Separate terminal loops in Gervis Place for services 20/24 and services 21–23	10 August 1947
	Extension of services 21–23 terminal loop in Gervis Place	17 August 1947
	Outbound wiring Royal Bath Hotel – Lansdowne via Bath Road introduced	7 April 1950
	New loop in Gervis Place for service 27	3 May 1953
	Loop last used	30 December 1956
	Equipment removed	October 1965
	Gervis Place terminal loops for services 20/24 and 21–23 combined into a single loop	14 May 1967
	Route B last used	20 April 1969
	Equipment removed	Apr. '69 to May '70
C	**Cemetery Junction – Castle Lane West (Broadway Hotel)** via Charminster Road including a turning circle at Five Ways (CL) (0.01 miles) and reversing triangles at the junction with Court Road and the junction with Luckham Road (2 miles)	Opened for traffic 23 August 1935
	Court Road reversing triangle removed	9 May 1961
	Route C last used	25 September 1966
	Equipment removed	Sep. '66 to Nov. '67
D	**Five Ways – Malvern Road** via Charminster Avenue with a reversing triangle at the junction of Malvern Road with Charminster Avenue (0.46 miles)	Opened for traffic 5 April 1937
	Route D last used	4 April 1965
	Equipment removed	Jul. '66 to Nov. '66
E	**Fisherman's Walk** one-way loop northbound via Southbourne Road and Parkwood Road from junction with Beaufort Road to junction with Seabourne Road (0.07 miles)	Opened for traffic 16 August 1948
	Last used by service trolleybuses in original form	27 September 1966
	Reopened for vehicles travelling in the opposite direction, i.e. southbound, as part of the Southbourne Traffic Management Scheme	5 October 1967
	Route E last used	20 April 1969
F	**Castle Lane** via Castle Lane West from junction with Wimborne Road to the junction with Charminster Road (Broadway Hotel) (0.67 miles)	Opened for traffic 19 October 1938
	Extension from junction with Charminster Road (Broadway Hotel) along Castle Lane West and East to junction with Christchurch Road, Iford (2.36 miles)	Opened for traffic 15 October 1951
	Strouden Park turning circle at junction of Holdenhurst Road with Castle Lane East (FQ) (0.13 miles) opened	23 May 1953
	Removed to permit roundabout construction	19/20 Dec. 1962
	Route F from junction with Wimborne Road to junction with Mallard Road last used	25 September 1966
	Equipment on this portion removed	Apr. '67 to Jan. '69
	Remainder of route F, Mallard Road – Christchurch Road, Iford last used	20 April 1969

FR	**Strouden Park** roundabout at junction of Holdenhurst Road with Castle Lane East:	
	North half for vehicles operating to Iford opened	21 April 1963
	South half for vehicles operating towards Charminster	19 May 1963
	East side (to enable vehicles from Charminster to turn)	19 May 1963
	West side (to enable vehicles from Iford to turn) opened	12 July 1963
	West side used only by learner drivers and wiring removed in connection with road widening on	23 September 1966
	Trail frog removed	12 March 1967
	Facing frog removed	26 March 1967
	Route FR last used	20 April 1969

G	Not used	

H	**Tuckton Bridge – Carbery Avenue** via Tuckton Road to junction with Carbery Avenue, including a turning circle at Carbery Avenue (HL)	Opened for traffic 5 October 1947
	Extension along Cranleigh Road, Beaufort Road and Beresford Road opened (1.56 miles)	16 August 1948
	Additional frogs at Carbery Avenue turning circle to enable vehicles from Fisherman's Walk to turn	26 September 1948
	Additional frogs added at the junction of Tuckton Road with Belle Vue Road enabling trolleybuses to proceed to/from Tuckton Bridge and Christchurch	1950
	New curve to turn right from Beresford into Seabourne Road opened for traffic (experimental traffic system)	27 October 1967
	Curve last used	10 February 1968
	Route H last used	20 April 1969
	Equipment removed	by September 1969

I	**Pokesdown – Iford Bridge** via Christchurch Road from junction with Seabourne Road to Iford Bridge turning circle	Opened for traffic 25 March 1935
	Extension along Christchurch Road and Barrack Road to the junction of Barrack Road with Stour Road, Christchurch	22 July 1943
	Jumpers turning circle, a one-way loop line (IL) along Oak Avenue and Stourvale Avenue opened (0.19 miles)	7 August 1944
	New frogs and wiring to enable vehicles to turn left from Stour Road into Barrack Road v.v. opened for traffic	1 August 1946
	Iford Bridge turning circle removed	19/20 May 1961
	New curve to turn left from Christchurch Road into Seabourne Road, Pokesdown, installed	22 December 1967
	Used by special party trolleybus	31 December 1967
	First opened for regular use (empty trolleybuses from Castle Lane Depot to take up service at Fisherman's Walk)	1 January 1969
	Route I last used	20 April 1969
	Equipment removed	April to Sept.1969

IR	**Iford Roundabout:** Junction of Christchurch Road and Castle Lane East:	
	South side, vehicles proceeding to Bournemouth Square opened for traffic	20 May 1956
	Entire roundabout opened for traffic	2 December 1956
	Additional frogs and wiring to enable vehicles to turn left from Christchurch Road into Castle Lane East opened	2 July 1965
	Route IR last used	20 April 1969

J	Used only as a Traction Pole Route suffix	

K	Not used	

L	**Lansdowne Roundabout:** Junction of Bath Road, Christchurch Road, Holdenhurst Road, Old Christchurch Road and Lansdowne Road:	Main construction 26 January 1947
	Opened for traffic (replacing a turning circle and junction)	27 January 1947
	Separate eastbound wiring around north side of roundabout from Old Christchurch Road into Holdenhurst Road (service 25)	12 March 1960
	Separate eastbound wiring last used	12 September 1965
	Separate eastbound wiring removed	27 March 1966
	Switch frogs in Old Christchurch Road, junction with Stafford Road (Trinity Church) removed	11 November 1965
	Facing frog on roundabout for Holdenhurst Road removed	26 May 1968
	Route L last used	20 April 1969
	Equipment removed	July 1969

M	**Richmond Hill – Moordown** via Richmond Hill, Wimborne Road to Moordown Depot including a turning circle at Cemetery Junction, a reversing triangle at Victoria Park Road and a one-way loop line (ML) at Winton via Crimea Road, Waterloo Road, Alma Road (Winton Banks).	All opened for traffic 7 June 1935
	Extension along Wimborne Road to Castle Lane East	11 March 1937
	Emergency reversing triangle at the top of Richmond Hill into Bodorgan Road opened	30 June 1945
	Reversing triangle Victoria Park Road last used	4 September 1946
	Equipment removed	29 May 1948
	Reversing triangle at Redhill Crescent opened for use	5 September 1946
	Redhill Crescent triangle replaced by loop inside Moordown Depot	14 August 1950
	Redhill Crescent triangle removed	11 November 1950
	Reintroduced	26 July 1953
	Last used for service buses	26 March 1956
	Cemetery Junction turning circle last used by service buses	25 July 1953
	Cemetery Junction turning circle removed in three stages	22/23 Oct.1960 5/6 Nov. 1960 19/20 Nov.1960
	Wiring removed at Cemetery Junction (from Lansdowne Road): Facing frog and crossover removed / Trail frog removed	6/7 October 1964 7/8 October 1964
	Route M last used	25 September 1966
	Equipment removed	Sep. '66 to Sep. '68
MFL	**Lawford Road**: One-way loop from the junction with Wimborne Road to the junction with Castle Lane West (0.2 miles) (including frog for Bear Cross extension)	Opened for traffic 11 March 1937
	Route MFL last used	25 September 1966
	Equipment removed	Jan. '67 to Oct. '68
MTR	Wiring re-aligned at junction of Wimborne Road and Talbot Avenue for new roundabout	18 March 1961
N	Not used	
O	**Holdenhurst Road – Cemetery Junction** via St. Paul's Road, Lansdowne Road (0.7 miles)	Opened for traffic 28 June 1935
	Route O last used	29 September 1963
	Equipment removed January/February 1964 except for ca. 50 yards at the Cemetery Junction end of Lansdowne Road retained for feeder purposes and removed	October 1964
P	**Bournemouth Square – Horseshoe Common – Lansdowne** via Old Christchurch Road one-way outbound to Horseshoe Common; via Fir Vale Road, St. Peter's Road and Gervis Place to the junction with Westover Road one-way inbound (PL); Horseshoe Common – Lansdowne via Old Christchurch Road in both directions	All opened for traffic 22 June 1934
	Extension Lansdowne – Pokesdown Station via Christchurch Road, including Boscombe (Pokesdown) Depot wiring	25 March 1935
	One-way emergency loop line Gervis Place to Old Christchurch Road	12 April 1941
	Emergency turning circle Horseshoe Common (PZ)	1 May 1942
	Separate eastbound wiring for services 25/25A along Old Christchurch Road, junction with Stafford Road (Trinity Church), across the Lansdowne and into Holdenhurst Road introduced	18 March 1945
	Separate wiring for services 25/25A in Old Christchurch Road and at Lansdowne removed and replaced by roundabout	27 January 1947
	One-way loop in Hinton Road (The Quadrant) from Old Christchurch Road into Gervis Place (PLZ) (0.04 miles) opened	1 August 1946
	Passing loop in Christchurch Road, Boscombe, to enable service 25 vehicles to pass those waiting at "main road" stop	26 April 1953
	Passing loop last used	12 September 1965
	Equipment removed	28 January 1968
	Emergency loop Gervis Place into Old Christchurch Road removed	2/3 May 1953
	Removal of wiring at Christchurch Road/Palmerston Road junction: Facing frog removed / Trail frog and crossover removed	13/14 Sept. 1965 14/15 Sept. 1965
	Separate eastbound wiring for service 25 along Old Christchurch Road, junction with Stafford Road (Trinity Church), across the Lansdowne and into Holdenhurst Road reintroduced	12 March 1960
	Separate eastbound wiring last used	12 September 1965

	Switch frog in Old Christchurch Road removed	11 November 1965
	Separate eastbound wiring removed	27 March 1966
	Frogs, crossover and redundant wiring at the junction of Portman Road with Christchurch Road, Boscombe, removed	14 January 1968
	Boscombe (Pokesdown) Depot junction and wiring last used	31 December 1967
	Frogs, crossovers and redundant wiring at Boscombe (Pokesdown) Depot junction with Christchurch Road removed	21 January 1968
	Route P last used	20 April 1969
Q	**Holdenhurst Road – Littledown Avenue, Queens Park Golf Pavilion** via Holdenhurst Road from the junction with Ashley Road to junction with Littledown Avenue including a turning circle at Littledown Avenue (0.18 miles)	Opened for traffic 20 October 1934
	Route Q last used	12 September 1965
	Equipment removed	Jan./Feb. 1966
R	**Bath Road (Royal Bath Hotel) – Bournemouth Square** via Bath Road, Bournemouth Pier Approach, Exeter Road from the junction with Westover Road to Bournemouth Pier in both directions, one-way from Bournemouth Pier to Bournemouth Square (0.55 miles).	All opened for traffic 7 April 1950
	Last used for service vehicles	23 August 1964
	Route R last used	20 April 1969
S	**Bournemouth Square**; Basic layout, turning circle for experimental trolleybus route to Westbourne opened for traffic	13 May 1933
	Through wiring to Old Christchurch Road and from Gervis Place with a turn back loop from the east added	22 June 1934
	Wiring to/from Richmond Hill, turn back loop and waiting loop at the end of Bourne Avenue added	7 June 1935
	Replaced by traffic roundabout thereby linking "main" and "side" route wiring at Bournemouth Square for the first time	30 March 1947
	Additional line for outbound "side" route services added on the west (Bourne Avenue) side of the roundabout eliminating the switch frog at the bottom of Richmond Hill	29 May 1960
	Removed	September 1966
	Rest of Route S last used	20 April 1969
	Equipment removed	May – July 1969
T	**Wimborne Road (Winton Banks) – Columbia Road** via Talbot Road, Talbot Avenue, Wallisdown Road, Kinson Road, including a turning circle at the junction of Kinson Road with Columbia Road,	Opened for traffic 15 April 1938
	Extension along Columbia Road, Ensbury Park Road to Wimborne Road at Moordown (TMJ) with additional switch frogs giving access to the Kinson Road turning circle	8 April 1939
	Route T last used	25 September 1966
	Equipment removed	Mar. '67 – Feb. '69
U	Not used	
V	Not used	
W	**Bournemouth Square – St. Michael's Church, Poole Road** via Commercial Road one-way outbound to Poole Hill; via the Triangle (west side), Avenue Road one-way inbound; Poole Hill – Seamoor Road, Westbourne via Poole Road in both directions (1.15 miles);	All opened for traffic 13 May 1933
	Triangle (east side) loop (WEL) between Commercial Road and Avenue Road, "passing" loop in Commercial Road and switch frog at the east end of Commercial Road for vehicles heading to the Triangle or Westbourne added	July 1936
	Four separate waiting loops in Avenue Road added	30 March 1947
	Loop through Triangle trolleybus parking area opened	23 May 1948
	Wiring in Seamoor Road, Poole Road, Poole Hill, Triangle (west side) and nearside kerb line in Commercial Road last used	12 September 1965
	This equipment removed	Nov. '65 – Feb. '66
	Switch frog at the east end of Commercial Road for vehicles heading to the Triangle or Westbourne removed	30/31 Oct. 1965
	Remainder of Route W last used	19 April 1969
WL	**Seamoor Road, Westbourne:** Westbound terminal loop following one-way road system used by all traffic from Poole Road (junction with Surrey Road South) to Poole Road (County Gates) along the entire length of Seamoor Road	Opened 13 May 1933
	Route WL last used	12 September 1965
	Equipment removed	Nov. '65 – Jan. '66

X	**Pokesdown Station – Fisherman's Walk** via Seabourne Road including a turning circle in Fisherman's Avenue (XFL)	Opened for traffic 21 November 1935
	Extension to Southbourne Cross Roads via Southbourne Grove, Southbourne Road, Belle Vue Road to a turning circle at the junction of Southbourne Overcliff Drive and St. Catherine's Road with Belle Vue Road, opened	23 December 1935
	Extension to Christchurch turntable via Belle Vue Road, Foxholes Road, Belle Vue Road, Stour Road, Bargates, High Street, Church Street, opened	8 April 1936
	Reversing triangle added at Tuckton Road	8 November 1943
	Reversing triangle removed (see Route H)	5 October 1947
	Trolleybus park added in Seabourne Road at rear of Boscombe (Pokesdown) Depot	12 March 1951
	Trolleybus park last used	30 September 1951
	Wiring removed	Spring 1952
	Trolleybuses adopted the one-way traffic system at "Pit Site", Barrack Road, Christchurch	28 August 1955
	"Pit Site" wiring modified to conform with roundabout changes for the new A35 Christchurch by-pass road	9 August 1959
	Additional east to south wiring added at junction of Christchurch Road with Seabourne Road, Pokesdown: Trail frog inserted outside Pokesdown Fire Station Junction frog inserted in inbound wiring	13 December 1967 6 December 1967
	Fisherman's Walk wiring changes for experimental one-way traffic management scheme completed by	8 October 1967
	Original Fisherman's Avenue turning circle (XFL) last used	4 October 1967
	Experimental traffic management scheme introduced	12 November 1967
	Experimental traffic management scheme discontinued	10 February 1968
	Trolleybuses reverted to two-way working	12 February 1968
	Route X last used	20 April 1969
	Equipment removed	June – Sept. 1969
XHR	**Tuckton Bridge Roundabout:** Roundabout at junction of Belle Vue Road, Stour Road, Tuckton Road on west side of Tuckton Bridge replacing a conventional three-way junction, opened	30 June 1963
	Route XHR last used	20 April 1969
	Equipment removed	June – Sept. 1969
Y	**Holdenhurst Road – Christchurch Road** via St. Swithun's Road, Southcote Road, through Central Depot, St. Clement's Road, Palmerston Road, using "interlaced" (common positive wire) wiring between Holdenhurst Road and the east entrance of Central Depot and for a short distance at the south end of Palmerston Road, and single bi-directional wiring in St. Clement's Road and the remainder of Palmerston Road (1 mile), including depot wiring (0.43 miles)	All opened for traffic 22 June 1934
	Route Y last used	7 June 1965
	Equipment removed	June '65 – Mar '66
Z	**Castle Lane West – Castle Lane Depot** via Mallard Road (0.1 miles), including all depot and workshop wiring (0.48 miles), opened	26 July 1953
	Note: the traction poles on this route never received their painted alpha-numeric codes	
	Depot lines reduced from three to two	November 1966
	Depot wiring last used	22 April 1969
	Wiring cut down	January 1971
	Some traction poles still intact 1998	

Post-Closure Wiring Removals

27 April 1969	Running wire and spans in Westover Road
1 May 1969	Outbound negative wire along Beaufort Road
4 May 1969	All running wires, frogs and spans in Gervis Place
23 May 1969	Following the removal of a traction pole just past the New Era Laundry, Pokesdown, outward wires had been slewed towards the inward wires. The span wire was now a pull-off
27 May 1969	Negative wires in Castle Lane from Iford roundabout to Holmfield Avenue. Positive wires in Christchurch Road from Iford roundabout to Warnford Road. Outward positive running wire Iford to Jumpers Wiring to and from Iford roundabout anchored off.
28 May 1969	Outward positive running wire Jumpers to Stour Road
29 May 1969	Inward positive running wire Stour Road to Jumpers
30 May 1969	Bracket arms Oak Avenue
2 June 1969	Inward positive running wire Jumpers to Iford
3 June 1969	Bracket arms Stourvale Avenue
4 June 1969	Pull-offs Barrack Road
5 June 1969	All wiring Stour Road junction to Bargates, Christchurch
6 June 1969	All wiring Christchurch turntable
8 June 1969	Bargates and High Street inwards to Christchurch, negative and positive running wire; also spans in High Street
9 June 1969	More pull-offs Barrack Road
10 June 1969	Outward negative running wire Iford to Stour Road
11 June 1969	Inward negative running wire Iford to Stour Road
12 June 1969	Spans Iford to Jumpers
13 June 1969	Avenue Road, all wiring from the Triangle to Fairlight Glen, also spans in Bargates
15 June 1969.	Bournemouth Square, all wiring from the south, east and west sides.
17 June 1969	Positive and negative outward running wire in Stour Road from Barrack Road to Bargates
18 June 1969	Spans, Barrack Road (MEXE to Jumpers)
19 June 1969	Negative running wire inward and outward on Stour Road from Tuckton Bridge to Barrack Road
22 June 1969	Avenue Road, all wiring from Fairlight Glen to Bournemouth Square
23 June 1969	Positive inward and outward running wire on Stour Road from Tuckton Bridge to Barrack Road
24 June 1969	Inward positive and negative running wire in Stour Road from Bargates to Barrack Road
25 June 1969	Part of Barrack Road/Stour Road junction
26 June 1969	Spans in Barrack Road (MEXE to Stour Road)
27 June 1969	More of Stour Road junction and spans in Stour Road from Tuckton to Barrack Road
29 June 1969	Remainder Stour Road junction and more spans in Stour Road
30 June 1969	Final spans in Stour Road and Bargates. Removal of last wiring in the Borough of Christchurch.
1 July 1969	Traction poles burned-off from Iford to Jumpers
2 July 1969	Pull-offs on Bournemouth Square north side
3/4 July 1969	Further traction poles Iford to Jumpers
6 July 1969	All remaining wiring Bournemouth Square
7/8 July 1969	Traction poles at Jumpers Corner
9 July 1969	Bracket arms in Westover Road
10/11/14-18 July '69	Poles in Barrack Road
21-24 July 1969	Poles in Barrack Road
13 July 1969	All wiring at Bournemouth Pier Approach
18 July 1969	Bracket arms in Gervis Place
20 July 1969	All wiring at the Lansdowne
25 July 1969	Bracket arms at the Triangle
27 July 1969	Trolley wire on Exeter Road
30 July 1969	Traction poles in Christchurch High Street
31 July 1969	Traction poles in Stour Road

1 August 1969	Spans in Exeter Road
10 August 1969	Bath Road, all wiring Bath Hotel Junction to Bournemouth Pier Approach
11/12 August 1969	Poles removed in Stour Road, Christchurch
13 August 1969	Poles removed in Bargates, Christchurch
14 August 1969	Clamps and straps removed from poles in Barrack Road, Christchurch
15 August 1969	Clamps and straps removed from poles in Stour Road, Christchurch
16 August 1969	Clamps and straps removed from poles in Bargates and High Street, Christchurch
18/19 August 1969	Poles removed in Bargates, Christchurch
20 August 1969	Running wire Bath Hotel to top of Bath Hill outwards
21 August 1969	Poles removed in Avenue Road
24 August 1969	Running wire Bath Road outwards from top of Bath Hill to the Lansdowne
26 August 1969	Running wire top of Beaufort Road outwards
27 August 1969	Running wire top of Beaufort Road inwards and also on Bath Hill inwards
28 August 1969	All wiring at the junction of Beresford, Parkwood and Beaufort Roads, Fisherman's Walk
29 August 1969	Running wire Bath Road inwards, Lansdowne to the top of Bath Hill and all spans in Bath Road
31 August 1969	Poles removed in Christchurch High Street
1 September 1969	Poles removed in Christchurch High Street
2 September 1969	Poles removed from Christchurch roundabout (the last piece of overhead equipment remaining in the Borough of Christchurch)
3 September 1969	All wiring in Beresford, Southbourne and Parkwood Roads
4 September 1969	Fisherman's Walk area anchored off.
5 September 1969	Running wire Pokesdown to St. James School outwards; also curve by Pokesdown Fire Station
7 September 1969	Running wire at the top of Old Christchurch Road outwards of the former service 25 passing loop
8 September 1969	Outward negative running wire Cranleigh Road and part of Carbery Avenue turning circle
9 September 1969	Pokesdown area anchored off
20 December 1969	Inwards and outwards positive and the inwards negative wires were tied off at Lascelles Road. By this date all other wiring on Pokesdown Hill had been removed. The outward negative wire had been removed all the way to Iford roundabout
21 December 1969	Pokesdown junction had been removed. All wiring in Christchurch Road between the Lansdowne and Pokesdown, and in Southbourne Road towards Fisherman's Walk, remained intact
12 January 1970	Seabourne Road pull-offs
13 January 1970	St. Peter's Road, poles stripped
14 January 1970	Bournemouth Square, poles burned-off
16 January 1970	Seabourne Road, inward positive
18 January 1970	Christchurch Road, outward negative Lansdowne to Boscombe Gardens
19 January 1970	Bournemouth Square, poles burned-off
21 January 1970	Seabourne Road, inward negative
22 January 1970	Bournemouth Square, poles burned-off
23 January 1970	Bournemouth Square and Gervis Place, poles burned-off
25 January 1970	Christchurch Road, outward negative Boscombe Gardens to Warwick Road
26/27 January 1970	Various poles in Bournemouth town centre stripped
28 January 1970	Christchurch Road, outward negative Warwick Road to Pokesdown
30 January 1970	Seabourne Road, spans
4 February 1970	Christchurch Road, inward negative Pokesdown to Wolverton Road
6 February 1970	Christchurch Road, inward negative Wolverton Road to Sea Road
11 February 1970	Christchurch Road, inward negative Sea Road to Boscombe Gardens
13 February 1970	Christchurch Road, inward negative Boscombe Gardens to Derby Road
February 1970	Underground feeders in Pokesdown, Iford, Southbourne
October 1970	Underground feeders in Bournemouth town centre
12-18 January 1971	All wiring at Mallard Road Depot, the last overhead remaining

Traction poles and some span wires in Christchurch Road, Boscombe, were retained at the request of the Boscombe Illuminations Committee, for illuminations purposes, until new street lights were installed. By 26 November 1970 only about 160 traction poles not required for street lighting purposes were still to be removed, and it was expected that these would be gone before the end of the financial year.

A street lighting modernisation in the winter of 1971/72 saw the removal of traction poles throughout the town centre and through Boscombe. Roads affected included Christchurch Road (Pokesdown – Lansdowne), Lansdowne roundabout, Old Christchurch Road, Fir Vale Road, St. Peter's Road, Gervis Place, Exeter Road, Avenue Road, Commercial Road, Triangle and part of Poole Road. The ornate traction poles and gantries were removed from Tuckton Bridge on 5–12 March 1972 and in the same month most of the section feeder boxes in Southbourne were also removed. That same winter, Christchurch Corporation erected new street lighting at the "Pit Site" roundabout, bringing the end of further poles.

Date	Vehicle	Comment
March 1957	MS2	Southern Counties Touring Society
21st July 1957		Southern Counties Touring Society
22nd July 1962		Southern Counties Touring Society
7th July 1963	212	Reading Transport Society; first vehicle to use newly-erected Tuckton Bridge roundabout wiring
16th November 1963	212	Handover of vehicle to Reading Transport Society for preservation, Castle Lane Depot
14th June 1964	200/201	Southern Counties Touring Society/H. O'Neill (two tours; vehicle allocation not recorded)
28th June 1964	200	Reading Transport Society
15th April 1965	291/294	M. P. M. Nimmo
23rd May 1965	202	Bournemouth Railway Club
30th May 1965	290/292	Reading Transport Society, last tour to Central Depot, Southcote Road
4th July 1965	202	National Trolleybus Association
12th June 1966	239/244	Reading Transport Society, including closed Wallisdown route (239 single staircase, 244 unrebuilt)
11th September 1966	234/246	National Trolleybus Association; farewell tour of Richmond Hill routes
25th September 1966	246	Bournemouth Railway Club, including Richmond Hill
12th March 1967	Portsmouth 313	Trials, including Horseshoe Common
30th April 1967	Portsmouth 313	National Trolleybus Association in conjunction with J. S. Reeves
18th May 1967	202	South Eastern Federation of Museums & Art Galleries (two separate tours, morning and afternoon)
17th September 1967	268	Reading Transport Society
17th September 1967	303	Southern Counties Touring Society
22nd October 1967	202/246	Castle Lane Depot confines only
5th November 1967	202/246	National Trolleybus Association & Maypine Trolleybus Company
31st December 1967	246	Boscombe (Pokesdown) Depot closure, in conjunction with R. S. Cromwell
21st January 1968	246	Transport Trust, in conjunction with R. S. Cromwell
21st April 1968	202/246	London Omnibus Traction Society/National Trolleybus Assn. in conjunction with R. S. Cromwell
19th May 1968	Glasgow TBS21	National Trolleybus Association; arrived Castle Lane Depot 9th May 1968
23rd June 1968	London 260	London Trolleybus Preservation Society
30th June 1968	London 260	London Trolleybus Preservation Society
28th July 1968	202	Bournemouth vehicle operated in Reading by National Trolleybus Association
17th September 1968	268	
24th November 1968	Huddersfield 631	
8th December 1968	Rotherham 44	National Trolleybus Association
29th December 1968	301	Reading Transport Society
29th December 1968	246	Bournemouth Passenger Transport Association
5th January 1969	246	R. S. Cromwell
26th January 1969	246	⎫ National Trolleybus Association and Maypine Trolleybus Company (Messrs Cromwell & Russell
26th January 1969	Reading 174	⎭ These two vehicles were both exhibited at the Commercial Motor Transport Exhibition, 1950.
26th January 1969	Maidstone 56	A. Stevens, in conjunction with National Trolleybus Association
16th February 1969	212	Reading Transport Society preserved vehicle
23rd February 1969	212	Bournemouth Passenger Transport Association, in conjunction with Reading Transport Society
20th April 1969	202	National Trolleybus Association preserved vehicle; last day of system
20th April 1969	212	Reading Transport Society preserved vehicle; last day of system
20th April 1969	246	R. S. Cromwell preserved vehicle, last day of system

Preserved Rotherham Corporation 44 (FET 618) on a National Trolleybus Association tour of the Bournemouth system on 8th December 1968. The vehicle is one of 46 Daimler CTE6 vehicles delivered as single-deckers in 1950. It and thirteen of its sisters were rebodied by Roe in 1956 to provide extra capacity. The Rotherham trolleybus system closed in October 1965. This view shows 44 in company with Bournemouth Sunbeam MF2B 272. *M. J. Russell*

This Appendix is divided into four sections:

1)   Bills and Acts of Parliament

2)   Statutory Rules and Orders

3)   Bournemouth Corporation Byelaws

4)   Transport Department Internal Instructions

Note: In view of the complex and dated terminology used in the original text, some explanatory additions have been made by the Author. These are shown in italics.

1)   BILLS AND ACTS OF PARLIAMENT

The authorisation of a new trolleybus route normally required the presentation and confirmation of a Provisional Order, as laid down under the Tramways Act, 1870. In 1945 a more flexible solution became available, based on the Statutory Orders (Special Procedure) Act, 1945. Where this Act applied, there was no fixed timetable for the Parliamentary stages; if an Order was unopposed, the introduction of a confirming Bill and the need for consideration of the Order and Bill on the floor of, or in Committee of, either House of Parliament was avoided; and if an Order was opposed the procedure was expedited. An example was Section 59 (2) of the Bournemouth Corporation Act, 1960.

Since the withdrawal of the trolleybuses, the Tramways Act, 1870, was rescinded and replaced by the Transport & Works Act, 1992, which provides for new tramway, trolley vehicle and guided transport installations.

1.1)   Poole, Sandbanks & Westbourne Railless Traction Bill

Sponsored by Clough, Smith & Co, Spencer House, South Place, London EC. Deposited 30th November 1913 by S Whittlestone (Wyatts, Parliamentary Agents). Solicitor: Messrs Wyatt & Co., Victoria Embankment. Published Maps and Diagram only.

First Reading (House of Lords) 19th February 1914. Objections noted from Bournemouth Corporation and from owners on or in the neighbourhood of the proposed trolley vehicle routes.

Second Reading 3rd March 1914.

Select Committee appointed on 31st March 1914 to look at the Bill and to hear witnesses. Bill examined on 1st and 4th May 1914.

Stephen Sellon, Consulting Engineer (formerly consulting engineer to the British Electric Traction Co) gave most evidence, including the following details of the scheme:

- Winter timetable would be a thirty minute service (route 1) for 12 hours a day, with an hourly service for 4 hours. Much more intensive service in summer

- Average of five passengers a journey would be expected in winter

- Likely operational costs of under 6d a mile (including contribution to wear and tear); average fares would be around 2d per passenger

- Maximum size of cars would be 28 passengers; five required for service, one for spare

- The routes would use the Cedes Stoll overhead collection system; route 1 would probably have separate sets of wires for each direction, but route 2 would probably only have one set of wires (passing vehicles would exchange trolley carriages)

- County Gates to Haven Hotel would be a 4d fare, with only 2d to Canford Cliffs.

It was conceded that there would possibly be congestion in the County Gates area, but much was made of the ease of turning Cedes vehicles.

Harry Webber (General Manager of Keighley Corporation) gave strong evidence for the compatibility of trolley vehicles with rural areas with expensive houses. However, Sellon was unable to convince their Lordships that his own experience at Aberdare was in any real way relevant to the character of the proposed route. Evidence from several prosperous landowners was against having trolley vehicles, and the Bill was not received favourably.

Bill not proceeded further with on 5th May 1914.

Route No. 1: County Gates, The Avenue, Western Road, Haven Road, Flaghead Road and West Road, to the Haven Hotel (Banks Road) Sandbanks (4 miles 4.23 chains).

Route No. 1A: Ravine Road (south) from Western Road (3.78 chains).

Route No. 2: from the junction with route 1 (West Road Sandbanks) via Shore Road, Lilliput Hill Road, Sandbanks Road to the junction with the existing tramways of Bournemouth Corporation at Parkstone Road (2 miles 3 furlongs 4.9 chains).

Route No. 2A: connection from Shore Road to West Road to allow access to route 1 northbound (1.82 chains).

1.2)   The Bournemouth District Railless Traction Bill

Deposited 30th November 1913 by A. Locke of Bakers (Parliamentary Agents). Solicitor: Messrs Baker & Sons, Westminster. Published maps a diagram and a copy of the Gazette Notice were provided.

Gazette Notice included:

"To incorporate a Company to provide, equip and maintain, work and run mechanically propelled vehicles (hereinafter called trolley vehicles) ..."

"Also to run omnibuses in connection with or substitution for the trolley vehicles upon the said routes, or in prolongation thereof"

Powers were to include the building of a generating station at the rear of the west side of Charminster Avenue

Route No. 1: From Kings Road (Winton) via Charminster Road to Charminster Avenue (Junction with Malvern Road) (7 furlongs, 9.5 chains).

Route No. 2: From Crescent Road via Malvern Road to Moordown Tramway Depot (Wimborne Road) (4 furlongs, 9 chains).

1.3)   Bournemouth Corporation Act, 1930 (Ch. clxxxi.), (20 & 21 Geo. 5.)

Part IV: Trolley Vehicle Omnibuses and Tramways

90.

1.   The Corporation may provide maintain and equip (but shall not manufacture) trolley vehicles and may work the same along any street or road in the borough or in the county of Southampton *i.e. excluding Poole, Dorset,* along which tramways have been constructed by the Corporation.

2.   The Corporation may also work trolley vehicles along the following routes:-

In the borough –

(1)   Commencing in Bath Road at its junction with Christchurch Road *i.e. the Lansdowne* proceeding along Bath Road,

Bournemouth Pier Approach and Exeter Road to and terminating in the Square on the south side at its junction with Exeter Road;

(2) Commencing in Westover Road at its junction with Bath Road proceeding along Westover Road to and terminating at Bournemouth Arcade *i.e. Gervis Place* by a junction with the Corporation tramway route at that point;

(3) Commencing in Meyrick Road at its junction with Bath Road *i.e. the Lansdowne* proceeding along Meyrick Road and Gervis Road and terminating in Gervis Road at its junction with Bath Road;

(4) Along Gervis Place from its junction with Hinton Road to the junction of Old Christchurch Road and Gervis Place;

(5) Along Sea Road from its junction with Christchurch Road to the Boscombe Pier Approach;

(6) Commencing at the junction of Sea Road and Hawkwood Road proceeding along Hawkwood Road to Heathcote Road and along that road to its junction with Christchurch Road;

(7) Along Parkwood Road from its junction with Christchurch Road to the junction of Parkwood Road with Seabourne Road;

(8) Along Woodside Road from its junction with Seabourne Road to the junction of Woodside Road with Parkwood Road *i.e. presumably a one-way system was envisaged with Route (7) above, with inward trolleybuses travelling via Woodwide Road and outward via Parkwood Road.*

In the borough and rural district of Christchurch in the county of Southampton *i.e. Hampshire* –

(9) Commencing in the borough in Christchurch Road by a junction with the existing Corporation tramway in that road at Pokesdown Station proceeding along Christchurch Road to and terminating at Iford Bridge at the boundary of the borough of Christchurch:

In that borough –

(10) Commencing in Holdenhurst Road at the junction of that road with Ashley Road and proceeding along Holdenhurst Road to and terminating at the borough boundary in that road *i.e. Castle Lane East;*

(11) Commencing in Charminster Road at its junction with Capstone Road proceeding along Charminster Road to and terminating at the borough boundary in that road *i.e. at the Broadway Hotel, Castle Lane West;*

(12) Commencing at the junction of Charminster Road and Charminster Avenue *i.e. Five Ways* proceeding along Charminster Avenue and Malvern Road and terminating at the junction of Malvern Road with Wimborne Road *i.e. Moordown:*

In the borough and the rural district of Poole in the county of Dorset:–

(13) Commencing in the borough at the termination of the existing tramway in Wimborne Road proceeding along that road to and terminating at Bear Cross in the parish of Kinson in the rural district of Poole;

(14) Commencing in the borough in Talbot Road at its junction with Wimborne Road proceeding along Talbot Road and Talbot Village Road *(later named Wallisdown Road)* to and along Kinson Road and terminating therein at its junction with Wimborne Road in the parish of Kinson in the rural district of Poole;

and with the consent of the Minister of Transport along any other street or road in the borough or the said parishes of Holdenhurst and Kinson which the Corporation think it necessary or convenient to use for the purpose of providing a turning point or of connecting trolley vehicle routes or of obtaining access thereto from any depot garage building or work of the Corporation.

3. Before equipping any trolley vehicle route to include a turning point or before arranging for a new turning point on any route the Corporation shall submit plans of the turning point to the Minister of Transport for approval.

4. No turning point shall be provided upon any street or road belonging to or maintained by a railway company without the consent in writing of such company.

1.4) Proposed Bournemouth Corporation Bill, 1935 (not presented)

Provided for the operation of trolley vehicles over the Upper Parkstone tram route in Poole.

At a Special Meeting of the Council, 2nd April 1935

(1) Trolley Vehicles, Borough of Poole

Whereas at a Special Meeting of the Council duly summoned and held pursuant to the provisions of Part XIII of the Local Government Act, 1933, and on the 5th of March 1935, it was resolved by an absolute majority of the said Council that in the judgement of this Council and in the interests of the inhabitants of Poole it is expedient for the Council to promote in the present Session of Parliament a Bill for the purposes following or some of them (that is to say):–

To empower the Corporation to provide, maintain and run trolley vehicles upon the following route in the Borough of Poole, namely, a route commencing at County Gates and proceeding along Poole Road, Ashley Road, View Road, St. Peter's Road, North Road, Parkstone Road, Longfleet Road, High Street and terminating on the eastern side of the level crossing at Towngate Street on the Southern Railway and to confer on the Corporation all other necessary and incidental powers in relation to the said trolley vehicles and the route upon which the same may be run.

To empower the Corporation to borrow and to raise money for and in connection with the said trolley vehicles and route and for other purposes of the Bill.

To make provision for the abandonment of the light railways constructed under the powers of the Poole and District Light Railway Order, 1899.

To amend, vary, alter or repeal the provisions of the Local Acts and Orders in force in the Borough and any other Acts or Orders which would interfere with any of the objects of the Bill.

And whereas the said Special Resolution has since been duly published.

And whereas to give effect to the said Resolution a Bill intituled "An Act to authorise the Mayor, Aldermen and Burgesses of the Borough of Bournemouth to use trolley vehicles upon a route in the Borough of Poole in the County of Dorset and for other purposes" has been prepared and is being promoted by the Council and was on the 7th day of March, 1935, deposited in Parliament.

And whereas it is expedient that the propriety of the promotion of the said Bill which has been submitted to and considered by this Council and also the said resolution should be confirmed. Now therefore it is, on the motion of the Mayor (Alderman Edgecombe), and seconded by the Chairman of the Transport Committee (Alderman Summerbee).

Resolved: by an absolute majority the whole number of the said Council – That the propriety of the promotion of the said Bill be and the same is hereby confirmed and the same Bill is hereby approved and adopted.

This proposed Bill was withdrawn due to the progress of the Poole Road Transport Act to Royal Assent on 2nd August 1935.

1.5) Bournemouth Corporation (Trolley Vehicles) Order Confirmation Act, 1938 (Ch. xxi.), (1 & 2 Geo. 6.)

Bournemouth Corporation Trolley Vehicles

3.

(1) Subject to the provisions of this Order and of the Act of 1930 so far as such provisions relate to trolley vehicles and trolley vehicle routes and are applicable to this Order the Corporation may work

and use trolley vehicles upon the following routes (in the borough except where otherwise stated) in addition to any routes upon which they are already authorised to use trolley vehicles (that is to say):–

Route No. 1 (1 mile 1 furlong 9.5 chains or thereabouts in length) commencing in Columbia Road at its junction with Kinson Road proceeding along Columbia Road and Ensbury Park Road and terminating therein at its junction with Wimborne Road;

Route No. 2 (1 mile 1 furlong 4.7 chains or thereabouts in length) commencing in Redhill Drive at its junction with Ensbury Park Road proceeding along Redhill Drive to and along Coombe Avenue and along Leybourne Avenue and Northbourne Avenue and terminating in the last-mentioned road at its junction with Wimborne Road;

Route No. 3 (3 miles 0 furlong 3.7 chains or thereabouts in length) commencing in Castle Lane at its junction with Lawford Road proceeding along Castle Lane and terminating therein at its junction with Christchurch Road i.e. Iford;

Route No. 4 (1 mile 4 furlongs or thereabouts in length) commencing in Alma Road at its junction with Wimborne Road i.e. Winton Banks proceeding along Alma Road and along Richmond Park Road and terminating therein at its junction with Holdenhurst Road;

Route No. 5 (1 mile 4 furlongs 4.8 chains or thereabouts in length) commencing in Tuckton Road at its junction with Bellevue Road proceeding along Tuckton Road and Cranleigh Road to and along Beaufort Road and Beresford Road and terminating in that road at its junction with Southbourne Grove;

Route No. 6 (1 furlong 3 chains or thereabouts in length) commencing in Parkwood Road at its junction with Seabourne Road proceeding in a north-easterly direction along Parkwood Road to and along Southbourne Road in a south-easterly direction and terminating in that road at its junction with Beresford Road;

Route No. 7 (1 mile 2 furlongs 6.5 chains or thereabouts in length to be situate in the borough and in the borough of Christchurch) commencing in Christchurch Road at its junction with Iford Lane proceeding along Christchurch Road and along Barrack Road and terminating therein at its junction with Stour Road Christchurch.

1.6) Extensions of time

On 9th December 1960 the Town Clerk applied to the MoT to extend for a further period of three years the time limited by Section 4 of the Bournemouth Corporation (Trolley Vehicles) Order, 1937 confirmed by the Bournemouth Corporation (Trolley Vehicles) Order Confirmation Act, 1938 as extended in 1943 and 1946, and the consents of the MoT dated 14th May 1949, 16th May 1952, 17th May 1955, and 8th November 1957 for the commencement of the use of trolley vehicles along routes 2 & 4 authorised by Section 3 of the said order of 1937, namely:–

Route No. 2 (1 mile 1 furlong 4.7 chains or thereabouts in length) commencing in Redhill Drive at its junction with Ensbury Park Road proceeding along Redhill Drive to and along Coombe Avenue and along Leybourne Avenue and Northbourne Avenue and terminating in the last-mentioned road at its junction with Wimborne Road;

Route No. 4 (1 mile 4 furlongs or thereabouts in length) commencing in Alma Road at its junction with Wimborne Road i.e. Winton Banks proceeding along Alma Road and along Richmond Park Road and terminating therein at its junction with Holdenhurst Road;

Formal consent was given on 1st May 1961. This was the last occasion that Bournemouth Corporation approached the legislative authorities in connection with their trolley vehicle system apart from the formal abandonment procedure.

2) STATUTORY RULES AND ORDERS

2.1) Statutory Rules and Orders 1933, No. 676

TROLLEY VEHICLE
Bournemouth Corporation System

ADDITIONAL REGULATIONS, DATED JULY 7, 1933, MADE BY THE MINISTER OF TRANSPORT AS REGARDS ELECTRICAL POWER ON THE BOURNEMOUTH CORPORATION TROLLEY VEHICLE SYSTEM

The Minister of Transport, under and by virtue of the powers conferred upon him in this behalf, does hereby make the following regulations for securing to the public reasonable protection against danger in the exercise of the powers conferred by Parliament with respect to the use of electrical power on the trolley vehicle system on all or any of the routes on which the use of such power has been authorised by the provisions of the Bournemouth Corporation Act 1930 (2-1 G.5c. clxxxi) and the applied provisions of the Bournemouth Corporation Tramways Order 1900 ((63-4 V.c. ccviii.) (hereinafter called "the routes"):–

And the Minister of Transport does also hereby make the following byelaws with regard to the use of electrical power on the routes.

REGULATIONS

I   Every trolley vehicle used on the routes shall comply with the following requirements, that is to say:–

(a) It shall be fitted with an apparatus to indicate to the driver the speed at which it is running.

(b) It shall be fitted with at least two independent brakes each capable of stopping and holding the vehicle on any gradient on the routes. One of the brakes at least must be applied by pedal.

(c) It shall be conspicuously numbered inside and outside.

(d) It shall be fitted with a bell, horn, gong, or other approved means for giving warning when necessary.

(e) It shall be so constructed as to enable the driver to command the fullest possible view of the road.

(f) It shall be equipped with an efficient fire extinguisher of a type suitable for dealing with electrical fires, and also a pair of rubber gloves.

II   No trailer vehicle shall be used on the routes except in case of the removal of a disabled trolley vehicle.

III   No passenger shall be allowed to travel standing on the steps, platform, staircase or upper deck of a trolley vehicle.

IV   During the hours of darkness, which expression means in summer time the time between one hour after sunset and one hour before sunrise and during the remainder of the year the time between half-an-hour after sunset and half-an-hour before sunrise, and at any time during fog, every trolley vehicle on the routes shall carry a lamp so constructed and placed as to exhibit white lights visible within a reasonable distance to the front and every such vehicle shall carry a lamp so constructed and placed as to exhibit a red light visible within a reasonable distance to the rear. The front lamps shall be fixed on opposite sides of the vehicle, be as nearly as possible of the same power and be fixed at the same height from the ground in such position that no part of the vehicle or its equipment extends laterally on the same side as the lamp more than 12 inches beyond the centre of the lamp. The rear lamp shall be fixed either on the centre line or on the off-side of the vehicle.

V   The speed at which the trolley vehicles may be driven or propelled along the routes shall not exceed the rate of:–

Thirty miles an hour –

> In Poole Road, between St. Michael's Church and the eastern end of Seamoor Road

Twenty miles an hour –

a) In Seamoor Road

b) In Poole Road, between its two junctions with Seamoor Road

Fifteen miles an hour –

a) When descending Poole Hill

b) In the Triangle

c) In Avenue Road

Ten miles an hour –

a) When rounding the curve from the Triangle into Avenue Road

Five miles an hour –

a) When turning from Poole Road into Seamoor Road

b) When turning from Seamoor Road into Poole Road

c) In the Square

At all other places not specifically mentioned the speed shall not exceed the rate of *twenty-five* miles an hour.

VI   The electrical pressure or difference of potential between the two overhead conductors used in connection with the working of the routes shall in no case exceed 600 volts. The electrical energy supplied through feeders shall not be generated at or transformed to a higher pressure than 650 volts, except with the written consent of the Minister of Transport, and subject to such regulations and consitions as he may prescribe.

VII   The interval between the supports to which the overhead conductors used in connection with the working of the routes are attached shall not, except with the approval of the Minister of Transport, exceed 120 feet, and as a general rule the overhead conductors shall in no part be at a less height than 20 feet from the surface of the street, except where they pass under railway or other bridges or at curves.

VIII Each positive overhead conductor shall be divided up into sections not exceeding (except with the special approval of the Minister of Transport) one-half of a mile in length, between every two of which shall be inserted an emergency switch so enclosed as to be inaccessible to pedestrians.

IX   Each separate insulator on the overhead conductors shall be tested not less frequently than once in a month, and any insulator found to be defective shall at once be removed and an efficient insulator substituted.

X   All electrical conductors fixed upon the trolley vehicles in connection with the trolley wheels shall be formed of flexible cables protected by india-rubber insulation of the highest quality, and additionally protected wherever they are adjacent to any metal so as to avoid risk of the metal becoming charged.

XI   The insulation of the electrical conductors from the metal work of each trolley vehicle shall be tested and recorded daily before the vehicle is used for passenger traffic with a testing pressure not less than 500 volts. No trolley vehicle shall be taken out for use if the leakage current exceeds 3 milliamperes.

XII   The hand-rails used by passengers on entering or leaving a trolley vehicle shall either be constructed of some non-conducting substance or be covered with a suitable insulating material.

XIII An emergency cut-off switch shall be provided and fixed so as to be conveniently reached by the driver in case of any failure of action of the controller switch.

XIV   If and whenever telegraph, telephone, or other wires, unprotected with a permanent insulating covering, cross above, or are liable to fall upon, or to be blown on to, the overhead conductors of the routes, efficient guard wires shall be erected and maintained at all places. Provided that this regulation shall not apply to Post Office over-road stay wires or other uncovered wires which are not electrical conductors where they are connected at each end to the negative conductor.

XV   The guard wires shall be connected to the negative overhead conductor at intervals of not more than two spans.

XVI   The poles carrying section switch boxes shall be efficiently connected with earth.

XVII Where on the routes there are two negative trolley wires these shall be cross-connected at intervals of not more than half a mile.

XVIII No gas or electric lamp bracket shall be attached to any pole unless triple insulation is provided between the pole and the positive overhead conductors.

In the case of any lamp suspended from the span wire carrying the overhead conductors that portion of the span wire from which the lamp is suspended shall be separated from that portion or portions on which the trolley wire or wires are carried by a suitable insulator.

(NOTE – The above-mentioned provisions with regard to triple insulation will not apply to the erection of lamp brackets in particular cases where the Minister of Transport is satisfied that adequate protection is attained by other methods of insulation an/or earthing approved by him).

Penalty

NOTE – The Bournemouth Corporation or any company or person using electrical power on the routes contrary to any of the above regulations is, for every such offence, subject to a penalty not exceeding £10; and also in the case of a continuing offence, to a further penalty not exceeding £5 for every day during which offence continues after conviction thereof.

BYELAWS

I   The bell, horn, gong, or other approved apparatus shall be sounded by the driver of the trolley vehicle whenever necessary as a warning.

II   The trolley vehicles on the routes shall be brought to a standstill as soon as possible whenever it is necessary to avoid impending danger and on all occasions immediately before commencing to descend Poole Hill.

III   A printed copy of these regulations and byelaws shall be kept in a conspicuous position inside of each trolley vehicle in use on the routes.

Penalty

NOTE – Any person offending against or committing a breach of any of these byelaws is liable to a penalty not exceeding forty shillings.

The provisions of the Summary Jurisdiction Acts, with respect to the recovery of penalties, are applicable to penalties for the breach of these regulations or byelaws.

> *Signed this 7th day of July, 1933.*
> *E. W. Rowntree, Assistant Secretary, Ministry of Transport.*

2.2)   Statutory Rules and Orders 1934, No. 909

TROLLEY VEHICLE
Bournemouth Corporation System

ADDITIONAL REGULATIONS, DATED AUGUST 16, 1934, MADE BY THE MINISTER OF TRANSPORT AS REGARDS ELECTRICAL POWER ON THE BOURNEMOUTH CORPORATION TROLLEY VEHICLE SYSTEM

The Minister of Transport, under and by virtue of the powers conferred upon him in this behalf, does hereby make the following regulations for securing to the public reasonable protection against danger in the exercise of the powers conferred by Parliament with respect to the use of electrical power on the trolley vehicle system on all or any of the routes on which the use of such power has been authorised by the provisions of the Bournemouth Corporation Act 1930 (2-1 G.5c. clxxxi) and the applied provisions of the Bournemouth Corporation Tramways Order 1900 ((63-4 V.c. ccviii.) (hereinafter called "the routes"):–

REGULATIONS

I   The speed at which trolley vehicles shall be driven or propelled along the routes shall not exceed the rate of:–

    1   *Twenty* miles an hour:

        (a)   in Old Chrischurch Road

        (b)   in Ashley Road, between the southern approach to the bridge over the Southern Railway at Boscombe Station and Christchurch Road

        (c)   in Portman Road

        (d)   in Gladstone Road

        (e)   in St. Swithun's Road, Southcote Road, St. Clement's Road and Palmerston Road

    2   *Fifteen* miles an hour

        (a)   in Fir Vale Road and St. Peter's Road

        (b)   in Gervis Place, between Hinton Road and Westover Road

    3   *Ten* miles an hour

        When passing over the bridge over the Southern Railway at Boscombe Station and the approaches thereto.

    4   *Five* miles an hour

        (a)   when traversing all turning circles and triangles

        (b)   when passing through all trolley wire junctions and crossings

        (c)   when turning from Palmerston Road into Christchurch Road

        (d)   when turning from Ashley Road into Christchurch Road

        (e)   when turning from Christchurch Road into Portman Road

        (f)   when turning from Portman Road into Gladstone Road

        (g)   when turning from Gladstone Road into Ashley Road

        (e)   when turning from Holdenhurst Road into Ashley Road and vice versa.

II   The insulation of the electrical conductors from the metal work of each trolley vehicle shall be tested and the leakage current recorded daily before the vehicle is used for passenger traffic with a testing pressure of not less than 500 volts. The arrangements for this test shall be such as to ensure that the whole of the high tension circuits of the vehicle, including any compressor or similar motor circuit, are subjected to the test pressure. If a high resistance instrument is used for the test, the scale shall be suitably calibrated to ensure that the resistance of the instrument itself does not affect the accuracy of the indication of the true leakage from conductors to chassis. No trolley vehicle shall be taken out for use if the leakage current exceeds 3 milliamperes.

III   Regulation XI of the Regulations and Byelaws made on the 7th day of July 1933 (S.R. & O. 1933, No. 676) is hereby rescinded.

These regulations shall be read with the Regulations and Byelaws made in this behalf by the Minister of Transport on the 7th day of July 1933 for the Bournemouth Corporation Trolley Vehicle System.

Signed this 16th day of August 1934.
E.W. Rowntree, Assistant Secretary, Ministry of Transport.

TROLLEY VEHICLE
Bournemouth Corporation System

REGULATIONS, DATED DECEMBER 21, 1936, MADE BY THE MINISTER OF TRANSPORT UNDER THE PROVISIONS OF SECTIONS 19 AND 24 OF THE BOURNEMOUTH CORPORATION TRAMWAYS ORDER, 1900, (confirmed by 63 & 64 Vict. c. ccviii) AND SECTION 99 OF THE BOURNEMOUTH CORPORATION ACT, 1930, 20 & 21 Geo. 5. c. clxxxi.) FOR REGULATING THE USE OF ELECTRICAL POWER; FOR PREVENTING FUSION OR INJURIOUS ELECTROLYTIC ACTION OF OR ON GAS OR WATER PIPES OR OTHER METALLIC PIPES, STRUCTURES, OR SUBSTANCES; AND FOR MINIMISING AS FAR AS IS REASONABLY PRACTICABLE INJURIOUS INTERFERENCE WITH THE ELECTRIC WIRES, LINES, AND APPARATUS OF PARTIES OTHER THAN THE BOURNEMOUTH CORPORATION, AND THE CURRENTS THEREIN, WHETHER SUCH LINES DO OR DO NOT USE THE EARTH AS A RETURN.

Definitions

In the following regulations –

    The expression "energy" means electrical energy.

    The expression "generator" means the dynamo or dynamos or other electrical apparatus used for the generation or conversion of energy.

    The expression "motor" means any electric motor carried on a trolley vehicle and used for the conversion of energy.

    The expression "wire" means any wire or apparatus used for telegraphic, telephonic, electrical signalling or similar purposes.

    The expression "current" means an electric current exceeding one-thousandth part of an ampere.

    The expression "the Corporation" means the Bournemouth Corporation, and includes their lessees, and any person owning, working or running trolley vehicles over the trolley vehicle system of the Corporation.

REGULATIONS

1   Any generator shall be of such pattern and construction as to be capable of producing a continuous current without appreciable pulsation.

2   (1)   The positive conductor used for transmitting energy from the generator to the motors shall be insulated from earth.

    (2)   The negative conductor shall be connected to earth at one point only, namely, at a generating station or at a sub-station, but shall elsewhere be insulated.

3   The insulation of the said positive and negative conductors, and of all feeders and other conductors, shall be so maintained that the leakage current shall not exceed one-hundredth of an ampere per mile of route. The leakage current shall be ascertained not less frequently than once in every week before or after the hours of running when the said conductors are fully charged. If at any time it should be found that the leakage current exceeds one-half of an ampere per mile of route, the leak shall be localised and the cause thereof removed as soon as practicable, and the running of the trolley vehicles shall be stopped unless the leak is localised and the cause thereof removed within 24 hours.

4   In the disposition, connections, and workings of feeders the Corporation shall take all reasonable precautions to avoid injurious interference with any existing wires.

5   The Corporation shall so construct and maintain their trolley vehicle system as to secure good contact between the motors and the said conductors.

6   The Corporation shall adopt the best means available to prevent the occurrence of undue sparking at the rubbing or rolling

contacts in any place and in the construction and use of their generators and motors.

7 The Corporation shall, so far as may be applicable to their system of working, keep records of the matters specified below. These records shall, if and when required, be forwarded for the information of the Minister of Transport.

Number of trolley vehicles running.

Length of routes.

Daily Records

- Maximum working pressure.

- Maximum working current.

Weekly Records

- Leakage current (vide Regulation 3).

Occasional Records

- Localisation and removal of leakages, stating time occupied.

- Particulars of any abnormal occurrence affecting the electric working of the routes.

8 The Regulations made by the Minister of Transport in this behalf, dated the 7th day of July, 1933, (S.R.&O.1933, No. 675) are hereby rescinded.

Signed this 21st day of December, 1936.
F.Gordon Tucker, Assistant Secretary, Ministry of Transport.

Subsequent Statutory Rules and Orders e.g. 1936 No. 1354, referred primarily to additional speed limits on new routes and revised speed limits on existing ones.

---

3) BOURNEMOUTH BYELAWS

BYELAWS

MADE ON THE THIRD DAY OF APRIL, 1951, BY THE MAYOR, ALDERMEN AND BURGESSES OF THE COUNTY BOROUGH OF BOURNEMOUTH, ACTING BY THE COUNCIL UNDER THE POWERS CONFERRED ON THEM BY SECTIONS 46 AND 47 OF THE TRAMWAYS ACT, 1870, SECTIONS 98, 118 AND 120 OF THE BOURNEMOUTH CORPORATION ACT, 1930, AND THE BORNEMOUTH CORPORATION (TROLLEY VEHICLES) ORDER CONFIRMATION ACT, 1938, WITH RESPECT TO THEIR TROLLEY VEHICLES AND CERTAIN PREMISES

---

1 In these Byelaws unless the context otherwise requires the following expressions have the meanings hereby respectively assigned to them, that is to say:-

"Corporation" means the Mayor, Aldermen and Burgesses of the County Borough of Bournemouth, acting by the Council.

"Trolley Vehicle" means any trolley vehicle owned and used by the Corporation for the conveyance of passengers.

"Trolley Vehicle system" means the system of trolley vehicles worked by the Corporation.

"Passenger" means any person other than an authorised person who has entered a trolley vehicle and travels thereon.

"Intending passenger" means any person waiting at a stopping place on a trolley vehicle route for the purpose of becoming a passenger on a trolley vehicle or who is about to enter a trolley vehicle for that purpose.

"Conductor" includes any officer or servant of the Corporation having the charge of or helping in the charge of a trolley vehicle.

"Driver" means any officer of servant of the Corporation driving or helping to drive a trolley vehicle.

"Authorised person" means any officer or servant of the Corporation (including the conductor) on duty upon or in connection with the trolley vehicle.

"Premises" means a cloakroom room or shed for the storage of bicycles tricycles and other vehicles or any shelter or other accommodation provided in connection with any service of trolley vehicles of the Corporation.

"General Manager" means the General Manager for the time being of the trolley vehicle system.

2 The Interpretation Act, 1889 shall apply to the interpretation of these Byelaws as it applies to the interpretation of an Act of Parliament.

3 When a trolley vehicle is carrying passengers or waiting to pick up passengers a passenger or intending passenger shall not -

(i) use obscene or offensive language or conduct himself in a riotous or disorderly manner;

(ii) enter or alight from the trolley vehicle otherwise than by the doors or openings provided for the purpose;

(iii) when entering or attempting to enter the trolley vehicle wilfully and unreasonably impede passengers seeking to enter the trolley vehicle or to alight therefrom;

(iv) enter or remain in or on the trolley vehicle when requested not to do so by an authorised person on the ground that the trolley vehicle is carrying its full complement of passengers;

(v) travel in or on the upper deck of the trolley vehicle unless he occupies a seat provided for that purpose, or in or on any part of the trolley vehicle not provided for the conveyance of passengers;

(vi) wilfully do or cause to be done with respect to any part of the trolley vehicle or its equipment anything which is calculated to obstruct or interfere with the working of the trolley vehicle or to cause injury or discomfort to any person;

(vii) when the trolley vehicle is in motion distract the driver's attention without reasonable cause or speak to him unless it is necessary to do so in order to give directions as to the stopping of the trolley vehicle;

(viii) give any signal which might be interpreted by the driver as a signal from the conductor to start;

(ix) spit upon or from or wilfully damage, soil or defile any part of the trolley vehicle;

(x) when in or on the trolley vehicle distribute printed or similar matter of any description or distribute any article for the purpose of advertising;

(xi) wilfully remove, displace, deface or alter any number plate, notice board, fare table, route indicator or destination board or any printed or other notice or advertisement in or on the trolley vehicle;

(xii) when in or on the trolley vehicle to the annoyance of other persons use or operate any noisy instrument or make or combine with any other person or persons to make excessive noise by singing, shouting or otherwise;

(xiii) when in or on the trolley vehicle throw any money to be scrambled for by any person on the road or footway; or throw out of the trolley vehicle any bottle, liquid or litter or any article or thing likely to annoy persons or to cause damage or injury to any person or property;

(xiv) throw any article from the trolley vehicle or attach to or trail from the trolley vehicle any streamer, balloon, flag or other article in such manner as to overhang the road;

(xv) wilfully obstruct or impede any authorised person;

(xvi) smoke or carry a lighted pipe, cigar or cigarette in or on any part of the trolley vehicle in or on which a notice is exhibited that smoking is prohibited;

(xvii) when in or on the trolley vehicle beg, sell or offer for sale any article;

(xviii) if his condition is such as to be offensive to passengers, or the condition of his dress or clothing is such that it may reasonably be expected to soil or injure the linings or cushions of the trolley vehicle or the clothing of other passengers, enter or remain in or on the trolley vehicle after an authorised person shall have requested him either not to enter or to leave the trolley vehicle and in such latter case shall have tendered to him the amount of any fare previously paid; provided that on trolley vehicles specially run for artisans, mechanics or daily labourers no passenger shall be prevented from entering or remaining in or on the trolley vehicle under the provisions of this Byelaw, on the grounds of the condition of his dress or clothing, if such condition is due solely due to the nature of his employment;

(xix) enter or travel in or on a trolley vehicle with loaded firearms, or any dangerous or offensive article or, except with the consent of an authorised person, bring into or on to the trolley vehicle any bulky or cumbersome article or place any such article elsewhere in or on the trolley vehicle than as directed by an authorised person;

(xx) bring any animal into or on to the trolley vehicle without the consent of an authorised person or retain any animal in or on the trolley vehicle after being requested by an authorised person to remove it or place any animal elsewhere in or on the trolley vehicle than as directed by an authorised person.

4   (a)   No passenger shall use or attempt to use:–

(i)   any ticket which has been altered or defaced, with intent to avoid payment of a fare; or

(ii)   any ticket which has been issued to another person if such ticket bears thereon an indication that it is not transferable; or

(iii)   any period or season ticket which has expired, with intent to avoid payment of a fare.

(b)   Every passenger shall –

(i)   unless he is the holder of a ticket in respect of that journey, immediately upon demand, declare the journey he intends to take or has taken and pay the conductor the fare for the whole of such journey and accept the ticket provided therefor;

(ii)   if requested by the conductor, leave the trolley vehicle on completion of the journey the fare for which he has paid;

(iii)   show his ticket, if any, when required to do so by any authorised person, or, if he fails so to show his ticket, pay the fare for the journey taken or to be taken by him;

(iv)   if required to do so surrender his ticket to any authorised person at the end of the journey covered by that ticket;

(v)   if required to do so surrender any period or season ticket held by him at the expiry of the period for which it was issued to him;

(vi)   if required to do so surrender any ticket held by him either on completion of the journey or journeys covered by that ticket or in exchange for a new ticket covering the journey or journeys he is still entitled to take.

5   Byelaw 3 (i) (ix) (x) (xi) and (xii) of these Byelaws shall extend and apply to the premises of the Corporation as if the words "when a trolley vehicle is carrying passengers or waiting to pick up passengers" were omitted therefrom and as if references to a trolley vehicle and to an intending passenger included references to those premises and to a person waiting on those premises respectively.

6   A passenger not being an artisan, mechanic or daily labourer, with the true intent and meaning of the statutory provisions relating to the Corporation shall not use or attempt to use any ticket intended only for artisans, or mechanics, or daily labourers.

7   No person except with the leave of an authorised person shall board or attempt to board a trolley vehicle which is disabled or otherwise not in service for the carriage of passengers.

8   No person shall commit any nuisance in, on, or against any trolley vehicle or premises used in connection with the trolley vehicle system.

9   (i)   Immediately before or on the termination of any journey, the conductor shall so far as practicable search the vehicle for any property accidentally left therein, and shall as soon as may be and in any case within twenty-four hours, hand such property together with any property found in the vehicle and handed to him by any other person, in the state in which it came into his possession, to the General Manager or his representative, who shall give the conductor a receipt for the property.

Provided that any property found by or handed to a conductor, may, if he goes off duty before the completion of the journey, either be dealt with by him in accordance with the provisions of this byelaw or be handed by him in the state in which it came into his possession, to the conductor who comes on duty in his place who shall give him a receipt therefor and deal with it in accordance with the provisions of this byelaw.

Provided also that if before such property has been handed to the General Manager or his representative, it is claimed by a person who satisfies the conductor that he is the owner, it shall be returned to that person forthwith without fee or reward on giving his name and address to the conductor who shall as soon as may be report the facts and give the claimant's name and address and a description of the property to the General Manager or his representative.

(ii)   Any property found in the vehicle which is not handed to the conductor in pursuance of sub-section (i) hereof and any property found in any shelter, or room used in connection with the trolley vehicle system shall be taken by the person finding the property in the state in which it came into his possession to the tramway office of the Corporation, and the General Manager or his representative shall give him a receipt for the property.

(iii)   The General Manager or his representative having the custody of property in pursuance of this byelaw shall retain the property in safe keeping for a period of at least six months, unless the property is previously claimed by the owner thereof.

Provided that official documents, including licences, passports and aliens' identity books, shall be returned forthwith to the appropriate Government Departments, local authority or other body or person by whom they were issued.

Provided also that where the name and address of the owner of any property, other than documents referred to in the preceding proviso, are readily ascertainable the General Manager or his representative shall forthwith notify him that the property is in his possession any may be claimed in accordance with this byelaw.

(iv)   If any property which has been handed to the General Manager or his representative be claimed and the claimant proves to the satisfaction of the General Manager or his representative that it belongs to him, it shall thereupon be delivered to him upon payment to the Corporation of a sum not exceeding 3d and in the case of property of a value exceeding 2/- an additional sum (up to an amount not exceeding £2) of 1/12th of the value of the property, any fraction of a penny being reckoned as a penny. For the purpose of this byelaw the value of the property shall be deemed to be such sum as may be agreed between the claimant and the General Manager or his representative, or failing agreement, such sum may be fixed by an appraiser. Any fee payable to such appraiser shall be paid by the claimant.

(v) If any property which has been handed to the General Manager or his representative appears to him to be of a perishable nature and it be not claimed and proved to his satisfaction to belong to the claimant within 48 hours from the time when it was found he may thereupon destroy or otherwise dispose of it as he sees fit.

Provided that any property which is or becomes objectionable may be destroyed or disposed of at any time at the discretion of the General Manager or his representative.

(vi) Where any property is forwarded to a claimant all costs of packing and carriage reasonably incurred shall be paid to the Corporation by the claimant.

(vii) Where any property is contained in a package, bag or other receptacle the General Manager or his representative may cause such receptacle to be opened and the contents examined if he deems it necessary to do so for the purpose either (a) of identifying and tracing the owner of the property, or (b) of ascertaining the nature of the contents.

(viii) Where any property is claimed by any person the General Manager or his representative may require the claimant to open any receptacle in which it may be contained and to submit the contents to examination for the purpose of establishing his claim to ownership.

10 A conductor shall to the best of his ability take steps whenever necessary to enforce these Byelaws and to prevent the breach thereof.

11 Any person contravening these Byelaws shall be liable to a penalty not exceeding forty shillings and may be removed from the trolley vehicle or premises as the case may be by an authorised person, or on the request of an authorised person, by any police constable.

12 There shall be placed and kept placed in a conspicuous position inside of each trolley vehicle and premises in use a printed copy of these Byelaws.

13 These Byelaws shall come into force on the first day of August 1951.

Given under the Common Seal of the County Borough of Bournemouth this third day of April One Thousand Nine Hundred and Fifty-one.

THE COMMON SEAL OF THE MAYOR
ALDERMEN AND BURGESSES OF THE
BOROUGH OF BOURNEMOUTH was
hereunto affixed in the prescence of

"A. LINDSAY CLEGG", *Town Clerk.*

I hereby certify that a true copy of the foregoing Bye-laws has, in accordance with the provisions of Section 46 of the Tramways Act, 1870, been laid before the Minister of Transport not less than two calendar months before such Bye-laws come into operation, and that such Bye-laws have not been disallowed by the Minister of Transport within the said two calendar months.

Signed this twenty-third day of July, 1951.
"G.F.STEDMAN"
An Under Secretary of the Ministry of Transport.

---

4) TRANSPORT DEPARTMENT INTERNAL INSTRUCTIONS

4.1) Speed Limits

BOURNEMOUTH CORPORATION TRANSPORT SERVICES

Speed restrictions – The speed at which the trolley vehicles may be driven or propelled along the routes shall not exceed the rate of 30 m.p.h. or such lower rate of speed as hereinafter specified

1) *Twenty five* miles per hour:–

   a) In Beresford Road

   b) In Tuckton Road between Belle Vue Road and Cranleigh Road

   c) In Southbourne Grove

   d) In Southbourne Road between Southbourne Grove and Belle Vue Road

   e) In Belle Vue Road between Southbourne Road and Cross Roads

   f) When ascending Commercial Road and Poole Hill

   g) In Castle Lane between Ibbertson Road and Throop Road

2) *Twenty* miles per hour:–

   a) In Exeter Road between its junction with Pier Approach and Terrace Road

   b) In Castle Lane between Holmfield Avenue and Christchurch Road

   c) In Belle Vue Road, Southbourne, between Cross Roads and Foxholes Road

   d) In Foxholes Road, Southbourne

   e) In Seamoor Road

   f) In Old Christchurch Road

   g) In St. Swithun's Road

   h) In Southcote Road

   i) In Wallisdown Road between its junction with Firs Glen Road and Talbot Road

   j) In Wimborne Road when rounding the curve at its junction with Talbot Avenue

   k) In Charminster Road from its junction with Alma Road to its junction with Richmond Wood Road

   l) In Charminster Road when rounding the corner at its junction with Maxwell and Hankinson Roads

   m) In Bath Road when descending the hill between Parsonage Road and the east side of Bournemouth Pier Approach

3) *Fifteen* miles per hour:–

   a) In Gervis Place

   b) When rounding the bend in Lansdowne Road at its junction with St. Paul's Road

   c) In the Triangle

   d) When descending Poole Hill

   e) In Avenue Road

   f) In Ensbury Park Road when rounding the curve at its junction with Highfield Road

   g) In Fir Vale Road

   h) In St. Peter's Road

   i) In Mallard Road

   j) When rounding the bend between Barrack Road and High Street, Christchurch

k)   In Ashley Road when passing over the railway bridge and its approach at Boscombe Station

l)   In Exeter Road between its junction with Terrace Road and the Square

m)   In the Square

4)   *Eight* miles per hour:–

a)   When descending Richmond Hill

b)   When turning from the Triangle into Avenue Road

c)   When passing over Tuckton Bridge

d)   When rounding Pier Approach

e)   In High Street, Christchurch, when passing the traffic island at its junction with Castle Street (outward journey only)

f)   When turning at either junction of Poole Road and Seamoor Road

g)   Whn passing through all trolley wire junctions and crossings

h)   When rounding all turning circles and right-angled turns

i)   At all reversing triangles

The above list represents the proposed new speed limits (abolition of 5 mph speed limits with restriction increased to 8 mph, and abolition of 10 mph speed limit with restrictions distributed to 8 and 15 mph) sent to Brigadier C. A. Langley, MoT, on 22 November 1956.

BYELAWS

The trolley vehicles on the routes shall be brought to a standstill as soon as possible whenever it is necessary to avoid impending danger, and on all occasions immediately before reaching the following points:-

a)   Richmond Hill (descending vehicles only) at (i) Richmond Gardens and (ii) The Church of the Sacred Heart

b)   Outside No. 23 Poole Hill (descending vehicles only)

4.2)   Instructions for Frosty Weather

BOURNEMOUTH CORPORATION TRANSPORT SERVICES

ARRANGEMENTS FOR DEALING WITH FROST
ON TROLLEY WIRES

It is most important that the first bus on all routes should run to time and in the event of frost, Night Superintendent Lacey, or his Deputy, must contact Castle Lane and Boscombe Depots, to ascertain what conditions prevail and, if necessary, will give instructions for the undermentioned staff to be called in for defrosting.

Should this be done, he must also contact the Engineer at the Christchurch Sub-Station, and ask him to make power available on the Christchurch Section.

Instructions must also be given for "Frost Heads" to be fitted on the early service vehicles, and in severe cases a special bus must be run before the services commence to clear the wires so that no delay is caused. The numbers of the vehicles so fitted, must be noted and a change over to normal heads made as soon as possible.

CENTRAL SECTION
Deputy Chief Inspector W. Biddlecombe
35 Athelstan Road
Southbourne   Telephone: Southbourne 1332

who will be in charge of this section.

Inspector C. Forscey
3 Swanmore Road
Boscombe East   Telephone: Southbourne 3344

The second man on all vehicles to be supplied from the Depot Staffs.

All vehicles to carry a spare head, spanners and a torch.

Trap doors over resistances must be taken up to allow resistances to cool as much as possible.

400 *i.e. AEL 400 – AEL 411 (72–83)* and 60 *i.e. ALJ 60 – ALJ 65 (84–89)* class buses have no trap doors and should not be used if others are available.

B.U.T. vehicles NOT TO BE USED UNDER ANY CIRCUMSTANCES

Separate sheets will be issued showing the routes to be taken, but these may be varied according to conditions.

14.9.53
E/L

BOURNEMOUTH CORPORATION TRANSPORT SERVICES

BOSCOMBE DEPOT

ROUTE NO. 1
Leave Boscombe Depot via No. 21 route. Proceed to Christchurch, return to Boscombe Depot via No. 20 route. Repeat until wires are cleared.

ROUTE NO. 2
Leave Boscombe Depot via No. 20 route. Proceed to Stour Road, return to Boscombe Depot via No. 21 route. Repeat until wires are cleared.

ROUTE NO. 3
Leave Boscombe Depot via No. 22 route for Tuckton Bridge. Proceed to Fisherman's Walk, via Cranleigh Road. Return via Cranleigh Road to Tuckton Bridge, then to Boscombe Depot via No. 22 route. Repeat until wires are cleared.

CENTRAL DEPOT

ROUTE NO. 1
Leave Central Depot and proceed to Portman Road, then No. 25 route to the Square via Old Christchurch Road then to Westbourne and return to Ashley Road, via 25 route. Return to Square by 25 Route unless different instructions are received.

ROUTE NO. 2
Leave Central Depot for Castle Lane via Portman Road and Pokesdown; turn at Mallard Road and return to Iford and repeat journey to Mallard Road from Iford until wires are clear, or other instructions are received from the Inspector at Iford.

CASTLE LANE DEPOT

ROUTE NO. 1
Leave Castle Lane Depot for Banks via Moordown, go up Talbot Road to Wallisdown and return to Banks via Ensbury Park Road. Turn at Banks and run in reverse direction, i.e. via Ensbury Park Road and Talbot Road to Banks, then to Square via 26 Route and return to Castle Lane Depot via 26 Route unless otherwise instructed.

ROUTE NO. 2
Castle Lane Depot to Iford, turn at Iford circle and return along Castle Lane to Cemetery Junction via Charminster; turn at Cemetery Junction and go to Luckham Road and back to Cemetery Junction; turn at Cemetery Junction and go to Malvern Road and from there go to Square via Lansdowne (No. 27 Route) and return to Castle Lane Depot via Charminster unless otherwise instructed by Inspector on duty.

4.3)   Trolleybus Driving Instructions

BOURNEMOUTH CORPORATION TRANSPORT SERVICES

In issuing these instructions, I do so realising that they are far from complete but as I wish them to be as short and concise as possible, much must be left to the discretion of the driver of the vehicle, at the same time they should serve as a useful guide to all the Traffic Staff.

IN THE DEPOT

Before starting from Depot, the following routine must be observed.

1. See that the trolleys are on the proper wire.

2. Test main lighting by turning on the main switch. (Important) Main lights must be switched off when in use, if trolleys are taken off or replaced on the overhead.

3. See that trolley dewirement buzzer is in the "on" position.

4. Set Circuit Breakers in "on" position, and bring reverser handle to "forward" position.

5. Test windscreen wiper and electric horn, and see that driving mirrors are in position.

6. The front exit door must be closed and locked before attempting to move.

7. On returning to Depot, place circuit breakers, all switches and reverser in "off" position. Open front door.

8. When leaving the vehicle, the handbrake must be firmly applied.

9. On commencing and completion of a duty, drivers and conductors must examine their vehicle and report on the form provided, all defects and damage, no matter how small, in order that it may receive immediate attention.

OPERATING TROLLEY BUSES IN SERVICE

All trolley buses are equipped with four forward brakes and one run-back electric brake.

These consist of: Hand, foot, regenerative, electric and run-back brakes.

(IMPORTANT) The electric brake must be used in the following manner:

Stop the bus at top of hill, place reverser handle in "brake", position as marked, and allow the bus to drift away. When changing to forward position the bus must be brought to a definite stop, otherwise serious damage will be caused to the electrical equipment.

RUN-BACK BRAKE

In the event of a complete brake and power failure, whilst ascending any hill, place one circuit breaker in the "off" position. This will check your speed to 2 mph.

The handbrake is for parking and emergency stopping, and should be firmly applied when leaving vehicle, and a scotch placed under a wheel. This especially applies when on inclines or declines.

The foot brake is vacuum assisted (*N.B. this refers to Sunbeam MS2 vehicles, the BUTs and Sunbeam MF2Bs having compressed air brakes*), and the gauge on the dash will show the amount in inches created.

The vacuum builds up when the bus is in motion, the usual amount being 23 ins. When the foot pedal is depressed a certain amount of vacuum is used at each application: about 1½ ins. It is, therefore, wrong to ride with the foot on the brake pedal. When the vacuum gauge shows less than 10 inches the driver should drive with great care, using the hand brake to assist in bringing the vehicle to a stop, and arrange for the vehicle to be sent into the Depot for attention.

POWER CONTROL OPERATION

There are 12 notches on the control panel, and when using the power pedal, the first five notches must be definitely felt for, but you should not dwell on numbers 1 to 5, as these are Resistance Notches and will quickly cause overheating of resistances. The following notches automatically come in as the pedal is depressed and full power is obtained.

For regenerative braking (*N.B. again this refers to Sunbeam MS2 vehicles only*), release the pressure on the control pedal slowly, until speed is reduced as required. For a smooth stop regenerate to 10 mph, when regeneration ceased, then fully release the power pedal, the bus can then be brought to a stop by means of the foot brake.

FROGS, CROSSINGS AND SECTION INSULATORS

The speed of trolley buses under ALL Frogs and Crossings must not exceed 5 mph.

Drivers must pass under all Breakers and Insulated Crossings with the Power Pedal in the "off" position. Failure to observe this instruction will cause flashing and damage to the overhead fittings.

DEWIREMENTS

If the trolley head leaves the wire, the driver must immediately bring the vehicle to a standstill, and must not apply power until the trolley head has been replaced and the proper signal to proceed received from the Conductor.

If the trolley head appears to have been damaged, the driver should use his own discretion as to whether he considers it advisable to proceed on his journey or wait until repairs have been carried out. If he does proceed, however, he should take steps to have the head inspected at the earliest possible opportunity.

Dewirements must be reported to the first Official on duty, also the exact time, place and pole number, and whether on the inward or outward journey.

In order to avoid dewirements at curves, the trolley bus must be driven so as to follow a curve greater that the curve of the overhead wires. Where this is impossible for traffic reasons, the speed must be further reduced.

When the driver of a trolley bus observes the Overhead Department's Lorry standing under the wires, he must not pass same until notified by the man working on the top of the lorry that everything is in order for him to proceed. (PASS WITH CARE)

* A special form must be made out for all dewirements

FLOODED ROADWAY

Trolleybuses must not be driven upon flooded roads at a speed exceeding 8 mph and must be kept as far as possible to the crown of the road.

TYRE PUNCTURES

In the event of a tyre being punctured the trolleybus must be parked immediately at the side of the road, in such a position as to cause as little inconvenience as possible to other road users. The conductor must then arrange for the transfer of passengers to other vehicles, and the driver must notify the Square Inspector (Phone Bournemouth 404).

ACCIDENT PROCEDURE

In the event of being involved in an accident causing injury to passengers or other personnel, obtain medical attention for the injured first, then the Inspector in the Square must be notified.

If involved in any accident, however slight or trivial it may appear to you, the following procedure is necessary at the time of the accident.

1. Under no circumstances admit liability or make a statement unless in the presence of the General Manager, Traffic Superintendent or an Inspector.

2. Obtain full particulars of all persons and property involved.

3. Names and addresses of witnesses.

4 Make a rough sketch of the scene of the accident.

REPORTING DEFECTS

Defects connected with the vehicle, body or fittings, are to be reported at the completion of duty on the driver's report sheet provided. Under no circumstances are drivers or conductors to give any information to the public regarding defects which may arise in their vehicles and they should be careful not to make any statement likely to be detrimental to themselves or the Department.

SERVICE RUNNING

When on service DO NOT DRIVE CLOSE BEHIND ANOTHER BUS and avoid grouping of vehicles which should be at least 200 yards apart.

UNATTENDED VEHICLES

Drivers and conductors are not to leave their vehicles unattended at terminal points or any particular stop. If it is essential for one to leave the other must be left in charge.

REVERSING

The driver must not reverse the vehicle until the "All Clear" signal is given. Reversing handle must not be moved until bus is stationary.

HIGHWAY CODE AND ROAD TRAFFIC ACTS

The Highway Code is a code of behaviour, based on courtesy, common sense and the Road Traffic Acts, laid down for the guidance of all users of the road.

Its strict observance at all times would greatly reduce the number of accidents. It is your duty to make yourself familiar with the Highway Code and such parts of the Road Traffic Acts as concern you and strictly conform to the regulations and advice contained in them. You, as a PSV (sic) driver, are conspicuous and should therefore, at all times, act in such a manner as to set an example to other road users.

4.4) BUT 9641T Additional Driving Instructions

BOURNEMOUTH CORPORATION TRANSPORT SERVICES

Instructions to drivers of BUT Trolleybuses which will be in service as and from Sunday, 1st October 1950

WHEN TAKING VEHICLE FROM DEPOT

1. Set circuit breaker in the "ON" position.

2. Close compressor control switch and wait for low pressure alarm to indicate that there is sufficient air pressure to proceed.

RHEOSTATIC BRAKING

The brake is actuated by the right pedal. A slight depression of the pedal brings in the first rheostatic brake notch, further depression of the pedal the second notch, and still further depression brings in the air brake with an intensity proportional to the amount depressed. (Please use with care to avoid passengers being thrown off balance).

It will be realised that however the brakes are applied to the vehicle, whether for normal service stop or under emergency conditions, the rheostatic brake is always brought into operation first. It is maintained in operation until the vehicle's speed falls to the low speed of 2 to 3 mph after which the vehicle is brought to rest by the air brake.

If at any time it is necessary to make an emergency brake application, the depression of the brake pedal, whilst the power pedal is also depressed, immediately cuts off the power. Under no circumstances is it possible to feed power from the line and at the same time apply the footbrake to the vehicle.

AIR PRESSURE ALARM

If the air pressure falls below a certain level, the low pressure alarm in the driver's cabin operates, a red signal arm is raised and a buzzer sounds. If this happens the driver should not proceed.

COASTING BRAKE

The coasting brake must be used in the following manner:-

Stop the bus at the top of the hill, place control handle in "BRAKE" position as marked, and allow bus to drift away. When changing to "FORWARD" position, the bus must be brought to a definite stop, otherwise serious damage will be caused to the electrical equipment.

WHEN LEAVING VEHICLE

When leaving the vehicle in Depot or Bus Park, make sure the circuit breakers are in the "OFF" position and that the compressor control is switched off.

ABOVE ALL, PLEASE REMEMBER YOU ARE DRIVING AN EIGHT FOOT WIDE VEHICLE.

W.D.REAKES, GENERAL MANAGER
WJG/BJB1.1.57

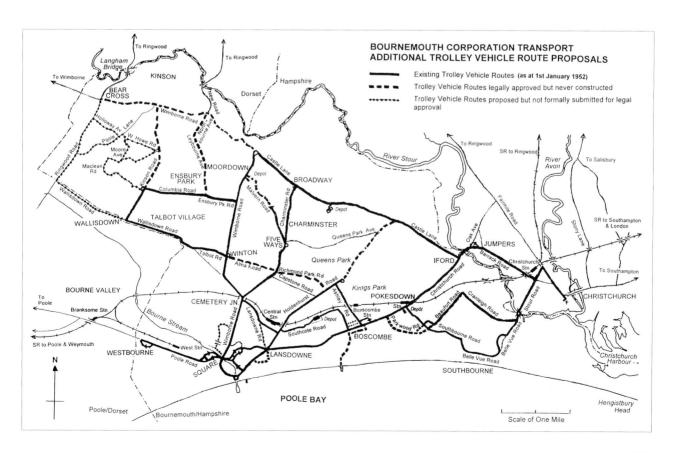

BOURNEMOUTH CORPORATION TRANSPORT
ADDITIONAL TROLLEY VEHICLE ROUTE PROPOSALS

———	Existing Trolley Vehicle Routes (as at 1st January 1952)
- - -	Trolley Vehicle Routes legally approved but never constructed
•••••••	Trolley Vehicle Routes proposed but not formally submitted for legal approval

Statistics

1. REVENUE STATISTICS

Year	Number of passengers per mile	Fare per passenger (pence)	Traffic revenue per mile (pence)	Working expenses per mile (pence)	Notes
1934	8.70	1.72	14.99	11.83	Tram, trolleybus and motorbus
1935	8.58	1.72	15.17	11.76	Tram, trolleybus and motorbus
1936	7.86	1.60	12.60	10.90	Tram, trolleybus and motorbus
1937	10.24	1.51	15.45	10.78	Tram, trolleybus and motorbus
1938	9.70	1.59	15.27	10.74	Trolleybuses only from this point onwards
1939	9.39	1.58	15.02	10.91	
1940	10.20	1.58	16.09	11.78	
1941	11.09	1.55	17.20	13.24	
1942	13.47	1.58	21.22	14.19	
1943	14.48	1.55	22.43	15.24	
1944	13.95	1.71	23.86	16.86	
1945	15.33	1.75	26.91	18.77	
1946	15.80	1.80	28.46	20.33	
1947	14.32	1.82	25.04	20.41	
1948	13.61	1.84	25.05	21.45	
1949	13.42	1.79	24.16	22.29	
1950	13.82	1.72	23.83	23.23	
1951	13.63	1.75	23.84	23.82	
1952	13.40	2.31	31.01	27.30	
1953	12.96	2.45	31.81	29.84	
1954	12.46	2.80	34.89	30.56	
1955	12.23	2.84	34.78	32.40	
1956	11.85	2.99	35.50	33.55	
1957	11.92	3.53	42.03	34.57	
1958	12.11	3.51	42.49	37.14	
1959	11.83	3.53	41.81	37.23	
1960	11.74	3.54	41.58	36.85	
1961	11.83	3.54	41.92	36.87	
1962	11.70	3.81	44.53	39.92	
1963	11.46	3.96	45.35	42.24	
1964	11.24	4.29	48.18	44.25	
1965	10.71	4.99	53.31	47.33	
1966	10.02	6.42	64.42	49.17	
1967	9.66	6.46	62.37	48.83	
1968	11.02	6.50	71.60	56.21	
1969	8.73	7.70	67.88	53.65	

2.   CAPITAL EXPENDITURE – MAJOR ITEMS

Year	Expenditure Item	Amount £	s	d	Incomes (write-offs)	Amount £	s	d	Comments
1934	Trolleybuses and equipment	10,008	8	5		—			
1935	Trolleybuses	63,691	11	3		—			
	Overhead equipment	28,369	17	11		—			
	Iford turning circle	2,250				—			
1936	Trolleybuses } Overhead equipment	177,448	16	1		—			
1937	Trolleybuses	17,097	14	1		—			
	Overhead equipment	7,165	5	0		—			
	Cables	4,236	12	5		—			
	Christchurch turntable	829	18	6		—			
	Parliamentary expenses	1,330	0	8		—			
1938	Trolleybuses	37	12	3		—			
	Overhead equipment	7,912	11	3		—			
	Cables	1	10	0		—			
	Christchurch turntable	45	13	8		—			
1939	Overhead equipment	6,314	3	6		—			
	Street improvements	5,838				—			
	Vehicles	154	19	10		—			
	Parliamentary expenses	1,103	17	6		—			
1940	Overhead equipment	3,547	8	0		—			
1941	Overhead equipment	136	17	0		—			
1942	Generating station	29,466	5	5	Trolleybus	1,450			single decker
1943	Electric coal conveyor	187	5	0		—			
	Superheaters (3)	516				—			
	Overhead equipment (Barrack Road extension)	2,923	7	11		—			from reserve fund
1944	Turbo generator	3,123	11	6		—			
	Overhead equipment (Barrack Road extension)	63	14	3		—			
1945	Turbo generator	1,755	14	2		—			
	Extension of overhead equipment	710	9	2		—			
1946	Turbo generator	288	9	3		—			
	Extension of overhead equipment	7	11	0		—			
1947	Overhead equipment	293	9	9		—			
1948	Overhead equipment	1,941	11	1		—			
1949	Overhead equipment	5,819	0	2		—			
1950	Overhead equipment: Pier Approach	4,753	16	0		—			
1951	Trolleybuses	147,599	19	3		—			
	Trolleybus equipment: Fisherman's Walk to Pier Approach extension	35	2	1		—			
	Castle Lane extension	7,731	13	10		—			
1952	Trolleybuses	860				—			
	Trolleybus equipment: Fisherman's Walk to Tuckton Bridge extension	583	5	9		—			
	Castle Lane extension	13,283	17	9		—			
1953	Trolleybus	257	7	11	Trolleybuses scrapped	39,680	10	0	
	Equipment, Castle Lane extension	737	16	1		—			
1954	Trolleybus equipment	3,448	17	6	Trolleybuses scrapped	13,299			
	Castle Lane extension	31,417	2	2		—			
1955	Electrical and cabling work at new substations	1,200				—			

Year	Expenditure Item	Amount £ s d	Incomes (write-offs)	Amount £ s d	Comments
1956	Electrical and cabling work at new substations	39,136	Power station plant scrapped	67,431	
1957	Electrical and cabling work at new substations	10,804		—	
1958		—	Trolleybuses scrapped	22,165	
1959	Trolleybuses	137,963	Trolleybuses scrapped	44,330	
	Trolleybus equipment	400		—	
1960	Trolleybuses	73,772	Trolleybuses scrapped	44,330	
1961	Trolleybuses	3,784		—	
1962	Trolleybuses	37,376		—	
1963	Trolleybuses	32,230	Trolleybuses scrapped	35,664	
1964	Trolleybuses	1,438	Trolleybuses scrapped	13,110	
1965		—		8,616	
1966		—		8,249	
1967		—		148,710	
1968		—		—	
1969		—		—	
1970	Abandonment: removal of system	7,045	Trolleybuses scrapped	284,858	
1971	Abandonment: removal of system	8,333	Abandonment	15,378	
			Equipment	221,058	
1972	Abandonment: removal of system	6,305	Abandonment	6,305	

3.   STATEMENT OF BORROWING POWERS AND ADVANCES

Purpose	Date of Act or Sanction	Repayment period (yrs)	Amount (£)	Advances made in the following years
Vehicles	Bournemouth Corporation Act 1930	10	300,000	1934, 1935, 1936, 1950, 1951, 1954, 1955
Equipment	Bournemouth Corporation Act 1930	20	157,000	1935, 1936, 1938, 1940
Iford, Land for turning Circle	06 July 1936	20	2,250	1935
Road works	Bournemouth Corporation Act 1930	20	47,000	1936, 1937, 1938, 1939
Parliamentary expenses	Bournemouth Corporation Act 1930	5	1,061	1938
Parliamentary expenses	Local Government Act 1931	5	227	1938
Parliamentary expenses	Bournemouth Corporation Act 1930	5	1,120	1939
Vehicles	Bournemouth Corporation Confirm. Act 1938	10	54,000	1951
Vehicles	21 October 1949	10	30,621	1951
Equipment (Castle Lane)	15 May 1950	25	31,296	1951, 1952
Equipment	15 July 1950	25	6,635	1951
Vehicles	20 March 1951	10	5,126	1951, 1952
Holdenhurst Substation	Bournemouth Corporation Act 1930	15	2,000	1953
Turning Circle	Bournemouth Corporation Act 1930	25	500	1954
Electric Cabling	23 April 1954	20	50,702	1955, 1956, 1957
Vehicles	11 February 1957	14	141,680	1959, 1960
Vehicles	14 January 1958	14	71,110	1960, 1961
Vehicles	24 February 1960	14	75,470	1962, 1963, 1964

4. OPERATING STATISTICS (In each case, for year ending 31 March)

Year	Number of passengers per mile	Fare per passenger (pence)	Traffic revenue per mile	Working expenses per mile	Working expenses per passenger	Net revenue charges per mile	Net revenue charges per passenger	Power units used	Power units per mile	Power cost per mile (pence)	Cost per power unit (pence)
1934-36			No separate trolleybus statistics available for this period								
1937	10.24	1.51	15.45	10.78	1.05			6,230,950	2.42	1.85	0.764
1938	9.70	1.59	15.27	10.74	1.11			6,607,590	2.37	1.99	0.840
1939	9.39	1.58	14.78	10.91	1.16			7,040,055	2.41	2.04	0.846
1940	10.20	1.58	16.32	11.78	1.16			6,807,441	2.43	2.14	0.880
1941	11.09	1.55	17.20	13.24	1.19			5,690,820	2.46	2.55	1.037
1942	13.47	1.58	21.22	14.19	1.06			6,833,720	2.49	3.41	1.369
1943	14.48	1.55	22.43	15.24	1.05			7,356,665	2.60	3.38	1.300
1944	13.95	1.71	23.86	16.86	1.21	2.99	0.21	6,826,060	2.69	3.15	1.171
1945	15.33	1.75	26.91	18.77	1.22	2.62	0.17	6,962,880	2.78	3.56	1.281
1946	15.80	1.80	28.46	20.33	1.28	1.76	0.11	7,363,995	2.86	4.03	1.409
1947	14.32	1.82	26.04	20.41	1.42	0.64	0.04	8,466,125	2.83	3.83	1.353
1948	13.61	1.84	25.05	21.45	1.57	0.60	0.04	8,601,255	2.70	4.05	1.500
1949	13.42	1.79	24.16	22.29	1.66	0.58	0.04	9,108,965	2.65	4.02	1.517
1950	13.82	1.72	23.83	23.23	1.68	0.59	0.04	8,890,755	2.60	4.15	1.596
1951	13.63	1.75	23.84	23.82	1.75	0.87	0.06	9,220,691	2.78	4.55	1.637
1952	13.40	2.31	31.01	27.30	2.04	2.52	0.19	8,864,705	2.92	5.35	1.832
1953	12.96	2.45	31.81	29.84	2.30	2.98	0.23	8,866,061	2.97	6.11	2.057
1954	12.46	2.80	34.89	30.56	2.45	3.47	0.28	7,908,790	2.86	6.20	2.168
1955	12.23	2.84	34.78	32.40	2.65	3.51	0.29	7,875,940	2.89	6.60	2.284
1956	11.85	2.99	35.50	33.55	2.83	3.68	0.31	8,495,130	3.13	5.44	1.738
1957	11.92	3.53	42.03	34.57	2.90	4.11	0.35	7,679,150	3.15	4.45	1.413
1958	12.11	3.51	42.49	37.14	3.07	4.22	0.35	7,190,670	3.22	4.69	1.456
1959	11.83	3.53	41.81	37.23	3.15	4.39	0.37	7,350,483	3.29	4.77	1.450
1960	11.74	3.54	41.58	36.85	3.14	5.96	0.51	7,081,660	3.20	4.51	1.409
1961	11.83	3.54	41.92	36.87	3.12	6.42	0.54	7,046,280	3.31	4.65	1.405
1962	11.70	3.81	44.53	39.92	3.41	5.00	0.43	7,120,885	3.39	5.02	1.481
1963	11.46	3.96	45.35	42.24	3.69	5.09	0.44	6,918,690	3.32	5.08	1.530
1964	11.24	4.29	48.18	44.25	3.93	5.36	0.51	6,998,480	3.34	5.19	1.554
1965	10.71	4.99	53.51	47.33	4.42	5.85	0.55	6,546,670	3.33	5.23	1.571
1966	10.02	6.42	64.42	49.17	4.90	7.82	0.78	4,910,862	3.21	6.06	1.887
1967	9.66	6.46	62.37	48.83	5.06	9.55	0.99	3,205,967	2.70	5.72	2.118
1968	11.02	6.50	71.60	56.21	5.10	5.53	1.15	2,334,350	3.24	6.43	1.985
1969	8.73	7.70	67.88	53.65	6.14	10.02	5.10	2,297,900	2.90	5.72	1.972

5. ABSTRACTS OF ACCOUNTS (In each case for year ending 31 March)

Year	Total Revenue £	s	d	Working Expenses £	s	d	Gross Balance (Profit before interest charges) £	s	d	Net Rev Charges (Loan & interest charges) £	s	d	Net Balance Profit (loss) £	s	d	To capital £	s	d	Capital Expenditure £	s	d	Sales (+) and write-offs (−) £	s	d	Note	Cumulative Capital Expenditure £	s	d	Miles run	Passengers Carried	No. of Vehs.
1934																			10,008	8	5					10,008	8	5			4
1935																			84,303	0	9					94,311	9	2			37
1936	114,871	2	5	77,653	2	2	37,218	0	3	23,455	0	0	13,763	0	3				177,448	16	1	34,000	0	0	1	305,760	5	3	1,857,984	18,973,849	106
1937	168,362	2	11	115,506	5	0	53,470	18	9	39,411	19	0	14,058	19	9				30,659	10	8					336,419	15	11	2,570,421	26,324,803	104
1938	180,018	11	7	124,586	10	11	55,549	0	1	41,145	0	0	14,404	0	1				7,997	7	2					344,417	3	1	2,785,462	26,994,490	104
1939	182,617	19	5	132,628	14	0	50,192	7	5	41,885	0	0	8,337	7	5				13,411	0	10	119,012	0	0	2	476,840	10	11	2,917,087	27,390,558	104
1940	190,071	3	7	137,145	0	0	53,069	0	11	41,929	6	11	11,139	14	0				1,321	8	0					478,161	18	11	2,794,812	28,494,985	104
1941	171,640	18	8	127,882	1	11	43,833	7	4	39,540	0	0	4,293	7	4				136	17	0					478,298	15	11	2,316,843	25,709,253	104
1942	252,016	17	1	161,906	13	10	90,372	11	3	67,487	0	0	22,885	11	3							1,450	0	0	3	476,848	15	11	2,738,982	36,775,895	104
1943	272,910	5	11	179,594	6	5	93,453	2	0	33,342	0	0	60,111	2	0				2,923	7	11	67,270	11	11	4	412,500	16	11	2,827,512	40,951,696	104
1944	261,063	2	7	178,160	0	5	83,221	2	2	31,901	0	0	51,320	2	2				63	14	3					412,564	11	2	2,535,435	35,361,965	103
1945	289,462	9	8	195,852	12	1	94,323	4	3	27,339	0	0	66,984	4	3				710	9	2					413,275	0	4	2,504,769	38,395,486	103
1946	311,980	7	6	218,010	16	5	94,785	2	7	18,932	0	0	75,853	2	7				7	11	0					413,282	11	4	2,573,489	40,665,391	103
1947	328,719	8	9	253,757	17	5	76,642	5	4	7,955	0	0	68,687	5	4				293	9	9	5,167	14	11	4	418,743	16	0	2,983,757	42,735,741	103
1948	338,650	10	9	285,823	9	2	54,145	7	10	8,031	0	0	46,114	7	10				1,941	11	1					420,685	7	1	3,197,703	43,512,250	103
1949	350,214	5	7	319,143	19	1	32,030	18	10	8,372	0	0	23,658	18	10				5,819	0	2					426,504	7	3	3,435,851	46,131,073	103
1950	342,816	7	9	330,719	7	0	12,426	9	11	8,457	0	0	3,969	9	11				4,753	16	0					431,258	3	3	3,417,963	47,255,913	103
1951	333,445	4	8	329,410	10	7	12,010	0	6	9,447	0	6	2,563	0	0				155,366	15	2					586,624	18	5	3,319,141	45,235,606	127
1952	396,458	19	0	345,782	12	4	50,676	6	8	31,938	4	11	18,738	1	9				22,507	2	10					609,132	1	3	3,040,327	40,740,388	127
1953	399,507	19	4	370,907	11	6	37,090	0	6	34,280	0	6	2,810	0	0	2,510	0	0	40,675	13	0	79,360	19	0	5	570,446	15	3	2,983,688	38,660,146	109
1954	406,547	12	0	351,422	8	10	55,163	16	7	39,949	4	6	15,214	12	1	2,572	0	0	3,448	17	6	13,299	0	0	5	560,596	12	9	2,759,805	34,390,263	103
1955	401,940	0	0	369,168	0	0	40,202	0	0	37,630	0	0	2,572	0	0	2,572	0	0	1,200	0	0					561,797	0	0	2,734,333	33,441,804	103
1956	409,299	0	0	378,851	0	0	41,532	0	0	38,947	0	0	2,585	0	0	2,585	0	0	39,136	0	0	67,431	0	0	6	533,502	0	0	2,709,685	32,114,997	103
1957	436,155	0	0	351,417	0	0	85,228	0	0	40,166	0	0	45,062	0	0	2,192	0	0	10,804	0	0					544,306	0	0	2,439,872	29,086,555	103
1958	404,932	0	0	345,784	0	0	61,519	0	0	39,812	0	0	21,707	0	0	1,872	0	0				22,165	0	0	5	522,141	0	0	2,234,470	27,053,030	93

Year	Total Revenue			Working Expenses			Gross Balance (Profit before interest charges)			Net Rev Charges (Loan & interest charges)			Net Balance Profit (loss)			To capital			Capital Expenditure			Sales (+) and write-offs (-)			Note	Cumulative Capital Expenditure			Miles run	Passengers Carried	No. of Vehs.
	£	s	d	£	s	d	£	s	d	£	s	d	£	s	d	£	s	d	£	s	d	£	s	d		£	s	d			
1959	397,853	0	0	346,434	0	0	53,006	0	0	40,770	0	0	12,236	0	0	1,670	0	0	138,363	0	0	44,330	0	0	5	616,174	0	0	2,233,197	26,427,978	100
1960	392,326	0	0	339,686	0	0	56,696	0	0	54,954	0	0	1,742	0	0	1,742	0	0	73,772	0	0	44,330	0	0	5	645,616	0	0	2,212,402	25,974,738	90
1961	382,160	0	0	327,160	0	0	59,326	0	0	57,685	0	0	1,641	0	0	1,641	0	0	3,784	0	0					649,400	0	0	2,129,572	25,196,802	90
1962	398,928	0	0	349,421	0	0	51,622	0	0	42,042	0	0	9,580	0	0	1,670	0	0	37,376	0	0					686,776	0	0	2,099,573	24,557,919	83
1963	402,434	0	0	366,716	0	0	46,034	0	0	44,406	0	0	1,628	0	0	1,628	0	0				3,414	0	0	5	683,362	0	0	2,083,612	23,875,422	83
1964	429,090	0	0	382,507	0	0	48,735	0	0	46,818	0	0	1,917	0	0	1,632	0	0				11,671	0	0	5	671,691	0	0	2,074,431	23,319,122	77
1965	447,673	0	0	387,817	0	0	62,202	0	0	50,259	0	0	11,943	0	0							8,866	0	0	5	662,825	0	0	1,966,430	21,057,307	73
1966	424,088	0	0	313,196	0	0	112,414	0	0	51,356	0	0	61,058	0	0							8,199	0	0	5	654,626	0	0	1,529,852	15,332,449	63
1967	317,014	0	0	241,359	0	0	77,235	0	0	48,746	0	0	28,489	0	0	1,172	0	0				148,710	0	0	7	505,916	0	0	1,186,210	11,456,601	29
1968	228,202	0	0	168,748	0	0	60,146	0	0	38,662	0	0	21,484	0	0	808	0	0								505,916	0	0	720,493	7,997,929	29
1969	232,674	0	0	176,615	0	0	56,776	0	0	33,703	0	0	23,073	0	0	1,124	0	0								505,916	0	0	790,037	6,899,945	29
1970																						284,858	0	0	5	221,058	0	0			
1971																						221,058	0	0	7	0	0	0			

Notes:

1 Tramway equipment sales.
2 Power station and tramway equipment sales.
3 Trolleybus withdrawn (single-decker).
4 Believed to apply to the write-off of the remaining tramway debt.
5 Trolleybuses scrapped
6 Power station plant scrapped
7 Overhead equipment abandonment

6.   TRACTION CURRENT USED

Year	Units generated for traction	Units bought	Traction Units	Power Units per mile	Power Cost per mile (pence)	Cost per Power Unit (pence)	Notes
1934	3,876,530	1,466,405	5,342,935	2.35			Tram/Trolleybus
1935	4,019,640	1,437,631	5,457,271	2.39			Tram/Trolleybus
1936	5,512,110	634,152	6,146.262	2.38			Tram/Trolleybus
1937	4,841,420	1,389,530	6,230,950	2.42	1.85	0.764	Trolleybus only from here on
1938	4,747,350	1,860,240	6,607,590	2.37	1.99	0.840	
1939	5,115,710	1,924,345	7,040,055	2.41	2.04	0.846	
1940	4,748,900	2,058,541	6,807,441	2.43	2.14	0.880	
1941	3,857,820	1,833,000	5,690,820	2.46	2.55	1.037	
1942	5,025,690	1,808,030	6,833,720	2.49	3.41	1.369	
1943	5,455,100	1,901,565	7,356,665	2.60	3.38	1.300	
1944	5,206,150	1,619,910	6,826,060	2.69	3.15	1.171	
1945	4,693,990	2,268,890	6,962,880	2.78	3.56	1.281	
1946	5,044,420	2,319,575	7,363,995	2.86	4.03	1.409	
1947	5,084,110	3,362,015	8,446,125	2.83	3.83	1.353	
1948	5,918,030	2,683,225	8,601,255	2.70	4.05	1.500	
1949	6,161,860	2,947,105	9,108,965	2.65	4.02	1.517	
1950	6,077,500	2,813,255	8,890,755	2.60	4.15	1.596	
1951	6,341,206	2,879,485	9,220,691	2.78	4.55	1.637	
1952	6,038,105	2,826,600	8,864,705	2.92	5.35	1.832	
1953	5,699,671	3,166,390	8,866,061	2.97	6.11	2.057	
1954	5,024,290	2,884,500	7,908,790	2.86	6.2	2.168	
1955	4,733,110	3,142,830	7,875,940	2.89	6.6	2.284	
1956	1,286,980	7,208,150	8,495,130	3.13	5.44	1.738	Generating station closed 31 August 1955
1957	—	7,679,150	7,679,150	3.15	4.45	1.413	
1958	—	7,190,670	7,190,670	3.22	4.69	1.456	
1959	—	7,350,483	7,350,483	3.29	4.77	1.450	
1960	—	7,081,660	7,081,660	3.20	4.51	1.409	
1961	—	7,046,280	7,046,280	3.31	4.65	1.405	
1962	—	7,120,885	7,120,885	3.39	5.02	1.481	
1963	—	6,918,690	6,918,690	3.32	5.08	1.530	
1964	—	6,998,480	6,998,480	3.34	5.19	1.554	
1965	—	6,546,670	6,546,670	3.33	5.23	1.571	
1966	—	4,910,862	4,910,862	3.21	6.06	1.887	
1967	—	3,205,967	3,205,967	2.70	5.72	2.118	
1968	—	2,334,350	2,334,350	3.24	6.43	1.985	
1969	—	2,297,900	2,297,900	2.90	5.72	1.972	

Bibliography

Title	Author	Publisher	Date	ISBN number
Books, Brochures and Pamphlets				
Book of Bournemouth	David & Rita Popham	Barracuda Books	1985	0 860232 19 0
Bournemouth and the Second World War	Michael A. Edgington	Bournemouth Local Studies Publications	1984	1 873887 03 5
Bournemouth Corporation Transport, Vol. 1	John W. Mawson	Advertiser Press	1967	
Bournemouth Corporation Transport, Parts 1 & 2	W. P. Ransom	Bournemouth Local Studies Publications	1982	0 96287 40 5 & 41 5
Bournemouth Trams and Buses	C. G. Roberts	Locomotion Papers	1972	
Bournemouth Trolleybuses 1933–1969	David L. Chalk	Bournemouth Corporation Transport	1969	
The Tramways of Bournemouth and Poole	R. C. Anderson	Light Railway Transport League	1964	
Bournemouth and Poole Tramways	R. C. Anderson	Middleton Press	1995	
85th Anniversary Bournemouth Transport	David L. Chalk	Bournemouth Transport	1987	
Bournemouth Transport 75 Years	David L. Chalk	Bournemouth Transport	1977	
Transport Department Diamond Jubilee 1902–1962	–	Bournemouth Corporation Transport	1962	
Brighton Corporation Transport – Fleet History	R. Knight	E.L.P.G. Enterprises	1971	
History of the British Trolleybus	Nicholas Owen	David & Charles	1974	0 7153 6370 0
Llanelly Trolleybuses	Geoff L. Griffiths	Trolleybooks	1992	0 904235 15 7
Silent Service	David L. Chalk	Omnibus Society	1962	
Trolleybus Trails	J. Joyce	Ian Allan	1963	
The Trolleybuses of Brighton and Hove	David Kaye & Martin Nimmo	Reading Transport Society	1967	
The Trolleybuses of Newcastle upon Tyne	T. P. Cannaux & N. H. Hanson	Trolleybooks	1974	0 904235 02 5
The Trolleybuses of South Shields	Geoff Burrows	Trolleybooks	1976	0 904235 04 1
Under Two Liveries	H. Brearley & D. T. Beach	West Riding Transport Society	1970	
The Walsall Trolleybus System	T. J. Brown	West Riding Transport Society	1971	
Newspapers				
Bournemouth Echo		Copies held at Bournemouth Reference Library		
Bournemouth Times		Copies held at Bournemouth Reference Library		
Times & Directory		Copies held at Bournemouth Reference Library		

Professional Periodicals

The Electric Railway, Bus and Tram Journal (particularly 16 June 1933 and 19 June 1936 issues)

Electrical Review (27 May 1960 issue)   W. D. Reakes

Passenger Transport (particularly 16 August 1950 issue)

Modern Transport (particularly 25 May 1946 issue)

The Tramway & Railway World

The Transport World (Particularly 19th July 1934, 7th November 1935, 14th May 1936, 18th June 1936 issues)

Enthusiasts' Periodicals				
Buses Illustrated (issues 30, 88,147 including Bournemouth trolleybus related articles)	Ian Allan		1949–70	
National Trolleybus Association Newssheet		National Trolleybus Association	1963–66	
Reading Transport Society Newssheet		Reading Transport Society	1963–66	
Journal of the Bournemouth Passenger Transport Association (known variously as Journal of the Bournemouth Heritage Transport Collection, Transbourne News, Trolley)		Bournemouth Passenger Transport Assn.	1969–95	
Trolleybus (Journal of the British Trolleybus Society)		British Trolleybus Society	1967–date	
Trolleybus Society Newssheet		Trolleybus Society	1954–55	
Trolleybus Magazine		National Trolleybus Association	1966–date	
Others				
Bournemouth Council Minutes		Copies held at Bournemouth Ref. Library	1912–72	
Transport Committee Minutes		Copies held at Bournemouth Ref. Library	1912–72	
Timetables, fare tables etc.		Bournemouth Corporation Transport		

Maps and Wiring Layouts

This appendix consists of two sets of maps:

• Eight overhead wiring layouts of the Bournemouth Square area, showing the changes over the life of the system.

• Seven overhead wiring layouts of the Lansdowne area, showing the changes over the life of the system.

Please refer also to the following maps:

• Fold-out map of the tramways system (inside back cover of book).

• Fold-out map of the trolleybus system, showing overhead wiring changes over the life of the system (inside back cover of book).

BOURNEMOUTH SQUARE

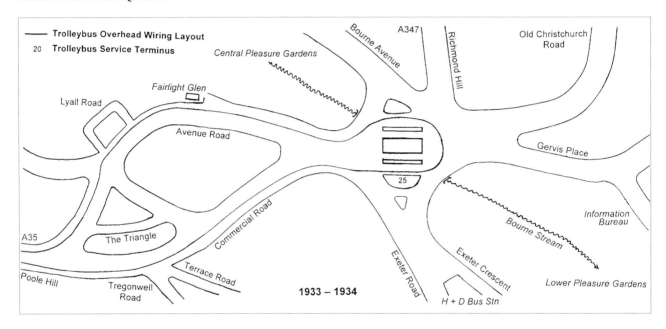

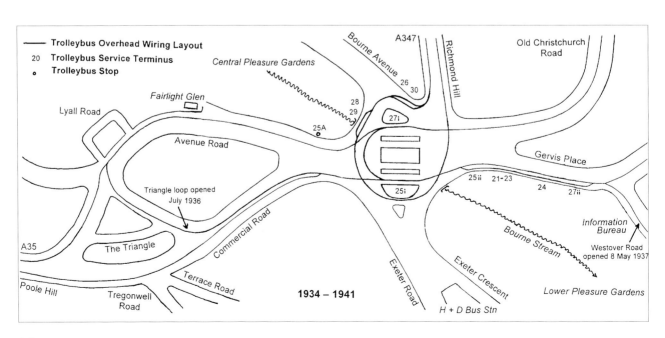

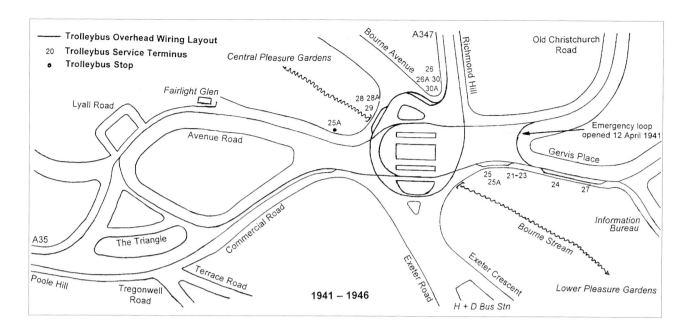

Trolleybus Overhead Wiring Layout
20 **Trolleybus Service Terminus**
•   **Trolleybus Stop**

Central Pleasure Gardens

A347

Bourne Avenue

Old Christchurch Road

Richmond Hill

Fairlight Glen

Lyall Road

26
26A 30
30A

28 28A
29

25A

Emergency loop opened 12 April 1941

Gervis Place

Avenue Road

25 21-23
25A

24   27

Information Bureau

A35

The Triangle

Commercial Road

Bourne Stream

Poole Hill

Terrace Road

Tregonwell Road

Exeter Road

Exeter Crescent

Lower Pleasure Gardens

1941 – 1946

H + D Bus Stn

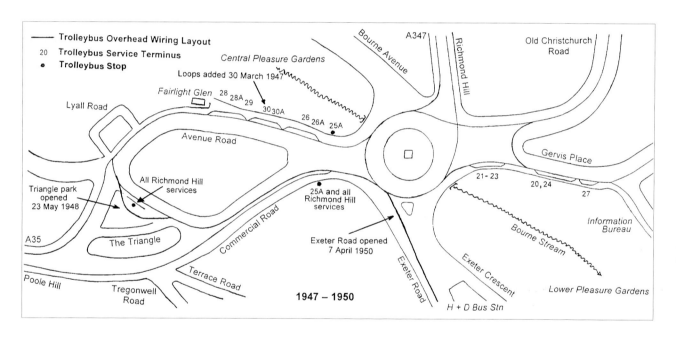

Trolleybus Overhead Wiring Layout
20 **Trolleybus Service Terminus**
•   **Trolleybus Stop**

Central Pleasure Gardens

Bourne Avenue

A347

Old Christchurch Road

Richmond Hill

Loops added 30 March 1947

Fairlight Glen

Lyall Road

28 28A 29
30 30A

26 26A 25A

Gervis Place

Avenue Road

Triangle park opened 23 May 1948

All Richmond Hill services

25A and all Richmond Hill services

21- 23

20, 24

27

Information Bureau

A35

The Triangle

Commercial Road

Exeter Road opened 7 April 1950

Bourne Stream

Poole Hill

Terrace Road

Tregonwell Road

1947 – 1950

Exeter Road

Exeter Crescent

H + D Bus Stn

Lower Pleasure Gardens

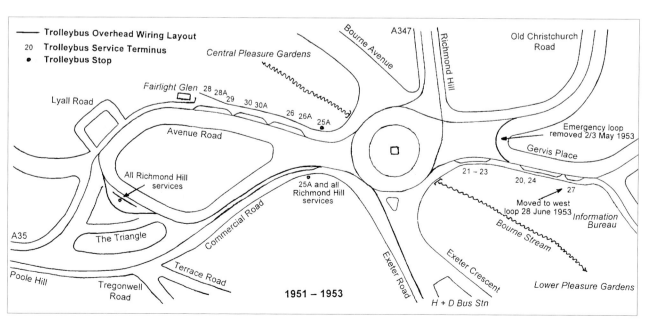

Trolleybus Overhead Wiring Layout
20 **Trolleybus Service Terminus**
•   **Trolleybus Stop**

Central Pleasure Gardens

Bourne Avenue

A347

Old Christchurch Road

Richmond Hill

Fairlight Glen

Lyall Road

28 28A
29   30 30A

26 26A 25A

Emergency loop removed 2/3 May 1953

Gervis Place

Avenue Road

All Richmond Hill services

25A and all Richmond Hill services

21 – 23

20, 24   27

Moved to west loop 28 June 1953

Information Bureau

A35

The Triangle

Commercial Road

Bourne Stream

Poole Hill

Terrace Road

Tregonwell Road

1951 – 1953

Exeter Road

Exeter Crescent

H + D Bus Stn

Lower Pleasure Gardens

Sunbeam MS2 123 (ALJ 997), one of the 1935 Park Royal bodied batch, seen at the Square on service 24, having just left Gervis Place. The curve of Old Christchurch Road is visible in the background while, at the top left of the picture, can be seen the wires coming in from Richmond Hill. Note, too, the motorcycle combination following the trolleybus.
J. R. Whitehead collection

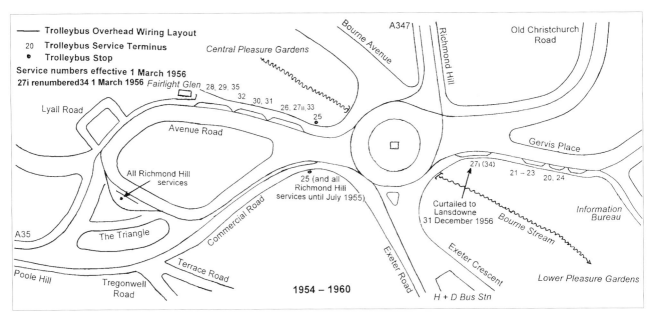

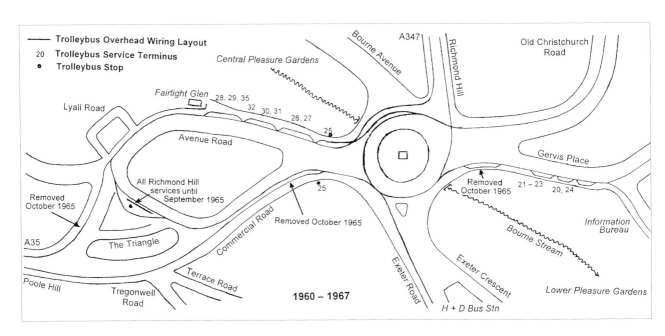

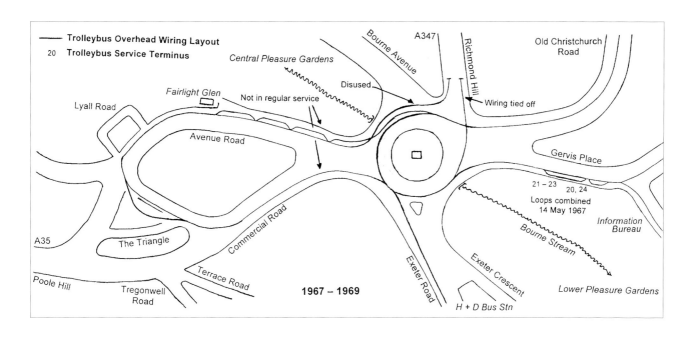

THE LANSDOWNE

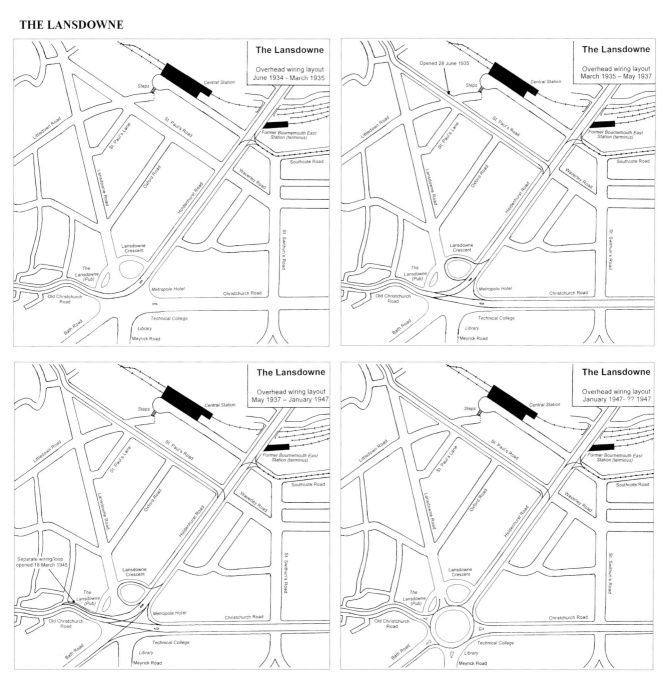

263

Sunbeam MF2B 258, the first of these vehicles to be delivered, is seen here at the Lansdowne during its first month in service, August 1958. It is waiting to enter the roundabout from Old Christchurch Road. The Lansdowne Hotel, after which this roundabout is named, is in the background.

Surfleet Transport Photographs
D. L. Chalk collection

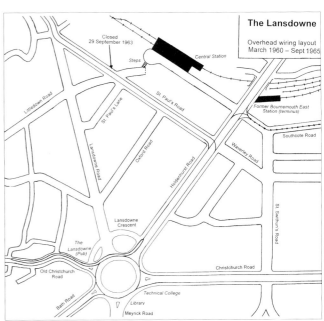